FIELDING'S
FAR EAST
SECOND REVISED EDITION

FIELDING'S BERMUDA AND THE BAHAMAS 1990
FIELDING'S BUDGET EUROPE 1990
FIELDING'S CARIBBEAN 1990
FIELDING'S EUROPE 1990
FIELDING'S MEXICO 1990
FIELDING'S PEOPLE'S REPUBLIC OF CHINA 1990
FIELDING'S SELECTIVE SHOPPING GUIDE TO EUROPE 1990

FIELDING'S AFRICAN SAFARIS
FIELDING'S ALASKA AND THE YUKON
FIELDING'S EUROPE WITH CHILDREN
FIELDING'S FAMILY VACATIONS USA
FIELDING'S FAR EAST 2nd revised edition
FIELDING'S HAVENS AND HIDEAWAYS USA
FIELDING'S LEWIS AND CLARK TRAIL
FIELDING'S LITERARY AFRICA
FIELDING'S MOTORING AND CAMPING EUROPE
FIELDING'S SPANISH TRAILS IN THE SOUTHWEST
FIELDING'S WORLDWIDE CRUISES 4th revised edition

FIELDING'S
FAR EAST
SECOND REVISED EDITION

BY
ANTOINETTE DELAND
WITH
ROBERT MILLER

Fielding Travel Books
c/o William Morrow & Company, Inc.
105 Madison Avenue, New York, N.Y. 10016

ISSN: 0739-0777

ISBN: 0-688-08046-4

ISBN: 0-340-48980-4 (Hodder & Stoughton)

Printed in the United States of America
Second Revised Edition

1 2 3 4 5 6 7 8 9 10

TO MOTHER

who opened the map and showed me the world . . .

ABOUT THE AUTHOR

Antoinette DeLand's interest in the Far East began at age ten, when she received a copy of Elizabeth Grey Vining's *Windows for the Crown Prince* as a Christmas present from her mother. In the past two decades, Ms. DeLand has been both a resident and frequent visitor to this exciting part of the globe.

During a five-year sojourn in Japan, Ms. DeLand studied art, history, and literature at Sophia University in Tokyo, worked with a local trading company, was program chairman of the College Women's Association of Japan, and originated a series of cultural seminars that are still one of the most popular winter events among the foreign community. She also wrote the weekly "Sunday Morning" page of the *Japan Times,* which chronicled the happenings in one of the world's most vibrant capitals.

The author spent two years in Hong Kong as associate editor of *Asian Hotels and Tourism.* When not overlooking some charming Chinese islands from a flat in Repulse Bay, she reported from Burma to Guam and all points in between. Her extensive travels around the Far East were enhanced by reading both fact and fiction about each country—a practice to which she still subscribes.

Antoinette DeLand is an alumna of Bryn Mawr College and the University of California at Berkeley. Her many articles appear in major publications both here and abroad. She is the author of the popular *Fielding's Worldwide Cruises*—considered the "bible" of the cruise industry. Ms. DeLand has her own production company to promote cruise and travel destinations. She has also created a *Master Chefs at Sea* series for the Public Broadcasting System—to be shown in 13 weekly installments during the 1990/1991 season.

Antoinette DeLand lives in New York City and Connecticut with her husband, Stephen Carter, an architect and designer. They have two Pekingese: Marco Polo and Genghis Khan.

CONTENTS

LIST OF MAPS

xvii

INTRODUCTION

As this revised edition of *Fielding's Far East* goes to press, we find few startling changes in the dozen countries and territories reviewed other than tourism numbers, which are in a constant state of flux. Hong Kong booms one season and softens the next, due to the hardening of China's internal policies. Thailand is finding its facilities stretched as a result of the overwhelming popularity of this beautiful country and people, and North Americans are slowly returning to the Philippines—to find themselves in good company with neighboring Asians. In fact, the most impressive change in the Far East in the 1980s is that Asians are visiting their neighbors—touring their countries, tasting their culture and enjoying their leisure activities. The beaches of Bali, once an enclave of young Western travelers, are now a potpourri of nationalities with as many Asian faces as Australian and North American.

Tourism is very important in the Far East, although some countries consider it a "necessary evil." In an effort to woo visitors (who were banned in 1988 following civil disturbances), Burma has extended the length of tourist visas to 14 days for the first time in decades. However, independent travel is not advised and there are several agencies that book tours to Burma from the United States and Bangkok. Burma, by the way, has changed its English name to the Union of Myanmar and its capital, formerly Rangoon, is now called Yangon. The new names are said to better reflect the ethnic diversity of the country. While the dominant group is Burman, that term excludes other ethnic minorities.

Revising a compendium like this is always a time-consuming project and I would like to thank Bob Miller for assuming the responsibility of Korea, Malaysia, Singapore, and Thailand. I would also like to thank the Hong Kong Tourist Association for its assistance in keeping the Hong Kong section current. The HKTA is among the finest and most efficient tourist organizations in the world and one can not applaud enough the dedicated people who work for it.

No edition of a Fielding's guide is complete without the mention of our editor and friend, Randy Ladenheim-Gil, whose good humor and wise comments are always welcome. I also salute my husband, Stephen Carter, whose photographs I always pinch, and my two Pekingese companions—Genghis Khan and Marco Polo—armchair travelers extraordinaire!

Antoinette DeLand
New York City

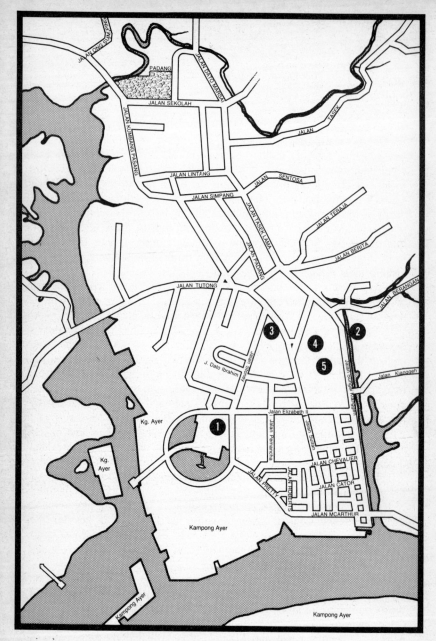

BANDAR SERI BEGAWAN

Key

1) Masjid O.A.S. (Mosque)
2) Pusat Belia (Youth Center)
3) Tugu Peringatan Churchill (Churchill Memorial)
4) Sheraton Utoma
5) Dewan Majlis (State Council)

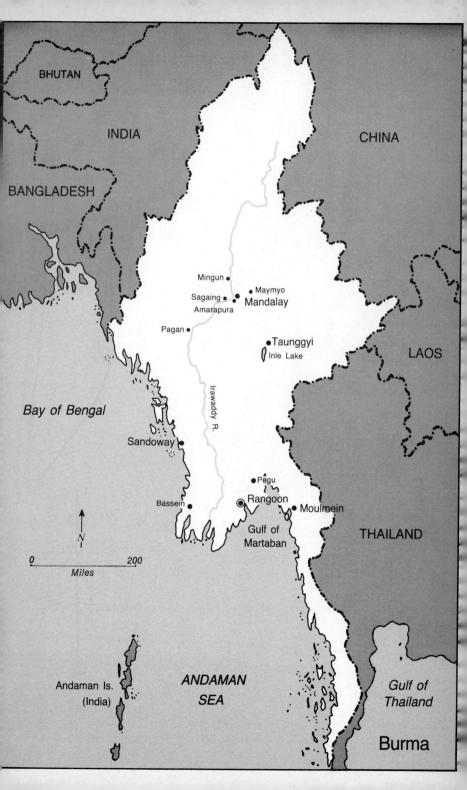

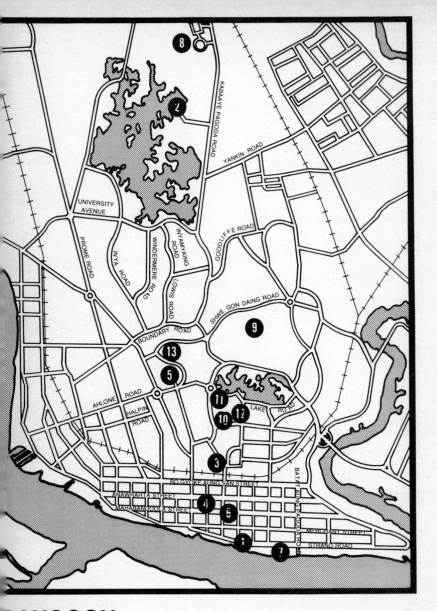

RANGOON

Key

1) Strand Hotel
2) Inya Lake Hotel
3) Thamada Hotel
4) Tourist Burma
5) Shwedagon Pagoda

6) Sule Pagoda
7) Botataung Pagoda
8) Kaba Aye Pagoda
9) Nga Htat Gyi Pagoda

10) National Museum
11) Zoological Garden
12) Horticultural Garden
13) Martyrs Mausoleum

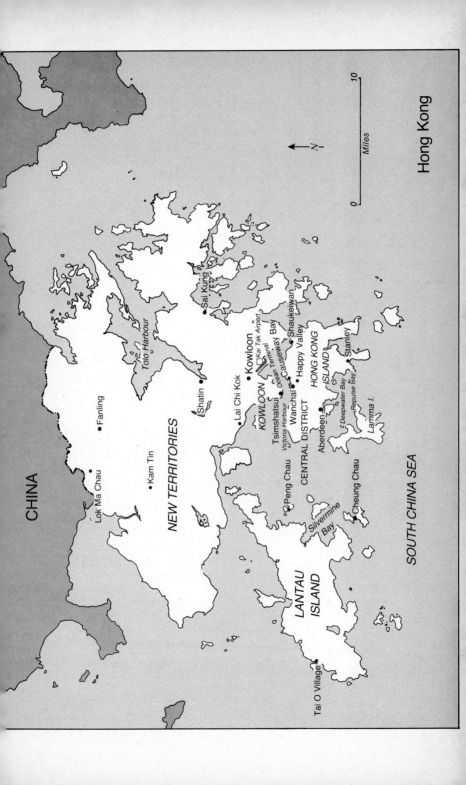

CHINA

Lok Ma Chau

Fanling

Kam Tin

NEW TERRITORIES

Sai Kung

Tolo Harbour

Shatin

Lai Chi Kok

Kowloon

Kai Tak Airport

KOWLOON

Tsimshatsui

Ocean Terminal

Causeway Bay

Shaukeiwan

Victoria Harbour

Wanchai

Happy Valley

Peng Chau

CENTRAL DISTRICT

HONG KONG

Aberdeen

ISLAND

Stanley

Deepwater Bay

Repulse Bay

Lamma I.

Silvermine Bay

Cheung Chau

LANTAU

ISLAND

Tai O Village

SOUTH CHINA SEA

N

Miles

0   10

Hong Kong

HONG KONG

Central

Key

1) Macau Ferry Pier
2) Government Pier
3) Outlying Islands Ferries Pier
4) Vehicular Ferry Pier
5) Blake Pier
6) Star Ferry
7) Queen's Pier
8) City Hall
9) Central Bus Terminal
10) Furama Hotel
11) Mandarin Hotel

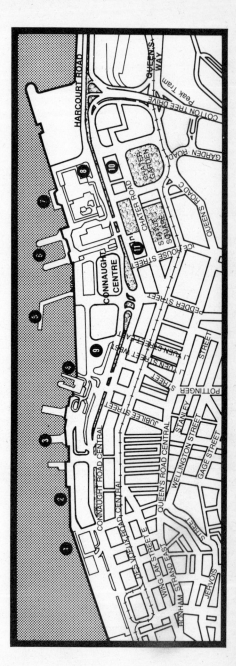

HONG KONG

Wanchi/Causeway Bay

Key

1) Wanchai Ferry Pier
2) Royal Hong Kong Yacht Club
3) Noon Day Gun
4) Wanchai Bus Terminal
5) Victoria Park
6) Excelsior Hotel
7) Lee Gardens Hotel

HONG KONG

Tsimshatsui

Key

1) Kowloon Park
2) Museum of History
3) Ocean Terminal
4) Star Ferry
5) Kowloon Public Pier
6) Space Museum
7) Prince Hotel
8) Marco Polo Hotel
9) Hong Kong Hotel
10) Hyatt Peninsula
   Hotel
11) Sheraton Hotel
12) Regent Hotel
13) New World Hotel
14) Holiday Inn
   Golden Mile
15) Holiday Inn
   Harbour View
16) Regal Meridien
17) Royal Garden Hotel
18) Shangri-La Hotel

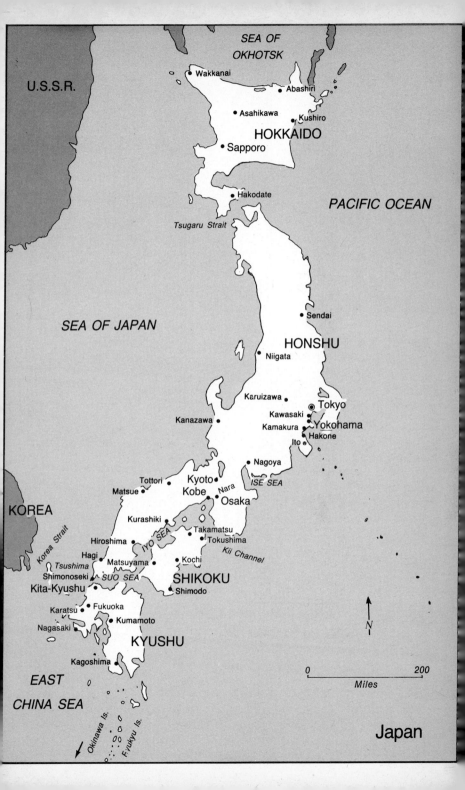

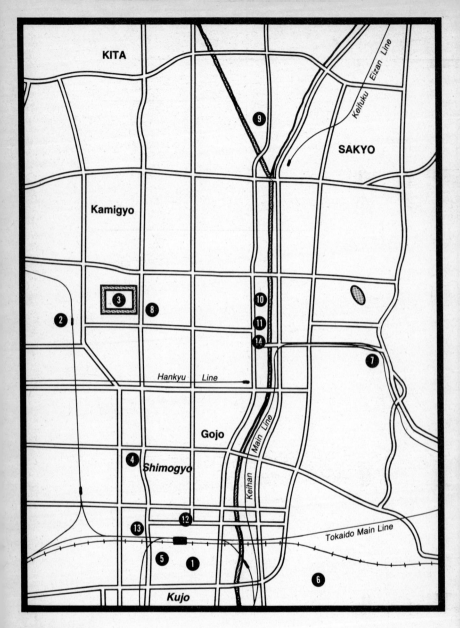

KYOTO

Key

1) Train Station (Shinkansen)
2) Nijo Station
3) Nijo Castle
4) Kyoto Tukyu Hotel
5) New Miyako Hotel
6) Kyoto Park
7) Miyako Hotel
8) International Hotel Kyoto
9) Kyoto Prince Hotel
10) Fujita Hotel
11) Kyoto Hotel
12) Kyoto Tower
13) Kyoto Grand Hotel
14) Kyoto Royal Hotel

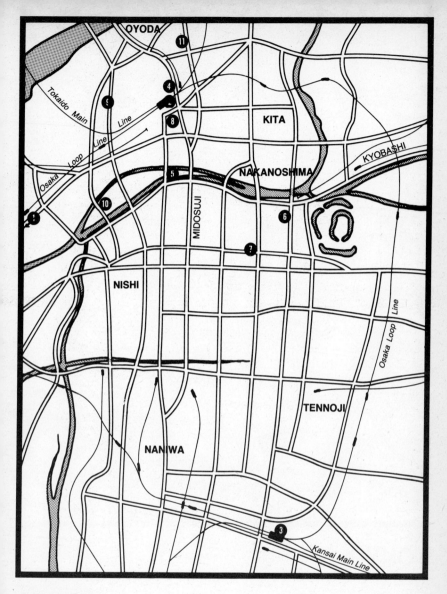

OSAKA

Key

1) Nishi-Kujo Station
2) Osaka Station
3) Tennoji Station
4) Hotel New Hankyu
5) Hotel Osaka Grand
6) Hotel Osaka Castle

7) International Hotel Osaka
8) Osaka Dai-ichi Hotel
9) Plaza Hotel
10) Royal Hotel
11) Toyo Hotel

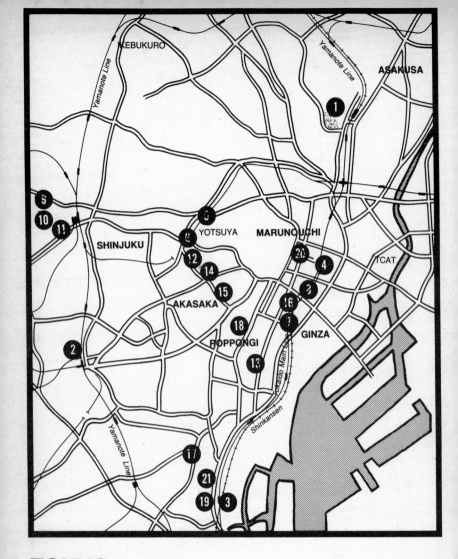

TOKYO

Key

1) Ueno Park
2) Shibuya Station
3) Shinagawa Station
4) Tokyo Station
5) Ichigaya Station
6) Yotsuya Station
7) Shimbashi Station
8) Yurakucho Station
9) Tokyo Hilton International
10) Century Hyatt Tokyo
11) Keio Plaza Inter-Continental
12) New Otani Hotel
13) Tokyo Prince Hotel
14) Akasaka Prince Hotel
15) Capital Tokyu Hotel
16) Imperial Hotel
17) Miyako Hotel
18) Hotel Okura
19) Hotel Pacific
20) Palace Hotel
21) Takanawa Prince Hotel

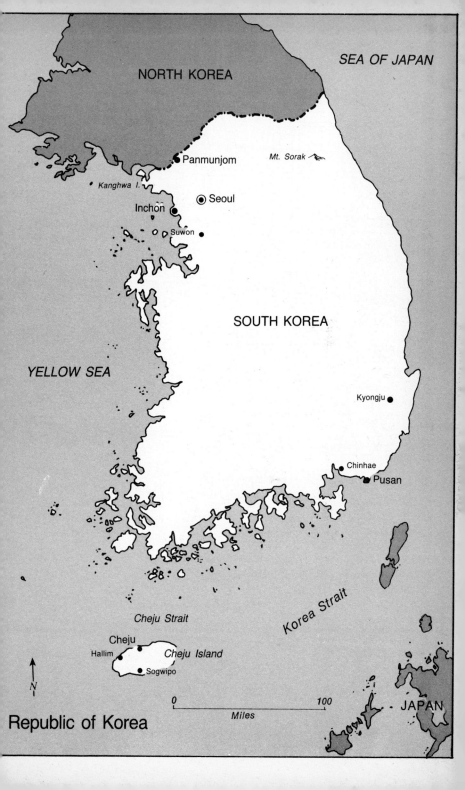

SEOUL

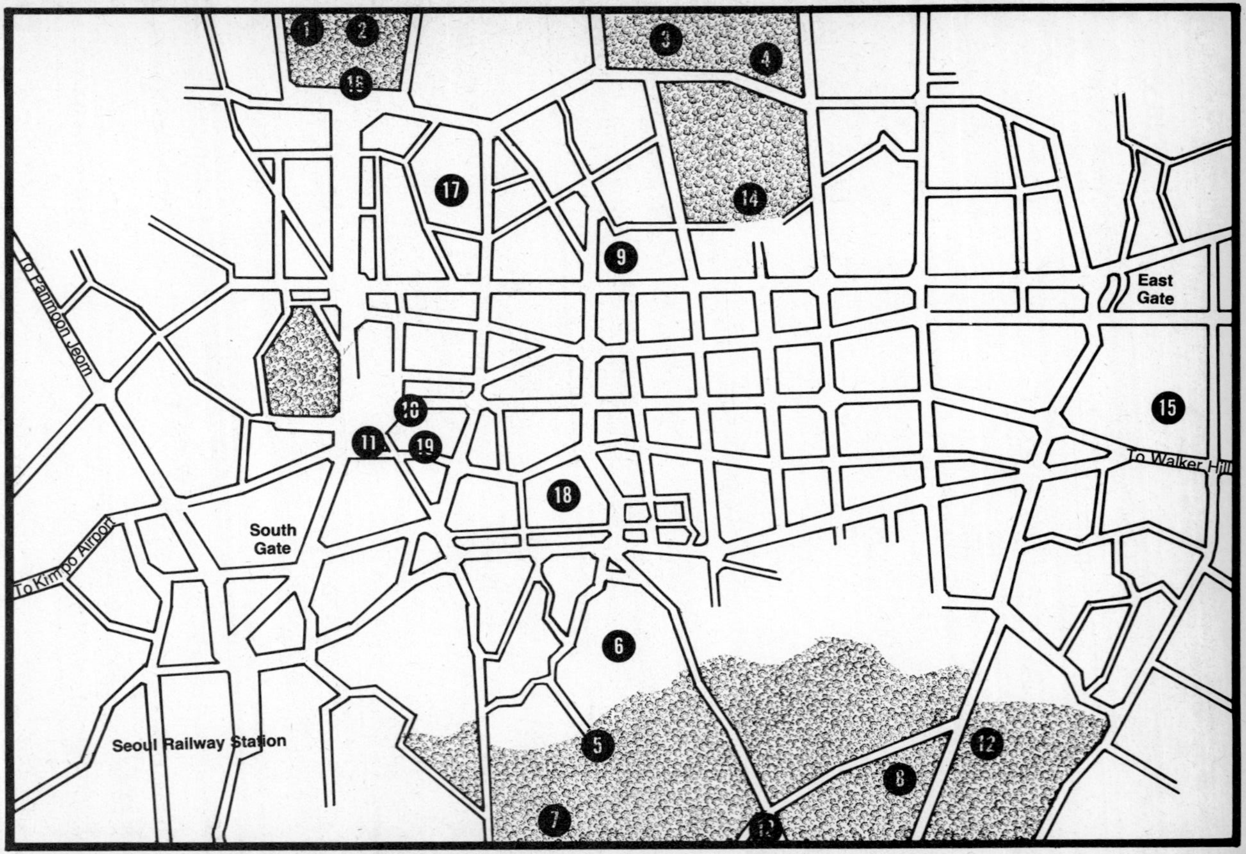

Key

1) National Museum
2) Folk Museum
3) Changdok Palace
4) Changgyong-won
5) Namsan Park
6) Namsan Dong
7) Nansan Tower
8) National Theater
9) Pagoda Park
10) Hotel Lotte
11) Seoul Plaza Hotel
12) Silla Hotel
13) Hyatt Regency Seoul
14) Chongmyo
   (Royal Shrine)
15) Seoul Stadium
16) Capitol Building
17) Chogye Temple
18) Cathedral
19) Chosun Hotel

East Gate

To Walker Hill

South Gate

Seoul Railway Station

To Panmoonjeom

To Kimpo Airport

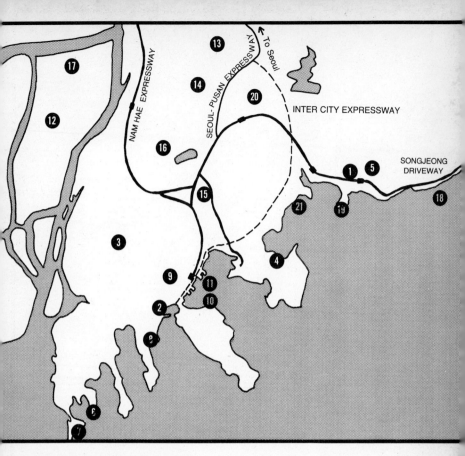

PUSAN (BUSAN)

Key

1) Haeundae Beach
2) Pusan Tower
3) Taejongdae Park
4) UN Memorial Cemetery
5) Chosun Beach Hotel
6) Dadaepo Beach
7) Molundae

8) Songdo Beach
9) Yongdusan Park
10) City Hall
11) Bukwan Ferry
12) Kimhae Airport
13) Beomeosa Temple
14) Geumgang Park

15) Seomyeon Tower
16) Seongjigog Park
17) Daeje
18) Songjeong Beach
19) Dongbaek Park
20) Chung-yol Shrine
21) Gwanganri Beach

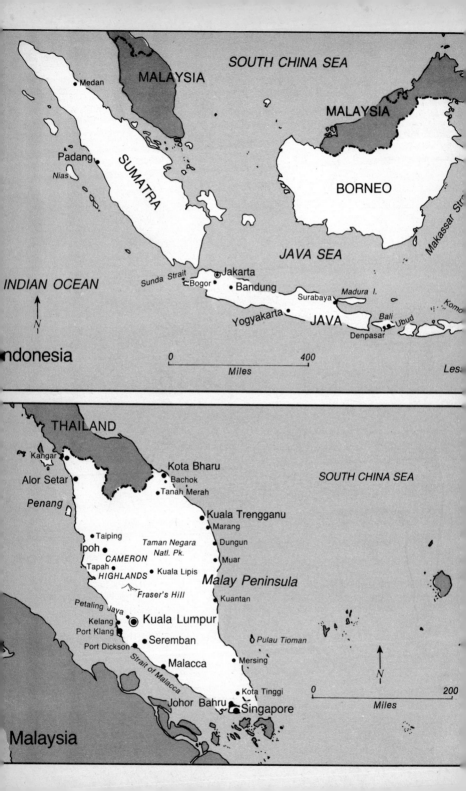

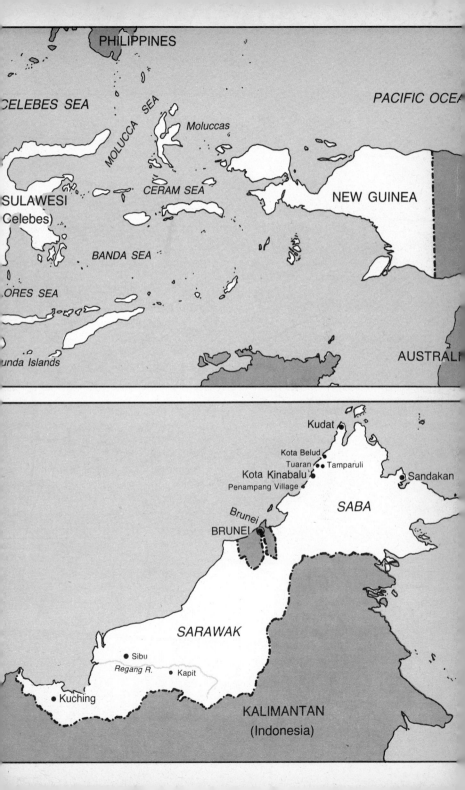

KUALA LUMPUR

Key

1) Lake Gardens
2) National Monument
3) Parliament House
4) National Museum
5) Kuala Lumpur Railway Station
6) Malayan Railway Adminsinstration Headquarters
7) Masjid Negara
8) Sultan Abdul Samad Building
9) Masjid Jame
10) National Museum of Art
11) Chinatown
12) Sri Mahamariamman Temple
13) International Buddhist Pagoda
14) Chan See Shu Yuen Temple
15) Merdeka Stadium
16) Istana Negara
17) Ming Court Hotel
18) Federal Hotel
19) Regent of KL
20) KL Hilton
21) Equatorial Hotel
22) Holiday Inn
23) KL Merlin Hotel
24) Shangri-La Hotel

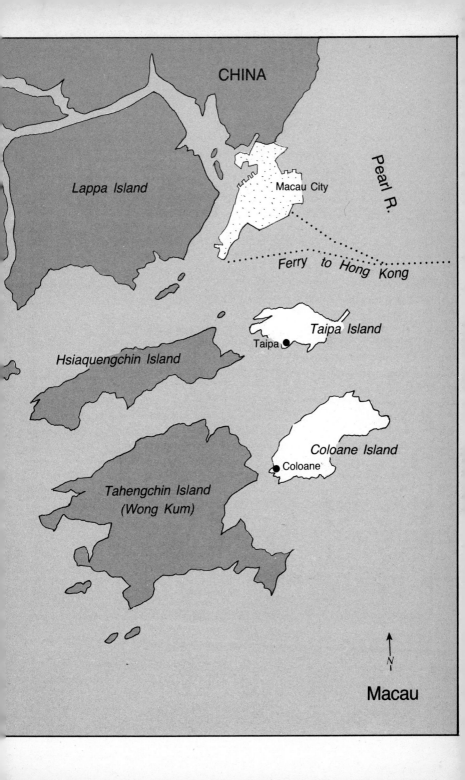

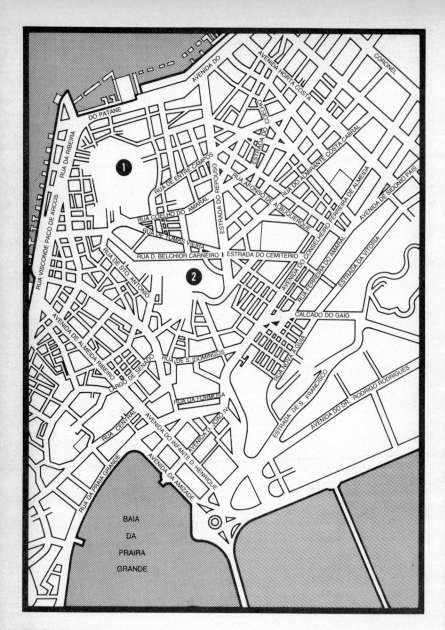

MACAU

Key

1) Jardim Luis de Camoes
2) Fortaleza do Monte

MANILA

Key

1) Cultural Center
2) Design Center
3) Folk Arts Theater
4) Fort Santiago
5) Malacanang Palace
6) Manila Hotel
7) Rizal Park
8) Century Park
   Sheraton
9) Holiday Inn
10) Hyatt Regency
    Manila
11) Manila Hilton
12) Philippine Plaza
13) Silahis International

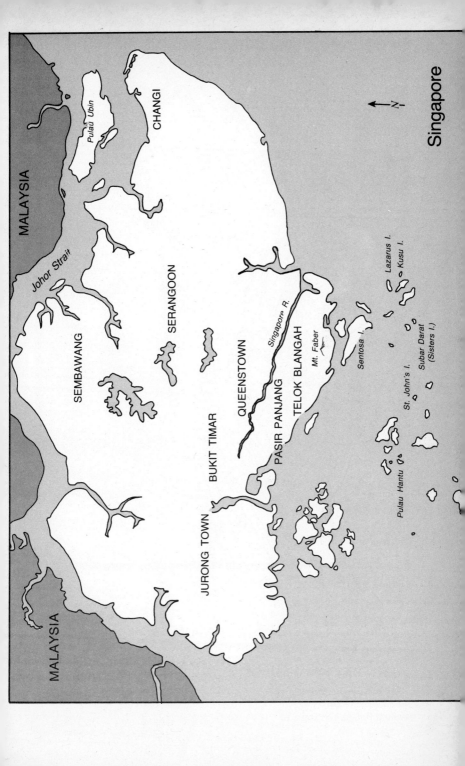

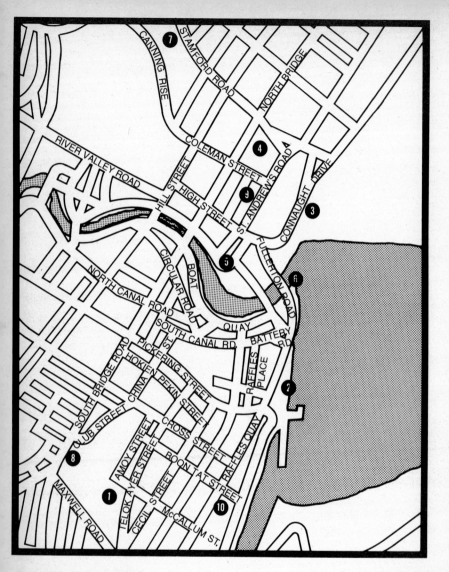

SINGAPORE

Key

1) Al-Abrar Mosque
2) Clifford Pier
3) Elizabeth Walk
4) St. Andrew's Cathedral
5) Sir Stamford Raffles Landing Site

6) Merlion
7) National Museum and Art Gallery
8) Sri Mariamman Temple
9) Supreme Court and City Hall
10) Telok Ayer

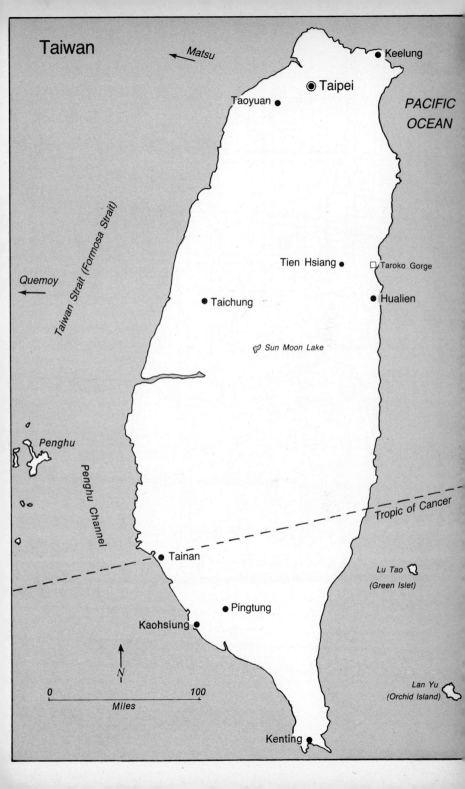

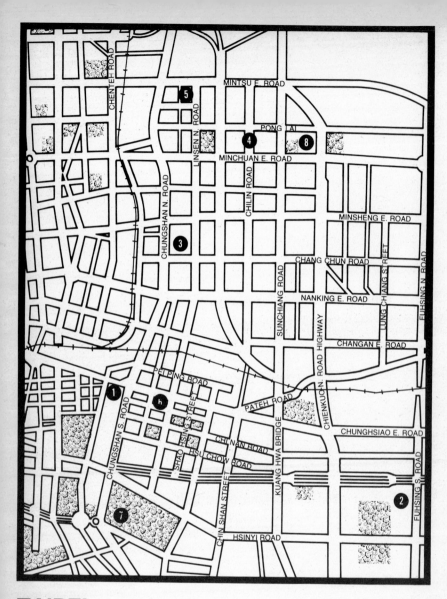

TAIPEI

Key

1) Hilton Hotel
2) Howard Plaza Hotel
3) Ambassador Hotel
4) The Ritz
5) President Hotel
6) Lai Lai Hotel
7) CKS Memorial Hall
8) Hsintien Temple

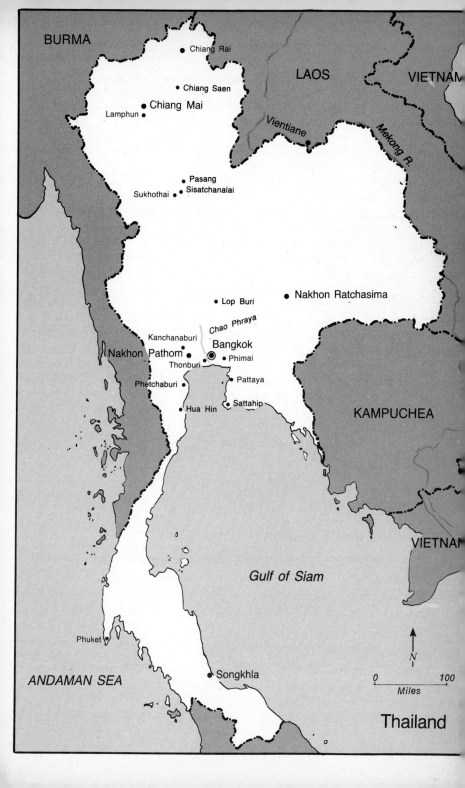

BANGKOK

Key

1) Chit Lada Palace
2) National Assembly Hall
3) Democracy Monument

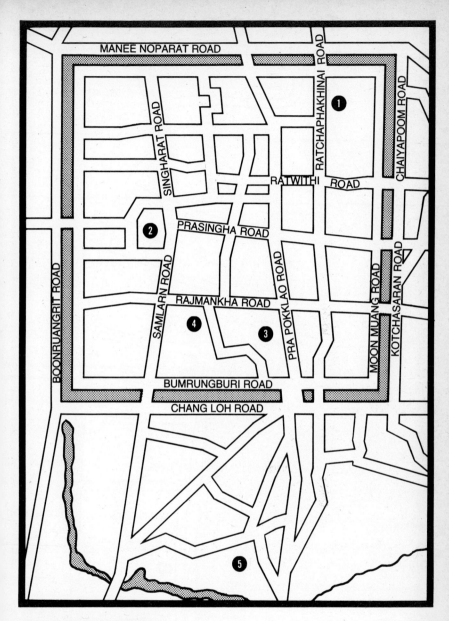

CHIANG MAI

Key

1) Wat Chiang Man
2) Wat Pra Singh
3) Chiang Mai Gate
4) Wat Meng Rai
5) Lacquerware Factory

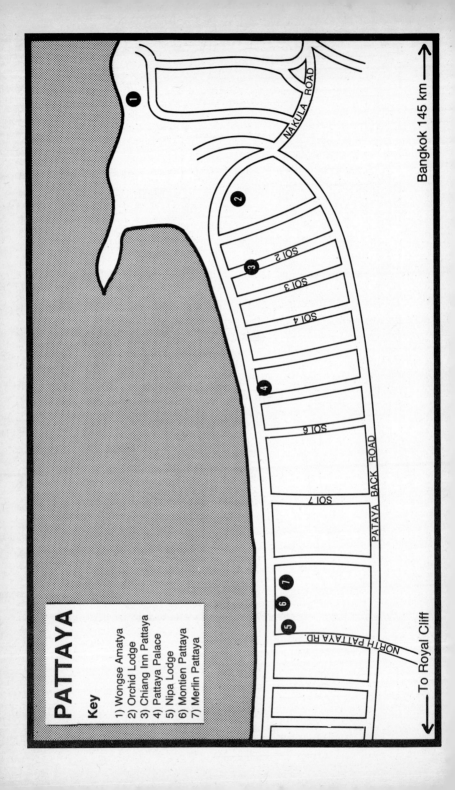

FIELDING'S
FAR EAST
SECOND REVISED EDITION

BRUNEI DARUSSALAM

HISTORY

The postage-stamp-size country of Brunei Darussalam became the world's 169th sovereign nation on January 1, 1984, ending nearly a century as a willing and loyal protectorate of the British. About the area of Delaware (some 2226 square miles), little Brunei Darussalam is a 500-year-old sultanate carved from virgin rain forests in Northern Borneo like a succulent filet mignon sandwiched between the East Malaysian states of Sabah and Sarawak off the China Sea.

Although tiny, the world pays considerable attention to Brunei Darussalam for it is oil and gas rich. Very rich, indeed. Per capita income is over $20,000, placing it among the world's wealthiest nations. To be sure, the $2 billion or so exports earned annually from oil/gas is far more than the government can possibly spend, even though all food is imported and beef arrives from the country's own cattle ranch in Northern Australia (the ranch is reputed to be larger than Brunei Darussalam itself)!

Brunei Darussalam is governed by the 44-year-old Sultan, Haji Hassanal Bolkiah Muizzaddin Waddaulah, who calls home the Istana Nurul Iman royal palace located on some 350 acres overlooking his capital, Bandar Seri Begawan (formerly called Brunei Town). The $300 million royal residence, considered the largest and most expensive in the world, was designed by Filipino architect Leandro Locsin (also known as "Lucky" Locsin because of his lucrative commissions).

The palace is Moorish-Islamic in design and flavor, with a private helipad, underground parking for 800 cars (of which the sultan owns 40 sports varieties), and his personal mosque, appropriately gold-domed. There are approximately 900 rooms in the family quarters for the sultan, his two wives and seven children, three brothers and their families. Landscaping is Japanese, the hardwoods are from the Philippines, the tiles from Italy, and the furniture American-bought.

An autonomous sultanate for centuries, Brunei's history is synonymous with that of Borneo. When Magellan's fleet dropped anchor off the port of Brunei Town in 1521, returning from the Philippines sans Magellan, this was the center of a sea-dominant empire stretching from

Sarawak to Manila. Brunei's power declined, however, during the 19th century until it was propped up by the first of the white British rajahs to arrive in North Borneo—James Brooke. The discovery of oil in the early 1900s brought quick prosperity. Today, the nation shares only the jungle climate and terrain of its neighbors—none of its 220,000 inhabitants know anything of poverty or internal political strife.

Completely Islamic, Brunei Darussalam means "Abode of Peace." Its people preserve traditional culture and tradition while enjoying every modern material convenience. It is defended by a military supplemented with some 1000 Gurkha troops, who helped squash an attempted revolt in 1962, presumably instigated from the outside. All is quiet now and whatever designs the neighbors considered are no longer viable.

Although tourism is certainly not a priority—the country hardly needs the hard currency—Brunei Darussalam is the newest, youngest, and richest of the Association of Southeast Asian Nations (ASEAN), which join together to promote economic and social progress as well as cultural development in the region. This joint cooperation is especially seen in the promotion of tourism. The other states in the association are Thailand, Malaysia, Indonesia, Singapore, and the Philippines.

The 29th sultan is an absolute and benevolent monarch, who is said to have an easy sense-of-humor approach to life and his country. Educated at Sandhurst, the British military academy, he loves fast cars, polo, and piloting his own helicopters. He shares the state's oil wealth with his subjects, in the form of electric, water, fuel, and basic staple subsidies. Medical care and schooling is free, and the state picks up the tab for university study abroad, pilgrimages to Mecca, and junkets to England for many civil servants. There is no such thing as a personal income tax, and interest rates are less than 1%!

Although the oil wells are presumed to run dry early next century, no one is worried because the sultan has invested wisely abroad and has some $20 billion in currency reserves—more than Britain or Switzerland. Hence, he can present easily $1 million to the United Nations

---

BRUNEI IN A CAPSULE

2226 square miles of an autonomous sultanate . . . smallest, richest, and youngest sovereign nation in the Far East . . . 240,000 population, 70% Malay, sizable Chinese and tribal communities . . . capital is Bandar Seri Begawan (BSB) on banks of Brunei River . . . Muara major port . . . oil and gas rich . . . per capita income over $20,000 . . . Malay is national language . . . English second . . . hot and humid tropical climate . . . interesting blend of traditional and modern.

Children's Fund on the occasion of his country's becoming the 159th member of that world body.

The sultan can also listen to his religious wise men, who picked February 23rd as his country's new National Day.

PLANNING AHEAD

BRUNEI INFORMATION BUREAU, Economic Development Board, Ministry of Finance Bandar Seri Begawan, Brunei (Tel: 31794) is unfortunately the only official tourist information center. Check plans also with local consulates in New York and Washington, and airlines serving the country.

VISAS are required of United States citizens at this writing, but always double check with your carrier for the latest in this regard. If visas are required for just a short touristic stay, go elsewhere.

INOCULATIONS are not required for entry and local health officials claim the country is cholera free; however, Americans are advised to have a valid cholera certificate upon arrival.

ENTRY is through Bandar Seri Begawan's international airport via Royal Brunei Airlines from Singapore, Hong Kong, Bangkok, Manila, and neighboring East Malaysian states. Other Far East/Asian airlines also serve the area. A coastal highway links Brunei to the Malaysian state of Sarawak. Taxis to and from the capital are reasonable, but take the Sheraton Utama car service if you are staying at the only international hotel in the country.

DEPARTURE is via BSB International Airport, which can become congested during Haji, the annual period of pilgrimages to Mecca. There is a duty-free shop at the airport, but liquor is not sold as this is a strict Muslim country. (Drinks are available to visitors in the restaurant here, however, except during Haji.) There is no departure tax.

DUTY FREE applies only to personal effects, including 200 cigarettes, ½ pound of tobacco, and 1 quart of liquor (frowned upon). Customs officials are strict on imported items like small electrical appliances and cameras, so declare equipment at airport.

CURRENCY in Brunei Darussalam is the Brunei dollar ($B), which consists of 100 cents. Brunei notes are in denominations of 1, 5, 10,

50, 100, 500, and 1000 dollars. Coins are in 5, 10, 20, and 50 cent pieces. The exchange rate is approximately $B1.98 to US $1. The Singapore dollar is on a par and circulates freely; the Malaysian rianggit has a slightly lower rate. There is no limit on foreign or local currency imported or exported.

LOCAL TIME in Brunei is Greenwich Mean Time plus 8 hours (13 hours in advance of Eastern Standard Time). Brunei is in the same time zone as Manila, Singapore, Bangkok, and Kuala Lumpur.

LOCAL CURRENT is 230 volts/50 cycles. The populace has all types of fancy, modern equipment and electrical power is good. The PAL system is used by the local television network.

LOCAL WATER is not potable from the tap in most cases. Drink bottled liquids or request boiled water.

OFFICIAL LANGUAGES in Brunei are Malay, with English widely utilized and understood in business circles. Do not expect to carry on long conversations upriver, however.

BUSINESS HOURS in Brunei are 7–8 a.m. to 4 p.m. Monday through Thursday, with a half day on Saturday. Friday is the official Muslim holiday and offices are closed on Sunday. Banks have slightly reduced hours, with lunchtime closing from noon to 2 p.m. Local markets are open from dawn and small shops stay open in the evening.

TIPPING varies from person to person, place to place, in this prosperous nation. Tip according to services rendered and the circumstances. Hotels add a 10% service charge.

TELEPHONE AND TELEX are good if you are in Brunei on business and stay within the confines of BSB. Upriver, do not expect worldwide communications. Brunei does have its own color television station, and even longhouse dwellers in the jungle have their own TVs (and personal generators) provided by the government. There is a limited amount of reading matter on the country, but the weekly English-language *Bulletin* attempts to keep visitors informed about the outside world.

WHAT TO WEAR in Brunei is cool and comfortable clothes in this hot and humid climate. Unless you are invited to the palace, you will not need dressy or smart attire. Safari suits for men are fine throughout the day; women should not wear shorts or anything too revealing in respect of Muslim tradition.

LOCAL TRANSPORTATION by taxis, buses, and boat is excellent. There are some self-drive cars available, but traffic is British style (left-hand drive) and can be confusing. An International License is required and minimum age is 23. Hotels will arrange airport transportation with prior notice.

FESTIVALS AND HOLIDAYS in Brunei are primarily Muslim but Chinese, Hindu, and Christian holidays are also observed. Public holidays are marked with an asterisk (*).

*January 1 • *New Year's Day.*

*January/February • *Chinese New Year celebrations.*

Variable • *Hari Raya Haji* • celebrated by Muslims to commemorate sacrifice of Prophet Abraham.

Variable • *First day of Hijrah (Muslim New Year).*

*Variable • *Maulud (tenth day of New Year).*

*February 23 • *National Day.*

*May 31 • *Anniversary of Royal Brunei Malay Regiment.*

*July 15 • *The sultan's birthday.*

*Variable • *First day of Ramadan (fasting month).*

*Variable • *Anniversary of Revelation of the Koran.*

*Variable • *Hari Raya Puasa* • two days' feast at end of Ramadan.

*December 25 • *Christmas holiday.*

WHAT TO SEE AND DO

Bandar Seri Begawan

Brunei History Centre • established in 1982 . . . here visitors can trace the genealogy of the Sultans of Brunei and history of the Sultanate.

Brunei Museum • An attractive structure four miles from the center of BSB . . . opened by the sultan and Queen Elizabeth II in 1972 . . . has spectacular views of Brunei River . . . plus fine collection of bronzes, Chinese porcelains. . . . Malay kris (inlaid swords) . . . artifacts of Borneo life . . . and antique Brunei brass . . . for which the sultanate was famous . . . Visit also the **Aquarium** next door . . . small but memorable.

Government Buildings • Just because they're there . . . Language and Literature Bureau Office with its mosaic mural . . . Youth Center and Parliament House . . . all attractive and well landscaped.

Kampong Ayer • Brunei's water village. A city within the city . . . home to some 30,000 people . . . actually a series of connecting villages where people live together in houses on stilts (each with its own TV antennae), and sometimes commute to the more modern metropolis . . . reached by small motor launches . . . a fascinating view of how people have lived for centuries . . . these folk just have a few more modern conveniences than others . . . ask about the antiques shops and the last of Brunei's brass workers.

Omar Ali Saifuddin Mosque • focal point of Brunei. Named after the late sultan . . . built on reclaimed land beside the Brunei River . . . with imported materials . . . exemplifies the fierce tradition of Muslim worship in an elegant atmosphere made possible only by petrodollars . . . don't miss lagoon in which floats the Mahligai (stone boat).

Royal Tomb and **Royal Palace** • pleasant sighting while boating on the river. The royal tomb is less than a mile to the west . . . the royal palace can be viewed in the distance . . . inquire discreetly if palace tours are actually on . . . there is talk.

Sir Winston Churchill Memorial Museum • in city center. The late Sultan Sir Omar Ali Saifuddin was a great admirer of Sir Winston . . . hence, this fine collection of memorabilia on the last days of the empire. Also pay a visit to the Constitutional Museum, although the Churchill Museum is the gem in town.

Upriver • the jungle. It is possible to hire boats for excursions to the longhouse people . . . Ibans from Sarawak . . . Dusun, Muruts, and Settled-Punan also live in villages upriver from BSB . . . but don't expect too much exotica . . . they also enjoy the material prosperity of Brunei.

Downriver • beautiful beaches along the South China Sea coastline. Good swimming . . . while watching the offshore oil rigs . . . there are few organized tours available . . . so be creative.

HOTELS

Sheraton-Utama Hotel • *P. O. Box 2203, Jalan Bendahara, Bandar Seri Begawan. Tel: 27272. Cable: SHERATON BRUNEI. Telex: (809) BU2306* • 170 rooms including 14 suites. Located opposite Parliament buildings, Churchill Memorial and Park . . . transportation arranged from airport . . . just four miles away . . . Coffee Shop . . . The Heritage continental restaurant . . . cocktail lounge . . . outdoor pool . . . meeting facilities . . . parking . . . air conditioning . . . color TV and refrigerator in all rooms . . . 24-hour service . . . gourmet shop . . . beauty salon, gift shop and florist . . . in short, the only recommended hotel in BSB.
Manager: C. Bachran. *Reservations:* Sheraton Int'l.

Other hotels include Ang's Hotel, the Brunei Hotel, and the National Inn in Bandar Seri Begawan; the Seaview Hotel and Sentosa Hotel in Kuala Belait. Reservations can be made through participating airlines.

WINING/DINING/ENTERTAINMENT

Don't expect much entertainment in BSB, other than a friendly chat with other tourists at the Sheraton or the Royal Brunei Yacht Club—if you happen to know a member! As this is a strict Muslim country, liquor is served only at designated places and strictly to tourists. The oilfield set have their own private clubs and entertainment, but these are hardly for the casual visitor.

There is plenty of good and interesting food in Brunei, including that succulent beef from Australia! Local dishes run the gamut from Malay curries and rice to Chinese noodles to excellent steaks and local seafood. There are also open-air stalls along the Brunei River opposite Kampong Ayer, which offer a tantalizing array of satay sticks and such, but these are not advised for most delicate American stomachs. Exercise judgment at these and other stalls throughout Asia—or have your lomotol handy!

Aside from the coffee shop, bar, and Heritage continental restaurant at the Sheraton, visitors should inquire of the hotel concierge about good local places to try. There are several, like the Chayo Phaya in Klasse Department Store (Thai Muslim dishes) and the Rasa Sayang for reasonable Chinese (next to the Chinese Temple).

If you plan to spend a day at one of the lovely beaches, a short drive from BSB, be sure to take along your own food and drink. The Sheraton can pack a lunch and it also has a nice gourmet shop for snack items. (Be sure to include sunscreen and some insect repellent as well, for obvious reasons.)

There are also several private sporting clubs that serve meals, some of which welcome visitors by invitation. They are the Brunei Tennis Club, the Royal Brunei Yacht Club and the Pantai Mentiri Golf Club—all located in the environs of Bandar Seri Begawan. Brunei Shell Petroleum has two clubs in Seria—the Panaga Club and the Shell Recreation Club—that extend a welcome to visitors who have an introduction. Membership in the posh Jerudong Park Polo Club is by invitation only. Polo happens to be a passion of this Sultan.

SHOPPING

Locally made handicrafts include brass cannon and ornamental kris (the Malay knife), and rattan furniture is also tempting if you can figure out how to get it home! Muslims are terrific gold dealers and 24-carat jewelry is a good buy here, especially in gold bangles. Dealers are honest, as they sell it by weight according to the world market price.

The main shopping area is in the Seri complex in BSB with its department stores, supermarkets and boutiques, which accept all major credit cards. Do pay a visit first to the Brunei Arts and Handicrafts Training Centre in BSB, where weaving, silver and bronze work, kris and kain songket (handwoven cloth) can be viewed and purchased.

BURMA

HISTORY

"The best thing a Burman can wish for a good Englishman is that in some future existence, as a reward for good works, he may be born a Buddhist and if possible a Burman." These words were written over a century ago (1882) by Shway Yoe—pen name for a young Scotsman who was just beginning his adult life as a teacher, journalist, and colonial administrator in Burma. The words apply today for all of us. Burma is the most enchanting, fascinating, delightful, and exotic of all Far Eastern countries to visit . . . and still the best kept secret in the travel world! A seven-day tour of Burma is comparable to stepping back several decades of the 20th century, assimilating some 2500 years in cultural history.

Burma means "first inhabitants of the world." Records do show that the Mons people laid the cornerstone for the Shwedagon Pagoda in 588 B.C. on a site that was already considered sacred. Rebuilt over the ensuing centuries, it has become the most important living monument in the Buddhist world. It not only dominates Rangoon, the capital city, but the entire country. This is the Land of Pagodas . . . many of them with brilliant golden domes and *hti* (umbrellas) encrusted with precious stones on their flight to heaven. Some say the Burmese practice the purest form of religion—Theravada Buddhism—as it permeates the everyday life of 80% of the people.

That the Socialist Republic of the Union of Burma is "socialist" can be readily affirmed; however, it has been anything but a "union" since its inception. Situated on the crossroads between the Indian subcontinent and the Indo-Chinese peninsula, the country has been trampled upon, fought among and over for far more than 25 centuries. Even today, it consists of many separate ethnic minorities—including the Chins, Kachins, Shans, Karens, Kayahs, Mons, and Arakense. These are only some of the over 60 racial groups present and the 200-plus languages spoken. I wonder what our friend Shway Yoe meant when he wrote, "It is a common belief that no one can speak Burmese well, till he chews betel (nut)." Add to all this the post-war influx of Indians and Chinese and you have quite a mixture of different factions.

9

The territory of Burma is the third largest in mainland Asia, after India and China, and boasts the mighty Irrawaddy River, which flows some 1350 miles from the foothills of the Himalayas down to the Andaman sea. The Irrawaddy, together with its tributaries the Chindwin and Mu rivers, is the heartland and powerplay of the country. It provides access from China to the rest of the world. The first kingdom was founded along its banks, and its overflow provides for both an abundant rice and bread bowl.

Burmese history becomes intriguing only in A.D. 1057, when King Anawrahta conquered the neighboring Mons capital of Thaton and returned with enough "loot" to establish the first Burmese Empire in Pagan. Among the 30,000 prisoners—including monks, craftsmen, and builders, the king brought to the banks of the Irrawaddy River in Upper Burma a culture, a new language, and Theravada Buddhism. As a fresh convert, the king began what was to become "the most remarkable religious city in the world." In just 200 years, no less than 13,000 sacred monuments were erected on this fluvial plain as successive monarchs tried to "win merit" in the eyes of Buddha and their own predecessors.

A hundred years ago, Shway Yoe wrote . . . "Jerusalem, Rome, Benares, none of them can boast the multitude of temples, and the lavishness of design and ornament that make marvellous this deserted capital on the Irrawaddy . . . for eight miles along the river bank and extending to a depth of two miles inland, the whole space is thickly studded with pagodas of all sizes and shapes, the ground is so thickly covered with crumbling remnants of vanished shrines that according to the popular saying, you cannot move foot or hand without touching a sacred thing."

The glory lasted until A.D. 1284, when the Emperor of China sent a vast army to avenge the murder of an ambassador, and Pagan's King Narathihapate "pulled down a thousand arched temples, a thousand smaller ones, and four thousand square temples to strengthen the fortifications." Unfortunately, however, he lost his courage and fled to the south. Pagan has been a deserted capital since. Today, less than 2000 of these magnificent structures are standing—due to both man-made and natural devastations (including a disastrous earthquake in 1975)—but it remains a place of pilgrimage for travelers from all over the world.

The founding of Mandalay, at a bend in the Irrawaddy in Upper Burma in 1857, represents another colorful chapter in the country's history. According to legend, Gautama Buddha and his disciple Ananda visited Mandalay Hill and proclaimed that on the 2,400th anniversary of his teaching, a great metropolis of Buddhist learning would be established there. King Mindon found this irresistible, and moved his palace from nearby Amarapura to a spot below the sacred mount of Mandalay Hill.

Between 1859 and 1885, when King Thibaw surrendered the "Golden City" to the British and went into exile, several dozen ambitious monuments to Buddhist teachings were erected. Mandalay became not only the capital of Upper Burma but the cultural center of the entire country. Unfortunately, most of its structures were built of teak, exquisitely carved and decorated by local craftsmen, but very few are standing today. All that remains of the renowned royal palace are the walls (1½-miles long) and the moat. The magnificent teak pavilions turned to ashes during the Second World War. Mandalay today is a shadow of its former self, although it is still a center for Buddhist teachings and many of the country's indigenous crafts.

On January 1, 1886, the independent kingdom of Burma ceased and became a province of British India. From that day until full independence on January 4, 1948, Burma was under British colonial rule, although the country was granted some sort of self-government in 1923 and became a separate colony (no longer annexed to India) in 1935. In 1941 the Japanese invaded Burma and persuaded the Burmese Liberation Army, led by Aung San, to help them drive the British back to India.

What ensued were perhaps the bloodiest and bitterest campaigns of the entire war—most of it in the treacherous jungles of Upper Burma. Somehow, all the "biggies" arrived at this crossroads of Asia and most lived to record their own brand of jungle warfare. There were "Vinegar Joe" Stilwell and the 114 Chinese soldiers he got safely to Delhi; General Wingate and his famous "Chindits"; General Claire "Old Weatherface" Chennault and his "Flying Tigers"; General Frank Merrill and his "Marauders," not to forget those who built the Ledo Road. This 500-mile stretch, through territory man never dared attempt before, was to connect with the famous Burma Road; it was never completed. Nonetheless, it is said to have cost exactly "one man per mile."

At the turning point in the raging conflict, Aung San transferred his troops and his allegiance to the Allies and the Japanese surrendered on August 28, 1945. Intense feelings about the "Burma Campaign" have not been mollified very much with time. In fact, Queen Elizabeth's uncle, Lord Mountbatten (whose other title was 1st Earl of Burma), specified that no Japanese representative be allowed at his funeral a few years ago. After 30 years, he was still incapable of forgiving the fate of British troops in Burma.

According to a local astrologer, the most auspicious moment for Burma to become independent (once and for all) was at exactly 4:20 a.m. on January 4, 1948. And so it happened, with Burma the first former colony to sever ties with the Commonwealth. Unfortunately, the nation's premier leader, Aung San, and six of his future ministers were assassinated just months before independence and were placed in a marble mausoleum near the sacred Shwedagon Pagoda in Rangoon. Since

1962, General Ne Win has been the Number One figure in Burmese politics and is now the Chairman, while U San Yu has assumed the presidency. Although isolated and introverted since independence, Burma has not been without its world statesmen—like U Thant, secretary-general of the United Nations in the 1960s.

The abrupt resignation of U Ne Win during the summer of 1988 followed a period of political, social and economic unrest as well as a number of truths that were finally told. The general has bankrupted the country during the past two and a half decades while amassing a reputed US $1 billion-plus stronghold in Europe for himself and his six wives; his ministers are said to also be multi-millionaires. During the general's tenure, Burma has disintegrated from one of the world's great rice producers to just bare subsistence for its own people. Its famous teak wood and gemstones are not part of the GNP (although the general is said to have had first pick) but smuggled out of the country by a select group for markets in Thailand.

Another fallacy: There is no such thing as a Burmese cat, which is actually a Siamese cross-breed available only in Thailand. The infamous "Golden Triangle" falls largely in Burma's Shan Sate, although it covers parts of Thailand, Laos and some of China's Yunan province. This is where the raw material for opium and heroin is grown, and it is definitely not a good place to visit at the moment.

Following the unrest of the summer of '88, the Burmese government closed its doors to visitors—especially journalists. However, a desperate need for hard currency prompted a slight opening on tours of 5-, 7-, or 8-days paid for in US dollars (see below). Visitors are watched carefully and advised *not* to make contact with the local populace. A change of government with democratic elections is promised—especially to the youth of Burma—but whether it will take place is another matter.

A Word About Pagodas

According to our friend Shway Yoe, the word *pagoda* is derived from the Sanskrit to mean "relic shrine" and is "properly allied only to a monument raised over some of the remains of the Lord Buddha." These include pieces of flesh, hair, teeth, bone, or sacred items used by the Teacher. Somehow, the Burmese seem to claim more personal relics of the Lord Buddha than could have possibly existed. The number of pagodas raised in Burma far exceeds those built by pious Buddhists in Sri Lanka (Ceylon), Tibet, or China. It is said that a Burman does not notice the multitude of religious edifices in his country . . . until he leaves it and sees how sparing other people have been.

There is a reason: no work of merit is so richly rewarded as the building of a pagoda, according to the form of Buddhism practiced by the Burmese. Actually, the word *pagoda* does not exist in the Burmese language. Such a structure is called a *zedi,* meaning offering place or place of prayer; but the expression *payā* is most frequently employed in reference to the more famous places of worship in this country. The greatest and most venerated of all the payās in Burma is the Shwedagon in Rangoon, followed by the Shwemawdaw (lotus-shrine) in Pegu, the Shwesandaw (depository of the sacred hair) at Prome, and the Maha-myatmuni (temple of the most exalted saint) at Mandalay. All were founded by individuals who received strands of the great Master's hair.

Another reason for the proliferation of religious shrines throughout this country is that one only gains "merit" from building anew, not from repairing those that are crumbling. In fact, the pious Burman felt it was enough to gratify the feeling of the moment, and therefore, most religious monuments were built of crumbling, sun-dried bricks that had no business lasting as long as they did!

As the people, language, and culture of Burma differ from north to south, east to west, so does the architecture of the *payas*. In Lower Burma, the forms are simple, patterned after the rice-heap or lotus-bud. They are solid, pyramidal cones of undistinguished design (except when covered with solid gold leaf) and topped with those lyrical *hti,* or um-brella spires formed of concentric rings from which bells or precious stones sway in the breeze.

The architecture of the Pagan temples is completely different in styles from all other parts of Burma. In fact, they differ one from an-other—some even resemble Christian shrines, laid out as they are in the form of a Greek cross. The earliest ones, built by King Anawrahta, who established the city, were modeled exactly after monuments built in Thaton—the kingdom he had previously conquered. (No wonder, since Anawrahta brought all the craftsmen and builders with him as booty.) Later monuments show a continued sophistication of the designs begun by Anawrahta, as well as Chinese and Indian influences.

The Upper Burma area of Ava, Amarapura, and Mandalay have quite different monuments altogether. Native teak—and local crafts-men—were abundant, and the temples were shrines of merit to all who labored upon them. Unfortunately, only the stone portions remain and even they take some imagination to recall their rightful glory. Of all, the Kuthodaw or Royal Merit House, built by King Thibaw's uncle, is one of the most compact and tastefully adorned of all the pagodas. The texts of Buddhist Scripture it contains are considered the best extant. This truly is the Land of Pagodas, and everywhere you turn is another delightful surprise and memorable travel experience.

BURMA IN A CAPSULE

A socialist state about the size of Texas . . . approximately 34 million inhabitants who populate seven regions: Irrawaddy, Magwe, Mandalay, Pegu, Rangoon, Sagaing, and Tenasserim . . . as well as seven minority states: Arakan, Chin, Kachin, Kawthule, Kayah, Mon, and Shan . . . Burmese people known for gentleness and graciousness, deeply nationalistic and devoted to their Buddhist doctrines . . . now in political turmoil . . . a country that tries to keep peace with its neighbors China, India, Bangladesh, Laos, and Thailand . . . opening its doors just a crack at a time to the outside world.

PLANNING AHEAD

TOURIST BURMA, also known as the Burmese Hotel and Tourist Corporation, is the country's only official tourism agency and tour operator. Headquarters is 77-79 Sule Pagoda Rd. in Rangoon (Cable: ENVOY; Telex: 21330 HOTOCO BM; Tel: 78376, 80321). There are also branch offices in the three main tourist areas: Mandalay, Pagan, and Taunggyi. Tourist Burma personnel try very hard to be helpful, but I've found, are often held back by bureaucracy and lack of inherent initiative.

Tourist Burma does not offer foreign visitors independent tours, due to the current political situation. However, it cooperates with a few appointed travel agents in providing tours, guides, transportation and meals for inbound traffic. The best-known and most knowledgeable is **Diethelm Travel,** Kian Gwan Building, 1/F, Wireless Rd., Bangkok (Tel. 255–9150), which has been sending tourists to Burma for several decades and knows what it is doing at every turn. Tours depart Bangkok several times weekly for 5, 6 and 8 days, and rates could not be more reasonable. In New York, **Journeyworld International,** 1061 First Ave., Room 2A, New York, NY 10022 (Tel: 212–752–8308) offers one-week tours from Bangkok. In 7 days, you will have a chance to visit Rangoon, Mandalay, Pagna, Taunggyi, Inle Lake and the Pindaya Cave, and possibly the beach resort of Sandoway (previously off limits). **Eastquest,** another tour operator based in New York City, also specialized in Southeast Asia and offers packages to Burma in combination with other destinations.

However, the U.S. State Department (spring 1989) has issued a travel advisory for Burma and suggests American citizens planning a visit contact the department's Citizens Emergency Center (Tel: 202–647–5227) in Washington, DC. Travelers should also contact the U.S.

Embassy in Rangoon (Tel: 82055, ext. 223) upon arrival, or the U.S. Embassy in Bangkok (Tel: 252–5040, ext. 2212). The State Department has also advised Americans not to fly via Burma Airways (or Union of Burma Airways), especially during the rainy season, because of four recent fatal crashes. Thai Airways flies between Rangoon and Bangkok and is a superior airline, anyway.

There are no Tourist Burma offices abroad but information concerning travel to the country can be obtained from the Embassy of the Socialist Republic of the Union of Burma, 2300 S St. NW, Washington, DC 20008 (Tel: 202–332–9044) and the Consulate General (mission to the United Nations), 10 East 77th St., New York, NY 10021 (Tel: 212–535–1310) between the hours of 9 a.m. and 1 p.m. weekdays.

VISAS   are required of all travelers to Burma, aged seven years and above, for a stay of up to seven days only. Tourist visas are not extendable but are easily obtained with plenty of notice—at least two weeks. If you are in Bangkok and planning to travel via a Diethelm tour, a visa will be forthcoming in two days' time for about $38. Once inside Burma, a business visitor may possibly apply for an extended visa with the invitation and recommendation of a state enterprise.

INOCULATIONS   for smallpox are not required for entry. If you arrive within six days from an infected area, certification of immunization against cholera and yellow fever is required.

ENTRY BY AIR   into Burma is via Rangoon's **Mingaladon Airport,** the country's only international gateway. There are daily flights that take less than an hour between Bangkok and Rangoon. Thai International offers far superior service than Burma Airways between the two capitals but only three times a week. There are also direct flights available from Singapore, Calcutta, Kathmandu, Dacca, Moscow, and Beijing on a variety of third-world airlines.

Mingaladon Airport is situated about 19 kilometers northwest of Rangoon, and there may or may not be a BAC bus to transport passengers into the major hotels. If you are traveling on a package tour, transfers are definitely provided. Expect to pay about $6 if using local taxis (and don't forget to bargain a little).

DEPARTURE BY AIR   from Burma is definitely more organized than arrival, especially if your visa is running out. BAC buses will transport passengers from city hotels to the airport for flights in good time for baggage inspection (black market goods and many artifacts may not be exported), foreign currency conversions, and what duty-free shopping is available.

Departure tax is included in tour package prices.

ARRIVAL BY SEA is the only other option available, since the land borders along Burma have long been closed and are considered extremely unsafe. Rangoon is the country's major port and it lies at the mouth of the Irrawaddy River. Visitors are welcome to travel upriver on private cargo ships or conveyances owned by the government-run Inland Water Transport Corporation to either Mandalay or Nyaung-U (for Pagan). The journey is hot, picturesque, and overly time-consuming for those with only a seven-day visa in hand.

Cruise ships in the Far East area often schedule calls at Rangoon but thus far, no company has been successful in arranging regular visits. A pity, because the best way to visit this still exotic country would be from the comfort of your own cruise vessel!

DUTY FREE is an expression the Burmese have not yet learned. Bona fide visitors may import 200 cigarettes, 50 cigars, or a half-pound of tobacco; one quart of liquor; and one pint of perfume or toilet water, for personal use only. Customs inspection is lengthy and tedious upon arrival, and all valuables (jewelry, cameras, tape recorders, typewriters, radios, etc.) must be listed in detail, and the list must be attached to your passport. Be sure to carry enough film and batteries for the entire tour. *Video cameras are strictly prohibited in Burma.* All foreign currency and credit cards should be included, and everything must be exported or you will be requested to show cause. Although it is very tempting to buy semiprecious gems on the flourishing black market, they cannot be exported without a receipt from the government-owned store. Be careful also of many artifacts, which may not be allowed out of the country (despite assurances from the seller). Emptor caveat, as they say.

CURRENCY of Burma is the kyat (pronounced chat) which is divided into 100 pyas. The official rate of exchange is approximately 6.1 ks. to U.S.$1. Notes are used in denominations of ks. 1, 5 and 10; make sure markings are in both Burmese and Arabic numerals. Coins are available in denominations of 1 kyat, and 1, 5, 10, 25, and 50 pyas. Coins are difficult to decipher because they are marked only in Burmese numerals.

Unlimited amounts of foreign currency, whether in cash or traveler's checks, may be brought into the country. But remember that what is declared upon entry must be accounted for upon departure. There are plenty of taxi drivers and tourist guides eager to offer a "better than official rate" for your dollars, so proceed at your own risk. Keep the currency conversion form with you at all times and present it to the customs officials upon exit. Loss of this document can be very troublesome. Unless your entire tour has been prepaid in U.S. dollars outside the country, your hotel may demand payment in foreign currency or by credit card. Keep the receipt as an extra precaution.

It is illegal to carry Burmese currency in or out of the country (despite the terrific exchange rates available in Hong Kong, Singapore, and Bangkok), and the government does not deal lightly with found offenders. Unspent kyats can be reconverted to U.S. dollars at the time of your departure.

LOCAL TIME in Burma is Greenwich Mean Time plus 6½ hours. Rangoon is half an hour behind Bangkok, 1½ hours behind Hong Kong, and 2½ hours behind Tokyo. If it is noon today in Burma, it is 12:30 a.m. today in New York and 9:30 p.m. the night before in California.

LOCAL CURRENT is 200-250 volts, 50 cycles. It is best not to count on using fancy electrical gadgets in this country as you may blow out the entire hotel. Try being *au naturel* for a week.

LOCAL WATER should not be consumed unless it has been boiled or properly treated. Local fruits and vegetables should be avoided unless peeled with your very own (clean) hands and/or cooked. You should also contact your physician for anti-malarial medicine and take it regularly before and after your stay in Burma. Experienced travelers also carry their own mosquito coils for use at night. They are available at any Southeast Asian street stall.

OFFICIAL LANGUAGE is Burmese, spoken by 80% of the population, with a script derived from Sanskrit. Chinese, Tamil, Hindi, and minority state dialects are also spoken throughout the country. However, the most important Western language employed is still English, and many official signs are left from the colonial period.

There are two English language daily newspapers in Rangoon, *The Working People's Daily* and *The Guardian,* which provide some news of the world outside (if you don't expect an impartial opinion). The Burma Broadcasting System offers daily programs in English at 8:30 a.m., 1:30 p.m., and 9:30 p.m. There is no television. Books and periodicals in English can be found in the large libraries and universities as well as at both American and British embassies.

BUSINESS HOURS in Burma are generally from 9:30 a.m., although banks do not open to the public until 10 a.m. The Burma Socialist Program Party and the military begin at 8 a.m. Everyone closes early, so try to do the important business in the morning. Offices are open half-day on Saturdays. No one except private shopkeepers seem to work on Sunday. The only closing problem in Burma is at dinnertime, because most restaurants finish service early—8 or 9 p.m. The

Burmese eat early and apparently retire early. There is no "nightlife" in this country.

TIPPING is not expected in Burma although service people who are exposed to the major hotels may have heard about the practice. A 10% service charge in the government-run hotels will be added to your bill and nothing else is expected. Helpful guides and taxi drivers frankly prefer new ballpoint pens, lighters, and other tools of Western decadence.

TELEPHONE AND TELEX service in Burma does exist, but expect delays and frustration. Overseas calls can be made from Rangoon but must be booked in advance and placed in order. For some reason, calls to North America are not accepted on Sundays! The Central Telegraph Office in Rangoon is located at the corner of Pansodan St. and Maha Bandoola Rd. They're open from 7 a.m. to 8 p.m. and Telex services are available.

The **General Post Office** is located on Strand Road and Bo Aung Gyaw Street in Rangoon, and operates during normal business hours. Mail for North America and Europe leaves the country twice weekly, on Monday and Friday nights. Another post office at Mingaladon Airport will receive all but registered letters 24 hours daily. The GPO also sells very attractive stamps.

WHAT TO WEAR in Burma is a wardrobe of cool, comfortable, and conservative clothing. The Burmese dress simply in sarongs and sandals; footwear is prohibited in religious monuments. Since many of the touristic sites are temples and other places of worship, visitors are expected to dress with respect. Short skirts and short shorts should not be worn sightseeing. The Burmese are a gentle and sheltered people, "unsophisticated" in the Western sense, and are deeply offended by flashy dress. Their long sleeves and long skirts or slacks are also considered excellent defense against the sun and mosquito bites. (Watch out for deadly snake bites, too—which occur more in Burma than any other country worldwide.)

Be sure to pack plenty of toilet tissue and other necessities (wash and drys, etc.) of travel for a country that has progressed from having little to almost nothing in consumer goods.

LOCAL TRANSPORTATION in Burma consists of vintage vehicles for bumpy roads, the train, and the domestic arm of BAC. Somehow, the Burmese have a way with 30-year-old cars and trucks that should have gone to their peaceful rest long ago but still manage to make yet another trip. So have faith, you too will be transported in relative comfort from here to there! In Pagan it is possible to find a guide with a jeep or land rover. If all else fails, there is still the romance of the horse and buggy (**tonga**) in this country as well as plenty of bicycles with sidecars. These **trishaws** are inexpensive, and a wonderful way to enjoy the local scenery. **Taxis** have red license plates and can usually be found outside major hotels, but make sure to agree on the fare before setting off.

City **buses** are overly crowded and not recommended for Westerners, who tend to take up too much room and cause a terrible commotion if they don't understand something. Tourist Burma operates buses from Rangoon upcountry, but the journeys I've taken have been tortuous and take too much precious time. For example, a Tourist Burma bus leaves Mandalay at 4 a.m. and arrives in Pagan ten hours later (maybe); another bus leaves Mandalay at 5 a.m. and arrives in Taunggyi about 12 hours later (lucky passengers). True diehards should inquire at Tourist Burma for complete schedule, and always reconfirm the information. Departing and arriving on time is not a virtue of this country's local transportation system.

There are two **trains** daily from Rangoon to Mandalay, departing the capital at 7 a.m. and approximately 7 p.m. Both are "express" (only four intermediate stops) and travel time is about 11 hours. There is an Upper Class for about $14, but carry your own food and drink. Some trains have sleeping accommodations and you'll save a whole day if you travel through the night.

Unfortunately, the best way to travel between Burma's tourist centers is via BAC, the state-run airline that offers daily flights from Rangoon to Mandalay, Pagan, Taunggyi, and Sandoway aboard Fokker Friendship equipment. Air tickets must be purchased in foreign currency and are slightly cheaper if booked abroad—but *reconfirm* again and again, because the state often sees no reason to inform its visitors of a change in schedule. Passengers may also be hit with a jet surcharge, but it's only a few dollars and not worth arguing about. As flights are often delayed throughout Burma, it is wise to carry good reading material along with some snacks and spirits—to keep *you* in good spirits!

CUSTOMS in Burma are similar to those in Thailand and the same do's and don'ts apply. Visitors are expected to respect the national flag, the socialist state, the deep religious feeling that permeates the country and the people themselves. Burmese are extremely polite to one another and employ several different pronouns denoting rank before their names. *U* is a title of respect for a man and used before one's proper name (as in U Thant). *Bo* is a title used for members of the military, *Kodaw* when addressing monks, and *Ko* for men and *Ma* for women of the same rank.

As yet, there are no family or surnames among the Burmese, but this may change when modernization sets in and the people need a stronger identification. So far, names are bestowed upon newborns by soothsayers, who apparently consult the heavens and their own consciences. That completed, parents begin by addressing their young with *Maung* which means "inferior" or *Ko Maung* (if the given name is just one syllable). Like the Thais, the Burmese enjoy spouting a mouthful of words whenever they must speak.

FESTIVALS in Burma revolve around the many renowned pagodas. There are plenty of pagodas, as well as plenty of national and regional holidays, so plan to encounter at least one colorful celebration during your seven-day stay in this country. Religious events are guided by the lunar calendar and change from year to year, while political commemorations are dictated by the Roman calendar and therefore take place on the same date annually. Public holidays are marked with an asterisk(*).

*January 4 • *Independence Day* • Marks Burma's independence from the British in 1948 . . . nationwide sports events and other festivities.

*February 12 • *Union Day* • Marks the country's union in 1947 through efforts of Bogyoke Aung San . . . week-long political rally and festival.

February/March • *Enshrinement of hair relics of Lord Buddha in Shwedagon Pagoda more than 2500 years ago* • Occurs on the day of the full moon of the lunar month *Tabaung* . . . special *htamane* rice dish offered to monks and Buddhist images.

*March 2 • *Peasants' Day* • Similar to our Labor Day.

*March 27 • *Armed Forces Day* • Commemorates Burmese resistance against the Japanese . . . military parades and evening fireworks display.

*April • *Burmese New Year* • *Thingyan* (water festival) lasts three to four days with great merriment . . . throwing of water denotes good luck.

*April/May • *Kason Lunar Month* • Triple celebration of Buddha's birth, enlightenment, and attainment of Nirvana upon his death . . . major ritual at Shwedagon Pagoda.

*May 1 • *May Day* • Workers' holiday in the socialist world.

*June/July ● *Waso Festival* ● Marks the beginning of Buddhist Lent . . . three-month period of abstinence.

*July 19 ● *Martyrs Day* ● Commemorates 1947 assassination of Bogyoke Aung San and cabinet . . . memorial wreaths laid at Martyrs Mausoleum.

*October ● *Thadingyut (Festival of Lights)* ● Occurs on full moon in the lunar month of *Thadingyut* and marks the end of Buddhist Lent . . . much dancing, feasting, and merriment.

*November ● *Tazaungdaing Festival* ● A festival of lights . . . all-night weaving contest at Shwedagon Pagoda

*December 25 ● *Christmas Day.*

BACKGROUND MATERIAL   *Burma* by Wilhelm Klein and photography by Gunter Pfannmuller, Apa Productions (HK) Ltd., first edition 1981. A wonderful memento of your trip. Well written and beautifully photographed.

Burma Through Alien Eyes by Helen G. Trager, Asia Publishing House, 1966. Missionary views of the Burmese in the 19th century. Available in Rangoon.

Burmese Days by George Orwell, available in paperback. Novel about British rule and written in the 1930s. Good atmosphere of colonialism.

Burmese Proverbs by Hla Pe, a UNESCO publication. A charming source of Burmese wisdom. Available in Rangoon.

Historical Sites in Burma by Aung Thaw, Director of Archaeology. Published by the government and available in Rangoon. Bad reproduction but the best offered.

Harp of Burma by Michio Takeyama (translated by Howard Hibbett), a UNESCO collection of contemporary works published by Tuttle in paperback. If you read nothing else, don't miss this beautiful story of Japanese POWs in Burma. The novel is among recommended world literature classics for high school students.

Rangoon: A Guide for Tourists and *Mandalay and Environs,* published by U.S. Embassy in Rangoon and written by the American Women's Association. Excellent and practical.

Road Past Mandalay by John Masters, Penguin Books, paperback. Memorable account of young British officer during World War II.

Stilwell and the American Experience in China 1911–1945 by Barbara W. Tuchmann, available in paperback. A great document of the Burma campaign by one of our best historians.

The Burman by Shway Yoe (also known as Sir James G. Scott), His Life and Notions. Available in paperback in Rangoon. Author spent over 30 years as a British civil servant in Burma and captures the essence of the country, even a full century after it was first written.

The Great Railway Bazaar: By Train Through Asia by Paul Theroux. Available in paperback. Thoroughly entertaining train experiences by a popular writer.

We Burmese by Helen G. Trager, Ph.D. and former visiting professor at the University of Rangoon. Published in New York by Praeger. This book explains a great deal about Burmese life and culture.

RANGOON

___ RANGOON IN A CAPSULE ___

Capital of the Socialist Republic of the Union of Burma . . . over 3 million people live tranquilly along the edge of Irrawaddy River delta . . . city surrounded by water on three sides . . . Pazundaung Creek on the east . . . Rangoon River on the south . . . Hlaing River on the east . . . city has an ambience of yesteryear, of 19th-century colonialism left by the British . . . the writings of Rudyard Kipling and Somerset Maugham still ring true . . . landscape dominated by one of Buddhism's most important monuments . . . 2500-year-old **Shwedagon Pagoda** whose golden dome glistens from dawn to dusk . . . a visit here is refreshment for one's soul.

WHAT TO SEE AND DO

Botataung Pagoda ● A 20-minute walk directly east of the Strand Hotel . . . original monument more than 2000 years old destroyed by Allied bombs in 1943 . . . contains relics of Buddha as well as several hundred bronze statues.

Chauk Htat Gyi Pagoda • Another contemporary Buddhist monument . . . several hundred monks live and study here . . . known for enormous reclining Buddha image.

Independence Monument • In the center of **Maha Bandoola Park** . . . represents Union of Burma with five former semi-autonomous states . . . Shan, Kachin, Karen, Kayah, and Chin . . . faces Supreme and High Court building erected by British.

Kaba Aye Pagoda • 1950s monument built by U Nu (independent Burma's first prime minister) just north of Inya Lake . . . dedicated to the cause of world peace . . . contains relics of two Buddhist disciples . . . U Nu also built **Maha Pasan Guha** (great cave) on the grounds.

Koe Htat Gyi Pagoda • Located on Campbell Road . . . huge sitting Buddha image some 5 stories high.

Martyrs Mausoleum • Just north of Shwedagon Pagoda . . . contains **Tombs of Aung San,** father of Burma's independence, and seven other statesmen assassinated with him in 1947 . . . country's most important nationalistic monument.

National History Museum • Located on southern shore of Royal Lakes . . . country's flora and fauna . . . area also encompasses Horticultural and Zoological gardens and Rangoon Zoo where visitors can ride camels and elephants every afternoon.

National Museum • Located a few minutes' walk behind Strand Hotel . . . interesting display of artifacts . . . most renowned item is Lion's Throne from the royal palace at Mandalay . . . other beautifully carved teak pieces from King Thibaw's reign.

Rangoon Arts and Science University • Located on southern shore of Inya Lake . . . boasts some 10,000 students . . . and an impressive library.

Royal Lakes • Tranquil spot in middle of city . . . features **Bogyoke Aung San Park** and statue of the country's most revered martyr.

Shwedagon Pagoda • One of Buddhism's most important and impressive monuments . . . should be visited at least three times . . . at dawn, midday, and dusk . . . center of life for all Burmese . . . said to boast more gold than the Bank of England . . . as well as precious stones from local mines . . . sun strikes a huge emerald on its dome at first ray . . . full of vitality, with worshipers and traders . . . no foot-wear allowed in compound . . . visitors should dress with respect . . . a climb of over 100 steps to the sacred compound . . . many important temples and pavilions along the way . . . look for the massive bronze bell that the British tried to steal in 1824 but the Bur-mese saved it through native ingenuity . . . every visit of Rangoon should begin and end at this site . . . and ask the stewardess which side of the plane will offer the best view when flying out of the country.

State School of Music and Dance • Located on Shwedagon Pa-goda Rd. . . . visitors may observe classes in traditional Burmese dances and music here during weekdays . . . also special performance on weekends . . . inquire at Tourist Burma.

Sule Pagoda • Located in the heart of the city . . . tallest struc-ture in the midtown area . . . originally called **Kyat Athok** . . . supposed to contain a hair from the Lord Buddha . . . second most important religious monument in the capital . . . busy with devotees and merchants.

Rangoon Environs

Until recently, the Burmese government kept Western travelers from visiting certain specific touristic areas to prevent potential harm that might come from warring minority factions within Burma. This is still in effect today in the famous Golden Triangle/opium dealing states. However, government policy has become considerably relaxed and vis-itors who wish to tour places of definite historical and cultural signifi-cance may do so by applying to Tourist Burma in Rangoon and persisting with a gentle firmness.

Bassein • Largest town in the Irrawaddy delta (after Rangoon) . . . a 30-minute flight due west or an 18-hour river journey from Rangoon . . . inhabited today by Karen and Akan tribes . . . some Christian converts . . . famous for three pagodas: **Shwemokhpaw, Tagaung,** and **Thayaunggyaung** . . . a sleepy town known for colorful umbrella cottage industries as well as exports of rice and jute.

Moulmein • Located at mouth of Salween River . . . a 40-minute flight southeast from Rangoon . . . once the country's major teak port . . . visitors can travel into the forests to see the elephants at work . . . noted for **Kyaikthanlan Pagoda** which Kipling immortalized . . . splendid views of city and port from the hilltop . . . see also **Uzena Pagoda** and caves of **Hapayong** and **Kawgaun** with Buddhist images . . . an hour south of the city near the town of **Thanbyuzayat** is an

Allied war cemetery that commemorates POWs who died constructing the infamous Thailand-Burma railway system for the Japanese.

Pegu ● Easy 50-mile road or train journey north of Rangoon . . . daily tours available from Tourist Burma . . . ancient capital of Mon people . . . 270-year Golden Era from mid-11th to late 13th centuries . . . country's greatest seaport in 16th and 17th centuries . . . river changed course and silted up . . . magnificent landmark is **Shwemawdaw (Great Golden God) Pagoda** which contains two Buddha hairs . . . destroyed by earthquake in 1930 but rebuilt in early 50s . . . also impressive is **Shwethalyaung** (Reclining Golden Buddha) considered the country's most beautiful and largest reclining Buddha image . . . look for the **Mahazedi (Great Stupa) Pagoda** that dates from 1560 but has been extensively reconstructed . . . en route between Pegu and Rangoon is **Kaikpun Pagoda** built in 15th century and a lovely spot to picnic . . . detour also to the British War Cemetery where 27,000 Allied soldiers are buried.

Syriam ● 45 minutes by ferry across the Pegu River . . . small industrial town southeast of Rangoon . . . worthy of a daytrip only if you've seen everything else . . . center of Indian life in the country . . . great trading center in 18th century . . . now just an oil refinery and People's Brewery (the local beer) . . . but 2 interesting pagodas in the vicinity, **Kyaik Khauk** and **Kyauktan.**

Sandoway ● Beach resort on southeastern side of Bay of Bengal . . . a few hundred miles northeast of Rangoon . . . daily flights via BAC . . . lovely stretches of sand as well as some interesting pagodas . . . a few decent hotels . . . no one travels to Burma for beach life, but if you have the time an entirely different experience awaits you here.

HOTELS

Dagon (Orient) ● *256-260 Sule Pagoda Rd. Tel: 71140. Cable: CAFETERIA* ● 12 rooms . . . inexpensive . . . in center of town . . . great in a pinch.

★**Inya Lake Hotel** ● *Kaba Aye Pagoda Rd., P.O. Box 1045. Tel: 50644. Cable: INYA LAKEHO. Telex: BM21520 INYAHO* ● 222 rooms . . . built by the Russians . . . out of town and difficult to get back and forth . . . lovely setting but no atmosphere.

Facilities: Western/Oriental dining room. Coffee shop. Two bars. Swimming pool (if it works). Putting green and tennis court.
Managers: U Tin Yi. *Reservations:* Tourist Burma.

Thamada (President) Hotel • *No. 5, Signal Pagoda Rd. Tel: 71499. Cable: THAMADAHO* • 58 rooms . . . situated in the center of town . . . in-between accommodations.
Facilities: Burmese/Chinese/European dining room. Bar. Coffee shop.
Manager: U Myo Khin. *Reservations:* Tourist Burma.

★★**Strand Hotel** • *92 Strand Rd. Tel: 81533. Cable: STRANDHO* • 100 rooms . . . very old world . . . the only place to stay . . . spirit of Somerset Maugham still hangs heavy . . . one of the great old colonial edifices of Southeast Asia . . . worth the whole journey . . . helpful staff.
Facilities: Old-world dining room serving Burmese/Chinese/European food. Great bar where locals come to visit. Entertainment of sorts.
Manager: J. Aungkhine. *Reservations:* Tourist Burma.

WINING AND DINING

Burmese food leans heavily on a vast number of different curry dishes ranging from sweet to mild to quite hot that accompany the daily portion of rice. The Burmese eat everything: fish, fowl, available meats, and plenty of fruits and vegetables. Some dishes can be more spicy than others, but visitors do not have to worry about the danger of chili overkill that is so prevalent in neighboring Thailand. In fact, the curry dishes are more reminiscent of Indian recipes than of anything else, and plenty of bland sticky rice helps soothe your stomach. Some of the most popular local dishes that visitors seem to enjoy are *hinga,* a sweet and sour soup of vegetables; *sibyan,* a fish or meat stew with mild sweet flavoring; and *mohinga,* rice noodles with bits of fish, egg, onions, and banana leaf. Condiments, or little side dishes, like *nagapi* or *ngapigyaw* or *balachaung,* should be tried with some trepidation for they all have a chili and fish base and do not always appeal to the Western palate.

Tea is, of course, the national drink and should be quite safe since the water has been boiled. Bottled sodas and People's Brewery Mandalay Beer (tasty and potent) as well as locally made rum, gin, and whiskey are available where tourists gather. However, frequent visitors stick to the local beer or bring in their own name-brand spirits.

Western food is available in the dining rooms of the Inya Lake and Strand hotels but I thought most of it was BB (bad British) and tasted as if it were prepared in the last century. (I have always said that the British should have taken their recipes back when they returned independence to these countries.) However, Chinese cuisine and real Indian curries and breads are excellent here.

Bamboo House • *3 Thapye Nyo St., near President Hotel compound in West Rangoon* • Noted for Burmese dishes in pleasant setting.

Burma Kitchen • *141 Shwegondaing Rd. Tel: 50493* • Respected for local dishes and frequented by Westerners.

Dagon Hotel (Orient) • *256-260 Sule Pagoda Rd. Tel: 11140* • One of the best for authentic Indian cuisine.

Inya Lake Hotel • *Kaba Aye Pagoda Rd. Tel: 50574* • Burmese, Chinese, and Western food in socialist setting . . . worthy of a detour for one night only, in my opinion.

Karaweik Restaurant • *Located on eastern shoreline of Royal Lake. Tel: 52352* • A great experience for Burmese, Oriental, and Western dishes.

Myananda Restaurant • *Across from Strand Hotel* • Open only in the evening and operated by Strand . . . great for simple Indian dishes in the open air.

Strand Hotel • *92 Strand Rd. Tel: 11533* • Dining room never turned the century . . . good Chinese food here though . . . Western cuisine just passable . . . Old World atmosphere . . . a memorable experience.

Thamada Hotel • *5 Sule Pagoda Rd. Tel: 71499* • Excellent Chinese dishes . . . located in town center.

MANDALAY

MANDALAY IN A CAPSULE

Golden City founded by King Mindon in 1857 . . . who moved his capital from nearby Amarapura . . . tradition says that Buddha prophesized that a great center of Buddhism would spring up at the foot of Mandalay Hill in the 2400th year of his religion (A.D. 1857) . . . most extant monuments date from mid-19th century . . . Mindon built a magnificent fortified city . . . was succeeded by King Thibaw in 1878 . . . but British annexed upper Burma in 1885 . . . city soon lost its cultural glory . . . devastated by the Second World War . . . heavy fighting when Japanese took area . . . later when British took it back . . . fire in May 1981 destroyed many existing monuments and left 35,000 homeless . . . today Mandalay is a sleepy town of approximately 600,000 . . . full of cottage industries where the arts still flourish.

WHAT TO SEE AND DO

Atumashi Kyaung • Known as the Incomparable Monastery before destroyed in 1890 . . . only foundation and stairway left . . . once famous for its beauty and intricate carvings.

Eindawya Pagoda • Built in 1847 . . . in the midst of the city . . . lovely shrine with Buddha image carried back from India.

Kuthodaw Pagoda • "Royal Merit House" located at base of Mandalay Hill . . . known as world's largest book . . . known for **Maha Lawka Marazein Pagoda** . . . over 700 surrounding *pitaka* pagodas built to house marble tables on which entire Buddhist canon Tripitaka were inscribed by some 2400 monks who worked 6 months . . .

dates from 1857 when King Mindon founded Mandalay and 1872 when the 5th Buddhist Synod (ecclesiastical council) was called here.

Kyauktawgyi Pagoda • Located near southern base of Mandalay Hill . . . dates from 1853–78 . . . known for marble Buddha and portrait of King Mindon.

Mahamuni Pagoda • Located a few miles south of Mandalay . . . on the road to Amarapura . . . pagoda also called **Arakan** or **Payagyi (Great Pagoda)** . . . originally built in 1784 . . . destroyed by fire and rebuilt a century later . . . famous for **Mayamuni Buddha** . . . a 12-foot bronze seated figure now covered thickly with gold leaf . . . figure has been to and fro during local wars . . . legend says that Lord Buddha meditated under bodhi tree in the back garden for an entire week . . . stalls full of interesting artifacts line route to temple.

Mandalay Hill • Focal point of the city . . . begin your sightseeing with a pilgrimage up the 1700-plus steps to the top (barefoot, please) past merchants, soothsayers, and local school children . . . stone walk is covered and cool . . . plenty of places to rest . . . small temples and statues line the way . . . **Shweyattaw Buddha** points to site of royal palace . . . statue dates from before 1857 . . . also **Sanda Moke Khit** statue of a woman said to be reborn as King Mindon of Mandalay . . . view from the top well worth the climb . . . only a plaque tells of the heavy losses suffered here by British and Indian troops during World War II.

Mandalay Palace • Dominates city . . . but only a few walls and the moat remain . . . built in 1860s by King Mindon . . . renowned in 19th-century writings for exquisite teak carvings and buildings . . . conquered by British in 1885 . . . devastated in 1945 during heavy fighting between British/Burmese troops and Japanese . . . today known as Mandalay Fort and serves as headquarters for Burmese Army . . . King Mindon's Mausoleum and watchtower still extant.

National Museum and Library • Located near **Shwe Kyi Myint Pagoda** and West Moat Rd. . . . artifacts and historical documents salvaged from the turbulence that has prevailed in this Golden City.

Sandamuni Pagoda • Located near **Kuthodaw Pagoda** . . . built over spot where King Mindon's younger brother, Crown Prince Kanaung was assassinated in 1886 . . . site also where Mindon lived during construction of royal palace . . . contains Buddha image cast in 1802 and over 1700 marble slabs inscribed with Buddhist canons.

Setkayathiha Pagoda • located along Shweta Canal . . . dates from 1814 . . . contains huge bronze Buddha image cast in nearby Ava . . . bodhi tree planted by independent Burma's first prime minister, U Nu.

Shweinbin Kyaung • Monastery contains 13th-century teak carvings . . . some of the few still exist.

Shwe Kyi Myint Pagoda • Built by King Minshinzaw of Pagan in 12th century . . . one of few extant religious monuments to predate founding of Mandalay . . . Buddha image dedicated by the king . . . known for other images in gold, silver, and crystal . . . salvaged from royal palace during British occupation in 1885.

Shwenandaw Kyaung • Located just east of **Atumashi monastery** . . . built by King Thibaw in 1880 . . . materials came from apartment owned by King Mindon . . . renowned for fine carvings and scenes from the 10 great Jataka . . . one of friendliest monasteries in Mandalay!

State School of Fine Art, Music & Dance • Located near Royal Palace along East Moat Rd. . . . visitors may attend rehearsals as well as performances.

Mandalay Environs

Amarapura • Immortal City founded by King Bodawpaya in 1781 . . . served as capital of Upper Burma until 1882 . . . located just a few miles south of Mandalay and reachable by taxi or public bus . . . original city a perfect square with moat surrounding walls of brick . . . little left of citadel today . . . most bricks dismantled and moved to Mandalay by King Mindon . . . still standing are 4 pagodas: **Kyauktawgyi Pagoda** built by King Pagan in 1847 . . . **Patodawgyi Pagoda** built by King Bagyidaw in 1820 and the twins on the bank of the Irrawaddy River . . . **Shwekyetyet** and **Shwekyetkya pagodas** . . . both built in 12th century . . . U Bein Bridge over Taungthaman Lake is considered oldest bridge in the country . . . Amarapura known today for its fine weavers.

Ava • City of Gems (Ratnapura) . . . located where Irrawaddy and Myitnge rivers meet in Upper Burma . . . just east of Amarapura by bus from Mandalay . . . founded in A.D. 1364 and seat of a kingdom until 1841 when abandoned in favor of Amarapura . . . in ruins today but **Maha Aungmye Bozan Monastery** worthy of a detour . . . beautiful white structure with an eerie air . . . also **Htilainshin Pagoda** built by King Kyanzittha during Pagan era . . . south of city are **Lei-**

tutgyi and **Lawkatharaphu pagodas** and **Ava Fort** . . . modern Ava Bridge in northern section was built by British in 1934 . . . they blew it up in the retreat of 1942 . . . reconstructed in 1954 . . . still the only bridge that crosses Irrawaddy River.

Inle Lake ● Reachable by daily flights from Mandalay or Rangoon . . . often included in 1-week tours of Burma . . . beautiful area located in Shan state . . . main attractions are famous Shan leg-rowers on lake, who maneuver long boats with one leg wrapped around the oar . . . local weaving industry famous but handwoven Shan shoulder bags often cheaper elsewhere . . . highly controlled by government here.

Maymyo ● Hill station some 2½ hours by road northeast of Mandalay . . . popular with British colonials . . . breathtaking views at 3500 feet and pleasant temperatures . . . boasts an Old World hotel called Candacraig and 175-acre Botanical Garden . . . also golf and waterfalls for swimming and picnics . . . strictly 19th-century atmosphere . . . known as **Pyinulwin** by the Burmese . . . relax and enjoy in horse-drawn carriages.

Mingun ● Boasts largest ringing bell in the world . . . town one hour by boat from Mandalay . . . King Bodawpaya took temporary residence on island in Irrawaddy River here while building **Mingun Pagoda** on west bank between 1790–97 . . . unfortunately never finished and now considered largest pile of bricks in the world . . . 90-ton bell was cast for the pagoda . . . still impressive and visitors can strike it . . . Mingun is a popular place for day outings for Mandalayans.

Sagaing ● Capital of Shan kingdom from A.D. 1315 until it moved to Ava in 1364 . . . located on right bank of Irrawaddy River . . . south of Mandalay . . . just across Ava Bridge . . . beautiful landscape dotted with religious monuments . . . at least 600 monasteries and 5000 monks live here . . . the air is alive with the ringing of bells and chanting of prayers . . . notable pagodas include 15th-century **Htupayon** . . . **Hsinmyashin** built by King Monhyin of Ava in A.D. 1429 but destroyed by an earthquake in 1955 . . . still contains some valuable images and votive tablets . . . the **Kaunghmudaw (Rajamanicula)** built by King Thalun in 1636 which enshrines a tooth relic of Lord Buddha . . . the **Aungmyelawka** erected in 1782–1819 and the **Ngadatkyi** built in 1657 . . . also the **Ponnyashin Zedi** which contains 2 relics of Buddha and **Onhmin Thonze (30 Caves) Pagoda** . . . **Tilawkaguru cave temple** built about 1672 with rare artifacts of Ava period.

Taunggyi • Hill station north of Inle Lake . . . reachable by daily flights from Mandalay or Rangoon to Heho . . . then by bus . . . only for those with plenty of time . . . local museum is worthy of visit.

HOTELS

Htun La Hotel • *27th Rd. Tel: 21283. Cable: HOTEL-MANDALAY* • 10 rooms . . . some with air conditioning and private bath, some without . . . restaurant serving Burmese, Chinese, and Western food . . . beer garden and swimming pool (when functioning) . . . 5 minutes from Mandalay Hotel.
Manager: C. T. Johns. *Reservations:* Tourist Burma.

★**Mandalay Hotel** • *26 B Rd. Tel: 21004, 22499. Cable: MANHOTEL* • 68 rooms . . . best hotel in town . . . across from Royal Palace . . . reserved for tourist groups . . . comfortable motel-like accommodations . . . restaurant serving Burmese, Chinese, and Western food . . . bar and beer garden.
Manager: U. Tun Kyaw. *Reservations:* Tourist Burma.

WINING AND DINING

The best plan in Mandalay is to stay with the menus available at the Htun La or Mandalay hotels for Burmese, Chinese, and Western dishes. Both hotels also offer a plentiful supply of Mandalay Beer from the People's Brewery. Nyaung Bin Yin on 29th Rd. is a local Burmese restaurant that caters to Western palates, and there are some good Chinese establishments in town—someone at either hotel will guide you to a favorite.

Needless to say, there is no nightlife in Mandalay.

PAGAN

PAGAN IN A CAPSULE

Deserted capital on the Irrawaddy . . . seat of kingdom of Burma from A.D. 1057 to 1284 and center of Burmese Buddhism. . . . 10,000 religious monuments built during its Golden Age . . . now only a few thousand left on a plain 8 miles along the river bank by 2 miles inland . . . structures have suffered ravages of war, time, and natural disaster (including devastating earthquake in 1975) . . . area thought to have been settled as early as 2nd century A.D. . . . and known by classical name **Arimaddana-pura** . . . today just a dusty plain with many breathtaking vistas . . . reachable by daily flights from Rangoon and Mandalay to small airport near Nyaung-U . . . then a half-hour ride to the banks of the Irrawaddy.

WHAT TO SEE AND DO

Abeyadana Temple • Located in Myinkaba village (just 2 km south of Pagan's city walls) . . . named after wife of Pagan's King Kyanzittha (1084–1112) . . . the site is where she waited when he fled the wrath of his brother King Sawlu (1077–1084) . . . resembles Nagayon nearby . . . red brick with perforated windows . . . bell-shaped stupa and interesting frescoes.

Ananda Temple • Whitewashed structure that dominates landscape . . . built by King Kyanzittha to resemble snowcapped Himalayas . . . golden pinnacle of tapering pagoda glistens in the sun . . . plan like a perfect Greek cross . . . 4 large corridors and many narrow passages lit naturally . . . upper terraces decorated with 389 scenes illustrating last 10 great **Jatakas** . . . largest collection of glazed plaques found on any shrine . . . colossal Buddha enshrined within structure . . . plus many, many smaller images . . . earthquake damage restored by Burma's archaeology department . . . ask to see upper terraces for views . . . especially near sunset . . . 2 Buddha footprints.

Bupaya Pagoda • Located on banks of Irrawaddy River . . . thought to be first pagoda built in Pagan . . . commissioned by King Pyusawti during 2nd century A.D. . . . bulbous shape of dome definitely predates King Anawrahta and the Golden Age of Pagan.

Dhammayangi Temple • Pagan's largest shrine . . . built by King Narathu (1167–1170) to atone for past sins . . . one of best preserved . . . resembles Ananda Temple in plan . . . brilliant masonry but structure never completed . . . Narathu assassinated by Indian prince . . . located southeast of city walls.

Gawdawpalin Temple • Located near the Irrawaddy . . . built in Burmese style by King Narapatisithu (1173–1210) . . . one of area's most impressive monuments . . . 2 stories of splendor . . . unfortunately badly damaged during 1975 earthquake . . . under reconstruction.

Htilominlo Temple • Located between Pagan and Nyaung-U . . . constructed by King Nantaungmya (1210–1234) whose other name was Htilominlo . . . considered the last Burmese-style temple built in Pagan . . . of a class with Sulamani Temple.

Kubyaukkyi Temple • Located in Myinkaba village, near Pagan . . . built by Rajakumar on death of father King Kyanzittha in A.D. 1112 . . . has features of early Pagan temples . . . dark corridors lit by perforated stone windows . . . excellent example of its period . . . fine Jataka prints and Buddha images inside . . . as well as Mayazedi Stone inscribed in four languages: Burman, Mon, Pali, and Pyu.

Kyaukku Umin • Cave temple near Nyang-U . . . built against side of deep ravine . . . long tunnels excavated . . . huge seated Buddha faces entrance . . . attributed to King Kyanzittha . . . upper stories date to King Narapatisithu's reign (1174–1211).

Lokananda Pagoda • One of 3 pagodas built by King Anawrahta . . . erected in A.D. 1029 . . . graceful white stupa with tall, cylindrical golden bell . . . 3 octagonal terraces . . . lower 2 can be ascended by stairs on all 4 sides.

Mahabodhi Temple • Constructed during reign of Nantaungmya (1211–1234) . . . exact replica of Indian temple where Buddha achieved enlightenment . . . only architectural style of its kind in Burma . . . unfortunately damaged in 1975 earthquake . . . now reconstructed.

Manuha Temple • Built in A.D. 1059 by King Manuha of Thaton, whom Anawrahta deposed and captured . . . was brought to Pagan along with numerous Mon architects, artists, and craftsmen to begin the Golden Age of construction . . . Manuha worried he would become a temple slave, so built this monument to gain heavenly merits . . . unfortunately, 2nd story collapsed during 1975 earthquake but was restored . . . known for 4 large Buddhas in shrine, one reclining . . . very cramped.

Mimalaungkyaung Temple • Located near south gate of old city . . . built in A.D. 1174 by King Narapatisithu . . . small and square structure . . . tall spiral pagoda . . . Narapatisithu avenged his brother, then-king . . . murdered him for wife-stealing . . . then ascended throne (1173–1210).

Mingalazedi Pagoda • Located just south of Pagan . . . last of great stupas built during Golden Age . . . construction said to precipitate fall of Pagan . . . built by King Narathihapate in A.D. 1284, but his arrogance dethroned him . . . was forced to tear down many fine temples in area to rebuild fortifications . . . army of Kublai Khan was on its way . . . nonetheless this monument represents the pinnacle of Burmese architecture . . . noted for unglazed Jataka plaques around its terraces.

Myinkaba Pagoda • Located on banks of Myinkaba River in village of same name . . . marks spot where Anawrahta killed half-brother Sokkate in A.D. 1044 and took monarchy . . . Anawrahta erected temple to expiate his crime . . . low round terraces and elongated bell . . . almost cylindrical in shape . . . very early style.

Nagayon Temple • Stands on site where Kyanzittha hid from brother Sawlu, his predecessor on Pagan throne . . . here he was given protection by a naga . . . structure has elegant form . . . corner stupas on all terraces and graceful pinnacle . . . lovely paintings in corridors and double lifesize Buddha image under hood of an enormous naga (serpent).

Nanpaya Temple • said to have been captive King Manuha's residence in Myinkaba . . . converted to temple . . . very early style . . . brick faced with stone . . . perforated stone windows . . . crenelated roof line . . . great place for house arrest.

Nathlaungkyaung Temple • Constructed in A.D. 931 by Taung-thugyi . . . dedicated to Hindu god Vishnu . . . was Pagan's great Hindu temple during Golden Age . . . only main hall and superstructure still standing . . . exterior of building and porch now lost . . . famous central **Vishnu statue** seated on Garuda was carried off to Berlin Museum at the turn of this century . . . a standing image of **Siva** in Pagan Museum may have belonged here.

Ngakywenadaung Pagoda • Attributed to King Taungthugyi . . . constructed in 10th century . . . definitely belongs to pre-Anawrahta period . . . similar in style to Bupaya Pagoda . . . bulbous-shaped structure on cylindrical base . . . unaesthetic pile of bricks.

Pagan Museum • Located near Thiripyitsaya Hotel . . . contains displays of what Burmese have managed to salvage of the artistic wealth of area . . . statues, paintings, architectural embellishments, etc. as well as votive panels collected in the region . . . written in Burmese, Mon, Pyu, Pali, Tamil, Thai, and Chinese . . . quite a meeting of Asian minds.

Pebingyaung Pagoda • Constructed in 12th century . . . noted for Sinhalese type of stupa with square chamber between bell and finial . . . confirms close ties between Ceylon and Burma during this period . . . King Anawrahta sent ships and supplies to squelch Hindu Cholas attempted invasion of Ceylon . . . also sent monks to strengthen future of Theravada Buddhism in Ceylon.

Pitakat Taik • King Anawrahta's library . . . built to house elephant loads of scriptures brought to Pagan from Thaton following his conquest . . . 51-feet square and 60-feet high . . . entrance on east with 3 perforated stone windows on other sides . . . interior conforms to plan of early Pagan temples . . . one of few secular structures preserved in Pagan . . . unfortunately altered in 1783 by King Bodawpaya . . . had finials added to corners of 5 roofs.

Sarabha Gateway • Eastern gateway into Pagan from Nyaung-U . . . only section of King Pyinbya's 9th-century city walls still standing . . . Pagan's guardian spirits, Nga Tin De and sister Shwemyethana, have prayer niches here . . . most important spirits in Burma after King of Nats, Thagyamin.

Shwegugyi Temple • Situated up road to Nyaung-U . . . built by King Alaungsithu in A.D. 1131 . . . the king died in the temple at grand old age of 81 . . . temple faces north toward former royal palace site . . . stands on brick platform . . . hall and inner courtyard lit by large windows and doors . . . denotes Burmese style architecture that evolved here.

Shwesandow Pagoda • Erected by King Anawrahta in A.D. 1057 following victorious return from Thaton . . . stupa enshrines hairs of Lord Buddha sent to Anawrahta by King of Pegu . . . also called **Ganesh Temple** because elephant-headed Hindu god images stood at corners of all 5 terraces.

Shwezigon Pagoda • One of most venerated in all Burma . . . begun by King Anawrahta (1044–1077) . . . finished by Kyanzittha (1084–1112) . . . most important shrine in Pagan . . . Buddha's collar bone, frontlet bone, and tooth here . . . pilgrims from throughout Burma arrive every autumn for Shwezigon Pagoda Festival . . . one of most popular in the country . . . considered prototype of later Burmese stupas . . . elegant structure with golden dome and *hti* despite many renovations from subsequent rulers . . . a favored place to visit.

Sulamani Temple • Located midway between Pagan and Minnanthu village . . . one of Pagan's fine 2-storied monuments . . . built by King Narapatisithu (1173–1210) 10 years after ascending the throne . . . upper story sits on pillar . . . seated Buddha images on all 4 sides of lower floor . . . also some 18th-century paintings.

Thandawgya Image • Huge seated Buddha built by King Narathihapate in A.D. 1284 . . . almost 20-feet high . . . hands signify moment of enlightenment . . . has a slightly jaundiced appearance but nonetheless important to the Golden Age monuments . . . located near Thatbyinnyu Temple.

Thatbyinnyu Temple • Temple of omniscience . . . tallest structure in Pagan . . . built by Alaungsithu (1112–1167) . . . structure consists of 2 enormous cubes . . . upper story reached from inside staircase . . . Buddha image here as well as wonderful view of Pagan plain . . . resembles Ananda Temple but not designed in Greek crossstyle . . . small **Tally Pagoda** nearby built from same bricks . . . ruins of bell pillars in former monastery nearby.

HOTELS

Irra Inn • *located near Bupaya Pagoda about a mile from Thiripyitsaya Hotel. Tel: 24* • 27 rooms . . . singles, doubles, and a suite with private bath . . . no air conditioning.

Facilities: Restaurant with Burmese, Chinese, and Western menu. Bar.

Manager: U Win Pe. *Reservations:* Tourist Burma.

★**Thiripyitsaya Hotel** ● *located overlooking Irrawaddy River in the midst of the ruins. Tel: A28* ● 36 rooms . . . modern resort hotel style . . . large clean rooms with air conditioning and private bath . . . only place to stay in Pagan.

Facilities: Restaurant with Burmese, Chinese, and Western menu. Bar. Gift shop. Nice grounds. Accepts Amex card.

Manager: U Myo Khin. *Reservations:* Tourist Burma.

WINING AND DINING

The best bet in Pagan is the dining room of the Thiripyitsaya Hotel. Otherwise there are a number of inns scattered among the ruins: the **Irra** near Bupaya Pagoda, the **Cooperative** near Gawdawpalin Temple, the **Moe Moe** near Mimalaung-kyaung, the **Burma Rest House** near the BAC office, and the **Aung Mahaya Lodge** near Shwegugyi Temple.

Visitors to Pagan are grateful for the lack of nightlife, for fatigue sets in soon after dinner from all that walking among the ruins!

SHOPPING

Burma may be an isolated, so-called third-world country, but inveterate shoppers will find a treasure trove here of local handcrafts and natural resources. Some of the world's finest semiprecious and precious stones are mined in Burma's soil, including Blood Ruby and Imperial Jade (which even the Chinese admit is superior in quality to anything found in their country). Other splendid gems available for adornment include sapphires, aquamarine, topaz, emeralds, amethysts, and lapis lazuli. Indeed, the abundance of such gifts from nature explains why the annual February **Gems and Pearl Emporium** at the Inya Lake Hotel in Rangoon is an exciting event and draws dealers from all over the world to bid upon what the government-controlled industry places in auction.

If you are not an expert gemologist but still plan to make some major purchase in unset stones, the government advises that visitors not stray from the **Diplomatic Shop** on Sule Pagoda Rd. (and its various branches throughout the country). Here, in something that resembles the Friendship Stores in the People's Republic of China, are cases and cases of gems in full range of brilliance, quality, and weight. The prices are set by the government, and payment must be in hard currency (U.S. dollars or traveler's checks). Street peddlers and relatives of your driver and/or guide will have stones at better prices, gems so well-made that even top jewelers often cannot tell that they are synthetic. Artificial stones are *everywhere* in Burma, and there is no such thing as a bargain-basement authentic ruby!

The Diplomatic Shop should be everyone's first stop, for it gives a general view of what beautiful handcrafts are available throughout the country: exquisite lacquerware from the Pagan area; gold leaf and teak carvings from Mandalay; silverwork from Sagaing; copper and brass items from Mandalay; beautiful handwoven material lengths and embroideries; and the popular Shan shoulder bags. Although prices are higher in this state-run store, the one-stop shopping is convenient. With all the sightseeing that you may wish to pack into a seven-day stay (not to mention the transportation delays), you'll find there is often not enough time to do extensive shopping while touring. Fortunately, there is a small branch of the Diplomatic Shop at the airport for last-minute items, but the secret of departing Burma with invaluable souvenirs is to buy what you simply can't live without when you first see it.

Market people will love the sights and sounds of the vast local outdoor emporia in both Rangoon and Mandalay. In addition to imported consumer items (most of them smuggled over the border from Thailand), there are stalls and stalls of foodstuffs and local craftsmen selling their artistry. Rangoon's largest and most prosperous marketplace is the **Bogyoke Aung San,** which the British always called the Scott Market. It is located across from Rangoon's red-brick moorish-style railway station, at the corners of Sule Pagoda Rd. and Bogyoke Aung San St., and it has *everything!* A great place for photographers as well as for a little bargaining.

Other spots of interest for frenetic activity and lots of local color are the **Open Air Market** off Shwedagon Pagoda Rd. and the **Thein Gyi Zei** (also known as the Indian Market) which has mainly fruits and vegetables. If your nostrils can take the pungent odors, it's worth a walk through. Rangoon also has a large Chinatown section, and the **Chinese Market** can be found on Lan Ma Daw Rd. not far from the Chinese Temple.

Around Mandalay's Diamond Jubilee Clocktower (erected in honor of Queen Victoria's 60th year as Monarch) is the **Zegyo Market,** which brings together the varied ethnic groups of Central and Upper Burma. At night, the Zegyo Market has the flavor of Istanbul's great bazaar and about as much variety in goods for sale. And since Mandalay was created as the artistic and religious center of Burma, you can find beautiful handcrafts as well as curios and antiques. Shan shoulder bags can be bought here cheaper than where they are made, and the renowned teak carvings of Mandalay are less expensive here than in the Diplomatic Shop. In any event, the Zegyo Market is about the only diversion in Mandalay during the evening hours, so you should not miss it.

Pagan has no great market, but the area is full of lacquerware cottage industries where you can pick up gold-leaf wedding baskets and such. Local guides will be delighted to act as agent/interpreters for a nice tip, of course. In any event, save some money for shopping in Burma—and enjoy the experience!

HONG KONG

HISTORY

The territory of Hong Kong, previously known as a British Crown Colony and later as simply a "colony," still sits precariously on the edge of China (now known as the People's Republic of China) "existing on borrowed time in a borrowed place," according to Eurasian author Han Suyin (*Love is a Many Splendored Thing,* etc.). Although much has changed in Hong Kong since the original edition (1983) of this guidebook, a great deal has stayed the same. There is still no place quite like it on this earth. As a destination, Hong Kong sells itself through contented shoppers, sightseers and gourmands who return home extolling the experience of a few days spent in frantic pursuit of pleasures around the perimeter of the world's most exciting harbor.

What Lord Palmerston, Queen Victoria's Foreign Secretary, once called a "barren rock" has become one of the 20th century's most astounding products. Its prosperity and vitality epitomizes the modern age in which we live, unhampered by tradition and able to bend with the political winds from all directions. Great fortunes are made almost daily, as the only two things that matter here are money and land. There is an obvious disregard for "culture," although the majority of Chinese do take the time to see that their ancestors are kept content (lest they cause misfortune to the living). Hong Kong is the great melting pot for all Asia, and never ceases to be a fascination to all visitors.

The fact that Hong Kong exists at all is due to the silting up of the Pearl River in the early 1800s, which caused the Portuguese territory of Macau to lose its status as the primary trading post between China and the West. Heung Gung, that "fragrant harbor" just 40 miles to the east, was a natural replacement for the British to establish their *hongs* (trading companies) and *godowns* (warehouses). It had a sheltered and defendable harbor, and was still convenient enough to Canton to handle the transport of "foreign mud" (opium) that gave the white man such clout.

So the British forced the cessation of Victoria Island "in perpetuity" in 1842; won the tip of Kowloon Peninsula (the Tsimshatsui area) and Stonecutters Island "in perpetuity" in 1856; and leased for 99 years some 350 square miles of New Territories and 234 other islands. Nine-tenths of Hong Kong's land reverts to China on June 30, 1997, in a contract the present regime has never acknowledged as valid (because it was made under a previous government and probably under duress), although Beijing does accept annually the token U.S.$1,000 "rent."

Sophisticated Sinologists agree that Hong Kong will remain the same, even if most of its land area falls under the jurisdiction of Beijing. Like bamboo, the most stalwart and reliable of Asian flora, Hong Kong has always bounced back from its travails and appeared somehow stronger than ever! It has survived several wars and pestilence during its less than a century and a half of existence, including the Christmas Day 1941 invasion by the Japanese Imperial fleet. It has absorbed hundreds of thousands of illegal Chinese immigrants and Cultural Revolution–inspired riots of the late 1960s.

However, the economy of Hong Kong is resilient, and Beijing has agreed to a "hands-off" policy for several decades. It is easy to remember the 1967 hysteria when the people of Hong Kong panicked following a period of left-wing rioting and to recall the stock market crash in 1973 when the Hang Seng fell from a peak of 1774.4 to 146—when many of the "new riche" found themselves just plain folks once again. This still is the third busiest port in the world and its work force has created the largest "emporia" in Asia, as items from back alley sweatshops flood the many multistory merchandise marts. "If you can't find it in Hong Kong, and for less, it doesn't exist" is the motto of experienced shoppers everywhere.

Unfortunately, however, many of Hong Kong's noteworthy landmarks have *not* survived. After years of bitter controversy, the Peninsula Group tore down the beautiful old Repulse Bay Hotel, where lunch on the terrace was a time-honored tradition. (Alas, the developers retained the facade and lunch is still served "al fresco," but it is just not the same.) That bastion of colonialism itself, the famous Hong Kong Club, also lost out and was replaced with a member-supported office high rise. Even the familiar Hong Kong and Shanghai Bank, that symbol of financial stability, saw the wrecker's ball and a new structure (said to be the costliest building in the world) now stands on the site. Alas, even the Bank of China has a new and stylish personality in a glamorous structure designed by Chinese-American architect I. M. Pei.

Tsimshatsui, Kowloon and the New Territories have changed so much that only The Peninsula stands as bastion of what once was (albeit from a recent US $20 million restoration project). It is said that you could sit in the lobby of The Pen and eventually run into everyone you know. Still true, but meanwhile most of the world passes by that you haven't yet met! From the landmark Star Ferry tower, you can walk up both sides of Tsimshatsui, past elegant hotels and condominiums, shopping arcades, and restaurants to tempt every palate.

Hong Kong is booming again and its business aggression has returned following the lease agreement between Britain and China that calls for the return of territory to the mainland in 1997. Indeed, tourism officials feel that the settlement of the lease will have a positive effect on Hong Kong tourism for it is such an important gateway to travel in China. In fact, the Excelsior Hotel in Wanchai, overlooking the famous Noon Day Gun, is accepting reservations for June 30, 1997, when it is expected the gun will salute Hong Kong's return to China.

More than one-quarter of all tourist arrivals in Hong Kong are from North America, according to officials, and shopping is still the number-one interest, although day trips to China are also popular. With the opening of a superhighway through the New Territories, China will become an even more attractive extension of Hong Kong visits. The building of more and more first-class hotels and lower transpacific air fares also adds to Hong Kong's appeal as the second most popular destination on Orient tour programs.

The decade of the 90s promises to be one of Hong Kong's more interesting and eventful as the territory prepares not to become independent, as the British have generally left their former colonies, but a "special autonomous region" of the most populated country in the world— with its own laws, currency, and guarantees of individual liberties. While the British are leaving a stable and prosperous (many of them have made fortunes here over two centuries) situation, what they are not leaving is any form of democracy as the western world knows it. Such lack of a more representative government for the Hong Kong Chinese has been a source of some debate the past few years, and one suspects that, as the world is turning, China will accept a far different Hong Kong than what we know now.

Meanwhile—and for the next decade—there will be no other place quite like it in the world!

HONG KONG IN A CAPSULE

1067 square kilometers of of a so-called "territory" . . . center of capitalistic endeavor in the Far East . . . 500 Rolls Royces registered in the colony . . . land area consists of Kowloon Peninsula, New Territories, Victoria Island, and several other islands in the archipelago . . . Britain's lease on the New Territories terminates in 1997 . . . present population of Hong Kong is 5.6 million . . . 98 + % are Chinese but practically every other nationality is represented here . . . Cantonese and English are official languages . . . subtropical climate . . . hot, humid, wet summers and springs . . . cool, dry, sunny winter months . . . beautiful harbor . . . exciting tourist destination.

PLANNING AHEAD

HONG KONG TOURIST ASSOCIATION (HKTA) is tops for encouraging travelers to visit this exciting city-port and then taking excellent care of them upon arrival. HKTA employees and members are *always* courteous and efficient; they dispense a number of continually updated publications as well as verbal information of quality and accuracy. Maps, shopping guides, walking tours, and special-interest folders are well researched and well written.

Headquarters and Information and Gift Centre of the HKTA is the 35th floor of Jardine House (that 50-story building that elicits the rude jokes). Telephone is 5–244191. There is an information center in Buffer Hall at Kai Tak Airport as well as charming young greeters who welcome you with a packet full of information as you clear immigration. Other centers can be found at G2 Ground Floor, Royal Garden Hotel, Tsim Sha Tsui East, and Star Ferry Concourse, Kowloon.

HKTA is bullish worldwide. In North America, the offices are in Suite 404, 360 Post St., San Francisco, CA 94104 (Tel: 415–781–4582); Suite 2323, 333 North Michigan Ave., Chicago, IL 60601 (Tel: 312–782–3872); and 590 Fifth Ave., New York, NY 10036 (Tel: 212–869–5008) and Suite 1220, 10940 Wilshire Blvd., Los Angeles, CA 90024 (Tel: 213–208–4582).

VISAS are not required for a stay in the colony of up to 30 days if travelers have a valid U.S. passport. Canadians with valid passports may stay up to three months sans visa.

INOCULATIONS for cholera are not required for entry unless you are arriving from an infested area. Check with your doctor or the Public Health Service for a current list of infected areas.

ENTRY BY AIR into Hong Kong is one of the great travel experiences, whether your plane arrives over Stonecutter's Island and New Kowloon or is brought in through the ''gap'' between Victoria Island and the New Territories. The thoroughly modern **Kai Tak International Airport,** with its 11,130-foot runway extending right into the harbor, is the hub of Far East traffic. At last count, 33 international airlines provided some 1320 scheduled flights weekly—and all this between the hours of 6:30 a.m. and midnight when the airport closes down for (among other things) noise pollution.

In Eastern Kowloon, Kai Tak is a 15- to 25-minute drive to the major hotels, and transport to and from the airport is plentiful. If your luggage is on the light side, the coach service to hotels in Tsimshatsui and Hong Kong-side is a bargain (about U.S.$1 to the farthest point). There is also a taxi stand, but be prepared to stand in line, especially if several 747s arrive simultaneously. If you are expected at one of the more luxurious hostelries in the colony, a Rolls or Bentley (at the very least, a super Mercedes) will be awaiting you at the exit marked "hotel transportation." The charge will be added to your hotel bill—but what a way to live!

Kai Tak is actually a well-organized international airport; it just seems chaotic because of the people who use it. There are large push-carts (that *you* push) to carry your baggage from the claim area through customs check to the transport terminus. Along the route you will pass an HKTA information center (for hotel reservations), an HKHA counter for hotel reservations, and a currency exchange window. Both do business concurrent with airport hours. There is also a left-luggage counter, upstairs in the departure hall, that offers inexpensive security for as long as you like. If you feel confused, make yourself heard above the din and one of the many security officers will point the way.

DEPARTURE BY AIR is something else again. Arrive early, because there always seem to be long lines ahead! Not to mention the mounds of cartons and crates that go along with the baggage. Be prepared to wait for check-in, immigration check, and the security clearance before you even see the departure lounge.

However, if you have arrived in one of those Rolls, Bentleys, or super Mercedes, chances are the hotel personnel at the airport will see you grandly through check-in. These fellows know their way around and are even adept at finding an empty airplane seat when an emergency situation arises for a guest.

Departure tax is HK$100 per person, HK$50 for children 2 to 12 years of age.

ARRIVAL BY SEA via one of the luxury liners that calls at Hong Kong is through the splendid **Ocean Terminal** at the southwestern tip of Kowloon Peninsula (catty-corner to the Star Ferry Concourse). This convenient passenger-ship terminal is an ever-expanding complex of shops, restaurants, and services stretching from Star House and the Hong Kong Hotel down Canton Road to the new Marco Polo Hotel. You need never see the light of day! Most cruise stays average about three days (good shopping spree time, by any standards), but some vessels are now drydocking in Hong Kong (where repairs are cheaper) while their passengers luxuriate in one of the nearby hotels.

If you wish to take a ship to Hong Kong, absolutely the *only* way to see the harbor at first hand, contact Cunard Line (for Sea Goddess ships and former NAC vessels), Princess Cruises, Royal Cruise Line, Ocean Pearl Cruises, Seabourn Cruise Line, Society Expeditions and Royal Viking Line. There are many other cruise ships coming afloat— those that sail down the Pearl River from Ghuangzhou (actually the port of Whampoa) or one of the many new arrivals from Japan. A new passenger pier is being built in Tsim Sha Tsui.

DUTY-FREE is the byword in the world's most famous duty-free port! Aside from asking about the usual compliment of cigarettes (200), cigars (50), tobacco (½ lb.), some perfume and "spirits" (1 liter), customs officials wave most travelers through. However, these same officials are very tough if they suspect gold or dope smuggling, since drug addiction is the colony's number one crime (and the gold goes without saying). It is also unwise to bring firearms into Hong Kong. They will be confiscated until your departure and you may become suspect of other things—just by association.

Children are okay but your loving pets are not, unless you wish to subject them to six-month quarantine under dubious supervision. Knowledgeable American veterinary specialists will suggest that you leave your pets behind during your Far East forays. For seeing-eye dogs, discuss the situation with your travel agent and the local HKTA office for procedure or write to the Department of Agriculture & Fisheries, 393 Canton Road, Tsimshatsui, Kowloon, Hong Kong (Tel. 3–688111).

CURRENCY of Hong Kong is the dollar (HK$). Each Hong Kong dollar is worth approximately U.S.$.128 (7.8 to 1), although the exact exchange rate fluctuates daily. Notes used are HK$10 (green), HK$50 (blue), HK$100 (red), HK$500 (yellow), and HK$1000 (orange), as issued by either the Standard Chartered or the Hong Kong and Shanghai Banking Corporation (known locally as the Honkers and Shankers). Careful with the coins as they can be confusing. They come in 10-, 20-, and 50-cent pieces as well as HK$1, HK$2, and HK$5.

The free market in Hong Kong extends to currency exchange; you may carry in, have on hand, and take out as much as you like. Money is often considered the "religion" of Hong Kong; the changers and lenders do big business—the former from their little cages by the side of the street, the latter in the glamorous halls of the banking corporations. It is possible to change any world currency in Hong Kong, often with just the wink of an eye, but watch out when you enter other Far East areas, as more stringent laws may prevail.

LOCAL TIME in Hong Kong is Greenwich Mean Time plus 8 hours. For our purposes, Hong Kong is exactly 13 hours ahead of Eastern Standard Time, 12 hours in advance of Eastern Daylight Time. Add another hour for each mainland U.S. time zone (add 5 for Hawaii). Hong Kong is in the same time zone as Beijing, Taipei, Macau, Kuala Lumpur, Singapore, Jakarta, and Manila, but 1 hour behind Seoul and Tokyo. It is 1 hour ahead of Bangkok and 1½ hours ahead of Rangoon.

LOCAL CURRENT is 200 volts/50 cycles, with the craziest assortment of plugs and sockets you ever saw. Electric razors can be used with most hotel multifitting bathroom plugs, and converters are available. However, the savvy hotels (Regent, Peninsula, and Hong Kong Hilton at this writing) have now added 110/120 sockets for flat American plugs so you need not leave home without your hair dryer and curling iron.

LOCAL WATER prides itself as being potable. Most reputable restaurants now serve bottled water, and elsewhere there is little problem. Use your discretion, however, in drinking the water served in out-of-the-way places (especially if from a communal cup).

OFFICIAL LANGUAGES in the colony are English and Chinese, with Cantonese the most widely spoken dialect. Mandarin, Shanghainese, Fukkienese, and other dialects are also spoken—loudly if not clearly. Many Chinese here tend to shout, especially when bargaining. Most signs, however, are bilingual and shopkeepers usually speak English, so you should have no problem finding your way around.

Of the four local English-language **newspapers,** I consider two as passable morning dailies—the *South China Morning Post* and the *Hong Kong Standard* (in that order). The *Asian Wall Street Journal* is put together in Hong Kong and ready in the early afternoon each day as is the Hong Kong edition of the *International Herald Tribune*. The Asian editions of *Time, Newsweek,* and *Reader's Digest* are also printed here. In addition, the *Far East Economic Review* and *Asiaweek,* also weekly magazines, originate in the colony.

There are two **radio** stations and two **television** channels devoted entirely to English-language programming. Check the local listings in the morning papers for news, music, and the back episodes of your favorite sitcom. For local color, the Kung Fu films on the Chinese television channels are great fun to watch; or you may want to catch a closed-circuit movie in your hotel.

Newsstands overflow with good reading material and the **bookstores** are excellent, especially **Swindon's** in Ocean Terminal and Ocean Centre and the **SCMP Family Bookshop** on the Kowloon side of the Star Ferry.

BUSINESS HOURS in Hong Kong range from 8 a.m. to midnight, depending upon whom your dealing concerns. The Chinese work hard and local services are open late. It is not unusual to have a late fitting for that Hong Kong suit. European-style concerns are the 9 a.m.–5 p.m. variety and banks have the usual "bankers hours." Expect many offices to close from noon to 2 p.m. (and the principals to return well after 2). Visitors can usually make their own hours, and a great deal can be accomplished later in the day. More deals are actually made in the Mandarin's Captain's Bar or the Lobby of the Peninsula than anywhere, I am told.

Local trade associations and multinational company offices are located easily through the English telephone directories. The **American Chamber of Commerce** is located in Swire House, Central District and the **American Club** is in Exchange Square. The famous **Foreign Correspondents Club** has moved to Ice House St. The **U.S. Consulate** is located at 26 Garden Rd. near the Peak Tram Terminal (Tel: 5–239011). The **Canadian Consulate** is at One Exchange Square, 11–14 floors, 8 Connaught Place, Central (Tel: 5–8104321).

TIPPING is a terminal problem in Hong Kong. Taxi drivers don't expect much, if anything, but everyone else does. In some hotels, porters will scoff at the change you have been able to muster up from the bottom of your bag. Baggage handlers usually expect HK$1 per piece, especially at Kai Tak International Airport (where porterage is billed as complimentary). Hotels and restaurants attach a 10% service charge to *everything,* but apparently it does not go to the service personnel. One hotel manager admitted recently that it was a tax "thing" (dodge), which explains a great deal about the system. Porters expect at least HK$3 per bag; washroom attendants at least HK$1; and waiters like to keep the "change." If service has been rendered with a smile, then a good tip is always in order. One friend, whose waiter slapped the bill down with "service is not included, Madam," replied, "As far as I am concerned, there wasn't any!" Of course, if you are riding in that Rolls or Bentley, HK$10 or $20 to the driver is expected. And for that fellow who found you a seat on the airplane . . . what is it worth to you?

TELEPHONE AND TELEX service in Hong Kong is superb. International direct dialing (IDD) from major hotels is easy and inexpensive as you are charged per second and no longer in minute increments. If you don't wish to pay the 10% service charge at your hotel, Cable & Wireless has public offices at Exchange Square (open 24 hours), Mercury House in Wanchai, at the Lee Gardens Hotel in Causeway Bay, and at the Passenger Terminal Building, Kai Tak Airport.

Telex services are equally good at major hotels or the above C & W offices. A businessman's center is also available in most hotels, with bilingual secretarial service, meeting areas, and complimentary coffee. Without fail, the personnel is attractive, helpful, and cheerful.

Local telephone calls are not charged to your hotel bill (yet), because subscribers receive unlimited calls. Although there is no long distance in Hong Kong, there are area codes for Hong Kong Island (5), Kowloon (3), and the New Territories (0), if calling from outside those areas. Public telephones (gray or pink) require HK$1 for the first three minutes. Dial 999 in case of emergency, no coin needed.

WHAT TO WEAR in Hong Kong is what you would wear in any thriving metropolis. Casual city clothes are the best bet for daytime sightseeing, shopping, and dining. In the evening, most European restaurants prefer a coat and tie for men (Hong Kong is the most dressy of the Far East cities). Beach wear is fine for the outer island tours, and cottons are best during the humid summer months (Apr. through Oct.).

Hong Kong is considered ''subtropical'' and therefore has a lovely, dry, winter season (Nov. to Mar.). A meteorologist may insist that there are actually four seasons in Hong Kong, but that's a matter of opinion; it's either hot and humid, or cool and fairly dry. For the cooler days, bring along a light coat and a few sweaters.

If your visit is scheduled from mid-March through September, bring along an umbrella! This is the rainy season and the tropical storm season, and so-called typhoons (big winds) can paralyze the place for a day or two. Hotel service continues unhampered, but tours and transportation stops and all small craft head for the nearest typhoon shelter. These storms are quite unpredictable, and there is nothing to be done but wait them out with good companionship and/or a good book!

LOCAL TRANSPORTATION throughout the colony has never been better or more varied. If you don't wish to spend your days languishing in the back seat of a hired car, or on a tour bus, grab your coin purse and expect some proper adventures!

You haven't been to Hong Kong until you have crossed the harbor via the **Star Ferry,** still the most romantic and inexpensive way to commute. Daily service between Edinburgh Place on Hong Kong Island and the clock tower-topped terminal in the Tsimshatsui section of Kowloon departs every five minutes from 6:30 a.m.–11:30 p.m. daily. This unbeatable ride takes seven to ten minutes, depending upon the weather and traffic in this busy port. By day, you are a participant in the world's third most active harbor; at night, you become an observer as the twinkling lights of prosperity enfold the harbor. All this for a mere HK80 cents for first class (top deck), HK60 cents for down below. Top deck is better for views and photographers but don't discount below, especially if you like to sit next to chickens and such. Automatic turnstiles have been installed, so save those coins up to $1.

The second most popular transportation experience is the **Peak Tram,** a cog-wheel railway departing from its very own station on Garden Road (just a short hike uphill from the Hilton Hotel). Since 1888 this funicular railway has been carrying local residents and breathless visitors to the top of this 1809-foot peak for the best view in town. There are five intermediate stops—so sit tightly—before a hideous structure (in my judgment) known as the Peak Tower. Have a good walk around the top of the peak before you settle down for tea. One way adult fare is HK$6, children HK$3, and there's a good path down for the energetic.

There are also 162 double-deck **trams** (in business since 1904) rambling noisily but regularly along the North Shore of Hong Kong Island only, from Kennedy Town (far west) through Western District, Central, Wanchai, Causeway Bay, and ending in Shaukeiwan at the eastern end. For a mere HK$.60 (in exact change), you can do the entire 9-mile, 65-stop trip in about an hour and a half and what a tour of the "real" Hong Kong. Avoid the rush hours and try to get a window seat on the top of a double-decker. And, if you're looking for an unusual party idea and have 100 friends in Hong Kong, you can rent a double-decker for approximately HK$300 per hour—plus the catering costs.

The English-style, double-decker **buses** that make their way around Hong Kong and Kowloon are rambling giants, too large for the thoroughfares and often too crowded. There is good airport service and Cross-Harbour Tunnel service (minimum fare HK$2.80), but most other modes of transportation are safer and more comfortable.

Taxis are plentiful and very inexpensive throughout the colony. Recognizable by their red/silver body and rooftop taxi sign, all are metered with a beginning fare of HK$6.50 for the first 2 km and HK$.80 for each subsequent ¼ km. (There is an additional charge of HK$20 each way for transversing the Cross-Harbour Tunnel, because Kowloon taxis are not allowed to pick up in Hong Kong, and vice versa.) Taxis also charge for "waiting time" and luggage (or large package). Taxis in the New Territories are green/white, and charge HK$5.50 for the first 2 km, HK$.80 for each subsequent ¼ km. There really is no beating the convenience of Hong Kong's 15,000 taxis, and most drivers do speak some English. However, also be prepared with addresses in Chinese if you plan to get somewhere complicated on time.

If you catch a glimpse of yellow/red minibuses darting in and out of the heavy traffic at rush hour, these are known as **Public Light Buses.** Not exactly for the first-time visitor, these minibuses are speedy and cheap but often difficult to board without some smattering of Cantonese. The 14-seater **maxicabs** (they have a green stripe on yellow) are somewhat easier to maneuver, as they serve specific areas. There is service from Central District (near City Hall) to the Peak (HK$3.50 one way), another route will take you to Ocean Park for the same amount.

For daytrips to the outlying islands, **ferries** depart frequently from the Hong Kong and Yaumatei Ferry Company terminal, about a ten-minute walk west from Edinburgh Place. The most popular islands to visit are Lantau, Cheung Chau, and Lamma, and the fares are a very reasonable HK$4–6.50 weekdays, HK$5–12 weekends and public holidays, for the vessels with air-conditioned salons. Telephone 5–423081 for information, or the HKTA.

If you wish to spend the day in the New Territories, why not take a ride on the old **Kowloon-Canton Railway** as far as it will take you (without a China visa). It is only HK$35 for the first-class journey of 22 miles to the end of the New Territories. Don't worry about not getting off (you will be firmly disembarked before the border). The new railway station is now in Hung Hom (its former spot is that awful Space Museum), a seven-minute drive from the Star Ferry in Tsimshatsui. **Note:** There are no "facilities" aboard this train, so plan ahead, though the new electric trains do have toilets.

For a sense of what this colony did for transportation before the motor age, take a **sampan** ride in Aberdeen.

For local color on land, look for a **rickshaw,** an endangered species on its way out. In fact, the only few left can be found lolling about in the Star Ferry concourses. If you want *only* a photograph, watch out! That's at least HK$20, if not more. The appearance of a tired old driver is deceptive—he can be stubborn and mean when it comes to money. The going rate is approximately HK$50–100 for a five-minute ride. Price negotiation beforehand is essential.

Modern Hong Kong is at its best in the new **mass transit railway** (MTR). Built in a record five years, the initial system of this $5 billion dollar (U.S.$) underground was opened in late 1979 to serve the Central District of Hong Kong Island, Nathan Road, East and North Kowloon. A Tsuen Wan extension and the Island Line are now completed. More expensive than bus or ferry, the MTR is speedy and clean and easy to use. Pick up the MTR guidebook, which explains everything well.

The HKTA publishes the complimentary booklet "Places of Interest by Public Transport," full of helpful hints, maps, route advice, etc. Ask for it by name at one of the information centers.

FESTIVALS AND HOLIDAYS are life in Hong Kong, where the major Western (Christian) and Chinese holidays are celebrated with equal fervor and time off from earthly chores. The Hong Kong Chinese are very serious about their superstitions and give proper attention to their annual festivals (which occur each year according to the lunar calendar). The festivities and preparations are all consuming, especially to the *tai tai,* or matrons. It is very important that good *joss* (luck) prevail throughout the year, and much attention is paid to appeasing the gods (and to the merchants who supply such things as joss sticks and other lucky items).

The Chinese in Hong Kong seem to celebrate their festivals with even more fervor than their counterparts in the rest of the Far East, but perhaps it only appears so because the colony is so confined. In addition to the great family gatherings, there is also much travel across the border to visit relatives on the mainland. This is a rather new and happy awakening of communications between extended families.

If you happen to be in the colony during one of the following holidays, it will be a colorful and memorable experience. But be aware that most businesses will close and services (except in the major hotels) will be scanty. Public holidays are marked with an asterisk (*).

*January 1–2 • *New Year's Day* • (Western style).

*February (early) • *Chinese New Year* • The most important festival in the lunar calendar. Lion dances and other celebrations are arranged by Kaifong Associations in residential areas. Long before the first *kung hei fat choy* (wishing you to prosper) is shouted, locals clear debts, and buy new clothes. This time of year barber and beauty establishments tend to charge double for their services—and get away with it. (Don't order any new clothes during this period, though, because the tailors are busy with local clientele.) Gifts are exchanged and red *laisee* envelopes are presented to children and young employees. The fifteenth day of the first moon marks the Lantern Festival, the end of the lunar New Year celebrations. This is not a public holiday but it is a colorful one, with lanterns lit in homes, temples, and restaurants.

Mid-January–mid-February • *Hong Kong Arts Festival* • A month-long cultural event that brings musical and theatrical artists from all over the world. Created in the fashion of the Edinburgh Arts Festival.

February • *Lantern Festival (Yuen Siu)*.

*April (early) • *Ching Ming Festival* • This marks the beginning of spring, and a time when Chinese visit their ancestors' graves to dust them off and make gifts of flowers and food. The whole event turns into a large picnic, and public transport is easily congested.

*March/April • *Easter holidays* • Don't expect to get any business done during this four-day weekend, as the Colony lies quiet.

April/May • *Birthday of Tin Hau, goddess of fishermen* • Fishermen gather at temples dedicated to this heavenly queen to ask for good luck in the coming years. The biggest celebration is at Joss House Bay, with lion dances and traditional rites. Launches and special ferries take residents and visitors to participate in the festival.

May • *Cheung Chau Bun Festival •* The dates for this festival on Cheung Chau Island are set only a few weeks before by the village elders. During the seven days of festivities there are religious observances, Chinese opera performances, and a definite carnival atmosphere. A procession of island folk in period costumes takes place on the third day, along with stilt walkers who maneuver through the attending crowds. You'll also see "bun hills" with lucky buns on top that bring islanders good fortune during the rest of the year. The festival derives from the days of buccaneers when villagers nervously appeased the gods for the many misdeeds and ill-fortune brought to the island. Launches and special ferry services are available to Cheung Chau Island during this period.

May • *Birthday of Lord Buddha •* The best place to enjoy the celebration of this great event is at the Po Lin Monastery on Lantau Island (good vegetarian lunches can be found here, too).

May • *Tam Kung Festival •* Commemorates the second patron saint of the boat people (after Tin Hau). The festival is celebrated with the most devotion and fanfare at the Shaukeiwan Tam Kung Temple; as a colony-wide festival it is minor.

June • *Dragon Boat Festival (Tuen Ng) •* This festival falls, usually in June, on the fifth day of the fifth moon, and therefore is known as the "double fifth" or Tuen Ng. It is probably the second most important Chinese festival in the lunar year, with colorful and spectacular dragon boats. The basis for this popular public holiday comes from the story of a young scholar named Chu Yuan who drowned himself to protest government corruption. The drum beating and paddling of dragon-boat rowers during the festival symbolizes the villagers' attempts to scare away fish who might devour the young man's body. According to this romantic legend, the villagers also threw dumplings into the water to goad the greedy fish. As a result, special dumplings are one of the delicacies served during Tuen Ng. Tickets and tours featuring the colorful Dragon Boat Festival can be obtained through your travel agent. You may also see international dragon-boat races around this time.

*June • Birthday of Her Majesty, Queen Elizabeth.

July • *Birthday of Lu Pan, the Master Builder •* Ceremonies sponsored by the builders' guilds are held at Lu Pan Temple in Kennedy Town, and dinners later celebrate the festival.

August • *Maiden's Festival or Seven Sisters Festival •* Held on the seventh day of the seventh moon, the origins of this festival are in Chinese folklore and spotlight girls and young lovers.

August • *Yue Lan or Festival of the Hungry Ghosts* • It is believed that ghosts roam the world on this day, and many Chinese in Hong Kong burn paper money, fruit, and offerings to appease these specters.

August/September • Hong Kong Food Festival.

*****August** • The Saturday preceding the last Monday in August.

*****August** • *Liberation Day* • Commemorates the colony's liberation from the Japanese troops in 1945. Last Monday in August.

September • *Mid-Autumn Festival* • Similar˙ to the many harvest festivals of the Western World. Moon cakes are a traditional food at this time, commemorating a 14th-century call to revolt against the Mongols. The message was transmitted on pieces of paper baked in these cakes. Another great family occasion for lighting lanterns.

*****September (mid)** • *Second day of the Mid-Autumn Festival and the end of the annual Lantern Carnival in Victoria Park* • This has become a celebration of lanterns, and shops throughout the colony display a varied selection from the traditional shapes to rabbits, airplanes, ships, buses, etc. In the evening, the lanterns are lit, and family groups parade through the park to gaze at the moon and eat the cakes filled with sesame seeds, ground lotus seeds, and occasionally a duck egg.

September (late) • *Birthday of Confucius* • Observances are held at the Confucius Temple in Causeway Bay.

*****October (mid)** • *Chung Yueng Festival* • Held on the ninth day of the ninth moon. Since the Han Dynasty, Chinese have moved to high places on this day to avoid impending disaster. Hence, a public holiday is necessary to free the public transport system for all these Hong Kong residents who move out to the New Territories or up to the Peak.

*****December 25–27** • *Christmas holidays* • Includes the English Boxing Day on December 26.

BACKGROUND MATERIAL   on Hong Kong is plentiful, especially in the exciting-fiction department. The colony has been the backdrop, indeed often the raison d'etre, for many an international intrigue bestseller. Most of the books listed below are available in paperback at your local bookstore.

Tai Pan by James Clavell (of *Shogun* fame). His best in my opinion. *Noble House* takes place in four hectic days in the modern era; if you can get through it without skipping the middle 500 pages (as I did), more power to you.

Dynasty by Robert S. Elegant. Beautifully written and full of power. The former *Los Angeles Times* correspondent has also made it big with *Manchu,* a hard-going period piece.

The Honourable Schoolboy by master spy author John le Carre. My all-time favorite. Old Craw, the catalyst, still occupies the same bar stool every evening at the Foreign Correspondents' Club and enjoys his notoriety.

Years of the Hungry Tiger by John Gordon-Davis. A former British police officer in the colony takes you back to the days of the 1967 Communist riots and border control. Exciting! (Probably not available outside Hong Kong.)

Hong Kong: Borrowed Place, Borrowed Time by Richard Hughes. The late Australian foreign correspondent and honorary Asian gives the best recap of what this place is all about. Hughes' keen observations are still impressive. He, by the way, is the model for Old Craw, above.

Love is a Many Splendoured Thing by Han Suyin. Autobiographical and a bit sentimental for these times, but still a good love story.

Hong Kong by Jan Morris. A recent (1988) account of this fascinating city by one of the foremost living travel writers.

An Insular Possession by Timothy Mo, a local author whose historical novel (1986) almost won Britain's prestigious Booker prize.

WHAT TO SEE AND DO

Hong Kong

Aberdeen • One of Hong Kong's oldest and most popular tourist attractions . . . some 600 junks house some 6000 of the colony's boat people here . . . take a sampan ride through "little Hong Kong" to see what it's all about . . . then enjoy a sumptuous (and over-priced) meal at one of the large floating restaurants in the harbor . . . visit the local Tin Hau Temple and little shops . . . HKTA's "Aberdeen" fact sheet gives a good walking tour.

Aw Boon Gardens and Memorial Hall • Often called the Oriental Disneyland . . . gardens are full of creatures from Taoist and Buddhist legend, artificial caves and grottoes and colorful pagodas . . . creation of a wealthy and ostentatious local businessman . . . contents of Memorial Hall a testament to family taste and culture . . . open during tourist hours . . . visit if you absolutely must.

Beaches • Public beaches on Hong Kong Island are: Deep Water Bay, Repulse Bay, Big Wave Bay, Middle Bay, Rocky Bay, Shek O (big surf), Turtle Cove, Hair Pin, Stanley Main, St. Stephen's, South Bay, and Chung Hom Kok. Lifeguards attend during summer season . . . watch red flag when swimming is dangerous.

Bird Watching • There are more than 370 species recorded in the colony, some of them very rare . . . local birds can be seen in the Botanical Gardens Aviary . . . there are birdwatching tours led by World Wilflife Fund of Nature, B/F, 1 Battery Path, Central (Tel: 5–261011). This organization has also created Mai Po Marshes near the Chinese border in New Territories—a conservation center of international importance . . . groups welcome . . . professional guides available.

Causeway Bay • Known as East Point when the British first settled here in the 1840s . . . high rises are here to stay, alas, taking away much of its picturesque, residential quality . . . 19-acre Victoria Park dominates the area . . . so do the Cross-Harbour Tunnel and new Aberdeen overpass . . . weekends, the Urban Services League brings performers to the park for free shows . . . at other times, you will see plenty of **tai chi** (shadow boxing), lantern carnivals, etc. . . . also of interest along the waterfront . . . Causeway Bay typhoon shelter (great place for hiring dinner sampans in summer) . . . Royal Hong Kong Yacht Club basin . . . famed Noon Day Gun, a well-known landmark once fired by Noel Coward, who also mentioned it in *Mad Dogs and Englishmen.*

Central and Western Districts • Get HKTA's "Central and Western District Walking Tour" for an enjoyable 3-hour walk around these areas . . . Central is full of sophisticated financial enterprises . . . elegant shops . . . high rises . . . Western is Old World . . . back alleys . . . food markets . . . lots of noise and confusion . . . and **Man No Temple** where giant incense coils burn constantly and the gods use sedan chairs.

City Hall • Complex of concert hall, theater, exhibition galleries, library, restaurants . . . Hong Kong Museum of Art on 10th and 11th floors (open daily, 10 a.m.–6 p.m. except Thurs.; 1–6 p.m. Sun. and holidays; free admission). Headquarters of Hong Kong Arts Festival each winter.

Cooking with Lucy • Towngas Centre, Basement of Leighton Centre, 77 Leighton Rd. . . . best show in town . . . Lucy Lo demonstrates real Chinese cuisine every Mon. from 2:30–4 p.m. Cost is a mere HK$50, or so . . . telephone Miss Aileen Tsing, 5–761535 for reservations.

Deepwater Bay • Known for some lovely mansions . . . and a pleasant 9-hole course at the Royal Hong Kong Golf Club, open to visitors during the week . . . can also see the more exclusive Hong Kong Country Club from the cable cars at Ocean Park . . . don't miss the world's largest oceanarium, if only for the spectacular cable car ride to the top.

Fung Ping Shan Museum • 94 Bonham Rd., Hong Kong University . . . Shang, Chou ritual bronze vessels . . . decorative mirrors of Warring States Period—Tang Dynasty . . . interesting ceramics, Ming/ Ch'ing paintings . . . some sculpture . . . open daily 9:30 a.m.– 6 p.m. Mon.–Sat. Closed on Sun. and holidays . . . free admission.

Golf and Other Sporting Events • Exchange privileges can be arranged at the 9-hole Royal Hong Kong Golf Club in Deepwater Bay or Fanling (see New Territories). Table tennis is also popular . . . there are many all-weather public tennis courts . . . boating fans might try the Hong Kong Boat Centre (5–223527) for charter rates . . . water-skiing is available in Deepwater Bay (Tel. 5–920391) . . . and bona fide yacht owners should definitely contact the Royal Hong Kong Yacht Club. . . . Join HKTA's "Sports & Recreation Tour" and visit the exclusive Clearwater Bay Golf and Country Club.

Hong Kong Convention and Exhibition Centre • Wanchai. A world-class facility with state of the art conference halls and meeting rooms . . . 4.4 million square feet of conference/exhibition space— largest of its kind in Asia and hoped to usher in new era of trade fairs and conventions . . . 1427 hotel rooms on-site at New World Harbour View and Grand Hyatt.

Hong Kong and Shanghai Banking Corp. • Also known as The Bank and the second most profitable public company in the territory . . . founded in 1864 . . . its familiar edifice in Central demolished in 1985 to make way for headquarters number three . . . most expensive office building ever erected and designed by English architect Norman Foster (who also worked on the controversial Georges Pompidou Centre overlooking Paris). Do not overlook this glass and steel contemporary structure with its famous lion guardians, Stitt and Stephen, still incumbent outside the main entrance.

Happy Valley Racetrack • Happy Valley. Hong Kong Chinese are inveterate gamblers . . . and here they all hang out! Racing season from mid-September to May, with 62 race meetings on weekends and Wednesday (many of them at night). Check with someone in the know (like a hotel concierge) for entry to the plushier parts.

Ocean Park • Brick Hill, Shum Sui Kok Peninsula (near Aberdeen). Fabulous U.S.$80 million Oceanarium on 170 acres of government-grant land . . . entry is at the Lowland Site . . . Italian-designed cable cars whisk 5000 people per hour to the top of the hill . . . a breathtaking ride with views of outlying islands and South China Sea . . . included in the family entertainment complex are a roller coaster, a "sensuround" cinema, and the largest outdoor escalator in the world . . . New attractions include 2000-bird **Aviary** with 150 species imported from Asia, South America and the UK . . . also featured are a Flamingo and Parrot gardens, Bird exhibition hall and 500-seat theater—a caterpillar-shaped **Butterfly House** is home to more than 1000 butterflies of 100 different species . . . and Middle Kingdom presents a journey through Chinese history from pre-historic through 13 dynasties to modern times. The 1989 opening of this ambitious project also boasts special displays of Chinese antiques and crafts, a restaurant, and a theater for opera, kung-fu and other cultural arts . . . visit the marine section (Atoll Reef, killer whale performance in Ocean Theatre, penguins in Wave Cove) . . . then head for 3-level restaurant where Chinese food catered by Miramar Hotel is excellent . . . Park open daily from 10 a.m.–6 p.m.; 9 a.m.–6 p.m. on Sun. and holidays . . . admission is HK$100 adults, HK$50 for children . . . avoid windy days when cable cars do not operate . . . call 5–5552222 for weather/events information.

Repulse Bay • named after HMS *Repulse,* which routed pirates in the mid-19th century . . . although some still insist it should be called repulsive bay because of the Monday morning garbage after summer crowds . . . lovely views of nearby islands and South China Sea, despite the new high rises that protrude everywhere . . . historic sites . . . avoid during summer weekends when traffic is terrible.

Royal Hong Kong Jockey Club • Happy Valley . . . established in 1884 . . . said to be 1 of the 4 most influential institutions in the colony (other 3 are Jardine Matheson, Hong Kong/Shanghai Bank, and the governor) . . . prosperous . . . draws some 15% of populace to off-track betting locations . . . races are held at Happy Valley Track or Chatin . . . most prestigious because racing began here in Wong Nei Chung not long after the British settled . . . night racing in season . . . call 5–8378345, or check with your hotel concierge.

Shaukeiwan • Eastern end of tram route and still only a HK$.60 ride . . . once a pirate's haunt, now residential and home of the colony's 2nd largest fishing fleet . . . **Tam Kung Temple** honors the 2nd saint of the boat people . . . nice festival in May during Tam Kung's birthday . . . **Shing Wong Temple** near tram terminus.

Stanley • a pirate hideout in the 1840s . . . formerly known as *ch'ek ch'u* (red pole), this small fishing village on the southern side of Victoria Island was named after the Secretary of State for the Colonies. Military cemetery full of markers from Japanese occupation . . . **Tin Hau Temple** represents a bit of old China here, especially during birthday celebrations in April . . . otherwise, the village is fairly quiet, known for **Stanley Prison,** its beachfront, Hong Kong Sea School, Stanley Market (for discounted jeans, sportswear, handicrafts), and Stanley Restaurant. Get HKTA's "Stanley" fact sheet for details.

St. John's Cathedral • Garden Rd., Central (behind the Hilton Hotel) . . . built in 1840s . . . a fine, old colonial edifice . . . seat of the Church of England . . . open daily.

Tai Chi Chuan • Literally "great ultimate fist" but often called shadow boxing . . . can be viewed early mornings (7:30–8:30 a.m.) in Chater Garden, Central District or Victoria Park, Causeway Bay . . . aficianadoes should call Recreation Amenities & Sports at 5–416405 for more details.

Tai Tam Reservoir • Tai Tam Rd., overlooking Repulse Bay . . . great place for Sunday morning hike . . . wonderful views during a 2-hour walk from Tai Tam Road to new Hong Kong Cricket Club grounds on Wongneichung Gap Road . . . spend the morning . . . pack a picnic.

Temples in General • There are over 600 in the colony . . . half of them Buddhist . . . most popular is **Tin Hau,** queen of heaven and protector of seafarers . . . worshiped by at least 250,000 people in 24 temples . . . **Kwun Yum** (goddess of mercy), **Kwan Tai** (god of war and source of righteousness), **Wong Tai Sin** (the Great Saga), and **Chai Tin Dai Sing** (monkey god) also important . . . Temples that combine Buddhism and Taoism are known as *Mius.*

AwBoon Haw Garden • Haw Par Mansion, Tai Hang Road, Causeway Bay . . . 8 acres of Chinese Disneyland . . . garish and a waste of time (my time, at least) . . . built with Tiger Balm medicine fortune . . . house has fine jade collection, if you can get in . . . contact the HKTA.

Victoria Peak • Almost 2000 feet straight up . . . the best view in the colony . . . take the historic **Peak Tram** (constructed 1888) from Garden Road to the Tower terminus (HK$6 for adults) . . . meals, snacks available in Peak Tower at 1350 feet . . . have a good walk around first . . . see handicrafts demonstrations at Peak Tower Village.

Wanchai • Suzie Wong is not forgotten . . . she's just older and more expensive . . . from the Korean through Vietnam wars, this area was notorious . . . all is quiet now as office towers rise where once cheong sams sat . . . still a great place for nightlife . . . and (lo!) cultural events daily at the Arts Centre on Harbour Road . . . exhibitions at The Museum of Chinese Historical Relics.

Wan Fu • The Hong Kong Hilton's 110-foot motorized brigantine is absolutely the best way to enjoy this famous harbor . . . sails directly from Blake's Pier daily . . . holds approximately 60 persons in great comfort . . . old-style 2-masted sailing ship, the *Wan Fu* means 10,000 felicitations! . . . good food and drink aboard from morning through night. Luncheon, sunset, dinner, and weekend sightseeing cruises, plus special breakfast outings on Wednesday and Friday mornings to Kowloon and Yaumati Typhoon shelter . . . return via Stonecutter's Island and Western district . . . for about $15, guests enjoy continental breakfast, fresh fruit juices, and unlimited bloody marys or bullshots. My, my. Full details from Hilton Int'l here or at home.

Zoological and Botanical Gardens • A bit of tranquillity in the midst of Central . . . harbor views on good days . . . shadow boxing (*tai chi*) in early morning . . . free.

Kowloon

Hong Kong Cultural Centre • opening next to Space Museum on Kowloon waterfront in Tsimshatsui. Across from Peninsula Hotel and offering variety of attractions and activities . . . concert hall, theater and studio . . . Chinese and European eateries and new home of Hong Kong Museum of Art. Check local listings for ticket information.

Hong Kong Museum of History • Kowloon Park, Tsimshatsui . . . open daily (except Fri.) from 10 a.m.–6 p.m.; Sun. and holidays from 1 p.m. . . . admission free . . . model junks collection . . . small historical display . . . worth a quick browse.

Lei Cheng UK Branch Museum • No. 41 Tonkin St., Sham Shui Po (on Lei Cheng UK Resettlement Estate) . . . open daily (except Thurs.) from 10 a.m.–1 p.m. and 2–6 p.m.; Sun. and holidays from 1 p.m. . . . small admission charge . . . site of the Han period (A.D. 25–220) tomb . . . discovered in 1955 . . . funerary wares, model clay houses . . . small but interesting.

Ocean Centre/Ocean Terminal/Ocean Galleries Complex • Several acres of shopping, eating, people-watching from early morning on.

Space Museum • Chatham Rd. across from the Peninsula Hotel . . . open daily for "space trips" . . . call 3–7212361 for English language times . . . admission: HK$15 for sky show . . . free for exhibition.

Sung Dynasty Village and Laichikok Amusement Park • Kau Wa Keng, Lai Chi Kok, Tel: 3–7415111 . . . owned by entrepreneur Mr. Chiu . . . Chinese wedding parade, acrobatic show, folk dances, a wax museum, and various craftsmen at work . . . I'd skip the expensive tour of the village . . . tacky and terrible food in my opinion . . . amusement park is more amusing.

Tai Chi Chuan • Practiced daily from 7–8 a.m. in Kowloon Park and King George V Park . . . call Yaumatei office of Recreation Amenities & Sports (Tel: 3–660998) for further details.

Temple Street Night Market • Temple St. Take Nathan Road to Jordan Road (MTR Station), turn left and walk 2 blocks—where teeming stalls offer every type of merchandise you never want to live without! A meal from one of the cooking stalls is not recommended, but the odors are memorable.

Tin Hau Temple • Market St. off Nathan Rd. . . . open daily from 7:30 a.m.–8:30 p.m. . . . dedicated to the goddess of fishermen and honored annually with a festival in April . . . open air market nightly.

Yaumatei Typhoon Shelter • Filled with boat people . . . great for seeing "the other side" of Hong Kong

Wong Tai Sin Temple • Upper Wong Tai Sin Estate . . . open daily from 7 a.m.–5 p.m. . . . small donation expected . . . a new temple in the old style . . . packed with devotees following ancient customs and superstitions . . . joss sticks, lucky charms, and fortunes at the nearby stalls.

New Territories

Beaches • Clear Water Bay is the best . . . others are Pak Sha Chau, Kiu Tsui, Hap Mun, Trio, Camper's, Silver Strand, Approach, Ting Kau, Lido, Casam, Hoi Mei, Gemini, Kadoorie, Cafeteria (Old, New).

Chinese University • Starting point for ferry trip around Tolo Harbour . . . villages of Shap Sze Heung, Sham Chung, Lai Chi Chong, Tap Mun, Kau Lau Wan, Chik Kang, and Tai Tan offer scenes of local interest. . . . 2 departures daily.

Ching Chung Koon • 21 Milestone, off Castle Peak Rd., Tuen Mun . . . Taoist temple retreat complex covering some 200,000 square feet . . . main worship hall dedicated to Lui Soon Yuen . . . summer pavilions . . . water-lily pond, stone lions . . . hundreds of bonsai for which the place is famous . . . most interesting times to visit are in May and Oct. . . . open daily . . . short walking distance from Castle Peak Hospital.

Fanling • One of the most beautiful market towns in the New Territories and home of the Royal Hong Kong Golf Club . . . visitors may play weekdays here . . . telephone Clubhouse at 0–901211 for details.

Kam Tin • Walled village . . . residents not so fond of tourists, but on the other hand . . . take care, here. Still, a regular stop on most tours . . . the 17th-century fortification has guard towers with slots for defending archers . . . admission is 50¢.

Lok Ma Chau • The lookout onto Mainland China . . . take the Kowloon-Canton Railway to the last station in the New Territories Sheung Shui, then a bus to the lookout point . . . a few old men with long beards for photographs . . . as a peek into China, it's lost popularity since the Bamboo Curtain opened.

Sai Kung Peninsula • Unspoiled area of Eastern New Territories . . . well known for walks and beautiful bays . . . Sai Kung Country Park . . . Hebe Haven for pleasure junks . . . Clearwater Bay . . . a Golf & Country Club . . . all worth the effort.

Sam Tung Uk • Tsuen Wan, New Territories. Hong Kong's largest folk museum . . . highlights culture and life of Hakka people . . . traditional village and exhibition hall.

Shatin Race Course • Most modern in the world . . . built in 1978 for U.S.$100 million . . . seating for 30,000 . . . European and

Chinese restaurants . . . Hakka women sweep litter . . . members' pavilion above . . . season from Sept.–May . . . a *very* Hong Kong spectacle . . . call 5–8378345 or check with concierge at your hotel.

Tai Po Market • Traditional Chinese foodstuffs more for looking than buying . . . visit also the **Tai Ping Carpet Factory** (by appointment) . . . **Tin Hau Temple** on Ting Kok Road . . . **Plover Cove Country Park,** a rural and peaceful view of Hong Kong.

Temple of 10,000 Buddhas • Shatin New Town . . . 328 steps to the top . . . thousands of gold-leafed Buddhas are gathered here . . . pink hexagonal pagoda nearby . . . open daily . . . free admission.

The Art Gallery • Chinese University, Shatin . . . open daily from 9:30 a.m.–4:30 p.m.; Sun. and holidays from 12:30 p.m.–4:30 p.m. . . . admission free . . . new art gallery of the Institute of Chinese Studies . . . main collection of 1300 items from Ming to modern . . . traditional Chinese garden in central courtyard . . . bronze seals of Han Period . . . rubbings and stone inscriptions of Han and Sung.

OUTLYING ISLANDS

Best Beaches • Recommended by the HKTA are Tung Wan and Kwun Yam Wan or Cheung Chau . . . ask for directions and enjoy the walk to the other coastline . . . explore a little on the way . . . you can't get lost.

Cheung Chau • Only 1 square mile on the surface, Cheung Chau houses at least 40,000 people in a potpourri of traditional 4-story Chinese shop/houses along an unending series of narrow, mazelike alleys . . . Cheung Chau people are fisherfolk and have a tenacious, independent reputation that borders on arrogance . . . a few hundred Westerners also live here defying the high rents in Central/Kowloon districts, and the commute by ferry seems to be worth the effort . . . there are a few cafes that cater to the Western palate with tea, beer, and sandwiches . . . if you're planning to spend the day at the beach though, bring along your own picnic and drinks . . . there is also a hotel with wind-surfing facilities.

Cheung Chau Bun Festival • This is the place to be during this annual event in May (the date set by village elders only a few weeks before) . . . come to the carnival, the parades, the bun hill and everything by special launch or ferry! . . . check HKTA for dates and times.

Cheung Sha Beach • On the southern coast, between Po Lin and Silvermine Bay . . . the best and brightest of all the beaches on Lantau . . . barbecue pits, snack stands, changing areas in season . . . prepare for crowds during the summer.

Discovery Bay • The talk of the town . . . 18-hole golf course designed by Robert Trent Jones Jr. . . . tennis/squash/swimming . . . restaurants/bars . . . only 25 minutes by special ferry from Central District.

Lamma Island • A favorite with the weekend boat trippers, Hong Kong residents who sail over to enjoy the deserted beaches and the lovely swimming bays . . . remnants of a previous civilization were discovered here, during archaeological excavations at Sham Wan Bay.

Lantau • The crown colony's most spacious and rural island in the outlying areas . . . home to some 30,000 who enjoy the 55-square-mile paradise just an hour from central Hong Kong . . . until recently, Lantau was just a favored day retreat for the masses who came by triple-decked, air-conditioned ferry, but tourism has really arrived and both town houses and resorts are being developed.

Pak Tai • The richest and most elaborate of Cheung Chau island's 9 temples . . . decorated with 1000-year-old sword brought from the sea by local fishermen in the last century . . . Taoist temple dedicated to the gods of the sea, since that has always been the island's livelihood.

Peng Chau • A tiny fishing settlement island on the ferry route between Hong Kong and Silvermine Bay . . . provides easy access to the **Trappist Monastery** on the hill about 10 minutes away by local boat . . . otherwise, just worthy of an hour's stroll through the noisy, crowded streets.

Po Lin Monastery • 60 acres straight up and under the shadow of 3064-foot Lantau Peak . . . richly decorated new buildings . . . Buddhist monastery dedicated to the "Precious Lotus" . . . visitors are welcomed . . . vegetarian lunches are served in the cafeteria or the retreat house (the latter is better) and a dormitory-style bed is available for a song (about HK$70 including meals per person) . . . the tallest outdoor Buddha statue in Southeast Asia is nearing completion here and reputed to cost US$3 million . . . constructed of 250 tons of gold-leafed bronze . . . in a Nanjing, China, factory . . . large enough to be seen from Macau . . . its platform altar based on Temple of Heaven in Beijing.

Silvermine Bay • The main ferry terminal on the eastern coast . . . the beach is just a short walk from the pier . . . fleets of buses and taxis will transport you over excellent roads to more interesting parts of the island.

Tai O Village • A 45-minute drive from Silvermine Bay and home to 20,000 of the island's inhabitants . . . still full of Old World shops selling every remedy possible . . . the oldest temple on the island is here . . . take a rope ferry across Five Cent River, which now costs HK$.20.

Trappist Monastery To Our Lady Of Joy • On the eastern side of the island and actually easier to reach by boat from Peng Chau (a 10-minute ride and then straight up the hill by foot) . . . the Trappists don't mind quiet visitors as they have taken a vow of silence . . . they keep their head above water by supplying fresh milk to the Hilton Hotel, I understand.

Tung Chung • On the northern side of Lantau island, the ramparts of an old fort dating back to 1817 and still standing . . . 6 cannons point straight out to sea to ward off attacks of pirates and barbarians.

Hong Kong Tours

Aberdeen and Harbour Night • 5½ hours nightly . . . tour to Peak for night viewing, Aberdeen for seafood dinner on floating restaurant, coach for tour of Hong Kong Island, relaxing cruise of harbor with unlimited free drinks . . . HK$380.

City Tram/Dinner Tour • 4½ hours, daily at 6 p.m. . . . tram ride from Happy Valley to Western Market with drinks . . . bus to floating nightclub for Chinese dinner/show or to La Ronda (Furama Hotel) for revolving buffet . . . HK$410.

Grand Combined Tour • 8 hours by coach and junk . . . daily at 9 a.m. . . . Lei U Man, Aberdeen, Hong Kong Island tour by bus . . . HK$350.

Harbour Junk/Sung Dynasty Village • 7½ hours, weekdays only . . . Victoria Harbour cruise with lunch, afternoon tour of village . . . HK$290.

Hong Kong Island Tour • 3-4 hours by air-conditioned coach . . . morning or afternoon departures . . . Victoria Peak, Wanchai, Aw Boon Haw Gardens, Wongneichung Gap, Repulse Bay, Aberdeen, University of Hong Kong, Western and Central Districts . . . HK$80.

Hong Kong Island Night Tour • 4-5 hours, nightly . . . coach to Victoria Peak, Aberdeen for dinner on floating restaurant, nightclub, and perhaps open air night market . . . HK$285.

Kowloon and New Territories • 3-4 hours by air-conditioned coach . . . morning or afternoon departures . . . Tuen Mun, Kam Tin walled village, Lokmachau Lookout to China border, Fanling (Royal Hong Kong Golf Club), Taipo, Shatin, Lion Rock Tunnel . . . HK$80.

Sung Dynasty Village Tour • 2-3 hours by air-conditioned coach . . . 4 tours daily during week . . . HK$220 for luncheon and dinner tours (3) . . . HK$170 for afternoon snack tour.

Double-decker Bus Tour • 5½ hours by open-air double-decker bus . . . daily at 6 p.m. . . . , tour of Kowloon . . . unlimited free drinks . . . dinner aboard floating restaurant with Chinese or Western-style buffet . . . HK$345.

Hong Kong City Tour • 6 hours . . . visit a museum housing Chinese antiquities . . . Western District and Aberdeen . . . lunch on a floating restaurant . . . watch a jewelry-setting demonstration in a factory and tour the open air market at Stanley Village . . . shop for clothes and handicrafts . . . HK$150.

The Land Between • 6 hours, Mon. through Fri., except holidays . . . visit to a serene temple . . . Hong Kong's highest mountain in the New Territories . . . paddy fields, duck farms and fish ponds . . . Luen Wo Market (traditional Chinese) . . . trip to Luk Keug overlooking the Chinese border . . . Chinese lunch with views of scenic Tolo Harbour . . . HK$220.

The Star Ferry • one of Hong Kong's most famous sights offers Star Ferry Harbour Cruises. All last one hour (with unlimited drinks) and have such names as Noon Day Gun Cruise, Seafarer's Cruise, Seabreezes Cruise, Tea Cruise, Sundowner Cruise, Harbour Lights Cruise.

Outlying Island Tours

Cheung Chau Cruise • 4 hours daily at 9:10 a.m. (except Sun. or holidays) . . . air-conditioned ferry to Cheung Chau for 3 hours on the island . . . HK$130. With lunch, HK$245.

Launtau Tour • 6½ hours daily (no Sun. or holidays) . . . Silvermine Bay, Po Lin Monastery, Cheung Sha Beach, Shek Pik Res-

ervoir, Tai O fishing village . . . vegetarian or Western lunch . . .
ferry and coach . . . HK$270 for lunch. HK$230 for snack.

Outer Islands Escapade ● Full day or overnight weekdays only
. . . combination of Cheung Chau Island with Sea Ranch on Lantau
. . . HK$260.

Special Tours

Sports and Recreation Tour ● 9 hours, Tues. and Fri., except
holidays . . . visit the luxurious Clearwater Bay Golf and Country Club
on Sai Kung Peninsula . . . enjoy the exclusive sports facilities and
golf course . . . delicious western brunch . . . HK$240.

Horseracing Tour ● 6 hours . . . day and evening horse racing
during the season (Sept.–May) . . . transfer and tour guides . . . Chinese
meal and guest badge for members' enclosure at race course . . .
HK$250.

Day Tour of China ● 1-day tour to Shenzhen, Guangzhou, from
HK$350 to HK$850 per person . . . includes train tickets, city tour,
lunch, kindergarten visit, and shopping expedition . . . book 36 hours
in advance.

Macau Tours ● 6-8 hours or overnight daily . . . hydrofoil to Macau, embarkation tax, sightseeing tour, meals, etc. . . . HK$350 to
HK$700 depending on length of stay.

Walking Tours

Aberdeen ● Called Little Fragrant Harbour or Little Hong Kong
. . . home of the colony's floating population . . . take a No. 7 or 70
bus from Central to Aberdeen Main Rd. (opposite Tin Hau Temple)
. . . walk over to Tin Hau Temple . . . then circle back to Old Main
St. (east of Aberdeen Main Rd.) to see a Chinese wedding gown shop
and have a good view of the typhoon shelter from the Rest Garden . . .
turn right into Aberdeen Main Rd. to see Hung Shing Shrine, an herb
shop, and fishermen's hall . . . at the corner opposite the shrine is the
ferry pier to Ap Lei Chau, where you can see traditional wooden junks
built (there is also now a bridge) . . . U-turn and walk past the seafood
hawkers along Wu Nam St. . . . turn right into Cheng Tu Rd. for a
visit to Kwun Yin and Kwan Ti shrine . . . a favorite of the fisherfolk
. . . on Wu Pak St. are roadside stalls selling paper offerings, jade,
and fresh sugar cane juice . . . foodstalls can be found on Sai On St.

. . . a bird shop and outside barber on Lok Yeung St. . . . and up and down Tung Sing Rd. are other colorful sights including a shop where mahjong sets are crafted. (60 minutes)

Botanical Gardens and Bowen Road • Start early and visit Botanical Gardens before 8 a.m. to see the Chinese practice shadow boxing . . . exit past aviary into Robinson Rd. . . . follow roundabout to Magazine Gap Rd. and continue on to Bowen Rd. . . . the walk soon levels out and becomes a footpath with lovely views of the harbor . . . benches along the way . . . at the junction of Wanchai Gap Rd. you can turn left and climb up to see Pak Tai Temple . . . or you can turn right and descend to Kennedy Rd., past Lover's Stone, visited by maidens on the 6th, 16th, and 26th of each lunar month. (90 minutes)

Causeway Bay • Also known as Tung Lo Wan or Copper Gong Bay, a popular tourist and local area for shopping, eating, and entertainment . . . take the North Point or Shaukeiwan tram from Central District (HK$.60) and alight at the corner of Yee Woo St. and Pennington St. (theater on corner) . . . turn into Pennington St. to see a paper shop, Chinese medicine shop, pawn shop, and herbalist's teahouse (try a bowl if you want to clear out the system) . . . take a quick detour left into Irving St. to see the soya sauce and Chinese wine shops . . . then U-turn into Jardine's Bazaar for the many foodstalls, Chinese provision stores, and herb shops . . . turn left into Fuk Hing Lane and right into Jardine's Crescent for open-market shopping for locally made clothing, imitation jewelry, and other goods . . . pass over Percival St. (because you can't walk down to the waterfront anymore) and enjoy the fresh food markets of Russell St., most crowded between 9 and 11 a.m.; 4 to 6 p.m. . . . if you buy something, watch it wrapped in newspaper, tied with a piece of straw . . . turn right into Canal Rd. East for paper and coconut shops . . . cross Hennessy Rd. and turn into Lockhart Rd. for good local restaurants (it's time for a rest and snack) . . . right at Percival St. brings you back to Hennessy Rd. and the China Products Department Store, one of the best in the colony . . . catch the tram back to Central. (1–2 hours)

Central and Western Districts • This walk is best between 10 a.m. and 7 p.m. when the shops are open . . . begin from Des Voeux Rd. Central in the business district, past the banks and sophisticated boutiques . . . make a U-turn into Li Yuen St. (East & West) where the shops and stalls lining the narrow streets offer good bargains in locally made clothing and fabrics . . . back to Des Voeux Rd., wander through **Central Market** (open 6 a.m.–2 p.m.; 4:30–8 p.m.) where most of the produce, meat, poultry, etc. is purchased . . . a left at Wing On St. offers more good buys in the full gamut of fabrics . . .

right on Queen's Rd. Central takes you past some of the many gold and jewelry shops . . . right on Wing Sing St. shows you every variety of eggs sold from one day to 100 years old . . . left on Wing Lok St. offers a typical Hong Kong scene with herb, medicine, preserved seafood, and tea shops . . . take a left on Man Wa Lane if you want to have your name carved in a chop . . . left at Bonham Strand (known for printing shops) . . . right on Jervois St. and right on Hillier St. to see all the snake shops . . . left again on Bonham Strand and walk past wholesalers of Chinese medicinal herbs and ginseng . . . left on Des Voeux Rd. West, the center of dried seafood . . . left on Sutherland St. past foodstalls and small markets . . . left on Queen's Rd. West, famous for herbs and household goods . . . continue on into Hollywood Rd. where everyone flocks to curio shops, furniture factories, and coffin makers . . . pay a visit to the Man Mo Temple, oldest in Hong Kong, where giant incense coils burn all the time and 2 carved sedan chairs are for the exclusive use of the gods . . . continue into Lyndhurst Terrace for more curio, embroidery, and Cantonese Opera costume shops . . . turn right into Wellington St. for ivory and brassware shops (**Note:** This area is being developed and many of these shops may no longer exist.) . . . D'Aguilar St. and Theatre Lane will return you to Des Voeux Rd. Central . . . with boutiques and bakeries along the way. (3 + hours)

MacLehose Trail • Named after Hong Kong's former governor, Sir Murray MacLehose . . . series of walks linking 8 lovely parks and stretching for 100 km. right across mainland . . . starting at Pak Tam Chung in Sai Kung Peninsula, walks are split into 10 sections ranging in length from 5 to 16 km. and graded to suit activity level . . . ask for MacLehose Trail pamphlet at Hong Kong Government Publication Centre. (60 minutes to full day with stops)

Victoria Peak • Take the Peak Tram from Garden Rd. (departs every 15 minutes; HK$6 per adult) . . . disembark at Upper Peak Tram terminus . . . walk clockwise around Lugard Rd. to Harlech Rd. (or vice versa) . . . many benches upon which to rest and enjoy views of Hong Kong panorama, Kowloon Peninsula, Victoria Harbour, Green Island, Peng Chau, Lantau Island, Macau, Cheung Chau, Lamma Island, and Aberdeen . . . more energetic can take Mount Austin Rd. to former Mountain Lodge at 1802 feet . . . return to Peak Tower for refreshments . . . take Peak Tram back to Garden Rd. or catch 14-seat maxicab down to City Hall vicinity. (60 minutes)

Yaumatei and Jade Market • Walk up Nathan Rd. and turn left into Kansu Street where from 10 a.m.–3:30 p.m. one side is solid jade of all varieties and prices . . . walk the length of Canton Rd. to Saigon

St. . . . turn right for stalls . . . and then right into Battery St. for paper items . . . more paper shops left on Ning Po St. . . . then left again on Reclamation St. for a true local market scene . . . everything imaginable . . . turn right into Temple St. for a visit to Tin Hau Temple (open 7:30 a.m.–5:30 p.m. daily) . . . on the other side of the temple is Public Square St. that becomes a busy night-market daily . . . turn right to Nathan Rd. and take bus or MTR back to your destination. (2 hours)

Other Tours

Do-It-Yourself Ferry, Bus, and Train Tour of New Territories • Take the MTR to Tsuen Wan . . . catch No. 68M bus to Yuen Long, largest town in northern New Territories . . . wander about stores, markets, restaurants . . . take No. 76K bus to Lok Ma Chau turnoff . . . border lookout to China allows views of Shen Zhen River, villages and farms of southern Kwangtung province. . . . continue on to Sheung Shui on another No. 76K bus . . . wander up to the northern section of town to see the walled village of Sheung Shui Heung, home to the Liu clan for more than 6 centuries . . . despite new developments surrounding it now . . . catch Kowloon/Canton Railway at Sheung Shui Station for 30-minute ride back to Hung Hom Station in Kowloon . . . through rural Hong Kong, Tolo Harbour . . . Chinese University . . . Shatin . . . and through tunnels back to one of the world's most populous areas. (Allow at least 6 hours)

For Joggers Only • 600-meter jogging trail winding through trees round central picnic area in Victoria Park (Causeway Bay) . . . flat area of Bowen Rd. in mid-levels (closed to traffic) . . . running clinic every Sun. at 7:30 here (Tel: 5–736261 ext. 357) . . . Lugard Rd. around the Peak (take Peak Tram up) . . . for the more hearty ones . . . from outside Hong Kong Cricket Club on Wongneichung Gap Rd. to reservoirs . . . (watch the heat, though) . . . Kowloon Park in early morning.

HOTELS

Hong Kong

★★★**The Excelsior** • *Causeway Bay. Tel: 5–767365. Cable: CONVENTION HONG KONG. Telex: HX74550* • 923 rooms (24 Suites) . . . huge, noisy convention hotel . . . connecting to the 42-story World

Trade Centre . . . out of way from central areas . . . not recommended for individual travelers. A Mandarin International affiliate . . . shuttle service between hotel and Central District . . . a splendid US $12.5-million renovation has just been completed of guest rooms and public areas.

Facilities: Live cabaret in 34th floor Talk of the Town. Windmill Coffee Shop overlooking Royal Hong Kong Yacht Club and typhoon shelter. Garden lounge and espresso coffee bar in Upper lobby area. Dickens Bar (pub) on basement level for drinks, snacks, lunches, and dinner. Excelsior Grill. Health club on 3rd floor. Fully equipped business center.

Trade Centre facilities: Noon Gun Grill and Cafeteria. Maxim's Palace Chinese restaurant. Palace Theatre seats 1000. World Trade Centre Club. 2 indoor air-conditioned tennis courts.

Gen. Manager: Hendrick-Jan Bosch. *Reservations:* LHW.

★★★**Furama Inter-Continental** • *1 Connaught Rd. Tel: 5–255111. Cable: FURAM H.X. Telex: HX73081* • 522 rooms . . . tries to be more deluxe than it really is (I think) . . . half the rooms have unobstructed harbor views . . . smaller than average accommodations (furniture doesn't quite fit) . . . good location between former Cricket Club and Queen's Pier . . . easy walking to Central District . . . flanked by Sutherland House and Hutchison House. . . . new Fitness Center.

Facilities: La Ronda revolving restaurant on 30th floor for buffet at luncheon and dinner with 360-degree views. Rotisserie French/Continental and lounge (2nd floor). Third-floor banquet facilities. Lau Ling and lobby bars. Island (Cantonese) restaurant. Coffee shop on ground level. Secretarial assistance.

Gen. Manager: Jean-Pierre Marcadier. *Reservations:* IHC.

★★★★**Grand Hyatt Hotel** • *Wanchai.* • 575 rooms. Located adjacent to Hong Kong Convention and Exhibition Center . . . opened late 1989 . . . jury still out.

Facilities: Specialty and Chinese restaurants. Cafe. Lounge and bar. Entertainment Center. Tennis and Squash courts. Fitness Center. Indoor/outdoor swimming pools. Banquet rooms and grand ballroom.

Gen. Manager: P. Jentes. *Reservations:* HYATT.

★★★★**Hong Kong Hilton** • *2 Queen's Rd. Central. Tel: 5–233111. Cable: HILTEL HONGKONG. Telex: HX73355* • 755 rooms . . . headquarters of Hilton International in the Far East . . . celebrating 2 decades of good hospitality and good food . . . well-trained and most courteous staff, full of many familiar faces . . . well-appointed and ample-size accommodations, many still with harbor views . . . recently renovated . . . two full floors for executives only.

Facilities: The Eagle's Nest on the 25th floor with set Chinese menu, great views and romantic ambiance. Jade Lotus (2nd floor) for sumptuous breakfast and luncheon buffets, a la carte dinners. The Grill (2nd floor), a longtime favorite. Lobby and Dragon Boat bars (2nd floor), among the most lively in town. Espresso Restaurant and Cat Street Coffee Shop (ground floor). Outdoor pool and barbecue area. Men's health club. Superb businessman's center. *Wan Fu* brigantine for harbor cruises.

Gen. Manager: J. Smith. *Reservations:* HILTON.

★★★★**Hong Kong Marriott** • *Queensway, Central. Tel: 5–8108366. Telex: 66899 MARTTT HX* • 605 rooms (44 suites). This brand-new hotel (1989) comprises 27 floors of a 48-story retail/office complex . . . its very existence in Hong Kong has provoked considerable controversy . . . Marriott is strictly a non-union shop and adheres to the five-day work week . . . unheard of in Southeast Asia . . . hotel features "atrium" service suite apartments as well as 199 king rooms.

Facilities: Man Ho Cantonese-style restaurant. JW's Grill continental restaurant. Marriott Cafe. Bar/Piano Lounge. Business Centre.

Gen. Manager: R. Wungler. *Reservations:* MARRIOTT.

★★**Lee Gardens Hotel** • *Hysan Ave., Causeway Bay. Tel: 5–9853311 Cable: LEE GARDENS. Telex: 75601 LEGAR* • 800 rooms . . . in the midst of Causeway Bay . . . within walking distance of large department stores, Happy Valley, and Excelsior Hotel . . . very group oriented . . . fairly spacious but rather nondescript guest rooms . . . a good moderate hotel under local management. . . . 15 new executive suites.

Facilities: Okahan Japanese restaurant (ground floor). The coffee shop (off main lobby). Pavilion Restaurant (luncheon buffets and a la carte dinners) on lobby level. Rainbow Room Chinese restaurant. Yum Sing Bar overlooking Hysan Avenue.

Gen. Manager: S. Shang. *Reservations:* UTELL.

★★★★★**The Mandarin Oriental** • *5 Connaught Rd., Central. Tel: 5–220111. Cable: Mandarin Hong Kong. Telex: HX73653* • 547 rooms (58 suites) . . . acknowledged as one of the world's great hotels for almost all of its 25 years . . . personal European-style service guided by top-rate managers . . . beautifully refurbished guest rooms and mini-suites (most with balconies) . . . top executives love the atmosphere . . . located in the middle of Central District . . . attached to Prince's Building by a "bridge" over Chater Rd. . . . does take some groups now, conservatively. The hotel group is offering clients the Mandarin Oriental Goldcard through Hong Kong Bank . . . but does one remit payment in HK or US dollars?

Facilities: Pierrot French restaurant on 24th floor, complete with red velvet and Picasso prints. Mandarin Grill (1st floor), one of the best in the Far East. Man Wah Restaurant (Cantonese) on the 25th floor. Causette Coffee Shop (ground floor, separate entrance). Marquee Coffee Shop (across the bridge in the Prince's Building). Harlequin Bar (24th floor, good views). Captain's Bar (ground floor; full of regulars and very popular). The Chinnery (1st floor), males only for pub lunches. The Clipper Lounge, winds around the mezzanine and great people place. Roman-style indoor pool with health center for both sexes (fabulous).

Fwn. Manager: J. Tuscher. *Reservations:* LHW.

★★★**The Park Lane Hotel** • *310 Gloucester Rd., Causeway Bay. Tel: 5–8903355. Cable: PARKLANE. Telex: 75343 PHL EX* • 850 rooms. Formerly known as The Plaza Hotel . . . renovated and under new management . . . located in heart of Causeway Bay . . . overlooking Victoria Park and harbor . . . near tunnel entrance and new subway.

Facilities: International Buffet at rooftop restaurant. Lobby Lounge. Gallery Bar and Lounge. Promenade European bistro. Parkview European/Oriental gourmet dishes. Starlight disco. Private meeting rooms. In-house movies.

Gen. Manager: K. Mullins. *Reservations:* Distinguished Hotels.

★★★**Victoria Hotel** • *Shun Tak Centre, Connaught Rd., Central. Tel: 5–407228. Cable: HOTELVC. Telex: 86608 HTLVT HX* • 540 rooms (62 suites). Elegant new high rise located above Shun Tak Centre Macau Ferry Terminal . . . located in central district right on waterfront . . . guestrooms begin on 26th floor for spectacular harbor views . . . Star Ferry a 5-minute stroll on elevated walkway . . . ferries to Cheung Chau and Lantau just 2 mintues.

Facilities: Mistral Mediterranean restaurant (mezzanine level) with harbor views. Belvedere French (specializing in fresh seafood) restaurant with harbor views. Golden Carp Lounge off lobby. Executive club floor for business travelers. Rooftop pool and health club.

Gen. Manager: Uwe Boeger. *Reservations:* HOLIDEX.

Kowloon

★★**Holiday Inn Golden Mile** • *46–52 Nathan Rd. Tel: 3–693111. Cable: HOLIDAYINN HONG KONG. Telex: HX 56332* • 599 rooms (9 suites) . . . regional headquarters for Holiday Inn in the Far East . . . has set occupancy records since 1975 opening . . . popular with large groups . . . in heart of Nathan Road's "golden mile" of hotels, shops, entertainment . . . dark interiors . . . very busy.

Facilities: Cafe Vienna coffee shop (M/F). The Baron's Table and

Baron Tavern (1st level). Inn Bar (lobby level). The Delicatessen Corner (basement). Rooftop pool and health club.

Gen. Manager: Jean-Marc Charpenet. *Reservations:* HOLIDEX.

★★★**Holiday Inn Harbour View** • *70 Mody Rd. Tel: 3– 7215161. Cable: INNVIEW. Telex: HK38670* • 597 rooms . . . showplace of Holiday Inn in Asia . . . 60% of guest accommodations overlook the harbor . . . spacious rooms . . . nice interiors . . . shuttle bus service to Golden Mile hotel.

Facilities: Minstral Mediterranean restaurant (mezzanine level) with harbor views. Belvedere French (specializing in fresh seafood) restaurant with harbor views. Golden Carp Lounge off lobby. Executive club floor for business travelers. Rooftop pool and health club.

Gen. Manager: Uwe Boeger. *Reservations:* HOLIDEX.

★★★★**Hyatt Regency Hong Kong** • *67 Nathan Rd. Tel: 3– 3111234. Cable: HYATT HONG KONG. Telex: HX43127* • 763 rooms (14 suites) . . . headquarters of Hyatt International in the Far East . . . Nicely refurbished . . . back to life again after 2½ years and US $20-million renovation . . . located in heart of Kowloon's Golden Mile of shops and nightspots . . . Popular Regency Club on two floors with exclusive lounge, concierge and every business amenity.

Facilities: Hugo's gourmet restaurant and lounge (2nd floor). Cantonese restaurant. Nathan's for luncheon buffet and snacks. International Cafe. Chin Chin lobby bar. Business Centre.

Gen. Manager: L. Tchou. *Reservations:* HYATT HOTELS.

★★★**The Kowloon Hotel** • *19–21 Nathan Rd. Tel: 3–698698. Cable: KLN HOTEL HX. Telex: 47604 KLNHL HX.* • 708 rooms (33 executive rooms) . . . newest of the Peninsula Group hotels in Hong Kong . . . built on a site behind the famous Pen . . . built for the business traveler . . . only 32 rooms have harbor views . . . 17 stories high . . . a limited number of ''studios'' available with fold-up beds for day use as office . . . opened early 1986 . . . guests encouraged to use restaurant facilities of The Pen.

Facilities: The Window Cafe. Pizzeria. Wan Loong Court Chinese restaurant. MIddle Row bar.

Gen. Manager: A. Poon. *Reservations:* SRS.

★★★★**Kowloon Shangri-La Hotel** • *64 Mody Rd. Tel: 3–7212111. Telex: 36718 SHALA HX.* • 719 rooms (30 suites) . . . one of nine Shangri-La International properties in Asia . . . a huge edifice with an overzealous diptych entitled ''Shangri La Valley'' as you enter . . . geared to the top-scale businessman . . . as well as incentive and special-interest groups . . .good views from generous-size accommodations of eastern end of harbor . . . only Shangri-La International hotel managed by Westin.

Facilities: Shang Palace Chinese restaurant and Nadaman Japanese restaurant (lower level). Lobby lounge with good harbor views. Steak Place for U.S. beef. Margaux gourmet restaurant (M/F). Coffee garden. Tiara Lounge (21st floor). Indoor swimming pool and health center. Executive center. 54-guestroom 11th floor is strictly non-smoking for health-conscious clients!

Gen. Manager: G. Angelini. *Reservations:* WESTIN HOTELS.

★★★**New World** • *New World Centre, 22 Salisbury Rd. Tel: 3–694111. Cable: NWHOTEL. Telex: HX35860 NWHTL* • 719 rooms (41 suites) . . . well-designed, moderately priced hotel in the New World complex of shops, offices, residences, etc. . . . excellent location on the waterfront . . . somewhat confusing to find your way around in the maze of activity . . . good value . . . on top of plenty of action!

Facilities: Patio coffee shop (4th level). Promenade bar/club/disco off main lobby. The Penthouse (18th floor) with views. Panorama continental restaurant (4th floor). The Patio (4th floor). Magnificent 40,000 square feet of poolside terrace, landscaped gardens, etc. Lovely pool. 18 executive suites with own elevator.

Gen. Manager: H. Stettler. *Reservations:* UTELL.

★★★**Omni Prince Hotel** • *Harbour City, Kowloon. Tel: 3–7361888. Cable: OMNIPH. Telex: 50950 OPHX HX* • 401 rooms (51 suites). Also located in the new Harbour City development area . . . just a few minutes' walk from the Star Ferry terminal . . . interlinked by air-conditioned walkways to more than 600 shops and boutiques. Geared for the business traveler . . . three function rooms . . . guests can use swimming pool at Omni The HongKong Hotel and other facilities in Omni Marco Polo Hotel nearby.

Facilities: The Rib Room. The Coffee Shop. The Tavern with traditional pub food at lunch. The Lobby for light refreshments.

Gen. Manager: W. A. Reich. *Reservations:* SRS.

★★★**Omni The HongKong Hotel** • *Harbour City, Kowloon.Tel: 3–7360088. Cable: OMNIKH. Telex: HK 43838* • 610 rooms (85 suites) . . . Originally operated by The Peninsula Group . . . now a member of the Omni Hotel Asia-Pacific chain. . . . terrific location between Star Ferry and Ocean Terminal . . . at the head of the new Harbour City complex down Canton Rd. . . . many guest rooms have lovely harbor views . . . a very popular hotel since 1969 opening.

Facilities: Gun Bar and coffee shop (ground floor). Bagatelle Boulevard Cafe (1st floor). Tai Pan Grill (6th floor). The Bauhinia Room (6th floor). Swimming pool and roof garden (6th floor). Spice market

(Ocean Terminal). Golden Unicorn (Cantonese) and Eastern Palace (Chiu Chao) Chinese restaurants. Non-smoking floors available.
Gen. Manager: D. Loewe. *Reservations:* SRS.

Omni The Marco Polo • *Harbour City, Kowloon. Tel: 3–7360888. Cable: OMNIP HONG KONG. Telex: HX 40077* • 439 rooms (55 suites). 10-minute walk from Star Ferry along Canton Rd. . . . in new Harbour City development . . . never have to leave the air-conditioned area . . . large guest rooms with queen or two double beds each . . . beautiful suites . . . The Silk Rooms for private functions.
Facilities: La Brasserie French provincial restaurant. The Festival cafe at top of the staircase. The Patisserie. Swimming pool at Omni The HongKong Hotel available to guests. The Coffee Mill on lower ground floor. The Tartan Bar off lobby. Excellent Business Centre.
Gen. Manager: B. Simeoni. *Reservations:* SRS.

★★★★★**The Peninsula** • *Salisbury Rd. Tel: 3–666251. Cable: PENHOTE. Telex: HX43821* • 181 rooms (19 suites) . . . THE landmark hotel in Hong Kong and the grande dame of the Far East . . . a memorable experience to stay here . . . had been allowed to become a bit shabby . . . but now under the good care of a new manager . . . tied to the colony's history since 1928, so "The Pen" must survive . . . The lobby is the crossroads of the East . . . enormous guest rooms, although many have now lost their lovely views . . . ask for the 6th floor front . . . there's an aura here that can't be beat . . . a US $20-million renovation makes the 60-plus-year-old lady look very grand, indeed . . . and a US $1.5-million fleet of 8 Silver Spirit Rolls Royce limousines boast telephones, programmed music and menus for meals as soon as you arrive!
Facilities: The Lobby for light meals, snacks, and people watching. Chesa Restaurant (Swiss, 1st floor). Inagiku Japanese restaurant designed on two levels to resemble a private Tokyo club. Verandah Restaurant (continental, 1st floor). Gaddi's Restaurant (gourmet, entrance off lobby). The Club (disco) with separate entrance on Nathan Road. Eight Silver Shadow Rolls for airport and private transportation.
Gen. Manager: E. Waldburger. *Reservations:* SRS.

Ramada Renaissance Hotel • *8 Peking Rd., Kowloon. Tel: 3–3113311. Telex: 81252 RAMDA HX* • 502 rooms (27 suites). Located in the business and commercial section of Tsimshatsui . . . three Ramada hotels in Hong Kong . . . caters to business travelers . . . boasts five on-site all-purpose officers for rent by day, week or month with secretarial services and all amenities. Renaissance Club (72 rooms and 4 suites) on 11th and 12th floors features limos, private lounge, concierge, fax machines, gold bathroom fixtures, etc.

Facilities: Capriccio Tuscan-style Italian restaurant. T'ang Court Cantonese Bostonian Seafood restaurant and raw bar. Sun's Cafe. Lobby Lounge. Poolside bar and grill. Health club, glass-sided squash court, heated swimming pool, sauna and massage on roof with magnificent harbor views. Non-smoking floor. Mitsukoshi department store. Ballroom/theater and banquet rooms.

Gen. Manager: A. Hepburn. *Reservations:* Ramada Int'l Hotels.

★★★**Regal Airport Hotel** ● *30–38 Sa Po Rd. Tel: 3–7180333. Cable: HOMRA. Telex: HX 40950HOMRA* ● 384 rooms (11 suites) . . . Hong Kong's first hotel at Kai Tak Airport . . . linked by air-conditioned walkway . . . China Traders Centre with reference library . . . flight information in guestrooms . . . on-site offices for rent.

Facilities: Five Continents continental restaurant. Regal Cantonese seafood restaurant. La Plantation Coffee Shop. China Coast Pub. Sushi Bar. Lobby Bar. Promenade Cafe. Pub for English-style lunches and snacks. Flying Machine Bar. Conference and banquet rooms.

Gen. Manager: J. Halbherr. *Reservations:* UTELL.

★★★**Regal Meridien** ● *71 Mody Rd., Tsimshatsui. Tel: 3–7221818. Cable: HOMRO. Telex: HX40955HOMRO* ● 623 rooms (35 suites) . . . the first hotel in the colony with a French accent . . . joining the Tsimshatsui East waterfront area . . . deluxe rooms for women travelers . . . all amenities of home and two of the best French dining rooms in the territory, so book well in advance and enjoy a lovely evening!

Facilities: Le Restaurant de France (haute cuisine) and La Brasserie (French provincial cooking). Regal (Cantonese) seafood restaurant. Nishimura Japanese specialties. Le Grand Cafe. Hollywood East disco. Manhattan Transfer for live jazz music. Le Rendezvous for live music nightly. Bagatelle lobby lounge. Business Center. Non-smoking rooms. Health spa.

Gen. Manager: S. Pfeiffer. *Reservations:* MRI/AIR FRANCE.

★★★★★+**The Regent** ● *Salisbury Rd. Tel: 3–7211211. Cable: REGENTEL, HONG KONG. Telex: HX37134* ● 602 rooms (71 suites) . . . most spectacular hotel in the Far East . . . nothing but success and awards since the fall 1980 opening . . . sits right on the harbor . . . no structure in Hong Kong has more dramatic views . . . superb service throughout . . . everyone smiles and *no one* has his hand out (although tips are well in order here) . . . spacious, beautifully designed guest rooms with sunken baths and separate showers . . . 5 fabulous suites on 16th and 17th floors with own saunas . . . nearly perfect this place, with its glass-encased lobby . . . new Health Centre . . . own fleet of Daimlers.

Facilities: Harbourside Coffeehouse, lower level at water's edge.

The Steak House, lower level. Mezzanine Lounge for late night views. Lobby bar for drinks and snacks. Plume (nouvelle cuisine) on two levels with fabulous views and one of Asia's most renowned wine cellars. Also Lai Ching Heen Cantonese restaurant and pool bar. Hotel selected by International Order of Wine Tasters as having finest wine selections for 1981.

Gen. Manager: R. Greiner. *Reservations:* REGENT INTERNA-TIONAL.

★★★★**Royal Garden** • *69 Mody Road, Tsimshatsui East. Tel: 3–7215215. Cable: ROYALHOTEL. Telex: HX39539* • 433 rooms (33 suites) . . . an absolute delight of a hotel . . . bright, airy, and charming . . . lovely, uplifting interiors by American Howard Hirsch . . . a small hotel opened this decade and loaded with personality . . . interior atrium effect and public spaces on several levels . . . guest rooms on the smallish side but most appealing . . . highly recommended . . . glass elevators . . . balcony-type corridors.

Facilities: Restaurant Lalique with Champagne Art Deco bar (3rd floor). The Royal Falcon (split-level pub) on 1st and 2nd basement levels. The Greenery (coffee shop) on 3rd floor. The Balcony (overlooks atrium on 4th floor) for snacks and tea. The flower Lounge Cantonese restaurant (ground floor). Business center with impressive board room.

Gen. Manager: R. Pfisterer. *Reservations:* LHW

★★★**The Royal Pacific Hotel & Towers** • *33 Canton Rd., China Hong Kong City, Kowloon. Tel: 3–7361188. Telex: 44111 ROPAC HX* • 650 rooms (23 harborview suites). Part of the new China and Macau ferry terminal . . . 50% of hotel clientele from neighboring Asian nations . . . tower has more upmarket accommodations and service, with one executive floor with concierge . . . rooms twice the size of those in the hotel.

Facilities: Business Centre. Conference and banquet rooms. Reflections Bar. Cafe on the Park California-style all-day cafe. Pier 33 Parisian-style cafe. Safari Bar. The Chalet Swiss restaurant. Flavours delicatessan. Fitness Centre and squash court. Access to Country Club for golf, tennis and swimming.

Gen. Manager: J. Girard. *Reservations:* Direct.

★★★**Sheraton Hong Kong Hotel & Towers** • *20 Nathan Rd. Tel: 3–691111. Cable: SHERATON HONG KONG. Telex: HX45813* • 860 rooms (151 suites) . . . prime location at the top of Nathan Rd. . . . excellent management . . . headquarters of Sheraton in the Far East . . . loyal clients since 1974 opening . . . good-size guest rooms, although the view is less than before . . . recently refurbished . . . 2 bullet-shaped elevators on the exterior . . . fabulous shopping mall . . .

the first to put in duplex suites . . . recommended . . . Towers is actually an executive club on the two top floors—designed as a hotel within a hotel.

Facilities: Coffee shop (lobby level). Great Wall Bar (lobby level). Grandstand Grill (4th floor). Pink Giraffe supper club and Sky Lounge (top floor). Cantonese restaurant (1st & 2nd floors). Unkai Japanese restaurant. Clark Hatch Health Club and rooftop pool. Business center.

Gen. Manager: B. Loeke. *Reservations:* ITT SHERATON INTERNATIONAL.

DINING

Hong Kong boasts something like 30,000 (according to Jan Morris in her latest book, *Hong Kong*) restaurants scattered about its 1067 square-kilometer area. You can safely say that eating is serious business here. Although most of these restaurants are Chinese/Cantonese style, you can eat well in any language, and almost every ethnic group is represented here . . . Shanghai, Beijing, Szechuan, Hangzhou, Chiu Chow and Hakka (the boat people from southern Chain). You will be able to find terrific Indian/Malay curries of varying strengths, Indonesian satays, the flat bread and tandoori-style meats of India, Vietnamese, Thai and Burmese dishes, Korean grills, Singaporean steamboats, Japanese teppanyaki or tempura, freshly made pasta with bel cantos in the phonograph at Italian places, nouvelle cuisine with kir champagne cocktails in the most spectacular settings, American-style steak houses with salad bars, English roast beef on the wagon, chicken Kiev, Scotch salmon, bagels imported from Beverly Hills, and an unfortunate number of fast-food chains . . . at any hour of the day.

CHINESE FOOD

The Chinese have an oft-repeated and much beloved saying: The best place to be born is Soochow . . . where the girls are pretty; the best place to live is Hangchow . . . where the weather is pleasant; the best place to eat is Kwangchow . . . where the food is freshest; and the best place to die is Lauchow . . . where the wood makes fine coffins.

Kwangchow, or Cantonese, cuisine is by far the most popular of all Chinese food because its emphasis is on freshness, and each dish is cooked to retain the original taste of the raw ingredients. Cantonese dishes come in an endless variety; the quick stir-frying method allows any combination of foods to be put together and keeps the dishes coming in steady succession . . . and nicely hot!

Some of the better known Cantonese dishes include chicken with corn soup, crabmeat omelet, beef with oyster sauce, combination mushrooms (three or four types), chicken with cashew nuts, and fried rice. The fried rice is often served at the end of the meal to alleviate that "too full" feeling. Some waiters suggest starting with a cold-meat platter, which I find not too tasty and rather costly (priced according to the time it took cook to create). Desserts are very light, with fruit and almond jelly prevailing. And if you find any fortune cookies, they must have fallen out of the U.S. shipment!

Dim Sum, or small chow that "touches the heart," is a ten-century-old tradition in Cantonese cuisine that is very popular with Hong Kong visitors. As waiters pass your table, you can point to your heart's content to little plates that the waiter will place on your table. Each plate contains savory items like shrimp and minced pork dumplings, spring rolls, barbecued pork buns, steamed chicken roll, hot custard

SAMPLE MENU

Har Gau	Shrimp dumpling
Shiu Mai	Meat dumpling
Pai Kwat	Steamed spare ribs
Ngau Yuk Mai	Steamed beef ball
Tsing Fun Kuen	Steamed shredded chicken
Kai Bao Tsai	Steamed chicken bun
Cha Siu Bau	Barbecued pork bun
Tsing Ngau Yuk	Steamed beef ball in lotus leaf
Chun Kuen	Fried spring roll
Woo Kok	Fried taro puff
Ham Sui Kok	Fried dumpling
Fun Gwor	Steamed dumpling filled with vegetables and shrimps
Daan Tat	Custard tart
Ma Tai Goe	Fried water chestnut sticks
Ma Lai Goe	Steamed sponge cake
Ma Yung Bau	Steamed sesame bun
Yah Chup Goe	Coconut pudding
Shui Tsing Gou	White fungus sweet dumpling
Chien Tsang Goe	Thousand layer sweet cake with egg-yolk filling
Tse Chup Goe	Sugar cane juice roll

Most dim sum dishes cost approximately HK $6 each, but one or two specialties can be considerably more.

tarts, and coconut snowballs. Dim sum is usually served from early morning to midafternoon but don't expect to eat in peace; the restaurants are crowded, noisy, and carnival-like in atmosphere as hungry patrons clamor for their chow and *cha* (tea). You pay according to the number of plates piled on your table at the end of the meal.

Szechuanese food is the most spicy, with chili peppers one of the primary condiments (if not, ingredients). Shanghainese food is less spicy and less interesting. Steamed freshwater crab served with a vinegar/sugar sauce is one winter specialty. Drunken chicken is another. Northern Chinese cuisine includes both the popular Peking duck and the Mongolian hotpots, a favored winter dish because you consume the broth or soup at the end of the meal.

You can also seek out Beijing-style cuisine (known for beggar's chicken), Hunanese food, Hakka dishes, and Chiu Chow restaurants. Chiu Chow is famous for bird's nest soup and that banquet standby shark's fin soup (costly but delicious when eaten with a few drops of vinegar to aid digestion). Chiu Chow meals always begin and end with Iron Buddha bitter tea, which also aids digestion.

Whatever your fancy, a Chinese meal in Hong Kong is bound to be an adventure, so order accordingly but don't be tempted by too many dishes—a great deal often goes to waste.

Hong Kong-Side

Jumbo Floating Restaurant • *Shum Wan, Wong Chuk Hang, Tel: 5–539111* • **Sea Palace Floating Restaurant,** *Tel: 5–527340* • Touristy . . . pick your seafood from the tank . . . once is enough . . . Cantonese.

Eagle's Nest • *Hilton Hotel, Tel: 5–233111* • Excellent Cantonese cuisine in romantic setting . . . dancing in the evening.

King Heung Restaurant • *59–65 Paterson St., G/F Causeway Bay, Tel: 5–771035* • Serves Peking duck and other specialties.

Luk Yu Tea House • *26–42 Stanley Street, Tel: 5–235464* • One of the traditional old teahouses . . . famed for its dim sum and local brand of characters . . . Cantonese.

Tai Woo Restaurant • *15D–19 Wellington St., Tel: 5–245618* • Another well-known dim sum place . . . Cantonese small chow.

Man Wah Restaurant • *Mandarin Oriental Hotel, Tel: 5–220111* • Classical Cantonese in sophisticated atmosphere . . . reservations a must . . . one of the best.

Maxim's Palace • *World Trade Centre, Tel: 5–760288* • Member of a chain . . . excellent quality . . . also serves dim sum.

Peking Garden Restaurant • *Excelsior Hotel, Tel: 5–777231; Alexandra House Central, Tel: 5–266456* • Excellent chain . . . known for Peking duck.

Red Pepper • *7 Lan Fong Rd., Causeway Bay, Tel: 5–768046* • Serves Szechuan-style . . . keep the teapot coming.

Riverside Restaurant • *Food St., Causeway Bay, Tel: 5–779733* • The most recommended among the 24 restaurants in this complex . . . Cantonese.

Siam Bird's Nest Restaurant • *55 Paterson St., Tel: 5–770967* • Chiu Chow cuisine . . . popular.

Wishful Cottage • *336 Lockhart Rd., Tel: 5–735645* • Known for its vegetarian Cantonese meals . . . if you are so inclined.

Yung Kee Restaurant • *36 Wellington St., Tel: 5–221624* • Reliable and reasonable . . . locals love it . . . Cantonese.

Kowloon

City Chiu Chow • *East Ocean Centre, Tsimshatsui, Tel: 3–7236226* • More delicate cooking than Cantonese . . . very fresh flavors . . . restaurant located on second floor.

Great Shanghai Restaurant • *26 Prat Ave., Kowloon, Tel: 3–668158* • You guessed it . . . Shanghainese.

Jade Garden • *one of five Star House, Tel: 3–7226888* • 1 of 5 locations . . . this is the best . . . fun to watch huge families out for Sunday lunch . . . Cantonese.

Lai Ching Heen • *Salisbury Rd., Tsimshatsui, Tel: 3–7211211* • Stunning water's edge restaurant on lower ground level of Regent Hotel . . . beautifully appointed . . . superb service . . . expensive but worth it.

New Home Hakka Seafood Restaurant • *19 Hanoi Rd., Tsimshatsui, Tel: 3–665876* • Hakka style . . . reputed to be very good.

Ocean City Restaurant & Nightclub • *Level 3, New World Centre, Tel: 3–699688* • Huge and always packed . . . like Ocean Palace and Oceania . . . Cantonese.

Shang Palace • *64 Mody Rd., Tsimshatsui East, Tel: 3–7212111* • In basement of Kowloon Shangri-La Hotel. In a league with Man Wah and Lai Ching Heen . . . elegant surroundings and prices.

Tien Heung Lau • *18C Austin Ave., Tsimshatsui, Tel: 3–689660* • Famous Beggar's Chicken is the speciality here . . . everyone should try it once—baked in the ground encased in clay and cracked open at table.

Ziyang • *45D Chatham Rd., Tsimshatsui, Tel: 3–687177* • A fine Szechuan-style restaurant for guests in the Regent and Kowloon Shangri-La hotels area . . . within walking distance.

NON-CHINESE FOOD

Non-Chinese restaurants fall into many categories: an abundance of Japanese restaurants (good and bad) which cater mainly to their fellow countrymen; a sprouting of Vietnamese restaurants due to recent settlers; and Korean, Malay, Indian, Indonesian, Singaporean, Thai, Filipino, and a few Middle Eastern restaurants. Most of them are as casual as most Chinese restaurants, and reservations are not really necessary.

Hong Kong-side

Ashoka • *57 Wyndham St., Tel: 5–249623* • **Bombay Indian Restaurant** • *50 Leighton St., Tel: 5–7950370* • Both good and long-time neighbors.

Chili Club • *68–70 Lockhart Rd., Wanchai, Tel: 5–272872* • Good, spicy Thai food by female chefs from Bangkok.

Chitose • *atop Sogo Department Store, Causeway Bay, Tel: 5–83290068* • Teppanyaki style of grills with Kobe beef (if you can afford it) . . . terrific Japanese specialties and Tokyo prices.

Cinta • *41 Hennessy Rd., Wanchai, Tel: 5–271199* • Indonesian and Filipino specialties at excellent prices . . . rattan-decorated basement setting.

Koreana Restaurant • *Kingston Mansion, 1 Paterson St., Tel: 5–775145* • Bulgogi, kimchee, and all the fixings.

Okahan • *Lee Gardens Hotel, Tel: 5–766188* • One of the best teppanyaki places in Hong Kong.

Rangoon • *265 Gloucester Rd., Causeway Bay, Tel: 5–8932281* • Burmese fish soup and other gently spiced fish dishes.

Silla Won • *47–49 Connaught Rd., Central, Tel: 5–458873* • Another Korean barbecue restaurant . . . order kim chee and bulgogi and feel at home . . . reasonable prices.

S.M.I. • *81–85 Lockhart Rd., Wanchai, Tel: 5–273107* • Satisfies all palates for Singapore, Indonesian, and Malay satays.

Spices • *109 Repulse Bay Rd., Repulse Bay, Tel: 5–8122711* • A sampling of Asian foods in a setting that tries to recall the glories of the good old days of the Repulse Bay Hotel . . . still, the atmosphere is quite colonial.

Tandoor • *75–77 Wyndham St., Central, Tel: 5–218636* • Stylish setting with food to match . . . tandoori oven emits wonderful breads and baked meats . . excellent value.

Kowloon

Golden Bull • *Level one, 17 New World Centre, Tel: 3–694617* • Vietnamese restaurant . . . another from the fast-growing fleet of Vietnam expatriates . . . nice setting . . . very large.

Java Rijsttafel • *38 Hankow Rd., Tel: 3–671230* • The full rice table . . . if you want it . . . lots of little dishes.

Manna Korea • *6 Humphrey's Ave., Tel: 3–682067* • Bulgogi . . . kimchee . . . and all that.

Nadaman • *Shangri-La Hotel, Tel: 3–7212111* • Very popular with Japanese visitors . . . expensive.

Cafe Adriatico • *89 Kimberly Rd., Tel: 3–688554* • Middle Eastern dishes . . . Greek wines . . . owner also operates **Alice's** down the road . . . very casual.

Spicemarket • *3200 Ocean Centre, Tel: 3–676238* • Southeast Asian cookery and as spicy as you like . . . operated by the Peninsula Group . . . casual with style.

WESTERN FOOD

Betwixt sumptuous Chinese banquets and tastings of neighboring Asian specialties, you will discover that Hong Kong is also considered the mecca for good European food in the Far East. Whether you dine elegantly in the Regent's **Plume** or casually at **Delicatessen Corner,** the food will be comparable to any available in a Western metropolis. Most of the top restaurants are found in the major hotels, because Hong Kong hotels take great pride in their food and beverage services. Furthermore, Hong Kong is a hotel town, and the colony residents bring much of their social and business life into these hotels—along with the demand for something of interest. Many of the following restaurants require coat and tie in the evening as well as advance reservations (if it's a room with a view, book early). All major credit cards are accepted throughout Hong Kong. If the restaurant you choose is conveniently located within your hotel, just sign the bill (although identification may be requested).

Hong Kong-Side

Amigo • *Amigo Mansion, 79A Wongneichung Rd., Happy Valley, Tel: 5–772202* • The pride of W. C. Yeung . . . very posh . . . the best in imported delicacies . . . excellent wine cellar . . . a total dining experience.

Chinnery Bar • *Mandarin Oriental Hotel, Tel: 5–220111* • Men only . . . for over-size drinks and roast beef lunches . . . closed in the evening.

Hilton Grill • *Hilton Hotel, Tel: 5–223111* • On a par with the Mandarin for loyal clientele . . . women now allowed for lunch.

Jimmy's Kitchen • *1 Wyndham St., Tel: 5–265293* • A long-time favorite in Central District . . . good food when the boss is in . . . chicken Kiev a specialty.

Landau's Restaurant • *2/F Sun Hung Kai Centre, 30 Harbour Rd., Wanchai, Tel: 5–8912901* • Same management as Jimmy's Kitchen . . . European food but in rather dark surroundings.

La Ronda • *Furama Hotel, Tel: 5–255111* • Good value for lunch/dinner buffet table and 360-degree views . . . banquet food.

La Taverna • *1 On Hing Terrace (off Wyndham St.), Tel: 5–228904, and 57 Wongneichung Rd., Happy Valley, Tel: 5–763435* • The first of a Far East chain . . . noted for seafood salad and chic crowd.

Mandarin Grill • *Mandarin Oriental Hotel, Tel: 5–220111* • No. 1 grill room in Hong Kong . . . business lunches and cozy dinners . . . top-rate chef and service.

Market Street • *19–27 Wyndham St., Central, Tel: 5–8107566* • New and different . . . no menu . . . select meat or fish and pay by weight.

Peak Tower • *Victoria Peak, Tel: 5–8497381* • Make the journey for the views . . . not the food . . . takes large groups for set meals.

Pierrot • *Mandarin Oriental Hotel, Tel: 5–220111* • Classical French cuisine . . . red velvet decor . . . Picasso prints . . . very chic and intimate.

Prince's Tavern • *Prince's Building, Connaught Rd., Central, Tel: 5–238989* • Cajun/Creole cooking . . . There had to be one!

Rigoletto • *Fenwick St., Wanchai, Tel: 5–277144* • Considered the best Italian restaurant in the colony . . . seafood soup and fresh tortellini . . . Verdi on the phonograph . . . very reasonable.

Rotisserie • *Furama Hotel, Tel: 5–255111* • Some prefer this grillroom . . . it's all a matter of opinion . . . features la cuisine du marche.

Stanley • *86 Stanley Main St., Stanley Village, Tel: 5–938873* • Small and fun, especially in good weather . . . worth the drive.

The Verandah • *109 Repulse Bay Rd., Repulse Bay, Tel: 5–8122722* • Not quite like the original . . . but for nostalgia and romance buffs . . . pepper steaks and double consomme.

Kowloon

Au Trou Normande • *6 Carnarvon Rd., Tel: 3–668754* • French provincial . . . a long-time favorite with locals . . . nice for a change.

Beverly Hills Deli • *New World Centre, Level Two, Tel: 3–698695* • Overpriced and over here . . . kosher food if you need it.

Brasserie • *Omni Marco Polo Hotel, Harbour City* • Modeled after the superb bistro-style restaurant at sister hotel in Singapore . . . looks like a winner.

Delicatessen Corner • *Holiday Inn Golden Mile (basement), Tel: 3–693111* • Homemade sausages . . . imported cheeses . . . good for a quick lunch.

Gaddi's • *Peninsula Hotel, Tel: 3–666251* • Still one of the best for an elegant meal . . . superb Swiss service.

Grandstand Grill • *Sheraton Hotel, Tel: 3–691111* • Good by any standards . . . never considered great.

Jimmy's Kitchen • *1st floor, Kowloon Center, 29–39 Ashley Rd., Tel: 3–684027* • The original of the group.

Lalique • *Royal Garden Hotel, Tel: 3–7215215* • Beautifully designed . . . champagne bar . . . Lalique crystal table service . . . classic French dishes . . . superb wines . . . a real treat.

Margaux • *Kowloon Shangri-La Hotel, Tel: 3–7212111* • Overly fancy gourmet restaurant, named after Nixon's favorite wine . . . female sommeliers!

Pink Giraffe • *Sheraton Hotel, Tel: 3–691111* • Luncheon buffets with a view . . . a la carte at dinner . . . supper club atmosphere.

Plume • *Regent Hotel, Tel: 3–7211211* • Fantastic views on two levels . . . beautifully prepared and served nouvelle cuisine . . . impressive table settings . . . award-winning wine cellar . . . may be the meal of a lifetime.

San Francisco Steak House • *101 Barnton Court, Harbour City, Tel: 3–7227576* • If you hanker for a piece of red meat . . . at reasonable prices.

Steak House • *Regent Hotel, Tel: 3–7211211* • Excellent steaks and chops . . . American-style salad bar . . . ask for a table with a view.

Tai Pan Grill • *Omni HongKong Hotel, Tel: 3–7360088* • Good, dependable menu . . . nice atmosphere.

The Belvedere • *Holiday Inn Harbour View, Tel: 3–7215161* • Good views . . . very ambitious menu . . . service needs a little jab.

The **Chesa** • *Peninsula Hotel, Tel: 3–666251* • The best Swiss-style restaurant in the Far East . . . cozy and very popular with locals.

The **Verandah** • *Peninsula Hotel, Tel: 3–666251* • Good, steady Peninsula food for three meals daily . . . views somewhat impaired by Space Museum . . . but the popularity of this place has not waned.

NIGHTLIFE

Hong Kong

Nightracing • Wed. evenings in season (Sept. to May) from 7:30 to 10:30 p.m. . . . at both Happy Valley racecourse and Shatin (New Territories) . . . limited number of guest badges available for about HK$50 per person . . . check with hotel concierge or call Membership Department, Royal Hong Kong Jockey Club (Tel: 5–7906321) . . . or join the HKTA's horseracing tour, which includes transfer, meal, and guest badge for members' enclosure at either race track.

Nightclubs • Don't expect much and you won't be sorry . . . **Talk of the Town** at the Excelsior Hotel has local entertainment and over-views of Kowloon . . . **Eagle's Nest** at the Hilton Hotel has good Chinese food and dance music . . . **La Ronda** at Furama Hotel has dinner buffet, dance music, and 360 degree views . . . coming up are a few places in Tsim Sha Tsui or Tsim Sha Tsui East that cater to local, up-market couples . . . ask around.

Discotheques • Constantly coming and going . . . **The Talk of the Town** at the Excelsior . . . **Disco Disco** . . . otherwise, **The Go-down** in Admiralty Centre is an enduring spot . . . going strong for over a decade.

Nightcaps • The **Captain's Bar** at the Mandarin Oriental Hotel perks up around 6 p.m. and never stops until closing . . . the **Dragon Boat Bar** at the Hilton is a popular hangout . . . for camaraderie but less class, the **Lau Ling** at the Furama and **Dicken's Bar** at the Excelsior . . . even further down scale are some of the spots (old and new) in The Wanch . . . try your luck, but watch out for "padded" bills and such . . . these places can be ruinous to your wallet.

Cinemas/Theater/TV • There is some legitimate theater in Hong Kong, but chances are you didn't come halfway around the world to see an amateur production . . . there are movie houses aplenty, but the greedy landlords have been known to cut the films down (in order to sneak in an extra showing per day). . . . best bet is on the TV screen in your hotel room . . . Hotelvision has 2 films daily and the choices are not too bad . . . otherwise, there are 2 TV channels in English, 2 in Chinese . . . take your pick.

Sampan Rides • Popular during warm summer nights . . . rent one by the hour and take a tour of the Causeway Bay Typhoon Shelter . . . some even offer a hot mahjong game . . . dinner bought from floating caterers . . . and drinks if you did not think to bring your own.

Rent-A-Tram • HK$300 per hour is small fare for your own personal tram tour . . . use it for the family or have a cocktail party with friends . . . not available during rush hours . . . best after 7 p.m. when the traffic slows . . . call or write to Traffic Officer, Hong Kong Tramways, Sharp St. East, H.K.; Tel: 5–8918765.

Kowloon

Night Market • From around 8 p.m. every evening in good weather, Temple St. (off Jordan Rd.) becomes a madhouse of hawkers and stalls . . . walk around for local color . . . a jumble of sense and smells . . . few bargains here for the visitor but fun . . . watch your wallets.

Nightclubs • The **Pink Giraffe** at the Sheraton has dinner and shows in a glamorous setting . . . for something less "sophisticated," try the very touristy **Ocean City Restaurant/Nightclubs** found in Ocean Terminal, Ocean Centre, and New World Centre . . . you'll be among friends.

Discotheques • The New World Hotel has the **Faces** . . . the Peninsula allows guests temporary privileges to **Le Club** (separate entrance on Nathan Rd.) . . . for what's new and crazy, head over to New World Centre where **Bar City** is a string of 7 bars/discos . . . operated by a fellow called Fast Francis who claims 2000 clients nightly . . . Holiday Inn (Golden Mile) has **Another World** . . . Kowloon Shangri-La has **Music Room** . . . newest swing-place is **The Falcon** at the Royal Garden Hotel . . . 2 floors of fun and music . . . for down-scale excitement after dark, take a stroll along Hankow and Peking roads for any number of bottomless/topless joints that cater mainly to Asian tourists in groups.

Nightcaps • The **Sky Lounge** at the Sheraton still has a pretty decent view . . . the **Mezzanine** at the Regent has a nice band . . . try also the **Tiara Lounge** at the Kowloon Shangri-La . . . the **Golden Carp** at the Holiday Inn Harbour View . . . but if you're not keen on coat and tie after dark, stay away from the hotel scene.

SHOPPING

Look around you at the success story: well-dressed Hong Kong Chinese—with 18K gold watchbands, designer clothing, status-symbol European-made handbags and attache cases, expensive cars. Is it any wonder that even the casual tourist succumbs to this overwhelming quest for material goods that pervades every aspect of life in the colony? Is it improbable to believe the HKTA statistics that some 4+ million or so annual visitors spend about U.S.$3 billion and approximately 54% of their time shopping in Hong Kong?

Hong Kong is still and always will be the shopping capital of the world, despite inflation and increasing competition from other Asian capitals. For quantity and quality, Hong Kong boasts every name worth mentioning in the fashion industry as well as in accessories, Swiss watches, cameras, precious jewelry, stereo and other electronic equipment, tailoring, etc. And, if what appears in the shop window or on the rack doesn't appeal to you, you can have what you want custom-made within hours or days. What man has not left Hong Kong without at least one new suit, if not at least an order of shirts and perhaps a smoking jacket? In fact, the best story around town these days concerns the American who had what friends thought were his initials in Chinese characters placed prominently on the breast pocket of each custom shirt. But, practical fellow that he was, the Chinese characters actually meant "No Starch."

Some things *have* changed in Hong Kong since the early 1960s, when Western visitors discovered what a shopping mecca this beautiful harbor/city is. The center of visitor shopping has changed from a high concentration along Nathan Road's "Golden Mile" to encompass the entire colony from the New Territories to Stanley Village. In addition, there are a dozen self-contained shopping complexes such as **Harbour City** (encompassing Ocean Terminal and Ocean Centre), **New World Centre,** and **The Landmark** in Central, where you never have to see the light of day to browse, buy, wine, and dine. Every major top-class hotel built in the past decade also has its own multistory shopping area. The Sheraton has a glass bird cage that whisks one up and down in style; the Regent spills over into New World Centre; and the Mandarin has been attached by bridge to the Prince's Building for years.

It is rather safe to say that just about every chic and elegant purveyor of nonessential items is represented somewhere in Hong Kong, and there was a time when you could buy most of these things more cheaply here. Not so anymore, considering the price of land and astronomical rents. However, the shops flooding the world with Gucci, Cardin, Cartier, and other name brands still abound, but they are filled today mainly with local success stories and Japanese tourists. Americans-in-the-know prefer to wait for after-Christmas sales back home or take advantage of the colony's fantastic ready-to-wear industry (the second largest producer in the world, after Italy). This industry now ranks with Paris, Milan, and New York, and offers some of the very best bargains in town! There are factory outlet stores for men, women, and children that will make you wish you had brought an empty suitcase!

Further temptations include gold watches (made in Switzerland but assembled in Hong Kong), the daily **Jade Market,** and handmade goods from the **China Arts and Crafts** stores that carry crafts from the mainland (embroideries, silks, carvings, etc.). Before you begin, however, pick up HKTA's most popular publication *The Official Guide to Shopping, Eating Out and Services in Hong Kong* at any Information and Gift Centre. Look for the HKTA red junk emblem when you shop (displayed on door or window) because it means reliability and accurate representation of products sold.

Shopping hours are generally from 9 a.m.–6 p.m., although many hotel arcade shops are open late. If you are patronizing a tailor or shoemaker, you can plan to have fittings as late as 9 p.m. Chinese shops may keep a 10 a.m.–7 p.m. regime, and stalls are open for business as long as there is some. Bargain if you revel in it, since most merchants will offer some discount on volume (or if the sale is necessary); be aware, though, that it is not polite to bargain in the "smart stores." But at night markets and along the stalls—enjoy, enjoy!

Cash will get you everywhere in Hong Kong; so will traveler's checks. Most credit cards are accepted, but plan for a surcharge of 5% to 7% (perhaps more)—although this is illegal, it happens.

There are some important guidelines by which all neophyte shoppers in Hong Kong should abide no matter how desirable the merchandise! Be a wee bit suspicious of all merchants in whatever circumstances. Check prices quoted and pay particular attention to the bottom line on your credit card slip (write in HK$ if necessary). Check merchandise, hidden costs, warranties and labels carefully (if a name is misspelled—forget it)! Check what your desirables cost at home; it may be more prudent to wait for a local sale. If you buy on the street, be prepared to pay for inferior products; deposit the bare minimum for goods to be rendered at a later date.

The following are some suggestions of the treasure trove that abounds in Hong Kong. None of the shops listed below is aware that its name will appear in this book. I succumb fully to the joys of shopping in the colony but I prefer to enjoy it incognito.

Antiques and Works of Art   Most respected and renowned is septuagenarian **Charlotte Horstmann,** whose good taste and keen eye after a lifetime in the Far East shows up in a two-level emporium in Ocean Terminal, has actually retired but Gerald Godfrey is three, trustworthy and ready to suggest that spectacular item. Two others are **Ian McLean Antiques** at 73 Wyndham St., and **Honeychurch Antiques** (run by reliable Americans) at 29 Hollywood Rd., both in Central. For more quality goods, visit **Eileen Kershaw** in the Peninsula, **I.D.L. Antiques** in Lane Crawford House (mainly European furniture, paintings, silver). Hollywood Rd. and Ladder St. are the traditional hunting grounds for curios, but only if you know your stuff. Walk around the back streets off Central District and Nathan Rd. to find your own specialties, or a17d the classified section of the *South China Morning Post* (always good for unusual items).

Cameras and Photographic Equipment   Often less than in country of origin: Agfa-Gevaert, Asahi Pentax, Avanar, Bauer, Beaulieu, Bell & Howell, Bolex, Braun Nizo, Bronica, Canon, Carl Zeiss, Chinon, Contax, Cosina, Elmo, Enna, Fuji, Gossen, Hasselblad, Kodak, Konica/Sakura, Leica, Metz, Minolta, Minox, Nikon, Olympus, Paximat, Polaroid, Praktica, Rollei, Soligor, Topcon, Universal, Vivitar, Voigtlander, Walt Disney (home entertainment films), Yashica, Zeiss Icon.

There is a camera shop on every street corner and competition is stiff, indeed. If you know what you want, you are way ahead of the pack—so price compare. My husband and other friends have found the best prices and service for Nikon equipment at **Fotoprint Service Ltd.** on the mezzanine level of the Mandarin Hotel, Hong Kong. Ask for Mr. Fong.

Carpets and Rugs   Excellent locally made carpets, old and new, in addition to China and Persian imports. **Chinese Arts & Crafts** in Star House is one of the best for carpets from the mainland. **Tai Ping Carpets** for the local variety made in New Territories, and **Hong Kong Oriental Rug Co.** and **Mandarin Carpet** in Empire Centre. Persian carpets can be found at **Azizi Sisters** in Gammon House or Ocean Terminal. Hard to resist!

Ceramics, China, Crystal   Buy a hand-painted set for 12 Chinese-style or your favorite European china. Wedgwood, Spode, Royal Doulton, Royal Worcester, Minton, and others are at often cheaper prices than in New York or London. **Rosenthal** has its own shop in the Prince's Building, and you can find Waterford, Lalique, Baccarat, and other fine crystal at shops like **Grenley's** in Gloucester Arcade, **De Silva** in Central Building, **Dodwell Wine & Spirits** in Union House Arcade and **Eileen Kershaw** at the Peninsula Hotel. Hoya and Noritake products from Japan are also available in the colony at low prices.

Department Stores   Most famous and expensive is **Lane Crawford** in Central District (branches in Peninsula Hotel, 74 Nathan Rd. and Windsor House, Causeway Bay); **Wing On** in Des Voeux Rd. Central is less chic and more practical; **Daimaru** is the big one in Causeway Bay; **Matsuzakaya** is on Paterson St. in Causeway Bay; some swear by **China Arts and Crafts** in Star House; others prefer the **Chinese Merchandise Emporium** on Queen's Rd. Central; there are also several branches of **China Products Co.** for all those mainland made items.

Electrical Appliances   You name it, you'll find it here! Akai, B&W, Bose, Dual, Grundig, Harman/Kardon, Kenwood, KLH, Marantz, Meridian, Nagra, Ortofon, Phase Linear, Philips, Pickering, Pioneer, Ronson, Sansui, Sony, Superscope, Teac, Technics, Thorens, Toshiba, Uher—for stereo equipment, tape decks, VCR machines, speakers, etc., etc. Be sure to get the right voltage and cycle if you plan to bring your purchases back to the U.S. But you can't miss the number of stereo shops in Wanchai, Causeway Bay, and along Nathan Rd. Price compare before you buy.

Fabrics   If you prefer to make your own garments, you will save plenty on nice fabrics here. Try **Kayamally's** or **King's Fabrics** on Queen's Road Central. Popular with the locals is Cloth Alley, actually Wing On Street, where the shops and stalls are filled with locally made materials. Nearby Li Yuen Streets East and West sell inexpensive accessories. Bargain here or you will look like a tourist! Chinese products department stores also have lovely handmade silks and brocades.

Furniture   You can have it custom-made or buy it off the showroom floor, but be sure it's kiln-dried or it will fall apart in a dry-heated home. Rosewood and teak are the two most traditional woods used, especially for Chinese-style designs. For the very best in custom-made try **Charlotte Horstmann** in Ocean Terminal or **Avant Garde,** 47 Wyndham St. For Chinese-style tables and chairs in rosewood, teak, or blackwood, **George Zee and Co.** in many of the hotel arcades is an old, established firm. Also try **Philip Chu** on Hankow Road, Kowloon. **China Arts & Crafts** in Star House has an interesting selection of furniture.

Gifts and Handicrafts   Unusual items for friends back home, try **Amazing Grace Elephant Co.** in Excelsior Hotel or Ocean Terminal; **Mountain Folkcraft** in Ocean Terminal; **Welfare Handicrafts; Temple Street Night Market.**

Jewelry   Precious and semiprecious stones and settings are excellent buys in Hong Kong, if you understand your gems. Again, anything you desire can be crafted, copied, or reset. If it's jade you prefer, consult an expert. For diamonds, consult the **Diamonds Importers Association** for their member firms and an introduction card, available from DIA, Rm. 1707, 17th floor, Lane Crawford House, Queen's Rd., Central (Tel: 5–235497). In general, patronize shops with HKTA membership displayed and always check gold hallmark. Always ask for a receipt and certificate of authenticity. Do not buy gold or gems on the street, and be wary of Cartier items not sold in the main store. Two good jewelery outlets are **Anju Jewelery** in Kaiser Estate, Hunghom and **Tse Sui Luen,** across the street in Summit Building. Both have on premises "factories" and will make anything to order. Good prices. Call HKTA (3–7225555) for more information on factory outlets.

It is not advisable to make an expensive pearl purchase in Hong Kong because the best quality tend to stay in Japan; seed pearls are a good buy here, however, if you like their ambience. Someone who has made a terrific name for herself, especially in the U.S., is the jewelry designer/socialite Kai Yin Lo, whose distinctive styles of semi-precious stones are worth every penny. Visit her gallerylike shops in the Mandarin and Peninsula hotels and compare prices with Bloomingdale's, Saks and Neiman Marcus.

Ready to Wear   Every name in British, French, or Italian fashion is represented here, often with its very own chic boutique. If you're looking for Dior, Cardin, Lanvin, Ricci, Hermes, Courreges, YSL, Jourdan, Gucci, Pucci, etc. you will find the latest rage in Hong Kong but be prepared to pay plenty! Since so much of fine ready-to-wear is now made in the colony, the latest shopping rage is to visit the factory outlet stores at least once weekly to see what's new. Many of these shops (cash only) are in the Kaiser Estate area of Hunghom, Kowloon. Try **Camberley Enterprises,** and **Four Seasons Garments,** to name a few. A list of these outlets is available from HKTA—watch also the *South China Morning Post* for advertisements. If you don't fancy the taxi ride out and back, visit **Shopper's World** at 104 Pedder Building, Hong Kong, plus **Camberley** in Swire House and **Lim Ying Ying** in Hung Hom. Try also the **Diane Freis** boutiques, where colorful no-wrinkle dresses cost less than half the U.S. price (beware of knock-offs, though, even from her own sister), the **Joyce Boutique** for no bargains but haute style; the **Ralph Lauren** outlet shops for some savings; and the **Miss O** (Oscar de la Renta) outlets for bargains at D'Aguilar Place, Central or 17 Hankow Rd. (Sands Building) in Tsimshatsui. If you are a knit freak, such well-known Italian designers as **Krizia** have their work down in Hong Kong (outlet is Sands Building—same as Miss O); the territory is also famous for cashmere sweaters, if you can bear to adorn your body with other than Pringle.

Designer jeans for a song can be found at **Stanley Market,** in Stanley Village, with blouses and cute tops to match. Here are Gloria Vanderbilt, Givenchy, and YSL at rip-off prices. Ceramics, rattan, and linens are also said to be cheaper here. But for dress-up time, why not try one of **Jenny Lewis's** lovely designs in silk, Chinese embroidery and beadwork. Ms. Lewis, a local designer of English origin, makes lovely garments for those very special occasions. Her boutiques in Swire House and the Regent Hotel arcade feature all-silk dresses, gowns, pantsuits, jackets, shawls, bags, belts, jewelry, and more for the total look. Lovely taste here. Shop carefully for an evening outfit you will keep for a lifetime.

Shoes and Handbags

Imported European-designed shoes are popular in Hong Kong but don't expect to find a selection in the larger sizes. If your feet are petite, then you can walk away with the latest in Charles Jourdan, Bally, Gucci, Pierre Cardin, Balmain, Dior, Ricci, and good English stock in men's wear. For locally made footwear, try **Diamond, Fairy, Nancy** and **Paris** in the shops that curve around Wongneichung Road in Happy Valley. Bargaining is allowed. Custom orders will take about a week. You can also have expensive European-designed handbags copied for a fraction of the original cost. Try **Dickson and Company** in Melbourne Plaza, and Vanity Fair in Central Building.

Tailors

And now it's the man's turn to indulge his fancy! Although the era of the 24-hour, U.S.$50 Hong Kong suit is long past, it is possible to have a custom-made suit ready in three days at a cost of about half the U.S. price (count on US$350 to $500 for good quality fabric and labor). There are many excellent tailoring shops on both sides of the harbor—whom you pick is whom you happen to like. Personality means a lot in this business! Shop around and listen to your instincts regarding fabric, styles, price, and number of fittings offered (the more the better). A few well-known names are **George Chen** in the Peninsula; **British Textile Company** in the Mandarin; **Jimmy Chen** in the Hong Kong Hotel shopping arcade; **Shirts N Shirts** on Haiphong Road, Tsim Sha Tsui. If you have just a few days, stick with the higher-priced shops in hotel arcades. Avoid the Indian-run establishments. Pay more and be happy with the results!

Watches Everywhere and less expensive than anywhere! Brands include Arlux, Audemars Piguet, Baume & Mercier, Bulova, Cartier (watch for fakes), Certina, Citizen, Continental, Ernest Borel, Girard Perregaux, Heuer, TWC, Jaegar Le Coutre, Longines, Movado, Omega, Piaget, Rado, Rolex, Seiko, Technos, Tissot, Tudor, Universal Geneve, Vacheron Constantin, Waltham. Patronize reputable shops and scrutinize your guarantee. Contact the **Swiss Watch Industry Information Centre** (Tel: 5–279621) for names of local agents, if you're planning on a major purchase. In the play category, Seiko watches are cheaper here than in Japan and their Rolex-copy models fool anyone from afar.

INDONESIA

HISTORY

Traders from China and India, who assimilated into the local animistic beliefs such religions from the East as Hinduism, Brahmanism, Vishnuism, and Mahayana Buddhism, were among the earliest outside influences on the Indonesian archipelago. This process of peaceful assimilation lasted for some six centuries and eventually engulfed the entire vast group of islands. For example, the Mahayana Buddhist kingdom of Shri-Vijaya in Sumatra came to power around A.D. 672 and reigned throughout the 13th century. During this period, the largest and most renowned monument extant to Buddha was erected—the vast stupa of Borobudur, which dates from the 9th century A.D. under Shri-Vijaya's Shailendra Dynasty. Other historic monuments that represent ambitious examples of the Hindu-Buddhist influence in the archipelago at this time are the temples at Prambanan, Pawon, Mendut, and Kelasan.

While trade was burgeoning during the 13th century (indeed, Marco Polo is said to have stopped by the Moluccas in 1292 and immediately called them the "spice islands"), yet another religion was introduced. This was Islam, which arrived in Sumatra as early as the 13th century and spread gradually through the archipelago for the next 200 years. As more and more Islamic "kingdoms" arose in Sumatra, Java, Sulawesi, Kalimantan, and the Moluccas, the Hindu era came to an end. Hence, many Hindu followers fled to Bali where they continued their religion in isolation. To this day, Bali is the only island in the chain where the greater part of the population embraces Hinduism.

That the Indonesian people can be considered among the most tolerant and peace-loving on this earth is understandable from their location between Asia and Australia and their fascinating history. Furthermore, they can rightfully boast the discovery in 1891 of the "Java Man" *(Pithaecanthropus erectus)* of the Pleistocene Era, proving that some sort of civilization occurred here on what was most likely still part of the Asian mainland (about 500,000 years ago), while sheets of ice still covered Europe and the Western Hemisphere. "Solo Man" was unearthed in the 1930s, not far from Trinil, and thought to be between 60,000 and 100,000 years old—of a Stone-Age culture.

The Portuguese conquest of Malacca brought Europeans into the region. These Portuguese were especially interested in the Moluccas, because they wanted their spices at the lowest prices possible! By the end of the 17th century, the Portuguese were being challenged by the Dutch and the British. The rivalry of the three powers culminated in the triumph of the Dutch East India Company, which had already established itself in Java in 1619 and renamed the principal port-city Batavia. Except for a few brief years during the Napoleonic Wars (1811–1815), when the English were in control and Sir Thomas Stamford Raffles was the much respected governor (and wrote the still worthy *History of Java),* the Dutch ruled Indonesia with an iron hand for about three centuries.

During colonial rule, a number of popular heroes challenged the unsympathetic policies that emanated from The Netherlands. Among them were Trunajaya, Surapati, Iman Bonjol (plenty of streets named after this one), Teuku Umar, and Prince Diponegoro. Leading the resistance prior to the Second World War were Mohammed Hatta and Achmed Sukarno, later considered "father of the country" and its first president. These two men were symbols of Dutch repression of the native Indonesian language, education for all, and work opportunities. Both were often jailed and even exiled. The Dutch were dispersed in 1942 as the Japanese arrived, bringing yet another occupation. But the Indonesians soon realized that this subjugation was only temporal; to ensure as much cooperation as possible, the Japanese espoused eventual independence from colonial rule.

Indonesian nationalism received a hefty boost between 1942 and 1945. The Japanese military regime relied heavily on local administrative and political support, reinstated the Indonesian language in schools, and renamed Batavia "Jakarta." The regime also recognized the ideals of both Sukarno and Hatta who, on the very day of the Japanese surrender to the Allies, issued their famous Proclamation of Independence. It was August 17, 1945, and it was one of the post-war shots "heard 'round the world."

Four long and arduous years followed as Indonesians fought a revolution to regain their land from the foreign devils who had occupied it for so long. It took world opinion and some discussion in the United Nations before the Dutch bowed and returned the sovereign rights of The Netherlands East Indies back to the new Republic of Indonesia. Queen Juliana finally signed the official document on December 27, 1949.

Achmed Sukarno became the new nation's first president, a post he held until deposed in 1965. He was a brilliant and charismatic man, whom his fellow countrymen called "Bung" (brother) Karno. Some said his manner was so mesmerizing that he could persuade and cajole just about anyone. However, in his later years of power he seemed to "run amok" and misuse the trust bestowed upon him by the people. He married a Japanese callgirl, who called herself Dewi (goddess), and lavished jewels and furs upon her while most of the country lived in poverty. He elected himself president "for life" and put forward a "guided democracy," against all that was written in the Constitution. He erected costly monuments to his glory and entered into an unnecessary confrontation with neighboring Malaysia. He withdrew membership of the Republic from the United Nations and espoused "Nasakom," an acronym for nationalism, religion, and Communism.

An attempted Communist coup in September 1965 failed but instigated more than a year of intense bloodshed, as Indonesians turned on each other in an attempt to rid the country of inside and outside Communist influences. Almost half a million lives were estimated lost— sometimes whole villages—before the Sukarno regime was deposed. The "father of the country" died a broken man, under house arrest. He was succeeded by Major General Suharto, who was installed as president of the Republic in 1968.

Under Suharto's leadership, the bankrupt and bereft country has reclaimed its place in the world. There are enviable natural resources (including plenty of gas and oil) and healthy foreign investments. However, there are still plenty of problems: immense poverty, too great a distinction between the classes, high illiteracy and infant mortality, factions between certain ethnic groups, and a rampant bureaucracy. Yet, visitors never fail to be overwhelmed by the beauty of the land and the people.

Tourist facilities are developing slowly but steadily, as the government understands how important this industry is. Travelers not only bring in much needed "hard currency"; they also offer an appreciation of the diverse cultures of the archipelago and the indigenous artistry inherent here. Worldwide concern for the restoration of Borobudur prompted IBM to offer computer technology, saving years of work and millions of dollars. At the same time, this concern brought focus to Yogyakarta—cultural capital of the country—and the preservation of such arts as batik, wayang plays, the ramayana ballet, silver-working, and other manifestations of the archipelago's colorful history.

Perhaps it is the women of Indonesia that make the country so vibrant in the eyes of Westerners, for they have never been anything but "liberated." Proud, beautiful, and forthright, they fought alongside their men in the struggle for independence and then took their well-earned place in the social and economic world. In addition to their beauty and feminism, Indonesian women are equal partners with the men in any business, profession, or trade they may wish to pursue. They also have the rare distinction of pointing proudly to a period in their history when a kingdom ruled by women flourished. (Even today among the Bataks of Sumatra, a multilineal society still prevails where inheritance and lineage are traced from the maternal line, and local issues are settled by a village council in consultation with women.) So, it comes as no surprise that one of modern Indonesia's greatest heroes is Ibu (Mother) Kartini, the little princess who advocated freedom and emancipation for all during the late 19th century.

INDONESIA IN A CAPSULE

Largest archipelago in the world . . . comprises some 13,677 islands . . . extends 3200 from east to west . . . 1100 miles from north to south . . . stepping stone along equator between Asia and Australia . . . primary islands are Java, Sumatra, Bali, part of Kalimantan, Sulawesi, and Irian Jaya (western part of New Guinea) . . . also Moluccas (which Marco Polo christened Spice Islands in 1292) and Nusa Tenggara Islands . . . 155 million Indonesians . . . fifth most populated country in world (after China, India, USSR, and U.S.) . . . inhabited as early as 5000 years ago . . . Java man discovered here is more than half a million years old . . . majority are Moslem . . . Bali is primarily Hindu . . . many ethnic groups represented . . . wondrous place and unforgettable experience.

PLANNING AHEAD

INDONESIAN TOURIST PROMOTION OFFICE for North America is located at 3457 Wilshire Blvd., Los Angeles, CA 90010 (Tel: 213–387–2078). Tourist information and visas are available at the Indonesian Embassy in Washington, DC, and Ottawa, Ontario; the Indonesian Consulate General in New York City, San Francisco, and Houston; and the Indonesian Consulate in Los Angeles and Vancouver. There is also an Honorary Consul for Indonesia in Hawaii (c/o Pacific Resources Inc. in Honolulu).

A **Visitor Information Center** is located in the Jakarta Theatre Bldg. at 9 Jalan M. Husni Thamrin, not far from the Hotel Indonesia (Tel: 354094). Other local information can be obtained from **NITOUR,** the National and International Tourist Bureau at 2 Jalan Majapahit and at offices throughout the country.

VISAS are not required of bona fide tourists holding valid U.S. and Canadian passports for a stay of up to two months for entry at Denpasar

(Bali), Jakarta, Medan, Biak, and Manado. Onward ticket is necessary and passport must be valid for at least six months after date of arrival.

INOCULATIONS for smallpox and cholera are required for entry and must be validated in an International Health Certificate if arriving from an infected area. Yellow fever inoculation may also be required if arriving from an infected area. Depending upon length of stay and itinerary, other inoculations you should discuss with your doctor are typhoid, paratyphoid, and gammaglobulin (for hepatitis).

ENTRY BY AIR is through the new **Cengkareng** (Soekarno-Hatta) **International Airport** in Jakarta, **Halim Hlp International Airport, Ngurah Rai International Airport** at Denpasar on Bali, or **Polonia International Airport** in Medan (Sumatra). Cengkareng is about 19 miles from Jakarta but the trip takes one hour. If you are not part of a tour and being taken care of, opt for a hotel limousine into the city. Taxis add a surcharge plus road toll so you need a fistful of rupiahs even before the door is closed. There are banks for changing currency and porterage service at all the airports. Be sure to save plenty of time for baggage handling, immigration and customs. Speed is not a virtue here!

EXIT BY AIR is normal procedure, provided you have not overstayed your welcome, your onward passage is confirmed, and you are not exporting Indonesian currency and/or valuable artifacts.

Departure tax is Rupiah (Rp.) 9000 per person for international flights, Rp. 3500 on domestic routes.

ARRIVAL BY SEA into Indonesia is possible through the international ports of Belawan (Sumatra), Denpasar (Bali), Jakarta (Java), Padang Bay (Bali), Surabaya (Java), and Padang (Sumatra). If you are planning to disembark your luxury cruise vessel or cargo ship in one of these ports, be sure to enlist the aid of the line's local agent to clear immigration and customs.

Among the lines sailing among the Indonesian archipelago are Pearl Cruises *(Ocean Pearl);* Salen-Lindblad Cruises *(Island Explorer);* Royal Cruise Line *(Golden Odyssey);* Society Expeditions *(World Discoverer);* and Travel Dynamics *(Illiria).* All these vessels have excellent itineraries and offer the best possible way to enjoy these islands.

DUTY FREE is not the byword here and the importation of consumer goods, other than personal effects, is carefully noted. Bona fide visitors may bring in the usual amount of alcoholic beverages (2 liters per adult), cigarettes (200), 50 cigars or 100 grams of tobacco, and a reasonable amount of perfume. Photographic equipment, typewriters, radios, and other accoutrements must be recorded and the serial numbers may be entered right into your passport. Since this is the usual practice in most controlled countries, travelers should not be offended but rather save time by entering the serial numbers themselves (the last page is best).

On the customs declaration, visitors will also be required to state the exact amount of foreign currency in their possession as well as amount of film (specify exposed or not). And avoid carrying pets, plants, or fruit.

CURRENCY of Indonesia is the Rupiah (Rp.). The approximate rate of exchange is around 1600 Rp. to U.S.$1. Coins in denominations of Rp. 5, 10, 25, 50, and 100 are circulated, and notes are Rp. 100, 500, 1000, 5000 and 10,000. Stick to the lower denominations outside major hotels, as change may not be available. Use the coins for tips and the many unfortunate ones you may encounter on the streets, who always have their hands out.

The best rate of exchange is through major banks, although it is more convenient in hotels. Rupiahs can be reconverted at the airport, provided you have receipts to prove the transaction. It is prohibited to carry Indonesian currency in or out of the country.

LOCAL TIME in most of Indonesia is Greenwich Mean Time plus 7 hours. Jakarta is exactly 12 hours in advance of Eastern Standard Time and in the same zone as Bangkok, Java, Bali, Sumatra, and Madura. It is 1 hour behind Hong Kong, Manila and Taipei and 2 hours behind Tokyo and Seoul. Since the Indonesian Archipelago is so vast, the islands of Kalimantan, Sulawesi, and Nusa Tenggara (not Bali) are on GMT plus 8 hours; and the islands of Maluku and Irian Jaya are on GMT plus 9 hours.

LOCAL CURRENT is 220 volts, 50 cycles, so travelers should pack convertors and extension cords (in case the plug is far, far away from the only mirror available).

LOCAL WATER should be avoided. Only bottled or boiled water should be used (supplied in major hotels). Ice in top tourist hotels is made with boiled water (or so they say), so use your discretion according to the sensitivity of your intestines. This is a country in which belly problems can be frequent.

OFFICIAL LANGUAGE in Indonesia is Bahasa Indonesia, although regional languages like Javanese, Balinese, and Chinese often take over in the outlying areas. English is widely spoken in major tourist centers, and oldtimers will remember the Dutch they were forced to learn in school. Bahasa Indonesia is based on Malay and contains many words of Sanskrit and Arabic origin. It was introduced as a national language in 1928, while the country was still under Dutch colonial rule, and spread rapidly as a matter of nationalist pride. The grammar is quite simple and it is rather easy to learn a few words during your stay.

There are some 25 major daily publications on Java, with two in English, the *Indonesia Times* and *Indonesian Observor*. They are available along with overseas publications (sometimes censored) in major hotels. There are almost 50 radio stations and one government-owned television station in the country. Some of the television programs broadcast in the evening will be familiar to Americans. Whoever would have dreamed that Indonesian was spoken in the Wild West!

Maps and small area guides in English are available from the Directorate General of Tourism in Jakarta as well as in hotel shops.

BUSINESS HOURS are generally from 8 a.m.–3 p.m. Mon. through Thurs.; until 11:30 a.m. on Fri. only; and from 8 a.m.–2 p.m. on Sat. Some firms close at 4 p.m. weekdays, with an hour off for lunch. Banks are often only open from 9 a.m. until noon weekdays; from 9–10:30 a.m. on Sat.; so always make your transactions early to be assured of service.

NOTE · · · It is best not to accept someone else's word for hours of business; find out for yourself.

There are plenty of local trade associations and multinational companies in Jakarta, especially for those in the business of oil, cement, or banking. The **American Chamber of Commerce** in Indonesia is located in the Citibank Bldg. (8th floor), 55 Jalan M. H. Thamrin (Tel: 354993; telex: 44368). The president is H. V. Ward. The INVESTMENT COORDINATING BOARD is located at 6 Jalan Jen. Gatot Subroto, Selatan, Jakarta (Tel: 512008; Telex: 44368). Anwar Nawawi is the promotion chief.

The **U.S. Embassy** in Jakarta is located at 5 Jalan Medan Merdeka, Selatan (Tel: 340001–9). The **Canadian Embassy** can be found at 29 Jalan J. Sudirman Kav (Tel: 584030).

TIPPING is becoming a practice in Indonesia, but it is still mainly in the Rp. 500 range for small services (taxi drivers, porters, bellboys, and barbers). If your luggage is especially cumbersome, another Rp. 100 is in order, per bag. Major hotels and restaurants add a straight 10% service charge to accommodation, bar, and restaurant chits but another 5% (equivalent) here and there doesn't hurt. (Be prepared for the 11% government tax on top of everything else, however.)

TELEPHONE AND TELEX service in Indonesia has improved somewhat in the past 15 years but never expect miracles. Always use the telex in your hotel so you can scream about payment when it gets messed up (some businessmen book hotels according to the integrity of the telex operators). Overseas telephone calls should also be made from your hotel and it is always better to call out than to receive (hotel operators in Indonesia are notorious for saying, "Sorry, he or she is not registered" when indeed you are sitting upstairs waiting). The local telephone system is not much better and usually out of order. Rely on the good services of your hotel for local calls and avoid unnecessary frustration.

Major hotels are also helpful in mailing letters and packages back home, but be sure to insist upon actually feeling the stamps (once bought and paid for) and attaching them yourself. Don't play the "all out" game; waiting another day for stamps will ensure delivery of your mail.

WHAT TO WEAR in Indonesia is what the Indonesians wear, the loveliest cotton batik in the world. As the archipelago actually straddles the equator, you can assume that the climate is exceptionally hot and sticky. It also rains frequently and fast, but the nights are blissfully cool. Synthetic fibers and pantsuits should be left at home. Here, you will need natural cottons that do not confine the body. Sport shirts and slacks are fine for the men, dresses and loose-flowing garments for the ladies. Life in Indonesia is casual and although local businessmen do don Western-style suits and ties, they need "dress up" only in the major hotels at dinnertime. Then, it becomes almost a necessity because the air conditioning is so cold.

Comfortable shoes are also a necessity here, because walking around in the heat will probably make your feet swell. Sunhats or parasols and plenty of sunscreen are also advisable because the rays are extra strong at this latitude. If your touring includes a stop at a tea plantation or a sacred mountain, the air will be quite cool so slacks and sweaters are in order. For beach and pool time, many visitors buy a length of batik and wear it as a sarong while walking through hotel lobbies and the like. In fact, the batiks are so irresistible that you may find a new wardrobe following you home!

LOCAL TRANSPORTATION throughout Indonesia varies from two- to four-wheeled vehicles to trains and an extensive domestic air service. **Taxis** are plentiful in the large metropolitan areas. In Jakarta, it is best to use the Bluebird taxi company fleet which has meters that work. In Denpasar (Bali), taxis often set fixed rates between town and the hotels. There are also pick-up taxis between Jakarta and resort areas, and each passenger pays according to the length of the ride. Major hotels have their own taxi service, which are air-conditioned and comfortable but more expensive. But passengers pay for the convenience of a driver who has been properly instructed and maneuvers carefully through the usually clogged city traffic. These cars can also be hired for the day, for visitors and/or business executives with a tight schedule.

Local **buses** are best left to the natives; they are uncomfortable and hopelessly overcrowded, and language is a problem. There are express buses linking major towns if you don't mind a bouncy ride. Cities linked by bus service in Java are Jakarta, Yogyakarta, Surabaya, Bogor, Cirebon, Semarang, Surakarta, Tegal, Purwokerto, Magelang, Malang, and Bandung. In Sumatra, bus service links Banda Aceh, Medan, Parapat, Sibolga, Padang, Bukittinggi, Pekan Baru, Jambi, Palembang, Bengkulu, and Tanjungkarang. One of the most widely used routes is between Surabaya and Bali.

For traveling short distances around the town, you can choose among the **oplet, bemo, becak, ojek,** or **tonga.** The **oplet** (actually **opelette**) is Jakarta's answer to the Philippine jeepney but lacks the colorful exterior. Cheap and handy, they ply regular routes like buses and even go as far as Bogor. The bemo is considered the poor-man's taxi; a three-wheeled motorized pedicab, it also runs regular routes although it can also be hired for individual purposes. The **bemo** seats one passenger in front and six in the back compartment. In Bali the **bemo** is a converted pick-up truck and seats about 10 passengers on wooden benches. The **becak** is a three-wheeled pedicab and only operates in Jakarta between the hours of 10 p.m. and 6 a.m. by law, although they operate freely in Yogyakarta and Denpasar. Fares are about Rp. 150 for the becak, versus about Rp. 50 for oplet and bemo. The ojek is a bicycle taxi, often motorized; the passenger sits behind the driver for a minimum fee of Rp. 100. The Tonga is a horsecart and in Indonesia is called a **dokar, delman,** or **sado.** It seats one passenger next to the driver and about three behind for a minimum fare of Rp. 200. They are most frequently found in the outlying areas, not in towns or cities.

Railway buffs may wish to try either the **bima** or **mutiara** train between Jakarta's Kota Railway Station and Surabaya via Yogyakarta. The bima is the better, with berths and a dining car. The mutiara has only reclining seats for the trip that takes from 15½ to 18 hours but passes some interesting countryside (although mainly in the dark). There are other trains in Java and Sumatra, but be prepared for primitive travel.

Domestic **air** service is frequent and inexpensive. Garuda Indonesia Airways links Jakarta with 30 domestic destinations using DC9 jets. Merpati Nusantara Airlines covers the smaller areas with smaller planes. Bouraq Indonesian Airlines has a large fleet for charter service only.

There is also **ferry** service available between Merak, Java and Padang, Sumatra, with six departures daily. Ferries between Ujungganyar (Java) and Kamal (Madura) depart every 30 minutes; those between Ketapang (Java) and Gillimanuk (Bali) depart approximately every 2½ hours. Fares are incredibly cheap to match the lack of luxury.

Finally, for do-it-yourself touring there are plenty of **rental cars** available from international companies (Avis, Hertz, National) but prices are high for chauffered-vehicles. Expect to pay more than U.S.$100 per day. Actually, the **motorcycle** is the favored beast of burden in Bali and Yogyakarta. Beachniks hire them by the day or week. They are practical, easy to manage, and totally ruin what is left of the atmosphere.

LOCAL CUSTOMS in Indonesia vary among the islands in the archipelago because so many ethnic groups inhabit this vast area. Despite a turbulent history and considerable bloodshed in the 20th century, the people are courteous and gentle. Westerners who dress immodestly, speak in loud voices, and use rude gestures are not appreciated. The Indonesians are very hospitable and visitors are expected to at least taste food and drink when offered. As in all Moslem countries (only Bali is Hindu), the left hand is considered unclean and should not be used to pass or eat food.

When visiting religious monuments and places considered sacred, proper dress should be worn and polite respect observed. Photographers should always ask permission before "shooting," especially in outlying areas where the imprint of one's image may be contrary to tradition and belief.

The Javanese seem to engage in rule by consensus and dislike outward signs of disagreement, so consider anything but a firm "YES" to be a silent "NO"—a word that will not pass their lips. And take along an extra supply of patience, for it takes a long, long time to accomplish anything in this country. Time means nothing here, despite the influx of digital watches from Japan and Hong Kong, and the waiting period for appointments is often lengthy. Of course, a little *baksheesh* (tip) will always pave the way and is the usual practice in this country.

FESTIVALS AND HOLIDAYS occur in Indonesia almost daily and are part of the charm of this country. In Bali, expect some type of temple celebration wherever you go (details available locally). The Ramayana Ballet Festival is held between May and October during the full moon at the Prambanan Temple near Jogyakarta. *Wayang kulit* (Indonesian shadow plays) are performed all year round in Yogyakarta at the Gedung Kiwo and the Ambarrukmo Palace Hotel. Public holidays are marked with an asterisk(*).

*January 1 • *New Year's Day.*

January 11 • *Sekaten* • Week-long Moslem fair in Yogyakarta and Surakarta that precedes the prophet Mohammed's birthday.

January 14 • *Galungan* • Most important event in the Balinese year. It symbolizes victory of good over evil with decorations, offerings, gamelan music, and dancing.

January 18 • *Grebeg Maulud* • Ceremonies in Yogyakarta and Surakata commemorate the birth of the prophet Mohammed. Music plays at midnight.

January • *Kunigan* • Offerings and religious ceremonies throughout Bali to honor ancestral spirits.

January/February • *Chinese New Year* • Noisy celebrations among Jakarta's Chinese population.

March/April • *Wafat isa Aimasih* • Christian Good Friday.

May • *Sedang Sono Pilgrimage* • Javanese Catholics make pilgrimage to Sendang Sono, a shrine dedicated to Holy Virgin.

May • *Waicak* • Commemorates Lord Buddha's birth . . . country's few Buddhists attend ceremonies at Borobudur.

May 30 • *Sarawati* • Commemorates the God of Knowledge in Bali with religious ceremonies at temples and reading the Veda book in homes.

June 3 • *Pagerwesi* • Religious rituals throughout Bali honor Sang Hyang Pramesti Guru, creator of universe, and offerings are made to ward off evil forces.

July 17 • *Balimu* • This ritual of purification falls prior to the month of fasting, especially at Negeri Pau and Durian Tinggi in West Sumatra, where you can see processions and a show of martial arts by young men of both villages.

*August 2 • *Idul Fitri* • End of Ramadan, the traditional month of fasting for Moslems. Two full days of holiday and feasting.

August 13 • *Galungan* • Repeat of January's festivities on Bali.

*August 17 • *Independence Day* • Parades, official ceremonies, and carnival atmosphere, plus decorated buildings in Jakarta.

August 23 • *Kuningan* • Same observances as January holiday, repeated throughout Bali.

September 23 • *North Sulawesi Anniversary* • Cultural performances, horse and bull racing events in Manado.

*October 8 • *Idul Adha* • Eve of Haj is marked by an annual pilgrimage to Mecca for Moslems. Cattle are slaughtered and offered to the poor.

December 23 • *Batara Turun Kabeh* • Temple ceremonies at Panataran Agung, Besakih in Bali.

*December 25 • *Christmas* • Celebrated throughout Indonesia.

December 31 • *Sekaten* • Repeat of January's festivities on Bali.

BACKGROUND MATERIAL   There are many fine books that discuss Indonesia, but few of them seem to have found their way into North American outlets. Check your local library for a bibliography. You can also pick up some books locally (Nirjosuparto and Kartini).

The Art of Indonesia by Frits A. Wagner, an Art of the World series book (Crown Publishers). Gives an excellent historical, sociological, and religious background overview.
The History of Java by Sir Thomas Stamford Raffles (Oxford University Press, 1965, two volumes). More history to enjoy.
Rama Stories in Indonesia by Sutjipto Wirjosuparto (Bhratara Publishers, Jakarta)
Letters of a Javanese Princess by Raden Adjeng Kartini, translated by Agnes L. Symmers (W. W. Norton). Ibu Kartini is one of the country's most beloved folk heroines.
Ring of Fire by Lawrence Blair with Loren Blair (Bantam, 1988).
Islands of Fire, Islands of Spice by Richard Bangs and Christian Kallen (Sierra Club Books, 1988).
The new *Indonesia Handbook* by Bill Dalton (4th edition) (Moon Publications, 1988).
Insight Guides for *Bali, Java, Indonesia* (APA Productions, Prentice Hall). Check for latest update.
Ramayana and *Mahabharata*—two originally Indian epic poems on which lie all Indonesian arts. Gods, kings, demons, and clowns in these tales are brought to life nightly by island's puppeteers.

INDONESIA TOURS

Jakarta and West Java

Angklung Tour • 3 hours, daily from Jakarta . . . visit bamboo musical instrument workshop in Padasuka village . . . southeast of city.

Bandung City Tour • 3 hours, daily . . . Biological Museum, Zoological Gardens, Institute of Technology.

Bandung Volcano Tour • all day . . . Tangkuban Prahu volcano and rim and Ciater hot springs . . . Lembang fruit market . . . Bogor Botanical Gardens and Puncak Pass.

Bandung Package • 2 to 4 days . . . visits Bogor and Puncak . . . Tangkuban Prahu and Ciater hot springs.

Bogor • 5 to 6 hours, daily . . . Botantical Gardens and Presidential Palace . . . 8-hour tour includes lunch at Puncak Pass.

Cirebon Tour • 6 hours, daily . . . Sultan's Palace . . . Princess Cemetery . . . batik cloth center.

Garut and Tasikmalaya Tour • 8 hours, daily . . . craft centers and hot springs.

Jakarta City Tour • 3 to 4 hours, daily . . . Presidential Palace, National Monument, Central Museum, Chinatown, Old Batavia restoration, Pasar Ikan (fish market), Senayon sports complex, batik factory.

Jakarta Night Tour • 4 to 6 hours, daily . . . Ancol Dreamland Park, jai alai stadium . . . dinner and cultural show.

Krakatoa/Ujung Kulon Package • 4 to 6 days . . . cruise to Krakatoa volcano in Sunda Strait . . . land on island it created . . . continue on to Ujung Kulon wildlife reserve.

Mini Indonesia Tour • 3 to 4 hours, daily . . . tour of Indonesia in miniature . . . bird park . . . Museum Indonesia . . . etc.

Yogyakarta and Central Java

Borobudur Temple Tour • 4 hours, daily . . . includes visits to Medut and Pawon temples . . . longer tour also includes Prambanan.

Yogyakarta City Tour • 3 hours, daily . . . visits Sultan's Royal Kraton . . . Sonobudoyo Museum . . . batik workshop and silver-works at Kota Gede . . . Taman Sari Water Castle substitute on Moslem holidays.

Prambanan Temple Tour • 3 tours, daily . . . includes Plaosan and Kalasan temples . . . evening tour to ballet performances during full moon nights from May to October.

Solo Tour • 4 to 5 hours, daily . . . also includes visit to Prambanan.

Surabaya and East Java

Bromo Sunrise Tour • 10 to 12 hours . . . departs at midnight by car . . . traverses Sand Sea by horse for sunrise at volcano's rim.

Madura Island Tour • full day . . . ferry crossing to island . . . drive, sightseeing and bull races in season.

Mentawai Islands/Bukittinggi Package • 7 days . . . visits all islands off West Sumatra coast . . . by boat.

Sukamade-Baluran-Mt. Bromo Tour • 7 days . . . visits wild-life areas in Mt. Bromo, Surabaya, Jember, Sukamade, Baluran, and Bayuwangi . . . begins in Surabaya . . . ends in Denpasar, Bali.

Surabaya City Tour • 3 hours, daily . . . governor's palace, zoo, Hero's Monument, and Jokodolok Statue.
Three Temples Tour • 6 hours, daily . . . calls at Singosari, Jago, and Kidal temples.

Bali

Bali Packages • 3 to 5 days . . . includes dance performances . . . Kintamani and Sangeh/Mengwi tours . . . 5-day package adds Besakih.

Bedugul Lake Tour • 6 hours, daily . . . stops at Mengwi, Bedugul, and Bratan Lake.

Besakih Tour • 6 to 10 hours, daily . . . combines Besakih with either Klungkung or Kintamani.

Dance Tours • varying lengths . . . view *barong* and *kris* . . . *kechak* and *legong* dances.

Denpasar City Tour • visits art and cultural center . . . Bali Museum and Le Mayeur Art Gallery . . . local market.

Kintamani Tour • 8 hours, daily . . . includes Celuk, Mas, Ubud, Bedulu, Penelokan, Tampak Siring, Kintamani, and Bangli.

Sangeh, Mengwi, Tanah Lot Tour • 4 to 8 hours, daily.

Singaraja Tour • full day to top of Bali . . . includes Mengwi, Bedugul, and Singaraja.

Trunyan Village Tour • 10 hours, daily . . . same at Kintamani tour . . . adds drive along Batur Lake to Trunyan.

Ubud Tour • 4 hours, daily . . . calls at Ubud, Mas, and Batuan.

Sumatra

Belawan Tour • 5 hours, daily . . . visit Medan's busy port . . . seafood dining and nightlife along Strait of Malacca.

Brastagi Tour • full day from Medan to Sembahe, Sibolangit Botanical Garden, Lawu Debuk-Debuk hot springs, and Batak Karo houses.

Baharok Orang-utan Reserve • 10 hours to 2 days . . . tour of Northern Sumatra reserve . . . special permit required.

Lake Toba Packages • 2 to 6 days . . . includes visits to Brastagi, Lingga, Prapat/Lake Toba, Pematang Purba, and Tomok.

Medan City Tour • 3 hours, daily . . . Grand Mosque, Palace of Sultan Deli, Heroes' Cemetery . . . shopping area.

Nias Island Package • full day to full week . . . includes visits to Teluk Dalam, Nias Village, stay at chief's house, stone jumping . . . can be combined with Lake Toba tour.

Padang City Tour • 3 hours, daily . . . Muara fishermen's village, open-air market . . . Chinese shine.

Padang/Bukit Tinggi Package • 2 to 4 days . . . visits Sicincin Padang Panjang, and Bukittinggi . . . longer versions also cover Maninjau Lake, Anai Waterfall, Ngarai Sianok . . . Bungus Bay, Karang Tirta, and Teluk Bayur Harbor.

South Sumatra Tour • 3 days . . . departs from Palembang . . . local tours and Musi River cruise.

Sulawesi

Toraja Land Package • 3 days in South Sulawesi . . . visits Lemo, Londa, Palawa, Siguntu, and Rantepao . . . 4 days adds other villages.

Ujung Pandang City Tour • 3 hours, daily . . . visits Fort Rotterdam, Bundt's Orchid House and Coral Collection, Pinisi Wharf, and local market.

Ujung Pandang Island Tour • 4 hours . . . visits fishermen's off Ujung Pandang.

Other Islands

East Kalimantan, Borneo Package • 3 to 9 days . . . visits Dayak tribal attractions . . . Mahakam River cruise . . . and Skedang River cruise.

Irian Jaya, New Guinea Package • 7 to 8 days . . . visits primitive areas of New Guinea . . . when safe.

Komodo Island Tour • 4 days from Bali . . . visits famous ''dragons'' (giant lizards) on Komodo . . . also Sumbawa Island.

JAKARTA

JAKARTA IN A CAPSULE

Capital of Republic of Indonesia . . . one of Southeast Asia's largest cities . . . population of about 8 million . . . located on northwest coast of Java . . . originally a Hindu-ruled settlement called Sunda Kelapa . . . conquering Moslem prince renamed city Jayakarta (City of Victory) in 1527 . . . Dutch East India Company seized city in 1619 and renamed it Batavia . . . colonial rule lasted almost 325 years . . . during Japanese-occupied period (1942–45), city was named Jakarta again . . . and it stuck . . . focal point of country's cultural, economic, and political forces . . . and a center for international business men and women.

WHAT TO SEE AND DO

Central Museum (Gedung Gajah) • located at 12 Jalan Medan Merdeka Barat . . . also known as National Museum because it's the largest and finest in Indonesia . . . Gedung Gajah means Elephant Building . . . bronze elephant statue in front . . . gift of King Chulalongkorn of Thailand on 1871 visit . . . museum contains wide collection of historical and cultural value . . . plus a library of social science . . . **Treasure Room** open on Sun. or by request only . . . open daily except Mon. from 9 a.m.–2:30 p.m., Fri. closing at 11 a.m., Sat. closing at 1:30 p.m.

Fine Arts Museum (Balai Seni Rupa) • Located on east side of **Fatahillah Square** . . . formerly office of Mayor of West Jakarta . . . houses fine painting collection of the Republic . . . includes contemporary works by Indonesians . . . plus collection donated by Vice President Adam Malik . . . hours same as Central Museum.

45 Generation Building (Gedung Juang 45) • Located at 31 Jalan Menteng Raya . . . place where revolutionary youth of Jakarta planned Proclamation of Independence in 1945 . . . event occurred immediately following news of Japanese surrender to allies . . . now a museum housing photographs from the revolutionary period.

Glodok (Chinatown) • Main square boasts good food . . . winding streets fun to wander.

Independence Pioneer Building • Located at 56 Jalan Proklamasi . . . original structure was simple house where late President Sukarno lived during Japanese occupation . . . Sukarno and General Hatta proclaimed Independence of Republic of Indonesia here on Aug. 17, 1945 . . . house replaced by high-rise . . . Proclamation Monument and Lighting Monument mark the historic spot.

Istiqlal Mosque • Located in Medan Merdeka area . . . said to be largest in Southeast Asia . . . very modern and fantastic sight . . . huge white dome and minarets tower above surroundings . . . visitors welcome . . . (please remove shoes) except during Friday prayers.

Immanuel Church • Located in front of Gambir station . . . massive domed structure (resembles Jefferson's Monticello) built in 1835 . . . was church for Governor General of the Netherlands Indies . . . used as repository for ashes of Japanese troops during World War II . . . present pulpit was formerly enclosure for Governor General and wife.

Jakarta Art Centre (Taman Ismail Marzuki) • Located at 73 Jalan Cikini Raya (Tel: 342605) . . . both traditional and contemporary arts here . . . dances, music, plays, poetry . . . regular performances for public . . . also cinema and planetarium here.

Jakarta Convention Hall • Located between city center and fashionable Kabayoran . . . a showcase of contemporary Indonesian art . . . works of sculptors Sidharta and Soenarjo . . . artists Pirous, Prijanto, and Sutanto and interior designer Adri Palar . . . fine marble relief . . . wood and copper murals . . . monumental sculptures influenced by traditions of Tanimbar, Nias, Central Java, and Bali . . . photographs of social and cultural life in Indonesia.

Jakarta Historical Museum (Fatahillah Museum) • Located on **Fatahillah Square** in Jakarta Kota area . . . museum collection depicts development of Jakarta since 18th century . . . maps, furniture, porcelain, paintings, etc. . . . building was original Stadhuis (town hall) and dates from 1626 . . . expanded in 1707 . . . played important role in Chinese massacre of 1742 . . . Prince Diponegoro was once imprisoned here before banishment to Makasar . . . hours same as Central Museum.

National Monument (Monas) • Medan Merdeka Square . . . towering gold-tipped obelisk . . . most eminent landmark in capital . . . memorial to Proclamation of Independence on Aug. 17, 1945 . . . eternal Flame of Independence on top : . . structure encompasses Museum of National History . . . Hall of Independence . . . viewing platform at top of obelisk and equestrian statue of Prince Diponegoro . . . open daily except last Mon. of each month from 9 a.m.–5 p.m. . . . admission charge.

Old Batavia (Taman Fatahillah) • Restored section of original Dutch-built city . . . Stadhuis and Jakarta Historical Museum . . .**Balai Seni Rupa** Jakarta (city's art gallery) . . . housed in Dutch period house . . . also Wayang Museum here . . . just northwest of Taman Fatahillah is picturesque old drawbridge over **Kali Besar** (great canal) . . . on the site of the old Kasteel (Batavia's venerable 17th-century fort) . . . it was unfortunately demolished in the 19th century.

Pasar Ikan (Fish Market) • Located just northwest again of **Kali Besar bridge** in old Batavia . . . area full of small lanes, warehouses and shops replete with articles made from the treasures of the sea . . . actual fish market has auctions early every morning.

Presidential Palace (Istana Merdeka) • Located on Jalan Merdeka Utara . . . official residence of head of state for Republic of Indonesia . . . formerly home of a Dutchman . . . became official residence for Dutch governors in mid-19th century.

Satria Mandala Museum (Armed Forces Museum) • Located at Jalan Jendral Gatot Subroto . . . formerly the residence of Dewi Sukarno, last and much despised wife of the late president . . . museum depicts armed struggles from Proclamation of Independence until present . . . 2 main buildings are General Sudirman Hall and General Urip Sumohardjo Hall . . . heavy armor exhibited on extensive grounds . . . open Tues. to Sun. from 9 a.m.–5 p.m.

Senayan Sport Centre • Near Jalan Pintu IX . . . one of biggest games complex in all Asia . . . includes Sports Palace, swimming arena, basketball hall, hockey, and softball fields . . . built during one of late President Sukarno's sprees . . . opened in 1962 for 4th Asian Games.

Sukarno-Hatta Monument • Located near Proclamation and Lightning Monuments . . . honors services of these two men to independence of Indonesian people . . . erected by order of President Suharto on Aug. 16, 1980.

Suropati Park • Located in front of National Development Planning Board at Jalan Imam Bonjo . . . contains monument to Raden Ajeng (Ibu) Kartini, Indonesia's most famous heroine . . . she espoused freedom in writings, "Letters of a Javanese Princess" . . . born in 1879 of noble family . . . died at age of 25 in childbirth.

Textile Museum • Located at 4 Jalan K. Satsuit Tubun . . . extensive collection of looms and other implements . . . batik and weaving . . . covers some 327 kinds of Indonesian batiks . . . historical data on process of production, preservation, designing, and other matters relating to textile industry . . . hours same as Central Museum.

Wayang Museum (Puppet Museum) • Located at 27 Jalan Pintu Besar Utara . . . houses wayang collections from Indonesia, China, Malaysia, and Cambodia . . . 2-story building formerly a protestant church built by the Dutch . . . performances every Sun. in museum . . . as well as all-night performances in square once a month . . . open Tues., Sat., and Sun., from 9 a.m. to 1 p.m., Fri. from 9 a.m. to noon.

Jakarta Environs / West Java

Bogor • Hill station less than a 30-mile drive south of Jakarta . . . renowned for Botanical Gardens (Kebun Raya) founded in 1817 . . . with 15,000 species of native flora and more than 5000 kinds of orchids . . . contains Grecian-style monument to Olivia Raffles (wife of Sir Stamford) who died in 1814 . . . Sir Stamford Raffles loved the place and was instrumental in designing the Botanical Gardens . . . Presidential Palace located within perimeter . . . built in 1745 by Baron Van Imhoff and restored in 1832 . . . used frequently by late President Sukarno . . . who also built weekend retreat called **Diah Bayurini** . . . palace has extensive painting and sculpture collection amassed by Sukarno . . . visitors welcome by prior arrangement.

Bandung • Commercial and cultural city 3 hours southeast of Jakarta by road . . . founded by Dutch in late 19th century . . . still has slight colonial atmosphere . . . called **Kota Kembang** (flowering city) and sometimes Paris of Java . . . center of Sunda culture . . . population nearing 3 million including environs . . . Sukarno went to Institute of Technology here . . . known for **Gedung Merdeka** (Concordia

Sociteir) built by Dutch architects in 1879 and site of Asia-Africa conference in 1955 . . . Also performances of *saung angklung,* music made from hollow bamboo tubes . . . other cultural attractions here are the mask dance, wooden puppet show, and ram fights.

Hero Monument (Pancasila Sakti Monument) • Located in small village of **Lubang Buaya** (Crocodile Hole) at Pondok Gede, near Pasar Rebo . . . dedicated to heroes brutally murdered during abortive Communist coup in fall of 1965 . . . official ceremonies held here on Oct. 1 every year.

Krakatoa • One of most famous volcanic islands in the world . . . located off the coast of Labuhan . . . volcanic erupted in 1883 killing more than 30,000 in the area . . . sending tidal waves across Indian Ocean to Africa . . . actually three islands now surround the new cone that rose in 1929 . . . scientists are fascinated by this area . . . day trips available for visitors from Labuhan, Carita, or Pasauran.

Marine Museum (Bahari Museum) • Located on Jalan Pasar Ikan, Sunda Kepala in North Jakarta . . . opened in 1977 . . . collection contains old maps, naval equipment, models of historic vessels . . . various woods used to construct ships . . . paintings of Tanjung Priok harbor . . . hours same as Central Museum.

Pulau Seribu (Thousand Islands) • About 60 small green islands with white sandy beaches located in Bay of Jakarta . . . **Pulau Melintang** and **Pulau Putri** becoming resort areas . . . with scuba and skin diving centers . . . amusement park for children . . . coral reefs and lovely beaches . . . reachable by boat or light plane.

Puncak • Summit of Mt. Gede . . . lies at almost 4000 feet . . . surrounded by tea plantations where winding road from Bogor to Bandung climbs . . . Puncak Pass Inn, Cibodas Botanic Gardens, and Cipanas Presidential Palace (built in 1750) all lie on slopes of Mt. Gede.

Ragunan Zoo (Taman Margasatwa Ragunan) • Situated at Pasar Minggu area about 10 miles south of Jakarta . . . favorite outings for Jakarta inhabitants . . . wonderful animals like Komodo dragon (lizards) and Bird of Paradise from West Irian . . . also lovely orchid park . . . **Taman Anggrek Ragunan,** where visitors can buy fresh orchid seedlings in bottles.

Taman Anggrek Indonesia Permai • Orchid Park located at Slipi (near Orchid Palace Hotel) . . . largest collection of orchids in Southeast Asia . . . garden divided into several sections . . . each styled with different tribal and traditional houses . . . gateway made in form of Candi Bentar, typical Balinese gate . . . a real treat for orchid lovers.

Taman Impian Jaya Ancol (Ancol Dreamland) • Located on former marshland between port of Tanjung Priok and harbor of Sunda Kelapa . . . more than 340 acres of recreation area . . . jai alai, bowling, hotels, and nightclubs . . . drive-in theater . . . Oceanarium, swimming pool complex . . . **Pasar Seni** (Art Market) . . . golf course and racing circuit . . . massage parlors and steambath . . . marina for yachts and motorboats . . . also Allied Troops' War Cemetery of World War II and 14th-century Chinese temple . . . every Sunday *reog ponorogo* (peacock dancers from East Java) perform . . . also *ondel-ondel*, gentle giant puppets.

Taman Mini Indonesia Indah (Beautiful Indonesia in Miniature) • Located a few miles south of Jakarta proper . . . pet project of Mme. Suharto despite intense opposition over cost . . . depicts all aspects of Indonesian culture on 400 acres . . . typical Indonesian houses . . . Orchid Garden . . . Bird Park . . . Museum Indonesia that houses many of the nation's cultural treasures . . . **Pancasila Flame Monument** to symbolize struggle for independence . . . and amusement facilities . . . takes a full day to visit.

Tangkuban Paraku Mount • Another famous volcano . . . visible from Bandung at dawn . . . 10 eruptions recorded . . . crater **Kawah Ratu** has shape of upside-down boat . . . still jets hot sulfur water.

Ujung Kulon • Nature reserve on southwestern point of Java . . . originally established to protect Java Rhino . . . white rhinoceros prized for its single horn . . . trip here takes 10 hours from Jakarta . . . traveling overland for 4 hours, then to seacoast town of Labuhan . . . watchtowers for observing animals . . . Javanese wild cattle, rusa deer, wild boar, peacocks, and over 250 species of jungle fowl . . . also canoe trips possible through jungle of nature reserve . . . can spend about a week here . . . stay at guest house in Pulau Peucang.

HOTELS

NOTE · · · The American Embassy in Jakarta advises all visitors to have CONFIRMED hotel reservations prior to their arrival in the capital. Occupancy levels at all major international hotels in that city have reached the saturation point, with no relief expected for several years.

★★★★**Borobudur Intercontinental** • *Jalan Lapangan Banteng Selatan, P.O. Box 329. Tel: 370108. Cable: BOROBUDUR IA. Telex: 44156 BDO IA* • 866 rooms . . . located on 23 acres of landscaped gardens . . . right in central Jakarta . . . sanctuary of Indonesian marble and polished teak . . . attractively furnished . . . adding 300-room extension (140 suites) . . . fitness center and nightclub . . . Javanese-style lobby . . . new shopping arcade.

Facilities: Business Center. Convention facilities for 2300 people. Jogging trail. Tennis, squash, mini-golf, swimming pool, and health club. Toba Rotisserie. Keio Japanese restaurant. Nelayan seafood restaurant. Bogor Brasserie (coffee shop). Pendopo lounge and bar.

Reservations: IHC.

★★★**Horizon Hotel** • *Taman Impian Jaya Ancol, Jakarta Utara. Tel: 680008. Cable: HOTELHORISON. Telex: 42824 HORIZ JKT.* • 350 rooms . . . major hotel at Ancol Dreamland . . . sports and recreation complex on beach in northern Jakarta . . . international standard . . . adjoins Copacabana Motel, restaurant and nightclub . . . avoid during local holidays.

Facilities: Coffee shop. Japanese restaurant, seafood and regional dishes. Swimming pool and all sports available. Children's playground.

Reservations: UTELL.

★★★★**Hyatt Aryaduta Jakarta** • *Jalan Prapatan Raya 44-46, P.O. Box 3287. Tel: 376008. Cable: ARYADUTA JAKARTA. Telex: 46220* • 220 rooms . . . located in downtown area . . . near Presidential Palace and government offices.

Facilities: Regency Club and business center. French, Italian, and Japanese-style restaurants. Coffee shop. Swimming pool. Closed-circuit video programs.

Reservations: HYATT INT'L.

★★**Hotel Indonesia** • *Jalan M.H. Thamrin 58, P.O. Box 54. Tel: 320008. Cable: INHOTELCOR. Telex: 44233 HIPA JKT* • 575 rooms . . . Downtown location . . . member of Hotel Indonesia International Group.

Facilities: Continental, Chinese, Indonesian, and Japanese restaurants. Coffee shop. Swimming pool and tennis courts. 5 bars. Secretarial services.

Reservations: INHOTELCOR.

★★★★**Jakarta Hilton International** • *Jalan Jend. Gatot Subroto (Senayan). Tel: 583051. Cable: HILTELS-JAKARTA. Telex: 46673*

Hilton IA • 468 rooms . . . spectacular 32-acre garden setting . . . minutes to downtown area . . . location adjacent to Jakarta Convention Hall . . . has Indonesian Bazaar on grounds . . . 30 typical ethnic houses for shops, handicraft, and art galleries around man-made lake . . . also Balinese Theatre . . . plus two residential towers.

Facilities: Executive club. Oriental club with Juliana's of London Disco. Taman Sardi Grill. Peacock Cafe, a 24-hour coffee shop. Kudus Bar. Swimming pool, sports, and health club. Pizzeria and Japanese restaurant. 31 executive lanai suites.

Reservations: HILTON.

★★★★★**Mandarin Oriental, Jakarta** • *Jalan M.H. Thamrin, P.O. Box 3392. Tel: 321307. Cable: MANDAHOTEL, JAKARTA. Telex: 61755 MANDA IA* • 455 rooms (19 suites) . . . oasis of elegance in heart of city . . . located at Welcome Monument Circle . . . impressive decor by Don Ashton.

Facilities: Captain's Bar. Clipper Lounge. The Marquee coffee shop. The Club Room. Spice Garden restaurant. Pelangi Terrace. Ballroom. Swimming pool, squash courts, and health club. Executive services.

Manager: M. Gibb. *Reservations:* LHW.

★★**Kartika Plaza** • *Jalan M.H. Thamrin, P.O. Box 2081. Tel: 321008. Cable: KARTIKAPLAZA. Telex: 45793 ROKAR IA* • 331 rooms . . . downtown location . . . next door to Hotel Indonesia . . . comfortable but not luxurious.

Facilities: Continental and Chinese/seafood restaurants. Bars. Swimming pool.

Reservations: UTELL.

★★★**Sahid Jaya Hotel** • *Jalan Jen. Sudirman 86. Tel: 587031. Cable: SAHIDHOTEL. Telex: JKT 46331* • 514 rooms plus 600-room extension . . . downtown location . . . attractive native decor.

Facilities: All rooms with refrigerator and minibar. Computer center. Mina's seafood restaurant. 24-hour coffee shop. Sahid Grill room. 2 bars. Swimming pool, tennis court. Business center. Executive Club.

Reservations: UTELL.

★★★**Sari Pacific Hotel** • *Jalan M.H. Thamrin, P.O. Box 3138. Tel: 323707. Cable: HOTLSARIPACIFIC. Telex: 44514 HTLSARI IA* • 500 rooms . . . downtown location . . . free airport transfer service . . . member of Japanese-operated Pan Pacific Hotel chain.

Facilities: Jayakarta grill. Fiesta Coffee Shop. Furusato Japanese restaurant. Melati bar. Pitstop disco. Swimming pool. Business center. Executive health center.

Reservations: UTELL.

WINING AND DINING

Indonesian cuisine revolves around the rice kernel as well as an abundant supply of coconuts, peanuts, native fruits, and vegetables and a treasure chest of tantalizing spices. No wonder Marco Polo called The Moluccas the Spice Islands in 1292 when he was the first European of a long tradition of traders lured by the taste of nutmeg, cloves, coriander, cardamon, cumin, ginger root, laurel, and lemongrass—not to mention the tiny, hot chili peppers that sprout like weeds throughout Java and Sumatra.

The Indonesian word for a meal is *nasi,* the same word for rice so it is not surprising to note that rice is the center of every meal. *Nasi goreng* is fried rice and delicious for breakfast when topped with a fried egg. *Nasi putih* is steamed white rice and served with a series of side dishes, and *sambal* (a fiery condiment made from mashed chilis and shrimp paste). Many of the side dishes have been simmered in coconut milk and then exquisitely spiced (the hottest sauces are made in Sumatra). One of the country's most delicious taste treats has Malayan origin—the *sate,* small pieces of skewered meat grilled over an open fire and then dipped into a spicy peanut sauce. Pure heaven!

It was the Dutch who dubbed ostentatious banquets in the palaces of the sultans *rijsttafel* (rice table) and the name has stuck. Indonesian restaurants throughout the world offer rijsttafel, a vast array of small dishes and condiments centered around a large bowl of rice. It's an excellent way to enjoy a variety of new food experiences and one should never pass up a proper rijsttafel, when offered. Some say that the rijsttafel today is only a shadow of its former self, but it's still a lovely way to enjoy an evening (especially when native music, dances, and wayang are included).

Chicken, goat, fish, beef, lamb, and egg dishes all accompany the rice, along with vegetables and fruits. Another important item is *krupuk,* shrimp paste potato chips. Pork is not served in Moslem society, and therefore it is only available on Hindu Bali. Soups often have a coconut milk base, and curried dishes are plentiful. A favorite salad among Indonesians is *gado gado* a mixture of bean curd and vegetables over which a peanut dressing is poured. (This one is definitely an acquired taste.) There is considerable Chinese influence on the local cuisine, and noodle dishes are very popular. Wheat or rice flour noodles are either fried and topped with bits and pieces of things, or served in a tasty broth.

Because the archipelago is actually more water than land, fish is an important part of everyone's diet. Seafood restaurants abound in Jakarta, and much of the fresh prawns, crab, eel, tuna, and other more unfamiliar species of fish are cooked Chinese-style. Spring rolls made with tiny shrimp are a local specialty and are scrumptious. Nature has also provided an abundance of succulent fruits: several varieties of bananas, from miniature to oversized; pineapples and papayas and mangoes; *rambutan* and *mangosteen; pomelos* and the smelly *durian* (that can make you quite ill if it's mixed in your stomach with alcohol).

Alcoholic beverages are both scarce and expensive in Indonesia, but the local beers (Anker and Bintang) are pretty potent. There are many different fruit juices too, a delightful fragrant tea, and strong coffee. It is best to avoid iced drinks outside the major hotels, so stick with bottled sodas and beer in the countryside. Wine by the bottle is available in the better restaurants, but European vintages are very, very expensive so why not give the Australians some business. (They are doing their best to ferment the grape.)

You can eat well indeed in Jakarta, as a metropolis of this size commands not only a great many good native restaurants but many quality European establishments. There are excellent Chinese, seafood, and an ever-increasing number of Japanese restaurants available. As in all major Asian cities, the most consistent in quality, service, atmosphere, and high prices are the food and beverage outlets in the top hotels. But don't leave town without spending at evening at the **Oasis,** located in a landmark Dutch colonial house formerly inhabited by an ambassador. Here, you can sip an aperitif in what was once the diplomat's chandeliered study and dine in the garden on either Indonesian or European cuisine. There is also romantic dancing under the stars. For years, the Oasis has been the smartest place in town—and well worth the price.

INDONESIAN RESTAURANTS*

Borobudur Intercontinental • *Tel: 370108* • Fri. evenings at poolside Kintamani garden bar . . . dinner and cultural show from 7 to 10 p.m.

Hotel Indonesia • *Tel: 320008* • Oriental Restaurant features 150 dishes from 27 Indonesian provinces.

Jakarta Hilton • *Tel: 583051* • Best food and shows in town . . . great foodstalls in Indonesian Bazaar daily . . . dance and musical per-

*Highly recommended by Directorate General of Tourism.

formances at 7 p.m. (except Mon.) weather permitting . . . free to hotel guests . . . also rijsttafel buffet for lunch and dinner in Peacock Cafe every Fri.

Jakarta Mandarin • *Tel: 321307* • Every Fri. *Kaki Lima* from 7 to 11 p.m. . . . named after Jakarta's street vendors . . . like local fair with food carts . . . troubadors serenade guests.

Kartika Chandra • *Tel: 511008* • Excellent local restaurant.

Lembur Kuring • *Jalan Pintu VIII, Senayan* • Rusticity on outskirts of town . . . freshly grilled fish . . . eat with hands . . . cultural dances entertain at both lunch and dinner.

Oasis Restaurant • *Tel: 326397* • Popular setting . . . wonderful for both Indonesian and European cuisine . . . smart place.

Putri Duyung • *Ancol Dreamland* • Special Indonesian buffet . . . great for visitors.

Sabang Metropolitan • *Tel: 354031* • Small local hotel . . . serves rijsttafel every Fri. evening.

Sahid Jaya • *Tel: 587031* • Mina's seafood restaurant the best in town.

Sayan Satay House • *Several locations* • Best barbecue specialties.

Spice Garden • *Jakarta Mandarin. Tel: 371208* • Szechuan cuisine.

WESTERN RESTAURANTS

Art and Curio Restaurant • *Jalan Kebon Binatang 111/8A (Cikini)* • Just that . . . good food among the antiquities . . . charming atmosphere.

Brasserie Le Parisien • *Hyatt Aryaduta Hotel. Tel: 376008* • French ambiance and menu.

George and Dragon Pub/Restaurant • *Tel: 345625* • Behind the Hotel Indonesia . . . pleasant and basic.

Le Bistro • *Tel: 347475* • Located in converted home . . . charming surroundings . . . limited but reliable Continental menu.

Oasis Restaurant • *Tel: 326397* • A superb dining experience . . . excellent European dishes too.

Pizzaria • *Indonesian Bazaar, Jakarta Hilton. Tel: 583350, ext. 613* • If you're craving for a slice . . . this is the place!

Rugantino Ristorante Italiano • *Tel: 714727* • Pasta and all that other stuff.

Swiss Inn • *Tel: 583280* • A nice spot for lunch or dinner in the Arthaloka building.

Taman Sari Grill • *Jakarta Hilton Hotel. Tel: 583350, ext. 251* • As in all Southeast Asian Hiltons, the top European food in town.

Toba Rotisserie • *Borobudur Intercontinental. Tel: 357611, ext. 2355* • Elegant dining in burnished copper setting . . . daily deliveries of specialties from the U.S. and Europe.

The Club Room • *Jakarta Mandarin Hotel. Tel: 371208* • Opulence galore . . . decor reminiscent of English club . . . Continental cuisine.

SEAFOOD/CHINESE RESTAURANTS

Arithya Loka • *Satria Mandala Museum. Tel: 582449.*

Coca Restaurant • *Tel: 775946.*

Dragon Gate • *Tel: 365293.*

Jade Garden • *Tel: 334104.*

King's Restaurant • *Tel: 357696.*

Mina • *Sahid Jaya Hotel. Tel: 584151.*

Perahu Bugis • *Horizon Hotel, Ancol Dreamland. Tel: 680008, ext. 111.*

Prince • *Tel: 345369.*

Ratu Bahari • *Tel: 774115.*

Yun Nyan • *Tel: 364063.*

Jakarta also has Korean, Indian, Thai, Japanese, and lots of fast-food chains. Grilled chicken, hamburgers, and ice cream are very popular here!

NIGHTLIFE

There is plenty of fast-paced nightlife in Jakarta these days as well as sophisticated supper clubs at the international hotels. Discos also abound but be sure you know the admission fee before you embark as tourists are easy prey. More magical and unforgettable is one of the many "wayang" theater performances where stories from the Hindu *Ramayana* and *Mahabharata* and *Bhagavad Gita* are played to the accompaniment of Gamelan music.

Wayang Museum • Wayang kulit (shadow puppets) performances Sunday mornings in Old Batavia and on second and last Saturday nights at Central Museum.

Aneka Ria Srumulat • *Jalan Pintu VII, Taman Ria Remaja Senayan* • Indonesian comedy daily from 7 to 9:30 p.m.

Bharata • *Jalan Kalilio* • Wayang Orang (human drama) nightly at 8 p.m. Ketoprak (an offshoot of Wayang Wong—also human drama) performed on Monday and Thursday with stories from popular folk legends and local history.

Taman Mini Indonesia Indah • cultural park outside Jakarta where regular drama and dance performances are scheduled.

SHOPPING

Shopping for Indonesian souvenirs is like taking an immersion course in the country's many cultural treasures. The most popular of the crafts to tempt visitors' purchasing power is **batik,** for it appears in the dress of everyday life throughout Java, Sumatra, and Bali. Few travelers leave without at least one **wayang** puppet to adorn a wall or niche. Silver items are also irresistible, especially the belts and bracelets made in Kota Gede, near Yogyakarta. More elaborate are the **kris,** or dagger with straight or wavey blade, whose scabbards boast local semiprecious stones (onyx, moonstone, jasper, agate, etc.). The art of carving is most prominent in Bali and some of the outer islands, and native baskets are also attractive. Antique buffs can find plenty of old Chinese porcelains, coins, and artifacts, although nothing more than 50 years old can be exported without permission.

The exact origin of the **batik** process, using drops of hot wax to create patterns on cloth, is rather vague and seems to have evolved from a pastime of court ladies to what has become a folk art. Today, the craft is also considered a "studio art," for framed batik paintings have become popular tourist items. The designs are from ancient interpretations of Hindu cosmology or modern abstractions of same, and many are made with light boxes behind for more dramatic viewing.

Needless to say, making batik demands considerable time and patience. The white factory-made bolts of muslin must be treated and dyed. Then the pattern is drawn on both sides and the hot wax applied, either by hand *(batik tulis)* or with a copper stamp *(batik cap)*. At least another month is needed for the dyeing and filling-in of the intricate designs.

The art of batik has become so refined that an educated eye can spot exactly which district in Java a particular piece was made. Most highly prized and best known are the designs from Yogyakarta and Solo, where the sultans preferred the colors of indigo, dark brown, blue, and maroon (a court color in any language). Brighter colors, like green or red or yellow are more prevalent in northern Java and on Madura Island, while light browns and golds on blue-black backgrounds can be found in western Java.

Shopping for authentic, handmade batik with traditional designs and colors is a rewarding experience if you are willing to spend both time and money in the selection of fine work. (Cheap imitations should be avoided.) A local Javanese who designs beautiful batik on both cotton and silk, then creates high-style fashions for both men and women is **Iwan Tirta.** A former lawyer turned couturier, Tirta has long been fascinated with the art of batik and has done much for both the craft and his country's fashion industry. He also has an excellent eye for antiques and serves as advisor to Mme. Suharto, First Lady of the Land, on many of her projects. Tirta's showroom and atelier is in his elegant old home at Jalan Panarukan 25 in central Jakarta (not far from the Mandarin Hotel) and definitely worth a detour.

Jakarta's Central and Textile museums are an excellent preview of the many other intricate fabrics found throughout the archipelago, especially *ikat*. This textile is made by either dyeing a pattern on the warp (long threads of the loom), or on the weft (thread woven across them), or on both, prior to the weaving. Warp ikat textiles are made by young girls with long, thin fingers and can be found on the islands of Sumba, Roti, Savu, Timor, Flores, and Laimantan, while many of the shawls (*selendangs*) in South Sumatra are products of the weft ikat technique.

From other islands come intricately woven tubelike sarongs worn by women and ceremonial shawls for men. Some are richly decorated, with gold or silver threads and covered with small mirrors and other metallic adornments. They can be framed or used as wall hangings, and are found in reputable shops in the main tourist centers. (But watch out for factory-made copies with synthetic dyes and threads.)

The most popular form of entertainment in Indonesia is the **wayang** or puppet play, that relates the many tales of the Ramayana. The moral of each episode performed is always the struggle of good against evil, with the former defeating the latter. Wayang performances can last all night and were originally a means of honoring one's deceased ancestors. The *dalang,* or puppeter, was considered the "medium" between the living and the dead and was treated as a holy person. Even today, the dalang is the producer, director, and every player as well as conductor of the accompanying *gamelan* orchestra.

The puppets themselves make interesting souvenirs. The *wayang kulit,* popular in Central and East Java, are flat leather figures intricately carved and painted. They are made to perform against an erected white cloth that serves as a shadow screen, so the audience on the other side sees only silhouettes (*wayang* means shadow). There are also *wayang golek,* three-dimensional puppets made of wood and bamboo (with batik garments), characteristic of West Java. They make lovely doll gifts.

Indonesian silversmiths produce delicate lacelike **silver** filigree in butterfly and flower shapes in objects that range from jewelry to belts, coffee sets, and candlesticks. Silverwork centers thrive where the Hindu influence was once (or remains) very strong, like Bali, South Sulawesi, Sumatra, and the seaports of Java. The best known center is Kota Gede near Yogyakarta, but the fine works from Kendari on Sulawesi and Kota Gadang on Sumatra find their way into the tourist center shops.

Carvings and **paintings** from Bali are just about irresistible, especially if you take time to visit the villages where a single craft is the local cottage industry. Ubud is the center of Balinese painting and visits are encouraged to the studios of artists in residence. Ubud is also the home of the **Museum Puri Lukisan** (post 1920 paintings) and gallery. Mas and Peliatan are villages where carvers begin very early to make masks and winged garuda statues out of jackwood and ebony. Celuk is good for silver and goldsmiths; Bangli and Tampaksiring for carvings of bone and horn; Batubutan, Blaju, and Gianjar for woven goods; and Puaya for puppets. Or you could just stop by the **Abian Kapas Art Center** in Denpasar to appreciate and purchase modern Balinese art. For serious buyers, Irishwoman Linda Garland (married to a Balinese) is a great help, and her shop has the best of Bali. For an appointment, telephone 28946 for a most enjoyable and rewarding time and good direction for other island galleries.

After Bali, Yogyakarta offers the best shopping opportunities, for this is still the cultural capital of the country and cottage industries thrive throughout the area. The **Batik and Handicraft Research Center** on Jalan Kusumanegara is a good place to begin one's research. Good shopping is also found on Jalan Malioboro, between the Sultan's Palace and the Pasar Beringharho market. Enticements include some antiques, batik, *wayang* kulit, brass, and silver items.

Shopping in Jakarta can be fast and efficient if you stick to the fixed-price stores, but be prepared to pay more for the convenience. The **Sarinah Department Store** on Jalan Thamrin, **Ancol Dreamland's** so-called art market, and the Hilton Hotel's **outdoor bazaar** offer wide selection of crafts. Antique buffs should stroll along Jalan Agus Salim, Jalan Majahpahit, and Jalan Surabaya for old coins, Ming kitchen china, and porcelains. **Pasar Baru** offers fabrics at a steal; **Pasar Burung** is famous for birds and birdcages; and **Taman Anggrek** is the most convenient center for orchid cuttings. Large general markets full of goods and local color are **Pasar Cikin** and **Pasar Minggu** (watch your wallets and packages).

Java's ancient capital, Solo, offers excellent shopping opportunities for the more traditional items. **Pasar Trewindu** is the city's flea market and known for interesting artifacts as well as brass oil lamps that sell for a song. **Pasar Klewer** has an overwhelming amount of batik in the traditional cream, brown, and indigo colors of central Java. There are also a number of batik "factories" in the area where visitors are welcome and purchases can be made. There is a **Toy Market** on the grounds of **Radyapustaka Museum** where doll houses, miniature gamelan sets, and amusing paper items can be found. If luggage is no problem, fine furniture reproductions are made along **Jalan Slamet Riyadi** (Toko Parto Art) and **Jalan Kemasan** (Mirah Delima), with artisans said to be the best in the country.

The island of Sumatra has its own regional specialties that include embroidered shawls from Bukittinggi, silver items from Kota Gadang, carvings and hand-woven Ulos cloth made by the Bataks around Lake Toba, and wonderful figures made from "old" coins that can be nicely framed.

BALI

— BALI IN A CAPSULE —

Formerly called **Pulau Dewata** . . . also known as the "Morning of the World" . . . whose people believe their island is just a loan from God . . . a 90-mile long beauty full of rice terraces and holy Mt. Agung . . . abode of the gods . . . a Hindu culture that supports 20,000 temples . . . 60 religious holidays a year . . . some 2000 different dance troupes . . . includes a Holy Monkey Forest where hundreds swing from trees to temples undisturbed . . . even the preparation of food here is a ceremony and an art form . . . no longer unspoiled . . . Bali still has an atmosphere in which visitors revel . . . life here is a continual festivity . . . and completely offbeat.

WHAT TO SEE AND DO

Bat Cave (Goah Lawah) • Located between Kusambe and Padang Bai . . . sinister sight . . . walls covered with bats . . . cave said to extend all way to base of Mt. Agung . . . eerie but considered holy place.

Batubulan Stone Carvers • Statues of divinities and demons line edge of road through this village just northeast of Denpasar . . . area also full of beautiful temples . . . especially **Pura Puseh.**

Batukau Mountain and Temple • Coconut Shell Mountain and Shrine . . . many shrines in area (straight north from Denpasar) . . . modestly decorated but dedicated to deities associated with **Batukau.**

Batur Temple and Volcanic Lake • People of **Batur** building almost 300 shrines at foot of volcano . . . began ambitious rebuilding of **Pura Ulun Danu Temple** in 1927 . . . people of **Trunyan** village near

Lake Batur consider themselves the original Balinese as descendents of
the aboriginals who lived on Bali before the Majapahit invasion. . . .
very private and proud settlement. Not recommended to visit on your
own . . . will probably experience hostility and hustling.

Bedugul Mountain Village • Northwest from Denpasar through
Mengui . . . beautiful landscape surrounding lake in ancient crater of
Mt. Bratan . . . Bedugul people honor **Dewi Danu** . . . goddess of
the waters . . . in temple **Ulu Danau** above lake . . . colorful flower
and vegetable market beneath village.

Bedulu Elephant Cave (Goah Gadjah) • Mysterious cave with
carved entrance . . . a former Buddhist hermitage . . . name taken
from nearby Elephant River **(Lwa Gadja)** . . . located near village of
Bedulu where mid-14th century king was known as He Who Changed
Heads . . . village lies in shadow of holy volcano Gunung Agung.

Besakih Mother Temple • Most holy of all temples on Bali . . .
thought to have been established in the 11th century . . . before Hinduism even arrived . . . built to house holy spirit of **Gunung Agung**
. . . today considered royal ancestry sanctuary . . . principal state temple
. . . venerates Hindu trinity . . . in large temple complex . . . watch
for many festivals here.

Celuk Gold and Silver Works • Craftsmen have inherited the skills
of their forebears in this tiny village . . . not far northeast of Denpasar
. . . intricate designs and delicate artistry here . . . lovely stop en
route elsewhere.

Denpasar Museum and Market • Name of Bali's capital means
''north of market'' . . . local museum built by Dutch government in
1932 . . . offers excellent survey of Balinese culture . . . architecture
of interest and depicts both temple and palace of Bali . . . visit also
Kokar Conservatory of Instrumental Arts and Dance for student performances . . . don't miss festival at **Pura Djagatnata Temple** every
full moon (next to museum).

Gillimanuk • Small port in northwest of island which connects to
Java . . . daily ferries available.

Gunung Kawi (Hindu Balinese Sanctuary) • Ancient burial towers hewn from solid rock . . . thought to have been constructed as
royal memorials to King Udayana and family . . . dates from around
the 11th century.

Karangasem • One of original kingdoms of **Gelgel** dynasty . . . cooperated with Dutch at turn of century so kept monarchy . . . palace of last *radja* **Puri Kanginan** very European . . . another moated water palace located on beach of Udjung.

Kintamani • Mountain village where colorful bazaar held every third morning . . . local dances here are full of trancelike movement . . . quite unique to this village.

Klungkung • Seat of **Gelgel** dynasty which ruled Bali for over three centuries . . . **Kerta Gosa Hall of Justice** known for **klungkung** style of painting and architecture . . . fantastic ceiling vignettes . . . Klungkung also good for antique shops and stalls . . . nearby is Gelgel, early capital of old kingdom.

Kubutambahan • North coastal town . . . site of **Pura Medrwe Karang** . . . Temple of Owner of the Land . . . honors Mother Earth and the sun . . . folksy carvings.

Kusambe Fishing Village • Located on east shore . . . opposite Nusa Penida island . . . visitors can travel to island from here.

Kuta Beach • Popular beach resort on southwest coast . . . known for good surfing . . . has become quite commercial . . . still sunsets here are something special.

Kutri • Site of statue of **Mahendradatta,** or **Queen Gunapriya,** who died in A.D. 1006 . . . statue now defaced . . . found in rubble of 1926 earthquake . . . but full of ancient rhythms and vibes.

Mas • Village famous for woodcarvers . . . first Hindu priest in Bali settled here . . . many claim descendancy from him . . . **Pura Taman Pule Temple** has frequent festivals . . . many statues carved here by young boys . . . good shopping.

Mengwi Temple • State temple of **Pura Taman Ajun** . . . former members of royal family pay respect to forebears here . . . temple in a moat . . . *taman* means "garden with a pond" . . . fine carvings on wooden doors.

Padang Bai • Small harbor on eastern coast . . . cargo and passenger vessels depart here for Lombok Island.

Pedjeng • Considered center of early Balinese dynasties . . . an ancient bronze drum dates from 300 B.C. . . . called the Moon of Pedjeng because local Balinese legend says it fell from sky one night . . . 40 ancient temples in the area . . . also government archaeological office.

Sangeh Monkey Forest • Also called **Bukit Sari** . . . home of hundreds of monkeys . . . sacred place with moss-covered temple in center . . . monkeys apparently dropped to earth during Ramayana epic times . . . have stayed . . . one of most popular spots on island . . . take along a bag of peanuts.

Sangsit • Town in northern Bali . . . known for **Pura Bedji** . . . subak temple dedicated to **Dewi Sri,** goddess of agriculture . . . pink sandstone and carvings of mythical animals . . . **naga** snakes guard entrance.

Singaradja • Capital of Buleleng district along Java Sea (in the north) . . . important commercial center since early times . . . Bali under Javanese rulers in 14th century here . . . Dutch arrived in 19th century . . . interesting variety of influences here . . . cosmopolitan town.

Tabanan • Rice belt of southern district . . . also known as home of famous gamelan orchestras and dancers . . . a little like Denpasar but much more unspoiled . . . lovely beaches here.

Tampaksiring • Holy spring of **Tirta Empul** . . . dates from legendary times . . . waters said to have curative powers . . . Balinese make annual pilgrimages here for purification . . . primary festival occurs on full moon of 4th month . . . temple restored in late 1960s . . . late President Sukarno built himself a palace above here in 1954.

Tanah Lot Temple • Temple suspended on huge rock off southwestern shore . . . one of Bali's most famous shrines . . . odd placement in the sea . . . Balinese believe a huge snake dwells within . . . casts a true Oriental quality when seen in late afternoon.

Tenganan Village • Walled town . . . most conservative village . . . said to date from pre-Hindu times . . . interesting dance rituals here . . . also women weave famous cloth which protects wearers from evil vibes . . . a traditional and friendly Bali Aga village.

Ubud • A must for every visitor . . . village of painters and galleries and studios . . . don't miss **Museum Puri Lukisan** (Palace of Fine Arts) founded in 1954 . . . excellent collection of modern Ba-

linese work . . . some of the most renowned are Ida Bagus Made Po-
leng, A. A. Gede Sobrat, and I. Gusti Ketut Kobot.

Yeh Pula ● Ancient ruins . . . small temple walled by long frieze
. . . reliefs excavated in 1925 . . . believed to date from 14th century
but exact meaning of carved figures unknown.

BEACHES

Bali's beaches have been famous with Asian hopping backpackers
for several decades, even though the Balinese themselves (the older
generation, to be sure) stay away because they feel an affinity with their
mountains, from which good emanates. Aside from the fishermen, who
must do their duty, Balinese feel that evil lingers beyond the smooth,
palm-fringed sands.

Indeed, during the Hippie Age of the '70s, Kuta Beach was one of
the three must Ks (the other two were Kabul and Kathmandu) for group-
ing and other activities. Kuta is still a favorite for most visitors but no
longer the enclave of indigent westerners from Australia and America;
it is now a potpourri, consisting of young Indonesians and Balinese who
want to mingle with visitors from all over the world. All three of the
well-known beaches—Kuta, Sanur, and Nusa Dua—are in the south of
the island and feature both excellent surfing and stunning sunsets. Each
one, however, has a distinct personality and draws its own type of crowd.
Each of the beaches boasts major resorts as well as small hotels, a
plethora of restaurants, shops, and local villagers just doing their own
thing.

The legendary **Kuta** boasts both upscale properties as well as the
many budget guest houses that have sprung up over the past three decades. Pertamina Cottages is located at the southern end of the beach
away from most of the action. Closer in are Kartika Plaza's cottages
and the Natour Kuta Beach Hotel, while the Bali Oberoi's villas are at
the very end—at Kayu Aya on Legian Beach. Between are clothing and
souvenir shops, vendors aplenty, and restaurants serving everything from
satay to burgers!

Sanur Beach is more stylish and quiet—known for the many artists and musicians who live in the area as well as for small inns, gracious restaurants, and art shops. Sanur boasts the Bali Beach, the island's first major resort hotel, the Bali Hyatt, and the Hotel Sanur Beach
(the last major hotel allowed). Balinese bungalow resorts include Segara
Village, the popular Tandjung Sari, and Bali Sanur Bungalows.

Nusa Dua Beach is a government experiment in resort planning—looked upon with some disdain by the locals, who feel it does not belong on Bali. Once an unpopular and inhospitable area on the east coast, the beach now is thriving with hotels, restaurants, tourist facilities, and shops—all built in the past decade. The area's first major property was the Nusa Dua Beach Hotel, followed by Hotel Bali Nusa Dua, Hotel Bali Sol, and a Club Med.

HOTELS

★★★★**Bali Beach** • *Sanur, Denpasar. Tel: 8511. Telex: 035129 HBB DPR* • 605 rooms . . . one of the first luxury hotels . . . high-rise right on beach . . . still one of the best.
Facilities: Baruna (seafood) Pavilion. Tirta bar. Bali Kopi shop and Beringin Coffee shop. Bali Hai supper club and lounge. Raja Room (Indonesian and Chinese). Swiss restaurant. Baris piano bar. Extensive watersports. 3 swimming pools. Tennis. Golf. Bowling. Health club. Heli-pad. $3.6 million renovation completed.
Reservations: UTELL.

★★★★**Bali Hyatt** • *Jalan Tanjung Sari, P.O. Box 392, Sanur. Tel: 8271–7. Cable: BALIHYATT. Telex: 35127* • 387 rooms . . . set on 36 acres at water's edge . . . in structures no higher than a palm tree . . . a popular spot with Americans.
Facilities: Regency Club with special amenities. Indonesian buffet and dance performances nightly. Seafood restaurant. 24-hour coffee shop. Disco. Watersports. Tennis. Golf. Health club.
Reservations: Hyatt Int'l.

★★★★★**Bali Oberoi** • *Jalan Kayu Aya, Legian Beach, Box 351, Denpasar. Tel: 51061. Cable: BALIOBEROI. Telex: 35125* • 75 rooms . . . guests stay in private cottages . . . like a Balinese village . . . a relaxing 34-acre resort . . . Villas have own patios, atriums, and garden bathrooms . . . favorite with visiting celebrities.
Facilities: Dining room. Coffee shop. Bar. Cultural shows in amphitheater. Swimming pool. Tennis. Watersports. Health club.
Reservations: LHW.

★★★**Bali Sanur Bungalows** • *Jalan Raya Sanur, Denpasar. Tel: 8421. Cable: BALI BUNGALOWS. Telex: 35178 Griya BSB DPR* • 161 rooms . . . located right on beach . . . avoid months of July, August, December, and January.

Facilities: Seafood, American, Chinese, European, and Indonesian restaurants. 5 bars. Swimming pool and watersports. Rental bicycles. *Reservations:* Direct.

★★★**Kuta Beach Hotel** ● *Kuta P.O. Box 393, Denpasar. Tel: 51461. Cable: KUBEHOT* ● 32 rooms . . . Balinese-style bungalows adjacent to beach . . . operated by Natour Ltd.
Facilities: Dining room. Bar. Swimming pool and watersports. Barong and Ketchak dances upon request.
Reservations: Direct.

★★★★**Nusa Dua Beach Hotel** ● *Nusa Dua Beach, P.O. Box 1028, Denpasar. Tel: 71210. Telex: 35107* ● 450 rooms . . . located right on beach in new development area . . . four-story hotel spread over 20-plus acres . . . Operated by Aerowisata and a favorite conference venue. Hotel Bali Nusa Dua (425 rooms) is operated by Hotel Indonesia International . . . Hotel Bali Sol (500 rooms) is a joint venture between Indonesia and Spanish Sol chain . . . also a Club Med.
Facilities: Restaurants. Airline and travel offices. Banks. Post office. Art shops. Meeting halls and performance stage. Swimming pools. Tennis courts. Watersports.
Reservations: UTELL.

★★★★**Pertamina Cottages** ● *Kuta Beach P.O. Box 121, Denpasar. Tel: 51161. Cable: PERCOT DPS. Telex: 35131* ● 178 rooms . . . just 5 minutes from airport . . . owned by state-run oil conglomerate. Began as an executive retreat. Now a property with extensive grounds and tourist facilities.
Facilities: All suites. Dining room. Coffee shop. Bar. Disco. Cocktail lounge. Swimming pool. 3-hole golf course.
Manager: H. Taryoto. *Reservations:* Direct.

★★★**Sanur Beach Hotel and Seaside Bungalows** ● *P.O. Box 279, Denpasar. Tel: 8011. Cable: AEROPACIFIC. Telex: 35135* ● 320 rooms . . . main high-rise structure . . . with individual bungalows in midst of palm trees . . . convention facility hotel. $2 million renovation.
Facilities: 4 restaurants. 24-hour coffee shop. Bar. Tennis. Putting green. Windsurfing. Cultural shows. Watersports.
Reservations: UTELL.

Segara Village Hotel ● *Jalan Segara Ayu, Sanur, P.O. Box 91, Denpasar. Tel: 8407. Telex: 35143* ● 100 rooms. Owned and operated by the Kompiang family . . . who pioneered tourism to Bali at Sanur Beach in 1956 . . . atmosphere of Balinese village with bungalows in shape of rice storage barns . . . connected by stone pathways . . . lush gardens full of orchids and singing birds . . . very personable . . . owners join guests for lunch.

Reservations: Direct.

★★★★★**Tandjung Sari Hotel •** *P.O. Box 25, Denpasar. Tel: 8441. Cable: TANDJUNGSARI. Telex: 35157* • 24 two-story bungalows . . . charming seaside resort . . . a favorite of Bali aficianados . . . full of tropical gardens and private courtyards.

Facilities: Indoor/outdoor restaurant with best rijsttafel on the island. Swimming pool. Tennis and golf. Watersports. Horseback riding.

Manager: E. Kalumata. *Reservations:* Direct.

WINING AND DINING

The foods of Bali are quite different from the rest of the Indonesian archipelago, for this is the only Hindu island in the large chain. Life on Bali is dominated by what the gods may think and every meal is considered a blessing from above. Because of the many festival days in every calendar year, food is constantly being prepared for presentation at the local temple. So a frequent and most attractive sight is a string of Balinese beauties carrying tiers of colorful rice on their heads as offerings to the gods.

Because the Balinese follow Hinduism, pork is not prohibited and no proper feast is prepared without a tiny suckling pig roasted slowly over a fire of wood. The succulent meat of the *babi guling* is flavored with a mixture of shallots, red peppers, garlic, coriander, lemongrass, Chinese celery, and that ever present shrimp paste, while the skin crackles with crispness. Pork is also used widely here in the *sate,* skewered bits of meat grilled over coals and dipped into a spicy peanut sauce.

Another local specialty used for feasting as well as in soups and sate is the sea turtle, which is cajoled to dry land for fattening and eventual slaughter. An endangered species in other parts of the world, the sea turtle is considered quite a delicacy by the Balinese. However, since both suckling pig and the sea turtle are festival foods and affordable only on special occasions, the primary diet throughout the island consists of rice, chicken, duck, fish, and the most wonderful array of fruits and vegetables that are definitely gifts from the gods.

The terraced rice fields of Bali are famous and so is the fluffy rice they produce. In fact, the Balinese insist that their two harvests annually offers no parallel in taste and fluffiness! So it is quite natural that one of the best rijsttafel (rice table) available in all of Indonesia can be found on a Saturday evening at Bali's **Tandjung Sari Hotel** on Sanur beach. Hotel food throughout the island is excellent and one can savor Indonesian, Chinese, Indian, Continental, and American (hamburgers) foods. But no one seems to combine the best of all worlds better than the Bali **Hyatt's Spice Islander** specialty restaurant which features a Balinese-style banquet along with dance performances.

NIGHTLIFE

Bali has an interesting nightlife because of the many different types of people that are drawn to the charms of this island life. You can wander into native restaurants and spend the evening tasting local dishes and speaking with all kinds of fellow travelers. Or you can spend the evening hours in the various villages, enjoying the performances of dances, plays, and wayang kulit (shadow puppetry). Evening comes swiftly on Bali—precisely at 6 p.m. year-round—and the nighttime hours are best for experiencing a cultural life that is unique to these people.

Dance Performances • Hotel shows are fine for offering a pot-pourri of what the different dances are, but attending performances in the village temple compounds is far more memorable and certainly worth the effort.

Baris • Traditional war dance . . . word means a line or file (of soldiers) . . . good baris dancer must be well coordinated and supple . . . dance was originally a religious rite . . . now just dramatic glorification of Balinese warrior.

Djanger • Popular among villagers . . . brings a dozen young men and young women together in song and dance . . . action ranges from sublime to frenzied.

Djauk • Classic demon dance . . . renowned for solo performances . . . dancer wears frightening mask and long fingernails . . . movements resemble baris dancer.

Kebyar • A most involved solo dance . . . performer becomes infused with the music . . . must know every instrument intimately . . . **kebyar duduk** (seated) is most popular in southern Balinese villages.

Ketjak • Most dramatic of all Balinese dances . . . 150 men simulate sounds of gamelan . . . also called Monkey Dance because drama related to ramayana.

Legong • Classical dance of divine nymphs . . . one of most subtle and beautiful of all . . . girls learn movements at age 5 and retire in their early teens! . . . **legong kraton** (of the palace) is the most beautiful and popular . . . exquisite costumes and headdresses.

Oleg Tambulilingan • Modern dance choreographed for young men and women . . . cat and mouse play with a happy ending.

Ramayana Ballet • Traditional tales with modern humor . . . introduced to Bali by Kokar, Conservatory of Instrumental Arts and Dance . . . very popular . . . especially the fanciful animals of the forest.

The Balinese are also fond of folk drama, in which tales of passion, intrigue, military prowess, romance, and adventure are acted out to the accompaniment of gamelan orchestra. Some of the plays may be difficult for visitors to appreciate and comprehend, but the Balinese love them—especially the ever-present clowns who provide comic relief and never fail to send the audience into gales of laughter!

Ardja • Popular folk opera which begins around midnight and ends in the daylight hours . . . when the lovers are invariably reunited . . . one of the best . . . so stop by for an hour or so.

Barong and Rangda • Typical triumph of good over evil . . . Barong is a mythical forest creature danced by two young men . . . as his life is threatened, so is that of the village . . . Rangda is eventually defeated.

Barong Landung • Giant Barong . . . considered sacred and can exorcise harmful influences when necessary . . . interesting and sometime raucous performances . . . giants striding around temple compound.

Tjalon Arang • Story of magic . . . often performed to appease magical powers of **tjalon arang** . . . and keep village safe.

Tjupak • Bali's notorious glutton . . . good over evil again . . . quite an adventure play . . . full of comic relief.

Topeng • Mask play . . . also called chronicle play of Bali . . . stories taken from old aristocratic families around the island . . . good topeng actors use 30 or 40 masks and create many diverse characters.

The wayang kulit are also popular on Bali and the performances are full of raucous clowns as well as the usual good and evil chasing each other around the forest.

YOGYAKARTA

Visitors who go nowhere else in Java must not miss Yogyakarta, also affectionately known as "Yogya" (pronounced Jogja), for this is one of three special districts of Indonesia—the heart and soul of the country. The exact antithesis of noisy, bustling Jakarta (less than an hour away by air), Yogya boasts a calm and peaceful atmosphere where life is rather slow and laid back. Indeed, here the sign of a cultured and refined person means slowness in movement, speech, and dance. (Westerners take note!)

The city is located at the foot of the active volcano Merapi and stretches to the Indian Ocean in the south. It is the main gateway to central Java, and its fertile plain was the seat of the mighty Javanese empire of Mataram during the 16th and 17th centuries. It is still a Sultanate, now under the jurisdiction of Sultan Hamengku Buwono IX, a dynasty dating from 1755, when the Mataram empire was divided. Due to its location and history, the arts flourished in Yogyakarta and are nourished today through the patronage of the Sultan and his Kraton, or palace, which is the hub of the area's traditional life.

Yogya is a place to relax and let the variety of its traditional arts—gamelan music, classical and contemporary Javanese dances, Wayang Kulit puppet theater, craftsmen of batik, silver and leather—cast a spell. Although its hotels (other than the Ambarrukmo Palace) and restaurants are not memorable, all is forgiven in the wonderful shops and the many spectacular places to visit both in the city and the environs.

The Sultan's palace is the center of life in Yogya. Here, visitors (with passes obtained from the local tourist office) may watch dance and music classes as well as the making of musical instruments and puppets for the wayang kulit. In fact, there are performances of the traditional arts daily throughout the city—either free or for a nominal charge. (Abbreviated versions of wayang kulit and *Ramayana* ballet are presented to guests at the Ambarrukmo Palace Hotel, and gamelan music can be enjoyed at lunchtime in the lobby.) Batik and silver artistry are also popular with visitors, and there are plenty of places to enjoy both the making and the buying!

A visit to Yogya takes at least three days because there is so much to see both in town and outside. The magnificent Shivaite temple of Prambanan is located in the village of the same name, about 10 miles east. Dating from the 9th century, this Hindu temple (in the center of the most popular Muslim country in the world) boasts parapets adorned with bas-relief depicting the legendary *Ramayana* story. Among its eight shrines are those dedicted to Shiva, Vishnu, and Brahma. Prambanan is impressive by day but spectacular under a full moon from June to October, when performances of the *Ramayana* ballet are staged with the temple as backdrop.

Approximately 25 miles northwest from Yogya is the world's greatest Buddhist monument—Borobudur—truly an outdoor museum. Built between the 8th and 9th centuries A.D., it is believed to predate Angkor Wat by 300 years, and its exact purpose is not clear because it is definitely not a temple (there is no interior access). It is estimated that more than 80,000 people worked on the more than 2 million pieces of stone and some 1500 relicf sculptures carved into its walls. A visit to Borobudur—a spiritual experience and architectural achievement—is often the reason many travelers put central Java on their Far East itinerary.

YOGYAKARTA IN A CAPSULE

Cultural capital of central Java . . . many centuries old . . . between 5th and 9th century A.D., center of Hindu-based civilization . . . that constructed Prambanan Temple complex . . . just 25 miles away is largest Buddhist temple in the world . . . Borobudur, a "mountain" of carved stones and shrines . . . city is home of Indonesia's greatest university, Gajah Mada . . . and many other cultural institutions . . . Kraton or Sultan's Palace still plays important role in region . . . just 40 miles east is Solo . . . another ancient capital and thriving port . . . 25 million live in Central Java area.

WHAT TO SEE AND DO

Affandi Museum • Located on airport road. Home of Indonesia's best-known painter. . . . private museum of his own paintings and those of his daughter, Kartika.

Batik Research Center • located on eastern outskirts of city. Interesting permanent exhibition of batiks in both classic and modern designs . . . both hand-drawn and hand-stamped process of batik can be seen.

Kraton ● Palace of the Sultan of Yogyakarta . . . formal name is **Kraton Ngayogyakarta-Hadiningrat** . . . city within a city . . . surrounded by 4 walls about ½-mile long each . . . pulse of cultural life here . . . some of the structures used by **Gajah Mada University** . . . others for continuing native crafts . . . compound dates from 18th century and some of the buildings are European roccoco . . . don't miss **Bengsal Kencono** or Golden Pavilion . . . open to visitors most days . . . especially charming on Tues. and Fri. when hundreds from wayang kulit collection of the Sultan are "aired" . . . shadow play performances offered on second Sat. of every month . . . can also see Ramayana ballet taught and performed here . . . a place not to miss.

Masjid Besar ● Great Mosque next to the Kraton . . . very important to religious and political life of palace and city.

Sonobudoyo Museum ● Also situated near Kraton . . . fine collection of central Javanese artifacts . . . see gamelan and wayang kulit figures . . . museum designed by Dutch architect (1935) in traditional Javanese style.

Taman Sari ● Water castle . . . located slightly west of Kraton . . . once a fine castle designed by European descent architect . . . now eerie ruins . . . destroyed by earthquake in 1865 . . . but worth a stop . . . many studios here selling curios, batiks, and batik paintings . . . bird market at the north wall.

Environs

Borobudur ● Monastery on the Hill . . . located about 35 miles from Yogyakarta . . . largest Buddhist monument in the world dates from 9th century . . . reopened (Feb. 1983) after an 8-year, $20-million restoration project . . . built some 3 centuries before construction of Angkor Wat (Cambodia) . . . by Sailendra dynasty . . . but a mystery why this site . . . temple has 504 statues of Buddha and over 1300 carved panels depicting scenes from his life . . . 432 alcoves and 1472 stupas . . . about 1½ miles of carvings . . . some of the artwork gone will never be replaced . . . restoration could not have taken place in such a short time without help of technology . . . IBM provided computers to aid in the reassembling task . . . 10,000 workers cataloged fallen stones and then matched them correctly . . . monument should be seen in moonlight as well as by day.

Dieng Plateau ● A full day trip to altitude of 7500 feet . . . breathtaking scenery and oldest temple complex in Java . . . also **Gun-**

ung Merapi . . . one of Java's most volatile volcanoes . . . erupts with regularity every 5½ years . . . known as "Mt. Fire" by Javanese.

Imogiri Tombs • Burial spot of Sultans since mid-17th century . . . located about 12 miles south of Yogyakarta . . . beautiful spot to visit . . . a pilgrimage up some 345 shaded steps . . . lovely view from top . . . must rent formal Javanese dress to enter sacred compound . . . available for a few Rupiahs at the top . . . why not.

Kasongan • village just southwest of Yogya. Known for artistic pottery and earthenware utensils . . . local artists sell their wares at reasonable prices.

Kotagede • Village famous for silver shops . . . located just about 4 miles southeast of Yogya . . . supposedly founded in 16th century by founder of second Mataram dynasty . . . his former Kraton now occupied by a garden cemetery . . . and don't forget the silver shops.

Parang Tritis Beach • seaside resort about 16 miles from Yogya. Important in Javanese mythology . . . Sultans make special offerings here in beachside ceremony called "Labuh."

Prambanan • Ancient Hindu Temple complex . . . located some 10 miles east of Yogya . . . built in 9th century . . . deserted 100 years later . . . restored between 1918 and 1953 . . . most famous now for Ramayana ballet performances from May to October during full-moon nights . . . a lovely experience . . . so should be visited during day and at night.

Solo • Ancient city located 40 miles east of Yogya . . . famous today for **Kraton,** sleepy pace of life and excellent shopping for antiquities . . . visit **Kraton Surakarta Hadiningrat . . .** also **Mangkunegaran Palace** and **Royal Museum . . . Radyapustaka Museum** . . . good wayang wong performances at **Sriwedari Park** . . . also annual festivals at 2 Kraton (palaces). There are two hotels in Solo.

HOTELS

★★★**Ambarrukmo Palace** • *P.O. Box 10, Yogyakarta. Tel: 88488. Cable: HOTELAMBAR. Telex: APHYO GYA 25111* • 251 rooms . . . hotel has been through many lives (InterContinental, Sheraton, etc.) . . . now is owned and operated by Hotel Indonesia Corp. . . . still most convenient to sightseeing . . . and most comfortable in the city.

Facilities: Pavilion restaurant in original building. Coffee shop. Borobudur restaurant with evening buffet and *Ramayana* dances. Cocktail lounge. Bar. Swimming pool. Tennis courts. Meeting facilities. Former palace.
Reservations: Direct.

Garuda Hotel • *72 Jalan Malioboro, Yogyakarta. Tel: 2112–4. Cable: GARUDA* • 120 rooms. Originally built in 1911 with cottages around a courtyard . . . now two wings with a series of fine rooms and suites . . . a truly historic place . . . accessible to major attractions.
Facilities: Garuda Bar and Restaurant. Rooftop pool with good view of volcanic Mt. Merapi.
Reservations: Garuda Airlines.

★**Mutiara Hotel** • *P.O. Box 87, Yogyakarta. Tel: 3272. Cable: MUTIARA HOTEL YOGYAKARTA* • 90 rooms.
Facilities: Dining room. 2 bars. Coffee shop.
Reservations: Direct.

★★**Puri Artha Cottage** • *Jalan Cendrawasih 9, Yogyakarta. Tel: 3752. Telex: 25147 ARTHA YK* • 60 rooms . . . located in Javanese garden setting . . . outside city . . . only partial air conditioning in some accommodations.
Facilities: Dining room. Bar. Swimming pool.
Reservations: Direct.

★★**Sri Wedari Hotel & Cottage** • *Laksamana Adisucipto, Yogyakarta. Tel: 88288. Cable: SRI WEDARI HOTEL. Telex: 25148 Srwhot* • 70 rooms.
Facilities: Indonesian, European, Chinese dining room. 2 bars. Cocktail lounge. Swimming pool. Native entertainment.
Reservations: Direct.

Solo

★★**Kusuma Sahid Prince Hotel** • *P.O. Box 20, Solo. Tel: 6356. Cable: SAHIDPRINCE. Telex: 22274 KSPH SOLO* • 100 rooms.
Facilities: Dining room. Bar. Coffee shop. Swimming pool.
Reservations: Direct.

★★**Mangkunegaran Palace Hotel** • *Istana Mangkunegaran, Solo. Tel: 5683. Cable: PURI SALA INDONESIA. Telex: HIPA JKT 44233* • 50 Rooms.

Facilities: Indonesian and Continental restaurant. Bar. Swimming pool.

Reservations: Direct.

WINING AND DINING

Andrawina Loka Gudegbu Tjitro • *Jalan Adisucipto (km 9)* • Indonesian.

Ayam Goreng Candi Sari Kalasan • *Candi Sari Kalasan* • Indonesian. Known for fried chicken specialty.

Garuda Bar & Restaurant • *72 Jalan Malioboro. Tel: 2113* • Indonesian, Chinese and Japanese.

Dewi Sri • *1 Jalan Solo C.T. XIV. Tel: 3599* • Indonesian, Chinese, Japanese, European.

Gita Bujana Snack & Steak House • *52A Jalan Diponegoro. Tel: 3742* • Everything!

Puri Artha Restaurant • *Puri Artha Hotel. Tel: 5934* • Everything.

Sintawang • *9 Jalan Magelang. Tel: 2901* • Everything.

Srikandi • *Arjuna Plaza Hotel. Tel: 3063* • Indonesian, French.

Srimanganti • *63 Jalan Solo. Tel: 2881* • Indonesian, European.

Wisma LPP Restaurant • *8 Jalan Demangan Baru. Tel: 88380* • Indonesian, European, Chinese.

SOUVENIR AND ARTSHOPS

Amri Gallery • *67 Gampingan* • Paintings, batik.

Ardiyanto • Many shops throughout Yogya. Batik.

Arjuna Art Shop • *110 Jalan Sala* • Statues.

Ganeca Art Shop • *69 Jalan Ambarrukmo.*

H.S. Silver Store • *Jalan Mandongan, Kotagede* • Silver items.

Indonesia Arts & Crafts • *Jalan Kemasan No. K6V, Kotagede* • Silver handicrafts.

Jul Shop Curio & Antiques • *29, Jalan Pangeran Mangkubumi* • Wayang, wood carvings, kris, masks.

Naga Art Shop • *61 Jalan Malioboro* • Paintings, statues, basketry.

Pak Djaelani • *Kadipatenkulon KPI/300* • Distant member of royal family who has made leather puppets for decades . . . prices range from $10 to several hundred.

Pasar Klewar • Batik market ner Kraton Hadiningrat in Solo

Sidamukti Art Shop & Batik Painting • *103 Jalan Taman Kampung III* • Paintings, carvings, wayang.

Toko Terang Bulan • *Jalan Malioboro/Jalan Jenderal Yani 76* • Batik at fixed prices.

Tom's Silver • *Jalan Kotagede* • Paintings, silver handicrafts.

SURABAYA

SURABAYA IN A CAPSULE

Indonesia's second most important industrial area after Jakarta . . . 2½ million inhabitants . . . located on Kali Mas River . . . northern coast of East Java . . . Tanjung Perak Harbor important for exports to Europe, Asia, and the Western Hemisphere . . . honored as the City of Heroes . . . Battle of Surabaya began less than three months after Proclamation of Independence had been read in Jakarta . . . not known for many cultural facets . . . but known for interesting excursions from the city . . . especially to Madura Island for the bull races . . . and Mt. Bromo.

WHAT TO SEE AND DO

City Tour • The best way to enjoy Surabaya is via a quick tour . . . Government House . . . **Jogodolok Statue** . . . Hero's Monument . . . Arab sector . . . Chinatown . . . **Tanjung Perak Harbor** . . . zoo.

Environs

Madura Island • 35-minute ferry ride across harbor . . . famous for monthly bull races on first Sun. . . . with Grand Bull Race in September following harvest . . . everyone must observe this colorful and ridiculous pastime if in the area.

Mt. Bromo • Home of God of Fire . . . you can visit crater from **Ngadisari** . . . through Sea of Sands via horseback . . . also popular for watching sunrises from the crater . . . en route you can stop by **Tenggerese** people who maintain ancient Buddhist beliefs with no temples.

Penataran Temple Complex • Built between A.D. 1200 and 1450 . . . full day trip from Surabaya . . . considered the creation place for Hindu Javanese kings of Kediri . . . temples show culture of Kediri kingdom . . . era of famous King Airlangga.

Tretes Mountain Resort • Magnificent air and views a few hours' drive away . . . just 40 miles south of Surabaya . . . area famous for **Candra Wilwatika** open air theater . . . where classical dances performed from May through October during full moon . . . with **Gunung Penanggungan** (almost perfect volcanic cone) in the background.

HOTELS

★★★★Bumi Hyatt • *124–128 Jalan Basuki Rakhmat. Tel: 470875. Cable: HYATTSURABAYA. Telex: HYATT BUMI 31391* • 268 rooms.
Facilities: Coffee shop. Chinese and gourmet restaurants. 3 bars. nightclub. Swimming pool and health club. Squash and jogging track.
Reservations: Hyatt Int'l.

★★★Jane's House • *100 Jalan Dinoyo. Tel: 67722. Cable: JANE'S HOUSE. Telex: 31459* • 50 rooms.
Facilities: Restaurant and bar. Interesting Javanese and Chinese antique decor. Dance performances. Secretarial services.
Reservations: Direct.

★★Mirama Hotel • *68–74 Jalan Raya Darmo, P.O. Box 232. Tel: 69501. Cable: MIRAMA HOTEL. Telex: 31485 MIRAMA SB* • 123 rooms.
Facilities: Coffee shop. Pub. Swimming pool. Korean and Japanese restaurants. Entertainment.
Reservations: Utell.

★★Ramayana Hotel • *67–69 Jalan Basuki Rakhmat. Tel: 46321. Cable: RAMAYANAHOTEL. Telex: 31202* • 100 rooms.
Facilities: Dining room. Coffee shop. Chinese restaurant. Bar. Swimming pool. Tennis nearby.
Reservations: Direct.

WINING AND DINING

Arumanis Terrace • *Hyatt Bumi Hotel. Tel: 470875* • Indonesian.

Cendana • *Cendana Hotel. Tel: 42251* • Indonesian, European, Chinese

Ceshiang Garden • *Hyatt Bumi Hotel. Tel: 470875* • Chinese

Chez Rose • *12 Jalan Panglima Polim, Tel: 45669* • Indonesian, European, Chinese.

Delby • *145 Jalan Raya Darmo. Tel: 66641* • Indonesian, European, Chinese.

Hugo's • *Hyatt Bumi Hotel. Tel: 470875* • European.

Mandarin • *93 Jalan Genteng Kali. Tel: 40222* • Indonesian Chinese.

Mirama Korean & Japanese Food Restaurant • *Mirama Hotel. Tel: 69501* •

Peninsula • *Ramayana Hotel. Tel: 45395* • Indonesian, European, Chinese.

Wijaya International • *1–7 Jalan Bubutan. Tel: 44088* • European, Chinese.

Zed Corner • *1 Jalan Setail. Tel: 68703* • Indonesian Chinese.

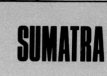

SUMATRA

SUMATRA IN A CAPSULE

Indonesia's largest island . . . fifth largest island in the world . . . stretches some 182,859 square miles from Andaman Sea in the north to Sunda Strait in the south . . . lies opposite southern flank of Malay Peninsula . . . forms southern boundary of long and strategic Straits of Malacca . . . island represents some 25% of Indonesia's land area . . . and 18% of its population . . . capital city is Medan . . . but Lake Toba is most popular tourist attraction . . . island known for almost unlimited oil resources . . . most major American oil companies have joint ventures here.

WHAT TO SEE AND DO

Brastagi • Mountain resort between Medan and Lake Toba . . . home of **Batak** tribesmen . . . native architecture features longhouses built high on stilts . . . have most distinctive high-peaked roofs . . . most Batak now Christians so many churches in countryside . . . look for tribespeople en route to church every Sunday.

Bukit Tinggi • Nestles on plateau on lower slopes of **Bukit Barisan** mountain range . . . known for center of **Minangkabau** people . . . skilled in woodcarving, weaving, and metal-working . . . also for *silat* dance . . . considered a form of self-defense . . . town lies at altitude of 3000 feet . . . can see great peaks of **Merapi** and **Singgalang,** both at 9000 feet . . . beautiful caves of **Ngalau Kamang** with enormous stalactites and stalagmites nearby.

Lake Toba • One of great tourist attractions on Sumatra . . . crater lake some 3000 feet above sea level and surrounded by mountains . . . 50 miles long and about 110 miles south of Medan . . . once sacred domain of local tribesman . . . outsiders once met with death if caught gazing at its dark and mysterious waters . . . now a tourist resort and refreshing hill station from the plains of Medan.

Medan • Bustling capital city of Sumatra . . . today full of American and Japanese traders dealing in oil, rubber, palm oil, tea, cocoa, sisal, and Deli tobacco . . . all exported from nearby port of Belawan . . . visitors should see only **Palace of Sultan of Deli** (built in 1888) and great mosque **Mesjid Raya** . . . built in 1906 and considered one of country's finest.

Monkey Tour • About 60 miles from Medan . . . sanctuary where hundreds of monkeys roam freely . . . considered a holy place . . . many people come here to worship.

Padang • Seaport in West Sumatra . . . main port along this coast during 18th century . . . used then for shipments of gold and pepper . . . now expanding area . . . known for **Nirwana** beach resort and camping facilities . . . important trading center on this island.

Parapat • Resort village overlooking Lake Toba . . . lakeside accommodations can be found here at Parapat Hotel and Danau Toba Hotel . . . main activities are swimming, waterskiing and antique hunting . . . late President Sukarno was in house arrest here . . . many tourists take a boat from Parapat to Samosir Island in Lake Toba . . . village houses on Samosir are characterized by sway-backed roofs . . . facades elaborately carved and painted.

HOTELS

Medan

★★**Danau Toba International Hotel** • *17, Jalan Imam Bonjol. Tel: 327000. Cable: HOTEL DANAU TOBA. Telex: 51167* • 300 rooms.
Facilities: Coffee shop. Japanese restaurant. Swimming pool. 4 Bars.
Reservations: Direct.

★★**Dirga Surya** • *6, Jalan Imam Bonjol. Tel: 323645. Cable: HOTELDIRIGASURYA MEDAN* • 60 rooms.
Facilities: Coffee garden. Bar. Restaurant with Indonesian, Chinese, and European cuisine. Traditional dances.
Reservations: Direct.

★★Dharma Deli Hotel • *Jalan Balai Kota. Tel: 327011. Cable: GAPLAZATEL. Telex: 516 GMC* • 103 rooms.
Facilities: Dining room. Bar. Swimming pool. Disco.
Reservations: Direct.

Tiara Medan • *Jalan Cut Mutia, Medan. Tel: 51600. Cable: GAYA MEDAN. Telex: 51721 GRIYA MEDAN.*

Parapat (Lake Toba)

★★Hotel Danau Toba • *Jalan Pulau Samosir. Tel: 41583. Cable: DANAU TOBA. Telex: 51157 HDTI MEDAN* • 50 rooms.
Facilities: Dining room. Japanese restaurant. Bar. Weekly entertainment.
Reservations: Direct.

★★★Hotel Parapat • *Jalan Marlhat. Tel: 410121. Cable: HO PAR* • 75 rooms.
Facilities: Dining Room. Bar. Folk entertainment. Tennis courts. Canoes and watersports. Lake resort.
Reservations: Direct.

★★★Hotel Patra Jasa Parapet • *Jalan Siukar 1, Parapet. Tel: 41766. Cable: PATRAJASA PARAPET* • 34 rooms.
Facilities: Dining Room. Bar. Entertainment. Swimming pool. Tennis. 9-hole golf course. Children's playground. Heli-pad. Boats. Stables. Waterskiing.
Reservations: Direct.

WINING AND DINING

Medan

Bali Plaza • *Jalan Kumango. Tel: 321164* • Chinese.

Cape Demarati • *Jalan Gatot Subroto. Tel: 29141* • European.

De'Bour • *Dharma Deli Hotel. Tel: 322210* • Indonesian, European, Chinese, Seafood.

De'Plaza • *Garuda Plaza Hotel. Tel. 326255* • Indonesian, European, Chinese.

Fuji • *Danau Toba Inn. Tel: 22700* • Japanese.

Hawa Mandarin • *Jalan Mangkubumi. Tel: 27275* • Everything.

Kuala Deli • *Dirga Surya Hotel. Tel: 323433* • Everything.

Polonia • *Jalan Jendral Sudirman. Tel: 27380* • Everything.

Toshiko Yokohama • *Jala 7 Palang Merah. Tel: 322319* • Japanese.

Parapat

Wisma Danau Toba • *Jalan P. Samosir* • Indonesian, European, Chinese.

Rantau Parapat

Lapaloma • *Jalax Imam Bonjol/Jalan Gatot Subroto* • Indonesian, European, Chinese.

Metro • *Jalan Jendrai Sudirman* • Everything.

OTHER AREAS

Irian Jaya • Eastern most territory of Indonesia . . . not yet a tourist center . . . first discovered by Portuguese, then Spanish who named it Nueva Guinea . . . Dutch renamed it Nieuw Guinea but returned island to Indonesia in 1963 . . . now 200 to 300 primitive tribes live here . . . certain villages can be explored by the adventurous interested in sociology or photography . . . most popular places are Biak, tiny island off north coast . . . Jayapura near Lake Sentani . . . Baliem Valley, discovered in 1938, where about 30 Dani tribes live . . . to enter Irian Jaya, special permission must be obtained from **Markas Besar Kepolisian (MABAK)**—department of police in Jakarta—or from local tour operator.

Komodo Island • Located in Flores Sea, east of Bali . . . famous
Komodo dragon (Scientific name is *Varanus Komodoensis*), the largest
lizard in the world, makes his home here . . . island sparsely populated
. . . people outnumbered by about 300 counted dragons . . . now considered a game preserve . . . a dragon sanctuary, if you will . . .
Komodo Dragon discovered in 1912 . . . recorded weight up to 300
pounds and length up to 12 feet . . . scientists say dragon/lizard has
remained unchanged for 5000 years or more while other lizards in world
have undergone genetic changes . . . must travel from Bali to Bima or
Sumbawa to charter boat to island . . . permission to visit must be
obtained from **MABAK** in Jakarta (see above) or from **CAGAR ALAM**
office in Bogor . . . try tour operator first.

The Moluccas • The fabled Spice Islands lie in all shapes and sizes
midway between Sulawesi and Irian Jaya . . . 900 to 1000 bits and
pieces of land of volcanic origin . . . capital and main tourist attraction
is **Ambon** . . . an island 14 by 30 miles filled with abundant clove and
nutmeg trees . . . heavenly smells! . . . September through January
are ideal for coral-viewing, snorkeling, and skindiving here . . . the
provincial capital, Ambon town, is situated on rocky coastline . . . has
several tourist hotels and well-stocked shops, beautiful old homes and
two jewel-like museums . . . 200 miles away are villages of **Liang** and
Waai, whose inhabitants welcome visitors to their homes . . . the fish
in Waai's river are reputed to be so tame that visitors can stroke them!
Hila is a smaller village through the jungle where drying mace and
nutmeg fill the air . . . also boasts an ancient fort called Nieuw Amsterdam and a wooden church dating from 1797. Pepper corns, nutmeg,
clove, and mace are plentiful, as well as ebony statues and handwoven
fabrics from Tanimbar Islands.

Nias • Situated off west coast of Sumatra . . . a remote and secluded island with a Stone-Age culture . . . just 30 by 80 miles . . .
a 12-hour boat journey from Sumatra and light years away . . . people
are primarily Batak . . . has one of largest megalithic cultures in the
world . . . no journey here complete without a truck ride up to fortress
of **Bawomatalowa** to see the sun set at 1300 feet above sea level . . .
ancient dances performed on site . . . an esoteric place but gradually
becoming a tourist attraction. Islands like Nias are best enjoyed aboard
a Society Expeditions' cruise ship.

Sulawesi • formerly called the Celebes . . . lies just east of Borneo at the equator . . . beautiful, lush, tropical island nourishing lovely
and rare wild orchids . . . capital city of South Sulawesi now called
Ujung Pandang (formerly Makassar) . . . more than half a million

inhabitants and old Fort Rotterdam one of great colonies sites. Ujung Pandang is also home of seafaring Buginese whose handmade two- and three-masted schooners constructed entirely of teak are still used in thriving inter-island trade. . . . but the Toraja hanging graves are most remarkable on island . . . Torajaland—land of the heavenly kings—is located about 300 miles north of Ujung Pandang . . . reached by jeep or mini-bus . . . through villages of Palawa, Marante, Nanggala, and Siguntu . . . Torajas eagerly welcome visitors . . . boat-shaped houses richly ornamented with geometric designs . . . funerals known as Festivals of Joy . . . deceased displayed openly in hanging graves at Lemo, Longa, and Ke Te . . . interesting and colorful. South Sulawesi also has resort and nature reserve at **Bantimurung,** where thousands of exotic butterflies can be seen against a background of high cliffs and waterfalls. North Sulawesi has colorful ports, spice plantations, lakeside resorts, and hot springs . . . capital, Manado, is a pleasant place to stay.

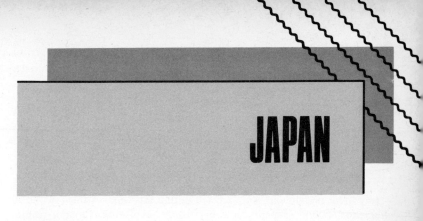

JAPAN

HISTORY

The Chinese called it **Jih-pen** or "Land of the Rising Sun," and its cultural history is totally absorbing if you like the intrigues of court life, swashbuckling samurai, religious zealots who set fire to rival factions, a sprinkling of sex, such charming pastimes as poetry contests, catching fireflies, and moon viewing—while Shinto deities play games overhead!

According to Japan's earliest recorded history, the 8th-century *Kojiki* (Record of Ancient Matters) and *Nihongi* (Chronicles of Japan), the archipelago was formed by brother and sister gods named **Izanagi** and **Izanami**—who married and bore a great many important gods and goddesses. Among them was **Amaterasu,** the Sun Goddess, who gave birth to the nation's first emperor on a mountain peak in Kyushu. The first **Mikado** (august gate) was born in 660 B.C. and called **Kamu-Yamato-Iware-Biko,** but posthumously named **Jimmu Tenno.**

According to Basil Hall Chamberlain in *Japanese Things,* the Japanese have always preferred Chinese titles like *Tenno* (the Heavenly Emperor) or *Shujo* (Supreme Master) to the distinctly Japanese-sounding *Mikado.* And, although 2000-year tradition insists that the emperor is directly descended from the ancient Sun Goddess, the late emperor, Hirohito, renounced this theory after the war. Whether anyone, but General Douglas MacArthur, took this pronouncement seriously is a moot point. The present generation pays little attention to the imperial family; indeed, many of them went off skiing during the late emperor's funeral as it was a public holiday.

Early history is vague for Japan but, according to the *Kojiki* and *Nihongi,* the monarchs seemed to have lived a very long time—occasionally over a century! The most important date at this time is A.D. 552 when emmissaries of the ancient kingdom of **Paekche** in southern Korea brought both Buddhism and a written language as a gesture of friendship. Both originated in China, which also introduced mathematical instruments, calendars, sericulture (raising silk worms), weaving, metal-casting, and brewing.

The most important early leader was Prince Shotoku (A.D. 573–621), who sanctioned Buddhism and drew up Seven Articles in which he instructed the nation to obey commands of the emperor and have a reverence for the gods, framed various administrative systems, and encouraged culture and education. Shotoku is also noted as an able sculptor and left some masterful self-portraits as well as religious imagery at Nara and Kyoto temples. Because of political intrigues and often too powerful priests, it was the custom for new emperors to change capitals. A permanent court was established at Nara around A.D. 661 and remained there until 784.

Called the Nara Period (A.D. 661–784), Buddhism flourished and many great monuments were erected during this time. Around A.D. 670 the name Nihon (Japan) came into usage, replacing Yamato (central plain) or Mi-kuni (great august country). This era also witnessed the rise of the powerful Fujiwara family who, for almost 400 years (670–1050), would have sons in important government positions and daughters married to emperors. During the Nara Period, the devout Emperor Shomu commissioned the **Daibutsu** or Great Buddha cast in bronze for **Todaiji** (Great Eastern Temple), and the *Man-yoshu* (A Collection of Ten Thousand Leaves) containing some 4500 poems was produced.

Alas, Emperor Kammu (A.D. 737–806) found the plains of Nara a bit uncomfortable and moved his court first to Nagaokakyo in 784, and then to a new and beautifully designed city he called **Heian-kyo** in 794. For the following four centuries, Kyoto (as it was later named) became the imperial capital. The famous Heian Period ensued (A.D. 794–1192) during which everything flourished: court intrigue, the Fujiwara family, Buddhism, and the arts. Temples couldn't be constructed fast enough, commissioned by this emperor, that empress, the regent, and such. If one seemed too much in imperial favor, a temple might be burned by a jealous rival or raided by the priests up on Mt. Hiei (who felt that all below should be kept in place).

Classical writers such as Sei Shonagon produced a collection of essays called *Makura-no-Soshi* (the Pillow Book) and Murasaki Shikibu completed the mammoth *Tale of Genji*, still the most important literary work of Japan. Heian court life was like being in heaven—gentle days filled with poetry contests, palaquin or boat rides, furtive glances across the chamber at a possible sexual partner. Nights were equally stimulating, with more poetry contests, catching fireflies, moon viewing, and more furtive glances. Emperors who fell from grace retired to spend their last days in prayer (as well as to avoid being deposed or assassinated), while their wives or widows fled to local nunneries. Toward the end of the Heian Period, corruption in government was endemic, and the rise of the military caste clan of Taira (Heike) to influential posts was the envy of other aristocrats. They were eventually overthrown in 1185 by Yoritomo Minamoto (Genji clan), who became Japan's first shogun and formed a military government that would endure for almost 700 years.

Yoritomo Minamoto moved to Kamakura with his counselors, *shugo* (guards), and *jito* (squires) at the permission of the emperor in A.D. 1185. He was appointed sei-i-taishogun (generalissimo for the subjugation of barbarians) in 1192, ending the Heian Period. The shortened term was Shogun. In contrast to the Heian Period's effeminate pursuits, the Kamakura Period (A.D. 1192–1333) was decidedly masculine—with written narratives detailing the rivalries between various clans (**Genji** and **Heike** are the most famous). Sculptoral generations such as Unkei, Tankei, and Kaikei gave vigor to Japan's masterpieces. Weapons, armor, and swordsmiths, *emakimono* (scroll paintings) were all in favor. During the Kamakura Period, two attempted invasions of Kyushu by Kublai Khan were repulsed, the latter by the appearance of a *kamikaze,* or divine wind (actually, it was a typhoon). None of this lessened the new virile national spirit of the Japanese, nutured by the *bushido,* or way of the warrior.

During the entire long shogunate period, the emperor was always the theoretical head of state even though he was powerless and often just a small baby in someone's arms. Still, he was there and his authority was only delegated to the shogun. Unfortunately, Yoritomo's descendants did not prove to be worthy of him and for over a century, the country was ruled by regents of the Hojo family, who managed to banish an emperor or two to some offshore island.

Kyoto again became the imperial capital in A.D. 1336 when Takauji Ashikaga established a *bakufu* (camp office) there. The Ashikaga shogunate was known as the Muromachi Period (A.D. 1336–1573). However, neither Takauji, nor his son Yoshimitsu, nor his grandson Yoshimasa, were very good administrators as they preferred to lead the luxurious life. Yoshimitsu built the Kinkaku or Gold Pavilion, while Yoshimasa built the Ginkaku or Silver Pavilion. This was the age of landscape artist Sesshu, Motonobu Kano, Zen Buddhism, tea ceremonies, flower arrangements, *renga* (linked verse) and *Kyogen (Noh* farces). While the arts flourished, the country was in a hundred years of civil strife as *daimyo* (feudal lords) and their samurai made their districts battlefronts. The weapon industry prospered greatly.

Nobunaga Oda (A.D. 1524–1582) set about uniting the country until he was assassinated by one of his own generals. He was succeeded by Hideyoshi Toyotomo (1536–1598), who is remembered for persecuting the Christians in Nagasaki and being the strong leader the country needed. He unfortunately died during a campaign in Korea against Chinese forces. Azuchi-Momoyama is the name of the period from A.D. 1573–1598, after the name of the Nobunaga and Hideyoshi castles. Castle construction and decorative painting were popular during this time. Both

Nobunaga and Hideyoshi developed a passion for the *chanoyu*, or tea ceremony, and the great master Rikyu raised it to the highest art form. *Bunraku* (puppet plays) and *kabuki* (all male dance-drama in period dress) were all born during Azuchi-Momoyama Period.

Ieyasu Tokugawa (A.D. 1542–1616) was the third and greatest of Japan's long shogunate. Upon Hideyoshi's death, he defeated his main rival in the famous Battle of Sekigahara of 1600 (Gifu prefecture) and was appointed shogun in 1603. He established his *bakufu* in Edo (old Tokyo) the same year, thus beginning the long Edo or Tokugawa period (A.D. 1603–1867). Ieyasu has been called the "maker of modern Japan" for he consolidated various administrative systems and established a consistent social structure. The feudal system was firmly entrenched, with about 270 *daimyos* with individual domains. Ieyasu continued Hideyoshi's policy of persecution against the Christians but not quite so strictly. He received foreigners, but they were becoming an increasing problem.

Iemitsu, the third Tokugawa shogun, closed the ports in A.D. 1639 and the country remained in isolation until 1853 when Commodore Perry arrived at Iraga to demand the ports be opened to world trade. The *bafuku* completed a Treaty of Amity with the United States at Kanagawa, opening Yokohama, Hakodate, and Shimoda. Similar pacts were signed with Great Britain, Russia, and the Netherlands, ending a policy of seclusion that had lasted over 200 years.

The Meiji Restoration of 1868 restored the emperor to his rightful position, abolished the feudal system, and centralized the power of the government. Emperor Meiji (1868–1912) changed Edo to Tokyo, making it the capital of the country. A parliamentery system was adopted and a constitution completed. Western ideas in politics, science, and economics flowed into Japan and two wars were fought with neighbors—Russia and China.

Emperor Taisho ascended the throne in 1912 and is remembered as being a rather pale monarch. He was succeeded in 1926 by the late emperor, Hirohito, whose official era was known as Showa (meaning peace) and lasted some 63 years. Hirohito was a highly respected botanist who lived through a revival of militarism, during which his country occupied much of Manchuria and waged war most brutally against the United States and the entire Pacific region. He accepted defeat and the occupation of his country in a manner that returned respect to his people. Ill from cancer for quite some time, the late emperor passed away at 6:33 a.m. on Saturday, January 7, 1989 (Japan time) and was buried in late March outside Tokyo. He is succeeded by the fiftyish former Crown Prince, now Emperor Akihito, whose era will be known as Heisei, which has been translated to mean "continued peace," "peace with honor," or "peace with prosperity." (It seems that few agree on the exact meaning!)

Through all this modernity runs a deep reverence for the past and a fervent belief in traditions, which makes travel throughout Japan a very positive and rewarding experience.

JAPAN IN A CAPSULE

Archipelago of 4 main islands and thousands of small islands lying between Pacific Ocean and Japan Sea . . . extensive variety in geographical features . . . extremely mountainous in areas . . . many active volcanoes . . . less than 75% of the land is arable . . . population of about 120 million . . . only natural resources are rice and water and people, according to a local journalist . . . highly industrialized nation . . . maintains its inherent traditions in a modern world . . . monarchial society several thousand years old . . . emperor directly descended from Sun Goddess Amaterasu-Omikami . . . main religions Buddhism and Shinto, many followers subscribing to both . . . language is Japanese, with 2 basic syllaberies, *kata-kana* and *hira-gana,* both derived from *kanji* (Chinese characters) . . . a proud and very regulated people . . . difficult to penetrate unless there has been some association with the outside world . . . country can be extremely expensive for Americans . . . one of the most rewarding travel experiences.

PLANNING AHEAD

JAPAN NATIONAL TOURIST ORGANIZATION has information centers which can be found at 6–6 Yurakucho 1–chome, Tokyo (Tel: 03–502–1461); the Airport Terminal Bldg., Narita (Tel: 0476–32–8711); and in the Kyoto Tower Bldg., Higashi-Shiokojicho, Shimogyo-ku, Kyoto (Tel: 075–371–5649).

There are 15 branches of the JNTO worldwide, six of them in North America. They are located at 630 Fifth Ave., Suite 2101, New York, NY 10111 (Tel: 212–757–5640); 333 North Michigan Ave., Chicago, IL 60601 (Tel: 312–332–3975); 1519 Main St., Suite 200, Dallas, TX 75201 (Tel: 214–741–4931); 360 Post St., San Francisco, CA 94108 (Tel: 415–989–7140); 624 South Grand Ave., Los Angeles, CA 90017 (Tel: 213–623–1952); and 165 University Ave., Toronto, Ontario M5H 3B8 (Tel: 416–366–7140).

JNTO issues over 50 different brochures, maps, and short guides to attractions throughout Japan, most of which are updated annually.

VISAS are no longer required of all travelers holding valid U.S. passports for a stay of up to 90 days. Four-year multiple-entry tourist visas are available gratis at any Japanese Consulate upon presentation of valid passport and proof of travel plans. Short-term commercial visas for up to 180 days are also available. Travelers with valid Canadian passports do not need visas.

INOCULATIONS for smallpox and cholera are no longer required for entry, unless you are coming from an infected area.

ENTRY BY AIR is most likely into Tokyo's modern International Airport in the northern suburb of Narita, about 90 minutes from the capital. Limousine bus service departs every 15 minutes for the downtown Tokyo air terminal (about $20-plus per person) and every 30 minutes for Shinjuku Station and area hotels (about $20-plus per person). Taxis from the airport to downtown Tokyo hotels cost more than $150 MINIMUM, and if you arrive on the Sunday evening of a lovely weekend, the fare could double as you sit in bumper-to-bumper traffic all the way into the capital.

Osaka International Airport is an alternate consideration for visitors to the Osaka/Kyoto/Kobe area. It is an excellent facility and far less hectic than Narita. The airport is not more than half an hour from central Osaka (about $3 by airport bus), more than an hour from Kyoto (about $7 by airport bus), or 40 minutes from Kobe (about $5 by airport bus).

Departure tax for international flights is ¥2000.

ARRIVAL BY SEA is generally via Yokohama or Kobe, the two most popular passenger ports in Japan. Several cruise lines call at these ports on their annual global voyages, such as Cunard Line, Crystal Cruises, P & O Line, Pearl Cruises, Royal Cruise Line, and Royal Viking Line.

DUTY FREE is applicable to the usual items of a personal nature (not for sale), plus three bottles of liquor, 100 cigars or 400 cigarettes or 500 grams of tobacco, two ounces of perfume, two watches valued under $110 each. Prohibited items include: narcotics of any kind, counterfeit notes or securities, obscene or immoral materials, articles that infringe upon registered trademarks and patents, and arms.

Travelers may purchase items duty-free at specified shops, provided a ''Record of Purchase of Commodities Tax Exempt for Export'' is attached to your passport and surrendered to a customs official upon departure from Japan. Items available for tax-free purchase are precious stones and metals, watches, camera equipment, and television and radio sets.

CURRENCY of Japan is the **yen** (¥), and there are approximately ¥125–130 to U.S.$1, although the rate fluctuates widely. Coins in circulation are 1, 5, 10, 50, 100, and 500 yen pieces. Bank notes utilized are in 500, 1000, 5000, and 10,000 values. You can purchase yen at any bank or authorized money exchange, upon presentation of your passport. Japanese currency may be imported and exported, up to a limit of five million yen.

As Japanese currency is one of the strongest in the Far East, it is impractical to reconvert it into U.S. dollars upon departing the country. Exchange your Japanese yen at the next destination, and save at least one brokerage fee. You may also get a better ''rate'' when exchanging yen for the currency of a neighboring country.

LOCAL TIME in Japan is Greenwich Mean Time plus 9 hours. Tokyo is 14 hours ahead of Eastern Standard Time, 17 hours in advance of Pacific Standard Time. It is in the same time zone as South Korea, but 1 hour ahead of Hong Kong, Beijing, Taipei, Macau, and Manila; 2 hours ahead of Bangkok and Jakarta.

LOCAL CURRENT is 100 volts, 50 cycles in eastern Japan (including Tokyo), 60 cycles in western Japan (including Kyoto and Osaka). Most hotels offer both 110 and 220 volts for shaving equipment. If you plan to take along your exercise videos or other how-to's, Japanese VHS and Beta machines are run on the same system as the U.S. equivalents.

LOCAL WATER is extremely potable throughout the country.

OFFICIAL LANGUAGE is Japanese but English is widely spoken in major tourist centers and hotels. It is, however, sparingly understood in the countryside. Street and subway signs in Tokyo, Yokohama, Kyoto, Osaka, Kobe, and Sapporo are in Romanji (Roman letters) but don't expect such luxury in smaller cities or even on major highways.

The Japanese can boast one of the world's highest literacy rates and scores of daily newspapers are published, including four in English. These are: *The Japan Times* (thought to be the official word), *The Mainichi, The Yomiuri,* and the *Asahi Evening News. The Asian Wall Street Journal, The International Herald Tribune,* and other news periodicals in English are readily available at hotel newsstands and bookstores.

There are some cable TV programs in English shown on closed circuit in major Tokyo and Osaka hotels. The Far East Network (FEN 810 KHz) is a popular English-language radio station operated by the

U.S. Armed Forces in Japan. Its news, weather, and music are very comforting while traveling in Japan.

Bookstores abound in any hotel arcade, and it is impossible to pass them by, for they are full of beautiful publications on every aspect of Japan—from coffee table picturebooks to paperback translations of contemporary writers. Japanese novels, especially, provide immediate insight to the people and culture.

BUSINESS HOURS in Japan are from 9 a.m.–5 p.m. for most commercial establishments, from 9 a.m.–3 p.m. for banks (until noon on Sat.), and from 10 a.m.–6 p.m. for department stores. Small shops keep their own hours and may remain open until 7 or 8 p.m. Travelers planning to use public transportation should avoid the morning rush hours when it is estimated that over three million commuters come into Tokyo each day—and a proportionate amount to the other metropoli.

Local trade associations and multinational company offices are located easily through the English-language Japan Times Telephone Book as well as the Yellow Pages. The **American Club,** 1–2 Azabudai 2–chome, Minato-ku (Tel: 583–8381) can put visitors in touch with the **Chamber of Commerce, Rotary,** and **Lions International.** The **Foreign Correspondents' Club of Japan** (FCCJ) is located in the Yurakucho Denki Bldg., 7–1 Yuraku-cho 1–chome, Chiyoda-ku (Tel: 211–3161), and smiling Mary is there to greet one and all. The **American Embassy** is just down the road from the Okura Hotel, at 10–5, Akasaka 1–chome, Minato-ku (Tel: 583–7141). The **Embassy of Canada** is at 3–38 Akasaka, 7–chome, Minato-ku (Tel: 408–2101).

TIPPING is not a nuisance in Japan because most establishments add a 10% to 20% service charge the minute you arrive, and the Japanese consider it impolite to accept cash that has not been properly wrapped. Taxi drivers and beauty salon attendants do not expect tips, but hotel porters often do. Have plenty of yen in your pocket upon arrival (and departure) at the airport because it will cost a FORTUNE for porter service (about ¥250 to ¥300 per bag and they count every little piece). Despite the official government policy, Japan is **expensive** and everything costs—and it keeps adding up and up and up! A hotel or restaurant charge will be 25% to 30% more than anticipated, because of added tax and service charges.

NOTE · · · Since April 1989, there is a 3% sales tax on just about everything in Japan, so keep plenty of small change at hand.

TELEPHONE AND TELEX service throughout Japan is excellent and one can quickly communicate with anywhere on Mother Earth. NTT (Nippon Telegraph and Telephone Public Corporation) handles domestic telegrams and KDD (Kokusai Denshin Denwa Co.) takes care of all international communications. It also handles all overseas telephone calls (dial 0051) in Tokyo.

Domestic calls still cost only ¥10 and can be made from public telephones of red, blue, or yellow color. The red phones accept only up to six ¥ coin pieces; the blue up to ten; and the yellow up to ten as well as up to nine ¥100 coin pieces. Confusing? Best to make long-distance calls from your hotel room, although it will certainly be more expensive because surcharges are usually added. Ask the operator about night discounts and be sure that she awards you the same. Domestic calls of between 60 and 320 km are reduced by 40% between 7 and 8 p.m. From 9 p.m. to 6 a.m., calls greater than 320 km are discounted 50%. Sundays and holidays are also less. Direct-dial international calls after 11 p.m. and before 5 a.m. are discounted 40%. Be aware of these rules when you review hotel bills.

Another service is the nationwide Japan Travel-Phone, which offers English-language assistance and information from 9 a.m. to 5 p.m. daily. In both Tokyo (502–1461) and Kyoto (371–5649) city limits, the phone call costs 10 yen for 3 minutes; outside, dial toll-free (0120–222800) for eastern Japan, (0120–444800) for western Japan to reach a Tourist Information Center (TIC).

Major hotels throughout Japan are equipped with telex machines and the call number is easily obtained (see hotel listings). Use the front desk for both convenience and confidence that your English is being understood and your message is relayed properly.

WHAT TO WEAR in Japan depends upon the season. The country lies in what is called the North Temperate Zone and there are four distinct seasons each year. Autumn (Sept.–Nov.) is best for traveling because the days are warm and sunny, the nights cool and crisp. The fall foliage is very beautiful in places like Nikko, Hakone, and Kyoto, and the Imperial Crest, *kiku* (chrysanthemum) is in abundance everywhere. Light woolens and several layers are the suggested clothing at this time. Winter is cold and fairly dry except in northern Honshu and Hokkaido, where the snow is several feet deep. In Tokyo, nary a snowflake falls during the winter months (Dec.–Feb.) and the days are crisp. Warm woolens and socks are very important, and some private homes also use an extra pair of socks on their Western-style toilet seat!

Springtime is lovely throughout Japan (March–May), although it tends to be extremely rainy (I once counted 40 days nonstop). However, in between showers one can enjoy the almond blossoms in Atami and the *sakura* (cherry blossoms) in Kyoto, Kamakura, and Tokyo's Meiji Park. The Prime Minister always hosts a ''cherry blossom party'' under the trees in March, and all the distinguished guests would freeze to death if it were not for the hot *sake* served! Again, lightweight woolens and several layers, a raincoat and hat, rubber boots, and a few fold-up umbrellas are suggested.

Summer (June–Aug.) is hot and humid and it seems to arrive quite abruptly around our Memorial Day. The Tokyo and Kyoto climates (geographically midway between Washington, D.C., and Atlanta) are quite enervating during the summer months so pace yourself. Most buildings are over-air-conditioned, so be prepared.

Visitors can cool off, however, in one of the country's many beautiful mountain resorts: Kamikochi, Karuizawa, Lake Nojiri, Nikko, Hakone, Fuji Five Lakes district, and Unzen, where the air is considerably drier and more refreshing. Since four-fifths of Japan is composed of mountains, and a chain runs through each of the main islands, it is not difficult to find a higher altitude encompassing major tourist attractions. Japan also has an unusually long seacoast, the best known of which is the **Seto Naikai** or Inland Sea, and some lovely stretches of white sandy beaches.

LOCAL TRANSPORTATION is excellent throughout the country. The formerly government-operated Japan National Railroad was privatized into 7 different corporations in 1987, with no change in train names or schedules. Now known as **Japan Railways (JR),** the Japan Rail Pass is still valid nationwide. In addition to the frequent commuter services, which carry several million passengers a day to and from Tokyo, there is the high-speed train *Shinkansen* (new trunk line) that will eventually cover the distance from Hakata and Kagoshima in Kyushu to Sapporo in Hokkaido. The *Shinkansen* has two systems: the *Hikari* (light) train that is super-express; and the *Kodoma* (echo) that makes intermediate stops. The cars are exactly the same and the rides are super-smooth, even at speeds of 220 km per hour. The trains have buffet cars as well as plenty of snacks peddled by sweet little girls, and there are even telephones in case you want to call your friends as the countryside whizzes by. A word of warning though: the only nonsmoking car is the No. 1 (unreserved), so if you are allergic to fumes (the Japanese are very heavy puffers), find the No. 1 on the platform and run for it! The trains stop only a minute in each station, so one must be very agile in boarding.

A new era for the famed bullet train arrived with double-decker cars! On daily runs (first class is upstairs) between Tokyo and Hakata (Kyushu), these glamorous trains will be incorporated among the entire bullet system within a few years. They feature first-class spacious seats above, a restaurant, and private compartments below. In addition, an electronic board advises passengers distance to the next station as well as availability of dining seats and restrooms. It takes less than 6½ hours to travel the 730 miles between Tokyo and Hakata (Fukuoka).

Tokyo's huge Ueno Station is the new terminus for bullet train service of the Tohoku and Joetsu Shinkansen to the northern regions of Japan's main Honshu island. The Tohoku Shinkansen links Tokyo to Morioka, some 330 miles northeast, in just 2 hours and 45 minutes. The Joetsu Shinkansen links Tokyo with Niigata on the western coast in two hours. This line takes travelers through the famed "Snow Country" of Yasunari Kawabata's novel.

Ueno is now Japan's largest underground station; the Shinkansen platform is located on the fourth basement level—quite a change from the original wooden station built over a century ago!

JR has a very fine railpass system for 7, 14, or 21 days of unlimited travel in either Ordinary car or Green car (first class) and you can reserve seats in advance, at no extra cost. Vouchers must be purchased in the U.S. prior to arrival, and then exchanged for the rail passes at JR travel centers at 13 locations throughout the country (including Narita Airport). The passes are nontransferable, and often you will be obliged to show your passport when entering the platform area because they are available for non-Japanese tourists visiting Japan from abroad for sightseeing purposes under entry status 4-1-4. Your travel agent can assist you in purchasing them through the Japan Travel Bureau or Nippon Travel Agency. However, there are a few private railroads in Japan that do not honor them, including the train to Nikko and several lines out of Osaka to Kobe.

The railpass is also good for Tokyo's *Yamanote* Line, the "loop line" that makes a continuous circuit around the heart of the capital and connects with major train and subway stations. The *Yamanote* is a quick, efficient and inexpensive way to get around Tokyo. It is also fun. Jean Pearce, longtime resident and *Japan Times'* columnist has written a charming book, *Footloose in Tokyo, the Curious Traveler's Guide to the 29 Stages (Stops) of the Yamanote Line* (available for about $10 at any hotel newsstand).

Japan's metropolitan **subway** systems are an alternative to traffic jams and expensive taxis, and the various lines are color coded so there is little chance of losing one's way. Fares are calculated according to distance and tickets are available from vending machines in all stations. (Keep your ticket as it must be surrended at final destination.) AVOID RUSH HOURS unless you wish to meet the famous "pushers," whose function is to pack the subway cars as tightly as possible at each stop. It's fun to watch them at work, but most Westerners do not do too well as sardines.

Local **buses** are also recommended, especially in cities laid out sensibly like Kyoto and Sapporo. (I have never been able to figure out the Tokyo bus system.) Kyoto and Sapporo have the only two remaining trolley cars left in the country (if you are staying at the famed Miyako Hotel in Kyoto, the trolley goes right past the front door). Express buses cover the popular tourist routes, Fuji-Hakone-Izu, Nikko, etc. and are certainly preferable to driving oneself as the highway signs are generally only in Japanese. Rental cars are available throughout the country, but driving is on the left and traffic is hazardous (especially in Tokyo).

Taxis are EXPENSIVE throughout Japan and it's easy to pay ¥2000 for a few blocks' ride. In Tokyo, most of the drivers seem to be ex-kamikaze pilots. (I'll never forget a tourist who hopped out of a taxi in front of the Imperial Hotel one day and said, "It's taking life in your own hands with this one!"—at which the taxi driver laughed gleefully.) However, in contrast to New York City, the taxicabs are all in top condition, and air-conditioned, and the passenger door is worked automatically by the driver. In addition to the horrendous fares, there are night, baggage, and extra person surcharges—so be prepared to part with lots of yen if you must travel by taxi.

There are three domestic **airlines** that cover the country: Japan Air Lines (JAL), All Nippon Airways (ANA), and Japan Air System (JAS) as well as a few local services in Okinawa and Hokkaido.

Since Japan is surrounded by water there is regular coastal **steamship** passenger service between Hokkaido and Honshu, Shikoku and Kyushu and in Ise Bay. **Hydrofoils** and more luxurious liners are available at the main tourist routes, especially through the Inland Sea National Park between Kobe and Beppu—a 13-hour journey and one of the highlights of any tour. **Hovercraft** service connects Gamagori with Toba, where most of Japan's cultured pearl farms are located and tourists can watch the women divers work the oyster beds.

NOTE · · · Japan railpass holders ride free on the Aomori-Hakodate and Uno-Takamatsu ferries, which are part of the JR system.

LOCAL CUSTOMS in Japan can seem charming and quaint but are often exasperating, frustrating, and misunderstood by Westerners. In fact, scores of books and articles are written constantly in an attempt to explain business and social practices in Japan to the rest of the world. One wonders if the Japanese also are trying to understand the outside world in which they have recently become such a powerful economic force. But that is doubtful, for this homogeneous and isolated people of approximately 120 million people have few doubts that they are unique and that foreigners are usually barbarians. The very word for foreigner in Japanese, *gaijin,* means outside person. Japan is not just another small Asian country; it is an entirely different process of thinking, and foreigners are not even considered human beings. The Japanese have no feeling of *honne* for outsiders and are extremely nervous and self-contained in their presence.

Decision-making in the Japanese business world is based on consensus, a slow process that begins in the lower ranks and works its way to top management. During the *ringisho,* or decision-making process, a document outlining the "deal" passes through management levels to receive the *hanko,* or chop. Thus each person authorizes the top management to *yoroshiku,* or carry out the proposal. It has been known to take two years for a decision to be made, so Westerners must exercise extreme patience. The Japanese never say "no" outright—everything is "maybe"—because no one individual is authorized to make a decision.

The Japanese live in a crowded country in very small dwellings, often one atop the other. There are few street numbers, so one must first understand what (*ku*) ward, or section, the building is in and then the *chome,* or block. Foreigners living in Japan have a file in which maps of their friends' homes are kept, to be presented to taxi drivers when visiting. It's a crazy system, but you soon become quite accustomed to never leaving home without the proper map.

Japanese houses are primarily constructed of wood, with floors of *tatami* (straw mats). In fact, the size of a space is measured by how many mats it can contain. The rooms are separated by *fusuma,* sliding doors covered with thick paper or cloth, or *shoji* screens (with translucent rice paper stretched over a wooden frame). There is little privacy in a Japanese house, but often a small garden with miniature trees (*bonsai*) and a pond of good-luck goldfish offers some solace from the outside world. The more affluent will have European-style living areas, with furniture and rugs, as well as a *chanoyu* (teahouse) in the garden. The *o furo,* or deep bathtub, is the focal point of every Japanese home not only because the people are exceptionally clean but because it also provides much needed warmth during the winter months. Like everything else in Japan, the *o furo* has its own strict set of rules, and grandparents or papa get the first crack. You wash outside the bath, and just soak in the hot, soothing water.

Japanese men all dress alike in dark suits, white shirts, and very conservative ties, although designer clothes are very popular (the Japanese love to spend money for show). Japanese women dress beautifully in designer outfits and the children always impeccably adorned. However, on holidays and special occasions it is the women who provide interest and color, with the traditional *kimono.* This one-size-fits-all loose garment of handmade silk is very costly, and often passed down from generation to generation. It consists of four parts: the sleeves or *sode;* the body or *migoro;* the gussets or *okumi;* and the replaceable neckband or *kake-eri.* There has been little fundamental change in the form since the 8th century. It is worn unlined in summer and heavily padded in winter. A *haori,* or cloak, adds more warmth during the cold weather. The *kimono* is held by a very stiff belt, *obi,* which prevents even the slimmest woman from breathing easily. On the feet one must wear *tabi,* crisp white cotton slippers with the big toe separated, and sandals.

Lovely young maidens wear the most colorful *kimonos,* with long *sode*. The *sode* become shorter as one advances in age and marries. Traditional matrons have *kimonos* for outdoor wear, traveling, attending the theater, weddings, and funerals. The more formal *kimono* is black silk with the family crest imprinted, if there is one.

The equivalent dress for men is the *hakama,* a divided skirt of heavy silk, that has become largely ceremonial. In fact, the only man I know to wear *hakama* regularly is Davey Jones—when he presents the Pan Am cup to the *yokozuna* (grand champion) at the annual sumo wrestling matches each winter.

The Japanese work steadily (some say, industriously) but no one outpaces the other, because it is not acceptable to "stand out." Housewives dutifully fix *obento* (lunchboxes of cold rice and vegetables) each morning, and apportion their husband's spending money. After work, employees of the same rank repair to their favorite *nomiya* (drinking place) before staggering home. The children are adorable in their navy blue school uniforms and bright yellow or red book bags, and are allowed as much freedom as possible until time for the grueling examinations that will determine their future. Those who make it to the top universities (Todai is considered the Harvard of Japan) are guaranteed to be future company presidents and future leaders.

The Japanese are infinitely polite and considerate of all who enter the stream of their life. Foreigners are often embarrassed by the "largess" of gifts and expensive entertainment that are pressed upon them while doing business. Rank is extremely important and a *meishi,* or business card, is essential because it immediately identifies one's station and how he or she should be treated. Bowing is a time-honored tradition, and the lesser always bows a little longer and lower to the superior. (Just watch the "boss" depart from any train platform or airport and you will understand the system.)

This is also a country in which trees are wrapped for the winter in the finest of rice-straw coats, called *yukizuri,* because trees are revered and thought to have their own *kami,* or soul.

The Japanese are very practical about many matters. Love and marriage do not necessarily go together; however, marriage can breed a certain affection and devotion. Young men and women wishing to find a life partner often engage the services of a "go-between," or professional matchmaker. Pictures and curriculum vitae are exchanged, and finally the couple meet. If all goes well, a wedding date is set and the go-between gets her handsome fee. Weddings often take place at shrines (the Hie Shrine on Sanno Hill above the Capitol Tokyu Hotel is especially popular) with the bride and groom dressed in traditional costume. If the bride's family is affluent and "Western," she will wear a white gown for the ceremony and then change into traditional dress for the reception.

Weddings in Japan are very expensive, as they are always sit-down banquets in a top hotel or restaurant. No simple at-home champagne and wedding cake reception for the Japanese. Everyone dresses in Sunday best, the women in elegant black *kimono* with family crest. And, as the guests depart, shopping bags loaded with gifts are presented to everyone. The Japanese are great gift-givers and weddings are no exception. October is the favored month for most weddings, because one can be assured of good weather and the chrysanthemums (national flower) are at their best.

The young couple then set out to honeymoon, probably on the husband's new bonus (married men get a raise in salary). Kyushu is a popular domestic spot, but Guam and Hawaii are more exciting because they are the closest U.S. soil. The young couple return loaded down with presents for the family, bought with wedding-gift money. Divorce is shameful in Japan but there is no stigma against an older man keeping a young mistress (the literature is full of such themes) or of going on sex tours of Taiwan or Thailand with his colleagues.

Some young couples still move in with the husband's family, and Japanese mothers-in-law are just as bad as any other. However, the so-called "nuclear family" is slowly disintegrating as young people can afford to demand their own way of life. Since the end of the war, the Japanese have been extraordinarily successful in keeping their population growth at an intelligent level and families are morally restricted to two children (although the Crown Prince has three). As a matter of fact, in the late '60s Prime Minister Sato suggested raising the restriction to include a third child because he was concerned about the future work force. But few took him seriously because of the space and natural resource problems. Even most of the bean curd (*tofu*) consumed is imported from the U.S.

Scholars insist that the Imperial Chinese invented "prejudice" but the Japanese have carried the idea to new heights. The College Women's Association of Japan once tried to offer a scholarship to a Japanese-born Korean and the ranks were instantly divided between the Japanese and Western members. Some of us learned a memorable lesson in non-noblesse obilge and the way things were.

But there is much to learn from Japan that will influence your life forever. The natural beauty of the land, the changing views of Fuji-san (Mt. Fuji) and the variety of greens are never forgotten. The mere coping with daily life is commendable, and the making of "national living treasures" is simply exquisite.

FESTIVALS AND HOLIDAYS   Public holidays are marked with an asterisk (*).

*January 1–3 • *Ganjitsu (New Year Days)* **•** Japan's most important holiday marks a new beginning. Streets and shops are gaily decorated. House fronts are decorated with *kado-matsu* (pine boughs, plum tree sprigs, and bamboo) to symbolize vigor, longevity, and vim. *O mochi* (ceremonial rice cakes) are consumed, and people make *hatsu-mode* (first visit of the year) to shrines and temples. The best *kimonos* are worn, and visits are made on second and third day to relatives and employers.

January 6 • *Dezome-shiki* • New Year's parade of firemen in Harumi Chuo-dori, Tokyo. Acrobatic stunts atop bamboo ladders.

January 9–11 • *Toka Ebisu* • Festival of Imamiya Ebisu Shrine, Osaka. Thousands pray to patron of business and good fortune.

*January 15 • *Seijin no hi* • Adults' Day is dedicated to those who have just celebrated their 20th birthdays.

February • *Snow Festival* • One of Sapporo's greatest moments. Huge snow sculptures line main streets of the city.

February 3 or 4 • *Setsubun* • Bean throwing festival throughout Japan to mark "last day" of winter.

February 3 or 4 • *Lantern Festival, Kasuga Shrine, Nara* • More than 3000 lanterns make a spectacular sight.

*February 11 • *Kemkoku Kinen-no-hi (National Foundation Day)* • According to tradition, it is the day Japan's (first) Emperor Jimmu ascended the throne.

March 3 • *Hina Matsuri (Dolls' Day)* • Ceremonial dolls are displayed for several days in the best room in the house. Okura Hotel has most beautiful display in main lobby on many tiers of shelves.

*March 20 or 21 • *Vernal Equinox Day* • *Higan* week is when Buddhist temples have special services and people pray for souls of the departed.

April 8 • *Buddha's Birthday* • *Hana Matsuri* (Flower Festival) celebrated in all Buddhist temples to commemorate birth of Lord Buddha.

April 14–15 • *Takayama Matsuri, Hie Shrine, Takayama* • This traditional festival from 15th century includes floats and a procession.

*April 29 • *The late Emperor Hirohito's Birthday. Now called "Midori No Hi" or Green Day* • Beginning of Golden Week, with May

1, 3, and 5 holidays. Most businesses give employees time off during this week.

May 1 • *May Day.*

***May 3** • Constitution Memorial Day.*

***May 5** • Shobu no sekku (Boys' Day)* • *Koinobori* or kites in shape of carp are flown from bamboo poles for every boy in the family.

May 11 • *Opening of Cormorant fishing season* • On Wagara River in Gifu prefecture. Season continues until mid-October.

May 15 • *Aoi Matsuri* • Hollyhock Festival at Shimogamo and Kamigamo shrines, Kyoto. Features colorful pageant reproducing imperial procession of ancient times.

May 17–18 • *Grand Festival, Toshogu Shrine, Nikko* • Parade of over 1000 armor-clad people, including escorting three shrine palanquins through town.

June 1–2 • *Takigi Noh, Heian Shrine, Kyoto* • *Noh* plays on open-air stage offered after dark. Light is provided by blazing torches.

June 10–16 • *Sanno Festival, Hie Shrine, Tokyo* • Since Edo Period (A.D. 1603–1867), this festival is largest in Tokyo, and includes a procession of palanquins through busy streets.

July 7 • *Tanabata or Star Festival* • Stars Vega and Altair meet across the Milky Way once a year; they symbolize star-crossed lovers.

July 13–15 • *Bon Festival* • Feast of Lanterns for souls of the dead. *Odori* (folk dances) performed in *Yukata* (cotton kimono).

July 16–17 • *Gion Matsuri, Yasaka Shrine, Kyoto* • Historic city's most famous festival; it dates from the 9th century when the head priest of Yasaka Shrine allowed procession of palanquins to mollify the gods because a "pestilence" was ravaging city. On the 17th you'll see colorful floats on the city streets.

Mid-July • *Kangensai (Music Festival) at Itsukushima Shrine, Miyajima* • Colorful, sacred boats towed from famous red "torii" across channel, and classical *gagaku* (court music) performed aboard.

August 6 • *Peace Ceremony, Hiroshima* • Held at Peace Memorial Park in memory of A-bomb victims.

August 5–6 • *Waraku Odori, Nikko* • Folk dances performed during Bon season.

August 6–8 • *Tanabata (Star Festival) in Sendai* • Star-crossed lovers meet one month later in northern Japan.

August 16 • *Daimonji Bonfire, Mt. Nyoigadake, Kyoto* • Center of Bon Festival in Kyoto. Huge *dai* lit near summit of mountain.

Late August • *Bon Festival, Okinawa* • *Bon odori* dances, called *eisa*, in traditional style.

*****September 15** • *Respect for the Aged Day.*

September 16 • *Yabusame, Tsurugaoka Hachiman Shrine, Kamakura* • Horseback archery contest is a reminder of feudal times when samurai competed in all martial arts.

*****September 23 or 24** • *Autumnal Equinox Day.*

October 9–10 • *Takayama Matsuri, Hachiman Shrine, Takayama* • Festival dates from 15th century and features a procession of colorful floats.

*****October 10** • *Health-Sports Day.*

October 12 • *Oeshiki Festival, Hommonji Temple, Tokyo* • Commemorates Buddhist leader Nichiren (A.D. 1222–82).

October 17 • *Autumn Festival, Toshogu Shrine, Nikko* • Palanquin carried from main shrine to *otabisho*, sacred place, escorted by armor-clad devotees.

October 22 • *Jidai Matsuri (Festival of the Ages), Heian Shrine, Kyoto* • Commemorates founding of Kyoto in A.D. 794 and features over 2000 townfolk dressed in costumes representative of all eras in Japanese history.

*****November 3** • *Culture Day* • Also *daimyo gyoretsu* parade along old Tokaido Highway in Hakone. In Tokyo, traditional tour of private gardens to raise money for the International Ladies Benevolent Society (ILBS), one of the capital's poshest women's organizations.

November 15 • *Shichi-go-san* • Seven-five-three festival. Children of these ages are dressed in *kimono* or ''Sunday best'' to visit shrines with parents to express thanks for good health and pray for bright future.

*November 23 • *Labor Thanksgiving Day.*

December 17 • *On Matsuri, Kasuga Shrine, Kyoto* • Procession of people masquerading as courtiers, retainers, and wrestlers of days gone by.
*December 23 • *Birthday of Emperor Akihito.*

December 31 • *Okera Mairi, Yasaka Shrine, Kyoto* • Sacred fire in shrine precincts. Worshipers take home sparks to cook first meal of new year. Many Japanese eat noodles on this eve to ensure good health in coming year.

BACKGROUND MATERIAL   There are so many informative books published about Japan as well as English translations of brilliant Japanese novels that it is truly impossible to offer a complete list. So I shall be most undemocratic and begin with the books written or translated by my friends, and then if there is space . . .

The Tale of Genji by Murasaki Shikibu, translated by Edward G. Seidensticker (Knopf). Japan's No. 1 classic (written in the 11th century) and translated by America's No. 1 professor of Japanese Literature (Columbia University).

Toto-Chan, The Little Girl at the Window by Tetsuko Kuroyanagi, translated by Dorothy Britton (Kodansha). A most unusual and touching tale of a precocious little girl's progressive education before the war. It has sold several million copies and is being used by psychologists all over the world.

Five Gentlemen of Japan by Frank Gibney (Tuttle). Frank was a wartime correspondent, occupation translator, and is still an excellent interpreter of the Japanese scene.

Japan, Images and Realities by Richard Halloran (Tuttle). Dick was *New York Times* correspondent in Japan.

Japanese Antiques by Patricia Salmon (AI Publisher). Pat owns and operates The Gallery in Tokyo and knows her stuff.

Japanese Inn by Oliver Statler (Tuttle paperback). A delightful history of the old Tokaido Road by a fine writer who was in the Occupation Army.

The Japanese by Edwin O. Reischauer (Harvard University Press). This and other books by former Ambassador and Harvard professor Reischauer are scholarly but highly readable.

A Daughter of the Samurai by Etsu Inagaki Sugimoto. A charming story of a little girl in feudal Japan.

A Potter in Japan by Bernard Leach. The late British potter who did, indeed, bridge two cultures.

The Makioka Sisters by Junichiro Tanizaki (Tuttle). Translated eloquently by Edward G. Seidensticker, this is considered Japan's greatest postwar novel (I have read it three times).

Mishima, A Biography by John Nathan (Little Brown & Co.). About the fellow who wrote Byzantine novels, had his own private army, and committed *hari-kari (seppuku)* in front of the students at the Self Defense Force.

Snow Country and *Cranes,* two novels by Yasunari Kawabata (Tuttle). Both translated by Edward G. Seidensticker, prize winning postwar novelist.

Japan, The New Official Guide. Compiled by Japan National Tourist Organization and published by Japan Travel Bureau, Inc. (¥5000). Heavy and full of maps but worth it for serious travelers.

Kyoto, A Contemplative Guide by Gouverneur Mosher (Tuttle). Now in paperback and the only information available in English that offers insight to the beauty and mystery of Kyoto, with a cover by American wood block artist Clifton Karhu . . . a Kyoto institution since 1955.

The Life of Shogun Tokugawa Ieyasu, The Maker of Modern Japan by A. L. Sadler (Tuttle). Written in 1937 and still the best.

A Haiku Journey by Dorothy Britton (Kodansha). Dorothy Britton (Lady Bouchier) was born and raised in Japan and is one of its best interpreters. Photographs by Dennis Stock.

National Parks of Japan by Mary Sutherland and Dorothy Britton (Kodansha).

Japanese Lacquer, 1600–1900 by Andrew Pekarik (Metropolitan Museum of Art). Andrew is a scholar of some note.

The Vermillion Bridge by Shelley Mydans. A charming novel about the Heian court by a well-known American writer.

Windows for the Crown Prince by Elizabeth Grey Vining. The first book I ever read about Japan . . . by the nice Quaker lady who tutored Crown Prince Akihito after the war.

And many, many more . . . Donald Richie (*Japan Times* columnist and authority on Japanese films) suggests works in translation by Soseki Natsume (*Kokoro*), Ogai Mori (*The Wild Goose*), Naoya Shiga (*A Dark Night's Passion*), Toson Shimazaki (*The Broken Commandment*), Kenzaburo Oe *(The Catch)*, Junnosuke Yoshiyuki (*The Dark Room*), and others.

Access to the World: A Travel Guide for the Handicapped by Louise Weiss (Facts on File, 1983).

And three excellent cookbooks by Elizabeth Andoh: *At Home with Japanese Cooking* (Knopf, 1985); *An American Taste of Japan* (Morrow, 1985); *An Ocean of Flavor* (Morrow, 1988).

ACCOMMODATIONS

Japan is **expensive,** and there is little one can do to combat the rising Yen, especially when staying in deluxe hotels where prices for a double room are upwards of $200 a night, excluding meals and taxes. There are many beautiful **deluxe hotels** throughout the country, with exquisite decor and tranquil gardens to soften the blow. Service is impeccable, and expect to find a nice cup of hot tea upon arrival. Other room amenities include a cotton Yukata and slippers (which guests are not encouraged to steal). Room service is excellent—albeit on the slow side. If you opt for a suite, expect to be in big monetary trouble unless it is a business expense. Check prices before you order breakfast; it could cost as much as dinner in New York City. However, staying in a deluxe hotel means executive services, limos from the airport, and other amenities that make traveling more comfortable.

Business Hotels are clean and convenient but English may not be easily understood—especially outside the major metropoli—and room service may not be available. These hotels are used by local middle management. **Pensions** offer homelike lodgings, especially at ski or other resort areas, and often include two meals a day. Any Japan National Tourist Organization office has a printed list of over 230 pensions recommended for visitors. **Minshuku** are in-home lodgings throughout the country. They are very successful as those Japanese who open their homes to gaijin (strangers) are gregarious and helpful, and one often departs having made some new friends. JNTO has a recommended list of over 100 minshuku. **Youth hostels** are for the young and young at heart and there are over 500 scattered about. They are very clean and well run, but sleeping and the use of facilities is communal so be prepared for a separation of the sexes. I also presume they are drug-free because Japan is very, very, very strict and even one little whiff of marijuana can get you into deep trouble—*jail!*

Ryokan are the traditional inns in which shoes are left in the genkan and individual attention begins upon entry. Sitting and sleeping are accomplished on tatami mats and one takes his turn in the o furo (hot tub) although some ryokan in the famous hot springs still practice everyone all together. Ryokan are an acquired taste and can be rather uncomfortable in cold weather, in hot weather, and when it rains. Expect breakfast and dinner in your suite—and you eat when they serve. Prices are very, very high—exceeding $500 per day when taxes and service are added—and there is no communication with the outside world. There are more modestly priced ryokan, but it is best to check with a knowledgeable person in advance.

FOOD

Food in Japan is more than just sustenance; it is the culmination of yet another art form. The cooking and presentation of Japanese cuisine has as much to do with satisfying the soul, as with nourishing the body. Nowhere else in the world is such culinary sculpture constantly placed before the diner. The presentation of Japanese foods also has much to do with the development and power of Zen Buddhism, which evokes a spiritual attitude toward cooking and dictates that attention should be focused on one thing at a time.

Japanese restaurants may appear unsophisticated at first glance, but their pristine simplicity purposefully enhances the food and its presentation. Natural woods with inherent grain, bare floors and tables, shoji screens for a feeling of privacy, and a small garden to provide eye and thought refreshment are all part of the setting. The few decorations consist of *mingei,* or folkcraft pottery, and some well-placed *ikebana* (traditional Japanese floral arrangement) in the *tokonoma* (niche). Even the chopsticks, or *o hashi,* are a calculated addition to the scene. The fresh, grainy wood matches the environment, and they are always packaged in such a way that one can tie the wrapping in a bow and use it as a "stand" between courses.

As throughout the Far East, boiled white rice (*gohan*) is the staple of every Japanese diet and most still insist on a bowl three times a day. The rice bowl is usually porcelain and used as an interim, or catchall, between the other dishes on the table and the mouth. Japanese people pick up a piece of fish, meat, or vegetable with their chopsticks and place it on the bowl of rice. They then lift the bowl to their mouth to complete the eating process.

Soup, either clear *(suimono)* or with a soybean base *(miso),* is also standard at all three meals. It is served in a lacquered wooden bowl. One holds the bowl with both hands and sips, although chopsticks may be employed to collect the bits and pieces of custard, green onion, mushroom, or fishcake floating delicately in the broth. *Tsukemono,* or small pickled items, accompany every meal. The vegetables are fine but the tiny fishes, with their heads intact, sometimes cause a little hesitancy.

Being an island country, Japan has an abundance of succulent shellfish and other fruits of the sea, which are served raw as *sashimi* or *sushi,* deep fried in *tempura,* or grilled (*yakizakana*). Until the Meiji Restoration of the late 19th century, strict Buddhist laws forbade the eating of animal flesh. Even today, meat is not a frequent item in most Japanese diets—mainly because of its expense. Japan is noted for its tender beef, however, from Kobe or Matsuzaka. The animals are famous for being fed beer and massaged to soothing music, which produces a mouth-watering cut of meat marbled with the very finest grains of fat.

Most Westerners need no introduction to *sukiyaki* (pronounced ski-yaki), the most popular of Japanese dishes. Primarily a winter meal, sukiyaki is cooked in a thick iron pot on a hotplate in the middle of one's table. Thin slices of marbled beef, vegetables, chunks of *tofu* (bean curd), sliced green onions, and *shirataki* (thin strips of a tuberous root called "devil's tongue") are cooked in a salty soup of *shoyu* (soy sauce), *sake* and some sugar. The results of the pot are served with plain boiled rice and sometimes a raw egg dip, to improve the taste and prevent burning one's tongue.

Many restaurants in Japan specialize in sukiyaki. One in Tokyo substitutes wild boar meat for beef, but that is a once-in-a-lifetime taste treat as far as I am concerned. Lighter and often more satisfactory versions are *mitzutaki* and *shabu shabu*. *Mitzutaki* is food boiled in an earthenware pot using chicken, sliced pork, or beef and vegetables. It is eaten with a dipping sauce of vinegar, soup stock, *shoyu*, etc. to which horseradish and green onion are added according to taste. Tender thin slices of the best beef are held by chopsticks, swirled into a pot of boiling water and then dipped into a special sauce for *shabu shabu*.

Much of Japanese food is an acquired taste . . . and slowly at that. *Sashimi* is thin slices of very fresh raw fish served over a bowl of rice, and accompanied with *shoyu,* pickled ginger, and *wasabi* (a very, very potent green horseradish like paste guaranteed to unstuff your sinuses). *Sushi* is infinitely more fun, and more aesthetic from beginning to last tasty morsel. Sushi is raw fish, vegetables, or a sweetened egg custard artfully laid on tiny mounds of cold, vinegary rice. An assortment of sushi on a lovely lacquered tray will reveal *maguro* (tender lean tuna), *unagi* (eel), *ebi* (slightly cooked shrimp), *sanma* (mackeral), perhaps *tako* (octopus), and definitely some *ikura* (red caviar). The ikura and perhaps a few pickles packed in rice will be wrapped in *nori*— paper-thin pieces of seaweed, that is an important part of every Japanese diet. Nori can be seen drying along any seashore, is inexpensive, and provides important vitamins as well as iodine (I think the Japanese even consider it an aphrodisiac).

Tempura is another popular Japanese dish that appeals to the palate of Westerners. It consists of prawn, fish, vegetables, and dried seaweed coated with a mixture of egg, water, and wheat flour and then quickly deep fried. It is eaten very hot, with a dipping sauce of shoyu, *mirin* (sweetened sake), and as much wasabi as you dare to add. Eggplant, green pepper, gingko nuts, mushroom, potato, and even asparagus are the vegetables that acquire a new character in tempura.

Teppanyaki is both a very filling meal and a martial art. Diners sit around a large flat grill on which seafood, beef, and vegetables are chopped and cooked. The chef truly enjoys performing, and his artistry involves some swashbuckling with knives. He also enjoys watching Westerners squirm as live shrimp hit the hot grill. Fresh bean sprouts and onions are cooked last, and the whole combination is served with boiled rice. Avoid teppanyaki at lunchtime unless you intend to finish the day; the cooking odors permeate every thread of your clothing. (Be prepared to bring them to the nearest drycleaner immediately.)

Yakitori, grilled bits of chicken and vegetables on a skewer, is Japan's version of *sate* and the country's greatest contribution to worldwide cuisine. It is often treated more as a light lunch or early evening snack than a full meal. Yakitori is best enjoyed at sidewalk stalls and the wonderful pieces of chicken are alternated with bits of green onion. There is one restaurant in Tokyo, called **Heike,** that is managed by descendants of an old samurai family, that serves the best yaki ever and offers a variety of meats and vegetables on skewers that are to be washed down with brimming glasses of warm sake. (Ask a friend or guide about its exact location in the back alleys of Shimbashi station; it is easily recognizable by its wooden castle-like door.)

During the late summer *unagi* (eels) are grilled at streetside stalls and considered necessary nourishment to keep the body well and happy during the heat and humidity. Noodles are another necessity in the local diet, eaten hot in winter and cold in summer. *Soba* are made from buckwheat flour, *udon* from wheat flour. *Chasoba* are thin, vermicelli-like noodles and *harusame* are soy noodles. They are sold at any number of standup shops in train stations and major working areas, for less than a dollar a bowl and eaten very noisily with chopsticks. The broth is then gulped with gusto.

Pork does not appear often on Japanese menus, except in the guise of *tonkatsu*—a breaded cutlet deep-fried and served with a spray of fresh cabbage. Veal is one of the least expensive meats sold in the butcher shop, yet seems to have no raison d'etre in Japanese cuisine. However, those in the mood for the exotic will find and taste such things as *gobo* (burdock root), *takenoko* (fresh bamboo shoots), *na-no-hana* (rape flowers), *daikon* (white radish), turtle, snake, whale, quail, and tiny quail eggs. Carp is a highly prized item, not only as gifts for some spectacular achievement but also as a main dish. Blowfish, often considered poisonous, is also a considered delicacy, but one must feel very brave at time of consumption.

Kaiseki cuisine is the highest form of culinary art in Japan, as it accompanies the traditional and elegant tea ceremony. Kaiseki is influenced by Zen Buddhist precepts and originates from Kyoto. The ingredients are vegetables and fish (no meat), with seaweed and *shiitake* (mushrooms) as a seasoning base. Everything is prepared in such a way to preserve its natural color and flavor. Spare courses are arranged on exquisite porcelain dishes in many shapes, then set on a lacquered tray with feet. The whole makes for a truly memorable dining experience, even though one is apt to leave the table still quite hungry.

For dessert, the Japanese eat *mikan,* mandarin oranges (frozen in bags of five during the summer), *kaki,* persimmons, or *nashi* (the most delicious and juicy apple-pear fruit). Imported fruits like papaya, pine-apple, mango, kiwi, and melons are very, very expensive. Even fat, plump grapes from the wine-producing districts are about $100 a kilo. There are also a variety of very dry cakes and buns, many filled with a sweet reddish bean paste—not to everyone's palate. For snacks, there are plenty of dried, shredded squid in plastic packets, a strange dried beef product, and *arare* (a puffy rice cracker flavored with shoyu and other things).

Anyone wishing a quick immersion course into Japanese cuisine should visit the food halls of large department stores. These treasure troves are located on the lower (basement) level and are often the most interesting diversion in town. Here, you can sample to your heart's content and I have often had a most satisfactory "lunch" in these vast caverns. It's like the International Food Fair at New York City's Coliseum and once you have sampled, you're hooked forever. The food halls of the major department stores are my first stop in any Japanese city! They also have a large liquor department, so you can taste the latest offerings of local and imported spirits. Pure heaven!

All of the above does not mean that anyone desiring a pizza, hamburger, or hotdog will be denied such pleasures in Tokyo. EVERY-THING is available in approximately 500,000 restaurants. Tokyo, especially, is the land of plenty in variety of food and every culture is well represented. I have eaten Indian, Indonesian, French, Spanish, and Chinese in Tokyo, but the best Western food is at the American Club (by invitation only). Major hotels have their sushi bars (expensive) as well as fancy French restaurants (very, very expensive) and a Chinese banquet hall. Eating outside hotels is fun and much less expensive, especially in moderately priced Japanese restaurants where the specialties are displayed in plastic in the front window. One need only point and pay for a delicious meal. Be sure to remember taxes (3% on more than ¥2500 per person) and service changes when calculating the cost in your head.

Sake and beer are the national drinks and apt accompaniments to the local cuisine. Sake is generally served warm in thimblelike cups and one NEVER pours his own. Although only 17% alcohol, it hits hard so first timers should be careful. During the winter months, hot sake can be considered medicinal because it warms the bones in a country where central heating is not commonplace. The smoother blends are served cold and the taste is quite different. Beer is an excellent antidote for many things and **Kirin, Ashai,** and **Sapporo** are the favored brands.

The Japanese have also begun to make domestic wines in recent years and the results are not too bad. **Mercien** is the most popular and comes in three colors: red, white, and rose. It sells for about $10 in food halls. Some of the wines have French-style labels and are served proudly at banquets and receptions. Others come in German-style bottles and taste slightly of Liebfraumilch. The Japanese also make their own whiskey (**Suntory** is the most famous brand), brandy, champagne ("yuk"), plum wine (*umeshu*), and other semialcoholic beverages. Since "drinking" is pretty well confined to businessmen (who prefer imported brands), the products are not always satisfactory. Many ridiculous combination cocktails are offered in hotel bars that could make any jet-lagged visitor quite ill.

SHOPPING

Forget about cameras. They are more competitively priced outside the country. So are transistors, calculators, and tape recorders. And why buy a Seiko watch when you can get a Swiss one for the same price in Hong Kong (and probably 14k gold at that)? Japanese products are not necessarily less expensive in their country of origin, because the whole system depends upon export. This theory applies strictly to factory-made items, not pearls or handicrafts or contemporary art works.

Pearls: An excellent buy in Japan, especially in the early spring when the new crop comes into the retail shops. **Mikimoto** is the No. 1 name in Japan and you can always be assured of excellent quality at any of the many branches. However, **Uyeda** in the Imperial Hotel arcade (basement level) is also a favored source, and its personnel are very helpful to visitors. It will custom make pearl items in a few days and seems to offer the best "tax-free" prices. Uyeda is considered the Tiffany of Japan, and its jewelry is lovely but very costly.

Metalwork: Japanese handcrafts have a long history, most dating from the Heian Period (A.D. 794–1185) when metalwork became a necessary part of temple design and swordsmiths were highly prized. They were elevated to an unbelievable status during the Kamakura Period because the sword was regarded the "soul" of a samurai and swordguards became works of art, which many people collect today. Another metalwork that has become an art is the casting of tea ceremony kettles (*tetsubin*), terrific for boiling water quickly.

Japanese lacquerware: An ancient tradition and the best lacquer-ware in the world. Beautiful lacquer soup bowls and trays are used daily throughout Japan in restaurants and private homes. Many lacquer artists have made history, encouraged by the samurai's interest in tea cere-mony. Huge lacquer sake cups are used for ceremonial occasions, and decorated *inro* (medicine boxes) are collectors' items.

Ceramics: The Japanese have also developed a fine skill in ceramics, improving greatly on techniques introduced from China in the 13th cen-tury. One can find whole sets of factory-produced china and glassware, or concentrate on the carefully handcrafted folk pottery in the style of the late **Kanjiro Kawai,** the country's most famous potter. *Arita* ware from Saga prefecture, *Kyo* ware from Kyoto, and *Kutani* ware from Ishikawa prefecture are the best known, but every province has its kiln and potter. Mashiko, a small town north of Tokyo, is a potter's dream for this is the home of National Living Treasure **Shoji Hamada**—who has made folkcraft pottery respectable.

Cloisonne: Cloisonne ware, *shippo,* is also an ancient Japanese craft but its origins are not known. However, it seems to have been made since before the 8th century as there are some cloissone ware in the famous **Shoso-in** repository at Nara. Nagoya is the center of the art, but cloisonne ware is also made in Kyoto, Tokyo, and Yokohama.

Netsuke: Another handicraft that will tempt visitors, netsuke are small carved ivory objects that were tied to one end of a silk rope while the other end held *inro* or small pouches and suspended from the waist sash (much like the English watch and chain idea). They were popular during the Tokugawa period and were used by the merchant class. There are many fine collections of netsuke in private hands, and beautiful, coffee-table books have been published about the different figures extant.

Folk art: The appeal of Japanese folk art is a relatively modern phenomenon. Even its name, *Mingei,* is a 20th-century happening and the idea of potter Kawjiro Kawai who wanted his style to be placed in some sort of genre. Much of Japanese folk art is regional and developed because of necessity. In Yamagata prefecture on the Japan Sea coast, you can find *yukigutsu* (snow boots) made from rice straw, *monoge boshi* (cold weather hats), or *bandori* (mats used for carrying heavy items on the back). *Miharu* is famous for its colorful red wooden horses in many sizes. *Kokeshi* dolls are made in Akita, Yamagata, Miyagi, and Fukushima prefectures in northern Japan (Tohoku).

Nara prefecture is famous for handmade Japanese rice paper (*washi*) and writing brushes. Bamboo items and basketwork can be found in

Chugoku district and *uchiwa* (round fans) in Shimane prefecture. *Tansu* (chests of drawers) are made at Takamatsu, where *takenoko gasa* (hats of skin of bamboo shoot) are popular.

The island of Kyushu is known for its fine ceramics: *sake* bottles at Nishi Shimmachi; *koishiwara* ware at Sarayama; *agano* ware; *kuromuta* teapots; *onda* ware; and *ryumonji* ware. Japanese cottons and silks are made throughout the country (*bingata* is a cotton/linen/silk from Okinawa dyed in paper patterns) but, alas, the dyes are no longer washed in Kyoto's Kamo River and laid on the banks to dry. (Industrial pollution has assumed the upper hand.)

Visitors interested in Japan's world of Mingei should spend an hour or so in **Takumi,** the country's first and foremost folkcraft store. Takumi is located at 8–4–2 Ginza, Chuo-ku, Tokyo (Tel: 571–2017), just a short walk from Shimbashi station. Takumi is headquarters of the Japan Folkcraft Society and closely associated with the very charming **Mingei-kan** (Folkcrafts Museum) established by the late Muneyoshi Yanagi. Be sure to canvas all floors at Takumi, as interesting straw items, handwoven materials, and furniture are above. Handmade paper and souvenir items crowd the tables and shelves of the ground floor. **Toraya** (13–1 Minami Aoyama 5–chome, Minato-ku; Tel: 400–8121) also sells folkcrafts, but the shop is more "commercial" and the personnel not so helpful.

Kyoto is the cultural center of Japan and the place to shop for the more traditional arts. *Kumihimo* (plaited cord) and *fusa* (tassled braid) have been made here since the 8th century, and the Japanese are said to have more than 77 different uses for these things. *Kyo ningyo* (traditional doll figures) date from the 9th century and are what every little girl sets up for **Hina Ningyo** (the doll festival on March 3rd). *Kyo sensu,* small folding paper fans with decoration, are used for Japanese dances, tea ceremony, in *Noh* plays, and just to enhance one's party *kimono.* The fans have not changed in style or shape since the 9th century.

Kyo shikki is locally produced lacquerware, and Kyoto craftsmen have spent generations modifying and improving upon the early Chinese technique introduced in the 9th century. Layers of lacquer are applied and polished on cypress, cedar, or horse chestnut for tableware, furniture, and tea ceremony utensils. Tea ceremony items can also be found in **Kiyomizu Yaki,** colorful pottery made in the area of Kiyomizu Temple.

Kyoto is world famous as the center for silk dyeing techniques. *Kyo yuzen* is a process named after Miyazaki Yuzen, a 17th-century dyer, who integrated many ancient techniques into one process, making silk *kimonos* available to the general public. *Tegaki yuzen* is drawing by hand, while *katagami yuzen* means drawing with stencil. One can also find many beautiful antique kimonos in Kyoto and Tokyo to use as decoration or standing free—hung over a bamboo frame. If you like the idea of *yukata,* the cotton lounging or sleeping kimono provided by most hotels (please do not steal them), they are available for a few thousand yen at many tourist shops. *Happi coats* are another popular item for both men and women, and most useful as a cover-up over bathing suits.

Kyoto is also the center for local bamboo craft (*takekogei*), as well as textile weaving for obi, Noh costumes and Shinto priests' robes. *Damascene* is another craft developed through the centuries here, and can be found in all types of jewelry, cigarette boxes, and ashtrays. Beautiful screens and scrolls of the Maruyama and Momoyama periods are still available in the finer galleries of Kyoto and Tokyo (or visit **David Kidd** in Ashiya), but the prices are out of sight and they must be kept in strictly controlled conditions.

Japanese wood block prints need no introduction, and are one of the best mementos one can buy. The origin of *hanga* was probably during the Nara Period, but only became popular in the 17th century when *ukiyo-e* appeared. The *ukiyo-e* school showed the manners and customs of the common folk, first as storybook illustrations and then as independent prints. Two of the most famous *ukiyo-e* artists of the late 18th to mid-19th centuries are **Hiroshige** (the 53 stations of the old Tokaido Road) and **Hokusai** (101 views of Mt. Fuji), which are available in book form or as separate prints.

Modern Japanese print makers show immense variety in form and subject matter. One of the country's most talented and respected artists is, in fact, an American who has lived and worked in Japan since 1955. **Clifton Karhu** lives in Kyoto, and has become more Japanese then his fellow adopted countrymen. His studio is open by appointment only on Tuesday, Friday, and Saturday. It is located at Shimochojamachi-sagaru, Muromachi-dori, Kamikyo-ku (Tel: 415–0606), and an impressive stream of visitors passes through the gate to see and buy.

Karhu's good friend and dealer, Norman Tolman, owns and operates the very best gallery of contemporary prints in Japan. Known as **The Tolman Collection,** it is located in a former geisha house at 2–2–18 Shiba Daimon, Minato-ku, Tokyo (Tel: 434–1300). Mary and Norman have lived in Japan for about 25 years, were formerly with the United States Information Service, and speak fluent Japanese. They represent many, many fine artists, many of them exclusively. Furthermore, they do not allow customers to handle the prints, so you are purchasing a fresh work (not dog-eared as in most shops). The Tolman Collection is open daily from 10 a.m.–7 p.m. (call for directions; it's easy to find).

Travelers who are in Tokyo during mid-October and are interested in the contemporary art scene should not miss the annual print show organized by the College Women's Association of Japan. Now approaching its 35th year, the show offers exposure to both new and recognized artists. Prices are very, very reasonable and some of the purchase price goes into the CWAJ scholarship fund. Check *The Japan Times* for dates, times, and location of the show.

Most Japanese items are found in specialty shops, instantly recognizable by their *kanban*—traditional signs—or *noren*, the divided cloth curtain at entrance with house insignia. There are stores that specialize in just fans, dolls, silk, *washi* (Japanese paper), or toothpicks. On the other hand, Japanese department stores offer a huge variety of products from their basement food halls to the inevitable art gallery at the top. At every level, pretty young women with white gloves bow and murmur greetings as you ascend the escalator. The stores are generally open from 10 a.m.–6 p.m. but closed one day during the week (to compensate for business on Sun.). Don't miss **Wako, Takashimaya, Daimaru, Odakyu, Seibu, Mitsukoshi, Keio,** and **Matsuzakaya.** One just seems to be bigger and better than the other!

HOKKAIDO

HOKKAIDO IN A CAPSULE

Japan's northernmost island and second in size. Represents over 20% of the country's land area but just 5% of the total population . . . separated from Honshu by Tsugaru Straits and bordered by Pacific Ocean, Japan Sea, and Okhotsk Sea . . . world's largest undersea railway tunnel links Aomori to Hakodate . . . when Shinkansen Line completed, the capital Sapporo will be just under 6 hours from Tokyo . . . a popular tourist spot for its many scenic attractions . . . mountain peaks, volcanoes, valleys, and lush forests . . . clear lakes and lovely plains . . . climate corresponds to Canada's Quebec province . . . known for agriculture, forestry (72% of the land still forests), mining, and fishery . . . Hokkaido king crab world famous . . . farming is on a grand scale with American-style barns . . . original inhabitants Ainu aborigines who developed own special folklore and handicrafts.

HAKODATE

HAKODATE IN A CAPSULE

Gateway to Hokkaido and one of Japan's oldest open ports . . . Name means "box castle" . . . dates from 15th century when Kono clan built a box-like structure as fortress . . . city embraces Hakodate Bay, just north of Tsugaru Straits . . . lies at foot of Mt. Hakodate . . . port opened as a coaling station in 1855 . . . became one of 5 ports opened to foreign countries in 1859 . . . along with Nagasaki, Yokohama, Kobe, and Niigata . . . connected by train and ferry to Aomori, northernmost port on Honshu . . . main industry is fishing (July to Dec.) as well as shipbuilding, marine products, and food processing . . . port festival held every Aug. to commemorate the welcoming of foreign trade.

WHAT TO SEE AND DO

Goryokaku • Japan's first Western-style fort . . . built in pentagonal shape . . . hence the name . . . for defense of Ezo (former name for Hokkaido) . . . when area under Tokugawa shogunate rule . . . Goryohaku Park boasts 4000 cherry trees . . . ramparts registered as Important Cultural Property . . . Goryokaku Tower on premises offers panoramic views of area.

Hakodate Park • Located on east slope of Mt. Hakodate . . . known for beautiful flowering fruit trees in spring . . . municipal library and museum located in the park.

Hakodate Museum • Dates from 1879 . . . fisheries museum is original structure . . . also displays of archaeology, aborigines, local arts and crafts, geology and minerals, flora and fauna of the area . . . manuscripts of a famous local poet if you can read Japanese.

Mt. Hakodate • Called Telegraph Hill by U.S. sailors with Commodore Perry in 1854 . . . opened to the public after the war and now a popular hiking place . . . view from summit includes mountain peaks in Honshu, across Tsugaru Straits . . . monument to Thomas Wright Blakiston on summit . . . a British zoologist who lived in Hokkaido from 1861–84 and contributed much to the understanding of local fauna.

Trappist Convent • Located about 20 minutes from Hakodate . . . founded in 1898 by 8 French monks . . . about 70 Trappistine sisters run a dairy farm and produce excellent butter and candy offered for sale . . . don't miss!

Yunokawa Spa • Founded in 17th century and oldest hot-spring resort in Hokkaido . . . offers the weary sulfur and salt springs . . . many restaurants and about 100 *ryokans* situated on both sides of Matsukawa River.

Environs

Mt. Esan • Active double volcano at tip of Oshima Peninsula . . . crest can be reached by an hour's hike . . . slopes covered with alpine plants and azaleas.

Matsumae • Formerly known as **Fukuyama** and was early capital of **Ezo** (Hokkaido) . . . only castle town on the island and headquarters of samurai culture . . . **Matsumae Castle** last feudal castle built in Japan . . . first structure built by Yoshihiro Matsumae in 1606 but destroyed by fire . . . second completed in 1854 but was lost to fire in 1949 . . . present built in 1961 . . . site now a park with 5000 cherry trees.

Okushiri Island • Located about 50 miles off coast from Esashi . . . former penal colony . . . now popular for its mild climate and scenic beauty . . . ferry boats make the journey in about 2½ hours.

Trappist Monastery • About 15 miles from Hakodate . . . founded in 1895 . . . about 50 brothers farm and sell their butter and cheese to the public . . . may be visited by males only, with permission in advance.

HOTELS

★★**Hakodate Kokusai Hotel** • *5–10 Otemachi. Tel: (0138) 238751.*
CABLE: HAKODATE KOKUSAI HOTEL JAPAN. Telex: 9926–04
HAKUHO • 131 rooms.
Facilities: 3 restaurants. 2 bars.
Manager: K. Tsutsumi. *Reservations:* Direct.

★★★★**Hakodate-Ohnuma Prince Cottages** • *148 Nishi-Ohn-*
uma, Nanae-cho, Kameda-gun, Hokkaido 041–13. Tel: (0138) 67–3211.
Telex: 9925–11 ONPRIN J • 130 cottages (155 Rooms). Located on
idyllic sylvan setting . . . cottages built with pine logs imported from
Finland . . . refrigerators, color TV, and telephones . . . just over 2
hours by air from Tokyo.
Facilities: Main Dining Room. Sushi Restaurant. Bar. Lounge.
Coffee Shop. Japanese restaurant. Banquet Hall. Indoor swimming pool.
Sauna. 16 tennis courts. Cycling path. 2 golf courses. Ski Area.
Manager: Y. Nikura. *Reservations:* Prince Int'l.

★★**Hotel Rich Hakodate** • *16–18 Matsukaze-cho. Tel: (0138) 25–*
2561. Telex: 9928–15 • 88 rooms.
Facilities: Dining room. Coffee shop. Bar.
Manager: H. Kawai. *Reservations:* Direct.

SAPPORO

WHAT TO SEE AND DO

Ainu Museum • Dedicated to Dr. John Batchelor (1854–1944) who
wrote the classic *Ainu of Japan* . . . the English-style house built in
1891 was Batchelor's home for 40 years . . . was presented to Hokkaido University and moved to the Botanical Gardens . . . contains
some 20,000 items pertaining to the Ainu tribes . . . includes **Sakhalin**

SAPPORO IN A CAPSULE

Ainu word meaning "long dry river" (the Toyohira) . . . capital of Hokkaido since 1869 . . . city laid out American-style with wide streets intersecting at right angles . . . also divided into north, east, south, west sections so very easy to make one's way around . . . main street called **O-dori** (the street) along which giant snow figures are placed during annual winter Snow Festival in February . . . city known for its heated underground shopping malls . . . very comfortable during heavy winters . . . main products are food stuffs (Snow Brand dairy items and Furuya confectionaries), lumber, Sapporo beer, dried fish, and Ainu handicrafts and carvings . . . a very pleasant city—Hokkaido's largest . . . and site of the 1972 Winter Olympics.

Ainu costumes of fish skins . . . and **Kurile Ainu** costumes that resemble American Indian styles.

Botanical Gardens • Some 35 acres of forests and fauna . . . open from April to Nov. . . . lovely gardens and University Museum of local folklore and natural history . . . also 1300 birds from the collection of zoologist T. W. Blakiston . . . whose bust is on the summit of Mt. Hakodate.

Clock Tower • Russian-style structure built in 1881 . . . served as military exercise hall of Sapporo Agricultural College, now Hokkaido University.

Furuya Confectionary Company • Kita Rokujo, Higashi-ku . . . largest confectionary in Hokkaido and well-known brand . . . makes caramels, candy, chewing gum, cookies, etc. . . . may be visited weekdays from 8:30 a.m. to 4 p.m. upon request one day in advance.

Historical Museum of Hokkaido • located in Nipporo Shinrin Park (about 50 minutes by bus from Sapporo Station). History of Hokkaido . . . plus historical village . . . cluster of buildings dating from last century . . . lovingly restored.

Hokkaido Agricultural Experiment Station Livestock Division • On Hitsujigaoka or Observation Hill at Toyohira, about 7 miles southeast of Sapporo Station . . . farm open to visitors from May to Oct. from 9 a.m. to 5 p.m. . . . good view of Ishikari Plain from hill.

Hokkaido Shrine ● Dates from 1869 when city founded . . . present structure restored in 1964 . . . lovely cherry trees on grounds and annual festival on June 15.

Jozankei Spa ● Located in Toyohira River about an hour from Sapporo. . . dates from mid-19th century . . . many salt springs and beautiful area with *ryokan* built along banks of the river.

Maruyama Park ● Located at foot of Maruyama (hill) . . . contains zoological garden, public youth hostel, and flowering fruit trees . . . Maruyama Primeval Forest covers the hill . . . noted for many species of trees and plants . . . and Hokkaido shrine.

Mt. Moiwa ● Summit offers panoramic view of Teine, Eniwa, Tarumae, and Daisetsu mountains as well as Ishikari Bay . . . observation platform, Ezo Deer Park, aquarium, and amusement park . . . primeval forest on slope contains 60 different species of broad-leaved trees . . . a 1.2 mile scenic drive runs along the southern slope.

Nakajima Park ● Situated between Toyohira and Sosei rivers . . . contains Hassoan (teahouse) moved from **Kohoan Temple** . . . also Hoheikan, European-style "guest house" from the Meiji era.

Nakayama Pass ● Lies between Jozankei Spa and Lake Toya . . . panoramic views of surrounding mountains . . . popular tourist attraction.

O-Dori ● The Main Street . . . cuts through the heart of Sapporo . . . on eastern end is TV tower with observation platform for view of Ishikari Plain.

Sapporo Underground Shopping Center ● Consists of Pole Town and Aurora Town . . . Pole Town extends from Minami-O-dori to Susuki-no . . . Aurora Town stretches from O-dori San-chome to the TV Tower . . . most entertaining during the winter months when packed with people.

Sapporo Breweries ● Kita-Shichijo, Higashi-ku . . . oldest in Japan (1876) and visitors welcome 9 to 11 a.m. and 1 to 3:30 p.m. by appointment (Tel: 011–743–4368).

Ski Areas ● West suburbs have excellent ski grounds . . . Sankakuyama, Miyanomori and Maruyama . . . also former Olympic sites like Mt. Teine . . . Mt. Arai is for beginners and Mt. Moiwa for all classes.

Tanuki-Koji and Susukino • Former means Badger Alley, which is filled with small shops active in daytime . . . latter has over 3000 bars, etc. and is strictly a nighttime quarter of the city.

Environs

Ainu Village • Located on shores of Lake Potoro in Shiraoi (between Noboribetsu and Tomakomai) . . . about 130 families were relocated here in 1965 . . . they welcome visitors to see their homes, buy their handicrafts and pay a little for lectures on their ancient customs . . . village chieftain and wife wear traditional costumes and do the speaking . . . from about 40,000 Ainu in Hokkaido some 80 years ago . . . there are now only about 17,000 left . . . most of the young try to intermarry as quickly as possible to "gain respectability."

Chitose • About 30 minutes by express train from Sapporo . . . site of the U.S. Airforce in Hokkaido . . . main airport for Sapporo and environs.

Karurusu Spa • About 5 miles northwest of Noboribetsu Spa on the Chitose River . . . great hot springs . . . with baths made from rock beds along the ravine of the river . . . waters said to have same curative effect as those in Karlsbad Springs in Czechoslovakia.

Lake Toya • About 2 hours from Sapporo by train . . . located in Shikotsu-Toya National Park . . . lake has large island in middle (**Nakanoshima**) where a forestry museum exhibits the flora and fauna that inhabit here . . . Mt. Usu is active volcano just south of the lake . . . formed Showa Shinzan (new mountain of Showa era) in 1945 . . . has been designated Special National Monument.

Noboribetsu Spa • Most famous spa in Hokkaido . . . in all of Japan . . . dates from around 16th century . . . hot baths are wonderful here and many hotels have a choice of various waters in the tubs . . . mixed bathing is still "in" here in some hotels . . . it's a wonderful spot to spend a day . . . great old hotels and funny little souvenir shops . . . visit also **Jigokudani** (Valley of Hell) with Oyunuma lake of hot mud and boiling water . . . and Hiyoriyama peak steaming with sulfur . . . New Noboribetsu Spa was established in 1962 and has none of the charm of the original.

Toyako Spa • Situated on southwest shore of Lake Toya . . . Lovely area full of mountain views and comfortable *ryokan* . . . salt and sulfur springs to cure all ills . . . if the waters don't, the views will anyway.

Otaru • Means "river on a sandy beach" in Ainu . . . located about 45 minutes from Sapporo by train . . . on Ishikari Bay facing the Japan Sea . . . Originally inhabited by the Ainu involved in herring . . . today the 5th largest city in Hokkaido . . . see Otaru Park for nice views and Temiya Cave . . . with ancient inscription inside that anthropologists have not yet deciphered.

HOTELS

★★★★**Keio Plaza Hotel Sapporo** • *7–2 Nishi, Kita–5, Chuo-ku. Tel: (011) 271–0111. Cable: KEIOPLATEL SAPPORO. Telex: 933–271 KPHSPK* • *525 rooms.*
Facilities: Ambrosia Sky restaurant. Jurin Coffee House. Duet tea lounge. Cross Vault main bar. Page 1 sound spot. Nan-en Chinese restaurant. Pompelmo Mediterranean restaurant. Miyama Japanese restaurant. Tokyo Chikuyo-tei Japanese restaurant. Tachibana Sushi bar. Kitano-Izakaya Hokkaido Pub. Delicatessen. Eminence banquet hall. Indoor pool, health club and sauna. Shopping arcade, nursery and garage.
Manager: K. Todoroki. *Reservations:* Keio Plaza Tokyo.

★★★**Sapporo Grand Hotel** • *4 Nishi, Kita–1, Chuo-ku. Tel: (011) 261–3311. Cable: GRAHO SAPPORO. Telex: 932–613 GRAHO* • 521 rooms.
Facilities: Chinese and Japanese restaurants. Coffee shop. Cocktail lounge and bar. Japanese tea garden and tea ceremony room.
Manager: K. Otsuka. *Reservations:* JAL.

★★**Sapporo Park Hotel** • *3–11 Nishi, Minami-Jujo. Tel: (011) 511–3131. Cable: PARK HOTEL SAP. Telex: 932–264 PRKHTL* • 223 rooms.
Facilities: Dining room. Continental restaurant. 2 bars. Nightclub.
Manager: S. Osanai. *Reservations:* Direct.

★★★★**Sapporo Prince Hotel** • *11 Nishi, Minami-2, Chuo-ku. Tel: (011) 231–5310. Telex: 933–949 SAPPRI. Cable: SAPRINCEHOTEL* • 227 rooms.
Facilities: Dining room. Japanese and Chinese restaurants. Cocktail lounge. Coffee shop. Golf and skiing rentals.
Manager: T. Ohno. *Reservations:* Prince Int'l.

★★**Sapporo Royal Hotel** • *Higashi 1–chome, Minami 7–jo, Chuoku. Tel: (011) 511–2121. Telex: 932–330 SROYAL* • 88 rooms.

Facilities: 4 restaurants. Coffee shop. 2 bars. Tea ceremony room. *Manager:* M. Sakazaki. *Reservations:* Direct.

★★★**Sapporo Tokyu Hotel** • *Nishi 4–chome, Kita 4–yo, Chuo-ku. Tel: (011) 231–5611. Telex: 934–510 THCSAP* • 263 rooms. *Facilities:* Grill. Coffeehouse. Bar. Japanese restaurant. *Manager:* T. Kaneko. *Reservations:* Tokyu Chain.

NATIONAL PARKS

Akan National Park • Extends over districts of Kushiro, Abashiri, and Tokachi in the eastern part of Hokkaido . . . volcanic mountains including **Me-Akan** and **O-Okan** . . . 3 large lakes, Akan, Kutcharo, and Mashu . . . subarctic primeval forests . . . 2 passes with panoramic views of the lakes, Bihoro and Sempoku . . . good base for visiting the park is Akan Kohan Spa on the south shore of Lake Akan . . . also Kawayu Spa at the foot of Mt. Ito and not far from tip of Lake Kutcharo.

Daisetsuzan National Park • Largest mountain national park in Japan . . . located in center of the island . . . known as Roof of Hokkaido . . . includes 3 important volcanic groups . . . Mt. Asahi, Mt. Tomuraushi, and Mt. Tokachi . . . also 3 large rivers and 2 lakes . . . park popular with hikers in summer, skiers in winter . . . also hot spring resorts located along rivers which offer accommodations in *ryokans* and youth hostels . . . Sounkyo Spa lies in center of Sounkyo Gorge . . . Daisetsu Highway runs from the gorge to Onneyu Spa through Sekihoku Pass . . . about 2½ hours by bus . . . Sounkyo is also the base for 1 of 4 routes up the dozen peaks called Mt. Daisetsu . . . at the southwest end of the park is active volcano Mt. Tokachi which last erupted in 1962.

Niseko-Shakotan-Otaru Coast Quasi-National Park • Includes the Niseko Mountains, Shakotan Peninsula, and Otaru seaside park . . . located northwest of Sapporo facing the Japan Sea . . . includes lovely sandy beaches along the coastline . . . interesting anthropological findings in ancient mounds and caves with inscriptions said to be 1500 years old . . . main peak is Mt. Nisekoan-Nupuri . . . fabulous ski area and full of hot spring areas at the base . . . the whole park combines such natural beauty in sea, mountains and coast . . . boat trips available.

Onuma Quasi-National Park • Located on Oshima Peninsula just north of Hakodate . . . combines Mt. Koma with 3 dammed lakes— Onuma, Konuma, and Junsai . . . about 80% of park is water . . . Mt. Koma is an active volcano and encompasses 3 mountain peaks . . . also known as Oshima-Fuji because it looks somewhat like Fuji-san from the base . . . Shikabe Spa lies at the foot of Mt. Koma . . . facing Pacific Ocean . . . best view in park is from Konuma Hill between Konuma and Junsai lakes.

Rishiri-Rebun-Sarobetsu National Park • Located in northwest part of Hokkaido, just south and west of Wakkanai . . . covers Rishiri and Rebun islands as well as Sarobetsu Plain . . . islands known for wild birds and ferry service available from Wakkanai . . . Rishiri has a conic volcano called Rishiri-Fuji for its resemblance to Fuji-san.

Shikotsu Toya National Park • Combines Mt. Yotei, Lake Toya, and Jozankei-Shikotsu and Noboribetsu spas . . . one of Hokkaido's most popular parks . . . easily accessible from Sapporo . . . Lake Shikotsu is deepest lake in Hokkaido . . . Mt. Yotei is an extinct volcano that also resembles Fuji-san . . . a favorite with climbers . . . excellent bus service available through this park.

Shiretoko National Park • Located in northeastern part of Hokkaido. Covers Shiretoko Peninsula . . . with fine views of Okhotsk Sea, Kunashiri Island, and Nemuro Straits . . . includes Rausu, Io, and Shiretoko volcanic peaks . . . considered quiet by local standards . . . also encompasses Shiretoko-Goko (Five Lakes of Shiretoko) . . . excellent bus service through the area . . . also boat service for majestic views from the sea.

OTHER PLACES OF INTEREST

Abashiri • Situated on the eastern coast of Hokkaido, facing the Okhotsk Sea . . . a great fishing area . . . not only in the sea but in the many natural lakes in the area . . . Lake Abashiri is full of carp,

smelt and shrimp and forms center of Abashiri-Quasi National Park . . .
near Abashiri River estuary is Moyoro Shell Mound . . . containing
tombs and relics of aborigines who lived here before the Ainu some
1500 years ago . . . Notor and Saroma lagoons are noted for their size
and excellent stock of fish . . . Abashiri plain is great agricultural center.

Asahikawa • Hokkaido's second largest city . . . name originated
from Ainu meaning "river of raging waves" . . . but Japanese translated it as "sun river" . . . city located in central Hokkaido in Kami-
kawa Basin . . . Ishikawa River divides city . . . serves as entrance
to Daisetsuzan National Park . . . Ainu Memorial Hall in Chikabumi,
a suburb, exhibits Ainu dwellings and customs . . . Kamuikotan about
12 miles west of Asahikawa is a canyon formed by the Ishikawa River
through the Yubari mountains.

Biratori Ainu Village • Located in Saru River basin, between Mu-
kawa and Hidaka-Mombetsu in southwestern Hokkaido . . . the oldest
and largest of Ainu communities on the island . . . traditional life is
pretty much intact here . . . Yoshitsune Shrine in the village is dedicated to Yoshitsune Minamoto . . . 12th-century warlord who allegedly
made the journey across the Tsugaru Straits of Ezo . . . shrine dates
from 1802 and is famous for its lovely cherry blossoms in mid-May.

Kushiro • On the southeast coast of Hokkaido, facing the Pacific
Ocean . . . name comes from the Ainu word for trout (Kutcharo) . . .
serves as base for deep-sea fishing because only one of two ports on the
island that never freezes (other is Wakkanai) . . . Lake Harutori is
designated National Monument . . . Natural Park for Japanese Cranes
with Red Crests on the right bank of Kushiro River is designated Special Natural Monument . . . some 200 cranes come every winter for
their bed and breakfast.

Wakkanai • Japan's northernmost city . . . the only other port
that does not freeze during the winter months . . . this port also boasts
more traffic in fish than any other—crab, herring, mackerel, salmon,
and scallops . . . U.S. Air Force has weather station here . . . which
offers tips via the Far East Network . . . an hour northeast is Cape
Soya . . . the northernmost point in Hokkaido . . . faces Soya Straits
separating the Japan Sea from the Okhotsk Sea.

HONSHU

CENTRAL MOUNTAIN AREA

CENTRAL MOUNTAIN AREA

Features Japan Alps . . . known as the Roof of Japan . . . this volcanic range is highest in Japan . . . extends from north to south through central and widest part of Honshu . . . area also encompasses Joshin-etsu Highland National Park . . . with renowned summer resort of Karuizawa at its southern entrance . . . the towns of Wajima and Fukui . . . and Yatsugatake-Chushin Highland Quasi-National Park.

WHAT TO SEE AND DO

Chubu-Sangaku National Park • Also known as Japan Alps . . . the country's No. 1 mountain range and park . . . noted for high peaks . . . Shirouma, Tateyama, Norikura, Kashima-yari, Harinoki, Renge, Eboshi, Kurodate, Tsubakuro, Jonen, Yari, Hotaka, and Kasa in the northern Alps . . . many lovely streams, gorges, and valleys . . . Kurobe, Azusa, and Sugoroku in particular . . . Kamikochi is a base for climbing such noted peaks as Hotaka, Yake, Kasumizawa, and Roppyaku . . . Azusa River offers clear waters . . . Kamikochi is about 3 hours by bus from Matsumoto . . . old castle town that is gateway to the Japan Alps . . . known for its 1504 castle designated National Treasure . . . Matsumoto is sister-city of Salt Lake City, Utah.

Joshin-Etsu Kogen (Plateau) National Park • Extends over Niigata, Gumma, and Nagano prefectures . . . divided into northern and southern sections . . . southern encompasses Mt. Tanigawa, active volcano Shirane, active volcano Asama as well as Shiga Heights and Sugadaira Plateau . . . in northern section are Mts. Myoko, Kurohime, Togakushi, and Izuma as well as popular summer retreat for both Japanese and Western hierarchy, Karuizawa (Crown Princess Akihito met his princess on the tennis court here) . . . Karuizawa is only 2 hours from Tokyo and many residents have summer houses in the area . . . Karuizawa has a refreshing climate . . . very, very social during the "season" . . . lovely man-made lakes, waterfalls, historic western buildings . . . hiking trails and a wild bird sanctuary . . . resort hotels impeccable and very expensive! Shiga Heights in the northern section is about 4 hours from Tokyo by train (change at Nagano) and very popular for skiing.

Minami (Southern) Alps National Park • Features magnificent Akaishi Range . . . located in southern part of Japan Alps . . . centers around Mts. Komagatake and Shirane . . . and great beauty in peaks, gorges, valleys, and rivers . . . waterfalls and cliffs . . . primeval forests and alpine flora . . . Nirasaki is the climber's base . . . about 2 hours by train from Tokyo . . . just under 2 hours from Matsumoto.

Yatsugatake-Chushin Highland Quasi-National Park • Sport and resort park area that extends over highlands of Tadeshina, Kirigamine, and Utsukushigahara . . . principal tourist attractions are Mt. Yatsu and Lake Matsubara . . . year-round vacation area . . . camping and hiking in summer . . . skating and skiing in winter . . . town of Chino is gateway to the park . . . just 3 hours from Tokyo by train . . . 1 hour from Matsumoto.

HOTELS

Karuizawa

★★★★★**Hotel Kajima No Mori** • 50 rooms. Resort hotel operated by Okura chain and noted for quiet elegance, service, and cuisine. Difficult to book during season.

★★★★★**Karuizawa Prince Hotel** • *1016–75 Karuizawa-machi, Karuizawa, Nagano Pref. 389–01. Tel: (02674) 2–5211* • 72 rooms . . . 168 cottages.
Facilities: Dining room. Bar. Golf. Riding. Skating. Skiing. Boating. Tennis.

★★★★★**Karuizawa Prince Hotel Seizan Honkan** • *1016 Karuizawa-machi, Nagano Pref. 389–01. Tel: (02674) 2–5211* • 68 rooms. . . . 231 cottages.
Facilities: Same as for the Karuizawa Prince Hotel.

★★★★**Karuizawa Mampei Hotel** • *925 Sakuranosawa, Karuizawa, Nagano Pref. 389–01. Tel: (02674) 2–2771* • 127 rooms.
Facilities: Dining room. Bar. Tennis. Golf. Riding. Skating.

FUJI/HAKONE/IZU

FUJI/HAKONE/IZU NATIONAL PARK

Japan's most famous national park and No. 1 tourist attraction . . . park covers 4 large districts . . . Mt. Fuji, National Mountain of Japan . . . and Five Lakes . . . popular hot spring resort of Hakone, wedged between Mt. Fuji and the Izu Peninsula . . . and the Izu Peninsula, full of seaside spas like Atami and lovely coastlines . . . golf resorts and places of historic interest . . . Ito is where first Englishmen set foot in Japan . . . Shimoda is port Townsend Harris opened and became first foreign diplomatic representative received in Japan . . . Seven Islands of Izu added later to the park area . . . entire region easily accessible from Tokyo by super-express Shinkansen to Atami or Odawara . . . excellent highways and local service.

MT. FUJI AND FIVE LAKES DISTRICT

Mt. Fuji • National Mountain of Japan . . . names comes from **Ainu** word meaning "fire" . . . but Japanese call it Fuji-san (papa Fuji) . . . dormant conical volcano . . . considered one of most beautiful in the world . . . Mt. Cotopaxi in Ecuador is a rival to its beauty . . . climbing season open from July 1 through Aug. . . . 5–9-hour ascent is a popular pastime to see sunrise on the summit . . . over 300,000 do so during the official season . . . post office on the top near the Sengen Shrine . . . 3 different trails up the peak . . . divided into 10 different stages . . . climbers buy a stick and have it branded at each station . . . travelers should be advised of plenty of company along the trail . . . change of weather from hot to rainy and cool . . . and no supplies . . . there are huts in which to rest a few hours.

Fuji Five Lakes District • Lies at northern base of Mt. Fuji. Lakes are Yamanaka . . . cool summer resort noted for Aug. 1 Lake Festival with thousands of lighted lanterns set afloat on the waters . . . Kawaguchi . . . noted for fine views of Mt. Fuji from northern shore . . . Saiko in a quiet setting . . . Shoji, the smallest of the lakes and facing Mt. Fuji from the northwest . . . and Motosu, the westernmost and deepest of the 5 . . . visitors admire beauty of its deep waters.

HOTELS

★★★★**Hotel Grand Fuji** • *8–1 Heigaki-Honcho, Fuji Shizuoka Pref. 416. Tel: (0545) 61–0360* • 25 rooms. 3 minutes by car from Fuji Station.

★★★★**Fuji-View Hotel** • *511 Katsuyama-mura, Minamitsuru-gun Yamanashi Pref. 401–04. Tel: (05558) 2–2211. Cable: FUJIVIEW KATSUYAMA* • 66 rooms.
Facilities: Dining room. Cocktail lounges. Bicycles. Tennis. Golf. Fishing.
Manager: G. Horiuchi. *Reservations:* Direct.

★★★★**Hotel Mt. Fuji** • *Yamanaka, Yamanakako-mura, Yamanashi Pref. 401–05. Tel: (05556) 2–2111. Cable: MTFUJI YOSHIDA* • 110 rooms.
Facilities: Dining room. Japanese restaurant. Grillroom. Bar. Swimming pool. Tennis. Boating. Stables. Bicycles.
Manager: S. Horikawa. *Reservations:* VIP Hotel Rep.

★★★**New Yamanakako Hotel** • *Yamanaka, Yamanakako-mura, Yamanashi Pref. 401–05. Tel: (05556) 2–2311. Telex: 3385–478 OMNIA J* • 66 rooms.
Facilities: Located near Lake Yamanaka. Western and Japanese cuisine. 2 bars. Swimming pool.
Manager: K. Nakazawa. *Reservations:* Direct.

★★★**Yamanakako Hotel** • *506–1 Yamanakako-mura, Yamanashi Pref. 401–05. Tel: (05556) 2–2511. Cable: YAMANAKAKO HOTEL. Telex: 3385–492 YAMHTL J* • 71 rooms.

HAKONE HOT SPRING RESORTS

Ashinoya • Located about 15 minutes by bus from Miyanoshita . . . 2 hot springs . . . base for climbing Komagatake, Futago, and Kami peaks.

Chokoku-No-Mori • The Woods of Sculpture . . . site of the Hakone Open-Air Museum . . . magnificent works by Henry Moore and others in hillside setting . . . located about 5 minutes from Kowakidani . . . open daily . . . until 6 p.m. in summer.

Dogashima • 10 minutes by foot below Miyanoshita . . . small hot spring on banks of Hayakawa River . . . restful and secluded spot.

Gora Spa • On slope of Mt. Sounzan . . . facing the spa is Mt. Myojo, famous for its Daimonjiyaki bonfire festival . . . Gora also home of Hakone Art Museum . . . with ancient art of Japan and China . . . cable car available from here up Mt. Sounzan.

Hakone-Yumoto • Oldest spa in area and gateway to Hakone National Park . . . located about 15 minutes from Odawara by bus . . .

at confluence of Hayakawa and Sukumo rivers . . . waters good for digestive diseases . . . site of Sounji, Zen Buddhist temple of Rinzai sect . . . established in late 15th century . . . once largest in eastern Japan . . . famous for Feudal Lord Procession every fall . . . 200 local townfolk dress as retainers of former lord Hojo whose portrait on silk in the temple is an Important Cultural Property . . . procession marches from Yumoto to Tonosawa and back.

Hakone Barrier • Established in 1618 during Tokugawa shogunate . . . stood on main road between Kyoto and Edo (Tokyo) . . . removed in 1869, year after Meiji Restoration . . . monument marks site . . . Hakone **Shiryo-kan** (Hakone Historical Materials Museum) near site . . . exhibits of life and customs of Edo period (A.D. 1603–1867).

Hakone-En • Located on eastern shore of Lake Ashi . . . has International Village of different architecture from many countries . . . ropeway to Mt. Komagatake . . . good views of Fuji and Izu Peninsula from the summit.

Hakone-Machi • A few minutes by bus from Moto-Hakone along the shores of Lake Ashi . . . lined with huge cedar trees . . . passes site of former Hakone Barrier . . . also site of one of Japan's most beautiful hotel properties . . . the modern Hakone Prince designed around a grove of cryptomeria trees at lake shore . . . architect was Togo Murano . . . historic Japanese-style annex known as Ryuguden . . . where famous have enjoyed *kaiseki ryori* (traditional dinners) and slept.

Kowakidani • Valley of Less Boiling . . . also called **Kojigoku** or Little Hell . . . bubbling sulfurous hot springs along Owakudani . . . good for nervous troubles and skin diseases, so they say . . . area known for flowering trees . . . and **Chisuji-no-Taki** (Falls of 1000 Threads) which is a favorite place for hikers.

Lake Ashi • One of Hakone's major tourist attractions . . . called Ashinoko and 11 miles around clear, sparkling water . . . known for inverted reflections of Mt. Fuji . . . best seen in autumn and winter from a red wooden *torii* of Hakone Shrine on the shore between Moto-Hakone and Hakone-machi . . . boats available from point to point around the lake.

Miyanoshita • Most popular of all hot springs in Hakone district . . . all roads lead here . . . home of famous Fujiya Hotel, Japan's oldest foreign-style hotel . . . a rambling wooden structure with Victorian ambiance . . . founded in 1878 and extensively rebuilt due to earthquakes and other natural disasters . . . one of the country's most enjoyable hostelries . . . Miyanoshita is full of charming shops selling *imari* and other expensive antique porcelain ware . . . excellent base for exploring Hakone.

Moto-Hakone • No. 1 town on Lake Ashi and major tourist center . . . buses from here to Atami and Odawara and boats across the lake . . . entrance to Hakone Shrine, founded in 8th century . . . dedicated to 3 Shinto deities . . . one of largest shrines in central Japan . . . warlord Minamoto took refuge here in 1180 during battle with the Taira clan . . . red *torii* on the lakeshore is known for **Sakasa-Fuji** . . . inverted views of the volcanic peak . . . annual festival here the last week in July . . . in honor of 9-headed dragon . . . believed to be spirit of the lake.

Owakudani • Valley of Greater Boiling . . . also known as **Ojigoku** or Big Hell . . . if you enjoy sulfurous fumes and bubbling hot springs . . . this is the place . . . located near Owakudani Station of Hakone Ropeway between Souzan and Togendai . . . Natural Science Museum of local flora and fauna established here . . . also good views of Mt. Fuji.

Sengokuhara • Popular resort about 15 minutes by bus from Miyanoshita . . . encompasses 6 different spas with waters piped in from Owakudani . . . Fujiya Hotel's 18-hole golf course located here also . . . extensive area that borders Lake Ashi on the south.

HOTELS

★★★★**Hotel De Yama** • *80 Moto-Hakone, Hakone-Machi. Tel: (0460) 3–6321. Telex: 3892–734* • 93 rooms.
Facilities: Lakeside resort. Dining room. Bar. Japanese garden. Tennis, boating, fishing, skating, and golf.
Manager: A. Shinohara. *Reservations:* Direct.

★★★★★**Fujiya Hotel** • *359 Miyanoshita, Hakone-machi. Tel: (0460) 2–2211. Cable: FUJIYAHOTEL. Telex: 3892–718 FUJIYA J* • 150 rooms.
Facilities: Old-world charm. Dining room. Grillroom. Kikka-so restaurant. Bar overlooking goldfish pond. Swimming pool. Golf course. Lovely grounds and traditional gardens.
Manager: T. Akiyama. *Reservations:* Direct.

★★★**Hakone Hotel** • *65 Hakone-machi. Cable: HAKONE HO-TEL. Telex: 3892–765. Tel: (0460) 3–6311* • 34 rooms.
Facilities: Restaurants. Boating. Fishing. Waterskiing. Tennis. Skating.
Manager: T. Toyama. *Reservations:* Direct.

★★★★★ + **Hakone Prince Hotel** • *144 Moto-Hakone, Hakone-machi. Tel: (0460) 3–7111. Telex: 3892–609 HAKPRI J* • 154 rooms.
Facilities: One of Japan's most beautiful hotels. Exquisite setting overlooking Lake Ashi. French restaurant. Continental buffet. Coffee shop. Japanese restaurant. Bar. Nightclub. Swimming pool. Tennis. Golf. Boating. Ancient Japanese-style annex and 142 private cottages on vast grounds.
Manager: H. Ohiba. *Reservations:* Prince Hotels Int'l.

★★★★**Hotel Kowaki-En** • *1297 Ninotaira, Hakone-machi. Tel: (0460) 2–4111. Cable: HTLKWK. Telex: 3892–730 HAKKWK J* • 257 rooms.
Facilities: Western, Japanese or Chinese nouvelle cuisine. Bars. Nightclub.
Manager: K. Inaba. *Reservations:* FUJITA.

★★★**Odakyu Hakone Highland Hotel** • *940 Shinanoki, Sengo-kuhara, Hakone-machi. Tel: (0460) 4–8541* • 60 rooms.
Facilities: Restaurant. Bar. Japanese garden. Tennis. Golf. Boating. Fishing. Skating.
Manager: K. Nishio. *Reservations:* Direct.

★★★**Yumoto Fujiya Hotel** • *256 Yumoto, Hakone. Tel: (0460) 5–6111. Telex: 3892–631 YUFUYA J* • 100 rooms.
Facilities: Western and Japanese restaurants. Bar. Golf. Fishing. Swimming pool.
Manager: S. Saitoh. Reservations: Fujiya.

IZU PENINSULA AND SEVEN ISLANDS

Atagawa Spa ● 30 minutes by train from Ito . . . hot spring resort by the sea . . . great for female diseases and other things . . . a few minutes away is Imaihama Spa . . . another seaside resort with waters piped in from Mine Spa across the mountain.

Atami ● One of largest and most famous spas in Japan . . . located at entrance to Izu Peninsula . . . name means Hot Sea . . . easily accessible to Tokyo via super-speed Shinkansen . . . excellent as interchange for Hakone . . . a town of over 50,000 inhabitants . . . known for lovely *ume,* or plum blossoms in the spring . . . has fine art museum and thousands of ryokans and shops . . . popular tourist area with the Japanese.

Cape Iro ● Located at end of Izu Peninsula . . . observation tower, meteorological station, and lighthouse on cliff . . . views of Seven Isles of Izu . . . also **Iro Shrine** where sailors worship.

Ito ● No. 2 spa in Izu Peninsula after Atami . . . over 700 hot springs in area . . . one active for more than 3 centuries . . . Yoritimo Minamoto banished here by Taira clan in 1160 . . . priest Nichiren also exiled here to Butsugenji, temple of the Nichiren sect . . . painted picture of his vision of paradise in 13th century . . . Englishman William Adams lived here between 1605 and 1610 . . . called **Anjin Miura** by the Japanese . . . set up a shipyard and constructed 2 large European-style vessels during this period . . . Adams Monument marks the site . . . Kawana Golf Course is just 10 minutes from Ito . . . also Lake Ippeki known for its shiny surface and small islets.

Izu-Nagaoka Spa ● Good for nervous ailments . . . located at foot of Mt. Katsuragi which offers fine views of Mt. Fuji and Suruga Bay.

Mito ● One of most attractive spots on west coast of peninsula . . . a few minutes by bus from Izu-Nagaoka Spa . . . fine views of Mt.

Fuji from beach . . . excellent fishing area . . . Mito Natural Aquarium on beach features dolphins and giant turtles in own habitat . . . also Pearl House.

Mt. Amagi ● Group of dormant volcanoes . . . occupies central section of Izu peninsula . . . includes high peaks . . . lush forests and popular for hunting wild boar from Nov. to mid-Feb. . . . lovely flowering bushes and trees in the spring.

Shimoda ● Main port at southern tip of Izu Peninsula . . . ferry service from here to coastal islands . . . famous for being first port opened to American shipping . . . and arrival of Townsend Harris as first American envoy in 1856 . . . negotiated Treaty of Yedo that opened Japan to the outside world in 1858 . . . Harris actually lived at **Gyokusenji,** small temple in village of Kakisaki . . . **Kurofune Matsuri** or Black Ship Festival held here mid-May every year . . . commemorates first landing by Commodore Perry . . . **Ryosenji,** a temple in the western section of Shimoda famous for a meeting between Commodore Perry and a representative of the Tokugawa government at which a treaty was concluded for U.S.–Japan Amity.

Shuzenji Spa ● 3rd most popular resort on Izu Peninsula . . . perched in valley of Katsura River . . . about 2 hours by bus from Shimoda . . . popular for hiking and hunting.

Seven Islands of Izu ● Recent addition to National Park . . . most popular are Hachijojima at southern extremity of chain . . . about 11 hours by boat from Tokyo . . . has 2 extinct volcanoes . . . and Oshima, just 4 hours by boat from Tokyo . . . famous for fauna and active conical volcano named Mt. Mihara . . . recreation spot with many facilities . . . other 5 islands are Toshima, Niijima, Kozu, Miyake, and Mikura.

HOTELS

Atami

★★★**Chateau Tel Akanezaki** ● *Aza Akane, Kamitaga, Atami. Tel: (0557) 67–1111. Telex: 3927–631* ● 550 rooms.
Facilities: French, Chinese, and Japanese restaurants. Bar. Nightclub. Swimming pool. Health club. Beach. Fishing. Boating.
Manager: S. Mizuno. *Reservations:* JTB.

★★★**New Fujiya Hotel** ● *1–16 Ginza, Atami. Tel: (0557) 81–0111. Cable: NEFTEL ATAMI. Telex: 3917–681 NEFTEL J* ● 320 rooms.

Facilities: Chinese and Japanese restaurants. Theater restaurant. Nightclub. 3 Bars. Swimming pool. Spa and sauna.

Manager: H. Shiotani. *Reservations:* JTB.

Kawana

★★★★★**Kawana Hotel** ● *1459 Kawana, Ito-City, Shizuoka Pref. Tel: (0557) 45–1111. Cable: KATEL ITO* ● 140 rooms.

Facilities: Japan's finest golf resort. 2 18-hole courses. Fuji Course has view of Mt. Fuji. Oshima Course overlooks Oshima Island and active volcano. Tennis. Swimming pool. Dining room. Japanese restaurant. Bar. Game room. Conventions. A very fine member of the Hotel Okura chain.

Manager: Y. Yoneyama. *Reservations:* Distinguished Hotels.

Shimoda

★★★**Shimoda Prince Hotel** ● *1547–1 Shirahama, Shimoda. Tel: (05582) 2–7575. Telex: 3929–754* ● 135 rooms . . . beach resort.

Facilities: Dining room. Bar. Nightclub. Swimming pool. Health club.

Manager: Y. Seto. *Reservations:* Prince Hotel Int'l.

★★**Shimoda Tokyu Hotel** ● *5–12–1 Shimoda. Tel: (05582) 2–2411. Cable: TOKYUTEL SHIMODA. Telex: 3929–732* ● 120 rooms.

Facilities: Grillroom. Sushi restaurant. Garden barbecue. Bar. Public bath.

Manager: M. Komatsubara. *Reservations:* Tokyu.

JAPAN SEA COAST

WHAT TO SEE AND DO

Hagi ● Fishing center of western Japan Sea . . . noted for production of *kamaboko* (boiled fish paste) and 4 centuries tradition of **Hagi-**

JAPAN SEA COAST IN A CAPSULE

Extends entire length of Honshu from Tohoku through Chugoku districts . . . among the most noted spots are Oga Peninsula in Akita prefecture, the Noto Peninsula in Ishikawa prefecture and Sotomo Beach in Fukui prefecture . . . Oki Islands of Daisen-Oki National Park are also famous for their scenic beauty . . . Kanazawa in the central seacoast region is known for its development of such traditional arts as *Noh,* tea ceremony and flower arrangement . . . Hagi is the entrance to Akiyoshidai Quasi-National Park.

---

yaki pottery . . . **Shoin Shrine** is dedicated to famous loyalist Shoin Yoshida executed by Tokugawa government . . . Kita-Nagato Coast Quasi-National Park encompasses some 60 offshore islands, including Omishima . . . known for its ancient **Saienji** Buddhist temple and pomelos . . . Chomonkyo Gorge an hour by bus from Hagi is another scenic spot . . . Hagi is entrance to Akiyoshidai Quasi-National Park which includes Japan's largest tableland . . . limestone grottos like Aikyoshi Cave great tourist attractions.

Kanazawa • Popular city on the Japan Sea and capital of Ishikawa prefecture . . . formerly a small town called Tamazaki, Kanazawa became headquarters of Maeda clan from 1580 until Meiji Restoration . . . developed as important cultural, administrative, and industrial center . . . noted for silk textiles, **kaga-yuzen** (colorfully dyed silks) and **kutani** ware (porcelain) . . . Kenrokuen Park is former site of Lord Maeda's mansion . . . considered one of three most beautiful landscape gardens in Japan (along with Kairakuen at Mito and Korakuen at Okayama) . . . laid out in 1819 with nice views of Mt. Utatsu, Japan Sea, and Noto Peninsula . . . Oyama Shrine dedicated to a Maeda ancestor and has nice views of the area . . . **Noh Theater** is one of most famous in the country . . . one of the few castle towns still remaining in Japan . . . has great scenic beauty . . . Sai and Asano rivers flowing through . . . fine museums—Ishikawa Prefectural Museum of Handicraft . . . Ishikawa Prefectural Traditional Arts and Crafts Museum and and Honda Museum (the Hondas were chief retainers of the ruling Maeda lords) . . . visit also Ninja-dera (Temple of the Secret Agents) . . . city has excellent tourist/cultural centers for info, especially Ruth Stevens' *Kanazawa: The Other Side of Japan* . . . serious visitors should use it diligently. Kanazawa is entrance to Hakusan National Park . . . with its 5 famous peaks . . . and Noto Peninsula . . . noted for its wild and beautiful scenery . . . Yuwaku Hot Springs on outskirts is famous for Edo Mural . . . partly restored Edo period (1600–1868) villages . . . dwellings of Samuarai, farmers, craftsmen, and merchants . . . local crafts on display at Dampuen, a nearby village.

Matsue • Old castle town in heart of Izumo province . . . called "City of Water" because it lies where Nakaumi Lagoon joins Lake Shinji . . . also closely allied to ancient myths of Japan's Age of Gods . . . **Matsue Castle** on Kamedayama Hill constructed by one of Hideyoshi's generals in 1611 . . . reconstructed in 1642 and has lovely views from summit of Lake Shinji and Mt. Daisen . . . Englishman Lafcadio Hern lived in Matsue for 7 months in 1890 and wrote of the area in his "Glimpses of an Unfamiliar Japan" . . . Matsue is less than an hour from Izumo Taisha Shrine, said to be Japan's oldest . . . dedicated to Okuninushi-no-mikoto, Shinto deity credited with the introduction of science, medicine, sericulture, and farming . . . main shrine in ancient architectural style dates from 1744 and designated National Treasure . . . long rectangular structures on east and west said to house Shinto gods who meet annually every autumn . . . called **Kamiarizuki** (month with gods) in Izumo province . . . **Kannazuki** (month without gods) in rest of Japan.

Noto Peninsula • projects into Japan Sea. West coast is rugged . . . calm and sheltered eastern coastline . . . inland mountainous . . . major city is **Wajima** . . . noted for Wajimanuri lacquerware . . . can observe process dating back six centuries at Wajima Lacquer Hall as well as small shops within walking distance . . . city also known for lacquered floats (on view at Kirko Kaikan on outskirts) . . . pulled through streets between August 23 and 25 every year. Sosogi coastline has dramatic beauty (45 minutes by bus) and Wakura Spa at tip of Cape Benten is one of most famous in Japan . . . boasts some 50 ryokan.

Tottori • Thriving spa town on western part of Japan Sea . . . lies on lower reaches of Sendai River . . . known for raw silk, pears, and Japanese paper . . . has interesting folk art museum and Oochidani Shrine dedicated to Ieyasu Tokugawa . . . Tottori Sand Dunes are famous for their conical shapes and belong to San-in Coast National Park . . . entrance to Daisen-Oki National Park . . . includes Shimane Peninsula, Oki Islands, Mt. Sambe, and Hiruzen Plateau . . . Mt. Daizen is called "Hoki-Fuji" because resembles Mt. Fuji's cone when viewed from the west . . . Oki Islands are among most beautiful of Japan Sea coast . . . were used for Imperial exiles during Kamakura period.

HOTELS

Hagi

★★★**Hagi Grand Hotel** • *25, Huruhagi-cho, Hagi, Yamaguchi Pref. 758. Tel: (08382) 5–1211* • 150 rooms.
Facilities: Dining room. Bar. Revolving restaurant. Golf. Boating. Tennis. Beach.

Kanazawa

★★★**Kanazawa Holiday Inn** • *1–10 Horikawa-cho, Kanazawa-shi. Tel: (0762) 23–1111. Telex: 5122–288* • 180 rooms.
Facilities: The Raspberry Restaurant. Teppanyaki and Kaga provincial specialty restaurant. Japanese Pub. Coffee Shop and bar. No charge children under 12. Parking. Banquet and convention rooms.
Manager: K. Anasawa. *Reservations.* HOLIDEX.

★★★★**Kanazawa Miyako Hotel** • *6—10 Konohanacho, Kanazawa, Ishikawa Pref. 920 Tel: (0762) 31–2202. Telex: 5122–203 MIYAKO J* • 192 rooms.

★★**Kanazawa New Grand** • *1–50 Takaoka-machi, Kanazawa, Ishikawa Pref. 920. Tel: (0762) 33–1311. Telex: 5122–357 KANGHL J* • 122 rooms.

★★**Kanazawa Sky Hotel** • *15–1 Musashi-machi, Kanazawa, Ishikawa Pref. 920. Tel: (0762) 33–2233. Telex: 5122–716 KSKYHL J* • 137 rooms.

★★★★**Kanazawa Tokyu Hotel** • *2–1 Korinbo, Kanazawa, Ishikawa-den. Tel: (0762) 312–411* • 250 rooms.
Facilities: Bar Marble. Sky Lounge Square. Temari Coffee Shop. Schloss French Restaurant. Pochette Tea Salon. Ooshima Japanese Restaurant. In heart of Kanazawa. Within walking distance of Kenrokuen— one of three most famous gardens in Japan.
General Manager: S. Ishida. *Reservations:* Tokyu Hotels.

Matsue

★★**Hotel Ichibata** • *30, Chidoricho, Matsue, Shimane Pref. 690. Tel: (0852) 22–0188* • 138 rooms. Hot springs.

Tottori

★★★**The New Otani Tottori** ● *2–153, Ima-machi, Tottori City 680. Tel: (0857) 23–1111* ● 143 rooms.

KOBE

KOBE IN A CAPSULE

No. 1 gateway to Japan since the 3rd century . . . originally called **Hyogo,** the port has prospered for centuries with world trade as well as international passengers . . . several luxury liners embark passengers in Kobe today for China cruises . . . city is a favorite with westerners because of its beauty . . . home visits arranged through the tourist section of the Kobe City Government (Tel: 331–8181, ext. 2381) are very popular . . . area dominated by the Rokko mountain chain which provides splendid panoramas of the Inland Sea, the Bay of Osaka, and Awaji Island . . . hydrofoils and ferry boats depart frequently from Kobe for ports situated along the Inland Sea National Park . . . one of Japan's most popular tourist attractions . . . Kobe also famous for its excellent sake and tender beef, from animals that have been hand massaged . . . Kobe was extensively destroyed during the war . . . and reconstructed.

WHAT TO SEE AND DO

Arima Onsen ● Health resort located on north side of Mt. Rokko . . . one of Japan's oldest hot springs . . . said to cure female diseases and heart disorders . . . among other things . . . lovely surroundings and many charming ryokan in the area.

Fukushoji ● Temple founded in 886 by order of Emperor Koko . . . located near Sumadera Station . . . headquarters of Shingon sect . . . noted for its beautiful cherry trees and 11-headed Kannon from the Muromachi Period.

Hakutsuru Art Museum • located at the foot of Mt. Rokko on Sumiyoshi River . . . founded by distiller of Hakutsuru Sake . . . Momoyama style architecture . . . contains Chinese bronzes, ceramics, lacquer, and ancient Japanese art . . . open from early March to late May, late Sept. to late Nov. Visit also Hakutsuru Sake Brewery Museum . . . located near Sumiyoshi Subway station (Tel: 392–0020 for directions).

Hon-Sumiyoshi Shrine • Shinto shrine said to have been founded in A.D. 202 but moved to Osaka . . . annual festival here on May 13.

Ikuta Shrine • Dedicated to mythical deity Wakahirume-no-Mikoto, guardian of Kobe citizenry . . . said to have been founded in 3rd century by Empress Jingu upon her return from Paekche, ancient kingdom of Korea.

Kobe City Hall • Constructed in 1957 . . . totem pole on north side presented by citizenry of Seattle . . . Kobe's sister city.

Kobe City Art Museum • *24 Kiyomachi, Chuo-Ku* • Collection of East West history of the city.

Maiko Park • Located along waterfront at western end of Kobe . . . boasts black pines some 500 years old . . . offers lovely views of Awaji Island across Akashi Straits . . . wood block artist Hiroshige made famous The Beach of Maiko here . . . has Sumaura Park on east and Akashi Park on west.

Meriken Observation Tower • *Meriken Pier* • Named after American sailors who landed here in 19th century. Landmark shaped like Japanese drum . . . has revolving deck . . . boat tours leave from here . . . visit also Kobe Maritime Museum in park at foot of tower.

Minatogawa Shrine • Also known as Nanko Shrine . . . dedicated to Masahige Kusunoki (A.D. 1294–1336) . . . a martyr in the struggle between Emperior Godaigo and Ashikaga . . . founder of the Ashikaga shogunate . . . shrine founded in 1692 by Mitsukuni Tokugawa.

Mt. Maya • No. 2 peak in the Rokko mountain chain . . . site of Toritenjoji . . . Buddhist temple of the **Koyasan-Shingon** sect . . . has 11-headed Kannon and Maya Hall dedicated to **Maya-Bunin,** mother of Lord Buddha . . . summit of mountain has recreation areas and youth hotels . . . nice view of Kobe at night.

Mt. Rokko • No. 1 peak in Rokko mountain chain . . . popular with visitors for views of Bay of Osaka and Inland Sea . . . summit reached by cable car or Rokko Drive . . . recreation areas, hotels, and Japan's oldest golf course (1903) . . . also a number of private summer villas.

Motomachi • Kobe's most popular shopping street . . . Daimaru and Mitsukoshi department stores located here . . . along with small shops and restaurants.

Nagata Shrine • Dedicated to **Kotoshironushi-no-Mikoto,** Shinto deity in charge of personal fortune and prosperity . . . very popular shrine . . . especially crowded at New Year . . . on Setsubun (early Feb.) and on annual festival days (Oct. 18 and 19).

Namban Art Museum • Kumachi-cho, 1–chome . . . Western-style paintings by Japanese artists . . . some depicting early Europeans . . . some registered as Important Art Objects.

Port Island • 642 acres reclaimed from the sea. Reached by computer-driven Portliner monorail . . . innovative architecture houses businesses, shops, hospital, mixed-income apartments, luxury hotel, conference center, and amusement park . . . also port industries . . . impressive area.

Sannomiya • Station where three train lines meet . . . contains Sanchika Town underground shopping arcade . . . and popular shops above ground.

Suma Beach Park • Situated at mouth of Myohoji River . . . contains recreation facilities, yacht harbor, fishing center, and municipal aquarium.

Sumaura Park • Encompasses slope of Mt. Hachibuse, beach, and some 1000 cherry trees . . . said to be site of famous battle fought in 1184 between rival Minamoto and Taira clans . . . ropeway to summit for views of Suma, Maiko, and Akashi beaches plus Awaji Island.

Taisanji • Temple of Tendai sect . . . founded in A.D. 716 by a member of the Fujiwara family . . . the most influential family in Japan during the Heian Period and whose daughters often married future Emperors . . . full of beautiful treasures that are aired annually on June 25 (of the lunar calendar) . . . can be viewed by public then . . . temple setting lovely with trees, stream, and falls . . . popular with hikers.

Takarazuka • Located along Muko River . . . most popular resort in Kobe/Osaka area . . . home of famous all-girl revue and 45-acre recreation area.

Zenshoji • Temple of the Rinzai sect . . . located at foot of Mt. Takatori . . . founded in mid-14th century and famous for 11-headed Kannon and **momiji** . . . small-leafed maple trees . . . also called **Momijidera** (Maple Temple).

HOTELS

★★★★★**Hotel Okura Kobe** • *48 Hatoba-cho, Chuo-ku, Kobe 650. Tel: (078) 333–0111* • 491 rooms (16 western suites, 5 Japanese suites). Luxurious 35-story hotel on seafront of Meriken Park . . . views of harbor, city, mountains, and Inland sea . . . with international conference facilities . . . Merikan Park banquet hall accommodates 2000 persons . . . Okura-style graciousness and atmosphere. Opened June 1989.
Facilities: Top-floor restaurant and bar. Coffee Shop. Terrace restaurant. Chinese, Japanese, and Teppanyaki restaurants. Health club with gymnasium, indoor/outdoor pools, tennis courts. Business center. Tea ceremony room. Shopping arcade.
Reservations: LHW

★★★★**Kobe Portopia Hotel** • *10–1, 6–chome, Nakamachi Minatojima. Tel: (078) 302–1111. Cable: PORTOPIA KOBE. Telex: KOPTEL J 5622112* • 533 rooms.
Facilities: Located on Port Island offshore from Kobe, across from International Conference Center. French, Chinese, Teppanyaki, and Japanese restaurants. Coffee shop. Sky lounge restaurant. 2 bars. Swimming pool, tennis, health club.
Manager: T. Nakauchi. *Reservations:* JAL.

★★**New Port Hotel** • *6–3–13 Hamabe-dori, Chuo-ku. Tel: (078) 231–4171. Cable: NEPOTEL KOBE. Telex: 5623–058 NEPTEL J* • 208 rooms.
Facilities: Dining room. Revolving restaurant. Chinese restaurant. Snack bar. 3 bars. Nightclub.
Manager: M. Iwase. *Reservations:* Direct.

★★★**Oriental Hotel** • *Kyomachi 25. Tel: (078) 331–8111. Cable: ORIENT KOB. Telex: 5622–327 J* • 190 rooms. Built in 1882 in colonial style and famous throughout Japan. Featured in Tanizaki's great novel *The Makioka Sisters,* who visited on special occasions to view the lush flora of Mt. Rokko in spring and fall.

Facilities: Sky Restaurant. 2 bars.

Manager: R. Kohno. *Reservations:* UTELL.

RESTAURANTS

Alan Chapel Restaurant • *Portopia Hotel, Port Island. Tel: 302–1111* • French nouvelle cuisine overseen by the French chef himself on bi-annual visits . . . lovely views . . . expensive.

Iroriya • *3–33 Kitano-cho, Chuo-ku. Tel: 231–6777* • Traditional Japanese serving Kobe beef (priced currently about $75 a pound) in shabu-shabu and sukiyaki dishes.

Misono • *1–7–6 Kitanagasa Dori, Chuo-ku. Tel: 331–2890* • Well-known chain throughout Japan. Kobe beef. Expensive!

Sky Restaurant • *Oriental Hotel. Tel: 331–8111* • Japanese/French and a favorite with locals who can afford it. Overlooks city, port, and Inland Sea . . . expensive.

Yamada-no-kakasi • *3–9–6 Sannomiya-cho Tel: 391–0363* • Popular for kushikatsu . . . skewered bits of this and that grilled . . . some 25 different combinations . . . very tasty and served with special sake from nearby Nada.

KYOTO

There is no place on earth that rivals Kyoto as a living cultural center, which it became in the 8th century and has continued unabated through the 20th—despite pestilence, civil, religious, and world wars that all threatened its existence but not its soul. Kyoto must be toured in the most calm manner possible so that "spirit of place" (a phrase borrowed from Lawrence Durrell) can be absorbed in the most gentle way and assimilated permanently. If you are short of time, bypass To-

---

KYOTO IN A CAPSULE

Classical capital of Japan and center of the country's civilization
for more than 10 centuries . . . founded in 794 by Emperor
Kammu, Japan's 50th emperor . . . laid out in checkerboard fashion
following Chinese custom . . . originally named **Heian-kyo** or
peaceful, tranquil capital . . . later named **Miyako** (imperial capital) . . . then **Kyoto** (capital city) . . . boasts more than 200
Shinto shrines, 1500 Buddhist temples and some 60 of Japan's
finest gardens . . . was saved from destruction during World War
II by American scholar Langdon Warner who argued that no industry of significance was centered here . . . although many
Buddhist temples founded early in Kyoto's history . . . most have
been rebuilt through the centuries because of natural disasters as
well as warring factions among the sects . . . a city of elegance
and tradition where the arts still flourish . . . **nishijin** silk weaving dates from 8th century . . . **yuzen-zome** process of dyeing
fabric created in 17th century . . . local embroidery work introduced from China and Korea . . . Kyoto lacquerware dates from
Momoyama Period A.D. (1558–1637) . . . other crafts include
Japanese dolls, **shippo** (cloissone), and **sensu** (folding fans) . . .
today a modern industrial city also known for machinery and metals, chemicals, sake, beer, and pastries . . . Kyoto is just under
3 hours from Tokyo by super-express Shinkansen.

---

kyo (that hurly-burly of wealth and power) and spend your days in Kyoto,
where the quality of life is tenfold more appealing and its atmosphere
encourages visitors to walk and browse, to enjoy an "o bento" (lunch
box) at riverside, and to understand a bit how Zen Buddhism has been
the underlying influence on Japanese culture for centuries.

Unlike Tokyo, Kyoto is a wonderful place to walk, and the local
Tourist Information Center has excellent maps and suggested routes.
One course is along my favorite route—from Ginkakuji Temple to Nanzenji Temple beside an old canal whose path is called Philosopher's
Walk and lined with charming shops selling papier-mache products. Another suggested course is between the Heian Shrine and Kiyomizu Temple. Also recommended is between Kinkakuji (gold pavilion) and Ninnaji,
with a stop at Ryoanji (noted for its "karesansui-style" rock and sand
garden). All take about an hour—more if you choose to meander. In
the outskirts of Kyoto is a former excursion area for Heian period (794–
1192) emperors and still popular with locals. This is Arashiyama, and
it is an hour bus ride from Kyoto station. Still the 90-minute-or-so walk

between Tenryuji Temple and Kameyama Park is a good hike, spectacular for spring and fall foliage.

Avoid tour groups in Kyoto because they spoil the ambience. Ask for all the literature the tourist information office can supply and buy a copy of *Kyoto, A Contemplative Guide* by Gouverneur Mosher (Tuttle paperback)—essential for understanding the city and touring on your own. Note: arrive at the places you most want to visit *early* to avoid the crowds. And enjoy this very special place on earth.

WHAT TO SEE AND DO

Choin-In ● Headquarters of **Jodo** sect and one of largest and most renowned temples in all Japan . . . founded in A.D. 1234 . . . followers of Jodo recite **Namu Amida Butsu** many times daily . . . to ensure a future life in the western paradise of **Amitabha** . . . 2-story **Sanmon** is one of most impressive temples gates in Japan . . . Assembly Hall known as Hall of 1000 mats (there are actually only 360) . . . *fusuma* (sliding screens) in Superior's quarters from the Kano school . . . many treasures in the temple complex . . . including a 48-volume biography of **Ho-nen** (A.D. 1133–1212), the founder of the sect.

Choboji ● Buddhist temple founded in A.D. 587 by Prince Shotoku . . . noted because **Ikebono** flower arrangement style created here . . . by priest of the same name in the 15th century . . . also known as **Rokkakudo** (hexagonal hall).

Daitokuji ● **Rinzai Zen** monastery . . . founded in A.D. 1324 and known for magnificent buildings . . . present ones date from 15th century . . . more than 20 subtemples on grounds, including **Daisen-in** (great hermit temple) and **Koto-in** (high paulownia temple) . . . also noted for 16th century **San-mon** (triple gate) and 17th-century **Butsuden** (Buddha hall) . . . complex contains many National treasures and traditional Zen landscaping.

Ginkakuji ● Silver pavilion temple . . . built by Yoshimasa Ashikaga in 1482 as retirement villa . . . reverted to Zen temple after his death in 1790 . . . noted for beautiful gardens . . . especially **Ginshadan** (silver sand beach) and simple 2-story **Ginkaku** (silver pavilion) with **Kannon** image by Unkei, famous Kamakura-period sculptor . . . Ginkakuji is a very pleasant 45-minute walk along the canal from the Miyako Hotel . . . **Jodo-in** or Pure Land Temple stands to left of Ginkakuji entrance . . . has image of **Kobo Daishi,** founder of rival **Shingon** sect.

Gion-Machi ● Traditional geisha quarter of Kyoto . . . situated on east bank of Kamo River . . . near **Shijobashi** (bridge) . . . geisha houses, bars, restaurants, cabarets, and theaters located in the area . . . also Gion Corner where visitors can enjoy a taste of the traditional arts in a few hours—tea ceremony, flower arrangement, bunraku puppetry, *kyomai* (Kyoto-style dances), koto music, *gagaku* (court music), and *kyogen* (classic farce) . . . all this for about ¥2000 . . . **Yasaka Shrine** or Gion Shrine is located at eastern end of Gion-machi . . . known mainly for **Gion Matsuri** . . . one of Japan's three great festivals and dates from 9th century . . . lasts from July 16 to 17 and full of colorful floats and parades . . . difficult to find accommodations in city at this time.

Heian Shrine ● Famous Shinto shrine located in **Okazaki Park** . . . new by Kyoto standards . . . built in 1895 to commemorate 1100th anniversary of founding of the city . . . dedicated to **Kammu** and **Komei** . . . first and last emperors of the imperial capital . . . noted for crimson-colored structures and flowering trees . . . also site of Jidai Matsuri (Festival of the Ages) each year on October 22 . . . more than 2000 townfolk parade from Imperial Palace to Heian Shrine dressed in ancient costumes . . . in Okazaki Park are also Kyoto Prefectural Central Library, Public Hall, Modern Art Gallery, and Zoological Gardens.

Higashi-Honganji ● Located near Kyoto Station . . . good views of grounds from New Miyako Hotel . . . is Otani school headquarters of Jodo-Shinshu sect . . . only Main Hall and Founder's Hall open to public . . . admission to other buildings by application a day in advance . . . temple buildings founded in 1602 but present structures from 1895 . . . among treasures is an image of **Amitabha** said to have been carved by Prince Shotoku. Shoseien Garden, or **Kikokutei,** is a villa of abbot of **Higashi-Hoganji.** Located east of the temple . . . once surrounded by a hedge of *kikoku* (orange bush) . . . some of Hideyoshi's Fushimi Castle brought here . . . landscape gardens by well-known 17th-century designers.

Hokoji ● Once called **Daibutsuden** (Great Buddha Hall) . . . image ordered by Hideyoshi in 1586 but nothing remains . . . repeated fires and an earthquake . . . just south of temple is Hokoku or Toyokuni Shrine . . . dedicated to Hideyoshi in 1599 . . . tomb on the precincts with 5-story pagoda restored in 1897, the 300th year of his death.

Honen-In ● Temple founded by Abbot Honen in 13th century . . . structures from Hideyoshi's former **Fushimi Castle** brought here . . . Fushimi apartments famous for Kano school paintings and beautiful garden.

Katsura Rikyu • Katsura Imperial Villa . . . located on Katsura River a short train ride from Kyoto . . . built in 1602 for Prince To-shihito, brother of Emperor Goyozei with beautiful gardens and pavil-ions . . . a perfect spot for photographs, especially in spring and fall . . . visitors must apply in advance to Imperial Household Agency (in Kyoto Imperial Palace) for written permission to tour the grounds . . . a pain but worth it . . . open weekdays and Sat. morning.

Kawai Kanjiro's House • Gojazaka, Kyoto (Tel: 561–3585) . . . beautiful memorial to Japan's most famous modern potter (d. 1966) . . . a real poet and endless searcher for perfection. Call for directions.

Kinkakuji • Temple of the Golden Pavilion . . . located at foot of Kinugasa Hill . . . originally built in 1392 as villa for a court noble but greatly improved by Shogun Ashikaga who retired here . . . built golden pavilion and laid out garden . . . became Buddhist temple named **Rokuonji** upon his death . . . arson destroyed pavilion in 1950 but reconstructed in 1955 . . . one of Japan's most photographed monu-ments, especially after a rare snowfall . . . Mishima's novel, *Temple of the Golden Pavilion,* describes how the arson could have occurred.

Kitano Shrine • Located near Nishijin silk weaving district . . . known as **Kitano Tenjin** . . . dedicated to Michizane Sugawara, court scholar who was exiled to Kyushu in A.D. 901 when he fell out of favor with the Emperor . . . upon his death in 903, Kyoto suffered such natural disasters . . . that subsequent Emperor commissioned shrine to appease the gods . . . Michizane later deified as Tenjin . . . present structures date from Hideyoshi's orders in 1607 . . . grounds contain Michizane's favorite plum *(ume)* trees which are lovely in spring . . . several festivals held here . . . nearby is 17th century Hirano Shrine . . . famous for cherry trees and architecture.

Kiyomizu-Dera • Clear water temple . . . Buddhist temple of the **Hosso** sect . . . brought from China in A.D. 655 . . . predates found-ing of Kyoto although the temple is said to have been established in 798 . . . officially recognized in 805 and called **Seisui-ji** . . . most buildings date from 17th century because site of fires caused by many warring factions among Buddhist sects . . . one of Kyoto's most im-portant shrines and number 16 on the 33-temple pilgrim route . . . elegant tea ceremony porcelains sold in shops that line the route up to the temple complex.

Kodaiji • Buddhist temple located just north of 5-story **Yasaka Pagoda,** built in 1440 by Shogun Ashikaga . . . Kodaiji built in 1606 by Hideyoshi's widow . . . dedicated to the shogun . . . noted for lacquer work and landscape garden . . . Place of Historical Importance and Outstanding Scenery.

Koryuji • Shingon sect temple founded in A.D. 622 for the repose of Prince Shotoku's soul . . . lecture hall built in 1165 and 2nd-oldest surviving structure in Kyoto . . . wooden statue of the prince at age 33 (self-portrait) in **Taishido Hall** . . . another self-portrait at age 16 in **Hakkakudo . . . Miroku-Bosatsu** considered to be oldest piece of sculpture in Kyoto . . . may also have been carved by Prince Shotoku.

Kyo-O-Gokokuji • Toji or East Temple . . . founded in A.D. 796 by Emperor Kammu and presented to **Kobo Daishi,** founder of **Shingon** sect of Buddhism, in 823 . . . main hall rebuilt in 1603 by Hideyoshi's son, Hideyori, and considered largest Momoyama structure extant . . . Shogun Iemitsu built 5-story pagoda in 1644 . . . highest in the country . . . temple is full of structures and objects designated as National Treasures.

Kyoto Gosho • Imperial Palace . . . located on over 30 acres in center of city . . . original palace built by Emperor Kammu was near Nijo Castle . . . **Shinsen-en Garden** is all that remains of the grounds . . . only a few swans on the pond . . . present palace dates from 1855 . . . consists of several pavilions . . . **Shishinden** (Ceremonial Hall) . . . **Seiryoden** (Serene and Cool Chamber) . . . **Kogosho** (Minor Palace) . . . plus lovely gardens and a stream with water drawn from Lake Biwa . . . visitors welcome weekdays and Sat. morning by applying directly to Imperial Household Agency located on the grounds . . . a palace guard escorts small groups and lectures.

Kyoto National Museum • Located southeast of **Hokoji,** across from Kyoto Park Hotel . . . contains over 2000 rare works of historic, religious, and traditional art . . . many taken for safekeeping from local Buddhist temples and Shinto shrines.

Kyoto Tower • Located in front of Kyoto Station . . . has two observation platforms plus Tourist Information Center . . . home visits can be arranged here (Tel: 371–5649).

Kyoto University • Second oldest and one of largest universities in Japan . . . located just west of **Ginkakuji** . . . Faculty of Literature museum has interesting historical and archaeological documents . . . just north of the university is **Chionji,** also called **Hyakumamben** (1 million times) a temple where in 1331 the abbot recited 1 million **Namu Amida Butsu** in succession . . . to appease the gods during an epidemic . . . 2 Chinese scrolls by famous artist of Yuan dynasty here.

Maruyama Park • Kyoto's most beautiful park . . . located at foot of **Higashiyama** (East Hill) . . . several temples once here but all destroyed by fires . . . cherry trees famous here . . . especially for **Gion-no-Yozakura** . . . night-viewing of Cherry blossoms in the spring . . . very festive when illuminated.

Momoyama • Peach Hill . . . site of tombs of Emperor Meiji and consort Empress Shoken . . . Hideyoshi once built a famous castle here . . . noted for abundant peach trees . . . name given to rise to Azuchi-Momoyama Period (A.D. 1573–1598) because of 2 castles owned by generals Nobunaga and Hideyoshi . . . *chanoyu* or tea ceremony and flowery style in painting (Kano school) were popular during this period.

Myoho-in • Tendai sect temple located across from the museum . . . known for **Ume-no-ma** or Plum Chamber . . . decorated with paintings from Kano school and treasures connected with Hideyoshi . . . temple originally built in 9th century and said to have been transferred here from Mt. Hiei.

Myoshinji • Headquarters of **Myoshinji School of Rinzai** sect . . . built in A.D. 1342 but rebuilt during Momoyama Period . . . **Butsuden** (Hall of Buddha) contains Japan's oldest bell, cast in 698 . . . has many subordinate temples with **Taizo-in** and **Keishu-in** noted for fine gardens and paintings . . . Motonobu Temple famous for paintings by Motonobu Kano.

Nanzenji • Headquarters of **Nanzenji School of Rinzai** sect of Buddhism . . . temple founded in 1293 but most structures from 17th century . . . paintings in superior's quarters from Kano school . . . 17th-century garden called **Karesansui** is one of most celebrated in Kyoto . . . several subordinate temples in the complex . . . **Nanzen-in** has 14th-century garden . . . landscape garden attached to **Konchi-in** also famous.

Nijo-Jo • Famous castle built in 1603 by Tokugawa Shogun Ieyasu . . . grounds cover some 70 acres surrounded by an outer moat . . . noted for many fine pine, hawk, and cloud paintings from the Kano school . . . also for **Uguisubari** (bush warbler floor) . . . squeaks when walked upon . . . so palace guards could hear intruders . . . visitors can tour **Ni-No-Maru,** 5 pavilions connected by covered corridors . . . including **Ohiro-ma** or Grand Audience Chamber where Emperor Meiji abolished the shogunate regime in 1868 . . . last Tokugawa shogun, Keiki, resigned in the **Kuro-sho-in** or Black Parlor in 1867 . . . **Ni-No-Maru gardens** originally designed without trees . . . because sho-gun did not want to be reminded of the transitory life from falling leaves

. . . inner moat surrounded the **Hon-maru** or central building . . . originally moved from Fushimi Castle but burned in 18th century . . . present Hon-maru is former 19th-century town mansion of Prince Katsura . . . moved here in 1870s.

Nijo Jinya • Encampment House for Nijo Castle . . . privately owned building by appointment only (tel: 84–0972) . . . fine example of ingenuity in design . . . concealed fortifications . . . fireproofing devices . . . owned by Ogawa family . . . whose ancestor was private retainer to Shoguns Nobunaga and Hideyoshi . . . very interesting to tour . . . usually with student guides . . . perfect for a rainy day.

Ninnaji • Headquarters of **Omuro School of Shingon** sect of Buddhism . . . formerly known as Omuro Palace . . . founded in A.D. 886 by Emperor Koko and completed by Emperor Uda who succeeded him . . . until Meiji Restoration, temple always had an "imperial prince" as superior . . . noted for **Kondo Hall** and **Nio-mon** (gate), and for cherry blossoms in spring.

Nishi-Honganji • Headquarters of **Honganji School of Jodo-Shinshu** sect . . . located about a 10-minute walk from back of Kyoto Station . . . sect originated here and temple considered finest existing example of Buddhist architecture . . . visits permitted 4 times daily by applying at temple office . . . **Hondo** (main hall) is Important Cultural Property . . . interior painted by Kano school master . . . **Daishido** (Founder's Hall) is also important Cultural Property . . . gate in front one of finest in Kyoto . . . **Daishoin Hall** brought from **Fushimi Castle** in 1632 and **Kara-mon** (gate) both National Treasures . . . inner chambers have many paintings by Kano school . . . 2 *Noh* stages . . . one transferred from Fushimi Castle and considered oldest in Japan . . . **Hiunkaku Pavilion** is a National Treasure . . . apparently even bathroom full of exquisite Kano paintings . . . **Honkokuji,** one of 4 head temples of Nichiren sect, close to **Nishi-Honganji** . . . shrine to General Kiyomasa Kato on grounds . . . he was a devotee of Nichiren and always carried his banner into battle for safety.

Ryoanji • Dragon Peace Temple . . . formerly an estate of a branch of powerful Fujiwara family . . . became Zen temple in 1473 and member of Rinzai sect around 1500 . . . main attraction is rock garden attributed to landscape architect So-ami (1472–1523) . . . 15 stones placed inside a fence of oil and mud . . . many meanings offered to their placement . . . some say meant to outline a dragon, whose head is at the east and tail at southwest . . . try to visit temple early to enjoy garden in solitude.

Saihoji • Also called **Koke-dera** or Moss Temple . . . founded in A.D. 731 by priest Gyoki . . . reconstructed in 1339 by priest **Muso-Kokushi,** who used 40 different types of green and yellow moss for a "stroll garden" . . . belongs to Rinzai sect.

Sambo-In • Belongs to **Daigoji,** headquarters of **Daigo School of Shingon** sect . . . established by Shokaku, Daigoji abbot in 1115 and present structures built by Hideyoshi . . . many beautiful paintings from Kano school . . . landscape garden considered one of finest in Japan.

Sanjusangendo • Also known as **Rengeo-in,** temple belonging to **Myohoi-in** . . . name comes from 33 spaces between pillars of elongated structure . . . Thousand-handed **Kannon** is a National Treasure . . . carved in 1254 by noted sculptor Tankei . . . 82 years old at the time . . . annual archery contest here in Japan.

Sanzen-in • Located in village of Ohara, about 40 minutes by bus from Kyoto . . . branch temple of one founded on Mt. Hiei in A.D. 788 . . . became temple residence of the abbot around 1698 . . . only named **Sanzen-in** in late 19th century . . . known for finely preserved image of **Amida** carved by priest Eshin in 985 . . . **Kyuku-den** (Guest Palace) built in 1587 . . . faces lovely small pond and garden in Heian court style . . . temple very popular with Buddhist pilgrims.

Shimokamo and Kamikamo Shrines • Located not far from each other and both predate founding of Kyoto in A.D. 794 . . . both are noted for **Aoi Matsuri** (Hollyhock Festival) on May 15 each year . . . festival reenacts Imperial processions made as hommage in feudal times.

Shoren-In • Also known as **Awata Palace** . . . was residence of head abbot of **Tendai** sect . . . in pre-Restoration days he held rank of "imperial prince" . . . present structures date from 1895 but *fusuma* (sliding screens) of Kano school . . . garden jointly designed by well-known landscape architects Soami and Enshu . . . one of best in Kyoto.

Shugakuin Rikyu • Shugakuin Imperial Villa . . . a detached palace built in 1654 as retreat for former Emperor Gomizumo-o . . . over 70 acres of beautiful gardens and three large villas . . . known as Lower, Middle, and Upper . . . Middle Villa adjoins **Rinkyuji,** a temple with fine landscaped garden . . . large lake with several small summer pavilions . . . one, called **Rin-untei,** has excellent view of Kyoto . . . visitors must obtain permission in writing in advance from Imperial Household Agency (located on grounds of Kyoto Imperial Palace) . . . Shugakuin Rikyu open weekdays and Sat. morning.

Tofukiji • Headquarters of **Tofukiji School of Rinzai** sect . . . founded in A.D. 1236 . . . known for rare paintings . . . and long *kakemono* (scroll) called **Sakyamuni's Entry into Nirvana** . . . exhibited to the public on March 15, when memorial service for Sakyamuni occurs.

HOTELS

Kyoto has many fine hotels and *ryokan*. The most famous ryokan are Tawaraya (located on Fuya-machi in Nakagyo-ku) where royalty has slept, the traditional Hiragiya with two buildings, and Yoshikawa Inn (located at Tominokoji, Oike-sagaru in Nakagyo-ku section) which invites nonguests to dine on traditional meals. The adventurous can also be accommodated in *shukubo*, or temples that take overnight guests. One such is **Myokenji** (located at Shinmachi Nishi-hairu, Teranouchi-dori in Kamigyo-ku section). Guests have private *tatami* rooms with futon (mattress) and are served breakfast only. There is generally one Western-style toilet, a communal tub and it may or may not be suggested that 6 a.m. prayers are in order—with the novitiates, of course.

Listed below are the top-rated hotels in Kyoto.

★★★**International Hotel Kyoto** • *284 Nijo Aburanokoji, Nakagyo-ku. Tel: (075) 222–1111. Cable: INTERHO KYOTO. Telex: 5422–158 INTCHO* • 332 rooms.
Facilities: Across from Nijo Castle. Starlight Bar. Japanese garden bar. Horikawa Japanese restaurant. Azalea Western restaurant. Swimming pool.
Manager: J. Mikoshiba. *Reservations:* FUJITA.

★★★★**Hotel Fujita Kyoto** • *Kamo Riverside, Nishizume, Nijohashi, Nakagyo-ku. Tel: (075) 222–1511. Cable: HOTELFUJITA KYOTO* • 195 rooms.
Facilities: Best lobby bar in town. Kamogawa Japanese restaurant. Sekisui grillroom. Chidori restaurant. Sekisui bar. Same management as International Hotel.
Manager: J. Mikoshiba. Reservations: FUJITA.

★★**Kyoto Hotel** • *Oike, Kawara-machi, Nakagyo-ku. Tel: (075) 211–5111. Cable: KYOHO KYOTO. Telex: 5422–126* • 507 rooms.
Facilities: Dining room. Steak house. Grillroom. Bianca ristorante. Japanese and Chinese restaurants. Seafood restaurant. Coffee shop. 2 bars.
Manager: K. Kanda. *Reservations:* JAL.

★★★★★**Kyoto Grand Hotel** • *Horikawa Shiokoji, Shimogyo-ku.*
Tel: (075) 341–2311. Cable: KYOTOGRAND KYOTO. Telex: 5422–
551 KYOGRA • 577 rooms.
Facilities: Top of Kyoto revolving restaurant. Katsura French res-
taurant. Tachibana teppanyaki grill. Tachibana French gourmet restau-
rant. Mimosa coffee shop. Kitcho and Tsuruya Japanese restaurants.
Tankuma Kyoto cuisine and Hakuho Chinese. Starlet and Granada bars.
Maiko lounge. Indoor swimming pool. Lovely hotel. New favorite! Shuttle
service to Kyoto Station.
Manager: T. Imai. *Reservations:* Royal Hotels.

★★★**Kyoto Royal Hotel** • *Kawaramachi Sanjo. Tel: (075) 223–*
1234. Cable: KYOTOROYAL, KYOTO. Telex: 5422–888 ROYALH •
395 rooms.
Facilities: 7 restaurants. Coffee shop. 4 cocktail lounges. Laundry.
Manager: S. Hosoya. *Reservations:* KLM.

★★★★**Kyoto Park Hotel** • *644–2 Sanjusangendo, Mawari-ma-*
chi, Higashiyama-ku. Tel: (075) 525–3111. Cable: KYOTO PARK. Telex:
5422–777J PARKHTL • 307 rooms.
Facilities: Built on site of 12th-century Go-Shirakawa Park. Lovely
gardens and across the street from National Museum. Versailles dining
room. Champs Elysees coffeehouse. Ohno-ya Japanese restaurant. Ten-
shin Fandian Chinese cuisine. Rogen Bar. Concorde lobby lounge.

★★★★**Kyoto Tokyu Hotel** • *Horikawa, 5 Jyo-Ave; Shimogyo-ku.*
Tel: (075) 341–2411. Telex: 5422459 THCKYO • 433 rooms.
Facilities: Lobby with waterfall. Tea Lounge. La Riviere French
Restaurant. Cascade Main Bar. Mitsuwa Kobe Steak Restaurant. Tank-
uma Kyoto specialty restaurant. Mishima-Tei sukiyaki restaurant. Chung
Kuo Soochow/Shanghai restaurant. Swimming pool. Banquet facilities.
Underground parking.
Manager: K. Murayama. *Reservations:* Tokyu Hotels.

★★★★★**Miyako Hotel** • *Sanjo-Keage, Higashiyama-ku, Kyoto*
605. Tel: (075) 771–7111. Cable: MIYAKO KYOTO. Telex: 5422–132
MIYAKO J • 480 rooms.
Facilities: Most famous hotel in town. 8 restaurants. Bar. Coffee
shop. Lounges with entertainment. *Noh* play and tea ceremony. 4 swimming pools. Health club. Book old wing for Japanese-style rooms.
Manager: R. Harada. *Reservations:* Distinguished Hotels.

★★★**New Miyako Hotel** • *Across from Kyoto Station: Tel: (075)*
661–7111. Telex: 5423–211 NEWMYK • 715 rooms. Hotel designed by
Togo Murano.

Facilities: Pompadour Grill. Kurumi restaurant. Ronde coffee shop. Hachijo Japanese restaurant. Shisen Chinese restaurant. Lagoon Bar. *Manager:* O. Yoshimura. *Reservations:* Distinguished Hotels.

★★★★★ + **Takara-ga-ike Prince Hotel** ● *Takargaike, Sakyo-ku, Kyoto-Shi, Kyoto 606. Tel: (81–75) 712–1111. Telex: 542–3261– KYTPRHJ* ● 322 rooms. Situated in lush grounds on northern edge of city . . . one block from Kyoto International Conference Hall . . . complimentary shuttle from hotel to railroad station 30 minutes away . . . beautiful building . . . spacious rooms with lovely views and all amenities. A Westin-operated hotel.
Facilities: Beaux Sejours French restaurant. Tohen Chinese restaurant. Sushi Bar. Charyo Japanese teahouse. Bar and lobby lounge. Jogging trail. Business Service Center. Meeting rooms.
Manager: K. Awazu. *Reservations:* WESTIN.

RESTAURANTS

Ashiya Steak House Restaurant/Gallery ● *3–172–13 Kiyomizu Matsubara, Higashiyama-ku. Tel: 541–7961* ● Japanese atmosphere . . . and garden . . . a wonderful experience . . . worth *every* penny.

Hiun (Cantonese) ● *Kiya-machi Sanjo Agar. Tel: 231–0253* ● Claims to be the best . . . only accepts group orders of 4 or 5 . . . closed Sun.

Hamasaku ● *Tominaga-cho, Yamato-oji Higashi. Tel: 561–693* ● *Also 3rd floor, Miyako Hotel. Tel: 771–7111* Kansai cuisine . . . high quality.

Hyotei ● *Nanzenji, Kusakawa-cho, Sakyo-ku. Tel: 771–4116* ● Old inn serving *kaiseki ryoir* (tea ceremony food) . . . vegetarian . . . 14th generation.

Jubei ● *Shimbashi-agaru, Nawate-dori, Higashiyama-ku. Tel: 561– 2698* ● Top-class sushi . . . Clif Kahru brings friends here to dine.

Juidanya Honten ● *Gion Hanami-koji, Higashiyama-ku. Tel: 561– 0213* ● Munkata prints on the walls . . . mizutaki on the table (or shabu-shabu).

Kitcho ● *Susukinobaba-cho, Saga Tenryuji, Ukyo-ku. Tel: 871– 5701.* ● Famous! Also at Kyoto Grand Hotel.

Manyoken • *Higashi-iru, Fuyacho, Shijo-dori, Shimogyo-ku. Tel: 221–1022* • Kyoto's oldest and most respected French restaurant . . . presidents and royalty have eaten here.

Matsuno • *Nishi-iru, Yamato-oji, Shijo-dori, Higashiyama-ku.* • *Tel: 561–2786* • Famous for kaba-yaki . . . broiled eel . . . good for the health.

Minokichi • *Torii-machi, Awataguchi, Sakyo-ku. Tel: 771–4185* • Kyoto-style cuisine in country atmosphere . . . claims 250 years of existence.

Mishimatei • *Sanjo Tera-machi, Nakagyo-ku. Tel: 221–0003* • Sukiyaki served in old butcher shop surroundings.

Nanzenji Junsei • *60 Kusakawa-cho, Nanzenji. Tel: 761–2311* • 2-minute walk from Nanzenji . . . Kyoto-style cuisine . . . refined Zen dishes.

Nakamuraro • *Yasaka Jinja, Gion, Higashiyama-ku. Tel: 561–0016* • Nice setting near Yasaka Shrine . . . traditional food.

Okazaki Tsuruya • *Higashi-Tennocho, Okazaki, Sakyo-ku. Tel: 761–0171* • Traditional Japanese haute cuisine . . . serves presidents and royalty.

Shim-Hammamura Bekkan • *Oike-agaru, Kiyamachi, Nakagyo-ku. Tel: 541–5111* • Cantonese cuisine . . . try also Honten branch in Higashiyama-ku.

Shin-Miura • *Minamigawa, Giommachi, Higashiyama-ku. Tel: 561–3175* • Old Japan atmosphere . . . mizutaki the specialty here.

Suehiro Kyoto • *Shijo-agaru, Kawaramachi-dori, Nakagyo-ku. Tel: 221–7188* • A branch of the famous Suerhiro chain . . . noted for Kobe beef steaks.

Yoshikawa • *Tominokoji, Oike Sagaru. Tel: 221–5544* • Japanese Inn welcomes nonguests to lunch and dinner . . . good tempura.

Yotaro • *Sanjo-agaru, Nawate-dori, Higashiyama-ku. Tel: 561–9358* • Tempura is what they serve here.

Environs

Arashiyama • Also known as **Ranzan** . . . beautiful hillside facing Oi River . . . noted for **Daihikaku,** a temple located on the hill . . . contains image of thousand-handed **Kannon** (Goddess of Mercy) . . . Arashiyama Park associated with Emperor Kameyama . . . many ryokan and restaurants along banks of the river . . . excursion boats available, too.

Hozu Rapids • Famous for "shooting" from Kameoka to Arashiyama . . . trip in flat-bottomed boats takes about 2 hours . . . fun for the adventurous.

Lake Biwa Quasi-National Park • Includes Mts. Hiei, Hira, Ryozen, Ibuki, and places along Uji River . . . Lake Biwa is Japan's largest lake and looks like the traditional musical instrument called **biwa** . . . tradition says it was formed in 286 B.C. by same earthquake that formed Mt. Fuji . . . was important to history of the area and full of beautiful temples and gardens . . . many founded during Nara period . . . *ukiyo-e* artist Hiroshige visited here and painted the largest pine tree (now dead) in the country . . . many sightseeing tours of Lake Biwa available from Otsu, largest city . . . located on southwest shore and only about 10 minutes from Kyoto Station by train. Three very fine Prince hotels in Lake Biwa/Otsu area.

Mt. Hiei • Kyoto's most important peak and site of *Enryakuji,* one of most important temples in Japan . . . founded in A.D. 788 by Priest Saicho, who established Tendai sect . . . was founded by order of Emperor Kammu to protect Kyoto from evil spirits in the northeast . . . unfortunately monks from this temple considered themselves all-powerful and frequently made raids on other temples in the city (like Kiyomizu-dera) . . . temple destroyed by General Nobunaga but monastery restored by Hideyoshi and enlarged by 3rd shogun Iemitsu . . . easily accessible from Kyoto and lovely for walking tours . . . especially in autumn . . . watch the monkeys! The Mt. Hiei Hotel is very pleasant for a meal or an overnight . . . shuttle bus service from downtown Kyoto.

Uji • Located on Nara Line about 40 minutes by train from Kyoto . . . beautiful town on the banks of the Uji River . . . Uji Bridge is a favorite of painters . . . noted for **Byodo-in,** former Fujiwara villa converted to a temple in 1052 . . . **Ho-odo** (Phoenix Hall) built in 1053 and considered one of finest religious structures in Japan . . . temple belongs to **Tendai** and **Jodo** sects of Buddhism . . . image of **Amitabha** in Ho-odo attributed to 11th-century sculptor Jocho and designated National Treasure . . . bronze bell south of hall is 1 of 3 most famous bells in Japan . . . Kannondo (Hall for eleven-headed Kannon) is where Yorimasa Minamoto said to have taken own life in 1180 when defeated by Taira clan . . . beautiful grounds and pond in which Ho-odo reflected . . . lovely to see in autumn . . . Agata Shrine near Byodo-in is dedicated to same Shinto goddess enshrined at Mt. Fuji . . . near Uji Bridge is stone monument dating from 646 when first bridge constructed . . . **Uji Shrine** allegedly dates from 313 but upper part of shrine dates from 10th century . . . beyond is **Koshoji,** first Buddhist temple of Soto sect in Japan . . . dates from 1233 . . . Uji is a charming town and perfect for a half-day tour . . . or a long stop en route to Nara.

NAGOYA

NAGOYA IN A CAPSULE

Japan's 4th largest city . . . called **Chugoku** or Middle Capital . . . was typical castle town of feudal Japan . . . located midway between Tokyo and Kyoto . . . city completely redesigned after war with wide streets intersected at right angles . . . just 2 hours from Tokyo by super-express **Hikari** train . . . industrial area and a pottery center since 13th century . . . also first in production of cloisonne in Japan . . . active harbor and port through which 90% of Japan's export china and 85% of its export woolen goods pass . . . an important rail and domestic air center.

WHAT TO SEE AND DO

Atsuta Shrine ● Most important Shinto shrine in Japan after Ise Jingu . . . name means "hot field" . . . derived from legend involving **Kusanagi-no-Tsurugi** (grass-moving sword) in shrine . . . along with the sacred mirror at **Ise Jingu** and crown jewels, the sword completed The Three Regalia of the Emperor . . . shrine founded in 3rd century and rebuilt in 1955.

Higashiyama Park • East Hill Park . . . contains botanical and zoological gardens, a zoo, science museum, insect hall, astronomical observatory, and cultural center . . . also **Kannon** (Goddess of Mercy) image.

Nagoya Castle • Originally built in 1612 by Ieyasu Tokugawa as a residence for his son . . . reconstructed in 1959 . . . has fine exhibition of *fusuma-e* (paintings on sliding doors) and observatory . . . good view of Pacific Ocean and Nobi Plain . . . 3-corner turrets undamaged by the war and designated Important Cultural Properties . . . castle great source of pride for Nagoyans . . . descendants of Tokugawa lived here until Meiji Restoration . . . near castle grounds is Aichi Shrine dedicated to Japanese servicemen.

Nagoya TV Tower • Observatory offers panoramic views from Japan Alps to Ise Bay . . . at ground level are Sakae Park and culture center . . . open from 10 a.m. to 5:50 p.m., Monday through Friday; 10 a.m.–9 p.m. Saturdays, Sundays, and holidays.

Nakamura Park • Contains small bamboo grove (**Taiko Yabu**) marking site of cottage in which Hideyoshi Toyotomi is said to have been born in 1536 . . . one of Hideyoshi's most successful generals, Kiyomasa Kato, was born nearby in Myokoji in 1559 . . . in a Buddhist temple.

Nanatsu Temple • Located in Osucho, Naka-ku . . . also called **Chofukuji.** Temple founded in 735 and moved to present site in 1611 . . . houses works from Heian period of Kannon (Goddess of Mercy) and Seishi Bodhisattva . . . listed as Important Cultural Properties.

Niitaiji • Buddhist temple located on Kakuozan Hill . . . nonsectarian and erected in 1900 . . . repository for **Golden Buddha** presented by King of Siam (Thailand) in 1900 . . . nice view from top of the hill . . . **Gohyaku Rakan Hall** nearby contains 500 images of Rakan . . . disciples of Buddha are quite different in features and repose . . . 18 Rakan in a special hall were carved by famous Netsuke artist Tametaka Kita.

Noritake China Model Plant Tour • *Tel: 052–562–5072 for reservtions* • 5 minutes by taxi from Nagoya station . . . complete process of porcelain making . . . museum.

Osu Kannon • Also known as Shimpukuji (temple) . . . located in center of Osu Amusement Quarter, Monzen-cho, Naka-ku . . . has many National Treasures.

Shiratori-No-Misasagi • (White Bird Mound) . . . located at Shiratori-cho, **Atsuta-ku** . . . one of two ancient tombs in the area . . . said to contain relics of Prince Yamato-Takeru . . . who was transformed into a white bird upon death.

Toshogu Shrine • Dedicated to Ieyasu Tokugawa . . . festival held here on April 16–17 each year . . . nearby is **Nagoya Shrine** founded in A.D. 911 by Emperor Daigo . . . annual festival on July 16.

Tokugawa Art Museum • Located at Tokugawa-cho, Higashi-ku . . . contains 10,000 documents of ancient emperors, armor, etc. as well as 43 sections of the famous picture scrolls of the Tale of Genji, Japan's No. 1 classic of the Heian Period . . . and picture scrolls of the Tales of Saigo, Buddhist priest and poet . . . many National Treasures here.

Yagoto Hill • Natural park in part of Higashiyama range . . . panoramic views from summit . . . also **Koshoji** (temple) with 5-story pagoda and 1000 Lantern Festival on night of harvest moon.

Environs

Gifu • Located on Nagara River, about 30 minutes by train from Nagoya . . . castle-town at foot of Mt. Inaba . . . noted for lovely scenery and **ukai** (cormorant fishing) on Nagara River every night from May 11 to Oct. 15 . . . Cormorants dive for *ayu* (river smelt) . . . popular tourist attraction.

Inuyama • Located on Kiso River . . . famous for white feudal castle built in A.D. 1440 on hill overlooking Kiso rapids . . . oldest fortress in Japan . . . shooting the **Kiso Rapids** from Imawatari to Inuyama is a great adventure . . . section forms the heart of Hida-Kiso River Quasi-National Park . . . just southeast of Inuyama is **Meiji-mura,** village-size museum extending over 250 acres . . . designed by Japanese architect Yoshiro Taniguchi . . . contains relics of the Meiji era . . . many Important Cultural Properties.

Ise-Shima National Park • Encompasses the sea, Japan's most important shrine, and the pearl industry . . . Spectacular seascapes and bays of Toba, Matoya, Ago, and Gokasho . . . **Ise Jingu** (the Grand Shrines of Ise) is the most sacred spot in all Japan . . . where the long Shinto tradition is considered most pure . . . more than 8 million Japanese make pilgrimages here annually . . . **Naiku** (inner shrine) dedicated to Sun Goddess **Amaterasu-Omikami,** mother of Jimmu Tenno (first emperor) . . . **Geku** (outer shrine) is dedicated to **Toyouke-Om-**

ikami, Goddess of Arms, Crops, Food, and Sericulture . . . custom dictates that shrines be razed every 20 years and new ones built on adjacent spots . . . Naiku contains the Mirror (**yata-no-kagami**) considered one of the three sacred treasures of the Imperial Court . . . **Ise-Shima Skyline Drive** links shrines with Toba City . . . offers panoramic views . . . **Mikimoto Pearl Island** in Toba Harbor is where Mr. Mikimoto produced his first cultured pearl (d. 1954) . . . has pearl museum and demonstrations of pearl gathering by women divers.

HOTELS

★★★**International Hotel Nagoya** • *3–23–3 Nishiki, Naka-ku, Nagoya 460. Tel: (052) 961–3111. Cable: INTERHOTEL NAGOYA. Telex: 444–3720 INTERH J* • 263 rooms.

Facilities: 5 restaurants serving French, American, Chinese, and Japanese cuisine. 3 bars. Entertainment.

Manager: M. Okano. *Reservations:* FUJITA.

★★★**Meitetsu Grand Hotel** • *2–4 Meleki–1–chome, Nakamura-ku, Nagoya 450. Tel: (052) 582–2211. Cable: MGHOTEL NAGOYA. Telex: 442–2031 HGHOTE J* • 242 rooms.

Facilities: Western and Japanese restaurants. Coffee shop. Cocktail lounge.

Manager: Y. Uyeda. *Reservations:* Direct.

★★★★**Hotel Nagoya Castle** • *3–19 Hinokuchi-cho, Nishi-ku. Tel: (052) 521–2121. Cable: HOTENACASTLE NAGOYA. Telex: J. 59787 CASTLE* • 253 rooms.

Facilities: European, Japanese, and Chinese cuisine. 2 bars. Entertainment. Swimming pool.

Manager: T. Umejima. *Reservations:* JTB.

★★★**Nagoya Kanko Hotel** • *1–19–30 Nishiki, Naka-ku, Nagoya 460. Tel: (052) 231–7711. Cable: KANHO NAGOYA. Telex: J5–9946 KANHO* • 505 rooms.

Facilities: French grill. Chinese and Japanese restaurants. Coffee shop. 2 bars. Cocktail lounge and tea lounge.

Manager: T. Uozumi. *Reservations:* JAL.

★★★★**Nagoya Miyako Hotel** • *9–10, 4–chome Meieke, Naka-mura-ku. Tel: (052) 571–3211. Cable: HONA MIYAKO. Telex: 442–2086 MIYAKO J* • 400 rooms.

Facilities: Western restaurant. 4 bars. Snack bar.
Manager: S. Suzuki. *Reservations:* MIYAKO Int'l.

NARA

NARA IN A CAPSULE

Cradle of Japanese civilization since first Emperor came to Yamato Plain . . . filled with ancient shrines and temples, most of them undisturbed for centuries and centuries . . . most revered is Horyuji in the southwest . . . founded in A.D. 607 by Prince Shotoku and boasts oldest extant wooden structures in the world . . . Nara offers a scenic and peaceful atmosphere . . . court life was thought to have been somewhat less politically intriguing than during the Heian Period (therefore not so many buildings were destroyed) . . . was first permanent capital of Japan . . . founded by Empress-Regent Gemmyo in A.D. 710 . . . lasted through 7 different Emperors . . . until Kammu transferred his administration to Nagaoka, southwest of Kyoto in A.D. 784 before founding Kyoto the next decade . . . known for its continuance of traditional Japanese arts and crafts . . . main products are brushes for calligraphy (writing), fans, dolls, and lacquerware.

WHAT TO SEE AND DO

Akishino • Temple founded in A.D. 780 by Emperors Konin and Kammu . . . Kondo (main hall) only original structure and National Treasures . . . other buildings fine examples of Kamakura period architecture.

Chuguji • convent near East Templle of Horyuji. Noted for Nyoirin Kannan . . . wooden Goddess image from 7th century.

Heijogu Palace Site • Located northwest of Nara Station (15 minutes by bus) . . . site of Imperial palace complex from A.D. 710 to 784 . . . nothing left but monument designating Special Place of Historical Significance.

Hokkeji • Buddhist temple established in 8th century by Empress Komyo . . . she intended to make it headquarters for all nunneries . . . empresses were always retiring to nunneries when their emperors lost the throne or died . . . site belonged to influential Fujiwara family . . . main hall dates from 1601.

Hokkiji • Established in A.D. 638 at final wishes of Prince Shotoku . . . also known as **Okamoto** because Prince had a palace here . . . has 3-story pagoda dating from 685 and fine example of 7th-century architecture of Nara/Buddhist period.

Horinji • ancient temple dating from 621. Located northeast of Horyuji . . . main object is seated wooden image of Yakushi-Nyorai in Kondo or Main Hall.

Horyuji • Oldest and largest existing temple in Japan . . . founded in A.D. 607 by Prince Shotoku by order of Regent of Empress-Regnant Suiko . . . considered cradle of Japanese art and culture . . . one of seven great temples of Nara . . . encompasses 45 structures dating from A.D. 607 to 16th century . . . 17 are National Treasures . . . rest are Important Cultural Properties . . . noted for **Nandaimon** (great south gate), **Kondo** (main hall), 5-story pagoda, **Shoryoin** (Sacred Spirit Hall), and modern storehouses which contain thousands of precious treasures . . . **Yumedono** (Hall of Dreams) considered most beautiful octagonal building in Japan . . . **Kannon** (Goddess of Mercy) carved by Prince Shotoku himself . . . on view twice annually . . . northeast of **Dempodo** (Sermon Hall) is **Chuguji,** nunnery with statue of **Nyoirin-Kannon** by Prince Shotoku and ancient embroideries . . . **Horinji** is another ancient temple nearby . . . founded in 621 by eldest son of Prince Shotoku . . . full of Important Cultural Properties.

Kairyuoji • Northwest of Nara Station (15 minutes by bus) . . . founded in A.D. 731 by Empress Komyo, consort of Emperor Shomu . . . site was property owned by her father, a Fujiwara . . . renovated in 12th century . . . 5-story pagoda is National Treasure.

Kasuga Shrine • Founded in A.D. 768 by a member of the Fujiwara family, part of the Imperial family by association . . . like the famous Ise Shrine, Kasuga was replaced every 20 years in early history . . . noted for some 3000 stone lanterns that line the route to Heiden (offering hall) . . . main shrine consists of 4 structures . . . all National Treasures . . . noted for **Kasuga Matsuri,** colorful festival on March 13 . . . nearby is **Kasuga-Wakamiya Shrine** . . . dedicated to a Shinto deity but built in same style . . . first construction in 1613 and many stone lanterns.

Kofukuji • One of seven great temples of Nara . . . originally known as Yamashina because first established in Kyoto in A.D. 669 by founder of the Fujiwara family . . . transferred to Nara by Fujiwara heir and named **Kofukuji** or "happiness-producing temple" . . . had as many as 175 buildings at height of prosperity but all burned . . . contains both 3- and 5-story pagodas . . . 2 octagonal halls and concrete treasure house full of National Treasures . . . shadow of **Kofukuji's** 5-story pagoda is reflected in Sarusawa Pond, just below Nara Hotel.

Mt. Kasuga • Several peaks that rise above the plain . . . considered home of the gods and full of sacred trees . . . lovely in spring and autumn and nice views from summit.

Nara National Museum • Located near entrance of Nara Park . . . modern building with excellent exhibits of works from Nara Period (considered to be from A.D. 645–784) . . . Nara Park is acres and acres of beautiful old trees and friendly deer who enjoy eating rice crackers . . . Sarusawa Pond is at right before entering.

Saidaiji (Great Western Temple) • Established in A.D. 765 by Empress-Regnant Shotoku and headquarters of **Shingon-Ritsu** sect . . . was once one of seven great temples of Nara . . . but fires destroyed the ancient structures . . . does boast 12 silk scrolls considered National Treasures.

Shin-Yakushiji • Founded in A.D. 747 by Empress Komyo, consort of Emperor Shomu, ill with eye infection at the time . . . only main hall is considered Nara Period architecture but contains some Important Cultural Properties.

Todaiji (Great Eastern Temple) • Constructed from A.D. 745 to 752 under supervision of Emperor Shomu . . . headquarters of **Kegon** sect . . . known for **Daibutsu** (Great Buddha) . . . **Nandaimon** (great south gate) is National Treasure . . . so are Daibutsu and great hall it occupies . . . octagonal bronze lanterns date from Nara Period . . . **Shosoin** or treasure house contains many precious objects from Emperor Shomu . . . whose consort donated them upon his death . . . many other statues in the temple considered National Treasures.

Toshodaiji • Headquarters of **Ritsu** sect . . . established in A.D. 759 by Chinese priest Ganjin of Tang Dynasty . . . **kondo** (main hall) considered one of finest Nara Period structures . . . both kondo and **kodo** (lecture hall) National Treasures . . . also Sutra Library.

Yakushiji • Headquarters of **Hosso** sect . . . founded in A.D. 680 and located here from previous site in 718 . . . was formerly one of seven great temples of Nara . . . but all structures now date from 13th century . . . except 3-story pagoda constructed in 698 and designated a National Treasure . . . also **Toin-do** (east hall) which contains many fine statues . . . **Bussoku-do** or Hall of Buddha's Footprint has print on stone dating from 753 and also National Treasure.

Yamato Bunka-kan • Museum located in Gakuen Minami section of Nara City . . . noted for fine collection of Far Eastern art . . . some 2000 works in all . . . exhibitions change . . . open daily (except Mon.) . . . call (0742) 45–0544 for directions.

HOTELS

★★★**Kikusui-ro** • *1130 Bodai-cho, Sanjo-dori. Tel: (0742) 23–2007* • 17 rooms . . . Japanese-style inn in elegant old mansion . . . located in a lovely garden on edge of Nara Park.

★★★**Hotel Yamatosanso** • *24–1 Kawakami-cho. Tel: (0742) 26–1011. Telex: 5522–202* • 51 rooms (majority Japanese-style).
Facilities: 3 dining rooms. Bar. Cocktail lounge. Near Todaiji.
Manager: H. Matsuo. *Reservations:* Direct.

★★★★**Nara Hotel** • *1096 Takabatake-cho, Nara 630. Tel: (0742) 26–3300. Cable: NARAHOTEL. Telex: 5522–108 NARAHO* • 107 rooms.
Facilities: Established over 70 years ago in Nara Park. Japanese palace architecture of Momoyama Period. 73 rooms in traditional structure with dining room, grillroom, and bar. 34 rooms in downtown annex in Kintetsu Station Building, with Sky Grill and bar.
Manager: K. Asada. *Reservations:* Miyako.

RESTAURANTS

For Western-style cuisine, stick with **Nara Hotel** dining room or Nara Hotel annex **Sky Grill**. There are plenty of interesting small eateries along Higashi-muki-naka-machi (arcade street right outside the station) or along Sanjo-dori . . . check the window displays for quasi-Japanese, Chinese, and Western dishes served.

OSAKA

OSAKA IN A CAPSULE

Japan's third largest city and third largest trading port . . . commercial and industrial center . . . shares control of Japanese economy with Tokyo . . . handles 40% of country's exports . . . Osaka merchants known for their business acumen . . . transportation hub of western Honshu in shipping, railway, and domestic air . . . city built on deltas formed by Yodo and former Yamato rivers . . . originally called Naniwa (rapid waves) . . . 5 emperors lived here between 4th and 8th centuries A.D. . . . became great commercial center during Tokugawa era . . . when Hideyoshi in mid-16th century persuaded merchants from neighboring towns to move to Osaka for business . . . for over 200 years until Meiji Restoration of 1868, Osaka was main distribution center for Japanese-made products . . . has retained its position as country's No. 1 commercial area . . . by super-express Shinkansen, Osaka is just over 3 hours from Tokyo.

WHAT TO SEE AND DO

Minami • Southern quarter . . . one of primary entertainment areas in Osaka . . . includes Dotombori along southern side of Dotombori

Canal . . . famous for 350 years as amusement quarter and site of **Asahiza Theater** where **Bunraku** performed several times a year . . . also Namba underground shopping center and Sennichi-mae . . . full of theaters, restaurants, and cabarets. Said to have more bars than anywhere else in the world!

Municipal Electric Science Museum • Founded in 1937 . . . exhibits all kinds of electrical apparatus and demonstration equipment . . . planetarium on 6th floor.

Nakanoshima • Civic center of the city . . . located on small island between Dojima and Tosabori rivers . . . contains city offices, hotels, festival hall, and Osaka University branch . . . Nakanoshima Park is oldest in Osaka.

Osaka Castle • Originally built in 1586 by Shogun Hideyoshi . . . noted for grand scale and granite requisitioned from Hideyoshi's generals . . . castle almost destroyed in 1615 by Tokugawa clan, who later reconstructed it, then burned it upon their retreat in 1868 . . . reconstructed in 1931 . . . offers fine views of city and historic exhibits . . . site now a park with Municipal Museum and Hokoku Shrine dedicated to Hideyoshi and family.

Osaka Merchandise Mart • 26 floors of locally made merchandise . . . one of the largest such marts in the world.

Scientific Transportation Museum • Located in front of Bentencho Station on JNR loop line . . . exhibits feature models of Shinkansen "bullet trains," electric trains, ships, automobiles, and airplanes.

Shitennoji • Temple founded by Prince Shotoku in A.D. 593 . . . popular name is Tennoji . . . said to be older than Horyuji near Nara . . . nothing left of original structures . . . but stone *torii* (gate) dates from 1294 and said to be oldest in Japan . . . temple headquarters of **Washu** sect . . . has many National Treasures, including some ancient Sutra and Prince Shotoku's swords.

Sumiyoshi Shrine • A popular Shinto shrine said to have been founded in A.D. 202 . . . dedicated to 4 different deities, 3 of which are guardians of sea voyagers . . . many stone lanterns donated by sailors and shipowners . . . **Rice Planting Festival (Otaue Matsuri)** celebrated here on June 14 . . . **Summer Festival** from July 30 to Aug. 1 . . . west of shrine is Sumiyoshi Park noted for pine and camphor trees.

Tennoji Park • Southwest of Shitennoji . . . second oldest park in Osaka and contains Municipal Art Museum, botanical gardens, zoological gardens, Chausuyama prehistoric burial mound, and Keitakuen Japanese garden.

Temmangu Shrine • Founded in A.D. 949 to honor Michizane Sugawara (A.D. 845–903), classical scholar exiled to Kyushu and deified as Tenjin . . . one of Japan's three greatest festivals celebrated here on July 24–25 . . . called **Tenjin Matsuri** . . . there is a boat procession on Yodo River . . . songs and dances on lantern-lit boats . . . sacred palanquin placed on decorated boat and carried upstream and back for several hours.

The Mint • Located east of the **Temmangu Shrine** on Yodo River . . . established in 1870 to unify Japan's coinage system . . . some coins still minted here . . . museum exhibits coins from all over the world . . . grounds of The Mint become a mall for viewing cherry trees each spring.

Umeda • Area around Osaka station for business and entertainment . . . Umeda Underground Center contains shops and restaurants and connects to a dozen buildings in the area . . . including **Hankyu** and **Hanshin department stores.**

Environs

Ashiya • Lovely residential area at foot of Mt. Rokko . . . about 20 minutes by train from Osaka . . . lovely climate and scenery . . . Japan's greatest postwar novel *The Makioka Sisters* by Junichiro Tanizaki is set here and in Osaka.

Expo Memorial Park • Site of 1970 World Exposition . . . contains huge Japanese Garden, Japan Folk Art Museum, EXPO Memorial Hall, EXPO land and amusement center.

Kongo-Ikoma-Quasi-National Park • Covers vast mountain district from Osaka to Nara prefectures . . . includes Ikoma and Shigi mountains . . . area of great beauty and historical interest . . . **Hozanji** or **Ikoma Shoten** is temple dedicated to **Shoten,** guardian deity of Buddhism . . . Shigi-Ikoma Skyline toll road offers lovely panoramic views . . . **Hiraoka Shrine** at foot of Mt. Ikoma is considered fountainhead of Kasuga Shrine in Nara . . . ancient pine grove in precincts and park noted for flowering bushes.

Koyoen Park • Lies at foot of Mt. Kabuto . . . nearby is **Kannoji,** Buddhist temple of **Shingon** sect said to have been founded by Kobo-Daishi . . . contains Important Cultural Properties from Heinan Period . . . precinct noted for cherry trees and nice views of Osaka Bay.

Nanki District • Southern part of Kii peninsula . . . scenic area accessible to Osaka . . . includes **Wakayama City** with castle built by Hideyoshi in 1585 . . . **Wakanoura** seaside resort about a half hour from the city . . . **Shirahama Spa** . . . most famous hot spring in the district . . . located about 2 hours along the coast south of Wakayama . . . and **Kushimoto,** a fishing port at the tip of the peninsula . . . noted for its charm . . . and **Oshima,** a pleasure island 10 minutes from the port by boat.

Toyonaka • Suburb north of Osaka . . . has Hattori Ryokuchi Park . . . which contains **Toyonaka Folk Museum** . . . with ancient structures moved from nearby areas.

HOTELS

★★International Hotel Osaka • *58 Hashizume-cho, Uchihon-machi, Higashi-ku. Tel: (06) 941–2661. Cable: INTERHOTEL. Telex: 529–3415 INTHTL J* • 400 rooms.
Facilities: Dining room. Japanese and Chinese restaurants. Steak house. 2 bars. Japanese garden.
Manager: M. Hatada. *Reservations:* Direct.

★★★Hotel New Hankyu • *1–35, Shibata 1–chome, Kita-ku. Tel: (06) 372–5101. Cable: NEWHANKYU, OSAKA. Telex: 523–3830 HTLNH J* • 1029 rooms.
Facilities: Steak house. Grillroom. Sushi/tempura restaurant. World cuisine buffet. 4 bars.
Manager: H. Chusho. *Reservations:* Direct.

★★★★Hotel New Otani Osaka • *4 Shiromi 1-chome, Higashi-ku. Tel: (06) 362–1111. Telex: J63068 OTANI OSK* • 610 rooms. New 18-story deluxe hotel situated next to Osaka Castle Park in Shiromi Higashi-ku . . . opened late 1986 . . . features western Japan's largest banquet hall . . . international conference hotel in major business center and Japan's second city.

Facilities: Large business center. Ho-oh-no-Ma Banquet Room. Four-story atrium lobby. Azalea restaurant. The Castle bar. The Lounge. Fitness Club with indoor/outdoor pools and tennis courts. Executive floors. Group floors. Family floors. Member's Club 808. Senba-Zuru Japanese cuisine. Taikan-En Chinese restaurant. A branch of Trader Vic's. Sakura dining room. Keyaki Teppan grill. Four Seasons Sky Lounge. Parking Garage.

General Manager: H. Kouda. *Reservations:* New Otani Int'l.

★★**Hotel Osaka Castle** • *2–35–7 Kyobashi, Higashi-ku. Tel: (06) 942–1401. Cable: HOTEL OSKCASTLE. Telex: 529–8505 CASTLE* • 90 rooms.

Facilities: Restaurant. Bar.

Manager: M. Nagano. *Reservations:* Direct.

★★★**Hotel Osaka Grand** • *3–18, 2–chome Nakanoshima, Kitaku. Tel: (06) 202–1212. Cable: OSAKAGRAND OSAKA. Telex: 522–2301 OGRND* • 358 rooms.

Facilities: Chikuyotei grill. Western, Chinese, and Japanese restaurants. Coffee shop. Bar.

Manager: T. Yamamoto. *Reservations:* JTB.

★★**Osaka Dai-ichi Hotel** • *1–9–20 Umeda Kita-ku. Tel: (06) 341–4411. Telex: 523–4423 ITHLO J* • 478 rooms.

Facilities: Japanese, Western, and Chinese restaurants. Grillroom. Coffee shop. Cocktail lounge.

Manager: M. Aota. *Reservations:* JTB.

★★★★★**Miyako Hotel Osaka** • *6–1–55 Uehonmachi, Tennojiku, Osaka 543. Tel: (06) 773–1111. Cable: MIYAKOHOTEL OSAKA. Telex: 527–7555 MYKOSA J* • 601 rooms.

Facilities: 14 restaurants/bars. Health Club with heated pool. Largest banquet facilities in western Japan. Airport limo service.

Reservations: UTELL.

★★★★★**The Plaza Hotel** • *ABC Center, 2–49 Oyodo-minami, 2–chome, Oyodo-ku. Tel: (06) 453–1111. Cable: PLAZAHOTEL OSAKA. Telex: 524–5557 PLAOSA J* • 575 rooms.

Facilities: Gourmet dining in Le Rendezvous Grill; Belvedere Continental restaurant with musical entertainment; Hanagiri Japanese; Sui-En Chinese; Yodo Teppan-yaki specialties; Plaza Pantry, 2 lounges; 3 bars. Outdoor swimming pool; Japanese garden; tea ceremony room; garage.

General Manager: H. Ohno. *Reservations:* LHW.

★★★**Royal Hotel** • *5–3–68 Nakanoshima, Kita-ku. Tel: (06) 448–1121. Cable: ROYALHOTEL OSAKA. Telex: J63350 ROYAL HTL* • 1500 rooms.
Facilities: 15 restaurants serving Western and Oriental cuisine. 4 bars. Entertainment. Swimming pool. Japanese garden. Health center. Nursery.
Manager: S. Hirose. *Reservations:* JAL.

★★★+**Osaka Terminal Hotel** • *3–1–1 Umeda, Kita-ku, Osaka 530. Tel: (06) 344–1235. Telex: 523–3738 OSATER J* • 671 rooms. Hotel located in terminal building.
Facilities: Terrace restaurant. Yamatoya Rinsen Japanese restaurant. Grill Moor. Tien-an Chinese restaurant. Coffee Shop. Several bars and lounges. Shops. Banquet Halls.

RESTAURANTS

Hachisaburo • *2–23 Namba-Shinchi, Minami-ku. Tel: 211–3201* • Sushi.

Honmorita • *1–7 Namba Shinchi, Minami-ku. Tel: 211–3608* • Sukiyaki.

Hiranomachi Suehiro • *3–24 Hiranomachi, Higashi-ku. Tel: 231–4773* • Sukiyaki and Kobe beef . . . Japanese or Western preparation.

Kikuya • *6–4–11, Nishi Temma, Kita-ku. Tel: 312–3196* • Tempura.

Kitcho • *3–23 Koraibashi, Higashi-ku. Tel: 231–1937* • Kaiseki Ryori.

Mimiu Honten • *5–36 Bingomachi, Higashi-ku. Tel: 261–7241* • Noodles.

Rokuban 39 • *Soemoncho, Minami-ku. Tel: 211–3456* • Teppanyaki.

Senba Suehiro • *13th floor, Itochu Bldg., 4 Kitakyutaro, Higashi-ku. Tel: 252–2140* • Sukiyaki and Kobe beef . . . Japanese/Western.

Suehiro Asahi • *1–5–2 Sonezakishinchi, Kita-ku. Tel: 341–1760* • Japanese/Western.

Tsuruya Honten • *5–9 Imabashi, Higashi-ku. Tel: 231–0456* •
Traditional.

Taikoen • *9–10 Amijimacho, Miyakojima-ku. Tel: 351–8201* •
Cantonese.

TOHOKU

TOHOKU IN A CAPSULE

Northeastern district of Japan . . . called Michinoku or Back
Country because of mountainous topography and heavy winters
. . . difficulty in tapping natural resources . . . now a major
tourist area because of natural parks . . . scenic beauty and many
hot springs . . . full of ancient folkcrafts . . . district extends
from Fukushima prefecture to Aomori . . . northern port on Honshu . . . also includes Akita, Iwate, Miyagi, and Yamagata prefectures . . . Sendai is major city and cultural, political, and
economic capital of Tohoku district . . . known for its famous
Tanabata Matsuri, Star Festival, held from Aug. 6–8 each year
. . . also noted for its beer and sake.

WHAT TO SEE AND DO

Aomori • Gateway to Hokkaido from northern Honshu . . . ferry
service several times daily to Hakodate across Tsugaru Straits . . . also
longest railway tunnel in Japan for Shinkansen . . . major tourist center
with Nebuta Matsuri (festival) Aug. 3–7, fashionable Asamushi Spa
some 30 minutes away . . . and **Natsudomari Peninsula,** with its many
swans from Nov. to March.

Bandai-Asahi National Park • second largest national park in Japan after Daisetsuzan in Hokkaido . . . extends from Yamagata and
Niigata prefectures along Japan Sea Coast . . . includes **Mt. Gassan**
and **Three Mountains of Dewa** . . . Asahi Range . . . Mt. Iide . . .

volcanic peaks of Mts. Bandai and Plateau, Mt. Azuma, and Mt. Ada-
tara . . . and Lake Inawashiro district . . . noted for **Bandai Azuma
skyline drive** and many flourishing spas.

Chokai Quasi-National Park • Extends along Japan Sea coast from
Yamagata and Akita prefectures . . . central peak is **Mt. Chokai,** called
Dewa-Fuji . . . peak resembles conal shape of Mt. Fuji . . . Tohoku's
most spectacular sight . . . view from summit especially spectacular at
sunrise . . . climbers begin from either Kisakata or Fukura.

Rikuchu Kaigan National Park • Extends along Pacific Ocean coast
in Iwate prefecture . . . Kitakami mountain range runs close to the sea
. . . great beauty . . . center of park is **Miyako,** noted for jagged
cliffs, lovely beaches, fjordlike bays, and rare flora and fauna . . . all
protected as Natural Monuments . . . sightseeing buses from Miyako.

Sado-Yahiko Quasi-National Park • Includes Mt. Yahiko on
mainland and 3 districts of Sado Island in Japan Sea . . . Sado Island
is 5th largest in Japanese archipelago (after Shikoku) . . . under administration of Niigata prefecture . . . reached from Niigata in 2 hours by
ferry . . . a very beautiful island known for **Toki,** a heronlike bird and
okesa ballads . . . was a place of exile in feudal times . . . also famous for its **Aikawa gold mine** in operation since 1600 and worked by
convicts during Edo Period . . . Mt. Kimpoku, Senkaku Bay, and Lake
Kamo considered part of national park . . . Sado is a lovely spot to
visit . . . especially during the summer months when the Japan Sea
between Niigata and the island is very pleasant . . . ferries crowded.

Sendai • Tohoku's largest city and cultural center for over 300 years
. . . formerly a castle town . . . now a thoroughly modern city surrounded by a range of low hills . . . **Osaki Hachimangu** (shrine) is a
National Treasure . . . originally built in 1607 . . . Momoyama Period
architecture . . . Sendai is base for visiting **Matsushima** or Pine Clad
Island, considered one of Japan's most scenic three . . . noted for its
Zuiganji (temple) founded in A.D. 828 . . . belongs to **Myo-shinji**
school of **Rinzai** sect . . . present 17th-century structures in Momo-
yama-style architecture are National Treasures . . . *fusuma* (sliding screens)
painted by Kano school . . . other smaller pine-clad islands in Matsushima Bay . . . best seen from Tomiyama, Otakamori, Tamonzan,
and Ogidani from 4 corners of the bay.

Towada Hachimantai National Park • extends over Aomori, Akita, and Iwate prefectures . . . comprises Hachimantai Plateau and Lake
Towada . . . as well as Mt. Koma and Mt. Nyuto . . . tourist attractions include Oirase Valley formed by Oirase River . . . pleasure boats

available on Lake Towada . . . third-deepest crater lake in Japan . . . tourist center of the lake is Yasumiya . . . Hakkoda mountains popular for camping in summer and skiing in winter.

Zao Quasi-National Park • Favored spot for skiers . . . **Zao spa** very chic and just a few hours by train from Ueno Station . . . then 45 minutes from Yamagata Station . . . also ideal retreat in summer and fall . . . during winter, trees covered with snow called "Silver Thaw."

HOTELS

Aomori

★★**Hotel Aomori** • *1–1–23 Tsutsumi-Machi, Aomori City. Tel: (0177) 75–4141. Telex: 812755 HTLAOM J* • 102 rooms.
Facilities: Dining room. Cocktail lounge. Golf. Fishing. Beach. Skating.
Manager: S. Inomata. *Reservations:* Direct.

★★★**Aomori Grand Hotel** • *1–1–23 Shin-machi, Aomori City. Tel: (0177) 23–1011* • 150 rooms.
Facilities: Continental and Japanese restaurants. Coffee shop. Bar. Golf. Skating. Fishing. Beach.
Manager: K. Miura. *Reservations:* Direct.

Niigata

★★★★**Myoko Pine Valley Prince Hotel** • *Okemi, Myoko-mura, Nakakubiki-gun, Niigata 949-22. Tel: 0255–82–4111* • 138 rooms. Small resort hotel located in midst of Myoko Valley. Guests have use of local country club with three 9-hole courses, 21 tennis courts . . . ski area nearby.
Facilities: 3 restaurants and lounge. Large public bath with hot spring and sauna. Game Room.
Reservations: Prince Hotels.

★★★★★**Naeba Prince Hotel** • *Mikuni, Yuzawa-machi, Minami-Uonuma-gun, Niigata 949-62. Tel: 0257–89–2211. Telex: 3238-370 NAEBA J.* 1444 Rooms. Open year-round for winter skiing, summer tennis and golf. Largest and most complete hotel in Naeba ski area (35 lifts) and Mikuni ski area (3 lifts). Has own golf course, 42 tennis courts, heated indoor swimming pool, and trout fishing pond.

Facilities: 17 restaurants (French, Japanese, Chinese, New York Steak/Seafood, Swiss, German) and 6 bars. Banquet hall.
Reservations: Prince Hotels.

★★★★★**Okura Hotel Niigata** • *6–53, Kawabata-cho, Niigata City 951. Tel: (0252) 24–6111. Cable: OKURAHOTEL NIIGATA. Telex: 3122–815 OKRNIT J* • 303 rooms overlooking Japan Sea.
Facilities: Japanese, French, and Chinese restaurants. Grillroom. Tea lounge. 2 bars.
Manager: J. Hasegawa. *Reservations:* Okura Int'l.

★★★**The Italia-Ken** • *7–1574 Nishibori, Niigata City 951. Tel: (0252) 24–5111. Telex: ITALIAKEN 3122–888* • 101 rooms.
Facilities: Japanese, French, and Chinese restaurants. Grill. Cafe. Bar. Golf. Skating, Boating. Beach. Tennis.
Manager: Y. Kurosaki. *Reservations:* JAL.

Sendai

★★**Hotel Rich Sendai** • *2–2 Kokubun-cho, 2–chome, Sendai 980. Tel: (0222) 62–8811. Telex: 853–483 RICHSB* • 242 rooms.
Facilities: Dining room. Bar. Coffee shop. Membership club.
Manager: K. Tsukamoto. *Reservations:* Hotel Rich Corp.

★★★**Hotel Sendai Plaza** • *2–20–1 Honcho, Sendai 980. Tel: (0222) 62–7111. Cable: PLAZA SENDAI. Telex: 852–965* • 221 rooms.
Facilities: Western restaurant and lounge. Chinese and Japanese restaurants. Coffee shop. Bar.
Manager: S. Aoki. *Reservations:* JAL.

★★★★**Sendai Tokyu Hotel** • *2–9–25 Ichiban-cho, Sendai 980. Tel: (0222) 62–2411. Cable: THCSEN. Telex: 852–393 THCSEN* • 302 rooms.
Facilities: French, Japanese, and Chinese restaurants. Coffee shop. Bar.
Manager: S. Hasegawa. *Reservations:* Tokyu Int'l.

TOKYO

————— TOKYO IN A CAPSULE —————

Japan's capital and most populous city in the world, after Shanghai and Mexico City . . . dates from end of 12th century A.D. . . . originally named Edo (Estuary) . . . selected by Shogun Ieyasu Tokugawa as administrative center in 1603 . . . became official Imperial capital at time of Meiji Restoration in 1868 . . . winds around Tokyo Bay and comprises 23 kus (wards), 26 cities, 6 towns, and 9 villages . . . a few million people commute into the city each business day . . . for government, commercial, financial, and cultural employment . . . one of the most expensive cities in the world, although recent official statistics insist it is only 16th most expensive . . . a city that has developed rapidly since 1945 . . . somewhat like a jigsaw puzzle . . . takes some doing to understand . . . excellent mass transit system that helps.

WHAT TO SEE AND DO

Akasaka • A favorite area with pleasure seekers . . . full of nightclubs, bars, and restaurants . . . **Roppongi** adjoining is more popular with Westerners . . . many fine restaurants catering to the foreign palate . . . a more individual crowd in Roppongi . . . diplomats from some 30 different missions, stage, and screen personalities, and other famous visitors.

Aoyama • A fashionable area where many foreigners live . . . Aoyama-dori is a wide street lined with elegant shops . . . **Togu Palace** in Aoyama is official home of Crown Prince.

Asakusa • Amusement center in one of city's oldest sections . . . site of **Asakusa Honganji Temple,** a branch of Higashi-Honganji in Kyoto . . . founded here in 1657 . . . **Kokusai Gekijo** (International

Theater) also here . . . headquarters of **Shochiku** All Girl Opera Troupe . . . **Asakusa Kannon Temple** is headquarters of **Sho Kannon** sect of Buddhism . . . dedicated to Goddess of Mercy . . . souvenir shops line the covered approach or Nakamise . . . temple founded in 7th century . . . one of the city's favorite.

Ginza • One of most famous shopping streets in the world . . . gin means silver . . . so silvershops must have lined this street in the early days . . . extends from Shimbashi to Kyobashi . . . several large department stores, traditional shops, restaurants, cabarets, bars . . . neon blazes in the evening . . . young couples like to *ginbura,* or stroll, the Ginza for fun . . . Ginza subway stations connect 3 lines . . . good interchange . . . just off the Ginza is the famed **Kabuki-za** where Kabuki is performed frequently.

Gokokuji • Headquarters of **Buzan** school of **Shingon** sect of Buddhism . . . temple founded in 1681 . . . largest in Tokyo and burial place for Imperial family . . . located in Toshimagaoka, Otsuka 5-chome . . . dedicated to Goddess of Mercy and Kannon image of amber from India . . . stone lanterns replicas of work from the Kyoto and Nara periods . . . Kamakura-period mandala.

Harajuku • Site of famed **Meiji Shrine** . . . one of holiest of pilgrimages in Japan . . . dedicated to Emperor Meiji (1852–1912) and his consort . . . pure Shinto shrine with large torii (gates) made of *hinoki* (Japanese cypress) said to be over 1700 years old . . . treasure house behind main shrine has articles used by Emperor Meiji, the monarch credited with opening Japan to the outside world . . . **Iris Garden** belonging to the shrine is considered best in Tokyo . . . lovely during summer . . . annual festivals at the shrine on Nov. 1 and 3, and May 3 . . . **bugaku** court dances performed on stage set up in front of sanctuary . . . not far from the shrine is **Yoyogi Sports Center,** created for the 1964 Olympic Games in Tokyo . . . includes 2 impressive structures designed by local architect Kenzo Tange . . . National Indoor Stadium and Olympic Swimming Stadium . . . ultra-modern.

Hibiya Park • Next to the Imperial Hotel in downtown Tokyo . . . site of former daimyo mansions . . . designed in 1903 to combine Japanese and Western philosophy . . . lovely in spring and fall . . . many festivals here.

Imperial Palace • All streets in the center of Tokyo lead around the palace moat . . . occupies grounds of former **Edo** or **Chiyoda Castle,** residence of the Tokugawa shogunate for 265 years . . . present structure is postwar . . . built of concrete in Japanese style . . . surrounded by a series of moats and approached by **Niju-bashi,** or a double-bridge . . . public may visit outer gardens only . . . twice a year visitors may enter precinct to sign a long scroll for congratulations on the New Year (Jan. 2) and on the Emperor's birthday (December 23) . . . otherwise permission must be received in advance from Imperial Household Agency.

Kanda • A student area in northeast section of Tokyo . . . known for its many schools and universities . . . and bookshops . . . **Kanda Myojin** is a Shinto shrine on the Kanda River . . . said to date from mid-8th century.

Kasumigaseki • Political district of Tokyo and Japan . . . National Diet Building stands on Kasumigaseki Hill . . . familiar landmark built in 1936 . . . foreign visitors may enter the gallery by signing their names at the information offices . . . National Diet Library is adjacent to the Diet Building . . . National Theater **(Kokuritsu Gekijo),** just north of the library, is noted for its bunraku performances . . . other large buildings in the area deal with transportation, construction, foreign affairs, home affairs, finance, economic planning, justice and the supreme court, agriculture and forestry, international trade and industry, etc.

Korakuen Garden • 5-minute walk from Suidobashi Station . . . one of Tokyo's most interesting landscape gardens . . . designed by Yorifua, 11th son of Ieyasu shogun, in 1626 . . . shows considerable Chinese influence . . . Full Moon stone bridge makes interesting reflection . . . garden designated Outstanding Scenic Place of Historical Importance . . . area adjoining the park is sports and amusement center . . . with 35,000-person stadium.

Keio University • Japan's oldest university . . . located in Mita district . . . established in late 19th century by leading educator Fukuzawa . . . noted for fine law, economics, commerce, medicine, and engineering.

Marunouchi • Tokyo's business district . . . centered around Tokyo Station, Tokyo Metropolitan Office (designed by Kenzo Tange), Central Post Office, JNR (Japan National Railway) and JTB (Japan Travel Bureau) buildings, and many, many offices with some of the most expensive rents in the world.

Nihonbashi • Bridge first constructed in 1603 and all distances in Japan were calculated from here . . . considered the hub of the city . . . name means Japan Bridge . . . only marker stands now . . . area around it is considered financial center of Tokyo . . . many banks and securities companies . . . just north of the bridge marker is Marunouchi 1–chome where William Adams, English pilot called **Anjin,** lived with his Japanese wife . . . Anjin was hired by the first Tokugawa shogun Ieyasu in early 1600s to teach him geography, mathematics, and foreign affairs . . . Anjin and his wife are buried in a cemetery in Yokosuka . . . where he also built a mansion.

Nezu Shrine ● Located near Nezu Station . . . dedicated to 4 Shinto deities as well as Michizane Sugawara, the famed scholar of Chinese classics exiled to Kyushu in A.D. 901 from the court of Kyoto . . . children make pilgrimages here for guidance, especially in the spring when more than 3000 azaleas are in bloom.

Shiba Park ● Formed in 1873 from the grounds of **Zojoji,** Buddhist temple next door . . . provides a bit of tranquillity in the area . . . Zojoji is Kanto district headquarters of **Jodo** sect . . . founded in 1393 and formerly family temple of the Tokugawa clan . . . 2-story Main Gate is a landmark and Important Cultural Property . . . commissioned by Ieyasu in 1605 and called Sammon (3 gates) . . . stands for the 3 sections as well as 3 ways to salvation . . . wisdom, benevolence, and Buddha . . . a delightful community of jizos (small statues) line the right-hand side of the grounds . . . temple's daimon (great gate) is a large red torii located in the midst of busy traffic . . . a symbol of times past . . . Zojoji and Shiba Park in the shadow of Tokyo Tower, an ugly monster that has absolutely no relation to the Paris monument . . . there are observation platforms if you are so inclined.

Shibuya ● A popular residential area in Tokyo . . . known for its many small shops and restaurants . . . once the site of a castle . . . now a bustling minimetropolis . . . 2 fine museums are located a short taxi ride from the station . . . the **Nippon Mingei-Kan (Japan Folkcrafts Museum)** and the **Tokyo Museum of Modern Literature** . . . the latter is on the campus of Tokyo University . . . alma mater of prime ministers and corporation presidents . . . and located in the former European-style mansion of the Maeda family, who auspiciously donated much of the property for the campus . . . Tokyo University grew from many educational institutions that existed since the mid-1800s . . . officially designated a state university in 1869.

Shinjuku ● Another popular residential area except for the fast-paced establishment around the station . . . Shinjuku Station boasts over a million commuters daily . . . around its perimeter are bars and cabarets (some of them gay), underground nightclubs and glamorous high-rise hotels . . . **Shinjuku Gyoen National Garden** is actually a short walk from Sendagaya Station (2 stops from Shinjuku) . . . about 150 acres of tropical and subtropical plants . . . on site of former daimyo mansion . . . best in spring (cherry trees) and autumn (chrysanthemums) . . . across the street is **Meiji Shrine Outer Garden** where the funeral of Emperor Meiji occurred in 1912 . . . actually no garden but an Olympic park . . . with stadiums and indoor swimming pool . . . **Memorial Picture Gallery** and **Meiji Memorial Hall** are also located here.

Shimbashi ● New Bridge . . . one of Tokyo's most easily found areas . . . Shimbashi Station allows exploring in several directions . . . the **Hama Detached Palace Garden** is just a 10-minute walk . . . over 60 acres that once belonged to the Tokugawa clan . . . still has atmosphere of feudal lords in Edo . . . scenic pond spanned by 3 bridges . . . perhaps a lucky view of the Sumida River and Tokyo Bay . . . lovely cherry blossoms in spring . . . a few minutes to the north is Tsukiji . . . reclaimed land from the Sumida River where foreigners were once forced to reside in isolation until 1899 . . . Behold! Fish have replaced foreigners, for this is now the wholesale fish district . . . the action begins about 4 a.m., but if you drop by around 6 a.m. you may still get some good pictures . . . before sneaking around the corner for the freshest sushi possible!

Shinagawa ● Another busy train center . . . all who travel to western Japan will pass through Shinagawa . . . the first station on the old Tokaido Road linking Edo with Kyoto . . . the area was once full of teahouses and inns . . . which have become enormous high-rise hostelries . . . even the Takanawa Prince Hotel, up the hill from the station, with its beautiful gardens offering peace and serenity, is now overshadowed by its own offspring . . . up beyond the hotel is **Sengakuji** . . . noted as the burial ground of the famous **47 Ronin** and a favorite place of pilgrimage for Japanese every winter . . . the Ronin (masterless samurai) plotted to avenge their daimyo, Asano, who was forced to take his own life for insulting one of the shogun's retainers . . . masterless . . . the 47 samurai vowed revenge and murdered the fellow Kira . . . they then placed his head on the fresh tomb of Asano and awaited punishment . . . the penalty was death at their own hands . . . all are buried in order of length of service to their master . . . a Kabuki play called *Chushingura* is presented every Dec. to mark the historic (and romantic) event of 1701 . . . a short walk from Sengakuji is **Tozenji** . . . used as a temporary residence of the British legation in 1861.

Ueno Park ● Tokyo's chief cultural center . . . borders the Sumida River and Asakusa . . . and is easily reached by trains and subway to Ueno Station . . . **Tokyo Metropolitan Festival Hall (Bunka Kaikan)** just across from the station . . . is the scene of many fine classical performances of music . . . there are 4 important museums in the park as well as Tokyo University's departments of fine arts and music . . . a large library and zoological gardens . . . south of the gardens is **Toshogu Shrine,** dedicated to the memory of Ieyasu Tokugawa in 1627 . . . with some 250 lanterns presented by different daimyos . . . a 5-story pagoda built in 1639 and formerly part of **Kaneiji** (Tendai sect temple that once owned the entire land of Ueno Park), a National Treasure and best seen from **Seiyoken Restaurant** on the edge of **Shinobazu Pond** . . . a whole day can be spent in Ueno Park (avoid Mon. when museums are closed) . . . there are plenty of places to rest and enjoy the scenery . . . and plenty of tempting snacks hawked at frequent intervals.

Yurakucho • A continuation of the Marunouchi district . . . many offices, restaurants, nomiya (small drinking establishments), theaters, and such . . . the **Sukiyabashi Shopping Center** (named for a bridge that once spanned a canal here) . . . **Yurakucho Food Center** . . . and Foreign Correspondents Club of Japan are located in the area . . . watch it during rush hour . . . very crowded.

Zempukuji • Temple of the Shingon sect said to have been founded by **Kobo Daishi** (great master) during early 9th century . . . located at Yamamoto-cho, near former Nihonbashi streetcar stop . . . famed as headquarters of American Townsend Harris, appointed Minister to Japan in 1859 . . . Harris retired in 1861, but his successors used the temple for another 8 years . . . structures all postwar . . . monument to U.S. envoys also replaced them.

Tokyo Museums*

Tokyo Metropolitan Teien Art Museum • *21–9 Shiroganedai, 5-chome (5-minute walk from Meguro station). Tel: 443–0201* • Former residence of Prince Asaka, the emperor's great-uncle . . . Teien means landscaped garden . . . now open to public for exhibitions. Closed second and fourth Wednesdays . . . unless national holidays.

Bridgestone Museum of Art • *1–10–1 Kyobashi, Chuo-ku. Tel: 563–0241* • Located on second floor of Bridgestone (the tire people) building . . . Japanese and Western art of 18th and 19th centuries . . . collection of company founder.

---

*All museums closed on Mondays unless otherwise noted.

Gotoh Art Museum • *3–9–25 Kaminoge, Setagaya-ku. Tel: 703–0661* • Ancient arts and crafts of Japan, China, and other parts of Orient . . . short stroll from Kaminoge Station.

Hatakeyama Collection • *2–20–12, Shiroganedai, Minato-ku. Tel: 447–5787* • Fine arts and crafts of ancient Japan, Korea, and China. Many objects relating to tea ceremony . . . 6-minute walk from Takanawadai Subway.

Idemitsu Art Gallery • *3–1–1 chome, Marunouchi, Chiyoda-ku. Tel: 213–3111* • Ancient arts and crafts of Japan, China, and other parts of Orient . . . short stroll from Yurakucho Station.

Japan Folk Crafts Museum (Nippon Mingei-Kan) • *4–3–33 chome, Komaba, Meguro-ku. Tel: 467–4527* • Founded 1936 by noted critic Soetsu Yanagi . . . full of lovely folk crafts and arts . . . mainly contemporary . . . closed Jan. 1 through Feb. (no heat, as I recall).

Japanese Sword Museum • *4–25–10 Yoyogi, Shibuya-ku. Tel: 379–1386* • Short walk from Sangu-bashi Station . . . ancient and modern swordsmiths' crafts.

Meiji Shrine Treasure House • *Yoyogi, Shibuya-ku. Tel: 370–0111* • 10 minutes from Yoyogi Station . . . objects related to Emperor Meiji . . . open daily.

Memorial Picture Gallery, Meiji Shrine • *Meiji Olympic Park, Shinjuku-ku. Tel: 401–7973* • 5 minutes from Shinanomachi Station . . . pictures of main events in reign of Emperor Meiji (1868–1912) . . . open daily.

Museum of Sumo • *2–1–9 Kuramae, Taito-ku. Tel: 851–2206* • 2 minutes from Kuramae Station . . . records, documents, history of sumo wrestling.

National Museum of Modern Art • *3 Kitanomaru Park, Chiyoda-ku. Tel: 214–2561* • Everything since 1907 . . . minutes from Takebashi Station. Visit also Crafts Gallery . . . contemporary Japanese handicrafts.

National Science Museum • *Ueno Park, Ueno Station. Tel: 822–011* • Contains exhibits in zoology, botany, geography, physics, chemistry, astronomy, meteorology, and oceanography.

National Museum of Western Art • *Ueno Park, Ueno Station. Tel: 825–5131* • Works of well-known Western painters and sculptors.

Nezu Institute of Fine Arts • *6–5–36 Minami-Aoyama, Mina-to-ku. Tel: 400–2536* • Omotesando Station . . . ancient arts and crafts from China, Japan, and Korea . . . may be closed in Aug.

Okura Shukokan • *Across from main entrance of Okura Hotel. Tel: 583–0781* • Late Baron Okura's collection of antiques from China, Japan, and India . . . very small Chinese-style building . . . few exhibits.

Ota Memorial Ukiyo-e Museum • *1–10–10, Jingumae, Shibuya-ku. Tel: 403–0880* • Large collection of Ukiyo-e woodblock prints acquired by Mr. Ota . . . 3-minute walk from Meiji-Jingumae Subway and Harajuku Station.

Paper Museum • *1–1–8 Horifune, Kita-ku. Tel: 911–3545* • Located in front of Oji Station . . . all sorts of Japanese paper, paper products, and utensils for making paper by hand . . . closed on national holidays.

Pentax Gallery • *Kasumich-Corp, 3–21–20 Nishi Azabu, Minato-ku. Tel: 401–2186* • Short walk from Roppongi Station . . . cameras and photos . . . one of a kind in Japan . . . operated by the camera people.

Riccar Art Museum • *2–3 6–chome, Ginza, Chuo-ku. Tel: 572–7211* • 5 minutes from Ginza Station . . . **Ukiyo-e** woodblock prints . . . fine arts of old Japan.

Suntory Museum of Art • *Tokyo Suntory Bldg. 1–2–3 Moto-Akasaka, Minato-ku. Tel: 470–1073* • Minutes from Akasaka-Mitsuke Station . . . art from all ages of Japan.

Takanawa Art Museum • *Across from Shinagawa Station left of Pacific Hotel. Tel: 441–6363* • Arts and crafts of ancient Japan and China . . . located on old Mori estate . . . built in 1962 by Seibu corporation.

Tokyo Central Museum of Arts • *Ginza Boeki Bldg., 2–7–18 Ginza. Tel: 564–0711* • Short walk from Ginza station . . . Japanese and Western paintings.

Tokyo Metropolitan Art Gallery • *Ueno Park, Ueno Station. Tel: 821–3726* • Contemporary Japanese artists and their works.

Tokyo National Museum • *Ueno Park, Ueno Station. Tel: 822–1111* • Largest museum in Japan . . . 86,000 objects from Japan, China, and India . . . exhibits changed periodically . . . Horyuji Homotsukan (treasure house) contains over 300 treasured objects from Horyuji in Nara . . . Hyokeikan contains art objects since Meiji era . . . Japanese garden behind the complex with 3 tea pavilions and pond.

Transportation Museum • *1–25 Suda-cho, Chiyoda-ku. Tel: 251–8481* • Short walk from Akihabara Station in heart of "electric" district . . . all means of transportation in Japan.

Tsubouchi Memorial Theater Museum • *Waseda University. Tel: 203–4141, ext. 300* • Short walk from Waseda Station . . . items and documents connected with the stage . . . erected in 1928 to honor one of Japan's most famous dramatists and translator of Shakespeare . . . Dr. Tsubouchi . . . closed Sun. and Aug. to mid-Sept.

Yamatane Museum of Art • *2–10 Kabuto-cho, Nihombashi, Chuo-ku. Tel: 669–4056* • Near Kayabacho Station . . . Japanese art since 1868.

Kamakura

An hour south of Tokyo by train . . . located on Miura Peninsula in a scenic valley . . . bordered by lush mountains and Sagami Bay . . . a mini-Kyoto with some 65 historic Buddhist temples and 19 Shinto shrines in the area . . . seat of shogunate government from A.D. 1192–1333 . . . a residential town with the majority commuting to Tokyo for business . . . definitely worth a day's visit . . . famous for **Kamakura-bori,** articles of wood lacquered in black or vermillion . . . fine artistry and durability.

Ankokuronji • Temple founded in A.D. 1274 by Nichiren . . . site of his original hermitage . . . copy of his treatise ("On Public Peace") is a treasure of the temple . . . Nichiren exiled once and almost executed another time for annoying the authorities . . . finally died of old age in Tokyo.

Daibutsu • Great image of Buddha . . . located in Kotoku-in, Jodo-sect temple just a short walk from Kamakura Station . . . cast in bronze in A.D. 1252 and only Todaiji Daibutsu is larger . . . but this is considered the better work of art . . . Kamakura's most famous attraction.

Eishoji • Jodo-sect nunnery founded in 1636 by Lady Eisho, consort of Ieyasu Tokugawa . . . Ieyasu considered the maker of modern Japan and founder of Tokugawa shogunate.

Engakuji • Located near Kita-Kamakura Station . . . founded in A.D. 1282 . . . a Chinese priest was the first abbot here . . . Rinzai sect . . . formerly among 5 great Buddhist temples in Kamakura . . . earthquake of 1923 destroyed most of building . . . bronze bell largest in town . . . many valuable art treasures and ancient documents contained here.

Hase Kannon • Located near Daibutsu . . . Jodo-sect temple famous for **11-headed Kannon** (Goddess of Mercy) carved in A.D. 721 by priest Tokudo . . . said to be from same piece of camphor wood as Hase Kannon south of Nara . . . temple bell cast in A.D. 1264 . . . nice view from grounds of coastline.

Jochiji • Rinzai-sect temple founded in A.D. 1283 . . . once was among 5 great temples of Kamakura . . . severely damaged by 1923 earthquake . . . **Jizo image** said to be carved by master sculptor Unkei and dates from Kamakura period.

Jufukuji • Rinzai-sect temple founded in A.D. 1200 by Masako, wife of shogun Yoritomo Minamoto . . . originally ranked third among 5 great temples . . . tombs of Masako and her second son are in the cemetery.

Kakuonji • Sen-yuji school of Shingon sect . . . founded in A.D. 1218 and located just north of Kamakura Shrine . . . famous for **Kuro (black) Jizo** said to prevent fire . . . visited by many believers each year.

Kamakura Municipal Museum • Located to left of Hachiman Shrine . . . houses more than 40 Important Cultural Properties and other objects of art from Kamakura and Muromachi periods . . . excellent changing exhibits . . . nicely designed and well lit . . . lovely setting overlooking lotus ponds.

Kamakura Shrine • Located northeast of the station . . . commissioned by Emperor Meiji in 1869 and dedicated to Prince Morinaga, who was assassinated on this site by order of a brother of the first Ashikaga shogun in A.D. 1335 . . . after unsuccessful attempt to restore government to imperial rule.

Kenchoji • No. 1 of 5 great temples of Kamakura . . . headquarters of Kenchoji branch of Rinzai sect of Buddhism . . . located near Hachiman Shrine . . . founded in A.D. 1253 for a Chinese priest known as Daigaku-Zenji . . . by a Hojo regent . . . has bronze bell cast in 1255 and designated a National Treasure.

Komyoji • Founded in A.D. 1243 by Regent Hojo . . . considered imposing center of Jodo sect . . . located away from city along coast road to Zushi . . . contains many National Treasures . . . tombs of samurai and the ashes of my Japanese dog named Akai (red).

Samponji • Tendai-sect temple that predates shogunate period in Kamakura . . . allegedly founded in 8th century . . . was starting place for pilgrimages of 33 Kannon temples in Kanto district.

Tokeiji • Located near Jochiji at Kita-Kamakura Station . . . known as Divorce Temple . . . founded in A.D. 1285 as refuge for wives ill-treated by husbands and mothers-in-law . . . was nunnery until late 19th century.

Tomb of Yoritomo Minamoto • Remains of first Kamakura shogun . . . located on hillside northeast of the shrine . . . overlooks site of Yorimoto's palace.

Tsurugaoka Hachimangu Shrine • Second most famous monument in Kamakura . . . a pleasant walk from the station along cherry-tree-lined **Wakamiya-Oji Street** . . . founded in A.D. 1063 and dedicated to Emperor Ojin who reigned from A.D. 270–310 . . . actually moved to this site in 1191 . . . present structures date from 1828 . . . known for many National Treasures and Important Cultural Properties . . . also Chinese-style bridge one must conquer to enter precincts . . . famous **Yabusame** (archery contest) held here every Sept. 16 . . . one of Japan's most charming festivals . . . other minor shrines on grounds . . . **Kamakura Museum** and **Shirahatasha** (White Flag Shrine) also on grounds.

Zeniarai Benten • Money-cleansing shrine . . . small but popular shrine especially on snake days in Oriental zodiac . . . if you wash your money, it may stretch . . . that's the theory!

Nikko National Park

Located about 100 miles north of Tokyo . . . noted for beauty of mountains and lakes . . . splendid architecture of **Toshogu Shrine** and refreshing climate . . . a pleasant day's journey by tour bus or train . . . comfortable accommodations available for longer stays.

Daiyuin Mausoleum • Dedicated to Iemitsu Tokugawa, third Tokugawa shogun . . . architecture resembles Toshogu Shrine but on a smaller scale . . . full of elaborately carved gates . . . many National Treasures . . . a dragon ceiling by the Kano school.

Futaarasan Shrine • Between Daiyuin Masoleum and Toshogu Shrine . . . oldest building in area . . . dating from 1617 . . . dedicated to 3 Shinto deities revered for their virtues . . . allegedly brought prosperity to the country . . . founded by priest Shodo in A.D. 784 . . . Inner, Middle, and Head shrines . . . umbrella pine allegedly painted by Kobo Daishi, priest who founded Shingon sect . . . Shinto dances often performed here.

Kegon Falls • Most spectacular in Japan . . . located about 30 minutes from **Chuzenji spa** . . . frozen in winter . . . impressive sight . . . elevator down to base to observe.

Lake Chuzenji • Part of Nikko National Park . . . lies at foot of Mt. Nantai . . . year-round holiday resort . . . lined with pleasant hotels and ryokans . . . Chuzenji was temple founded here in A.D. 784 by priest Shodo . . . town and lake named after it . . . other lakes in district are Yunoko, Sugenuma, Marunuma, and Kirikomi-Karikomi . . . many interesting **spas.**

Mt. Nantai • Second highest peak in park, after Mt. Shirane . . . open to climbers from May 5 through Oct. 5 . . . path straight up takes about 5 hours . . . considered sacred mountain and pilgrims often begin at **Chugushi Shrine** (middle of **Futaarasan Shrine**) . . . at edge of crater is inner shrine of Futaarasan . . . as well as **Takin-o Shrine** at summit.

Nikko Botanical Gardens • Belong to Tokyo University . . . in garden of former Tamozawa Imperial Villa and covering about 25 acres . . . over 3000 Nikko alpine flora varieties . . . also **Nikko Museum** with exhibits of natural history and fine arts of the area.

Nikko-Yumoto Spa • Located on northern shore of Lake Yunoko, about 30 minutes from Chuzenji Spa . . . year-round resort noted for quiet surroundings . . . other spas in the park worth visiting are Kinugawa, Nasu (with 11 hot-spring resorts at foot of Nasu range), and Shiobara (also 11 hot-spring resorts along Hoki River gorge).

Rinnoji Temple • Located along main approach to Toshogu Shrine . . . said to have been founded in 9th century . . . belongs to Tendai sect of Buddhism . . . **Sambutsudo** is largest structure in Nikko . . . erected in 1648 President Ulysses S. Grant stayed at Hombo, abbot's residence, for over a week in July 1879 . . . cherry tree over 2 centuries old in front of main hall is designated a Natural Monument . . . **Futatsudo** or twin halls were founded in A.D. 848, similar to buildings on Mt. Hiei above Kyoto . . . they are called **Hokkedo** and **Jogyodo.**

Sacred Bridge • Crosses Daiya River parallel to Nikko Bridge . . . also known as **Mihashi** or **Shinkyo** (Divine Bridge) . . . used for ceremonial occasions . . . marks site where priest Shodo crossed the waters on backs of 2 serpents to reach summit of Mt. Nantai . . . original bridge built in 1636 for shogun and imperial messengers when visiting shrines . . . present one dates from 1907.

Toshogu Shrine • One of largest and most spectacular monuments in Japan . . . dedicated to Ieyasu Tokugawa by his grandson, the shogun Idemitsu, in 1636 . . . approach is up a broad flight of steps and under a huge granite torii . . . vermillion structures decorated in splendor . . . architecture is combination Shinto/Buddhist . . . often difficult for the senses to accept . . . in fact, some visitors consider it awful! . . . nonetheless, the shrine is filled with National Treasures . . . the shrine was almost destroyed at the time of Meiji Restoration . . . you can spend several hours here . . . try to do so early in the morning before crowds of domestic travelers and students enter . . . annual colorful festivals held at Toshogu Shrine on May 18 and Oct. 17 . . . processions of people in ancient costumes, sacred music and dances, and portable shrines carried back and forth.

Yokohama

Just 30 minutes southwest from Tokyo by train, slightly more by highway . . . noted for its fine harbor . . . port opened in 1859 and No. 3 in the country in goods and traffic . . . passenger port for Tokyo and northern Japan . . . as a city, not much to offer . . . rather unattractive and totally industrial . . . satellite to Tokyo in commerce and commuter population.

Chinatown • Believe it not, one of the major attractions, especially for visiting sailors . . . more than 70 restaurants and some 30 exotic shops.

Sankeien • Three Glens Garden . . . laid out by local businessman in purely Japanese style . . . contains many flowering trees as well as historic structures . . . 3-story pagoda more than 500 years old . . . **Choshukaku,** a tea-ceremony house allegedly built by Idemitsu, third Tokugawa shogun . . . old farmhouse from Gifu prefecture . . . and small temple brought from courtyard of Daitokuji in Kyoto . . . said to have been erected by Hideyoshi Toyotomi in 1592 to celebrate his mother's longevity.

Santondai • Large excavation uncovered in 1961 . . . artifacts said to date from Jomon Period (3000–2500 B.C.) and **Archaeological Mu-**

seum on the site has earthenware, stonework, metal goods, glass, bones, shells, etc. on display . . . very interesting dig in Minami ward.

Shomyoji • Buddhist temple of Shingon-Ritsu sect . . . founded in A.D. 1260 as family temple for Kanazawa clan . . . who ruled the area . . . famous for its 1296 **Miroku Bosatsu** and bronze bell cast in 1269 . . . recast 1301 . . . library has over 20,000 rare books . . . some National Treasures.

Sojiji • Soto sect of Zen Buddhism temple . . . one of two head monasteries . . . over 250 novitiates here . . . also high schools and colleges for girls on the premises . . . monastery originally founded in A.D. 1321 . . . present buildings date from 1911 . . . some friends and I spent a New Year's Eve here . . . it was mighty cold until we discovered a vendor selling bottles of hot sake behind the third shrine . . . everyone felt very cozy after that . . . we were encouraged to attend midnight service of sutra reading . . . the bell strikes 108 times . . . most interesting experience . . . the breakfast was a bit spare . . . but Zen teaches you to do without.

Yamashita Park • Extends from South Pier to Yamashita River . . . most attractive park in Yokohama . . . contains fountain presented by sister city San Diego . . . also **Hikawa Maru** ocean liner and **Marine Tower.**

Yamatemachi • Hills above city called **The Bluff** by foreigners . . . has international cemetery with remains of Westerners who contributed to Japan . . . also Motomachi shopping street and hill with good views of the harbor.

HOTELS

There are several dozen fine hotels in the Tokyo area, but the list below reflects the top names familiar to travel agents and tour operators in the U.S. Some hotels are very difficult to book, especially from March to May and Sept. to Nov. Hotel Okura—considered one of the finest hotels in the world—regularly receives guest bookings as much as a year in advance, and even its new addition is not sufficient to satisfy the many pampered travelers from all over the world who wish to stay here.

Those with the time and desire for a more intimate experience should consider **Minshuku,** private homes where foreign guests are treated to a true family experience. Minshuku reservations are available from any JNTO office in the U.S. and Japan. Chances are your "host" will meet you at the nearest train station, take you sightseeing, and engage you in plenty of English conversation. His wife will arrange your *futon* (floor bed), and serve two delicious meals (dinner and breakfast). It is somewhat like staying in a **ryokan** (traditional inn) but far more personal, and when you depart you will have made new friends.

★★★★★**Akasaka Prince Hotel** • *1–2, Kioi-cho, Chiyoda-ku, Tokyo 102. Tel: 234–1111. Cable: PRINCEAT TOKYO* • 761 rooms. (123 suites)
Facilities: New 40-story V-shaped high rise opened spring 1983. Designed by award-winning architect Kenzo Tange. All guest floors have an executive business meeting room. 12 restaurants including Le Trianon, Napoleon Lounge, steak house, cafe terrace, lobby lounge, and sushi, tempura, and Chinese restaurants. VIP services and Prince Club.
Manager: A. Nakai. *Reservations:* WESTIN INT'L.

★★★★**Capitol Tokyu Hotel** • *10–3, Nagata-cho 2–chome, Chiyoda-ku, Tokyo 100. Tel: (03) 581–4511. Cable: CAPITOL TOKYU-TEL. Telex: 24290* • 479 rooms (18 suites). Former Tokyo Hilton . . . situated adjacent to Sanno shrine . . . within walking distance of Akasaka district . . . well-known and popular property.
Facilities: Origami Coffee House. Keyaki Grill. Genji Japanese restaurant. Star Hill Chinese Restaurant. Tea Lounge. Lip Bar. Garden Cafe. Misao Lounge. Business Center. Banquet rooms.
General Manager: M. Nakajima. *Reservations:* Tokyu Int'l.

★★★★**Century Hyatt Tokyo** • *2–7–2 Nishi-Shinjuku, Shinjuku-ku, Tokyo. Tel: 349–0111, Cable: CENHYATT. Telex: J29411 CENHYATT* • 762 rooms.
Facilities: Lofty, 7-story atrium lobby. Regency club on 26th floor. Chenonceaux French restaurant. Hugo's Continental restaurant. Kamogawa Japanese food. Jade Garden Chinese cuisine. Boulogne coffee shop. Caterina Italian restaurant. Tradewind pub. Eau de Vie bar. Rhapsody nightclub. Samba disco. Stephanie coffee lounge.
Manager: Y. Murakawa. *Reservations:* HYATT INT'L.

★★★★★**Imperial Hotel** • *1–1–1 Uchisaiwai-cho, Chiyoda-ku, Tokyo. Tel: 504–1111. Cable: IMPHO TOKYO. Telex: 222–2346 IMPHO J* • 1133 rooms.
Facilities: New 31-story tower opened March 1983. Features 6 new restaurants, indoor swimming pool, sauna, and 70 boutiques in arcade. Also Fontainebleau French restaurant. Old Imperial Bar. Prunier. Nadaman Japanese restaurant. Peking Chinese cuisine. Nakata sushi bar.

Grillroom. Rainbow room and lounge. Tea ceremony room and garden
Manager: J. I. Inumaru. *Reservations:* SRS, UTELL.

★★★**Hotel Kayu Kaikan** ● *8–1 Sanban-cho, Chiyoda-ku, Tokyo
102. Tel: 230–1111. Cable: KAYUKAIKAN TOKYO. Telex: 232–3318*
● 128 rooms.
Facilities: Same management as Okura Hotel. Kasuga tempura and
teppanyaki restaurant. Lilac Room Continental restaurant. Ascot Bar.
Yamato Room. Celebrating a successful decade of service!
Manager: Y. Mochizuki. *Reservations:* Hotel Okura.

★★★★**Keio Plaza Inter-Continental Hotel** ● *2–1 Nishi Shinjuku, 2–chome, Shinjuku-ku, Tokyo 160. Tel: 344–0111. Cable: KEIO-
PLATEL Tokyo. Telex: J26874 KOPTEL* ● 1500 rooms.
Facilities: 20 restaurants. 9 bars. 30 party rooms on 42nd and 43rd
floors. Branches of Inagiku (tempura) and Okahan (sukiyaki) restaurants. Kyubei sushi bar. Ambrosia French cuisine. Prunier seafood.
Polestar spaceship lounge. Member's Only Club. Menuet restaurant/lounge
on 54th floor of adjacent Shinjuku-Mitsui building. Superb views of
Meiji Shrine and Imperial Gardens. South Tower's top 5 floors for ex-
ecutives.
Manager: S. Suzuki. *Reservations:* IHC.

★★★★★**Miyako Hotel** ● *1–50 Shiroganedai, 1–chome Minato-
ku, Tokyo 108. Tel: 447–3111. Cable: MIYAKO TKY. Telex: 242–3222
MYKTKY-J* ● 500 rooms.
Facilities: Elegant 12-story hotel designed by Minoru Yamasaki
and Togo Murano on 5½ acres. 8 restaurants and bars, all with lovely
garden views. Grand ballroom. Indoor swimming pool, sauna, and steam
baths. La Clef d'Or grillroom. Yamatoya-Sangen Japanese restaurant.
Shisen Chinese cuisine. Miyako cafe. Silver Hill coffee shop. Crystal
Lobby Lounge and Tudor main bar. Adding 4-story convention center.
Manager: Y. Saeki. *Reservations:* Distinguished Hotels.

★★★★★**New Otani Hotel & Tower** ● *4–1 Kioi-cho, Chiyoda-
ku, Tokyo. Tel: 265–1111. Cable: HOTELNEWOTANITOKYO. Telex:
J24719 HTLOTANI* ● 2047 rooms.
Facilities: 25 restaurants. 9 bars. 10-acre garden with 3 pavilions
serving barbecue specialties. Chinese revolving buffet on 17th floor.
Indoor and outdoor swimming pool, 4 tennis courts, 3 racquetball courts.
48 banquet rooms. 110 shops. Tour D'Argent restaurant.
Manager: K. Okada. *Reservations:* Hotel Otani.

★★★★★+**Hotel Okura** ● *10–4 Toranomon 2–chome, Minato-ku,
Tokyo 105. Tel: 582–0111. Cable: HOTELOKURA TOKYO. Telex:
J22790 HTLOKURA* ● 910 rooms.

Facilities: Considered one of Asia's finest hotels. Located across from American Embassy. Executive Service Salon (even prints meshi or namecards). 8 restaurants. 4 bars. Indoor and outdoor swimming pools. Health club. Japanese garden. La Belle Epoque French restaurant. Yamazato Teppanyaki Corner. Toh Ka Lin Chinese restaurant. Orchid Room (seafood restaurant). Continental Room. Camellia Corner coffee shop. Terrace restaurant. Bar Highlander and Starlight Lounge. Okura also manages several other fine hotels in Japan plus Hotel Okura Amsterdam. Affiliates are Hotel Shilla in Seoul and Halekulani in Honolulu.

Manager: T. Goto. *Reservations:* LHW, Distinguished Hotels, Hotel Okura.

★★★★**Hotel Pacific Meridien Tokyo** • *3–13–3 Takanawa, Minato-ku, Tokyo 108. Tel: 445–6711. Cable: HOTELPACIFIC TOKYO. Telex: J22861 HOTELPAC* • 954 rooms.

Facilities: Across from Shinagawa Station. Blue Pacific 30th-floor sky lounge. RoLan Chinese restaurant. Oshima Japanese cuisine. El Vencedor cellar bar. Boeuf d'Or sky restaurant. Kan-en Beijing buffet. Ukidono garden restaurant. Fontana swimming pool. Suomi sauna and steambaths.

Manager: H. Sato. *Reservations:* Meridien Hotels.

★★★★**Palace Hotel** • *1–1 Marunouchi 1–chome, Chiyoda-ku, Tokyo. Tel: 211–5211. Cable: PALACEHOTEL TOKYO. Telex: 222–2580 PALACE* • 407 rooms.

Facilities: Overlooking Imperial Palace Plaza. In center of business district. Crown restaurant. Grill Simpson. Swan terrace restaurant. Viking Room buffets. Wadakura Japanese restaurant. Zuirin Chinese (Shanghai) cuisine. Crown Lounge. Royal Bar. Pub restaurant.

Manager: M. Yoshihara. *Reservations:* UTELL.

★★★**Roppongi Prince Hotel** • *2–7 Roppongi 3-chome, Minato-ku, Tokyo 106. Tel: 03–587–1111. Telex: 242–7231 RPNPRH J* • 216 rooms. Located adjacent to Roppongi-Akasaka entertainment and shopping areas . . . also convenient for business travelers as many embassies, government offices, and companies are in this area.

Facilities: Italian and Japanese restaurants. Coffee Shop. Two bars. Indoor swimming pool. Meeting rooms.

Reservations: Prince Hotels.

★★★★**Shinagawa Prince Hotel** • *4–10–30 Takanawa, Minato-ku, Tokyo 108. Tel: 440–1111. Telex: 242–5178 SNAPRH J* • 1273 rooms. Located across from Shinagawa station. Unequalled sports facilities on the luxurious grounds . . . recommended for young, budget-minded travelers . . . not so expensive as other Tokyo hotels.

Facilities: Japanese, Chinese, American, and European restaurants and snack shops. 13 banquet halls. 2 ice skating rinks. Bowling center. 9 indoor tennis courts. Gym classes. Supermarket, book shop, bakery, drugstore on premises.

Manager: S. Kurosu. *Reservations:* PRINCE HOTELS INT'L.

★★★★**Shinjuku Prince Hotel** • *1–30–1 Kabukicho, Shinjuku-ku, Tokyo 160. Tel: 205–1111. Telex: 232–4733 SHIRPRH* • 571 rooms. Located in heart of Shinjuku entertainment district. Quite reasonably priced for location and facilities.

Facilities: Le Trianon and Chatelaine French restaurants. Bayern German food. Alitalia Italian restaurant. Several Japanese snack areas. Over 70 shops in Prince Promenade Pep and American Boulevard, which offers American-"inspired" merchandise (but don't expect to be able to afford anything!).

Manager: T. Haba. *Reservations:* PRINCE HOTELS INT'L.

★★★★**Takanawa Prince and New Takanawa Prince Hotel** • *3–13–1 Takanawa, Minato-ku, Tokyo 108. Tel: 447–1111. Cable: PRINSOTEL. Telex: 242–3232 TAKPRH* • 1510 rooms.

Facilities: New and older buildings on a 10-acre hilltop location across from Shinagawa Station. New 1000-room annex with international conference hall and 5000-person banquet hall. Slightly overgrown for modest tastes. Swimming pool and garden. Le Trianon French restaurant. Katsura steak house. Kokiden Chinese restaurant. Several other Japanese restaurants and snack areas. Member's Club night spot. Tea-ceremony house.

Manager: S. Furukawa. *Reservations:* PRINCE HOTELS INT'L.

★★★★★**Tokyo Hilton International** • *6–6–2 Nishi-Shinjuku, Shinjuku-ku, Tokyo 160. Tel: 344–5111. Cable: HILTELS, Tokyo. Telex: HILTON J2324515* • 842 rooms.

Facilities: Part of a high-rise complex of offices and shops, overlooking Shinjuku Central Park. Two blocks from Shinjuku Station. Fitness center, gym, sauna, indoor pool, and tennis courts with pro shop. Imari Restaurant, featuring displays of antique porcelain. Japanese restaurants surrounding traditional garden. Chinese restaurant, cafe, English-style pub, patisserie and cocktail lounges. Conference facilities (to accommodate up to 1800) and business center. Shopping arcade and Golden Key Club (for executives; almost a hotel-within-a-hotel).

Manager: R. Handl. *Reservations:* (Tokyo) 213–4053.

★★★★**Tokyo Prince Hotel** • *3–1 Shiba Park 3–chome, Minato-ku, Tokyo 105. Tel: 432–1111. Cable: HOTELPRINCE. Telex: 242–2488 TYOPRH* • 510 rooms.

Facilities: In the shadow of Tokyo Tower. Beaux Sejours French restaurant. Maronnier Chinese cuisine. Gotoku sushi and Fukusa tempura restaurants. Ascot bar. Prince Villa restaurant. Swimming pool. Several lounges.
Manager: T. Motoi. *Reservations:* WESTIN INT'L.

Kamakura

★★★**Kamakura Park Hotel** ● *33–6 Sakanoshita, Kamakura, Kanagawa Pref. 248. Tel: (0467) 25–5121* ● 41 rooms.
Facilities: Golf. Boating. Sailing. Beach. Riding. Skating.

Nikko National Park

★★★**Chuzenji Kanaya Hotel** ● *2482 Chugushi, Nikko, Tochigi Pref. 321–6. Tel: (0288) 5–0356. Cable: CHUZENJI KANAYA* ● 32 rooms.
Facilities: Boating. Sailing. Fishing. Closed Dec. to March.

★★★**Nikko Kanaya Hotel** ● *1300 Kami-Hatsuishi, Nikko, Tochigi Pref. 321–4. Tel: (0288) 4–0001. Cable: KANAYA NIKKO. Telex: 3544–451 KANAYA J* ● 82 rooms.
Facilities: Japanese garden. Swimming pool. Skating. Skiing.

★★★★**Nikko Lakeside Hotel** ● *2482 Chugushi, Nikko, Tochigi Pref. 321–6. Tel: (0288) 5–0321* ● 100 rooms.
Facilities: Japanese garden. Golf. Skating. Skiing. Boating. Sailing. Tennis. Beach. Fishing.

★★★★**Nikko Prince Hotel** ● *Shobugahama, Chugushi, Nikko, Tochigi Pref. 321–16. Tel: (0288) 5–0661* ● 60 rooms, 18 cottages.
Facilities: Tennis. Golf. Boating. Fishing. Swimming pool. Skiing. Skating. Restaurant. Lounge. Bar.

DINING

JAPANESE RESTAURANTS

Listed below are just a few of the taste experiences in Tokyo. There are so many restaurants that the specialty restaurants in major hotels are not included here (see hotel listings).

Akasaka Misono ● *In front of Akasaka TBS-kaikan. Tel: 583–3389* ● Known for teppanyaki garden . . . one of the first . . . expensive.

Ana ● *3–15–8 Soto Kanda, Chiyoda-ku. Tel: 253–3311* ● Serves snake in many forms.

Aoshima ● *Akasaka Sanno Grand Bldg. B1. Tel: 592–1533* ● Shabu shabu.

Au Bec Fin ● *CI Plaza 2–3–1, Kita Aoyama, Minato-ku. Tel: 470–5596* ● Kobe beef . . . teppanyaki . . . closes early.

Benihana of New York ● *1–1 Nihombashi, Muromachi, Chuo-ku. Tel: 571–9060* ● Teppanyaki . . . touristy.

Chinzan-so ● *2–10–8 Seikguchi, Bunkyo-ku. Tel: 943–1111* ● Garden restaurant in old estate . . . large grounds and imported fireflies.

Edogin ● *Tsukiji 4–chome, Chuo-ku. Tel: 541–9236* ● One of the oldest and best sushi places . . . convenient to the Kabuki-za and Tsukiji.

Furusato ● *3–4–1 Aobadai, Meguro-ku. Tel: 463–2310* ● Located at top of Dogenzaka hill in Shibuya . . . 300-year-old wooden house.

Goemon ● *1–1–26 Hon-ko Magome, Bunkyo-ku. Tel: 811–2015* ● 9-course *tofu* (bean curd) meals . . . reasonable.

Happo-en ● *1–1–1 Shiroganedai, Minato-ku. Tel: 443–3111* ● One of Tokyo's most traditional and famous restaurants . . . run by retired geisha.

Hassan ● *Roppongi 6–1–20, basement Denki Bldg. Tel: 403–9112* ● Looks like interior of Sukiya-zakuri (tea ceremony house) . . . shabu shabu.

Imaasa ● *Shimbashi Ekimae Bldg. 2nd floor. Tel: 572–5286* ● Known for excellent sukiyaki for over 8 decades . . . expensive.

Inakaya ● *Akasaka Social Bldg. 2nd floor. Tel: 586–3054* ● Robata-yaki . . . fish, meat, vegetables broiled on open hearth . . . also 2 Roppongi branches.

Inagiku • *Nihonbashi Kayabacho 2–6. Tel: 669–5501* • Known for great tempura . . . other branches throughout city . . . reasonable.

Kujiraya • *2–29–22 Dogenzaka, Shibuya-ku. Tel: 461–9145* • Whale meat only, in many forms.

Kushihachi • *Roppongi, 3–chome. 3rd floor of Kentucky Fried Chicken Bldg.* • Best yakitori in town . . . small and cozy . . . let chef Kato-san cook you the full course . . . U.S. presidents ate here.

Matsuri • *Roppongi 7–16–5, 3rd floor of Toda Bldg. Tel: 402–2570* • Popular yakitori restaurant . . . open late . . . try kushiyaki dishes.

Minokichi • *Roppongi Roi Bldg. Basement level. Tel: 404–0767* • Country-style cooking . . . specializes in Kyoto dishes . . . Kaiseki ryori at reasonable prices.

Mon Cher Ton Ton • *3–12–2 Roppongi, Seryana Bldg. Basement level. Tel: 402–1055* • An old favorite for Kobe beef . . . even served as sashimi.

Murakami Suppon Hompo • *4–2–2 Higashi Ueno, Taito-ku. Tel: 841–9831* • Specializes in turtle cuisine . . . if you feel adventurous.

Sasa No Yuki • *2–15–10 Negishi, Taito-ku. Tel: 873–1145* • Known for its many varieties of tofu . . . reasonable, even with sake.

Seryna • *3–12–2 Roppongi, Minato-ku. Tel: 402–1051* • Shabu shabu . . . open until 2 a.m.

Suehiro • *Ginza 4–chome, Churo-ku. Tel: 562–0591* • Known for Japanese beef in steaks or sukiyaki . . . familiar with tourists . . . many branches throughout Kanto plain.

Tenichi • *Ginza 6–chome, Chuo-ku. Tel: 571–1271* • Best and most popular of tempura restaurants . . . branches all over town.

Tesshu-an • *3–2 Negishi, Taito-ku. Tel: 874–3893* • Noodles.

To Rigin • *5–5–7 Ginza, Chuo-ku. Tel: 571–3333* • Best yakitori in town . . . good prices, but only cash accepted.

Tung • *3–20–8 Akasaka, 2nd floor Rinsui Bldg. Tel: 586–7092* • Considered a samurai barbecue restaurant . . . decorated with swords.

Yabu Soba • *2–10 Kanda Awaji-cho, Chiyoda-ku. Tel: 251–0287* • Only fresh soba in broth.

Zakuro • *TBS Kaikan Bldg. 3–3 Akasaka 5–chome, Minato-ku. Tel: 582–6841* • A favorite with tourists . . . known for excellent shabu shabu . . . expensive.

NON-JAPANESE RESTAURANTS

Ashoka • *9–18, Ginza 7–chome, Chuo-ku. Tel: 572–2377* • Tandoori chicken and eye-watering curries.

Bofinger • *Roppongi 3–10–5, Minato-ku. Tel: 479–1123* • Nouvelle cuisine . . . related to restaurant of same name in Paris . . . so they say.

Castle Praha • *Roppongi 6–chome 2–31, Minato-ku. 2nd floor of Tokyo Nissan Bldg. Tel: 405–2831* • Czechoslovakian decor and cuisine . . . left from EXPO in Osaka . . . very popular with foreign community.

Chardonnay • *16–15, Roppongi 3–chome, Minato-ku. Tel: 584–0954* • Cozy Mediterranean atmosphere . . . French menu.

Double Ax • *10–4, 3–chome Roppongi. Koshi Bldg. Basement level. Tel: 401–7384* • Greek chef . . . Greek food . . . Greek atmosphere.

Gandhara • *8–13, Ginza 5–chome, Ginza Five Star Bldg. 4th floor. Tel: 574–9289* • Only Pakistani restaurant in town . . . shish kebab.

Gaslight • *5–7, Azabudai 3–chome, Minato-ku. Tel: 585–3390* • Victorian decadence and fat slices of American roast beef . . . next door to Russian Embassy.

Henry Africa • *Hanatsubaki Bldg. 2nd floor, Roppongi. Tel: 405–9868* • All the way from San Francisco . . . branches in Akasaka, Harajuku, Ginza, and Shinjuku . . . if you can stand the rhino horns and Tiffany lamps.

Indonesia Raya • *Yurakucho 1–chome, Chiyoda-ku. Tel: 591–0897* • Across from Hibiya Theatre . . . sate and mild curries . . . branch at Renga-Dori, Shimbashi.

Jade Garden • *1–8 Shinbashi, 4–chome, Minato-ku. Tel: 431–6701* • Cantonese cuisine straight from Hong Kong . . . wonderful.

Les Vincennes • *Shibuya 1–16, Metro Plaza Bldg. 1st floor, Shibuya-ku. Tel: 406–0675* • French cuisine from Japanese chef . . . with 15 years experience.

Lohmeyer German Restaurant • *3–14 Ginza 5–chome, Chuo-ku. Tel: 571–5024* • 3rd generation establishment . . . frequented by famous German spy Sorge during the war . . . branch in Akasaka.

Maxim's de Paris • *3–1 Ginza 5–chome, Sony Bldg. Basement level, Chuo-ku. Tel: 572–3621* • A copy of the real thing . . . French chef and Maitre d'hotel . . . expensive . . . fresh delicacies flown in daily.

Nancy Chin Ma's Chinese Restaurant • *Chateau Mita, 7–1, Mita 2–chome, Minato-ku. Tel: 453–7092* • Very chi-chi for Chinese food . . . she has written a book or 2.

New Hama Steak House • *2–10, Roppongi 7–chome, Minato-ku. Tel: 403–1717* • Fairly reasonable . . . for good steaks.

Nicola's • *12–6, 3–chome Roppongi, 3rd floor Roppongi Plaza, Minato-ku. Tel: 401–6936* • A favorite hang-out for pizza, pasta, and other Italian specialties.

Prunier • *Tokyo Kaikan, 2–1 Marounouchi 3–chome, Chiyoda-ku. Tel: 215–2111* • Excellent for fresh fish . . . open Sun.

Red Baron • *7–11 Akasaka, 3–chome, Minato-ku. Tel: 583–8860* • Owned and operated by American named Ken . . . hamburgers and steaks.

Rengaya • *Kashima Bldg., 7–19 Ginza 6–chome, Chuo-ku. Tel: 573–0456* • Cuisine of Lyons . . . supposedly supervised by Paul Bocuse . . . branches in Shibuya and Setagaya.

Russian Restaurant Volga • *5–14, Shiba Koen 3–chome, Minato-ku. Tel: 433–1766* • Decor straight from Catherine the Great . . . different and fun . . . I spent a memorable Christmas Eve here once.

Sanno Chinese Restaurant • *12–4 Nagata-cho 2–chome, Chiyoda-ku. Tel: 581–2451* • Great for banquets.

Shido • *TBS Kaikan Bldg., 3–3 Akasaka 5–chome, Minato-ku. Tel: 582–5891* • One of the city's first . . . and best . . . French restaurants.

Mr. Stamp's Wine Garden • *Kyowa Bldg. 1st floor, 4–2 Roppongi 4–chome, Minato-ku. Tel: 479–1390* • Al Stamp serves good, reasonable food.

Tokyo Swiss Inn • *Tokyo Bed Bldg., 1–16 Roppongi 4–chome, Minato-ku. Tel: 584–0911* • There are others now . . . but this was the original.

NIGHTLIFE

Tokyo is a nighttime town. When the lights go on, every section of the vast city assumes a new character. No one, it seems, ever goes home until well after midnight when the last trains depart. Why go home to your six-tatami room when you can walk the Ginza, famous for its network of neon, have a few beers, or sake, and plenty of delicious snacks? Businessmen head straight for their favorite drinking establishments, many of which are "bottle clubs" (where the Suntory whiskey is under lock and key until the next visit). Young couples seek the multitude of coffee shops, where the lights are low and the music usually very American. Top management frequents the expensive geisha houses to entertain or be entertained. There are fabulous nightclubs a la the Copacabana, hostess bars, discos, and cocktail lounges with romance and views atop every major hotel. You'll also find many cultural activities, some of which begin around 11 a.m. and last until midnight.

Bunraku, ningyo joruri, is Japan's puppetry theater that has been a tradition for over four centuries. Beautifully handcrafted dolls, manipulated by live puppeteers dressed in black, tell tales of sacrifice, heroism, *giri-ninjo* (passion in conflict with duty), and loyalty, often with charming vignettes of comic relief. The dolls weigh from 10 to 50 pounds each and assume mesmerizing life and character on the stage to the accompaniment of lute (*biwa*) and *shamisen* players. Home base of traditional bunraku is the **Asahi-za Theatre** in Osaka, but the troupe makes four annual appearances at **Tokyo's National Theatre.** This particular troupe has been designated an Important Cultural Treasure (*bunka-zai*), and recently made a very popular appearance at the Japan Society's headquarters in New York City.

Kabuki is Japan's most famous theatrical tradition and evolved from a dance during the Tokugawa Period (A.D. 1603–1867). The verb *kabuku* means to deviate from the normal custom and do something absurd, and that is what kabuki actors do: they assume the costume and mannerisms of women. For this is an all-male world and certain players pride themselves on their *onagata* or female roles. Kabuki themes are either historical (with very complicated plots), or everyday problems of the commonfolk (sex, sin, money, relatives, and the like). The plays are performed on a revolving stage with *hanimachi,* an extension into the left-hand side of the audience proper. Entrances and exits along the hanimachi are most dramatic, with much foot stamping, preening, and expected audience approval.

Kabuki is best enjoyed at the famed **Kabukiza Theatre** (4–12–5 Gina, Chuo-ku, Tokyo. Tel: 541–3131) for about 25 days a month from 11 a.m. until about 10 p.m. The theater is a huge structure, rebuilt after the war in the traditional style, and the seats are less expensive the higher you climb. At all levels, there are restaurants and foodstalls; snacking between acts is part of the fun. The two leaders of Grand Kabuki are **Nakamura Kanzaburo XVII** and **Nakamura Utaemon VI,** both designated Living National Treasures by the Japanese government. A few years ago, we also had the thrill to watch veteran Koshiro VIII relinquish the stage name he inherited from his father and pass it to his oldest son (becoming himself Hakuo), while Somegoro took over the name Koshiro IX. Kabuki actors belong to several traditional clans, whether real sons or adopted, and the passing of names is like a religious rite.

Because Kabukiza is so huge (there are other theaters but this is the best), tickets are usually available at the box office for same-day performances. However, remember that the stars come forth as the day grows long (the program is published in the daily newspapers) so gauge your attendance accordingly. Only true kabuki nuts spend all day in the theater.

Noh are masked dramas that developed from **bungaku,** a court dance popular during the Heian Period. There are over 200 different dramas extant in Noh repertory today, and they are divided into five different categories. There are god pieces (*kami mono*), male pieces (*otoko mono*), female pieces (*onna mono*), mental derangement or frenzy pieces (*kyoran* or *kurui mono*), and demon pieces (*oni mono*). Noh is characterized as "symbolic, solemn, static, yet elegant and graceful." It is not to everyone's taste. Noh is performed regularly in Tokyo, Kyoto, and Osaka; if you enjoy interesting masks and beautiful costumes, check the local papers.

Shimpa and **shingeki** are more modern Japanese dramas, originating in the late 19th century as a rival to kabuki. But the traditional arts of both kabuki and bunraku have enjoyed a resurgence in popularity in the past few decades and well deserve their National Treasure status.

The **geisha** house is alive and well in Japan, but you must be introduced properly through a regular patron. Japanese and multinational corporations all have their own accounts at the best and oldest establishments, and some Kyoto night tours will feature dinner at a geisha house (but rest assured it is not a traditional one). From time to time, Western women are included in the "parties," but most find them rather dull—what with antiquated parlor-type games and such.

Hostess bars are everywhere and heavily advertised in tourist handouts. If you are planning to barhop as a couple, inquire first because you may be both embarrassed and impoverished at the end of the evening. **Shinjuku** area is known for its homosexual bars as well as places operated by the Japanese mafia. It is one of the most swinging areas in the city, and quite overwhelming in the evening. Tokyo is one of the safest cities in the world (weapons are unlawful to private citizens), but watch your purses and the other paraphernalia anyway. Nobody's perfect.

Tokyo has its share of Las Vegas-style nightclubs, where you can dine, drink, be cuddled by a hostess, and watch a cabaret. The **Copacabana** (3–6–4 Akasaka, Minato-ku. Tel: 585–5811) is one of the oldest and considered the flashiest. Also in the neighborhood are the **Golden Getsusekai** (3–10–4 Akasaka, Minato-ku. Tel: 584–1151), which means Golden Moon World; the **Mikado** (2–14–6 Akasaka, Minato-ku. Tel: 583–1101), which has bare-breasted beauties swinging from the ceiling; and the **New Latin Quarter** (2–13–8 Nagata-cho, Akasaka, Minato-ku. Tel: 581–1326) in the basement of the Hotel New Japan. You could spend a month's salary within a few blocks, as these entertainment emporia have stiff cover and drink charges. Nightclub hostesses are among the better paid employees in Japan (many of them are foreign).

All-girl musical reviews are very popular in Japan, especially the famed **Takazuraka,** whose home base is near Osaka. However, the troupe plays Tokyo frequently at the **Hibiya Theatre** (across from the back door of the Imperial Hotel). Another group can be found at the **Kokusai Gekijo** (International Theater) near Ueno Station in Asakusa. Ueno is also the site of the beautiful and acoustically sound Festival Hall **(Bunka Kaikan)** where serious musicians perform often. In addition to the National Symphony, I have enjoyed the Juilliard Quartet, the late Arthur Rubinstein, and native-son Seiji Ozawa conduct Mahler's Ninth with full chorus. Maestro Ozawa is a Japanese citizen, although he was actually born in Shanghai, where his father was a physician during the occupation of the 1930s.

There are many other fine public halls where serious music is performed throughout Japan, but Bunka Kaikan offers a very special experience.

INLAND SEA

INLAND SEA IN A CAPSULE

Called Seto Naikai (Sea with Channels) by the Japanese . . . extends from Bay of Osaka on the east to Shimonoseki Straits on the west . . . actually 5 seas linked together and very shallow . . . geologists believe volcanic eruptions caused both Shikoku and Kyushu to separate from Honshu . . . thus forming the boundaries of the "sea" . . . there are more than 1000 small islands in the sea . . . enhancing its natural beauty . . . designated a national park in 1934 . . . water traffic continual from such major ports as Osaka, Kobe, Hiroshima, Beppu, Matsuyama, and Takamatsu . . . although smaller ports are also accessible . . . hydrofoils, day- and overnight-ferries available . . . best times for an Inland Sea voyage are summer and early autumn.

WHAT TO SEE AND DO

Akashi • Located on Akashi Straits separating Honshu from Awaji . . . Akashi Park has remains of former castle built in 1619 . . . **Gesshoji** (temple) on summit of Hitomaru Hill marks 135th-degree meridian by which Japan standard time is calculated . . . **Kakinomoto Shrine** here dedicated to 7th-century poet celebrated for works in one of Japan's greatest classics, *The Man-yoshu* . . . also **astronomical science museum** halfway up Hitomaru Hill.

Awaji • Largest island in the Inland Sea . . . accessible from Kobe by hydrofoil or ferry . . . largest city is Sumoto noted for production of buttons as well as onions and dried sardines . . . **Onaruto Bridge** linking Awaji to Shikoku . . . spans the famous whirlpools that roar through the Naruto Straits . . . **Onaruto Bridge Commemorative Hall** and **Whirlpool Science Hall** . . . also **Awaji Puppet Joruri Hall** . . .

500-year-old puppet theater, designated an important cultural property
. . . **Senkoji,** a temple of the Koyasan-Shingon sect stands atop Mt.
Senzan . . . dedicated to 1000-handed Kannon, Goddess of Mercy . . .
Goshikihama (5-colored beach) on west coast has lovely views . . .
touring buses (in Japanese only) cover island from March to Nov.

Himeji • Former castle town located in heart of Harima Plain, near
the Inland Sea . . . **Shirasagijo** or **Hakurojo** (Egret Castle) is considered to be the finest feudal structure in Japan . . . built by shogun
Hideyoshi in 1581 . . . became residence of a General Ikeda . . . **Na-
goyama Cemetery** has large pagoda erected in 1960 . . . contains ashes
of Lord Buddha . . . presented on a 1954 visit of late Indian Prime
Minister Nehru . . . Mt. Shosha has **Enkyoji** . . . temple of the Tendai sect founded in A.D. 966 and 27th of 33 holy temples in western
Japan . . . popular on the pilgrim route.

Hiroshima • Transportation center of western Inland Sea . . . site
of the first atomic bomb that was dropped at 8:15 a.m. on Aug. 6,
1945, because of extensive shipping and industry . . . **Atomic Bomb
Dome** is probably the world's most sobering monument . . . **Peace
Memorial Park** contains a museum, cenotaph for A-bomb victims designed by Kenzo Tange, 2 bridges over the Motoyasu River designed
by noted sculptor Isamu Noguchi, and auditorium . . . views of the
site can be seen from Hijiyama Park . . . a **Memorial Cathedral** for
world peace was constructed in 1954 under the guidance of a German
priest . . . **Hiroshima Castle** first built in 1589 was reconstructed in
1958 . . . **Shukkeien** (landscape garden in miniature) on the Ota River
is registered as a Scenic Place.

Iwakuni • Castle-town founded by the Kikkawa family in 1603 . . .
Castle destroyed in 1615 by Tokugawa shogun Idemitsu . . . finely
reconstructed in 1962 in southern European style . . . situated on top
of Shiroyama (hill) with fine views of the bay . . . **Kitani Bridge**
constructed in 1673 by another member of the Kikkawa family . . .
resembles an abacus, the traditional Japanese calculator . . . so called
Sorobanbashi by locals.

Miyajima • **Shrine Island** in Hiroshima Bay . . . red torii (gate)
that leads to **Itsukushima Shrine** is one of most photographed monuments in Japan . . . dedicated to three daughters of Susano-o-no-Mi-
koto, ancient Shinto deity and records date from A.D. 811 . . . torii is
largest in Japan and was erected in 1875 . . . in addition to Main Shrine
only entered by priests, complex encompasses **heiden** (offering hall),
haiden (hall of worship) and **haraiden** (purification hall) all designated
National Treasures . . . also **asazaya** (morning prayer room) with masks

and costumes on display . . . **senjokaku** (hall of one thousand mats) commissioned in 1587 by shogun Hideyoshi Toyotomi and new **shoso-in** (treasure hall) with over 4000 important objects . . . bronze and stone lanterns within inner shrine are beautiful at night when lit . . . colorful festivals here each year on June 17 and July 18 (both by the lunar calendar).

Okayama • Cultural center of Chugoku District and castle-town founded in 16th century . . . noted for production of Bizen stoneware . . . also **Korakuen Park,** one of three most famous gardens in Japan . . . designed by a local daimyo in 1700 after the Enshu school of landscape gardening . . . has tea ceremony pavilions, ponds, water-falls, and trees to match each season . . . Okayama is station for visiting Kurashiki, about 10 miles from Inland Sea coast . . . a flourishing rice storehouse town in feudal times, the old granaries have been made into shops and museums of folkcraft, archaeology, history, and small hotels . . . the new **Ohara Art Gallery** houses a fine collection of European, Persian, Turkish, Egyptian, and Japanese art . . . the **Old Quarter** is a popular tourist attraction.

Shimonoseki • Port at extreme western end of Inland Sea . . . lies across Kammon Straits from Kita-kyushu . . . weekly ferry service between here and Pusan, South Korea . . . famous battle of Dannoura took place along the beach in 1185 when Taira clan was literally exterminated by the Minamotos . . . another battle occurred in 1864 when Dutch, English, French, and American warships forced the reopening of the straits and provoked the Meiji restoration.

Shodo Island • Second largest of the small islets dotting the Inland Sea . . . lies off coast of Shikoku from Takamatsu . . . noted for olive groves and stone quarries . . . **Kankakei** (cold and misty gorge) is a popular tourist attraction, especially when autumn colors are brilliant.

Tomonoura • Considered the most beautiful bay in the Inland Sea National Park . . . also famed for **Homeishu** (sake) and **Abuto Kannon Temple** dedicated to Goddess of Mercy . . . stands on craggy spot above the sea . . . lovely view . . . port for Fukuyama whose 17th-century fortress was rebuilt in 1966 . . . Japan's only museum specializing solely in footgear is here.

HOTELS

Hiroshima

★★★**Hotel Hiroshima Grand** • *4–4 Kami-Hatchobori, Naka-ku. Tel: (0822) 27–1313. Cable: GRANDHOTEL HIROSHIMA. Telex: 652–666 HGH* • 385 rooms.
Facilities: Dining room. Coffee shop. Chinese and Japanese restaurants.
Manager: K. Koyanagi. *Reservations:* JAL.

★★**Hiroshima Riverside Hotel** • *7–14, Kaminobori-cho, Naka-ku. Tel: (0822) 28–1251. Telex: 652–554 HRH J* • 92 rooms.
Facilities: Western and Japanese restaurants. Bar. Entertainment.
Manager: S. Sakikoyama. *Reservations:* Direct.

★★★**Hiroshima Tokyu Inn** • *3–17 Komachi, Naka-ku. Tel: (0822) 244–0109* • 286 rooms.
Facilities: Dining room. Bar.

★★**Hotel New Hiroden** • *14–9 Osuga-cho, Minami-ku. Tel: (0822) 63–3456. Cable: HOHIRODEN. Telex: 653–884* • 353 rooms.
Facilities: Dining room. Bar.
Manager: T. Sakai. *Reservations:* Direct.

Kurashiki

★★★**Ivy Square Hotel** • *2–7 Honmachi* • 180 rooms . . . located in Old Quarter near toy museum.

★★★**Kurashiki Kokusai Hotel** • *1–44 Chuo 1-chome. Tel: (0864) 22–5141. Cable: KURAHOTEL. Telex: 5933–258 KKHTL* • 70 rooms.
Facilities: Dining room. Grillroom. Coffee shop.
Manager: T. Kishimoto. *Reservations:* JAL.

★★★**Mizushima Kokusai Hotel** • *4–20, Mizushima-Aoba-cho. Tel: (0864) 44–4321* • 74 rooms.
Facilities: Dining room. Bar. Tea-ceremony room. Tennis.
Manager: H. Nouno. *Reservations:* Direct.

Okayama

★★★**Hotel New Okayama** • *1–25, 1–chome. Tel: (0862) 23–8211.* *Cable: HOTELNEWOKAYAMA* • 82 rooms.
Facilities: Dining room. Grillroom. Bar.
Manager: T. Kobayashi. *Reservations:* Direct.

★★★**Okayama Kokusai Hotel** • *1–16 4–chome, Kadota Honmachi. Tel: (0862) 73–7311. Cable: OKAKOKU. Telex: 5922–669 OKAKOK* • 194 rooms.
Facilities: Western, Chinese, and Japanese cuisine. Bar. Swimming pool.
Manager: H. Otani. *Reservations:* Direct.

★★★**Okayama Plaza Hotel** • *116 Hama 703. Tel: (0862) 72–1201* • 85 rooms.
Facilities: Dining room. Tearoom. Golf. Boating. Beach.
Manager: Y. Fujiwara. *Reservations:* Direct.

★★★**Okayama Royal Hotel** • *2–4 Ezu-cho. Tel: (0862) 54–1155* • 198 rooms.
Facilities: Western, Chinese, and Japanese cuisine. Bar. Sauna.
Manager: S. Miwa. *Reservations:* Direct.

Shimonoseki

★★★**Shimonoseki Tokyu Inn** • *4–4–1 Takezaki-cho, Shimonoseki. Tel: (0832) 33–0109. Telex: 6823–15* • 128 rooms.
Facilities: Restaurant. Coffee shop. Bar.
Manager: T. Kishi. *Reservations:* Direct.

KYUSHU

KYUSHU IN A CAPSULE

Southernmost island in Japan's archipelago . . . third largest and connected to Honshu by 2 railway tunnels, a highway tunnel, and a suspension bridge over Kammon Straits . . . southeastern section considered to be "cradle" of Japanese civilization . . . Stone Age finds . . . mythical figures who descended from heaven here to parent first Emperor in 7th century B.C. . . . mountainous in central area . . . boasts world's largest volcano and several national parks . . . famous for sulfur springs and beautiful seacoasts . . . was gateway for ideas and influence from China and Paekche, Korea's southern kingdom . . . also target of Mongol invasions in late 13th century . . . island known for historic kilns in Karatsu, Okachi-yama, Arita, Mikawachi, and Bizen . . . north, central, and southern areas vary from industrial to subtropical with colorful scenery . . . 8 prefectures in Kyushu, now including neighboring Okinawan islands.

FUKUOKA

WHAT TO SEE AND DO

Fukuoka Art Museum ● Second largest in Japan . . . beautiful new building houses over 4000 works from both East and West . . . don't miss.

Fukuoka Castle ● Completed in 1607 for Kuroda clans . . . only a gate and turret survive . . . designated Place of Historical Importance.

FUKUOKA IN A CAPSULE

Kyushu's largest city (over 1.25 million inhabitants) and commercial capital . . . city divided by Naka River—Fukuoka proper is on the west bank while Hakata occupies the eastern side . . . was chief trading port of Japan in ancient times . . . scene of 2 attempted invasions by Kublai Khan . . . in A.D. 1274 and 1281 . . . second attempt ended in disaster because typhoon (kamikaze or divine wind) appeared and destroyed entire Mongolian fleet . . . modern city is most industrial in all Kyushu, producing textiles, electrical appliances, etc. . . . less than 7 hours by Shinkansen (super-speed train) from Tokyo . . . main train station is in Hakata . . . ferry service departs daily between Hakata and Pusan, South Korea.

Hakata Harbor • Considered one of most modern in Kyushu . . . located at mouth of Naka River . . . large ships connect to ports all over the world . . . smaller ones take sightseers to neighboring islands.

Hakozaki Hachiman Shrine • Shinto shrine founded in year A.D. 923 . . . one of most noted Hachiman shrines in Japan . . . although gate and main building are 16th century . . . shrine noted for many annual events including **hojo-e,** the setting free of captured pigeons during a religious service.

Higashi (East) Park • Monument commemorates attempted Mongol invasions of A.D. 1274 and 1281 . . . bronze statues of Emperor Kameyama and priest Nichiren (1222–82), founder of Nichiren sect of Buddhism.

Higashi Nakasu • Amusement quarter of Fukuoka . . . located between Naka and Hakata rivers . . . entertainment and restaurant facilities . . . very colorful in the evening.

Kashii • Location of **Kashii Shrine,** dedicated to Emperor Chuai and his Empress in 1801 . . . Important Cultural Property.

Kinryuji Temple • Contains tomb of noted Chinese classicist and herbalist Kaibara A.D. (1630–1714), said to have contributed much to the society of his time.

Nishi (West) Park • Located on Arato Hill, about 3 miles from Hakata station . . . noted for some 4000 *sakura* (cherry trees) in spring . . . fine views of Genkai Nada Sea.

Ohori Park • Located on the site of outer moats of former Fukuoka Castle . . . large lake with 3 islands connected by bridges . . . huge sundial.

Shofukuji • Temple founded in 1195 and boasts longest affiliation with Zen Buddhism in all Japan . . . actually belongs to Myoshinji School of Rinzai sect . . . temple built by priest Eisai (A.D. 1141–1215) who introduced Zen doctrines (and tea) into Japan after 4 years of study in China . . . temple said to have been sponsored by Yoritomo Minamoto, the first shogun of Japan, who established a long precedent of shoguns involved in Zen and the tea ceremony.

Sumiyoshi Shrine • Shinto shrine dedicated to guardians of sailors . . . grounds have fine old trees and view of Naka River . . . main shrine restored in 1623 and designated Important Cultural Property.

Tenjin • Largest shopping and business center in Kyushu . . . two large department stores . . . also amusement and nightlife area.

Uminonakamichi • A 7-mile stretch of sandy beach along Hakata Bay . . . runs from Fukuoka to Saitozaki . . . ferries cross the bay for tourists.

Environs

Futsukaichi • Fashionable spa about 20 minutes by train from Hakata . . . district famous for associations with Michizane Sugawara, famous Chinese scholar in court of Emperor Daigo . . . was exiled to Kyushu in A.D. 901 because of political rivalries . . . devoted himself to study until death in 903 . . . considered guardian of literature and revered by schoolchildren all over Japan . . . **Dazaifu Shrine** (15 mins. by bus from Futsukaichi station) established in 905 and dedicated to Michizane Sugawara . . . full of *ume* (plum blossoms) that are said to have followed him into exile . . . present shrine dates from 1590 . . . 2 colorful festivals here Sept. 23–25 and Jan. 7 . . . see also **Kanzeonji** . . . Buddhist temple of Tendai sect . . . originally founded in 746 to be largest Buddhist center in western Japan.

Genkai Quasi-National Park • Marine park in Genkai Nada Sea . . . extends over 50 miles between Fukuoka and Karatsu . . . encompassing white sandy beaches, *kuro matsu* (Japanese black pines) and some 20 coastal islands . . . midway is **Keya-no-Oto** (Great cave of Keya) . . . huge rock projecting into the sea with grotto . . . boat rides available inside . . . park is popular recreation area and beach resort.

Karatsu • Chief port of communication with Korea in ancient times . . . base for exploring Genkai Quasi-National Park from eastern end . . . known for **Karatsu-yaki** . . . ceramics made as early as 16th century for use in tea ceremony . . . also **Kinshoji** . . . Rinzai-sect Buddhist temple where Monzaemon Chikamatsu, Japan's most noted playwright, said to have been a novitiate.

Kita-Kyushu • Industrial town and port linked to Honshu by suspension bridge over Kammon Straits . . . also 3 tunnels . . . one used exclusively by the Shinkansen and second only to the Simplon tunnel between Italy and Switzerland in length . . . **Mekari Park** on Cape Mekari has **Peace Pagoda** donated by Burmese government in 1958 . . . for repose of souls from World War II dead . . . **Mekari Shrine** said to date from 3rd century when Empress Jingu returned from Korea . . . Shinto ceremony takes place here in the new year . . . just south of the city is **Hobashira Natural Park** . . . cable car to summit of Mt. Hobashira offers views of area and local steel works.

Kurume • Former castle town of Arima clan located on Chikugo River . . . Known for production of *kurume-gasuri,* cotton cloth with "splashed" patterns, and *rantai,* lacquerware made from split bamboo or wicker . . . also **Suitengu Shrine** on the river . . . dedicated to Emperor Antoku and founded in 1185 . . . thought to offer protection from water calamities . . . counterpart in Nihombashi, Tokyo . . . festivals held here in early May and Aug.

HOTELS

★★★★**Hakata Miyako Hotel** • *2–1–1 Hakataeki Higashi, Hakata-ku. Tel: (092) 441–3111. Cable: HAMIHO J* • 300 rooms.
Facilities: 2 Japanese restaurants. Bars. Lounge.
Manager: K. Hirao. *Reservations:* Miyako Hotels.

★★★**Hakata Tokyu Hotel** • *1–16–1 Tenjin Chuo-ku. Tel: (092) 781–7111. Cable: HAKATATOKYUTEL. Telex: 723–295* • 266 rooms. 168 rooms in annex.
Facilities: Dining room. 24-hour cafe. Bar.
Manager: N. Kubo. *Reservations:* UTELL.

★★★+**Kitakyushu Prince Hotel** • *3–1 Higashimagari-machi, Yahatanishi-ku, Kitakyushu-shi, Fukuoka 806. Tel: 093–631–1111* • 220 Rooms. First Prince Hotel in Kyushu . . . opened April 1989 . . .

designed as a city-resort hotel with athletics area, indoor and outdoor swimming pools, 23 tennis courts, and ice skating rink.

Facilities: French, Japanese, and Chinese restaurants. Patio coffee shop. Banquet hall.

Reservations: Prince Hotels.

★★★★**New Otani Hakata** • *Watanabe-Dori, Chuo-ku. Tel: (092) 714–1111. Telex: 726–567.* • 436 rooms.

Facilities: Continental, Chinese, and Japanese restaurants. Buffet. 3 bars. Indoor swimming pool. 34 shops.

Manager: K. Sugiura. *Reservations:* New Otani.

★★★**Nishitetsu Grand Hotel** • *2–6–60 Daimyo, Chuo-ku. Tel: (092) 771–7171. Telex: 723351 NGHJ* • 308 rooms.

Facilities: 4 restaurants. Coffee shop. 2 bars. 2 cocktail lounges. Swimming pool.

Manager: F. Miyata. *Reservations:* JAL.

★★★**Tokyo Dai-Ichi Hotel Fukuoka** • *2–18, Nakasu 5–chome, Hakata-ku. Tel: (092) 281–3311. Telex: 724–823* • 221 rooms.

Facilities: Japanese, Chinese, and Ikesu restaurants. Coffee shop.

Manager: T. Maruhashi. *Reservations:* Tokyo Dai-Ichi.

KAGOSHIMA

KAGOSHIMA IN A CAPSULE

Sometimes called the "Naples of the Orient" . . . 29 generations of the Shimazu clan ruled this castle-town for 695 years . . . until the Meiji restoration in 1868 . . . city situated on Kagoshima Bay . . . facing former island called Sakurajima . . . now a peninsula . . . port for passenger ferries to Satsunan Islands . . . products are silk textiles, tin ware, bamboo and pottery items, food stuffs, shochu liquor, and independent thinkers . . . Admiral Togo born here . . . also several leaders of the restoration movement.

WHAT TO SEE AND DO

Furusato • Hot-spring resort on southern coast of Sakurajima Peninsula . . . about a 20-minute ferry ride from Kagoshima port . . . fine view of Osumi peninsula mountains . . . mild climate with many citrus trees and famed sakurajima-daikon, a turnip-shaped white radish used often in Japanese cooking.

Ibusuki • Hot-spring area on southern tip of Satsuma Peninsula . . . known for *sunamushi* (hot-sand baths) . . . supposed to cure all ills . . . reachable by hovercraft from Kagoshima port.

Iso Park • On site of former villa of Shimazu clan . . . 17th-century villa stands in beautiful garden along coast called Iso . . . cable car to Isoyama (hill).

Kirishima-Yaku National Park • 160,000 acres embracing Kagoshima Bay, Mt. Kirishima, and Yaku Island . . . also includes Sakurajima, Ibusuki Spa, and tips of Satsuma and Osumi peninsulas . . . Kirishima range encompasses some 23 peaks as well as craters, lakes, waterfalls, forests, hot springs, and rare flora . . . some protected as National Monuments . . . Kirishima Spa has over a dozen hot springs with charming ryokan for overnight stays.

Lake Ikeda • Largest lake in Kyushu . . . a round caldron at the foot of dormant Mt. Kaimon . . . located about a 45-minute drive from Kagoshima . . . nearby is Nagasakibana Spit . . . a promontory into Pacific Ocean with views of Takeshima, Iojima, and Kuroshima islands.

Nanshu Shrine • Located in precincts of Jokomyoji . . . a Buddhist temple . . . dedicated to Takamori (Nanshu) Saigo, a 19th-century rebel associated with the restoration movement . . . tombs of Saigo and a few thousand others killed in the Satsuma Rebellion are nearby.

Sakurajima • Cherry Tree Island . . . formerly in the Bay of Kagoshima . . . now a peninsula owing to a 1914 lava flow of Sakurajima volcano.

St. Xavier's Memorial Church • Erected in 1949 on 400th anniversary of landing of St. Francisco de Xavier in Kagoshima . . . the Spanish Jesuit arrived from Malacca in 1549 . . . the first to teach

Christianity in Japan . . . later visited Hirado, Yamaguchi, Kyoto, and Oita before departing in 1551.

Shiroyama Park • On site of former Shimazu castle of 14th century . . . summit offers fine views of Kagoshima Bay, Sakurajima, and Kaimon volcanoes . . . behind hill is a cave where Saigo and friends committed hara-kiri (suicide by sword) when their Satsuma rebellion of 1877 collapsed.

Shoko Shuseikan Museum • Adjoins Iso Park . . . once a Shimazu factory . . . now a museum of 700 years of the Shimazu family.

Environs

Cape Toi • Located at southeastern end of Shibushi Bay . . . noted for wild horses grazing freely . . . and fern palms around **Misaki Shrine** . . . both flora and fauna listed as Natural Monuments.

Kirishimajingu • Shrine dedicated to Ninigi-no-Mikoto, said to be mythical grandson of deity Amaterasu-Omikami . . . the sun goddess who gave birth to Jimmu Tenno, first emperor of Japan . . . and founder of the so-called Yamato Court near Nara . . . shrine located on southwest slope of Kirishima River . . . with fine views of Sakurajima and Kaimon volcanoes.

Miyazaki • Birthplace of Japan's first emperor . . . Miyazaki Shrine dedicated to Jimmu Tenno . . . museum in shrine shows archaeological finds of *haniwa* (clay figures from Japan's Stone and Iron ages) . . . artifacts reveal the culture of the Jomon Period (until about 336 B.C.) and Yayoi (336 B.C. to A.D. 193).

Nichinan Kaigan Quasi-National Park • Extends along Pacific Ocean from Aoshima to Nichinan . . . tourist resorts and subtropical flora . . . **Udo Shrine,** about 30 minutes from Aoshima is one of most famous Shinto centers in Japan . . . dedicated to Ugayafukiaezu-no-Mikoto . . . one of the deities in the mythical realm . . . located in a cave . . . outer precinct experiences constant crashing of surf below.

HOTELS

★★★**Kagoshima Sun Royal Hotel** • *8–10, Yojiro 1–chome, Kagoshima. Telex: 7822–91* • 337 rooms in resort area.
Facilities: Dining room. Bar. Swimming pool.
Manager: S. Niimoto. *Reservations:* Direct.

★★★**Shiroyama Kanko Hotel** • *41–1 Shinshoin-cho, Kagoshima. Tel: (0992) 24–2211. Cable: SHIROYAMA KANKO. Telex: 7825–48* • 621 rooms.
Facilities: Japanese, Chinese, Korean, and French restaurants. 2 bars. Swimming pool. Saunas.
Manager: M. Nehara. *Reservations:* Direct.

Miyazaki

★★★**Hotel Plaza Miyazaki** • *1–1 Kawahara-cho, Miyazaki. Tel: (0985) 27–1111. Telex: 7779–77. Located on banks of Ohyodo River* • 183 rooms.
Facilities: Dining room. Sushi bar, 2 Japanese, and 1 western restaurants. 2 bars. Swimming pool. Watersports. Golf arranged.
Manager: K. Okazaki. *Reservations:* Direct.

★★★★**Sun Hotel Phoenix** • *3083 Hamayama Shioji, Miyazaki. Tel: (0985) 39–3131. Cable: SUNPHENIX. Telex: 7778–58* • 302 rooms. Resort Hotel.
Facilities: Entertainment. Swimming pool. Tennis. Dining room. Sushi bar. Golf course. Zoo. 194-room seaside Hotel Phoenix next door.
Manager: H. Nakamura. *Reservations:* Direct.

KUMAMOTO

KUMAMOTO IN A CAPSULE

Third largest city in Kyushu, after Kita-Kyushu and Fukuoka . . . located in west-central section of the island . . . noted as a powerful stronghold during the Tokugawa Period . . . founded by warlord Kiyomasa Kato about A.D. 1600 . . . a commercial city heavily bombed during World War II and extensively rebuilt . . . known for rice, pottery, bamboo, and inlaid work . . . 5 excellent institutions of higher learning located here . . . gateway through middle of the island via cross-Kyushu highway . . . extends through Aso National Park to Beppu on the Inland Sea . . . also known for ancient tombs thought to be from the fifth to seventh centuries A.D. in the surrounding area.

WHAT TO SEE AND DO

Fujisaki Hachimangu • Shinto shrine dedicated to Emperor Ojin, his mother Empress Jingu, and Suminoe-no-Okami . . . located about 2½ miles northeast of the station . . . noted for its **Hojo-e Festival** on Sept. 15 each year . . . mounted warriors in ancient armor escort 3 portable shrines.

Hanaokayama • Hill noted for pagoda on its summit which contains ashes of Buddha . . . erected in 1954 and dedicated to souls of World War II dead . . . ashes donated by Indian Prime Minister Jawaharlal Nehru . . . nice view of city from here.

Hommyoji • Buddhist temple of Nichiren sect . . . noted for containing tomb and many relics of Kiyomasa Kato (1562–1611), lord of the province.

Kato Shrine • Dedicated to Kiyomasa Kato, founder of the city . . . among the treasures contained are the warlord's helmet, sword, and war drum . . . fine view of city from shrine.

Kumamoto Castle • One of Japan's three most famous castles . . . others are in Osaka and Nagoya . . . originally built in 1607 by Kiyomasa Kato . . . located on **Chausuyama** (hill) and called **Gingko Castle** . . . because a large gingko tree at the entrance is said to have been planted by the warlord himself . . . burnt in a seige of 1877 and thoroughly destroyed during last war . . . rebuilt with ferroconcrete in 1960 . . . **donjon** houses a museum.

Misumi • Port town for steamers to Shimabara and Amakusa islands . . . along the seacoast is **Segonko-kofun,** one of many decorated tombs in northern Kyushu . . . 2 mounds with interesting motifs in red with blue or green . . . there are several such mounds in the area believed to date from fifth to seventh centuries A.D.

Rokka • About 20 minutes south of Kumamoto is **Iidera-Kofun,** a round tomb with stone chamber also decorated with red paint.

Suizenji Park • A 130-or-so-acre Japanese landscape garden . . . set in former property of Hosokawa clan, who succeeded Kato clan as rulers . . . contains **Izumi Shrine** dedicated to Hosokawa ancestors . . . also large manmade **Lake Ezu** and local **zoo.**

Tatsuta Natural Park • Site of **Taishoji,** family temple of the Hosokawas . . . famous for beautiful moss garden, pond, and cypress trees . . . contains **Koshiken,** a teahouse designed by Tadaoki Hosokawa (A.D. 1563–1645) . . . a reminder that warlords sought peace and tranquillity in tea ceremony and beautiful landscapes.

Environs

Aso National Park • One of Kyushu's main tourist attractions . . . several thousand acres in Kumamoto and Oita prefectures . . . contains volcanic Mt. Aso and Mt. Kuju as well as many other peaks in the Kuju chain . . . cross-Kyushu highway runs through park to Beppu . . . Mt. Aso is the collective name for one active (**Nakadake)** and four extinct volcanic peaks . . . the adventurous may climb to rim of Nakadake from **Aso Shrine** . . . said to have been established in A.D. 100 and dedicated to first aristocrat who settled in the area . . . **Sanjo Shrine** is at the rim . . . there are many hot springs and resort areas in the park . . . and Daikambo peak on the outer ridge is considered best spot to view entire region.

Beppu • Hot-spring resort at other end of cross-Kyushu highway, a 4½-hour drive from Kumamoto through Aso National Park . . . boasts 9 different types of spring waters, public baths, and some 600 different hotels . . . plus numerous *jigoku* (hell boiling ponds) that eject mud into the air . . . area includes 8 different spas . . . said to cure all ills . . . buses take believers from Beppu station to outlying sulfur springs . . . town also noted for its wild monkeys on **Takasakiyama** (hill) . . . and beautiful parks and gardens.

Yaba-Hita-Hikosan Quasi-National Park □ Several thousand acres covering Mt. Hikosan, Yabakei Gorge, and Hita sections . . . established in 1950 . . . Mt. Hikosan is another group of volcanic peaks, with a 7th-century Shinto shrine atop one of them . . . Yabakei Gorge lies along the Yamakuni River between Ayugaeri and Morizane-Onsen . . . gateway is **Ao-no-Domon** . . . a rock tunnel that took a Buddhist priest named Zenkai 30 years to cut in the 18th century . . . Hita is a basin city known for its beauty and serenity . . . often referred to as the ''Kyoto of Kyushu'' and popular as a summer retreat.

HOTELS

Beppu

★★★★**Kijima Kogen Grand Hotel** • *Kijima-Kogen, Beppu. Tel: (0977) 22–1161. Cable: BING HOTEL BEPPU. Telex: 7734 74* • 111 rooms.
Facilities: Hot-spring spa in mountains, about 9 miles from Beppu. Japanese-style restaurant and grill. Traditional entertainment. Bar and nightclub. 4 tennis courts. Golf course. Horses.
Manager: M. Konishi. *Reservations:* Direct.

★★★**Suginoi Hotel** • *Kankaiji, Beppu. Tel: (0977) 2401141. Cable: SUGINOI* • 606 rooms.
Facilities: Dining room. 4 cocktail lounges. Nightclub. Musical show. Swimming pool. Bowling. Ice skating. Sauna. Museum.
Manager: T. Watanabe. *Reservations:* Direct.

Kumamoto

★★★**Hotel Hokke Club** • *20–1, Torimachi Kumamoto-shi. Tel: (0963) 22–5001. Telex: 7626–76* • 152 rooms.
Facilities: Dining room. Bar.
Manager: K. Asami. *Reservations:* Direct.

★★★**New Sky Hotel** • *2 Higashi Amidaji-machi, Kumamoto. Tel: (0963) 54–2111* • 201 rooms.
Facilities: Restaurant. Coffee shop. Cocktail lounge.
Manager: S. Hoshiko. *Reservations:* Direct.

NAGASAKI

WHAT TO SEE AND DO

Dejima • Former manmade island in Nagasaki Bay where Dutch traders were confined from 1641 to 1854 . . . to prevent infiltration of

NAGASAKI IN A CAPSULE

Kyushu's fourth largest and most attractive city . . . situated on western coast of island, port was opened to trading ships from Holland, Portugal, and Spain in 1571 . . . remained center of Western ideas and learning until Meiji restoration (1868) . . . also center for Christianity in Japan until banned by military ruler Hideyoshi in 1597 . . . Spanish and Portuguese banished in 1639 and Dutch confined to Dejima Island in Nagasaki Bay . . . famous as gateway to Unzen National Park . . . a solace for Westerners living in southern China in early 20th century . . . now a popular honeymoon spot for young Japanese . . . bombed along with Hiroshima on Aug. 9, 1945, because of shipbuilding industry . . . completely restored and still boasts one of world's highest ship tonnage in building and supplies . . . a lovely city somewhat reminiscent of San Francisco with its hills and views of the bay.

Western ideas . . . landfill has now made it part of the mainland . . . scale model of the colony and municipal museum displaying objects from the Dutch times. . . . **Nagasaki Holland Village.**

Glover Mansion • Victorian mansion and former residence of William Glover, an Englishman behind the railway in this area . . . beautifully kept English gardens overlook harbor . . . statue of Madame Butterfly at end of series of terraces . . . this seems the perfect setting for the opera . . . although no evidence exists that Puccini ever visited here.

Kodaiji • Buddhist temple of Soto sect . . . contains tombs of some Japanese who introduced Western sciences (military and photography) into the country.

Meganebashi • Eye-glass bridge . . . double span across the Nakajima River that looks like a pair of spectacles . . . built in 1634 by a Chinese priest named Nyojo . . . oldest "foreign-style" bridge in Japan.

Mt. Inasa Natural Park • Located on Inasa-yama (hill) . . . cable car available to the top (5 mins.) . . . fine views of city and harbor.

Nagasaki Park • Formerly known as **Suwa Park** . . . banyan tree allegedly planted by General and Mrs. Ulysses S. Grant in 1879 during a visit . . . memorials to honor 3 Europeans who introduced medical and botanical sciences to Japan . . . also prefectural library with historical documents of the area.

Oura Catholic Church • Oldest Gothic-style wooden church in Japan . . . finished in 1865 under supervision of French Jesuit Petit Jean . . . to commemorate 26 Christians martyred nearby . . . designated National Treasure.

Peace Park • Dedicated to world peace and all war victims . . . exact spot where atomic bomb exploded at 11:02 a.m. on Aug. 9, 1945 . . . contains bronze statue of Peace sculpted by Seibo Kitamura . . . and **International Culture Hall** . . . also **Urakami,** where Christians reaffirmed their faith during Tokugawa Period . . . Urakami Church nearby was the largest in Far East until destroyed by the bomb.

Site of Martyrdom of 26 Saints • 20 Japanese and 6 foreign Christians were crucified at this site in 1597 when Hideyoshi banned the practice of this religion . . . legend says they stayed on their crosses for 80 days, looking like sleeping angels, while miracles happened throughout the neighborhood . . . place named **Nishizaka Park** in 1949 on the quadricentennial of Francis Xavier's arrival in Japan . . . this monument erected in 1962 on centenary of cannonization of all 26 martyrs . . . Christians come from all over Japan to pay their respects here.

Sofukuji • Also known as **Nankindera** (Chinese Temple) . . . built in 1629 as first temple of Obaku sect of Zen Buddhism . . . had Chinese priest . . . architecture said to be fine example of Ming Dynasty style . . . still favored by Chinese community who come here in mid-Sept. each year to observe *o bon* . . . Second Gate and Main Hall designated National Treasures.

Suwa Shrine • Adjoins Nagasaki Park . . . gate tower contains models of unusual Chinese shops . . . panoramic view of city and harbor from atop 73 stone steps.

Environs

Arita • Small town on Sasebo Line noted for production of white porcelain . . . a Korean potter named Li-San P'ing brought the art of ceramics to Arita in 1616 . . . Dutch traders from Dejima Island in Nagasaki exported large quantities to Europe . . . **Arita Ceramic Art Museum** in Chamber of Commerce and Industry Building has exhibit of old and new Arita ceramics . . . more than 400,000 come annually to annual ceramic fair from May 1 to 5.

Omura • Located about 27 miles from Sasebo . . . noted for **Omura Park** where ancient castle once overlooked the sea . . . town also second in pearl production (after Ise Bay near Nagoya).

Saikai National Park • A marine park reached from either Nagasaki or Sasebo . . . encompasses Kujukushima (99 islands) noted for subtropical flora . . . **Hirado Island,** which claims to be first port opened to foreign traders . . . **Saikai Bridge** that spans **Hario-no-Seto Straits** . . . and **Goto Islands** (5 islands) scattered off northwest coast of Kyushu . . . reachable by steamer from Nagasaki and Sasebo . . . famous for cattle breeding and coral production.

Sasebo • Thriving port city just north of Nagasaki . . . shipbuilding center as well as base for U.S. Navy in western Japan.

Unzen-Amakusa National Park • First national park ever designated in Japan . . . encompasses inactive volcano Mt. Unzen . . . several hot springs bubbling with sulfur beds . . . **Unzen Spa,** a summer resort situated at over 2000 feet above sea level . . . **Obama** summer and winter resort . . . lakes and waterfalls . . . and **Shimabara,** a small port known for its castle associated with Christian rebellion of 1637 . . . now contains a museum on Christianity . . . **Tsukumojimi** islands dot Shimabara port . . . formed by eruption of Mt. Mayuyama in 1792 and now covered with lovely pine forests and sandy beaches.

HOTELS

★★★★**Nagasaki Grand Hotel** • *5–3 Manzai-machi. Tel: (0958) 23–1234. Cable: NAGASAKI GRAND HOTEL* • 126 rooms.
Facilities: Main dining room. Italian restaurant. Grill.
Manager: S. Kaneko. *Reservations:* Direct.

★★★★**Nagasaki Tokyu Hotel** • *18–1 Minami Yamate-cho. Tel: (0958) 25–1501. Telex: 752762 THECNGA* • 225 rooms.
Facilities: Grillroom. Japanese and Chinese restaurants. Bar.
Manager: S. Ohta. *Reservations:* Tokyu Hotel Chain.

OKINAWA

OKINAWA PREFECTURE

Located off southern tip of Kyushu and one of its 8 prefectures . . . formerly called Ryukyu Islands with 4 main groups—Okinawa, Miyako, Yaeyama, and Daito—some 60 various sizes . . . settled as early as 12th century with own unique culture . . . site of bloody battlefields during World War II . . . came under U.S. jurisdiction in 1945 . . . only reverted to Japan in treaty of 1972 . . . Naha is cultural, political, and commercial capital and gateway . . . climate is subtropical and area famous for many different species of sea life . . . chief products are sugar, pineapple, and fish . . . traditional arts include bingata, a technique of dying cotton, linen and silk . . . Ryukyu ceramics . . . Ryukyu lacquerware using deigo wood . . . Ryukyu kasuri cloth . . . and tortoise-shell crafts . . . U.S. still maintains large Air Force base in Kadena, near Okinawa City (formerly called Koza).

WHAT TO SEE AND DO

Expo 75 • Site of International Ocean Exposition . . . featured ''The Sea We Would Like to See'' . . . includes pavilions of fish exhibitions . . . **Marine Life Zoo** . . . **Ethnic Studies and History pavilions** . . . **Aquapolis** and ship exhibits . . . many still standing and worth a visit.

Gyokusendo • **Stalactite cave** about 7 miles southeast of Naha . . . third largest in Japan . . . contains almost half a million stalagmites and stalactites . . . plus streams and bats . . . not for everyone.

Itoman • About 7 miles south of Naha . . . center of Pacific Ocean fishing industry . . . also noted for sugar production . . . **Haryusen boat race** held here every year in early May.

Iriomote National Park • Consists of several small islands—Iriomote, Kobama, Taketomi, Kurojima, Aragusuku, and Nakanokan—extensive virgin forests with wild animals and coral reefs . . . colorful tropical fish . . . rather inacessible but interesting.

Nago • Located at neck of Motobu Peninsula . . . known for sugar cane and pineapple cultivation . . . many typical examples of local architecture . . . not damaged during the war . . . ruins of **Nago Castle** built in 14th century . . . offers fine views of peninsula and Kunigami mountain range . . . **cherry blossom festival** held here every year.

Naha • Principal city . . . located just 15 minutes from **Kokusai O-dori international airport** . . . a few of the sights left are **Shurei-no-mon** (Shurei gate) built in early 16th century . . . typical Okinawan architecture . . . restored in 1958 . . . **Tamaudon tombs** of Sho family . . . rulers of Ryukyu kingdom and designated Important Cultural Properties . . . **Sonohiyan Utaki** built in 1511 for Ryukyu royal family prayers . . . **Benzaiten** (goddess of beauty temple) . . . and main gate of **Enryakuji** . . . and **Okinawa Prefecture Museum** . . . with exhibits of local culture and archaeological relics.

Nakagusuku • Located in south-central part of island . . . **Nakagusuku Park** has castle built in 1440 by most skilled architect on island (named Gosamaru) . . . also **Nakamura House** of 200 years ago . . . undamaged during the last war . . . noted for lack of nails . . . Important Cultural Property.

Okinawa City • Honky-tonk town . . . located near U.S. Air Force base and full of bars and bar girls . . . **Gushikawa** is about 5 miles northeast and known for local bullfights . . . also views of Kin and Nakagusuku Bays.

Okinawa Coast Quasi-National Park • Lovely beaches stretching from Nagahama Beach to Nago Bay . . . from Unten to Cape Hedo in north . . . clear waters and coral reefs.

Okinawa Kaichu (Marine) Park • Along southern tip of Nago Bay to Cape Busena . . . underwater observatory to view coral and tropical fish . . . also **Shell Exhibition Hall** . . . glass-bottom boats, etc.

Okinawan Old Battlefield Quasi-National Park • Located between Itoman and Gushikami . . . monuments and tower dedicated to war dead.

Miyako Island • An hour by plane from Naha . . . atmosphere of old Okinawa . . . with typical architecture . . . **Hirara** is political, economical, and cultural center . . . **Monument of Philanthropy** built by German Emperor Wilhelm I . . . **Tomb of Toyumiya** built in 15th century . . . **Tax Stone** used to levy taxes from 17th to 19th centuries according to height of inhabitants . . . tropical botanical garden nearby.

HOTELS

★★★★**Naha Tokyu Hotel** • *1002 Ameku, Naha. Cable: TO-KYUHOTEL NAHA* • 280 rooms.
Facilities: 2 restaurants. Bar. Disco. Swimming pool.
Manager: M. Fujita. *Reservations:* UTELL.

★★★★**Okinawa Grand Castle** • *1–132–1 Shuri Yamagawa-cho, Naha. Tel: (0988) 86–5454. Telex: 795375 OKAOGCJ* • 305 rooms.
Facilities: 4 restaurants. Theater restaurant. Disco. 3 lounges. Swimming pool.
Manager: H. Kobanawa. *Reservations:* JAL.

★★★★**Okinawa Miyako Hotel** • *40 Matsukawa, Naha. Tel: (0988) 87–1111* • 318 rooms.
Facilities: Bar. Dining Room. Swimming pool. 318 rooms.
Manager: T. Nishida. *Reservations:* Direct.

★★★★**Pacific Hotel Okinawa** • *3–5–1 Nishi, Naha. Tel: (0988) 68–5162* • 380 rooms.
Facilities: 6 restaurants. Bar. Cocktail lounges. Swimming pool.
Manager: S. Kuniyoshi. *Reservations:* Direct.

SHIKOKU

SHIKOKU IN A CAPSULE

Japan's fourth major island . . . name means "four provinces" . . . and island is divided into 4 prefectures: Tokushima, Kagawa, Ehime, and Kochi . . . which correspond to 4 former provinces of Awa, Sanuki, Iyo, and Tosa . . . island has own traditions quite apart from rest of Japan . . . famous for Buddhist pilgrims dressed in white kimonos, followers of Kobo Daishi (Great Master), who was born in Sanuki province in A.D. 774 (as Kukai) . . . about 100,000 pilgrims arrive annually to visit 88 sacred shrines scattered throughout the island, which takes from 45 to 60 days by foot (read Oliver Statler's *Japanese Pilgrimage*) . . . Shikoku also a popular tourist resort . . . with beautiful parks and views of the Inland Sea . . . reachable by air or ferry from southern Honshu . . . and by hydrofoil from Hiroshima, Kobe, and Osaka.

WHAT TO SEE AND DO

Kochi and Environs

Ashizuri-Uwakai National Park • Marine reserve established in 1972 along southwest seacoast between Minokoshi and Tatsukushi . . . glass-bottom boats for sightseeing along the reefs . . . 50,000 shells in **Exhibition Hall . . . Coral Museum** . . . breathtaking scenery.

Cape Muroto • Forms southeast corner of Tosa Bay on Pacific Ocean side of island . . . famous for **Muroto-Anan Coast Quasi-National Park** . . . and **Hotsumisaki Temple** (also known as **Higashi-dera**) . . . founded by Kobo Daishi in A.D. 807 and 24th of 88 sacred places . . . trees on property named Natural Monuments.

Ino • Small town a few miles west of Kochi . . . situated on Ni-yodo River . . . known for production of **Tosagami** . . . handmade paper from mulberry trees.

Kochi • Cultural seat of Kochi Prefecture . . . located at center of Tosa Bay . . . known for 18th century **Daimyo Castle** (Important Cultural Property) in Kochi Park . . . **Godaisan Park** with view from summit . . . **Chikurinju Temple** founded in A.D. 724 by priest Gyoki . . . 31st of 88 sacred shrines . . . just a mile south of city is Urado Bay and lovely beaches.

Kokubunji • Important Cultural Property . . . about 8 miles from Kochi . . . temple founded by priest Gyoki in A.D. 729 . . . 29th among 88 sacred places on Shikoku.

Kongofukuji • Temple located behind lighthouse on Cape Ashi-zuri . . . dedicated to thousand-handed Kannon . . . established in A.D. 822 by Kobo Daishi . . . magnificent views of cape and open sea . . . 38th of 88 sacred shrines.

Nakamura • 15th-century town . . . considered the ''Kyoto'' of old Tosa Province . . . situated on Shimanto River . . . Shikoku's second longest river . . . visit **Ichijo Shrine** on Atago Hill in center . . . dedicated to founder Norifusa.

Sakawa • About 15 miles west of Kochi . . . noted for sakura (cherry blossoms), sake, and **Seizan Library** . . . library contains works from Meiji restoration era (1868 onward).

Matsuyama and Environs

Cape Sada • Considered part of the Inland Sea National Park . . . Hoyo Straits off the Cape divides Inland Sea from Pacific Ocean . . . also lovely views here of Bungo Channel.

Dogo Spa • One of Japan's oldest spas . . . located about 1½ miles from Matsuyama Station . . . several hot springs with public bathhouse . . . also Imperial bathhouse (**Yushinden**) built in 1899 . . .

Dogo Park noted for sakura (cherry blossoms) in the spring . . . colorful festival and dances each year from March 19–21.

Imabari • Called the Osaka of Shikoku . . . many industries including towels . . . visit **Fukiage Park** on old castle grounds . . . **Chikamiyama Hill** for panoramic views of mountains, islands, and Kurushima Straits . . . narrow passage between Imabari and Oshima Island . . . noted for fast currents.

Matsuyama • Largest city on Shikoku . . . old castle-town, now center of culture and education for the island . . . **Matsuyama Castle** dates from 1602 . . . finely preserved and centered in city's main park . . . named Important Cultural Property and contains museum of weaponry belonging to daimyo (feudal lords) of Matsudaira clan.

Omogokei Gorge • Located on upper reaches of Omogo River . . . visitors can hike several miles through the gorge from Kammon to **Goraiko Falls** . . . also up Mt. Ishizuchi from Kumabuchi Bridge.

Ozu • Known as Little Kyoto . . . city noted for tissue paper and silk production . . . watch cormorants fish on Hiji River from June 1 to late Sept.

Takahama/Mitsuhama • Thriving ports for Matsuyama City . . . connections from here by sea with most Honshu/Inland Sea ports . . . **Gogoshima** is island just west of Takahama . . . covered with peach blossoms in spring and famous for **Funa Odori** (Ship Dance) held sometime in mid-Oct. (by lunar calendar).

Uwajima • Port city and cultural center 2 hours by express train from Matsuyama . . . **Uwajima Castle** built in 1665 is registered as Historic Site . . . **Uwatsuhiko Shrine** at foot of Atago Park noted for **Yatsushika Odori** (Eight Deer Dance) and **parade of Ushi-oni** (Ox Monster) . . . both held on Oct. 28–29 . . . **Tenshaen** is fine landscaped garden near train station . . . once owned by a retired daimyo of the area . . . **togyu** or bullfights held in bullring about 6 times annually . . . bulls lock horns and are not killed as in the Spanish style.

Takamatsu and Vicinity

Awa-Ikeda • Station for visiting famous **Iyadani Gorge** . . . scenic area along Iya River . . . remote valley in which descendents of the Taira clan live with own customs and dialect . . . **Iya-no-Kazurabashi** (vine bridge of Iya) made by clan members is considered Important Folk Material by government.

Kan-Onji • Known for **Kotohiki Park** on seashore . . . beautiful pine trees and *zenigata*, ditches along beach dug in shape of old coin . . . apparently dug by earlier inhabitants as reminder not to waste money . . . also **Kan-onji** temple at foot of Kotohiki Hill . . . belongs to Koyasan-Shingon sect of Buddhism . . . is 69th of 88 sacred places on Shikoku.

Kotohiragu Shrine • Located just west of Kotohira Station, half-way up Zozusan Hill . . . dedicated to Shinto deity Omononushi-no-Mikoto, protector of all sea voyagers . . . long climb to inner precincts of shrine through lovely cedar, pine, camphor, and flowering trees . . . *shoin* or parlor hall built in 1659 . . . *fusuma* (sliding doors) painted by landscape artist Okyo Maruyama in late 18th century . . . both structure and art named Important Cultural Properties . . . principal landing place for pilgrims is **Marugame** . . . where 1597 castle has been designated Important Cultural Property also.

Megishima • Island located about a mile from Takamatsu . . . allows nice views of Inland Sea . . . also known as **Demon's Island** . . . associated with popular fairy tale about Momotaro (peach boy).

Takamatsu • Shikoku's chief passenger port . . . castle-town dating from 1588 . . . seat of Matsudaira clan until 1868 . . . administrative center of island . . . also known for cotton, fans, lacquerware, tissue paper, medicines, and parasols . . . **Tamamo Park** near Takamatsu Pier . . . faces Inland Sea . . . site of **Takamatsu Castle** built in 1588 and taken over by Matsudaira clan . . . few remains left but turrets registered as Important Cultural Properties . . . **Ritsurin Park** also on site of a former Matsudaira clan residence . . . now beautiful park with zoo, folk art museum, and Japanese gardens.

Yashima • Former island now connected by causeway . . . about a mile from Takamatsu . . . **Yashimaji** Buddhist temple on summit of South Hill (on peninsula side) contains relics from battles between rival clans of Taira and Minamoto (Taira lost).

Zentsuji • Town where Kobo Daishi (A.D. 774–835) introduced Shingon sect of Buddhism into Japan . . . headquarters of Shingon is **Zentsuji temple** founded in A.D. 813, but reconstructed in 18th century . . . on land owned by the Great Master's father, Saeki . . . **shoso-in,** or treasure house, contains works by Kobo Daishi as well as gifts of previous emperors.

Tokushima and Vicinity

Chofukuji • Temple founded in A.D. 824 just a mile northwest of Sanuki-Tsuda station . . . on other side of station is **Kinrin Park** with more than mile-long grove of ancient black pines.

Kakurinji • Temple 7 miles southwest of Tatsue station . . . 20th of 88 sacred shrines on Shikoku . . . stands in grove of very old cedars.

Mt. Tsurugi Quasi-National Park • Contains second-highest peak in Shikoku plus 2 extensive gorges . . . pilgrims in white visit 2 shrines beside Fujinoike Lake at annual festival July 17 . . . **Tsurugikyo Gorge** runs along Anabuki River from Miyanouchi to Taniguchi . . . **Iyadani Gorge** between Kubo and Deai . . . the very healthy spend 3 nights hiking in this park

Muroto-Anan Coast Quasi National Park • Extends some 60 miles along southeast coastline from Anan City to Cape Muroto . . . dramatic views of Pacific Ocean . . . huge turtles and subtropical flora.

Naruto Straits • Connect Inland Sea with Pacific Ocean, plus separate Awaji (island) from Shikoku in northeast . . . also called **Awa-no-Naruto** (roaring gateway to Awa province) . . . heavy currents and whirlpools here . . . Naruto Hill offers fine views of straits.

Nyoirinji • Temple about 9 miles south of Tokushima station . . . headquarters of Hoju-Shingon sect of Buddhism . . . located halfway up Mt. Nakatsumiṇe . . . **Nyoirin Kannon** is Important Cultural Property.

Shido • Seat of famous **Shidoji** of Shingon sect . . . founded in 7th century . . . considered 86th of 88 sacred shrines on Shikoku.

Tatsueji • Temple just southwest of Tatsue station . . . considered 19th of 88 sacred shrines . . . contains painting of Lord Buddha . . . Important Cultural Property.

Tokushima • Cultural center of Tokushima prefecture . . . known for Awa-dori, local dance performed from Aug. 15–18 . . . and local bunraku puppetry with performances between planting and harvest because farmers work the puppets . . . Tokushima also last residence of Portuguese Wenceslao de Moraes, who married a local woman and is buried in **Cho-onji** . . . **Tokushima Park** has ruins of 1586 castle built for local feudal lord . . . also fine views of city . . . **Bizan Park** on slope of Otaki Hill has scenic views of Yoshino River, surrounding mountains and Inland Sea . . . Yoshino River is longest in Shikoku and its source is near Mt. Ishizuchi, the island's tallest peak . . . the river crosses 3 prefectures.

HOTELS

There are plenty of charming, small *ryokan* (traditional Japanese inns) scattered throughout Shikoku that offer 2 meals and a memorable experience. There are also many, many temples available for overnight stays, especially if you plan to join a group to visit all 88 sacred places (don't worry, it's hardly done on foot anymore). If none of this appeals to you, the hotels listed below have both Western and Japanese accommodations and are quite comfortable—although unmemorable.

Imabari

★★★**Imabari Kokusai Hotel** • *4–6 1–chome, Asahi-machi. Tel: (0898) 22–3355* • 142 Western, 2 Japanese rooms.
Sauna.

Kochi

★★★**Kochi Dai-Ichi Hotel** • *2–2–12 Kitahon-machi, Kochi City 780. Tel: (0888) 83–1441* • 120 Western rooms.

Matsuyama

★★★**Hotel Oku Dogo** • *267 Suemachi. Tel: (0899) 77–1111* • 226 Western, 77 Japanese rooms.
Hot-spring bath. Golf course.

Takamatsu

★★★**Keio Plaza Hotel** • *5–11, Chuo-cho. Tel: (0878) 34–5511. Telex: 5822–725 KPHT J* • 178 Western, 2 Japanese rooms.

★★★**Takamatsu Grand Hotel** • *10–5–1 Kotobuki-cho. Tel: (0878) 51–5757. Telex: 5822–557 TGRAND J* • 136 Western rooms.

Tokushima

★★**Hotel Astoria** • *2–26 Ichiban-cho, Tokushima 770. Tel: (0886)*
53–6151 • 24 Western, 1 Japanese rooms.

★★**Awa Kanko Hotel** • *3–16–3, Ichiban-cho, 770. Tel: (0886)*
22–5161 • 23 Western, 12 Japanese rooms.

★★★**Tokushima Park Hotel** • *2 Tokushima-cho, 770. Tel: (0886)*
25–3311. Telex: 5862–345 PRKHTL J • 75 Western, 7 Japanese rooms.

KOREA

HISTORY

Choson, Land of the Morning Calm, is the earliest name bestowed upon the Korean kingdom by its legendary founder Tan'gun. Morning freshness and calm has been recorded in paintings and the poetry of this east Asian peninsula, but not in the 5000 year history—which has been turbulent. The Koreans are a strong people, taller than most of their neighbors, and their distinctive character has been molded by centuries of domination by other nations. Even today, the 600-mile peninsula that includes 6000 miles of coastline is ideologically divided at the 38th parallel.

It is thought that the earliest settlers on this peninsula were Chinese intellectuals seeking refuge around 213 B.C. and later, laborers attempting to avoid the "draft" to build the Great Wall. Traditionally, the early history of Korea begins with the Three Kingdoms and every schoolchild learns the dates 57 B.C. for Silla, 37 B.C. for Koguryo, and 18 B.C. for Paekche. Koguryo was located in the north and therefore heavily influenced by China and the introduction of Buddhism. Paekche occupied the southwest corner and was most noted for its influence on Japan, to where a written language and Buddhism spread.

The Silla kingdom was the last to get itself together but proved to be the strongest. With the help of T'ang dynasty military prowess, Silla armies vanquished both Koguryo and Paekche and unified the peninsula. During the Unified Silla Period (A.D. 668–936), the country prospered and reached its "golden age" around the middle of the 8th century. The capital at Kyongju had an estimated one million inhabitants at this time, and great advances were recorded in science, philosophy, and architecture. Magnificent monuments to Buddhism were erected here, including **Pulguk-sa** (temple) and the great image in **Sokkuram** grotto. Both are considered among the country's greatest treasures, and tourist attractions, in this vast outdoor museum.

Unfortunately, infighting and lessening of the aristocracy caused the Silla Dynasty to weaken after the 8th century and its capital was sacked in the year 927. The Koryo Dynasty was established north of the Han River (936–1392), renowned for its highly prized bluish-green **celadon** ware and the **Tripitaka Koreana.** These 81,358 wooden blocks, on which the Buddhist scriptures have been carved, were commissioned during the 13th century by King Kojong. The king was in exile on Kanghwa Island and used the project to secure "divine favor" against the invading Mongols. The Tripitaka, one of the country's most important National Treasures, are now housed in the Haein Temple near Taegu.

Seoul became the country's capital during the Yi Dynasty (1392–1910) and Buddhism replaced Confucianism as the dominant force. **Hangul,** the Korean phonetic alphabet, was devised during the reign of King Sejong (A.D. 1418–50) and is considered one of the most precise writing systems ever invented. Sejong is recorded as having been a great cultural achiever, and his court left some impressive accomplishments in music, science, and other technology.

By 1592 the armies of Japanese General Hideyoshi were trampling the Korean peninsula en route to conquering China. However, General Yi and his iron-clad turtle-shaped vessels drove the Japanese back across the sea. Barely recovered from repulsing unwanted guests in the southern flank, the Koreans turned northward to watch the Manchu armies arrive twice—in 1627 and 1636. When peace was finally achieved, the country retreated into itself and was known as the "hermit kingdom" until 1876 when ports were opened (reluctantly) to Japan. In 1882 Korea and the United States signed a friendship and commerce treaty. This was followed by similar treaties with European nations.

The 20th century, however, has not been kind to Korea. The Japanese annexed the peninsula in 1910, having already murdered the popular and strong Queen Min and forced King Kojong to abdicate in favor of his son. Until 1945 the Japanese occupied the country and the Korean people were forced to abnegate their own national language, characteristics and culture. The country was divided at the 38th parallel at the end of World War II and the Republic of South Korea was born in 1948, with Dr. Syngman Rhee as its first president. Jubilation over independence was short lived, alas, when Communist forces from the north attacked in 1950 and took Seoul within three days.

The Korean Conflict lasted three bitter years. Brother was fighting brother, as the Communists captured every South Korean port and city but Pusan. Although the majority were certainly Americans, troops from 16 United Nations member countries joined the battle. The conflict was suspended in July 1953 but a peace treaty has never been signed, and negotiations still continue at the DMZ (Demilitarized Zone). It is a sad reflection on the nature of mankind.

The resilient Koreans have produced nothing short of a miracle in almost four decades, turning a beleagured nation into a vibrant force in not only Asia but the world. From the ashes of war have arisen a healthy, happy, well-educated people who have restored their national pride, great cultural heritage, and an economic future that few of their neighbors can match.

Once-drab Seoul has become a great and exciting metropolis, with elegant high rises by local architect Kim Soo Gun, chic new hotels managed by international names and full of expensive places to dine and sip, shops brimming with beautiful things, and renovated palaces still worthy of the kings who built them. Korean women, long famous for their quiet beauty and charm, have returned to their colorful native dress of billowing silk—**hanbok**—for festive occasions.

More and more international sporting events are being held in Seoul. The 10th Asian Games, in the fall of 1986, were expected to draw some 150,000 foreign visitors.

The big event, however, was the 1988 International Summer Olympics, for which the city of Seoul built a special sports complex and Olympic Village. In preparation, the government expanded the city subway system, coordinated new sightseeing programs, and built new access roads from Kimpo Airport. New hotels were constructed and major carriers provided air service from 21 countries.

The Seoul Sports Complex was the main venue for these 24th games. It has two gymnasia, an indoor swimming pool, baseball park and huge stadium. Olympic Park is just 4 kilometers from the complex, with a velodrome, three gymnasia, indoor swimming pool and tennis courts. Other Olympic venues are the Seoul Equestrian Park, Han River Regatta Course, Pusan Yachting Center; other venues for handball, hockey, wrestling and judo will be in Suwon, songnam and Yong-in, all within an hour's drive from Seoul. Since the Olympics, which were watched by 3 billion people worldwide and attracted athletes from 160 countries, plans for the sports facilities include other international competitions and use by the 10 million residents of Seoul. Olympic Village, where athletes and the press lived during the 24th Games, has become much needed housing for a booming metropolis.

This is more than the land of **kimchee** (pickled cabbage), **ginseng** (that mysterious root that portends to cure everything), and **ondol** (the heated floors in traditional homes). This is a land of ceremony and belief. The many historic Buddhist temples are full of the devout as well as visitors seeking peace—or a glimpse of tranquil beauty.

Perhaps it is the Korean flag—**taeguk**—signifying harmony that most exemplifies what 5000 years of cultural history has meant. The red upper portion represents *yang,* while the lower blue is the *yin* or *um.* It is a symbol often painted on gates of important structures and means that life is filled with opposites—good and evil, hot and cold, day and night, fire and water, male and female—and contradiction. This symbol also offers an endless source for contemplation and interpretation, and raises the spirit above earthly and mortal things.

KOREA IN A CAPSULE

Korean peninsula extends 600 miles south from the Asian continent . . . divided by 38th parallel into north and south segments . . . Republic of Korea has almost 40 million inhabitants, descendants of migrant tribes from central Asia . . . ancient history records three rival kingdoms here until Silla unification in 6th century A.D. . . . Koryo Dynasty succeeded from 10th to 14th centuries . . . Japan annexed Korea in 1910 and colonized the country until 1945 . . . Korean War lasted from 1950 to 1953 . . . 38th parallel division then established . . . official language is Korean, with English and Japanese widely understood . . . official religions are Buddhism and Confucianism, with about 5 million Christians . . . Islam has been introduced only recently . . . climate throughout the peninsula ranges from temperate in southern area and islands to harsh winters and hot summers in the northern sector . . . first impressions of Korea revolve around its rugged landscape and the individuality of its people.

PLANNING AHEAD

KOREA NATIONAL TOURISM CORPORATION (KNTC) does an excellent job of enlightening potential visitors to the Land of the Morning Calm, as this ancient country is called. As a result, Korea is among the top major tourist destinations in Asia, and has been welcoming more than a million visitors annually since 1978. Among the accomplishments of the KNTC were bringing the American Society of Travel Agents' world congress to Seoul in 1983 and scheduling the International Summer Olympic Games for September 17 to October 2, 1988, in Seoul.

Headquarters of the KNTC is 10 Ta-dong, Chung-ku, Seoul, or C.P.O. Box 903 (Tel: 757–6030). Tourist information is also available in the Arrival Lounge, 1st floor of Kimpo International Airport (Tel: 665–0086) and at Pusan's Kimhae Airport (Tel: 98–1100) and at Cheju's Airport (Tel: 42–0032). Seoul City Tourist Information Center is located directly behind Seoul City Hall, 31 1–ga, Taepyeongno, Junggu (Tel: 731–4337, 735–8688); the Pusan City Tourist Information Center is in the Tourism Section, Pusan City Hall (Tel: 22–7289); and there is an Information Center at Pulguk-sa Temple in Kyongju (Tel: 2–4747).

KNTC offices in North America are located in Korea Center Bldg., 460 Park Ave., Suite 400, New York, NY 10022 (Tel: 212–688–7543); 510 West 6th St., Suite 323, Los Angeles, CA 90014 (Tel: 213–623–1226); 205 N. Michigan Ave., Suite 2212, Chicago, IL 60601 (Tel: 312–346–6660). There are representative offices at 1188 Bishop St., Century Plaza PH1, Honolulu, HI 96813 (Tel: 808–521–8066); or the 4th & Vine Bldg. Seattle, WA 98121 (Tel: 206–441–6666).

VISAS are not required of tourists holding valid U.S. passports, for a stay up to 15 days in the Republic of Korea, if they are en route to another destination in the Orient. Business travelers are required to obtain a visa before entry from their local Korean Consulate Office. U.S. passport holders visiting Korea *only* may obtain multiple-entry visas valid for 48 months, without photographs or fee. Five-day landing permits are available at port of entry for visitors holding confirmed reservations (and tickets) onward. Aliens touring Cheju Island only may transit for five days without visas, and extensions can be arranged.

INOCULATIONS for smallpox and/or cholera are not required for entry, unless you arrive through or via an infected area.

ENTRY BY AIR into the Republic of Korea is generally through Seoul's modern **Kimpo International Airport,** a passenger terminal built for the 1980s. Security is very tight at Kimpo because a military airfield is nearby and because Seoul is situated just 20 minutes' flying time from the 38th parallel. Therefore, photographs of this area are forbidden and even loaded camera equipment is suspect. Kimpo is also the home of Korean Air Lines, one of the best national carriers in the region that offers topnotch pilots (often ex-air force) and good international service. There are nonstop flights from New York and Los Angeles.

Airport buses depart about every 20 minutes from Kimpo to downtown Seoul hotels as well to the Sheraton Walker Hill, the final stop. Plan to spend 30 minutes to one hour in heavy traffic. The cost is about U.S.$1. Some hotels (like Lotte) provide complimentary transportation for their guests. Taxis are plentiful and the meter rate from the airport should come to about U.S.$10. There is also regular city bus service between Kimpo and the capital, but I'd hardly recommended it on such occasions.

Kimhae International Airport serves the Pusan area, and Cheju Island now receives international flights from Japan as well as frequent daily domestic service. Taxis and airport buses are available.

DEPARTURE BY AIR via Kimpo International Airport can be time consuming, so allow for plenty of time! In fact, the luggage and bodily searches for some domestic flights take longer than the time spent airborne. International passengers are treated more lightly, but be prepared for a thorough inspection. Arrive with cameras unloaded and film packed tightly away, or you may be required to check through all your equipment (unwise in any country). There are also certain restrictions on goods carried out of the country by hand, including anything considered a "cultural property," more than 20 cuttlefish, five ladies' wigs and three men's wigs, 200 pairs of false eyelashes, or 100 phonograph records. Ginseng can also be limited, but several kilograms are permitted in most cases.

Departure tax is ₩5000 per person.

ARRIVAL BY SEA is possible from Shimonoseki to the port of Pusan, aboard the 952-passenger *Pukwan* ferry. The vessel departs Japan late afternoon (5 p.m.) except Saturday. The seven-hour journey brings passengers to Pusan in the wee morning hours. There are four classes of accommodations, with hot tubs, restaurant, and bars available. (Better to bring along your own snacks.) Call 738–0054 in Seoul, 463–3165 in Pusan, (03) 562–0541 in Tokyo. Fares range from $55 to $90 each way. A new ferry service is also now in operation between Osaka, Japan, and Pusan. The vessel, called the *88 Olympia,* departs from Osaka 1 p.m. every Wednesday and Saturday and from Pusan 5 p.m. every Monday and Thursday. Duration is approximately 21 hours and fares range from $90–200 each way, depending on the class of service.

DUTY-FREE items for personal use are allowed to be imported: two bottles of spirits, 400 cigarettes, 50 cigars, 250 grams of pipe tobacco, 100 grams of snuff, 100 grams of brick tobacco (or any combination of the above tobacco within 500 grams limit), and two bottles of perfume. Travelers planning to spend any time in the country should bring the maximum allowed, as all these items are very expensive locally. Those entering Korea with more than $5000 value in foreign currency are required to register the amount at customs. Upon depature, the amount of local currency allowed exchanged can not exceed U.S.$100.

CURRENCY of Korea is Ŵon (Ŵ), which is exchanged at just under Ŵ700 to U.S.$1. Notes are used in denominations of Ŵ1000, Ŵ5000 and Ŵ10,000. Coins can be found in denominations of 1, 5, 10, 50, 100, and 500 Ŵon.

LOCAL TIME in Korea is Greenwich Mean Time plus 9 hours. That makes the country 14 hours ahead of Eastern Standard Time, 17 hours in advance of Pacific Standard Time. It is in the same time zone as Japan and Okinawa, 1 hour ahead of Hong, Kong, Peking, Taipei, Macau, Malaysia, Singapore and Manila; 2 hours ahead of Bangkok and Jakarta.

LOCAL CURRENT in Korea is mainly 100 volts, sufficient to run electrical devices designed for 110 volts without loss of efficiency. About one-third of the rural areas now use 220 volts but major hotels provide dual voltage outlets. Power is in form of alternating current, according to international usage.

LOCAL WATER in most public places is potable. When in doubt in rural areas, drink bottled water, soda, or beer.

OFFICIAL LANGUAGE is Korean, a member of the Ural-Altaic family and considered closer to Hungarian, Finnish, or Turkish than to the other Oriental tongues. During the reign of King Sejong (1419–1450), the phonetic alphabet called Hangul was invented. This is viewed as the most brilliant achievement in the history of Korean culture. Romanizing the Korean language calls for some patience. For example, K is often replaced by G (Kyongju/Gyeongju) and T is replaced by D (Taegu/Daegu). P and B are frequently interchangeable (Pusan/Busan), CH by J (Cheju/Jeju) and inevitably R with L (Sorak/Seolag). A good imagination is often required in reading maps, road signs, and books; and the Ministry of Education apologizes for any confusion arising from inconsistency in Roman letters.

English is readily understood in all places of touristic interest. Indeed, it is the unofficial second language due to the visible presence of American military for the past three decades. In the rural areas, Japanese is understood by the older generation because they were schooled in the language through World War II.

There are two English language dailies available in the major cities: the *Korea Herald* and the *Korea Times* (but neither publishes a Mon. edition). There is also a weekly newsmagazine called *Korea Newsreview*, and a local edition of the U.S. military *Stars and Stripes*. *Time*, *Newsweek, The International Herald Tribune*, and the *Asian Wall Street Journal* are all available at newsstands in hotels and shopping arcades.

The U.S. Armed Forces Network operate eight transmitters and two FM stations with music, feature programs, and news. The U.S. military operates also AFKN-TV for its personnel and can be received on hotel sets throughout the country. The programs are terrible but the news is always welcome.

BUSINESS HOURS in the major cities run from 9 a.m. to 6 p.m. in good weather, until only 5 p.m. from Nov. through Mar. Government offices are open on Sat. from 9 a.m.–1 p.m. Banks open from 9:30 a.m. to 4:30 p.m. weekdays, until 1:30 p.m. on Sat. Foreign diplomatic missions are closed on Sat. and Sun. Major department stores

KOREA · · · 307

are open for business from about 10 a.m.–7:30 p.m. daily, street markets from early morning to late evening.

The **American Chamber of Commerce** is located on the third floor of the Chosun Hotel Building (Tel: 753–6471). The **World Trade Center Korea** houses 30 trade associations as well as the Trade Service Corner. It is located at 2–ga, Hoihyon-dong, Chung-gu, just a short walk from the Shinsegye Department Store. **KOTRA** (Korean Trade Promotion Corporation) also has an office here. Owner of the center is the Korean Traders Association (Tel: 28–8251), a nonprofit organization composed of all licensed traders in Korea.

TIPPING is not traditional in Korean custom, but times are certainly changing. Unless taxi drivers have helped with luggage or been asked to wait for you, they do not expect much of a tip (if anything). A 10% service charge is added to all hotel and better restaurant bills, and a 10% Value Added Tax is levied on most purchasable goods. Hotel and airport porters should get about ₩200 per bag. A good rule is always to reward when some service has been rendered.

TELEPHONE AND TELEX service in Korea is good. A direct-dialing system links Seoul with major provincial cities throughout the country, using the proper area code. International Direct Dialing (IDD), not yet available, is on its way. Meanwhile, dial (102) for assistance with calls to the U.S./Canada, Hong Kong, etc. Local calls can be placed from either red or green public phones, with a ₩10 coin piece (for 3 minutes). Yellow public phones accept ₩100 coin pieces, for direct-dial countrywide calls. Add more coins when you hear "pip-pip." Overages will be returned.

WHAT TO WEAR in Korea ranges from Dr. Zhivago-like overcoats and hats during the hard winter months to cool, cool cottons in summer. Chances are you'll want to avoid Seoul from December through February when it is snowy and so cold it almost hurts to breathe. During these months you should plan to dress very warmly for both outside and in. Korean homes and inns are ingeniously heated by *ondol* (hot floor), but the wicked wind manages to come through paper-thin windows and partitions. Wool socks, tights, long underwear, and a layered exterior is essential for this climate. Wear lighter woolens for the March to May springtime period. Summers are hot and humid, so lightweight cottons are recommended. Drip dries are fine for traveling, but the synthetic material is not very comfortable in humid weather. The autumn months (Sept. through Nov.) are the best in any northern hemisphere country, and Korea is no exception. The air is crisp and refreshing, the sunshine brilliant from a blue sky. Light woolens in layers are a good idea during these months, as early morning and later afternoons tend toward the cool side. Rain in both fall and spring can be harsh and bothersome. Pack proper gear, and remember that conservative clothing is the fashion here.

NOTE · · · the southern portion of the Korean peninsula and Cheju Island have a more temperate climate than Seoul. Winters are considerably milder, with summers drier and hotter. Cheju Island suffers from severe droughts, so much so that hotel swimming pools can be filled only during July and August.

LOCAL TRANSPORTATION is excellent throughout the country. In Seoul, there are two kinds of taxis: small and aging, and medium-size. Regular taxis charge ₩600 for the first 2 km and ₩50 for each additional 400 meters; the larger cars charge ₩800 initially with ₩100 for each additional 400 meters. Taxis also can be called from hotels and restaurants, with a basic fare of ₩1000.

The major cities have good local **bus** service, with an exact fare of ₩150 in coins (or a ₩140 token) no matter what your distance. There is no transfer system. Seoul also has a convenient **subway** system, with stations all an easy stroll from major touristic sites. The subway runs from the main railway station through the heart of the city to Cheongryangri (second most important railway station). It passes the Great South Gate (Namdae-mun) and Toksu Palace, turns right at Jongro. It stays underground past Great East Gate (Dongdae-mun) to Cheongryangri; there are seven 30-second stops between these two stations. In the southern direction, the train surfaces near the Han River and continues to Suweon or toward Inchon Port. Trains are scheduled every five minutes until midnight and fares start at ₩200 and increase according to the distance traveled. Three other subway routes are now under construction, and more are planned.

Korean National Railroads maintains an extensive network that connects the entire country. The super-express Saemaul runs between Seoul/Pusan (4 hrs. 50 min.), Seoul/Mogpo (5 hrs. 40 min.), and Seoul/Kyongju (4 hrs. 30 min.). The trains are clean, the service courteous, and the countryside lovely. But the stations have no good facilities, there are no porters in rural areas, and the embarkation platforms are always on the other side of several sets of stairs. DO NOT CARRY LUGGAGE INTO THE COUNTRYSIDE. Fares are reasonable and first-class tickets can be purchased up to ten days prior to departure.

The **highway** network is also excellent throughout Korea, and some ten express bus companies connect all major cities. For example, buses leave at one-hour intervals for Kyongju and the drive takes about four hours and 37 minutes. The cost is about one-third of the super-express train, and it's the same scenery. Ask your hotel concierge to help with ticket purchases.

Because the roads are so good, **car rentals** are not discouraged. (Most highway signs are in both Hangul and English.) Hertz Korean Rent-a-Car manages about 190 vehicles in Seoul, both self-drive and chauffeured. Drivers must be over 25 years of age, have a valid passport, and an international license. Charges change frequently but include a 10% VAT (Value Added Tax). (Tel: 585–0801, 798–0801, or 724–7465). There are about 30 cars for rent on Cheju Island, and the government has plans to provide rental cars at all tourist sites.

Korean Air Lines has the domestic monopoly, and it is just under one hour from Seoul to Cheju Island but it takes longer than an hour to pass through security and body check at Kimpo Airport. Domestic facilities and services are very poor, and watch out for excessive crowding.

There are passenger/car **ferries** daily between Cheju Island and Pusan or Mogpo, as well as summer trips between Pohang and Ulreungdo Island. A **hydrofoil** makes six trips daily between Pusan and Chungmu.

FESTIVALS AND HOLIDAYS in Korea combine the traditions of an agrarian society with somber remembrances of a people that has fought so long for freedom. Most of these events can be counted upon to be colorful sights, well worth a detour, for the native female costume is one of the most enchanting in all of Asia. Public holidays are marked with an asterisk(*).

*January 1–3 • *New Year's Day* • Also a reaffirmation of family ties.

*March 1 • *Samiljol or Independence Day* • Anniversary of the 1919 Independence Movement against Japanese colonial rule.

April • *Village Ritual of Unsan, Eunsan-gun, Chungcheongnam-do Province* • 13-day festival with ceremonies and processions led by farmers' bands. Ritual in honor of mountain spirit and certain generals. Designated Intangible Cultural Asset No. 9.

*April 5 • *Arbor Day* • Trees planted throughout countryside as part of reforestation program.

*March/April • *Buddha's Birthday* • Feast of Lanterns. Thousands of lanterns are displayed in temple courtyards and later carried in processions. (Note: Actually 8th day of the 4th lunar month.)

April (mid) • *Hansik-il or Cold Food Day* • Koreans visit ancestors' graves with offerings of cold dishes, meat, fruit, rice cakes, and wine.

May • *Chunhyang Festival, Namweon-gun, Jeonrabug-do Province* • Chunhyang is a Korean folk heroine, symbolizing distinguished beauty and conjugal fidelity. Pansori (narrative song) contests are held at the festival, where this native music originated.

*May 5 • *Children's Day* • Colorfully dressed children pack the parks and other attractions this day. Stresses the family as an abiding institution.

May 5 • *Arang Festival, Milyang-gun, Gyeongsangnam-do Province* • Another heroine distinguished for conjugal fidelity, this one from Silla Dynasty (57 B.C.–A.D. 935). Traditional ceremonies at Arang Shrine and contest for young woman exemplifying beauty and virtue, excellence in composition, music, painting, calligraphy, embroidery, and needlework. If she can be found!

June • *Kangnung Dano Festival, Gangneung, Gangweon-do Province* • A principal rural holiday, with traditional prayers for good harvest and dance processions of shamans and masks. Designated Intangible Cultural Asset No. 13.

June (early) • *Tano or Swing Day* • Summer festival when new food is offered to ancestors, and young girls gather in parks for "swinging matches."

***June 6** • *Memorial Day* • The nation's war dead are remembered with services throughout the country, most impressively at the National Cemetery.

***July 17** • *Constitution Day* • Commemorates proclamation of the Constitution of the Republic of Korea on July 17, 1948.

***August 15** • *Liberation Day* • Anniversary of Japanese acceptance of surrender to Allies and end of their domination in Korea. Also marks formal proclamation of Republic of Korea in 1948.

***August/September** • *Chusok or Korean Thanksgiving Day* • Harvest festival and full moon, so people offer food at ancestors' graves. (Note: Actually 15th day of 8th lunar month.)

September 28 • *Andong Folk Festival, Andong, Gyeongsangbug-do Province* • Warrior contests with Chajonnori (war of wagons), Hahoe

Mask Drama, and Girls' Bridge Crossing Game. Chajonnori is designated Intangible Cultural Asset No. 24.

*October 1 • *Armed Forces Day* • Parades, acrobatics, and honor guards are held at the May 16 Plaza on Yoido.

*October 3 • *National Foundation Day* • When legendary founder of the Korean Nation, named Tangun, established Kingdom of Ancient Chosun in 2333 B.C.

October 8 • *Mahan Folk Festival, Igsan-gun, Chungcheongnam-do Province* • Historical legends from Mahan to Paekche period as well as cultural relics are included in events of this festival.

October 8–10 • *Silla Cultural Festival, Kyongju, Kyongsangbug-do Province* • Folk festival held in ancient capital of Silla Dynasty. Concerts, poetry, dancing, praise to Buddha on grounds of Pulguk-sa Temple, archery, and photographic contest. All to revive spiritual and cultural activities pursued by people of ancient kingdom.

*October 9 • *Han'gul Day* • Celebrates anniversary of promulgation of Hangul, the national written language of Korea, invented under King Sejong in mid-15th century.

October • *Paekche Cultural Festival, Buyeo and Gongjiu, Chungcheongnam-do Province* • Held at both Gongju and Buyeo, last capitals of Paekche Kingdom, with rituals and processions and flower-crown dances.

October (mid) • *Moyang Castle Festival, Gochang-gun, Jeonra-bug-do Province* • Only castle festival in Korea, with 5000 women and girls praying for long life and ascension to heaven. Moyang Castle was completed in 1453, with labor of only women and girls.

October • *Halla Cultural Festival, Cheju-do* • Art contest, exhibitions, concerts, fireworks, lantern parade and bell ringing in temples and horn blowing on boats.

October • *Hansan Victory Festival, Chungmu, Gyeongsangnam-do Province* • Honors naval hero Admiral Yi Sun-shin's victory at Hansan Island during Hideyoshi's invasion of Korea in 1592. Ceremony commemorates eight treasures sent to Admiral Yi from king of China, lighting of sacred fire, and gun salute. Formal military parade, Chungmu victory and sword dances follow.

November (mid) • *Kaech'on (National Foundation) Art Festival, Jinju, Gyeongsangnam-do Province* • Contests in Chinese poetry, calligraphy, music, art exhibitions, and drama. Famous sword dances.

*December 25 • *Christmas Day* • Observed with great pomp in Korea due to large American military and other Western communities.

BACKGROUND MATERIAL on Korea is more varied and plentiful than you might expect from perusing the average hotel bookshop. Serious readers should visit the **Kyobo Book Center,** across from the big Sejong Cultural Center at Kwanghwamun intersection (in the new Korea Education Insurance Building). It is the biggest bookstore in Seoul and has a comprehensive foreign language section on Korea. An alternative and most rewarding shop can be found at the Korea branch of the **Royal Asiatic Society,** Christian Center Bldg., 136-46 Yun ji-dong, Chongno-ku, near Chong-no 5-ka (Tel: 763–9483). The RAS has been publishing lectures by its members since 1900, plus several books that were written locally. Visitors are also welcome to sign up for RAS tours as well as those conducted by the Korea Art Club.

Through Gates of Seoul by Edward B. Adams (two volumes, $10 each). The author was born in Taegu in 1934 and has spent most of his life in Korea. He probably knows it better and writes about it better than any of the longtime Western residents. These two volumes are informative and worthy of the finest coffee table.

5000 Years of Korean Art edited by Choi Sunu ($120). Only for those with very serious interests in the art of this country, published in 1979 to coincide with traveling exhibit in the United States.

Korean Chests by Michael Wickman. Anyone interested in buying antique chests should spend the $5 to read this guide. A good primer.

History of Korea by Han Woo-Keun ($14). Most readable single volume history, revised for Western readers by an American editor.

Korean Patterns by Paul S. Crane ($5 at RAS). Still the single, basic tome on what makes Korea tick. History and cultural background, sometimes oversimplified but easily understood.

Seoul Past and Present by Allen D. and Donald N. Clark ($12.50 at RAS). Comprehensive guide to the capital by long-time residents. Lots of background and history for those planning to stay around.

The Korean Cookbook by Judy Hyun ($10). Comprehensive and practical. Recipes written so Western ingredients can be used.

History of Korean Literature by James Hoyt. This soon-to-be-published anthology is translated and compiled by the former Cultural Attache of the U.S. Embassy, a charming fellow who has served his country well in several posts around the Far East. Jim was also a president of the Royal Asiatic Society. Worth waiting for, to understand a bit more of Korean culture.

WHAT TO SEE AND DO

SEOUL IN A CAPSULE

Chinese character means capital . . . City of Kings . . . chosen by Yi T'aejo in A.D. 1392 as seat of ruling dynasty that boasted 27 successive kings . . . until deposed by Japanese annexation in 1910 . . . gateway to Korean peninsula since country united . . . once enclosed by 10-mile-long city wall with 9 gates, of which 4 still stand . . . a miracle metropolis with 8 million inhabitants . . . a phoenix from the ashes with modern high rises just 3 decades after devastation following the Korean conflict . . . but the intrigues surrounding 5-century-old palaces still remain the focal point of city life.

Seoul

Capitol Building • Located in the square in front of Kyongbok Palace . . . built in 1926 by the Japanese as a government-general structure . . . a symbol of the heavy-handed architecture their long occupation left behind . . . utilized by U.S. military following World War II . . . burned beyond repair by Communist troops heading north in 1950 . . . finally rehabilitated during 1961 military coup . . . now used as a central government office building.

Changdok Palace • Palace of Illustrious Virtue . . . built in the reign of T'aejo (A.D. 1394) but burned and rebuilt several times since . . . used as a royal residence until 1910 . . . now a favorite of most visitors . . . watch for the **Tonhwa-mun** (Gate of Mighty Transformation) dating from A.D. 1404 . . . cross the famous **Kumchon-gyo** (Forbidden Stream Bridge) . . . visit the **Injong-jon** (Hall of Benevolent Government) first built in 1404 and rebuilt in 1804 . . . small museum here shows personal effects of royal family . . . also royal garage on premises, filled with antique autos . . . some members of the royal family still inhabit **Nakson-jae** . . . not open to public . . . but **Piwon** (Secret Garden) is . . . 78 acres of woodlands reserved for royal family during Yi Dynasty . . . one of Seoul's loveliest parks . . . 44 pleasure pavilions, bridges, ponds, and picnic areas throughout.

Changgyong-won ● To the east of the Secret Garden . . . formerly the site of **Changgyong** (Glorious Blessings) Palace . . . being restored for Olympics . . . flowering cherry trees in spring.

Chogye-sa ● Chief temple of Korean Buddhism . . . founded only in 1910 . . . located near Hankook Ilbo (newspaper tower) and American Embassy Compound No. 2 . . . easily accessible to visitors . . . main building moved up from a southern province by a mystic . . . festivities on Buddha's birthday (early May) very impressive here.

Chongmyo ● Royal Ancestral Tablet House . . . located in a wooded corner of Changdok Palace . . . ancestral tablets of Yi Dynasty kings and queens housed here . . . grounds open daily, but courtyards and main shrines only accessible during ceremonials.

Chongno Bell ● Originally cast in A.D. 1468 . . . originally rung every morning and evening as signal to open and close gates of the city . . . 33 times at daybreak for 33 heavens of Buddhism . . . 28 times at sunset for 28 principal stars in the heavens . . . too fragile to be even rung at the New Year now . . . hangs at intersection of Chongno and Namdaemun-no.

Independence Arch ● Erected in 1896 by members of the Independence Club . . . symbolized Korea's independence from China and establishment of Great Han Empire . . . later symbolized freedom from Japanese domination . . . now rather inconspicuous due to elevated highway overhead.

Kojong Memorial ● Erected in 1902 to honor King Kojon's 40th year on the throne . . . inside the **Mansei-mun** (Ten Thousand Year Gate) is a stone tablet indicating the distances in *li* to various sections of the country . . . located at northeast corner of Kwanghwa-mun intersection.

Korea House ● Established in 1956 by Ministry of Culture and Information . . . new facility completed in 1981 . . . largest single traditional Korean house in the country today . . . designed after Chagyongjon (residence of Yi Dynasty queens) of Kyongbok Palace . . . main hall has three traditional *ondol* (heated floor) rooms for meals and entertainment . . . buffet lunch and dinners also served in Sohwadang . . . exhibition and sale of traditional Korean handicrafts and art . . . performances of folk dances and music . . . located at 80-2 Pildong, 2-ga, Chunggu, Seoul . . . Tel: 267–8752) . . . open Mon. through Sat. (except holidays) from 10 a.m . . . Worth a visit.

Kyongbok Palace • Shining Happiness Palace . . . originally built in A.D. 1395 by Yi T'aejo, founder of the Yi Dynasty . . . devastated by the Japanese invasion of 1592 . . . again in 1868 . . . rebuilt for King Kojong . . . his queen allegedly murdered here . . . Kojong and crown prince fled in sedan chairs to nearby Russian legation . . . one of most historic sites in Seoul . . . **Kwanghwa-mun** (Gate of Transformation by Light) behind Capitol Building was original entrance . . . **Kunjong-jon** (Throne Hall) dominates entire area . . . still used for official receptions in honor of visiting dignitaries and statesmen . . . visit also **Hyangwon-jong** (Lotus Pavilion). . . . **Kuonghoe-ru** (Hall of Happy Meetings) . . . 13-storied **Koryo Pagoda** dating from 1348 and one of the monuments moved here by the Japanese . . . grounds also include **National Museum of Art** and **National Folk Art Museum.**

May 16 Plaza • On reclaimed land in the middle of the Han River . . . Named after date of military revolution in 1961 . . . used for armed forces parades and religious revival meetings . . . like Billy Graham.

Namdaemun • Great South Gate . . . designated National Treasure No. 1 . . . dates from A.D. 1448 . . . now dwarfed by high rises near Seoul Railway Station . . . proper name is Sungnye-mun or Gate of Exalted Ceremony and one of 9 entrances to the ancient city.

Nam-san • South Mountain . . . the No. 1 landmark in Seoul . . . rises from the center of the capital . . . signal fires atop Nam-san were important to the defense of the city in ancient times . . . **Seoul Tower** now stands on the highest peak . . . lower slopes are being built up with hotels and national structures . . . cable car available to top for hiking and picnicking in the park . . . 3 traffic tunnels through the mountain aid motorists in traversing the city.

National Assembly • Located on Yoido in Han River . . . assembly meets in a futuristic building on an island (at one time Seoul's airport) in the Han River . . . designed by Korea's leading architect, Kim Soo Gun, who is also responsible for the innovative **Space Center and Theater** . . . where music, dance, drama and art exhibitions take place.

National Folk Museum/National Museum • Kyongbok Palace grounds . . . open daily from 9 a.m. to 5 p.m. with small admission charge . . . the folklore museum displays the culture and crafts of rural Korea . . . including traditional articles in everyday use . . . National Museum of Seoul contains a fine collection of Paekche and Silla pottery, Yi Dynasty paintings and scrolls, Koryo and Yi porcelains.

National Theater/National Classical Music School • Located on the lower slope of Nam-san, en route to Shilla Hotel . . . watch for performances of students under Korea's National Living Treasures in the art of classical dance, drama, and music . . . Confucian court instruments also displayed here.

Pagoda Park • Commemorates Korean Declaration of Independence in 1919 . . . every March 1, the proclamation signed by 33 Korean patriots is read here . . . located on Chong-no . . . former site of a Buddhist temple . . . 13-story pagoda dates from A.D. 1464 and was transplanted from Wongak-sa (temple).

Russian Legation • Designated Community Cultural Relic No. 3 . . . ruins of old legation known as Yanggwan . . . originally built in 1890, although most destroyed during Korean War . . . historic landmark since King Kojong and the Crown Prince fled here in 1896 following murder of Queen Min . . . located in Chong Dong area of foreign residences . . . right next door to American Embassy Residence . . . and Seoul Club, where King Kojong lived after fire destroyed Toksu Palace in 1904.

Sajik Park • Site of the ancient altars to gods of earth and harvest . . . located between Capitol and Independence Gate . . . until 1897 the King would offer sacrifices in spring and autumn on behalf of the country . . . now a public park with swimming pool, children's library . . . and Pavilion of the Yellow Cranes . . . where archers use traditional implements.

Samchong Park • Named for the Three Pure Ones, a Taoist trinity . . . the site of the North Gate to the city . . . located about a mile north of the Capitol . . . worth the trek for its panoramic views.

Seoul Grand Park • New site of city's zoological gardens.

Seoul Railway Station • An unimposing but important landmark to all visitors . . . built by the Japanese in early 1900s and considered "brewery baroque " . . . withstood the ravages of 20th-century history . . . although there are plans to relocatē it on the south side of the Han River.

St. Mary's Cathedral • Oldest Catholic edifice in Korea . . . built in 1890s and a landmark in the Myongdong district . . . only building within miles left standing after Korean War . . . quaint interior . . . sanctuary only church in Seoul that boasts some real pipe organs . . .

A Chinese junk becomes many with a multiple lens.

The Star Ferry is a constant in everchanging Hong Kong . . .

. . . while a Singaporean elder transports himself.

The five-story pagoda is a symbol of Japan's cultural history.

The Mong children in Northern Thailand adore attention and flair pens.

Government buildings from Kuala Lampur's colonial period are Moorish-style grandiose.

A Cebu woman carries Filipino specialties aloft.

Fledgling Burmese monks and their dog pose in Mandalay.

Hindu ladies in Singapore greet wedding guests with jasmine petals and perfumed water.

A World War II cemetery lies beside the infamous bridge over the River Kwai.

The rock garden at Ryong-ji, attributed to landscape architect Soami, is one of Kyoto's many inspirational sites.

A walk through the morning calm of Korea's ancient Pulguk-sa temple complex.

Hand painted Thai umbrellas are an irresistible souvenir from Chieng Mai.

Macau may need a coat of paint but architectural details are impressive.

Two young Japanese dress as Ohara maidens during a local festival.

Raffles Hotel, named after the founder of Singapore, will reopen in 1992 following restoration.

what remains after Communist army took the majority for use as war materiel.

Temple of Heaven • 3-tiered pavilion located between Chosun and Lotte hotels . . . from 1897 to 1910, King Kojong (now Emperor Kwangmu) transferred harvest ceremonies from Sajik Altar to this new Altar of Heaven . . . all that remains of this fine edifice is the **Hwang-gung-u** (Temple of Imperial Firmament) . . . once contained a memorial tablet to spirit of Yi T'aejo, founder of the dynasty.

Toksu Palace • Palace of Virtuous Longevity . . . originally built as residence of Prince Wolsan, grandson of King Sejo, who reigned from A.D. 1455–68 . . . present name given in 1907 when King Kojong abdicated and went to live here . . . now home of National Museum of Modern Art . . . notice **Chunghwa-jon** (Hall of Central Harmony) . . . and **Kwangmyong-mun** (Bright Light Gate) . . . museum is at western end of palace grounds . . . gardens noted for peonies in the spring and chrysanthemums in the fall.

Tongdae-mun • Great East Gate . . . also known as Hunginji-mun (Gate of Uplifting Mercy) . . . shares National Treasure No. 1 designation with Namdaemun (Great South Gate) . . . present structure dates only from 1869, replacing original of T'aejo and Sejong reigns . . . distinctive feature is semicircular outside wall . . . entry only through well-defended narrow opening to the north.

Tong-myo • East Shrine . . . located about a quarter-mile's walk outside Tongdae-mun . . . shrine dedicated to Kwan-u, God of War, and contains some interesting . . . but dingy relics.

Yi Sun-sin • Admiral and master warrior . . . statue erected in 1968 to Ch'ung mu-kon (Loyalty-Chivalry Lord), the Admiral's posthumous and honorary title . . . used famous "turtle boat" to destroy Japanese fleet in 1592 . . . only major defeat suffered by Japan before World War II . . . country's favorite Admiral . . . well placed at Kwanghwa-mun intersection.

Seoul Environs

Inchon • Major port for Seoul . . . the landing here of General Douglas MacArthur in 1950 with U.N. Forces has become one of history's major military maneuvers . . . this port has played a major role in Korea's political life . . . first Westerners to ever visit the country passed through here in 1880s . . . Japanese and Russian navies fought here in 1904 . . . busy and modern port city . . . Yonan Breakwater famous for seafood . . . reachable from Seoul in less than one hour by subway.

Kanghwa-do ● Kanghwa Island . . . Korea's 5th largest island, just 1½ hours drive northwest of Seoul . . . important to country's history for over 4000 years . . . center of celadon pottery in 12th century . . . Kanghwa appears in legends from 2333 B.C. . . . when mythical founder of country, Tan'gun, thought to have erected an altar on island's highest peak Mani-san . . . **Samnang Fortress** said to have been built by Tan'gun's sons in a single day . . . **Chondung-sa** within is one of Korea's top 30 temples . . . visit also **Pomun-sa,** founded by Buddhist monk named Hoejong in A.D. 635.

Korean Folk Village ● Working, living village formed in 1974 . . . about 20 miles south of Seoul . . . offers a good overview of traditional rural life and crafts . . . approximately 200 large and small buildings around a 163-acre site . . . private dwellings representative of the whole country . . . shops, schools, municipal-like structures . . . gossip corners for the village elders, etc. . . . the inhabitants live and work under your gaze . . . open-air folk dances . . . simulated weddings and funeral services in season . . . open year-round . . . admission about $3.50 per person . . . dress appropriately for walking in the countryside . . . tours from Seoul available . . . about $35 per person, with lunch.

Kumgok-nung ● Royal tombs of last two Yi Dynasty rulers . . . located in Kumgok, about 13 miles east of the East Gate . . . Emperor-style tombs . . . Hong-nung is tomb of Kojong and wife, Queen Min . . . Yu-nung contains Sunjong, last ruler of Yi Dynasty . . . tomb built by Chinese craftsmen under Japanese supervision . . . considered the most magnificent of all Korean royal tombs.

Kwang-nung ● Tomb of infamous ruler Sejo (A.D. 1455–1468) . . . located about 20 miles north of Seoul in National Forest district . . . Sejo grabbed throne from nephew through murder . . . became devout Buddhist later in remorse . . . many temples and hermitages near his tomb here . . . pleasant walking tour in good weather.

Namhansan Castle ● Fortress with a 2000 year history . . . located some 15 miles southeast of Seoul . . . present 5 miles of preserved walls were originally constructed A.D. 1626 . . . spectacular view from top . . . visit also Yoju, with Silla Dynasty temple Shinrruk-sa located on South Han River . . . Young-nung contains royal tomb of King Sejong (1418–50), father of Sejo and considered one of the

more intellectual rulers . . . some 11 miles from here, village of Ichon
is famous for reproductions of Yi Dynasty porcelains at reasonable prices.

Onyang ● Popular spa dating from Koryo period (A.D. 918–1392)
. . . King Sejo stopped by in 1464 and found a cool "holy well"
among the hot-spring waters . . . visit also nearby Asan where shrine
of Hyon-ch'ung erected in 1706 now honors Admiral Yi Sun-shin, who
repressed Japanese fleet in 1592 with his famous "turtle boats" . . .
located about 60 miles south of Seoul.

Panmunjom ● Demilitarized Zone . . . 2½-mile wide area where
North and South Korea meet . . . Joint Security Area . . . Armistice
Commission building (where talks still take place) . . . Freedom Bridge
over which 12,773 Korean War prisoners walked . . . Bridge of No
Return . . . Freedom House . . . only way civilians can tour the area
is through Korean Travel Bureau . . . book 3 days in advance . . .
passports are required . . . children under 12 not permitted . . . no
photography allowed . . . a thoroughly sobering experience . . . even
30 years later . . . located less than 35 miles northwest of Seoul.

Suwon ● Walled city . . . designated National Treasure No. 403,
but worth only a scant visit . . . unless you wish to taste the local
kalbii or marinated broiled beef rib, or take the narrow gauge railroad
from Suwon Station to Songdo Station—a 2-hour and 40-minute trip
. . . through beautiful and rural countryside south of Inchon . . . Suwon itself is only about an hour's drive from Seoul . . . has popular
golf club for members and visitors . . . not far from Korean Folk Village.

Tonggu-nung ● East Nine Tombs . . . best known and most easily accessible of all royal tombs near the capital . . . contains the graves
of 7 kings, including Yi T'aejo, founder of the dynasty . . . around the
tombs are wooded hills and ravines . . . a lovely area just 8 miles
outside the East Gate.

MT. SORAK

MT. SORAK IN A CAPSULE

Snow Peak Mountain chain of over 5000 foot peaks near East Sea
. . . just a few miles south of Demilitarized Zone . . . dubbed
Switzerland of Asia . . . about 138 square miles of spectacular
forests, waterfalls and lakes, rugged peaks . . . area divided into
Inner Sorak and Outer Sorak . . . tallest peak is 5636-foot Tae-
chong-bong, Korea's 3rd highest . . . year-round sport area for
hiking, skiing, skating, tobagganing, golf, and fishing . . . still
relatively unknown to foreign visitors . . . beaches on East Sea
just a few miles from national park . . . also historic temples,
hermitages and shrines . . . park is just about 1 hour by air from
Seoul . . . over 5 hours by express bus along super-highway . . .
nearest city is Sokcho with 70,000-plus population . . . comfortable tourist hotels in park . . . country's largest hotel/condomin-
ium/recreation complex now under construction on some 400 acres
. . . slated to put this snow peak chain on the map of Asia.

Oe-Sorak (Outer Sorak)

Chonbuldong Valley • Imaginative outcroppings . . . valley noted
for craggy shapes and forms resembling praying monks and lions thousands of years old . . . like an exhibition . . . also many lovely ponds,
lakes, and falls.

Hindulbawi Rock • Rocking Rock . . . huge boulder north of
Sinhung Temple . . . average person can put rock into motion.

Kye jo-am • Hermitage near Heundeul Rock . . . stone Buddha
in small cave . . . legend says famous monks Wonhyo and Uisang
came here to practice asceticism.

Kumgang-gul • Cave about 2 miles from Sorak Village . . . findings of tools, utensils, and Buddha statues . . . indicate high monk

spent time here . . . possibly to attain enlightenment . . . 649 stairs upward.

Kwongum Fortress • 3600 feet high . . . Kwongum Cable car runs from Sorak-dong up to fortress . . . surrounded by over 6600-foot stone wall . . . constructed perhaps as early as Silla Dynasty . . . simple lodgings atop now available for climbers.

Piryong and Towang-song Falls • Located southeast of Sinhung-sa . . . favorites for beautiful rainbows created . . . like a silvery ribbon suspended between the falls . . . Piryong also known as Flying Dragon Falls . . . another name for both is Singwan, God's Light Falls.

Pison-dae Plateau • Flying Fairy Peak . . . legend says an angel ascended to heaven from here . . . after enjoying natural grandeur from Wason-dae Plateau . . . visitors, too, will enjoy the beauty and majesty.

Sinhung-sa • Temple built by God's Revelation . . . main temple in Outer Sorak area . . . first constructed on site by Priest Chajang in 632 A.D. . . . came from Silla Dynasty nobility . . . Chajang disobeyed call to Silla court . . . quoted as saying "I would rather die keeping laws of Buddha for only one day . . . than live for one hundred years while breaking them" . . . temple destroyed by fire in 1842 . . . rebuilt in present state in 1847 . . . now encompasses 7 buildings . . . stone carvings excellent for those interested in rubbings . . . large bell and some wooden blocks date from Yi Dynasty . . . temple just a short walk from Sorak-dong.

Sorak-dong • Tourist village . . . inns, hotels, restaurants, shops here . . . also starting point for most hikes into national park.

Ulsanbawi Rock • Mountain of granite, quartz, and mica . . . legend says a god was carrying huge rock bound for peaks of Mt. Kumgan-sun . . . also known as Diamond Mountains . . . now located north of DMZ . . . when he learned there were already 12,000 peaks . . . rock was dropped at this point . . . a spectacular outcropping.

Yangpok Falls • Positive/Negative . . . noteworthy because Koreans believe the yin and yang fall together here.

Nae-Sorak (Inner Sorak)

Changsu-dae Villa • Resting place for weary travelers . . . built in 1958 . . . commemorates victorious battle fought here during Korean conflict.

Madung-ryong Pass • Range dividing Inner and Outer Sorak . . . rises some 4500 feet above sea level.

Oknyotang • Legendary waterfall . . . tradition says an angel used to bathe at Taesung Falls . . . attacked by monster . . . fled to Oknyotang Falls . . . monster followed but angel saved by thunderbolt from gods.

Ose-am • Hermitage on southern edge . . . known for story of Monk Maewol . . . came here with young nephew for spiritual studies . . . child left in hermitage during severe winter weather . . . found dead but striking bell before statue of Buddha . . . listen for the hollow sound of bells.

Paektam-sa • Temple of One Hundred Pools . . . situated at gateway to Inner Sorak area . . . fine resting place for climbers . . . moved to present site by monks who gave attention to a revelation.

Pongjon-am • Highest hermitage in Korea . . . built during Silla Dynasty . . . on highest point in the country . . . rock named Pongbawi above it . . . records lowest temperatures in Korea.

Taesung Waterfall • One of 3 largest in Korea . . . rainbow here considered one of wonders of Mt. Sorak area.

Environs

Choksan Hot Springs • Just outside Sokcho City . . . features bathing facilities . . . both public and private . . . small hotels.

Chonggan-jong Pavilion • One of 8 wonders of Mt. Sorak area . . . graceful pavilion perched on wooded foothills . . . at juncture of Chonggan-chon Stream . . . from deep in Mt. Sorak . . . and East Sea.

Hajodae Pavilion • Near Naksan-sa Temple area . . . adjacent beach also popular . . . visit also Hanryon-am (hermitage).

Hwajinpo Beach • Most northern on East Coast . . . considered one of Korea's most beautiful beaches . . . and most unspoiled.

Kyongpo-dae Pavilion • Mirror Lake pavilion . . . stands on hills near Kyongpo-ho (lake) . . . known locally as Kyongpo Three Moons . . . moon pillars . . . moon pagoda . . . moon wave . . . among beautiful pine trees . . . lovely blossoms in season.

Naksan-sa • Built by great monk Evisang . . . according to a revelation following enlightenment at Hongryon-am (hermitage), the great monk built this temple . . . Haesugwanumbosalsang, 50-foot standing statue of granite . . . Buddhist Goddess of Mercy . . . looks down upon East Sea . . . popular as prayer site for fishermen's safe return.

Ojukhon • Former home of philosopher Yi Yulgok . . . great statesman and philosopher . . . Yi Dynasty figure . . . Ojuk means black bamboo . . . together with old pine trees create elegant and serene atmosphere around the house.

Sokcho • Major city on eastern seaboard . . . located about 10 minutes from Sorak National Park turnoff . . . population of over 70,000 . . . fishing port . . . now busy with park tourists . . . less than one hour by air from Seoul . . . 5 hours by express bus . . . don't forget to pay attention to fascinating fleet of fishing boats.

Uisang-dae Pavilion • A favorite of monk Euisang . . . located near Naksan-sa . . . strolling place of the monk . . . popular now for sun rises viewed over East Sea . . . plus natural beauty of old pine trees.

Woljong-sa • One of oldest temples of Silla Dynasty . . . nestled at foot of Mt. Odae . . . octagonal pagoda constructed by Monk Jajang of Silla period . . . temple itself often rebuilt because of fires . . . at gateway of Odae-san National Park . . . 180 square miles.

PUSAN

Chinhae • Beautiful natural harbor . . . headquarters of Korea's naval forces . . . just 24 miles from Pusan . . . hosts famous Cherry Blossom festival each spring.

Chinju • Ancient fortress on cliffs of South River . . . legend says that Nongae . . . Kisaeng entertainer . . . drove foreign general to edge of cliff . . . then took her own life . . . sacrifice in 1592 is recorded on Unirangam (Faithful Woman Rock).

PUSAN IN A CAPSULE

Korea's second largest city . . . until 1969 its principal port . . . present population about 3 million . . . a "special city" administered separately rather than part of a province . . . has been a cosmopolitan harbor since ancient times . . . only gateway to outside world during Korea's "hermit kingdom" . . . formally opened for trade by Japanese in 1876 . . . Japanese began construction of the railway north in 1904 . . . only major city in South Korea never in enemy hands during conflict . . . large United Nations Cemetery stands as reminder of the sacrifices . . . today Pusan a bustling, modern metropolis . . . located in a "cauldron" . . . beneath 2500-foot peaks . . . name dates from Koryo period . . . most temperate climate in the country after Cheju-do . . . terminus for ferry traffic to Japan, Hallyo Waterway, and Cheju-do.

Haein-sa ● One of jewels of Mt. Kaya area . . . temple founded in 802 A.D. . . . preserves important historic and artistic treasures . . . repository of Tripitaka Koreana . . . 80,000 wooden printing blocks engraved with most comprehensive compilations of Buddhist scriptures in all Asia . . . blocks carved by royal command in 13th century . . . temple complex encompasses about 4 miles . . . as many as 93 satellite temples, hermitages, and shrines in this area . . . but Tripitaka considered national treasure . . . and one of the great wonders of the ages.

Haeundae Beach ● Most beautiful beach in area . . . located about 11 miles northeast of center city . . . long and sandy beach in a gentle curve . . . bounded on west by Tongbaek-do . . . rocky, wooded islet . . . Chosun Beach Hotel only place worthy of a special detour.

Hallyo Waterway ● Stretches from Kojedo (island) . . . shimmering expanse of placid water . . . southwest of Pusan . . . past fishing village of Chungmu (named for Admiral Yi Sun-Shin's posthumous title) . . . onto refinery and industry port of Yosu.

Hansando ● Island famous as battle area in A.D. 1592 . . . Admiral Yi Sun-shin scored famous naval victory here . . . using world's first iron-clad ships . . . built in form of turtles . . . also site of renovated headquarters of Admiral Yi . . . military training hall . . . and Chungyolsa shrine . . . victory festival held every year on Oct. 27 . . . with sacred fire and gun salute.

Pomo-sa ● One of 3 greatest temples in southern province . . . located north of Tongnae . . . on eastern slopes of Mt. Kumjong . . . one of largest Buddhist temples in country . . . also known as Sanskrit Fish Temple . . . founded in A.D. 678 . . . present construction dates from 1717 . . . contains original 7th century stone pagoda and other carvings . . . number of shrines and hermitages scattered throughout wooded slopes . . . has beautiful approach via arched stone bridge . . . over babbling mountain brook.

Pusan Tower ● Observation point in Yongdusan Park . . . worth the view from this television-observation tower . . . Yongdusan or Dragon Head Mountain . . . overlooks city . . . see also statue of Admiral Yi.

Tongdo-sa ● Korea's largest monastery . . . located midway between Pusan and Kyongju . . . via super-highway . . . main temple complex consists of 35 buildings . . . plus 13 small hermitages in surrounding hills . . . founded in A.D. 647 by Chajang . . . one of Korea's greatest monks who traveled to China and returned with Tripitaka (Buddhist scriptures) and piece of Buddha's skullbone and tooth . . . Tongdo-sa is traditionally a Zen temple . . . name means "to save the world by mastering the truth" . . . watch for Four Heavenly Kings . . . and rainbow-shaped bridge . . . beautiful setting, especially in autumn.

Taejongdae Park ● Named after King Muyol . . . located on tip of peninsula overlooking sea on Yong-do (island) . . . named for Silla ruler who spent leisure time here after unification of Three Kingdoms . . . lighthouse stands on promontory.

Tongnae Hot Springs ● Noted for medicinal effects . . . located about 9 miles north of central Pusan . . . variety of hotels and inns offering curative baths . . . said to have been well known as spa since 17th century . . . very old town.

United Nations Cemetery ● Only one of its kind in the world . . . dedicated to members of armed forces of 16 Korean War allies . . . from conflict of 1950–53 . . . every faith represented . . . but American war dead repatriated to U.S. . . . impressive central plaza and chapel . . . Korean government maintains cemetery in appreciation of those who sacrificed their lives for the war.

CHEJU – DO

CHEJU-DO IN A CAPSULE

Island of the Gods . . . about 60 miles off southern Korean coastline . . . less than 1½ hours by air from Seoul or Pusan . . . another side of Korean culture . . . first under mainland control in 938 during Koryo . . . later conquered by Mongols who began horse and cattle breeding . . . a place of exile for Yi Dynasty political undesirables . . . first spot in Korea visited by Westerners . . . 36 shipwrecked Dutch sailors in 1653 . . . 700 square miles of fertile land and temperate climate . . . known for tangerine groves, fishing industry, cattle, barley, carrots, garlic and onions, sweet potatoes, and sesame . . . 400,000 population . . . now thriving tourism . . . mainly honeymooners from mainland and Japanese golfers . . . trademark of the culture is Tol Harubang . . . grandfather images carved from porous lava . . . entire island dominated by Mt. Halla . . . dormant volcano with huge lake in crater at summit.

Cheju-City ● Capital of the island . . . located midpoint of north shore . . . about 100,000 population . . . new and old city . . . visit **Kwandokchong Pavilion,** built in 1448 . . . used as training place by court-appointed magistrates . . . also **Folklore Museum** (new and better one promised) . . . **Sarabong Hill,** with good views of harbor . . . now a children's park . . . **Yongduam Rock** (Dragonhead Rock) in northwest corner of city . . . just east is **Yongyon Pond** and **Kurum (Cloud) Bridge . . .** which costs W40 to cross!

Cholbaum Rock ● Intriguing formation offshore . . . just 20 minutes south from Hallim . . . Tradition says represents fisherman's wife waiting for husband's return from the sea.

Chongup Village ● Designated cultural asset . . . located in eastern section of island . . . represents mountain people . . . 1000-year-old trees, small thatched houses . . . warm and friendly people.

Chungmun Beach • Spectacular sandy area . . . just east is Chonjeyon Waterfall . . . bathing place of celestial beings . . . two cascades but often dry in summer . . . Chungmun is terminal point of 2nd cross-island highway.

Mt. Halla • Korea's highest mountain . . . dominates Cheju Island . . . from 6397 feet . . . volcanic cone last active in A.D. 1007 . . . but 15 separate lava flows identified . . . large crater at summit with Paeknokdam or White Deer Lake . . . worth the 6-hour round-trip hike.

Hallim • West coast town in midst of fishing industry . . . visit the famous Hallim weavers . . . best excuse for making journey to Cheju-do . . . **Isidore Ranch** run by Catholic Church since 1955 raises sheep for wool . . . cottage industries run by sisters make Irish-style sweaters . . . call on Sister Rosarii for tour of handicraft center and shop . . . closed Sun.

Hamdock Beach • One of 4 fine beaches on the north shore . . . located about 25-minute drive from Cheju-City . . . also visit **Samyang** (about 10 min. away) . . . **Kimnyong** (being developed by inhabitants of local village) . . . and **Sehwari** . . . another 10 minutes east.

Hangpaduri • Dedicated to resistance against Mongols . . . historic monument located halfway between Hallim and Cheju-City . . . Mongol troops invaded island in A.D. 1232 . . . sacked whole peninsula later . . . occupied Koryo Kingdom on mainland from 1270 to 1294 . . . used island as pasture for their ponies.

Hwasun Beach • Memorial to the shipwrecked men of Dutch sailing ship *Sparrow Hawk* in 1653 . . . erected in 1980 in memory of the seamen . . . Hendrick Hamel and some survivors spent 13 years in southern part of Korean peninsula . . . Hamel escaped to Japan and recorded his adventures in 1668 . . . first account of Korea to appear in Europe.

Hyupjaegul Cave • On southern outskirts of Hallim . . . located near Hyupjae Beach . . . cavern of common Cheju lavatubes . . . sand from beach formed iciclelike stalactites and stalagmites.

Ilchulbong • Sunrise Mountain . . . located at eastern end of island . . . near fishing village of Songsanpo . . . also called Fortress Mountain Port . . . curious volcanic cone towers overhead . . . one of 360 parasitic volcanos that stud the island . . . trail leads up western side . . . helicopter rides also available . . . spectacular sight at sunrise.

Sagul • Cave of the Serpent . . . Manjang and Kimnyong are two most popular snake caves on island . . . **Manjang Lava Tube** is longest known in world (4.2 miles) . . . now has lighting system and refreshments for visitors . . . old belief that huge demonlike serpent lived in this lava tube . . . young virgin sacrificed every year to avoid disasters . . . practice ended in 1625 by killing of the snake by military officer . . . monument erected by his descendants in 1973 . . . tradition of snake cult on Cheju-do still lingers.

Sam Songhyol • Cave of Three Spirits . . . 3 gods said to have appeared on this site—Ko, Pu, and Liang . . . considered the island's forefathers . . . visitors should call here first to appreciate the mystical mood that permeates this island.

Sanbanggul-sa • Temple Grotto . . . located west of Chungmun Beach . . . seated Buddha image in cave . . . this hermitage once considered the dwelling place of Monk Hyeildaedog of Koryo Dynasty . . . good views from front of grotto.

Sogwipo • Main port on southern coast . . . located almost in direct line across island from Cheju-City . . . accessible in less than an hour by either of 2 cross-island highways . . . mild subtropical climate here year-round . . . thriving tangerine and pineapple industry . . . beautiful vistas from rugged coastline . . . important touristic center after Cheju-City . . . **Chongbang Waterfall** east of port . . . **Chonjiyon Waterfall** west of port . . . both popular with visitors . . . see also **Sogwipo Steps** . . . inclined exposure of sea bed of Late Pleistocene period . . . 10-minute drive west of Sogwipo takes you to **Oedolgae (Lonely) Rock** . . . through local grass and pine trees.

KYONGJU

——— KYONGJU IN A CAPSULE ———

Former capital of the Silla Dynasty . . . Korea's southern kingdom . . . for almost 1000 years (57 B.C. to A.D. 935) . . . called Kumsong or Golden City . . . considered one of the world's 10 greatest historic metropoli . . . 1 million inhabitants at its height of power . . . with structures all roofed of tiles . . . heated with charcoal . . . now a rather sleepy town of 100,000 . . . but the country's major tourist attraction . . . an open-air museum . . . ancient sites and recent excavations of Silla Dynasty tombs . . . Pulguk-sa (temple) and Sokkuram Grotto on Mt. Joham important pilgrimages for both Koreans and visitors . . . new Bonum Lake Resort complex about 15 minutes from city center . . . about 4½ hours from Seoul by express train or super-highway.

Anap-ji ● Pond of Geese and Ducks . . . originally constructed by King Munmu in A.D. 674 to commemorate unification of Silla Kingdom . . . designed in shape of total unified territory . . . located near Panwol-song, at one time most spacious palace garden in entire kingdom . . . rulers kept variety of exotic birds and animals here . . . alas, on this very spot the last Silla king surrendered to invading forces in 935 . . . and glorious dynasty ended.

Bomun Lake Resort ● Manufactured recreation center about 15 minutes from historic sites of Kyongju City . . . attempt to harmonize traditional heritage with modern tourist facilities . . . huge man-made lake for boating and water skiing . . . 36-hole golf course in the hills above . . . convention facilities for 1000 plus simultaneous translation . . . several new tourist hotels . . . shopping arcades, folk art performances, Silla earthenware copies, several restaurants . . . even a local hotel school . . . shuttle buses to train station or Kimhae Airport (Pusan).

Chomsong-dae ● Star Tower . . . one of the world's oldest monuments devoted to study of the heavens . . . constructed during reign of Queen Sondok (A.D. 632–646) . . . designated National Treasure

No. 31 . . . challenging construction with 12 stones at base, 30 layers, and a total of 366 stones in all . . . actual role in Silla culture still a mystery . . . perhaps how astronomers read the stars enabled kings to predict auspicious times for the planting, harvest and important ceremonial occasions.

Emille Bell • Considered one of most resonant bells in Asia . . . occupies place of honor on grounds of Kyongju Museum . . . legend says that the sacrifice of a child into the molten metal makes the unusual and beautiful tone.

General Kim Yu-shin Tomb • One of Korea's greatest military heroes . . . General Kim led the armies of Kings Muyol and his son Munmu in 7th century A.D. campaigns that unified the country . . . his tomb is more sophisticated in detail but smaller than King Muyol (visible in the distance) . . . stands on wooded bluff overlooking Kyongju . . . surrounded by Zodiac figures . . . very elegant in concept.

King Muyol Tomb • One of most spectacular sights in area . . . 29th King of Silla and originated move toward unification . . . turtle tablet in front of tomb designated National Treasure No. 25 . . . symbol of Muyol's great efforts to bring country together . . . splendid views of surrounding area from path behind the tomb.

Kwae-nung • Tomb belongs to Wonsong, the 38th king . . . located about 5 minutes from Pulsuksa train station . . . a quiet and seldom visited area . . . full of interesting statues of military guards, civil officials, lions, monkeys, etc. . . . military figures thought to represent Persian mercenaries serving Silla court . . . worth the detour.

Kyerim Glade • Cock Forest . . . shrine in this wooded area outside of the city marks sacred birthplace of Kim Alji, ancestor of the famed Kim clan during Silla Dynasty . . . legend says that King Talhae, 4th Silla ruler, found a baby here in a golden casket and named him Kim (gold) . . . Kim is now the most common surname in all Korea.

Kyongju National Museum • The country's most beautiful house of treasures . . . Main Hall contains priceless collection of Silla Dynasty artifacts . . . special **Tomb Gallery** devoted to displays of recent excavations . . . also thousands of treasures dredged from Anapji Pond in mid-'70s . . . worth more than one visit.

O-Nung • Five Tombs . . . a compound of 5 of the most ancient mounds in the area . . . among them the 2000-year-old tomb of the kingdom's founder, Pak Hyokkose, first king of Silla Dynasty . . . also memorial shrine of his birthplace nearby . . . small memorial in clump of bamboo and pines of spot where dynasty's 1st queen was born from rib of a dragon.

Panwol-song • Crescent Moon Castle . . . believed to be the site of the first known palace for Silla kings . . . a place once so vast that a pair of straw sandals would not last the tour . . . small shrine still maintained in honor of King Talhae (monarch who found the golden prince) . . . **Stone Ice House** is listed as a cultural treasure . . . worth a visit.

Posok-jong • Abalone Stone Pavilion . . . located on slopes of Nam-san (South Mountain) . . . former banquet garden of 10th century A.D. Silla court . . . Kyongae (55th Silla king) and his queen assassinated in 927 here . . . in midst of merriment . . . one of its kind in garden party realms . . . although records say that similiar places existed in China.

Pulguk-sa • One of Korea's 5 great temples . . . No. 1 tourist attraction in the country . . . first constructed in 535 during reign of Pophung, 23rd Silla king . . . redesigned and rebuilt during reign of Kyongdok, 35th Silla king . . . one of oldest surviving monasteries in the country . . . rebuilt by Kim Tae-song to honor his parents . . . a graceful and dignified structured that has outlasted devastating wars and natural events for the past 12 centuries . . . nonetheless, 23 reconstructions were recorded in 1973 . . . and now 1/10th the size of the original temple site of Silla . . . still a magnificent Buddhist complex in the Far East . . . with no less than 6 of Korea's National Treasures recorded here . . . legendary architect was Asadal, master craftsman from Paekche . . . lost his lovely wife Asanyo near Pulguk-sa and never returned . . . but his genius is characterized in the elegance and simplicity of lines throughout . . . a wander through the various gates, courtyards, and halls is symbolic of the progression toward "enlightenment" . . . spectacular settings from some areas . . . and views worth the entire trip.

Pulguk-sa Pagodas • Tabo-tap and Sokka-tap . . . National Treasures No. 20 and 21 . . . examples of the genius of Asadal's craftsmanship . . . Tabo-tap symbolizes elegance of Silla Dynasty artistry . . . richly symbolic with 4 stairways and 4 coarse pillars reaching for the Four Truths of Buddha . . . also called the Pagoda of Many Treasures . . . octogan symbolizes Eight Right Ways . . . as shown by round lotus blossom . . . 8-sided wheel of Buddhist law acts as shield until spirit ultimately rises above worldly attachments and enters sub-

lime heaven of complete purity . . . Sokka-tap equal in age but different style . . . symbolizes descent to earthly world . . . 8 lotus pedestals
seats for Buddhist angels . . . represents strong and masculine characteristics of Silla's neighbor Paekche Kingdom . . . but the 2 pagodas
complement each other . . . the simplicity of the Sokka-tap balances
the intricacy of Tabo-tap.

Punhwang-sa Pagoda ● Oldest datable pagoda in Korea . . . believed to have been built by Queen Sondok, same ruler who built Star
Tower, was found to contain personal effects of the queen during repairs in A.D. 1015 . . . boasts superlative carvings and guardian statu-
ettes . . . materials of construction were cut stones shaped to resemble
bricks . . . originally built of 9 stories . . . only 3 left . . . still an
impressive sight.

Sambul-sa ● Three Buddha Temple . . . discovered in 1923 . . .
triad located on west side of Nam-san . . . considered one of oldest
Buddhist remains in country . . . said to date from early 6th century
A.D. . . . display overall massive boldness of Koguryo style.

Sam-nung ● 4 small tombs . . . just a minute's drive from the 3
Buddhas . . . Tok-nung or "lone tomb" at end attributed to Kyongae
. . . 2nd to last Silla King . . . whole area here has unreal quality.

Sokkuram ● grotto shrine on Mt. Tohamsan . . . built by Kim
Tae-song . . . classical example of Silla stone sculpture . . . carved
Buddha image of great artistry . . . placed within domed rotonda . . .
overlooks spectacular countryside below . . . now unfortunately encased from the elements (both human and natural) . . . sad talk of
replacing statue with a plaster copy . . . to climb Tohamsan and reach
Grotto by sunrise was one of most rewarding pilgrimages in Buddhism.

Tumuli Park ● 20 ancient tombs . . . situated in center of Kyongju City . . . site of recently excavated Chonma-chong (Heavenly
Horse Tomb) and 2-mounded Great Tomb at Hwangnam . . . fabulous
Silla crowns found in these tombs . . . like no other in the world . . .
visit Heavenly Horse Tomb . . . reconstruction and displays very impressive . . . good place to begin tour of Silla Dynasty sites.

HOTELS

Seoul

★★★**Westin Chosun Hotel** • *87 Sokong dong, Chung-ku (CPO Box 3706). Tel: 771–05. Cable: WESTCHOSUN. Telex: K2456 Seoul* • 470 rooms . . . originally an Americana hotel . . . one of the 1st and best of the American-managed hotels in Seoul . . . now under Westin International . . . recently renovated and looks good . . . spacious guest accommodations with 75% king-size beds . . . full amenities with mini-bar and well-designed work spaces . . . difficult to figure out the room numbers because the building is curved . . . centrally located and one of the great survivors in the hotel industry.

Facilities: Ninth Gate Bar and French restaurant (off lobby level). Galaxy (luncheon buffet only) and Moon Palace Chinese restaurants on top floor. Dolls House coffee shop, Cafe Centro Italian cafe, Yesterday Italian restaurant on lower level. Outdoor swimming pool in season. Shopping arcade with 30 airline offices, 4 travel agencies. Businessmen's center. Executive Fitness Center. Underground passage to next door Lotte Hotel.

Manager: L. A. Martinelli. *Reservations:* Westin Int'l.

★★★★**Hyatt Regency Seoul** • *747–7 Hannam-dong, Yongsan-ku (CPO Box 3438). Tel: 797–1234. Cable: HYATT SEOUL. Telex: K24136* • 607 rooms . . . stunning to behold from outside and in . . . located right atop Nam-san (South Mountain) . . . spectacular views from every angle of the capital and the historic Han River . . . impressive decor throughout and plenty of Western comforts . . . shuttle bus service to city center, beginning at 8 a.m. . . . excellent lounges and restaurants . . . definitely worth a detour.

Facilities: Terrace Cafe and Delicatessen Corner off main lobby. Hugo's Grill (Continental and elegant), Akasaka (Japanese) and Dragon Palace (Szechuan/Peking) restaurants plus The Bar on lower level. Regency bar and lobby lounge for cocktails and small gatherings. Silhouette bar (live entertainment) and lounge (buffet breakfast and lunch; a la carte dinner of Continental and Korean specialties) on 20th floor with best views in town. Regency Club for members. Health club with 2 swimming pools (1 outdoor) and sauna. Tennis facilities and tournaments. Business center with full services in several languages. Nightclub with live entertainment.

Manager: P. Smith. *Reservations:* Hyatt Int'l.

★★★★★**Hotel Inter-Continental** • *159–1 Samsung-Dong Kang-nam-ku. Tel: 553–8181. Telex K34254* • 600 rooms, including 200 suites . . . Seoul's newest hotel and one of the most elegant . . . already a favorite among local and international business people, partly due to a location adjacent to the new Korea Trade Center complex . . . the hotel has a traditional and elegant Korean look, with most materials used in the construction coming from various regions of the country.

Facilities: Korean, Japanese, Italian, seafood restaurants with a formal Continental restaurant overlooking the city. A health club, business traveler's club, and three lounges plus a disco.

Manager: Giorgio Bagnasco. *Reservations:* 800–332–4246.

★★★★★**Hotel Lotte** • *1 Sokong-dong, Chung-ku (CPO Box 3500). Tel: 771–10. Cable: HOTELOTTE. Telex: K28313* • 1353 rooms . . . tallest building in Korea . . . largest hotel in Seoul . . . perfect as a convention center . . . adjoins huge Lotte shopping center and Chosun Hotel . . . joint Japanese venture with Korean candy company . . . considered "European style" because of greatly over-decorated *belle epoque* public areas . . . jars the senses a bit . . . ambiance exudes quantity rather than quality although touted as one of Seoul's most sophisticated hostelries.

Facilities: Posh Metropolitan Club (members only) on 38th floor. A grand total of 30 other restaurants and bars including Sky Cafeteria & Observatory (38th floor); La Seine and Maxim French restaurants (37th floor); Annabelle's Supper Club and Disco (37th floor); Cafe Gardenia (2nd floor); Peninsula Cafe, Windsor Bar, and lobby lounge with waterfall (1st floor); La Coquilla seafood restaurant, The Margaret Tearoom, The Prince Eugene Rotisserie, Toh Lim Chinese, Mu-gung-hwa Korean, Po-suk-jung Korean, Momoyama Japanese, Benkay (sushi/sashimi), Bobby London Pub, Mannari, Eve, Rendez-Vous, and Lotte Delicatessen all on first basement level (B1). Plus swimming pool (4th floor) with snack bar, indoor swimming pool, and sauna. Businessman's services. Only glass-exterior elevator in town.

Manager: K. Shin. *Reservations:* SRS/Hotel Lotte USA.

★★★★★**Ramada Renaissance Hotel Seoul** • *676 Yoksam-dong, Dangnam-ku. Tel: 555–0501/556–0601. Telex K34392 RAMDAS* • 500 rooms including 21 suites . . . One of Seoul's newest and certainly most glamorous and best-equipped hotels . . . spectacular fitness facilities and a Renaissance Club for the best of everything.

Facilities: Club Horizon for members only, Chinese, Japanese, Korean, Italian restaurants plus buffet and coffee shop. Fitness center includes tennis and squash courts, indoor swimming pool, and the latest in exercise and weight equipment. Convention facilities and a business center.

Manager: Johannes Jahns. *Reservations:* Ramada International.

★★★★★**Seoul Hilton International** • *395, 5–ka, Namdaemunro, Chung-ku. Tel: 753–7788. Cable: HILTELS. Telex: 26695* • 712 rooms (35 Suites) . . . 21-story building . . . looks like 3-paneled screen . . . 4-acre site near Great South Gate . . . walking distance to business and entertainment area . . . attractive Korean decor in public rooms and guest rooms . . . 2 top floors feature executive guest rooms with lounge and own concierge . . . solid Hilton International management.

Facilities: Coffee shop; Japanese, Chinese, and gourmet restaurants. Health club and 2 swimming pools (1 indoor heated). Triple-story glass-roofed Palm Court. Rain Forest discotheque. Businessman's corner in lobby. Free parking in underground garage for hotel guests.

Manager: Hans Hauri. *Reservations:* HILTON.

★★★★**Seoul Plaza Hotel** • *23, 2–ka, T'aep'yong-ro, Chung-ku. Tel: 771–22 Telex: K26215. Cable: PLAZA HL SEOUL* • 493 rooms . . . located in center city across from Toksu Palace.

Facilities: Bakery; Chinese, Japanese, and French restaurants. Bar and Sky Lounge. Steak House. Business center.

Manager: H. Kwon. *Reservations:* Loews

★★★★**Sheraton Walker Hill** • *San 21, Kwangjang-dong, Songdong-ku (CPO Box 714). Tel: 453–0121. Cable: Walkerhill. Telex: K28517* • 804 rooms . . . the showplace of Seoul . . . located on 139 acres outside of town . . . on summit of A-Cha mountain, once the site of a 6th-century fortress . . . dramatic hotel with 22-story tower, 6 low-level annexes, 26 secluded luxury villas, and a new convention/banquet center . . . not a convenient location for executives with business in town, although shuttle service daily every 20 minutes . . . spectacular setting for R and R, with plenty of diversions both inside and out . . . lovely views of surrounding wooded areas as well as Seoul . . . dramatic waterfall lobby area.

Facilities: The Crystal Room operated by Casino Continental—24-hour nonstop action (bring your passport). Kayagum Theater Restaurant, with lavish Las Vegas–style shows as well as Korean folk dances—one of the best in the East (5 and 7:30 nightly). Reflections Disco and Polynesian Restaurant on lower level. Pokpo Waterfall Lounge and Cascade Cafe (24-hour coffee shop) on ground floor. Celadon Bar and gourmet restaurant (Austrian/German/French chefs) on 2nd floor. Sarang-bang Lounge (17th floor) and Summit Broiler on penthouse floor, with luncheon buffets/fashion shows, and Swiss specialties at night. Great

views of Han River and lights of Seoul some 1111 feet below. Health center with swimming pools, saunas, gymnasium, and tennis courts. Golf facilities nearby. Walking and jogging trails, and other outdoor recreation. Biggest and most modern convention center in Korea.
Manager: Y. C. Sung. *Reservations:* Sheraton Hotels.

★★★★**Hotel Shilla** • *202, 2–ka, Changchung-dong, Chung-ku. Tel: 233–3131. Cable: Hotel Shilla. Telex: K24160* • 672 rooms . . . located at foot of Nam San (South Mountain) . . . next to the Yeong Bin Gwan (Shangri-La guesthouse) . . . and near Jangchung Park and Gym . . . shuttle-bus service to city center every 30 minutes . . . affiliate of Hotel Okura chain . . . but no comparison with that fine facility in Tokyo . . . lovely lobby area with traditional Okura-style Ikebana and Bonsai . . . excellent facilities throughout . . . refurbished for 1988 Olympics, including larger, U.S.–made beds . . . watch out for Japanese holidays when the place is jammed with groups of men on the make. . . . this frequent influx detracts from any deluxe ambiance here.
Facilities: Sky Lounge and Continental restaurant (23rd floor) with fine views. Yeong-Bin-gwan Shangri-La buffet restaurant and supper club. Club Universe Disco (basement level). Lobby Lounge, Rainbow Bar, and Azalea Coffee Shop on lobby level. Sorabol Korean restaurant, Ariake Japanese restaurant, Palsun Chinese (Cantonese/Szechuan) restaurant on 2nd floor. La Continentale French restaurant. Health club with indoor pool, gymnasium, sauna, outdoor pool, and 4 tennis courts, and businessmen's corner (5th floor). Member's bar for local VIPs on 2nd floor. Delicatessen/pastry corner and shopping arcade on basement level.
Manager: B. Kang. *Reservations:* LHW.

★★★★★**Swiss Grand Hotel** • *201, Hongeum-dong, Suhdai-moon-ku. Tel: 356–5656. Telex: K34322 SGHSEL* • 111 fully equipped residential suites in four buildings (400 rooms) . . . a brand-new Swiss-otel designed for the business traveler, in a secluded park with lagoons and waterfalls . . . a Swiss-chalet feel in the Far East.
Facilities: Suites with kitchens, 24-hour concierge service . . . business center and shopping facilities, 6 restaurants, and 2 bars.
Reservations: SWISSOTELS.

Pusan (Busan)

★★★★**Chosun Beach Hotel** • *737, Uil-dong Haeundae-ku, Pusan 607–04. Tel: 742–7411. Cable: Westchosun Pusan. Telex: Chosunb K3718* • 350 rooms . . . situated on Haeundae Beach in Korea's largest port . . . a most attractive property with bright decor and wonderful

views of the bay throughout . . . not far from city center or airport
. . . well worth the effort . . . nice facilities and well-managed.
Facilities: Ninth Gate French restaurant. Kuromatsu Japanese restaurant. Dongbaek American-style coffee shop. Paekche cocktail lounge,
with evening entertainment. Ondol rooms. Disco Disco nightclub on
lower lobby. Swimming pool in season. Jogger's map and sauna. Deli-
catessen/bistro off lobby. Tennis court. Health Club.
Manager: D. Hayden. *Reservations:* Westin Int'l.

★★**Commodore Dynasty Hotel** • *743–80 Yongju-dong, Chung-
ku (P.O. Box 407). Tel: 44–9101. Cable: Commodore Pusan. Telex
Comotel K3717* • 320 rooms . . . Australian-managed hotel with Korean architecture in midst of downtown . . . nice views of harbor . . .
if you are brave enough, try it . . . only a few minutes from ferry
terminal and railway station (by taxi) . . .
Facilities: Coffee shop. Cocktail lounge. Nightclub. Theater restaurant. Casino.
Manager: S. Han. *Reservations:* Commodore Hotels Ltd.

★★★★**Hyatt Regency Pusan** • *1405–16 Chung-dong, Haeun-
dae-gu. Tel: 797–7819. Telex: 52668* • 363 rooms . . . Part of Hyatt's
impressive expansion to regional cities throughout the Far East . . .
Opened in 1988 as resort and convention hotel.
Facilities: Continental, Japanese, Chinese, and Korean restaurants
and a large fitness center, with nearby casinos and golf.
Reservations: HYATT HOTELS.

Kyongju

★★**Kolon Hotel** • *111–1, Ma-dong, Kyongju, Kyongsangbukdo
(P.O. Box Kyongju 21). Tel: 2–9001. Cable: Kolht. Telex: K–4469* •
240 rooms . . . located just a stone's throw from famous Pulguk-sa
Temple, on 59 acres of spacious Royal Gardens . . . a spare hotel with
moderate rates . . . casino and live entertainment in nightclub . . .
convenience to town and ancient sites.
Facilities: Nightclub, bar, game room, casino. Tennis court and
fishing pond. Western, Korean, and Japanese restaurants on premises.
Manager: W. J. Pickring. *Reservations:* Odner.

★★**Kyongju Chosun Hotel** • *410 Sinpyong-dong, Kyongju-si,
Kyongsangbuk-do. (P.O. Box Kyongju 35). Tel: 2–9601. Cable:
ChosunKyo. Telex: K4467* • 304 rooms . . . located about 4 miles from
Kyongju City . . . on the shores of Bomun Lake . . . a newish, man-
made project that reminds me somewhat of Disneyland . . . offers plenty

of indoor/outdoor diversions . . . spacious rooms both Western and Ondol style . . . but I'd watch the service . . . no longer connected to Chosun/Westin group . . . hard to predict if deluxe standards will be maintained.

Facilities: Ninth Gate gourmet restaurant. Kohan Japanese restaurant. Surabul Korean/Western coffee shop with style. Pool cafe in season. Barbecue outdoor garden in season. Kaya Lobby cocktail lounge with piano music. Bomun Nightclub on lower level. Grand Ballroom used for extensive weekend buffets. Indoor/outdoor olympic-size pools. Bowling alley. Game room. Exercise room and saunas. Tennis courts. Golf/sailing/water skiing/boating/hiking/bicycling all within easy access. Shuttle bus to Pusan's Kimhae International Airport daily.

★★**Kyongju Tokyu Hotel** ● *410 Sinpyong-dong, Kyongju (P.O. Box Kyongju 6). Tel: 2–9901/6. Cable: Kyongju Tokyu. Telex: K4328* ● 300 rooms . . . situated also on Bomun Lake . . . right next to Kyongju Chosun . . . but this hotel caters to Japanese trade . . . very costly shopping arcade as a result of large groups from Japan . . . all the same outdoor activities as Kyongju Chosun Hotel above . . . Western and Korean-style guest rooms . . . many places to eat and be merry . . . rather a drab decor . . . not much for a soul feast here—for me.

Facilities: Cafe Terrasse coffee lounge. King's Arm main bar and dining room. Hojeong Japanese Restaurant. Hobanjang-Marina Restaurant for international buffets. Seven & Eleven Discotheque. Tennis courts, swimming pool, and plenty of activities on Lake Bomun.

Manager: K. Saito. *Reservations:* Utell Int'l.

Cheju Island

★★★**Cheju Grand Hotel** ● *263 Yon-dong, Cheju, Cheju-do (P.O. Box 45), Cheju-do. Tel: 7–2131/41. Cable: Chejugranhtl. Telex: K712* ● 522 rooms (200 more rooms by late 1983) . . . newest and grandest on the island . . . just 5 minutes from the airport, in the downtown section of "new" Cheju city . . . very comfortable public areas and rooms (both Western and Ondol) . . . pleasant restaurants . . . hotel-owned 36-hole golf course at Ora Country Club just 5 minutes by car . . . popular for local honeymooners . . . and the golf set from Japan . . . privately operated by Samho Development Company of Seoul.

Facilities: Fantasia Bar. Pokpo (Waterfall) Lounge. Samdajung Japanese/Korean restaurant. Azalea coffee shop. All on lobby level. Fontainebleau French restaurant on rooftop. Swimming pool in season. Hotel-owned Ora Country Club. Health center. Game/recreation room.

Manager: J. Hwan. *Reservations:* Odner.

★**Cheju KAL Hotel** • *1691–9, 2–do, 1–dong, Cheju, Cheju-do (CPO Box Cheju 62). Tel: 2–6151. Cable: K744* • 310 rooms . . . now the second best property in town by my standards . . . needs considerable refurbishing . . . popular with groups and gamblers . . . only casino on the island . . . if the Grand is full, you are likely to land here . . . otherwise, I'd avoid it.

Facilities: Revolving sky lounge on 21st floor with good views of Mt. Halla and Korean coastline. Kapaa Nightclub on lower level. Casino Continental on 3rd floor with Las Vegas and Eastern-style games (open from 2 p.m.–4 a.m.). Swimming pool in season and health club. Obsier House Korean/Japanese restaurant (2nd floor). Western coffee shop (1st floor). Lobby bar. Bowling alley and game room.

Manager: J. Kim. *Reservations:* KAL.

★★★★**Hyatt Regency Cheju** • *3039–1 Saekdal-dong, Seogwipo-si, Cheju-do. Tel: 33–1234. Telex: 66749* • 225 rooms. Located on Choongmoon Beach . . . south shore of Cheju Island . . . in Choongmoon tourist complex . . . overlooking Pacific Ocean . . . 11-story structure bisected by open-air terrace . . . 7-story penthouse with atrium lobby . . . 35 minutes from airport.

Facilities: Cafe-restaurant. Lobby bar with spectacular waterfall terrace. Grotto Bar and pool bar. Nightclub. Casino. Japanese and Korean restaurants. 2 swimming pools. 2 tennis courts. Squash courts. Jogging track. Fitness Center. Resort Center with variety of watersports. Business Center and ballroom.

Manager: E. Tai. *Reservations:* Hyatt Int'l.

Mt. Sorak National Park area, Kangwon Province

★★**New Sorak Hotel** • *106–1 Sorak-dong, Sokcho-si, Kangwon-do. Tel: Sokcho 7131–50. Cable: NEWSORAK HOTEL. Telex: K24893* • 120 rooms . . . located in the tourist town of Sorak-dong . . . on the edge of the beautiful national park . . . considered "first class" with comfortable but not luxurious Korean and Western rooms . . . very reasonable prices.

Facilities: Korean, Japanese, and French restaurants. Cafeteria. Sky lounge and nightclub. Skating rink. Sauna.

Manager: Y. Soh. *Reservations:* Tel. 771–92 in Seoul.

★★**Sorak Park Hotel** • *74–3, Sorak-dong, Sokcho-si. Telex: 24142* • 121 rooms . . . also considered "first class" accommodations . . . located near the New Sorak . . . on hill overlooking Sorak-dong . . . has only casino in Mt. Sorak area, if that is an important factor . . . comfortable but hardly luxurious here.

Facilities: Korean, Japanese, and Western restaurants. Nightclub. Game room and casino. Saunas.
Manager: I. Kim. *Reservations:* Tel: 7–7711 in Seoul.

Note: · · · The 132-room **Sorak Oncheon Hotel** near the Oncheon Hot Spring (972-12 San, Nohak-dong, Sokcho) is scheduled to open soon. Also under construction is a 400-acre, $54.5 million resort complex in the Mt. Sorak area. The site is about 7 miles from the National Park, between the East Sea and neighboring mountains. Called the **Myung Sung Sorak Hotel and Condominiums,** the project includes Korea's largest condominium complex (1080 rooms), a 75-room tourist hotel, country club, ski area, 18-hole golf course, zoo, children's park, riding trails, and bathing area. The financial source is a conglomerate of construction, tourism, manufacturing, and other companies.

WINING AND DINING

"A majestic view has no charm when the table is bare" notes one of Korea's most charming proverbs. The cuisine of this country offers the visitor a bountiful variety of dishes unchanged through the centuries. Although a few urban sophisticates may eat Western-style breakfasts, most Koreans enjoy three hearty, traditional meals each day centered around steamed rice. Whether accompanied by soup, meat, vegetables, or fish, no repast is complete without small dishes of *kimchee.* This highly seasoned and fermented pickle of cabbage, radish, or cucumber, is unique to the Korean diet and provides much-needed vitamins during the long winter months.

Kimchee is known throughout the world not only for liberal doses of garlic and red pepper, but also for the large brown-glazed pots in which the vegetables are fermented and stored, buried in the ground. Every proud Korean housewife has her own method for making kimchee, whether it's the winter variety made at harvest time or the summer type made on a day-to-day basis. Kimchee is an acquired taste, however, and foreigners must accept its virtues very slowly!

Probably the most popular local specialty among visitors is *pulgogi* (also spelled bulgogi or pulgoki), which is simply marinated strips of beef cooked over a brazier while you sit at table. The marination includes soy sauce, garlic, green onions, sesame seeds, and oil. Cooked to your taste, the meat is accompanied with boiled rice and kimchee, of course. *Pulkalbi,* or short ribs, are served in the same manner.

Other native dishes you may encounter are *kujolpan*—small, self-made pancakes filled with a variety of meats and vegetables; *sinsullo* or Angel's Brazier—a bubbling brazier filled with broth, chopped vegetables, meat, quail egg, gingko nuts and fish balls, or bean curd; *naengmyon*—a refreshing summer dish of cold noodles (made of wheat or potato flour) and topped with vegetables, eggs, and pieces of meat; *mandukuk*—soup with meatballs wrapped in dough; *hanjong-shik*—simple meal of the day in Korean inns, consisting of soup, plus side dishes of rice, vegetables, fish, meat, and kimchee.

The most popular local beverage throughout the country is beer, either Crown or OB brand. It is a satisfying accompaniment to the many spicy dishes. Tea, the traditional drink, comes in many flavors: ginger, ginseng, and barley are only a few. For Western meals, a very pleasing white wine called Majuang is most enjoyable. The price is a bit high for a local wine (about $10), but imported wines are rather exorbitant so this brand is the best alternative.

There are a number of good Western restaurants in the big cities throughout Korea. The better ones have sprung up in the many new international class hotels, since food and beverage is a mainstay of hotel life. For example, at least half of the Hotel Lotte's 31 specialty restaurants and bars cater to the Western palate, including the exclusive Metropolitan Club on the 38th floor. Unfortunately, the listing below is confined to the Seoul area, but the **Ninth Gate** at the Chosun Beach Hotel in Pusan is also recommended. The Kyongju equivalent, however, is under local management and not especially noteworthy.

WESTERN RESTAURANTS

Ban Jul • *Near Samil Bldg., Tel: 733–4432* • Popular with foreign community . . . must be good . . . crowded at both lunch and dinner . . . nice decor and service.

Bear House • *On picturesque Skyway Dr., Tel: 762–1448* • Best in good weather . . . rewarding view of city below . . . food okay . . . decor rustic . . . advertises live music.

The Baron • *Top of the new Hotel Inter-Continental. Tel: 553–8181* • On a clear day you can see all of Seoul and have formal dining as well . . . elegant, understated surroundings, with gorgeous woods and white linen.

Celadon Restaurant • *2nd floor, Sheraton Walker Hill, Tel: 444–9111* • One of city's most elegant restaurants . . . truly gourmet . . . boasts French, Austrian, and German chefs as a combo . . . beautiful table settings with celadon accessories, Bavarian china, hand-blown German crystal . . . superb menu and exquisite food.

Continental Restaurant • *23rd floor, Shilla Hotel, Tel: 255–3111* • Superb views . . . open for breakfast, lunch, and dinner . . . piano music in evening . . . cocktail lounge adjacent . . . fine food and service.

Diplomatic Club • *On secluded slope of Nam-san, Tel: 752–5629* • Another favorite with foreign community in Seoul . . . French cuisine in subdued atmosphere.

Firenze • *Hotel Inter-Continental. Tel. 553–8181* • Seoul's newest Italian restaurant in a glamorous new hotel . . . elegant and intimate.

Four Seasons • *Out the back door of the Chosun Hotel, on 15th floor of Samkoo Bldg., Tel: 752–8667* • Good variety of Western food . . . nominal prices . . . good Chinese and Japanese dishes also available here.

Hugo's Grill • *Lower level, Hyatt Hotel, Tel: 795–0141, ext. 161* • Masculine decor . . . excellent steaks . . . Continental specialties . . . executive chef Werner Meister, president of Chaine des Rotisseurs in Seoul, presides here.

La Coquilla • *1st basement level, Lotte Hotel, Tel: 771–10* • Mediterranean atmosphere . . . hand-thrown pizzas . . . fresh Italian pastas . . . seafood.

La Seine • *37th floor, Lotte Hotel, Tel: 771–10* • Luncheon and dinner buffets in nice settings . . . reasonably priced for all you can eat.

Maxim • *Across the hall from La Seine, Lotte Hotel. Tel: 771–5511* • Very small . . . very chic . . . table d'hote about $45 per person . . . set menu . . . worth the money, if you wish to spend it.

Metropolitan Club • *38th floor, Lotte Hotel, Tel: 771–10* • Very posh . . . for club members and guests . . . Bavarian china . . . Japanese silver . . . extensive wines . . . contains about 200 Korean members (at $5,000 per annum) and about 30 foreigners.

Ninth Gate • *Off the lobby, Chosun Hotel, Tel: 771–05* • Seoul's first French restaurant and still one of the best . . . a favorite with businessmen . . . convenient to downtown area . . . excellent meals and service at both lunch and dinner . . . try rack of lamb or chateaubriand.

Prince Eugene Rotisserie • *Lower level, Lotte Hotel, Tel: 771–10, ext. 156* • Restaurant re-creates splendor of Palais Belvedere and aura of most celebrated host of his time . . . beautiful menu . . . well prepared dishes . . . hard-to-resist desserts.

Silhouette Lounge • *20th floor, Hyatt Regency Hotel, Tel: 795–0061* • Open for buffet breakfast and lunch . . . sit-down dinners . . . best views in town. . . nice atmosphere . . . live entertainment in evening . . . adjacent Silhouette Bar.

Sky Park • *Top floor, UNESCO Bldg., Tel: 776–2955* • Sensational view . . . deluxe atmosphere . . . good Western menu . . . live entertainment and floor show in evenings.

Summit Broiler • *16th floor, Sheraton Walker Hill, Tel: 445–0181* • Penthouse restaurant overlooking hotel's 139 acres of landscaped grounds . . . city of Seoul far beneath . . . good steaks . . . Swiss chef . . . daily luncheon buffets and fashion shows.

Noblesse • *Ramada Renaissance Hotel. Tel: 555–0501* • One of the newest of the glamour restaurants in a rapidly growing city . . . formal dining with an elegant bar area.

KOREAN-STYLE RESTAURANTS

Bull Barbecued Rib House • *On Ulchi-ro, Tel: 777–1666* • Popular barbecued spare ribs place . . . good variety of other local dishes.

Dae Won Gak • *323, Songbuk-dong, Songbuk-gu. Tel: 762–0034* • One of Seoul's most popular traditional restaurants . . . located in the hills in a posh residential area overlooking the city . . . bungalows with individual service of the best of Korean cooking . . . very festive and delicious . . . extremely popular with Koreans as well as tourists.

Hanil Kwan • *In either Myong-dong and Chong-ro areas, Tel: 776–3388* • Restaurant chain . . . rated No. 1 by Koreans . . . reasonable prices . . . you won't be disappointed.

Hamhung Naengmyon • *Across from UNESCO Bldg., Tel: 776–1016* • A Poonsik Jip, or noodles restaurant . . . buckwheat noodle (momil kooksoo) served with sweet radish sauce . . . house specialty . . . in heart of popular shopping area . . . follow the talking bird.

Korea House • *80–2, Pildong, 2–ga, Chunggu, Tel: 266–9101* • Probably the best introduction to traditional Korean food and beverages

. . . Korean buffets at lunch and dinner . . . afternoon rice cakes, candies, and tea . . . formal multicourse Korean dinners . . . slightly elaborate and expensive . . . operated by Foundation for the Preservation of Cultural Properties.

Mugungwha • *Lower level, Lotte Hotel, Tel: 771–10* • Restaurant named after Korea's national flower . . . simple but good food served in cheerful setting . . . worth a visit.

Pine Hill • *Half-block east of Myong-dong Cathedral, Tel: 266– 4486* • Specializes in beef . . . inexpensive but excellent food . . . great atmosphere and often crowded . . . try beef with vegetables cooked at your table.

Sabiru • *Ramada Renaissance Hotel. Tel: 555–0501* • Elegant surroundings in which to try the delicacies of Korea . . . served with silver chopsticks . . . a favorite among business people, local and international.

Sasaroki • *In Myong-dong area, Tel: 220–8446* • Very popular with foreign residents in Seoul . . . good food . . . good prices.

Sorabol • *2nd floor, Hotel Shilla, Tel: 255–3111* • Hearty Korean cuisine . . . hot and spicy . . . dishes you won't easily forget . . . opt for the specialties prepared at your table.

OTHER ASIAN-STYLE RESTAURANTS

Akasaka • *Lower level, Hyatt Hotel, Tel: 795–0141, ext. 154* • Named after one of Tokyo's most popular areas . . . open for breakfast, lunch, and dinner . . . beautiful menu and setting . . . sushi, tempura, sukiyaki, and other specialties.

Ariake • *2nd floor, Shilla Hotel, Tel: 255–3111* • Great views over woodlands behind hotel . . . Kaiseki served here . . . delicately flavored cuisine of Kyoto.

Benkay • *Lower level, Lotte Hotel, Tel: 771–10* • Simple but well-appointed Japanese restaurant . . . specialties include tempura, sukiyaki, sushi, and shabu-shabu . . . excellent service.

Bright Moon Hall • *In Korean pavilion at Sheraton Walker Hill, Tel: 445–0191, ext. 1376* • Traditional Korean pavilion on hotel grounds . . . features northern Chinese specialties . . . good for groups or small parties at both lunch and dinner.

Dragon Palace • *Lower level, Hyatt Regency Hotel, Tel: 795–0141, ext. 163* • Very pleasant restaurant featuring both Szechuan and Beijing dishes . . . house specialty is candied apples for dessert . . . dip them first in cold water.

Kotobuki • *2nd floor, Seoul Plaza Hotel, Tel: 771–22* • Very attractive Japanese restaurant . . . sushi bar and tempura bar . . . beautiful private rooms.

Moon Palace • *20th floor, Chosun Hotel, Tel: 771–05* • Great views on a clear day . . . offers Chinese buffet everyday at lunchtime . . . northern Chinese and Beijing dishes . . . nice decor and very good service.

Palsun • *2nd floor, Shilla Hotel, Tel: 255–3111* • Serves delicacies of Middle Kingdom (Szechuan and Cantonese) in quiet setting . . . with overtones of yellow and white . . . very elegant.

Waebaek • *Across from the back exit of Chosun Hotel, Tel: 22–1010* • Beijing cuisine . . . pleasant decor . . . cocktail lounge . . . located in basement next to Choheung Bank.

Waewon • *Across from the back exit of Sejong Hotel* • Lovely Japanese restaurant with small garden . . . willow-shaded parking . . . steaks, sukiyaki, and other Japanese dishes . . . not too expensive.

BEER HALLS

For those wishing to partake in some of the "local color," seek out the many lively and inexpensive beer halls scattered around the metropolitan areas. Some feature live entertainment and some offer hostess/companions for a price. Be wary of ripoffs, especially near U.S. Army posts.

Choose from two types of Korean beer, Crown or OB (Oriental Brewery), available in large bottles or draft. You are expected to order some snacks, such as peanuts, dried fish (not to everyone's taste), or raw vegetables. And, unless you want a big surprise at the end of the evening, I recommend that you pay as you drink.

OB's Cabin • *4-story complex 2 alleys behind the UNESCO Bldg., Tel: 776–4784* • A longtime favorite with foreigners . . . live bands . . . the latest popular singers on stage.

Sansoo Gapsan • *About 100 yards behind Tiffany on the left, Tel: 777–3125* • Known as Seoul's "only classic music beer hall."

Green Villa • *Behind Tiffany, about 75 yards on the right, Tel: 777–4728* • One of the "common folk" beer halls . . . noisy on the ground floor . . . lots of action . . . quieter above.

Blue Villa • *Near South Gate, behind Seoul Plaza Hotel, Tel: 23–3694* • One of many beer halls along this alley . . . another one of the "common folk" variety . . . or so they say.

CASINOS

The South Korean government only frowns upon gambling if it does not get a percentage of the "take." There are several rather posh casinos located throughout the country, generally one per major tourist area but this may be changing. Most of the casinos are run by Casino Continental and offer several games of chance—roulette, blackjack, poker, baccarat, kendo, etc. You can find the No. 1 casino in Korea at the **Sheraton Walker Hill** resort complex; it is usually open around the clock. There are also casinos at the **Kolon Hotel** in Kyongju, the **KAL** (Korean Air Lines) **Hotel** in Cheju City, the **Paradise Beach Hotel** in Pusan, the **Songnisan Hotel** in Songnisan National Park Area, and the **Olympos Hotel** in Inchon. Another is planned for the new Mt. Sorak tourist complex.

NOTE · · · If you plan to gamble, always carry your passport for identification.

KISAENG HOUSES

What the famous geisha is to Japan, the kisaeng is to Korea. Although the true kisaeng—traditional palace entertainers who sang, or danced, or recited poetry—disappeared at the beginning of the 20th century, the spirit lingers on. Because an evening spent in a Kisaeng House tends to be very expensive—with food, wine, and much attention from beautifully trained women in colorful costumes—this type of evening is total immersion into the Korean culture; it should not be attempted, though, without the good advice of local friends or your hotel concierge (who appreciates your seriousness). Ask about **Jang Won,** near the U.S. Embassy (Tel: 72–8645), and other suggestions.

MAKKOLLI HOUSES

Considered the height of "local color," these traditional drinking man's establishments are a study in how the common men folk entertain themselves. Located in great abundance throughout the country, these houses are long on sociability and rather short on atmosphere. The main brew served is *makkolli,* a milky-white rice liquor that packs a mighty and rather unsuspecting wallop at the end of a session! You're expected to order an array of side dishes to make the drink all the more palatable. Try, for example, some *pindaedok* (pancake with vegetables), *maeuntang* (hot fish soup), *pachon* (fried leeks with clams in batter), *joge tang* (clam soup), or *rodorimook* (wild acorn gluten). The entire evening is an experience (just for people-watching) and not too costly.

More common even than makkolli is *soju,* "burned liquor," which is considered a popular accompaniment to beef and pork dishes as well as to green onions, garlic, and sesame leaves. Soju is renowned for giving an immediate "kick" and should be consumed carefully. Best survival method is to eat as much of the *anju* (snacks) as possible and go very slowly on the drink.

Tae Ryon • *Across street east of Samilro Bldg., Tel: 265–5349* • Try also **Chonggey-oke** • *Tel: 267–2744* • in same area. Known for great anju, especially the pancakes . . . go easy on the drink.

Posokchong • A well-known chain easily recognized . . . good for chogaetang (clam soup).

Chongil Chip • *Behind Kwanghwamun Theater, Tel: 75–7588* • Very inexpensive . . . noted for soju . . . stick with sogum-qui (grilled beef).

Pojang Macha • A tent wagon or pushcart . . . try the one up the alley beside Samilro Bldg. . . . order chogae (clam grilled on shell) and soju.

NIGHTSPOTS

Since the elimination of curfew years ago, nightclubs and discos now flourish as never before. However, as all are heavily taxed, the tab will be high no matter what you eat or drink. You can find the usual "disco" in most major hotels, but there are also excellent theater restaurants with sophisticated nightclub shows.

Kayagum • *Sheraton Walker Hill resort, Tel: 444–9111* • The biggest and the best . . . 2 shows nightly . . . classical Korean dances by Honey Bee Revue . . . plus Las Vegas-style extravaganza (lots of T and A).

Tiffany • *In the basement of Tongmin Bldg., opposite Kolon Arcade, Tel: 777–8901* • Club-style restaurant . . . features bright Korean talent.

World Cup ● *On Mugyo-dong, west of Samilro Bldg., Tel: 777–1081* ● Fairly decent food . . . with international variety show.

Hee Joon ● *Located in basement of Kukdong Bldg. on Toegye-ro, 1 block east of King Sejong Hotel, Tel: 265–0466.*

TABANGS

The tabang (tadang, tashil) is an institution unique to Korea. This very simple "tearoom" provides a focal point for the social life of the entire Korean population. You can find an entire cross-section of local society at a tabang—to meet friends, exchange information, even settle some business matter. There are more than 5000 tabangs in Seoul alone, each one with its own ambiance, decor, and clientele. Tea, coffee, and juice drinks are available, and lingering time is never noticed. The teas range from China to barley to ginseng to a thick, soupy walnut brew served sprinkled with pine nuts. Ask a friend or local guide about tabangs, and choose either a quiet place with classical music or a popular, noisy room crowded with young people. The largest variety of tabangs can be found in the Myongdong area.

SHOPPING

With five millennia of colorful history, Korea's cultural expression shines forth brilliantly in the many handcrafts and artifacts that will make every visitor unashamedly covetous. In addition to modern ceramics worthy of the once-famed Koryo celadon and Yi dynasty porcelains, there are so many other items to purchase as enduring memories of time spent in this country. Korean ginseng, one of the basic ingredients in the mystery of herbal medicines, is considered one of the best available. Semiprecious stones mined locally feature the amethyst and smoky topaz. Korean silk is renowned for its eloquent colors, especially in the traditional striped patterns. Brassware is found in abundance, from hand-crafted temple bells, ornate locks, jewelry, and furniture accessories. Bamboo and straw objects are skillfully conceived, with favorite motifs like plum blossoms, peonies, clouds, and Chinese characters. Lacquer-ware and mother-of-pearl inlaid items reached their apex in the 12th century and the technique has not been lost in translation to the modern age. Often found on boxes and chests is the inlay of painted transparent oxhorn on wood—a craft unique to Korea.

Dolls: Traditional dolls of mulberry bark paper, with real silk for hair and features, have become a new-found art. One of the most inspired young makers is **Kim Young-hee,** who brings the everyday labors of country folk to life. Her handmade dolls take from one to five weeks each, and have been exhibited at museums around the world.

Embroidery: Embroidered handkerchiefs, cushions and blankets, large screens, and ornamental knots for personal use all make splendid gifts. The *hanbok* or formal women's costume is a beautiful sight with its long graceful gown and short, rather flared top. Hardly suitable as everyday garb at home, it makes an interesting and striking evening dress. If you are so tempted, indulge; dressmaking and tailoring in Korea are both inexpensive and efficient. In addition to the local silks and synthetics, good quality woolens are available. The best (but very heavy) are those handcrafted by the **Hallim weavers** on Cheju Island.

Miscellaneous Items: One of the country's most popular exports is handmade wigs. These and long eyelashes are available to the casual visitor at considerable savings. However, remember not to overdo in this category, for not more than five ladies's nor three gentlemen's wigs may be exported on one's person. As far as eyelashes are concerned, chances are you are not planning to purchase more than 200 pairs, nor send more than 50 by post. Masks, fans, and kites of paper and papier-mache are also beautifully decorated, and there is no limit on these temptations as souvenirs.

Among some less traditional notables, sneakers and jogging shoes and equipment are another good buy. Many popular brands are manufactured here (Nike even has outlet stores in Korea) and can be purchased at less than half the U.S. price. Leather and suede products, especially eelskin, are popular and inexpensive, too. The Jindo Fur Company of Korea is the world's largest manufacturer of fur coats and jackets. These items are designed solely for export to foreign customers and must be purchased in foreign currency, either by cash or credit card. Arrangements for customs clearance, export notification, and delivery to your departing flight must be made with Jindo.

Antiques: Buying in this category is another matter and always somewhat risky for the purchaser. First, make sure what you buy is authentic—there are very good copies of Silla pots sold everywhere. Old chests, ceramics, scroll and screen paintings are displayed along the area known as **Mary's Alley** in Seoul, but always beware with whom you are dealing. If you happen upon a certified national treasure, it is not exportable. If you want to ship other authenticated ancient works, they must be accompanied by a government certificate, which may involve undue red tape. For costly purchases, always seek the advice of an expert—at the very least, someone who lives in the country and knows the language.

Myongdong: Shopping heart of Seoul and the nation's busiest area. Department stores, tailors, fashionable boutiques, top hotels, leather and silk shops are crowded but fun. Try **Lotte Shopping Center** and **Shinsegae, Midopa, Cheil,** and **Cosmos** department stores.

Itaewon: A 20-minute taxi ride from downtown Seoul. Known for its blocks of antique shops and some of lowest priced goods in Seoul. Haggling is expected here; start low to come out on top.

Insadong: **Mary's Alley.** Area located between Korea Times Building and Pagoda Park Arcade. Antique stores are in abundance, and you'll find many lovely private galleries and stationery, ceramic, and embroidery shops. A favorite place in Seoul.

Tongdaemun Sijang: **East Gate Market.** Located near the ancient East Gate on Chongro St. It's the biggest and most colorful bazaar in Korea, where the local residents shop. The market sprawls over 10 city blocks on both sides of Chonggyechon and Chongno. Bargain for best buys—shoes, books, umbrellas, clothes, furniture, bedding, sports equipment, cooking utensils, food, colorful fabrics, and sewing accessories. It's worth a visit if only for a touch of native color.

Namdaemun Sijang: **South Gate Market.** Located near South Gate, a block south of Namdaemun-ro (street), this is another popular place for local shoppers. A maze of alleys lined with stalls, the market also offers cut flower, fish, and produce.

Shopping Arcades: The last word in variety. The majority line pedestrian underpasses. Try Chosun, Shillo, and Plaza hotels in midtown and by the Tongbang and Daewoo buildings. You'll find aboveground arcades in Pagoda Park, Chonggyero, and Toegyero.

Duty-free Shops: Luxury items can be purchased in town. Visitors with proper identification can buy perfumes, lighters, pens, watches, liquor, scarves, leather goods, and some local products. Try **Lotte Duty Free Shop** (8th floor shopping center), **Nam Moon** at #5 Yang-dongin Chung-ku, **Ungchon Company** at 15 Insa-dong in Chongno-ku, **Tonghwa** at 1-41 Sajik-dong in Chongno-ku, and shops at **Kimpo Airport.**

Department Stores: Shopping here is the best way to get a feel for prices and quality of goods. No bargaining. Ask for English-speaking clerks. The stores are usually open from 10:30 a.m.–7:30 p.m. **Lotte** and **Cosmos** are closed Tuesday, **Shinsegae** is closed Monday, **Midopa** is closed Wednesday, and **Cheil** is closed Thursday. The **Korean Handicrafts Department Store** houses 40 shops of traditional wares such as celadon, china, ceramics, woodcraft, and lacquerware inlaid with mother-of-pearl. Some credit cards are now accepted.

Souvenir Shops: These are plentiful throughout the country. In Seoul, try **Arirang, Dabo, Samsung, Namsan, Samsong, Korea Folk Handicraft Center,** and **Yongbo.** In Pusan, the **Arirang, Kukdong,** and **Kaya Native Arts.** In Kyongju, **Minsokkwan, Kyongdo,** and **Chosun Hotel.** In Cheju-do, the **Grand Hotel** shop and **Korea Native Products.**

Favorite Shops: **Chosun, Lotte,** and **Shilla** Hotel arcades. Don't leave Seoul without at least one item from **Hallim Hand Weavers** (in Chosun Hotel arcade). My favorites are also lovely amethyst or smoky topaz jewelry, silk in traditional multicolored stripe pattern for a long skirt, heavenly ancient scroll paintings, and a Korean chest. Brass planters that never tarnish are also a must.

MACAU

HISTORY

Some travelers visit Macau and think of Venice—without the canals or Bridge of Sighs, of course. I prefer to consider Macau and Malacca as soul sisters. Both were settled by the Portuguese as Windows to the exotic East: Malacca on the west coast of the Malay peninsula, Macau on the southern coastline of China. Both have had glorious pasts, but neither fully recovered when their wealth and importance waned. The difference is: although Macau's rich and colorful past must still be attended and its monuments restored, business is booming and this tiny territory enters the 21st century as a meritous partner with the rest of Asia. It exports US $1 billion in manufactured goods and receives some 6 million visitors annually (albeit the majority Hong Kong Chinese who arrive each weekend and holiday to satisfy their compulsive gambling instincts).

The place name *Macau* derives from a legend of a beautiful Chinese goddess called A Ma or Ling Ma, who was revered by the fishermen around this village (previously known as Hou Kong or Hoi Keang). According to the story, A Ma came through a horrific storm one night and guided a fishing junk safely into harbor. When the boat landed in Hoi Keang, this lovely mortal from the heavens stepped ashore, walked to the crest of Barra Hill, and ascended whence she had come. A temple was dedicated on the very spot, and the port was renamed Amago—eventually shortened to Macau.

For over 400 years, Macau has flown the green-and-red banner of Portugal. Even during six decades of Spanish rule, no other flag was ever raised. So when independence was restored to Portugal on December 1, 1640, Macau was granted the official name "Cidade do Nome de Deus de Macau, Naho Ha Outra Mais Leal" or "City of the Name of God, Macau, There is None More Loyal."

From the beginning of the 16th century on, several trading posts were established around southern China. These centers were later consolidated as Macau, which began to enjoy a monopoly on trade between China, Japan, and Europe. (Canton was also an open port.) Although Portuguese influence in Malacca waned around 1641, the Portuguese territory of Macau remained at a prosperous high until the mid-19th century.

In addition to its commercial importance during the 16th and 17th centuries, Macau became a vital base for the infiltration of Christianity to China and Japan. Pope Clement XII created the Bishopric of Macau as early as 1575, to strengthen the power of the Church in the East. While one branch of Jesuits settled in Nagasaki to convert the Japanese, another group established a headquarters and a respected college in Macau. They supervised the construction of elegant monuments for the devoted and extended their influence to the Ming Court. In 1602 the cornerstone of the Church of the Mother of God (now known as St. Paul's ruins) was laid, and the church was finished within a few years by Chinese and Japanese (Christian) artisans. Annals described the edifice as "the greatest monument to Christianity in all the Eastern lands," and stories of such gilded magnificence found the crowned heads of Europe competing to give the most spectacular donation. During this same decade, the Jesuits added the college next door and built the Citadel of Sao Paulo do Monte (Monte Fort) on a nearby hill.

The glory of Macau at this time was not unnoticed by other ambitious seafaring nations from the West, in particular the Dutch, who attempted takeovers in 1604, 1607, 1622, and 1627. The 1622 attack gave the cannons at Monte Fort their renown. A most successful repulsion resulted, and St. John was considered responsible, since it occurred on June 24, the Feast of St. John the Baptist. He was promptly declared Patron of the city and his feast day has been a traditional public holiday ever since.

By the 18th century Holland and Portugal were allies, other European traders were spending their summers in Macau (to escape the bad air of Canton and elsewhere), and Chinese were arriving en masse. The port of Macau became one of the main arteries for opium smuggling along the coast—and a tempest in China's teapot. In the enduring battle between the British and the Chinese over the legality (and balance of payments) in the trade of this "foreign mud," Macau was caught broadsides. Finally, in 1839, the Chinese ordered all British subjects and their merchant ships out of the territory. So, they sailed but 40 miles out to a barren rock named Hong Kong situated on the easterly approach of the Pearl River estuary. The rest, one might say, is history. . . .

Although the tiny peninsula of Macau and two offshore islands called Taipa and Coloane were recognized by the Chinese as a proper Portuguese colony in the late 19th century, the fortunes of the area floundered as commerce began to favor Hong Kong. During the ensuing war years of the 20th century, however, Macau and Portugal remained neutral and thus became a haven for refugees fleeing both the Japanese and the Communist forces in China. The colony bounced back mightily just after World War II when it became one of the world's largest importers (and smugglers) of gold, which found its way into Hong Kong, China, and other Far Eastern ports. This healthy business ended in 1974, when the British colony revised its strict gold-import laws and China opened its own door to world trade. By this time, though, Macau had another scheme to keep herself afloat—legalized gambling—as in casinos, tracks, and Jai Alai.

The majority of visitors to today's no longer sleepy Macau arrive at the passenger terminal in the Outer Harbor and go directly to the largest casino in town, attached to the Lisboa Hotel. The Sociedade de Turisomo e Diversoes de Macau (STDM) holds the monopoly for casino gambling as well as for transporting visitors to and from the territory and interest in four leading local hotels. STDM has invested heavily in Macau since it won the gambling concession some 25 years and just a quarter million visitors ago. The consortium built two ferry terminals (one in Hong Kong, the other in Macau) and operates the largest Boeing jetfoil fleet in the world. It brought leading hoteliers (Hyatt, Mandarin Oriental) to the territory as well as an annual Grand Prix. Although gambling is on most visitors' minds (the stakes are about half a billion US dollars a year), STDM has created some diversity in spectator as well as participatory sporting events.

Macau's Department of Tourism and Information and STDM work in tandem in attracting more international and active visitors. A fabulous resort is now operated by Hyatt on Taipa Island and an even more comprehensive complex is planned for the island of Coloane. The local currency (pataca) now has an international standing. A deep-sea facility and an airport are on the drawing boards. And when the main trunk road to Guangzhou is completed, it will be the fastest means of getting to China's most promising industrial region so business travel is expected to multiply rapidly. Although Macau lacks one essential—a golf course—an 18-hole facility is just over the Chinese border in Zhongshan.

In political terms, the more Macau changes, the more it remains the same. The only land ever ceded by China to a foreign power, and never quite a proper colony because of an unratified 1862 Sino-Portuguese treaty, this area was until recently known as the Portuguese Overseas Province of Macau. Today, it is officially called a Chinese Territory under Portuguese rule. For the past four centuries Portugal has sent governors to rule the land. Chinese leaders, however, could easily have repossessed the area. Indeed, during the mid-1960s, the world watched as Red Guards rioted through city streets—disrupting Macau's precarious balancing act with China.

In 1974 the territory received another jolt; the newly arrived Portuguese governor offered to return Macau to China—no strings attached. He was flabbergasted when the offer was turned down. So the Portuguese government remains with tenuous rule and little control over the oldest European settlement in Asia. The future of Macau is now assured and stable, as issued in a joint communique signed in Beijing by China and Portugal. On December 20, 1999, Macau will become the Special Administrative Region of Macau and no major changes are foreseen in its economic climate. Its principles of private property, free market, and financial independence will be honored and maintained. So, since the official "founding" of the territory of Macau by the Portuguese in 1557, China accepts its return exactly 442 years later. A great many events turned the course of life in Macau during that time—and more is promised in the ensuing decade!

MACAU IN A CAPSULE

Chinese territory under Portuguese rule . . . 6 square miles of small peninsula and 2 islands . . . 40 miles west across the mouth of the Pearl River from Hong Kong . . . located on southeastern coast of China 70 miles below Canton . . . annual rainfall about 70 inches . . . average daily temperature 68°F with high humidity . . . officially founded in 1557 by Portuguese explorers . . . present population more than 400,000 . . . 5% living on board fishing junks . . . population mix is 95% Chinese, 3% Portuguese and other Europeans, 2% others . . . official language is Portuguese, although Cantonese is widely spoken (English is third) . . . majority of visitors are Hong Kong Chinese who take the 50-minute jetfoil weekly to try their luck in the casinos . . . overseas visitors are encouraged to stay a while in one of the lovely resort facilities and visit China from here.

PLANNING AHEAD

MACAU TOURIST INFORMATION BUREAU is located at Travessa do Paiva, Macau (Tel: 77218). In Hong Kong, the MTIB is situated at 305 Shun Tak Centre, 200 Connaught Rd., Central Hong Kong (Tel: 5–408180). This office is excellent for queries, free publications and maps, and directing you to the hotel and hydrofoil services. North American offices are located at 3133 Lake Hollywood Dr., P.O. Box 1860, Los Angeles, CA 90078 (Tel: 213–851–3402) toll-free in CA (800–331–7150); 608 Fifth Ave., Suite 309, New York, NY 10020 (Tel: 212–581–7465); P.O. Box 22188, Honolulu, HI 96822 (Tel: 808–

538–7613); Suite 304, 1385 West 8th Ave., Vancouver, B.C., Canada V6H 3V9 (Tel: 604–736–1095).

VISAS   are not required of travelers holding U.S. or Canadian passports. Nationals of the U.S. and Canada are required to have a valid passport for entry into Macau.

INTERNATIONAL INOCULATION CERTIFICATES   are not normally required unless cholera has been detected either in Hong Kong or Macau, or in the area recently visited by the arriving traveler.

ENTRY   is by sea, since Macau has no airport yet—although it is in the stars; so is 20-minute helicopter service via East Asia Airlines from Hong Kong via 8- and 10-passenger choppers to a helipad in Macau's Outer Harbour. Meanwhile, visitors arrive by jetfoils, hydrofoils, jetcats, ferries, and fast ferries from Shun Tak Centre, 200 Connaught Rd., Central, Hong Kong Island. There is also limited service from the ferry pier at Shamshuipo, Kowloon and planned service from Tuen Mun (formerly Castle Peak) in the New Territories because of heavy traffic.

Visitors holding Visa, AmEx, and Diners Club cards may telephone 5–8593288 to book jetfoils up to 28 days in advance; hydrofoils and jetcats may be booked up to 35 days in advance (5–232136). Cash sales are also available at several dozen outlets in Hong Kong and Kowloon (contact your hotel concierge for the nearest office).

Jetfoils cover the 40-mile journey in just under one hour in air-conditioned comfort. Half-hour departures begin at 7 a.m. daily and fares vary according to upper/lower deck, weekday/weekend and holiday travel. **Jetcats** carry 215 passengers and make 10 round trips daily; the 70-minute trip has a somewhat lower fare. The British-built **hover ferries** carry up to 250 passengers on 8 round trips daily from Shamshuipo; the 1-hour-plus trip is quite inexpensive. **Hydrofoils** take 75 minutes, **ferries** just under 3 hours, and **high-speed ferries** about 100 minutes.

All seacraft arrive at the spanking new ferry terminal in Macau's Outer Harbour, which has been designed to handle some 5000 passengers per hour by the early 21st century. The 3-level structure handles a variety of passenger vessels, has car and coach parks, restaurants, plus spectator stands and pits for the annual Macau Grand Prix.

Among the vessels calling at Macau's fancy new terminal is the 4200-ton *Macmosa,* which inaugurated passenger service from Kaohsiung, Taiwan, in September 1988. The vessel carries a total of 550 passengers (310 first class, 140 second class, 104 economy) and takes 24 hours between the two ports. Facilities on board include two restaurants, a 24-hour bar, disco, slot machines, video room, and duty-free shop. The *Macmosa* is operated by STDM, the giant Macanese tourism/gambling company.

NOTE · · · *Never* leave Hong Kong without your return ticket booked and in hand. Traffic to and from the small territory is considerable and you may be stranded longer than you wish. Also, be aware of the luggage limit of 20 pounds per person on jetfoils. There is no baggage limit on the new Hi-Speed Ferries, however.

Departure Tax from Hong Kong is HK$15. There is no departure tax from Macau.

DUTY FREE applies to Macau as well as to Hong Kong. Customs officials do not bother travelers very much and there are no export duties. However, Hong Kong customs authorities will only allow returning visitors to import one quart of wine, 200 cigarettes or 50 cigars or 250 gr. of tobacco into the colony. Hong Kong residents are allowed to bring only one quart of wine, plus 100 cigarettes or 25 cigars, duty free.

CURRENCY of Macau is the pataca, pegged by the government to the Hong Kong dollar at the rate of 104 to HK$100, with a permissible variance of up to 10%. The pataca comes in coins: 10, 20, 50 avos, and 1, 5 patacas; banknotes: 5, 10, 50, 100, 500 patacas. However, Hong Kong dollars are used freely here. There is no restriction on the amount of currency brought in or taken out (should you win BIG).

OFFICIAL LANGUAGES are Portuguese and Cantonese. English is third, used for trade, tourism, and commerce.

BUSINESS HOURS in Macau are similar to those in Hong Kong, although the pace is *much* slower. Macau enjoys its reputation as an R & R post.

TIPPING in Macau is less obviously courted than in Hong Kong, therefore more of a pleasure. Prices tend to be much lower anyway, for everything. Hotels and restaurants still add their 10% service charge, plus a 5% "tourism tax," but waiters still appreciate the extra change and even say "thank you."

TELEPHONE AND TELEX services are good in Macau, but better 40 miles away. A three-minute call to Hong Kong costs HK$10, plus service charges if placed through your hotel. Local calls cost three 10 avos coins from public phones, free at your hotel. The area code for Taipa is 070, for Coloane 080.

WHAT TO WEAR in Macau is the same as you would wear in Hong Kong, although the territory is slightly less dressy in the evening. Resort-type clothes would be in order at one of the new beach hotels.

LOCAL TRANSPORTATION consists of taxis, pedicabs, car rentals, and buses here. There are about 580 licensed **taxis,** all with meters and all painted black with a cream-colored roof. Fares run 4.5 patacas for the first 1500 meters, and 60 avos for every subsequent 250 meters. There are minimal surcharges to Taipa and Coloane islands by bridge.

For slightly slower but far more romantic means of transport, try the **pedicabs** or **trishaws,** on which fares must be negotiated in advance—from 10 to 40 patacas for a journey. There is also a fancy fleet of about a dozen based at the Lisboa Hotel. Uniformed drivers will offer one of three different itineraries, including a taped commentary on Macau's history and attractions. The itineraries and prices are fixed (from 20 minutes at about US $6.50 to 60 minutes for under $15), which enables visitors with limited time to enjoy this special type of sightseeing.

Public **buses** run from 7 a.m. to midnight; the fare is 70 avos per journey. The bus on Route 3 provides regular service between the jetfoil piers and the city center. From the bus stop near the Statue of Governor Ferreia do Amaral (in front of the Hotel Lisboa main entrance, near the bridge), you can go to Taipa (1.30 pataca), Coloane Village (1½ patacas) and Hac Sa Beach (2 patacas). Take the top deck in summer.

If you want to go exploring on your own, try renting a Mini Moke (a colorful hybrid somewhere between a jeep and a golf cart). You must be at least 21 years old and a licensed driver of not less than two years. Rates, which include insurance, are HK$280 per 24-hour weekday and more on the weekend. A weekend special, 6 p.m. Friday through 9 a.m. Monday, costs HK$500-plus. Macau Mokes, Ltd. is located in the Macau Ferry Terminal Building, Room 202, Outer Harbour (Tel: 78851). Reservations are recommended and can be made in Hong Kong (Tel: 5–434190).

FESTIVALS AND HOLIDAYS in Macau mean extravagant celebrations for both Portugal's national and religious holidays as well as for events determined by the Chinese lunar calendar. Although most holidays coincide with those honored in Hong Kong, some are purely Macanese like the **A Ma Festival,** the **Na Cha,** and Coloane Island's **Feast of Tam Kong.** During public holidays, Macau becomes extremely crowded as Hong Kong residents journey across to tempt Lady Luck. During these times it may be impossible for you to secure hotel or jetfoil reservations. It may not be as tranquil as most other times either, so take note. Public holidays are marked with an asterisk (*).

*January 1 • *New Year's Day.*

*January/February • *Chinese New Year.*

March • *Procession of Our Lord of Passos* • A moving spectacle only to be seen in Macau. It centers on the image of Jesus on the way to the Cross, which is usually kept on the altar of St. Augustine's Church. Following ancient tradition, the statue is taken at night from the church to the Cathedral (where an all-night Vigil is kept). The next day the statue is carried in solemn procession around Macau to the Stations of the Cross and then returned to St. Augustine's.

*April 5 • *Ching Ming Festival* • Chinese version of All Souls' Day.

*March/April • *Good Friday, Saturday, and Easter Sunday.*

April/May • *A Ma Festival* • Macau's most personal Chinese celebration. This festival revolves around A Ma's temple in the city center.

*April 25 • *Anniversary of the Portuguese Revolution (1974).*

*May 1 • *Laborers' Day* • Also Feast of the Drunken Dragon and the beginning of Coloane Island's spectacular Tam Kong Festival—a traditional procession held in honor of the patron saint of the fishermen—followed by a week-long celebration.

May • *variable; Feast of the Bathing of Lord Buddha/Feast of the Drunken Dragon/Tam Kong Festival.*

May 13 • *Process of Our Lady of Fatima* • A celebration of the religious miracle of Fatima in Portugal in 1917. Around 6 p.m. on this day an image of Our Lady of Fatima is carried from the Sao Domingos Church to Penha Church.

*May/June • *Dragon Boat Festival* • Dragon boat races take place in the bay of Praia Grande.

June 10 • *Camoens Day and Portuguese Communities Day.*

*June 24 • *Feast of St. John the Baptist, patron saint of the city* • A public holiday established in 1622 when the Dutch were defeated.

Early Summer • *Feast of Kuan Ti* • Offerings are made at a small temple near Senado Square, followed by a lion dance through the streets of the city around 11 a.m. Demonstrations of Kung Fu also popular.

Early Summer • *Feast of Na Cha* • Devotees gather at the temple beside the ruins of St. Paul's basilica to pay homage to their patron. Lion dance through the streets of the city.

*September/October • *Mid-autumn Festival* • Also known as Mooncake Festival.

*October 1 • *National Day of the People's Republic of China* • A day of celebration for Macau's Chinese community; many shops are closed.

*October 5 • *Republic Day* • Marks the establishment of the Portuguese Republic on October 5, 1910.

*October • *Festival of Cheung Yeung* • Chinese gather at their ancestors' graves to pray for protection from disaster for the coming generation.

*November 1 • *All Saints' Day.*

*November 2 • *All Souls' Day.*

November • *variable; Macau Marathon.*

*November • *Macau Grand Prix* • Biggest motor event in the Far East; included in FIA's Pacific Racing Championship. Production car and motorcycle races, and Grand Prix Formula III car race.

*December 1 • *Portuguese Independence Day* • Marks restoration of Portuguese independence on December 1, 1640, following six decades of Spanish domination.

*December 8 • *Feast of the Immaculate Conception.*

December 22 • *Winter Solstice.*

*December 25 • *Christmas Day.*

WHAT TO SEE AND DO

Barrier Gate • Portas do Cerco is Macau's only official checkpoint with China . . . located at northern end of Istmo Ferreira do

Amaral . . . beyond is No Man's Land . . . tourists now pass through this portal daily.

Canidrome • Located on Avenida General Castelo Branco . . . greyhound races several times weekly . . . bars, restaurants, and betting booths.

Casinos • Located in Hotel Lisboa, Macau (floating) Palace, Jai Alai Palace, and on Avenida Almeida Ribeiro (Chinese games only) . . . baccarat, blackjack, roulette, boule, fan tan, dai-siu, keno . . . also slot machines . . . minimum and maximum bets . . . don't expect Monte Carlo, but pretty high stakes are played, nonetheless.

Coloane Island • Former pirate base . . . last raid in 1910 . . . now connected to Taipa by 1½-mile causeway . . . still quiet 2½-square-mile retreat . . . chapel of St. Francis Xavier in Coloane village . . . **Coloane Park** . . . several acres of gardens and ponds with large walk-in aviary . . . Chinese-style pavilions have been built for rest areas along hillsides . . . open daily 9 a.m.– 7 p.m. . . . admission fee . . . buses from across Hotel Lisboa serve the park.

Guia Fortress • Stands on highest point in Macau . . . constructed 1637–38 . . . contains oldest lighthouse on China coast . . . plus dramatic chapel with vaulted ceiling . . . noted landmark.

Historic Archives • In restored mansion on Avenida de Conselheiro Ferreira de Almeida . . . letters, books, manuscripts relating to Portugal's exploration and Macau's relations with outside world . . . some 7500 items dating from 1587 to 1786 on microfilm.

Jai Alai Palace • Located on the Outer Harbor . . . 4500-seat stadium . . . games played nightly from 7:30 p.m. except weekends and holidays (when 2 p.m. matinees are played) . . . entrance fee . . . bars, restaurants, and betting booths.

Jorge A Vares Monument • First Portuguese to set foot in China in 1513 . . . arrived from Malacca and landed on small island of Lin Tin in Pearl River, returned several times, and is buried on Lin Tin . . . statue stands in front of Macau Administration Building.

Leal Senado • Municipal Council building . . . outstanding example of Portuguese colonial architecture . . . lovingly restored . . . one of few buildings in Macau with a proper coat of paint . . . lovely tiles and stone carvings . . . visit the library on the first level . . . copy of the famous institution at Coimbra in Portugal.

Lin Fong Temple • Situated near the Barrier Gate . . . elegant example of Chinese architecture . . . Mandarins stayed here on their visits to Macau . . . on Avenida do Almirante Lacerda.

Lou Lim Ieoc Garden • Former Chinese garden reminiscent of those found in Soochow . . . on Avenida Horta e Costa . . . laid out by a wealthy merchant . . . pavilions, miniature bridges, lotus ponds . . . lovely and tranquil . . . dates from 19th century and considered one of the most historic and interesting sites in Macau . . . typical of Chinese philosophy, where man and nature are meant to become one.

Luis De Camoes Museum • Former headquarters of East India Company Select Committee . . . building dates from 1770s . . . contains fine collection of Chinese and European paintings and porcelains . . . open daily except Wed. from 11 a.m.–5 p.m.

Macau Forum • The new cultural and sports complex has convention centers seating 400 and 4000 . . . located between Jai Alai fronton and the Mandarin Oriental, near the Ferry Terminal.

Macau Maritime Museum • Located opposite historic A-Ma Temple. New structure to be completed soon . . . on display several boats as well as working model of Guia Lighthouse . . . exhibits of Macau/Japan trade in 1640s . . . collection of model junks from China . . . aquarium and display of ship drawings and models by local schoolchildren. Open daily except Tuesday 10 a.m.–6 p.m. Admission free.

Monte Fort • Citadel of Sao Paulo do Monte . . . built around time of St. Paul's . . . sits at the central point of Macau's old city wall . . . greatest moment in 1622 when fortress guns aborted a Dutch invasion . . . now used as a weather observatory . . . reached by narrow cobblestone street . . . good views of the city and of China from the top . . . closed from dusk to dawn.

Noteworthy Colonial Architecture • Penha church and residence of the Bishop of Macau on Penha Hill . . . 1870 Military Club . . . historic 1872 Dom Pedro V Theatre on Largo de Sto Agostinho . . . Santa Sancha residence of the governor on Avenida do Republica.

The Old Protestant Cemetery • Located next to Camoes Museum . . . Sunday services in English conducted in the tiny Anglican Chapel . . . graves of China coast artist George Chinnery, Robert Morrison (compiled first English/Chinese dictionary), and Captain Lord John

Spencer Churchill, Commander H.M.S. *Druid* and ancestor of Sir Winston.

Ruins of St. Paul's • Only the facade and great staircase are left of this "greatest monument to Christianity in the East" . . . cornerstone laid in 1602 . . . designed by an Italian Jesuit and built by Christian Chinese and Japanese artisans . . . Jesuits attached to this church and teaching college held rank of Mandarin . . . Church of the Mother of God (original name) destroyed by fire in 1835 . . . still most famous landmark in Macau.

Sao Domingos Church • 17th century baroque . . . built by a Spanish order of Dominicans . . . located on Rua do Sao Domingos . . . contains image of Our Lady of Fatima . . . Fatima procession begins here every May 13 . . . church open afternoons . . . don't miss the small museum at the rear.

Sun Yat Sen Memorial Home • Founder of the "Chinese Republic," Dr. Sun Yat Sen practised medicine in Macau in 1892 . . . memorial home on Avenida Sidonio Pais was built by Sun family to house relics of the revolutionary leader . . . open daily except Tues. from 10 a.m.–1 p.m., weekends from 3 p.m.–5 p.m. also.

Taipa Island • Connected by a 1.6-mile bridge over the harbor . . . island measures about 1.4 square miles . . . known for firecracker factories and farms . . . 170-year-old **Tin Hau Temple** on edge of Taipa village square . . . **Pou Tai Un Temple** situated near the bridge . . . **Macau Horse Trotting Club & Track** raceway occupies 50 acres of reclaimed land west of village . . . Check Four Faces of Buddha Shrine at end of Trotting Club car park . . . only two others of its kind (in Bangkok and Los Vegas). Taipa Folk Museum is first of five structures to be cultural village . . . shows how Portuguese families lived in Macau a century ago . . . lovely colonial-style structure facing the sea. Taipa Island Resort adjacent to Hyatt Regency is first of its kind in Macau . . . multimillion-dollar facility boasts territory's largest swimming pool, whirlpool with swim-up bar, tennis and squash courts, fitness and health spa plus food and drink areas . . . worth inspecting for architecture and ambience of the Algarve.

Temple of the Goddess A Ma • Oldest Chinese temple in Macau . . . honors the goddess of seafarers and fishermen . . . A Ma came from Fukien Province, walked to crest of Barra Hill and ascended to heaven . . . temple erected on this legendary spot . . . Macau named after her.

Temple of Kun Iam ● Temple of the Goddess of Mercy . . . dates from Ming Dynasty (4 centuries ago) . . . first temple on this site may have been built some 600 years ago . . . entrance flanked by 2 huge stone lions (turn the balls in their mouth 3 times to the left for good luck) . . . look for the image of Marco Polo who is said to have converted to Buddhism in China . . . seek out the historic "treaty table" where the Chinese and Americans signed a trade agreement in 1844 . . . lovely Chinese garden and "lovers tree."

University of East Asia ● founded in 1981 in the tradition that Jesuits brought to Macau in 1572. In less than a decade, 1000 full-time students and 6000 part-time with the fastest growing section a graduate college offering MBAs . . . also a junior college and polytechnic. Quite a feat for this territory!

Vasco Da Gama Monument and Garden ● Greatest of all Portuguese explorers . . . monument situated in garden on Avenida Sidonio Pais (near Hotel Estoril) . . . bas relief carvings on base of statue chronicle da Gama's voyages of discovery.

Pre-Arranged Tours

There are many tours available daily to Macau from Hong Kong (Mon. through Thurs., that is), priced at under US $100 for 24 hours exactly. This includes travel by jetfoil, a city tour, dinner, half of a twin-bed room in a middle class hotel, dinner, and American breakfast.

If you get here on your own, a guided city tour is available that lasts about 3½ hours and includes: Barrier Gate, Kun Iam Temple, St. Paul's ruins, Sun Yat Sen Memorial House, Guia Circuit, Lou Lim Ieoc Garden, Museum, Penha Church and Bishop's Residence, Leal Senado, Floating Casino, and Jai Alai Palace. Island tours of Taipa and Coloane to see (what is left of) rural life take about two hours and include: Trotting Club, Taipa Village, Temple of Goddess Kun Iam, Junk-building Village, Coloane Village, St. Francis Xavier's relics, Tam Long Temple, Cheoc Van Resort, Hac Sa Village and Beach. It costs just a few dollars for the islands tour, about $15 including lunch for the city visit.

Most interesting and popular of all are the Macau/China tours which began when the border was officially opened to tourists in the fall of 1979. A day tour of China can be booked in Macau itself (if you are not part of a package from Hong Kong) at the **China Travel Service,** with passport, three photographs, and 36-hour notice. The cost from Macau is about U.S. $35 and includes either the Zhongshan circuit to Cuihang (birthplace of Dr. Sun Yat Sen) and Zhongshan Hot Spring Resort, lunch at Shiqi (the county capital), and a visit to a local commune or nursery; or the Zhuhai circuit with a visit to Cuihang, lunch and a visit to the Shijinghan Tourist Centre, and a visit to the Xiangshou fishing village. China Travel Service is located at 63, Rua da Praia Grande in Macau. Tel: 88812; cable: 9999.

There is also a new resort about a 30-minute drive from the Chinese border town of Gonbei. The 160 rooms built in traditional court style are distributed among five main low-rise blocks connected by covered walkways. There are 10 villas designed for family groups, with four bedrooms each plus a kitchen, sitting room, and a garden. Facilities at this time feature a coffee shop, teahouse, Cantonese restaurants, department store, swimming pool, bath house, artificial lakes, and open playground for children. Boating, tennis courts, fishing, and shooting are expected to be introduced. Rates range from about U.S. $35 per person, per day in a double room; U.S. $250 for one of the large villas. Arrangements can be made through China Travel Service in Macau.

Another small hotel is situated only about a 15-minute drive from Macau, on the southern part of Guangdong Province. The hotel has 61 air-conditioned rooms, a coffee shop and two-story Cantonese restaurant. Boating, horseback riding, tennis courts, and a golf course are available. Seeing is believing and rates are obtainable from the Macau-Zhuhai Tourism Development Co. Ltd., 22 Rua Dr. Pedro Jose Lobo, Macau. Tel: 76586.

From Hong Kong, the best tours are the three- and four-day (actually about 54 hours and 72 hours, respectively) visits of nearby towns in China via Macau. The longer tour includes one night in Macau; both provide a return on the "express" train from Guangzhou to Hong Kong. At this writing, the 72-hour tour of Macau/Chung San/Foshan/Guangzhou departs Hong Kong on Wed. and costs about U.S. $200. The 54-hour tour of Chung San/Foshan and Guangzhou (no stopping in Macau) departs Hong Kong on Thurs. and costs about U.S. $180 per person. Macau is certainly worth a visit along the way, especially for so little extra money.

China Travel Service offers a triangular tour from Macau to Guangzhou (Canton) and Hong Kong, but as the excursion is not scheduled daily bookings must be made 10 days in advance. The four-day, three-city tour costs about HK$1300.

Walking Tours

San Ma Lo • Chinese name for Avenida de Almeida Ribeiro ("New Street") . . . approach from Praia Grande and take left side of street . . . pass Nam Tung Bank, China Products store to Leal Seando (open 11 a.m.–5 p.m.) . . . look across at Santa Casa de Misericordia, oldest Christian charity foundation in Asia . . . continue along arcade section of street with many Chinese shops . . . turn left at Rua de Mercadores

leading via Travessa do Aterro Novo to some traditional shop houses
. . . see the sidewalk shrine on Rua de Felicidade (once the red-light
district of Macau) and continue on to the end of the street . . . opposite
is the Inner Harbour waterfront and the Floating Casino . . . cross over
and return on the other side of Avenida de Almeida Ribeiro . . . pass
the Grand Hotel . . . turn left into Rua de Cinco de Outubro to have a
look at facades of Farmacia Tai Ning Tong and Loc Koc Teahouse at
No. 159 . . . return to main street . . . turn into Travessa do Mastro
to see old mansion now restored as Associacao de Benefi-
cencia Tong Sin Tong . . . at juncture of Rua dos Mercadores take
left to Tercena, or continue back to Praia Grande . . . cross square
where Leal Senado located . . . past GPO . . . and steps to cathedral
. . . have a deserved rest and drink at Solmar on western side of Praia.
(30 minutes.)

Penha Hill • Take Praia Grande along the waterfront . . . the avenue of Banyan trees was planted over a century ago . . . to the right
is the pink/white Government House . . . walk past the shops and Col-
egio Ricci . . . after Helan Liang nursery, turn right up steep Calcada
do Bom Parto . . . on right is Escola Ricci on Rua do Chunambeiro
(named for cannon factory that furnished Macau and China during 18th
century) . . . follow road past Bela Vista Hotel to Rua da Boa Vista
. . . below good views of China across narrow channel . . . at top of
hill is Bishop's Palace and garden (open from dawn to dusk) . . . excellent views of Macau and South China Sea . . . return same way
. . . stop off at Bela Vista for a drink or meal on the veranda. (30
minutes.)

Tercena • In heart of old Macau . . . Also known as Ou Mun and
full of one-room factories and workshops . . . great for photographers
and bargain hunters . . . take Avenida Almeida Ribeiro to Mercadores
. . . turn right . . . then right after road curves . . . follow Tercena
along to Rua do Tarrafeiro . . . optional detour to Camoes Gardens
and Old Protestant Cemetery from top of the road . . . return through
Tercena on opposite side of road . . . take Travessa do Armazem Velho
to Travessa do Pagode with bird sellers and Veng Meng (one of Macau's leading antique shops) . . . enjoy the crowded streets full of
craftsmen and shops . . . ask first if you wish to take photographs. (30
minutes.)

Macau Peninsula • Where China and Macau meet . . . between
the Bay of Praia Grande and Inner Harbour . . . follow Praia along
waterfront for 2 blocks . . . turn right up steep Calcada de Sto Agostinho . . . cross street and walk up ramplike Calcada do Teatro . . .
to the left is the perfect bijou-type Dom Pedro V Theatre . . . first of

its kind to be built on the China coast (entry through green door to left) . . . across the square is St. Agostinho Church . . . also note Casa Ricci (a Catholic charity) . . . Robert Ho Tung public library and S. Jose Seminary . . . return down ramp and turn right along Rua Central . . . on right is S. Lourenco church . . . on left is Salesian Institute on former site of British East India Company offices during 18th century . . . continue along Rua do Pe. Antonio ahead . . . to a square with 3 huge Banyan trees and house with loft doors . . . continue along Rua da Barra . . . on the left are grand old houses on the Beco do Lilau . . . ahead is Marine Department's Harbour Office with turreted towers . . . down the cobbled street is waterfront . . . along the left is Ma Kok Temple, which gave its name to Macau . . . explore cluster of prayer halls and shrines and fine view from the top . . . walk along Inner Harbour and turn right at Avenue Almeida Ribeiro to central city. (60 minutes.)

St. Paul's and Monte Fort • Steep climbs but spectacular views from old Jesuit fort on Monte Hill . . . overlooks site of Jesuit college for missionaries and scholars going into China . . . St. Paul's is but a facade . . . but the most famous one in Macau . . . take Praia Grande or Avenida de D. Joao IV to Rua do Campo . . . to Calcada da S. Lazaro . . . climb steps at end of street . . . turn left and follow cobbled slope of Caminho dos Artilheiros to entrance of fort . . . old cannons and superb views . . . Macau's Meteorological Office now occupies only extant building . . . leaving fort take footpath to left for more views . . . narrow flight of steps leads across a field to the facade of St. Paul's . . . at foot of staircase is Rua de S. Paula . . . returning from facade, turn left at Rua da Palha with bazaar of cheap clothes . . . walk along and turn right at Rua de S. Domingos to visit one of the city's finest churches . . . opposite is Largo do Senado and Avenida Almeida Ribeiro . . . return to the Praia directly or take Travessa do Roquete to Rua da Se . . . note Chinese Acupuncture College opposite . . . to left is Cathedral . . . to right a cobbled street directs you to Praia. (60 minutes.)

Guia • Highest point in Macau . . . 17th-century fort contains oldest lighthouse on China coast (built 1865) . . . begin in square with Chinese Reading Room . . . with pink/white Military Club to the right . . . walk straight ahead through S. Francisco gardens . . . turn left and climb Estrada Visconde de S. Januario . . . pass hospital of same name . . . to left are good views of Monte Hill . . . to right is Guia Hill . . . turn left at Calcada do Gaio and continue on to Vasco da Gama garden and monument . . . turn right and follow Avenida Sidonio Pais . . . at Victory Garden in front of Perpetual Help College, cross avenue and take Estrada de Adolfo Loureiro opposite . . . just beyond intersection with Avenida do Conselheiro Ferreira de Almeida is Lou Lim Ieoc garden, constructed in classic Soochow style . . . turn left on Ferreira de Almeida noting restored colonial mansions which serve as government offices . . . turn right at Estrada do Cemiterio to visit Catholic Cemetery with chapel, Chinese graves, statue of local hero Mesquita . . . continue on and turn right at Calcada de S. Lazaro to see church and fine restored library . . . continue along avenue to Rua do Campo and back to Praia Grande . . . OR you can climb Guia Hill from Estrada de Cacilhas and walk along small lane that encircles fortress . . . very steep in places. (60 minutes.)

HOTELS

★**Bela Vista** • *8 Rua Comendador Kou Ho Neng, Macau. Tel: 573821. Cable: VISTA* • 23 rooms . . . expatriates living in Hong Kong consider the place Old World . . . a genteel shabbiness as they say . . . quiet though if you want to get away from it all . . . very popular, especially view from the terrace of Macau and the South China Sea. The local government announced plans to buy Bela Vista and restore it to former grandeur . . . to be operated like Portuguese pousada . . . we are still waiting . . . meanwhile, enjoy a drink or meal on the veranda and converse with the other guests . . . a place much beloved by locals.

Manager: A. P. Marques. *Reservations:* Direct.

★★★★★**Hyatt Regency Macau** • *Central P.O. Box 3008, Taipa Island. Tel: 27000. Telex: 88512 HY MAC OM* • 356 rooms. Resort hotel located on Taipa Island . . . Asia's first modular-built hotel . . . complimentary shuttle bus service from town center . . . just 5 minutes from Macau's main entertainment area . . . definitely the poshest place to stay and play in Macau!

Facilities: Afonso's (Portuguese) restaurant. Flamingo (Macanese) Kamogawa Teppanyaki restaurant. A Pousada Cafe. Atrio Lobby lounge. The Greenhouse and Fado's international Discotheque. Regency Club accommodations. Business Center/conference rooms. Outdoor pool. Fitness Center with jogging track. Tennis courts. Beaches, trotting track and casinos nearby.

Manager: J. DePabros. *Reservations:* Hyatt Int'l.

★★★**Hotel Lisboa** • *Avenida da Amizade, Macau. Tel: 77666. Telex: 88203 HOTELOM. Cable: Hotelisboa* • 750 rooms . . . Macau's largest existing hotel/casino complex . . . Las Vegas atmosphere . . . nonstop action throughout day and night . . . nice views of Taipa Island from harbor-side rooms . . . new circular tower features all deluxe suites from 9th to 17th floors and revolving restaurant on 20th.

Facilities: Several restaurants: Portas do Sol (Portuguese); Galera Grillroom; Chiu Chow, Cantonese, Furugato, and Tamaya (Chinese); Noite e Dia 24-hour coffee shop; Caesar's Palace restaurant and coffee shop. 6 bars. Sauna and health center. Bowling alley. Swimming pool and children's playground. 500-person Chinese restaurant in new wing. Everything available here in Las-Vegas, glitzy style, including the Crazy Paris Show performances.

Manager: P. Lobo. *Reservations:* Hong Kong Tel: 5–415680.

★★★★★**Mandarin Oriental Macau** • *Avenida da Amizade, Macau. Tel: 567888. Telex: 88588OMA OM. Cable: Oriental* • 406 rooms (32 suites) . . . $35 million facility managed by Mandarin Oriental Hotel Group . . . 21-story hotel on waterfront site near ferry terminal . . . rooms facing south, east, and west have unrestricted views of harbor and Taipa and Coloane Islands . . . all guest rooms in 17-story tower . . . with public areas on three-level podium.

Facilities: Business center and conference areas. Health center. Squash and tennis courts. Swimming pool. Poolside Terrace. The Grill (European) and Dynasty (Chinese) restaurants. Caravela Lounge. Cafe Girassol. Pastelaria sidewalk cafe. Shuttle bus service.

Manager: G. C. Balenier. *Reservations:* LHW.

★★**Pousada de Coloane** • *Praia de Cheoc Van, Coloane. Tel: 28143. Telex: 88690 PDC OM* • 22 rooms . . . located right on Cheoc Van beach . . . small and very attractive . . . nicely managed and popular . . . especially if you wish to avoid the "big time" . . . swimming in ocean . . . dining with sunsets.

Facilities: Charming restaurant and bar. Swimming pool and children's playground. Sauna. Transportation service. Meeting facilities.

Manager: F. Lucio. *Reservations:* Hong Kong Tel: 5–455626.

★★★**Pousada de Sao Tiago** • *Avenida da Republica, Macau. Tel: 78111. Telex: 88376 TIAGO OM* • 23 rooms . . . plans for 75 more . . . opened December 1981 . . . charming, small inn built inside stone walls of Fort of St. James of the Barrier . . . on a hill overlooking Macau's Inner Harbour . . . 1629 fort protected harbor from Dutch raids . . . local architect Nuno Jorge recognized by PATA for "sensitive use of a historic site" . . . and for "great style and comfort" in creating $3-million property . . . interiors beautifully decorated with furniture from Portugal . . . Old World ambience with modern amenities . . . very cozy.

Facilities: Cafe da Barra. Grill Fortaleza. Cascata Bar. Swimming pool and conference room.

Reservations: Hong Kong 5–8910366.

★★★**Hotel Presidente** • *Avenida da Amizade, Macau. Tel: 553888. Telex: 88440HPM OM* • 333 rooms . . . opened June 1982 . . . second largest property after Lisboa . . . 21-story tower sitting on yet another pedestal . . . south rooms overlook Pearl River estuary, Taipa and Coloane islands . . . north rooms view Guia Hill and lighthouse.

Facilities: A Casa (European), President (Chinese), and Korean-style restaurants. Skylight nightclub/disco. Sauna.

Manager: R. Kwong. *Reservations:* Hong Kong 5–416056.

★★★**Hotel Royal** • *Estrada da Vitoria, Macau. Tel: 552222. Telex: 88514 ROYAL OM* • 380 rooms . . . opened Feb. 1983 . . . 19-story hotel managed by Dai-Ichi group of Japan . . . not recommended for independent traveler . . . overlooks Vasco da Gama garden in central area . . . 4-floor podium topped by 15-story tower.

Facilities: Vasco da Gama (European), Ginza (Japanese), and Royal (Chinese) restaurants. Indoor swimming pool, athletic club, and squash courts.

Manager: M. Nakayama. *Reservations:* Hong Kong 5–422033.

DINING

For over four centuries, the Macanese have been mixing and matching ingredients from Europe, South America, India, Africa, Southeast Asia, and China. The early Portuguese settlers introduced a great many food stuffs to China, among them peanuts, sweet potatoes, green beans and lettuce, pineapples and papayas, shrimp paste, coffee, and wine. From China, they learned of tea, rhubarb, celery, tangerines, ginger root, soy, and the art of sealing flavors through fast cooking.

Macau can boast a distinctive cuisine that combines many contrasting kitchens. Its most famous dish is something known to all as "African chicken," which is cut-up fowl marinated in a spicy-garlic sauce and grilled over hot coals. (Perfection!) According to tradition, the dish was originally brought to Macau by African sailors and over the centuries modified by the Portuguese. Another popular Macanese specialty is piquant prawns, also marinated and grilled with peppers and chilis. Macau sole, local quail, pigeon, and duck as well as lovely fresh vegetables are featured on most restaurant menus. Portuguese dishes include *bacalhau,* the country's beloved codfish in all its guises, *caldo verde* and *sopa alentejana*—two well-known vegetable soups. From the Portuguese in Brazil comes the mighty *feijoadas,* a heavy stew of pork, potatoes, cabbage, spicy sausage, and kidney beans that is best consumed for Saturday lunch (so you can spend the remainder of the weekend recuperating).

To accompany the meal, Macau's bakers produce Continental-style bread and rolls, and Portuguese wines are not only plentiful but very inexpensive. Remember Mateus Rose? It retails here for about U.S. $3.50 (which explains why Hong Kong customs only allow one bottle per person). Other Portuguese red, white, and sparkling vino verde as well as ports and brandies can be found at remarkably low prices. Dining in general is much less expensive in Macau than almost anywhere in the Far East, and dress (except for hotel nightspots) is quite casual.

PORTUGUESE/MACANESE RESTAURANTS

A Galera • *Hotel Lisboa* • *Tel: 77666, ext. 124* • Fancy setting and prices . . . grilled prawns, steaks, African chicken . . . live music in the evening for dancing.

Algarve Sol • *41–43, Rua Comandante Mata e Oliveira. Tel: 89007* • Portuguese and Continental food in an Iberian setting.

Bela Vista • *Hotel Bela Vista. Tel: 73821* • Portuguese home cooking in hilltop setting . . . dine on the terrace. Very, very Macanese casual.

Cafe de Barra • *Pousada de Sao Tiago. Tel: 78111* • Lovely views and very romantic. A potpourri of dishes offered. Superb service.

Fat Siu Lau • *64 Rua da Felicidade. Tel: 573585* • Opened 1903 and oldest restaurant in Macau . . . known for roast pigeon, prawns, and crab.

Flamingo Restaurant • *Taipa Island Resort (adjacent Hyatt Hotel), Taipa Island. Tel: 27000* • Good Portuguese food in veranda setting. Excellent prices for being where it is. Specialty is *Macacheesa*, a pizzalike savoury more than ample for two!

Henri's • *4 Avenida da Republica. Tel: 76207* • Tables along the seafront popular in the evening . . . known for biggest spicy prawns in town . . . marvelous African chicken and prawn fondue.

Pinocchio's • *4 Rua do Sol, Taipa Island. Tel: 27128* • Take a table in the garden . . . marvelous roast quail, chili crabs, and roast suckling pig.

Pousada de Coloane • *Praia de Cheoc Van, Coloane Island. Tel: 08144* • Renowned Sun. luncheon buffet on terrace with panoramic views . . . also superb feijoadas, prawns, sardines . . . arrive early.

Solmar • *11 Praia Grande. Tel: 74391* • Not much atmosphere, alas . . . one of most popular places in town . . . superb seafood . . . African chicken.

The Grill • *Mandarin Oriental Hotel. Tel: 567888* • Continental food in hotel setting with fine service. Don't look for excitement or Macanese ambience here.

CHINESE RESTAURANTS

Chiu Chau • *Hotel Lisboa. Tel: 77666, ext. 82001* • Excellent Chiu Chau cuisine . . . deep-fried bean curd . . . prawn ball and bamboo soup . . . mushrooms stuffed with minced prawns.

456 Restaurant • *Hotel Lisboa. Tel: 77666, ext. 2090* • Shanghainese food . . . named after that well-known place in Shanghai.

Jade Garden • *Avenida Almeida Ribeiro. Tel: 88474* • Cantonese cooking . . . known especially for good dim sum . . . spring rolls, pork buns, shiu mai, and har kau.

Long Kei • *7 Largo do Senado. Tel: 73970* • Probably Macau's most popular and best Cantonese restaurant . . . Crowded.

Tong Kong • *32 Rua da Caldeira. Tel: 77364* • Known for its Hakka cuisine.

OTHER RESTAURANTS

Furusato • *Hotel Lisboa. Tel: 81581* • Japanese meals in traditional settings . . . caters to Japanese . . . expensive.

Malay • *Travessa do Pe. Soares. Tel: 83366* • Good satay and Malay-style curries.

NIGHTLIFE

When you need a respite from tempting Lady Luck in one of the casinos Macau is a nightlife town and there are plenty of choices. Sports fans may enjoy an evening of jai alai (weeknights at 7:30 p.m.), the greyhound races (several times weekly at 8 p.m.), or harness racing at the glamorous Macau Trotting Club on Taipa Island (Tel: 27211 for information).

The Crazy Paris Show in Mona Lisa Hall, Lisboa Hotel (8:30 and 10 p.m. weeknights; 8:30, 10, and 11 p.m. weekends) is slick and professional and very French. More local in color are the Portuguese folk dances at Portas dol Sol restaurant, Hotel Lisboa, with performances on odd calendar days at 9:30 p.m. Among the many nightclubs are **Paris** at Hotel Estoril, **Portas dol Sol** at Lisboa Hotel, **Skylight Disco** at Hotel President (with dancing show by European girls), **Ritz** on the top floor of Jai Alai Palace, and **Green Parrot** disco at Hyatt Regency. All have a minimum charge for drinks and open for action just after 9 p.m.

SHOPPING

Although the Macanese travel to Hong Kong for their "serious" shopping, you can have some fun exploring the byways of this tiny territory and even find a bargain or two. The popular purchases seem to be gold jewelry, Chinese "antiquities," porcelain and pottery, small electrical items, and locally made knitwear and clothing. For knittedwear and locally made clothing, try the street stalls near Senate Square in the morning, and in Rua de Palha. Do not expect to find something wonderful for a song at the souvenir stalls at St. Paul's, Border Gate, or Penha Hill. These enterprising entrepreneurs are peddling souvenirs and nothing else! Portuguese wines are still the best buy, but unfortunately you must consume all but the final bottle before embarking the jetfoil back to Hong Kong!

Until 1974, when Hong Kong eased restrictions on the import of gold into the colony, tiny Macau was a gold-lover's haven and quite obviously in the smuggling business. However, these romantic days are past and the **jewelry** shops you see on the Avenida Almeida Ribeiro (about every other step) or Rua dos Mercadores are charging the current market rate per ounce. These shops tend to be entirely Chinese-owned and patronized. Only the very clever should venture forth here (and it helps if you know the language). If you must buy an expensive item, ask for a receipt and a warranty card and don't be surprised if you get "stuck."

Chinese **"antiquities"** can be found in the lanes around St. Paul's Ruins as well as in the antique shops along Avenida de Almeida Ribeiro and the many side streets off this main boulevard. And if you run across a sweet old thing with gold front teeth, who wraps her goods in last week's San Francisco Chronicle—that's the very one who "took" me for several dollars once. I've been looking for her ever since! Actually, I rather enjoyed the pair of "valuable" vases I bought and was quite devastated when they broke.

MALAYSIA

HISTORY

It is impossible to describe the typical Malaysian, for he or she is every-man: a Straits-born Chinese Buddhist whose family is most likely involved in commerce and may even control one of the great export fortunes in rubber or tin or timber; a Moslem descended directly from one of the original Malay settlers; a Hindu whose ancestors were brought to the peninsula from India by the British for much-needed labor; or one of the almost one million tribal members living on the northern coast of Borneo, whose ancestors are said to have inhabited this area as early as 37,000 years ago.

Although Eastern man flocked to the Malay Peninsula very early after the birth of Christ (to confirm rumors of precious minerals in the ground) and the great Marco Polo boasted about his sail through the Straits of Malacca at the end of the 13th century, things really didn't begin to pop until the beginning of the 15th century. A favored date is 1403, when a Sumatran prince named **Parameswara** seems to have founded the city of Malacca—the city that became the primary trading post between India and China for over 300 years. The place was obviously destined for success because two years later, in 1405, the colorful Admiral Cheng Ho came to call and gave the port the blessing of the Ming Court.

China was so impressed by this new settlement that in the 1460s the emperor sent his daughter **Princess Hang Li Poh** to marry the reigning sultan, **Mansor Shah.** She did not come alone, so the sultan created a special residential area for her entourage of 500 ladies-in-waiting. Today **Bukit China** covers 160 acres and is the largest Chinese cemetery outside the mainland; many of the tombs date from the Ming Period.

By 1500 the Portuguese fleet was looking for some Eastern real estate; they took control of Malacca just over a decade later. Although they only held the port for a little more than a century, the Portuguese left their legacy in the Eurasian community that still exists and speaks a medieval dialect only its proud members can understand. The Portuguese were replaced by the Dutch in 1641 as the dominant force in

Malacca, and the architecture took on a pinky hue with bricks brought all the way from Holland.

The Dutch traded their booty to the British in 1786, the same year that Captain Francis Light claimed the island of Penang for the British Crown. The Straits settlements were falling into place, and Britain would control the destiny of the Malay Peninsula for the next 155 years. Kuala Lumpur, the "muddy estuary," was founded at the confluence of the Klang and Gombak rivers in 1864 on the notion that tin could be mined nearby. The town was unimpressive outback until the turn of the century when the British began to fill its swampland with colonial-style structures and made it the capital of the Protected Malay States.

Born administrators, the British also became planters on a grand scale. Some Brazilian rubber trees sent from Kew Gardens as an experiment became an unexpected bonanza; Malaysia is now the world's largest single supplier of the raw material. Tin mining is another lucrative export, and two-thirds of the land covered with jungle supplies much of the world's timber. Life was pleasant for all concerned and progressing nicely until the Second World War when two decades of jungle warfare ensued.

The Japanese sank a few British battleships patrolling the South China Sea and arrived at the northeast corner of the Malay peninsula on December 8, 1941—within minutes of their colleagues' attack on Pearl Harbor. From Kota Bharu, the army made its way south via anything with wheels (including bicycles) and took the seemingly impregnable island of Singapore within two months. While the British kept their big guns pointed in the other direction, the Imperial Army simply crossed over the causeway and marched most of the white population off to Changi POW camp. Meanwhile, the British on the peninsula fought beside Chinese and Malay in their own battle against the invaders.

The official war was over in 1945, but peace did not last long. A communist revolt began in 1948 that lasted 12 bitter years. The British called it "The Emergency" and used their considerable wit and intrigue to flush Communist guerillas from the Malayan jungles. Due to the absence of support from the other populace, the British Military Administration launched the Resettlement Programmes for villages near the jungles. The Emergency did hasten the independence of Malaya, however, for it took all purpose away from the CTs (communist terrorists) who claimed they were just attempting to rid the country of colonial imperialists.

As the fighting continued through the 1950s, the British could no longer hem and haw. Finally, on August 31, 1957, independence came to the Malay peninsula, and its 11 states were symbolized in a new flag with an 11-point star. On September 2, the new king and ruler of the Federation of Malaya kissed the blade of his gold *kris* (dagger) and took office. His official title was the **Yang di Pertuan Agong** and he would govern for a period of five years, after which one of the other ten sultans would be elected king. It is a most sensible and democratic solution, fair to the individuality and autonomy of each state and its sultan or ruling family.

Malaya became known as Malaysia in September 1963 when the former British colonies of Sabah, Sarawak, and Singapore joined the federation. But 14 states did not prove to be an auspicious number, and Lee Kuan Yew split Singapore away in December 1965, making it a fully independent republic. The prime minister and his Malay counterparts just never saw eye to eye, and historians now feel that an independent Singapore was his scheme all along.

With such a diversity of cultures and people living tolerably together, travel in Malaysia is a constant surprise. Visitors may come across an Islamic festivity, Chinese celebrants lighting *joss* sticks in a colorful Buddhist temple, or Indians chewing betel nut by the side of the road at the same time. Pork will be on the menu in a Chinese restaurant, but you will probably find only beef or chicken sate, and your favorful Indian curries are more likely to be vegetarian than not. From the Borneo chieftain to the sultan's daughter, the people of Malaysia cling tightly to their traditions and customs.

While the original inhabitants of the Malay Peninsula were aborigines (Senois, Negritos, and Temiars) as well as Malays, the 15th century Chinese arrivals resulted in a new group called the Peranakans. This is a mixture of Chinese/Malay in food, traditions, and language. When the Portuguese arrived in the 16th century, however, their offspring from marriage to the locals were and still are considered Eurasians. Today, there is relaxed intermarriage among the ethnic groups (something the British never encouraged)—especially betwixt professionals like administrators, politicians, and teachers.

The range of experiences for travelers in Malaysia may make many think they are actually touring several countries at once. You can join the Pesta Menuai festival in Sabah to welcome the rice spirit Bambaazon. Shop to your heart's desire at Kota Belud's famous *tamu,* or weekly open-air bazaar. Continue on to Sarawak for a trip upriver and a stay in one of the *dayak* long houses. Watch turtles lay their eggs along the East Coast beaches in peninsular Malaysia. Shoot the rapids in Taman Negara, the national park that spans three states. Lose a bundle at the Genting Highlands casino, or join the chic on the golden sands of Penang's Batu Ferringhi, or Foreigner's Rock.

You can revel in the colonial atmosphere of Kuala Lumpur and eat like a prince or princess, or relive the fiery past of Malacca where the oldest Anglican church in Southeast Asia still stands. You can visit the new industrial town of Petaling Jaya, an experiment in living and a national showpiece, or watch the tapping of rubber trees, a method unchanged for years. Tin mines, timber trucks bound for ships in the port of Singapore, batik, and kite-flying contests are also part of the Malaysian scene.

It is a colorful and fascinating tapestry that beckons the traveler to visit again and again. In fact, Malaysia expects to welcome more and more visitors annually and is preparing a great many new tourist facilities. In addition to more hotel rooms, Kuala Lumpur boasts one of Asia's largest convention centers, the Putra World Trade Center. The 12-acre site features a 35-story tower, exhibition hall, and hotel in an architectural design that combines the traditional cultural features of the country's many varied regions.

MALAYSIA IN A CAPSULE

A confederation of 13 separate states and almost 130,000 square miles of the Malay Peninsula . . . between southern Thailand and Singapore . . . plus Sabah and Sarawak on the northern coast of Borneo . . . name comprises *Malay,* the ethnic term for the Moslems of Indian origin who make up 50% of the 15 million population . . . plus *sia* for the 35% Chinese, 10% Hindu, and 5% others (Eurasian and European) . . . Malay is the official language but many others are widely spoken, including Cantonese, English, and Tamil . . . sultans remain ceremonial rulers and elect one of their kind every 5 years as king on a rotating basis . . . Islam is the official religion but tolerance of other beliefs is one of the country's most fervent manifestations . . . a beautiful and fascinating place to visit . . . full of surprises and charming people.

PLANNING AHEAD

THE TOURIST DEVELOPMENT CORPORATION   (TDC) of Malaysia is working hard to welcome more and more visitors every year. Major tourism projects have been included in the Fourth Malaysia Plan, the country's blueprint for development. Highway extensions, railroad improvements, more first-class hotel rooms in Penang and Kuala Lumpur, and a $7 million cultural zone in the capital are all scheduled for the future.

Headquarters for the TDC is 26th Floor, Menara Dato Onn, Putra World Trade Centre, Jalan Tun Ismail 50480, Kuala Lumpur (Tel:

2935188). Visit the regional offices—in Penang, Trengganu, Johor Bahru, Kota Kinabalu, and Kuching—for excellent maps and brochures.

Unfortunately, the only North American branch is the Malaysian Tourist Information Center, 818 West Seventh St., Los Angeles, CA 90017 (Tel: 213–689–9702).

VISAS are not required of travelers holding valid U.S. passports, for a stay of up to 14 days, which can be extended to three months. Proof of solvency, respectable dress, and airline tickets are necessary for receiving an extension.

INOCULATIONS are not required for entry, unless you are coming from an endemic area.

ENTRY BY AIR is probably into Kuala Lumpur's glamorous new airport at Subang, about a half-hour ride from the capital. There is also daily service to about 35 other domestic destinations, including Penang, Malacca, Kuantan, Kota Kinabalu, and Kuching. Kuala Lumpur is a mere 35 minutes by air from Singapore and about 80 minutes from Bangkok. Malaysian Airline System (MAS), which has extensive regional service and from North America, ranks as one of the best airlines for efficiency and service in Asia.

Departure tax is M$3 for domestic flights, M$5 for flights to Singapore, and M$15 for international flights.

ARRIVAL BY SEA is via the historic island of Penang or Port Klang (for Kuala Lumpur). Penang is the more popular of the two and several cruise lines call here annually on their global voyages, such as Cunard Line, P & O Line, Pearl Cruises, Royal Cruise Line, and Royal Viking Line.

ARRIVAL BY LAND offers many opportunities. There is **train** service between Bangkok and Singapore right through the Malay Peninsula, if you can bear to sit for two days straight. I took the train once from Bangkok to Penang (Butterworth) and it was a very, very long ride.

Better yet are shared **taxis** that run frequently between Johor Bahru and Penang on a pay-per-destination basis. Malaysia's road system is pretty good and you never know who your companions will be.

You can also rent a **car** in Singapore and drive to Kuala Lumpur or along the east coast, if you don't mind fighting with timber trucks that use the same route. In fact, be prepared to pay extra insurance if you tell the car rental people of your plans to drive into Malaysia. The roads along both coasts are generally excellent, and a new east-west highway has been cut into the main Range Mountains in the north and reduces travel from Penang to Kota Bharu from 621 miles to 225 miles. It also offers lovely views of formerly inaccessible areas. Driving in Malaysia is on the left.

DUTY FREE   are the usual items, but beware: pornography, narcotics, daggers, and walkie-talkies are prohibited.

THE CURRENCY   of Malaysia is the dollar or ringgit, and there are approximately M$2.50 to U.S.$1. although the exchange rate fluctuates slightly. The Malaysian dollar has the same approximate worth as the Singapore and Brunei dollar but is no longer interchangeable. Bona fide tourists may import not more than M$10,000 and export not more than M$5,000. The importation of traveler's checks, letters of credit, or cash in foreign currency is unlimited. Credit cards are accepted widely throughout the country, although some shops add a surcharge.

LOCAL TIME   in Malaysia is Greenwich Mean Time plus 8 hours, in the same zone as neighboring Singapore. The entire Malay Peninsula and the separate states of Sabah and Sarawak on Borneo were finally synchronized on New Year's Day 1982 as a symbol of unity.

LOCAL CURRENT   is 220 volts, 50 cycles, but don't expect appliances to work too well outside the leading hotels. You will probably even have a problem with razors in this country.

LOCAL WATER   is potable throughout Malaysia, which can boast an extremely high standard of living and excellent health facilities. There is an abundance of bottled water and soft drinks available for the timid.

THE OFFICIAL LANGUAGE   is Bahasa Malaysian, but Tamil is spoken by the Indian population and either Cantonese or Hokkien by the Chinese. English is still spoken widely by the educated class. Even in small towns, someone will be old enough to remember some English and be helpful.

There are three English language newspapers published daily, *The New Straits Times, The Star,* and *The Malay Mail;* they have to make do since it is difficult to find much outside reading material. Tune into the English broadcast on Radio Ibukota from 6 to 7 p.m. daily for weather, money exchange rates, music and local events in Kuala Lumpur. Most imported television programs are in English with Malay subtitles.

BUSINESS HOURS   differ widely throughout the Malay Peninsula. Government offices usually operate from 8:15 a.m. to 12:45 p.m. and from 2 to 4:15 p.m. (Mon.–Fri.) with a little extra time off on Friday noon for communal Jumaah prayers at the many mosques. Offices and shops open at 9 a.m. and close anywhere from 5 to 9 p.m. Saturdays are usually halfday for office work and Sunday is a holiday. However, the five states in the eastern part of the peninsula still maintain the traditional Moslem half-holiday on Thursday, full holiday on Friday (the holy day), and business as usual on Saturday and Sunday. The best rule is to always confirm appointments and check hours of business.

TIPPING   is not considered compulsory in Malaysia and a 5% service charge is added to most hotel and restaurant bills. However, you should still always reward service rendered with a smile.

TELEPHONE AND TELEX   service is quite good in Kuala Lumpur, not good anywhere else in Malaysia. The major hotels in Kuala Lumpur offer excellent services for overseas calls and telexes, or you can use the Central Telegraph Office located in Bukit Mahkamah, open 24 hours daily. There is also a Telegraph Office at the Kuala Lumpur International Airport, open from 7:30 a.m. to 11:30 p.m. daily.

Direct calls can be made from telephones with International Subscriber Dialing (ISD) facility to Australia, Japan, United Kingdom, Germany, Hong Kong, Switzerland, U.S., Italy, and Tahiti, but expect to pay heavily for this service. Self-dialing facilities are available to all cities within Malysia as well as to neighboring Singapore, and trunk calls (long distance) are charged at reduced rates between 6 p.m. and 7 a.m. Keep in mind, Jahatan Telekom Malaysia has just in the last year changed all telephone numbers in Selangor and the Federal Territory of Kuala Lumpur from six to seven digits long. If you need assistance or information regarding a new number, contact the Assistance Centre by dialing 1060 and give them the old number. Local calls within each city limit are M$.10.

WHAT TO WEAR   throughout Malaysia is what the Malaysians wear— cool, light, comfortable, and very conservative clothing. The local batik is lovely. In this country women may be requested to don a covering when visiting a mosque or other holy place. People ''dress'' in the evening in Kuala Lumpur, where a jacket and tie are expected for gentlemen, a long skirt or pantsuit for the women. However, batik sport shirts and casual clothes is the practice elsewhere.

It can really *rain* on the Malay Peninsula, so some sort of protection is suggested at all times. An umbrella is useless in these torrential storms that come from nowhere and leave after several drenching moments; a plastic wrap is more advisable. The country is hot and humid most of the time, but the luxury hotels and restaurants are over airconditioned, so carry a shawl or sweater when dining out. Sandals are worn by everyone, and are not a bad idea considering the rain and the fact that shoes are not allowed in Moslem monuments. Inexpensive straw hats are also helpful to those not accustomed to the hot tropical sun.

Dress in the highlands or hill resorts is quite different, as the temperatures drop very low at these heights and wool slacks are often necessary, especially in the evening. At some of the more colonial-style hostelries (e.g., Foster's Lakehouse in the Cameron Highlands), life is a bit formal and stuffy in the evening, so be prepared. Never venture toward the hill resorts without a few extra layers, as you will be very uncomfortable and definitely get a chill.

LOCAL TRANSPORTATION throughout the country is excellent and consists of constantly improved **railway** service, **highways** along both coasts connecting east with west, local **buses,** and share **taxis.** In the capital and smaller cities, there are local buses and taxis, even a few **trishaws** (three-wheeled vehicles). You should bargain in advance for the trishaws, which are terrific for sightseeing in Penang or Malacca. Catch them quickly, before they disappear forever!

A new multimillion-dollar bridge (the third largest in the world) now connects Penang to the mainland. Thirteen and a half kilometers in length, it has a lifespan of 400 years and was built to withstand earthquakes measuring up to 7.5 on the Richter scale.

In Penang a **ferry** operates around the clock between Georgetown (on the island) and Butterworth on the mainland. There are two terminals on each side, one for passengers and vehicles, the other for vehicles only. Departures are every 7 to 10 minutes during the day, every 10 to 30 minutes from 10 p.m. until 5:30 a.m. and rates are very reasonable (M$.40). Penang also has a **cog railway** that goes up to Penang Hill, with departures about every 30 minutes and rates about M$3 per adult (round trip).

Domestic **air** services are provided by Malaysian Airline System (MAS), Malaysia Air Charter Company, and Wira Kris Udara Malaysia. The latter two companies are headquartered at Kuala Lumpur International Airport in Subang.

FESTIVALS AND HOLIDAYS It almost seems that Malaysians celebrate every festival known to man, since their calendar includes holidays belonging to Christians, Hindus, Buddhists, and Moslems—as well as many local and national events. It is quite a calendar and visitors are certainly encouraged to participate in any celebration under way! (Public holidays are marked with an asterisk*.)

***January 1** • *New Year's Day* • (Not a holiday in the states of Johor, Kedah, Kelantan, Perlis, and Trengganu.)

January • *Gengguland Day* • The Orang Asli aborigines in South Perak lay a feast for the spirits and deities as well as for themselves.

January • *Thaipongal* • The first day of the Tamil month of Thai. Harvest Festival and *pongal,* or new grain, is cooked.

*January • *Birthday of Prophet Muhammad* • Born April 20, A.D. 571. Processions and chanting of holy verses held throughout the country. Also a large rally in Kuala Lumpur's Merdeka Stadium.

January • *Thaipusam* • A day of penance for Hindus, who offer milk, honey, and fruit carried on *kavadi* (a steel arch with long thin skewers attached) to shrines of Lord Subramaniam. Celebrations in Kuala Lumpur take place at Batu Caves with a colorful procession.

January/February • *Chinese New Year.*

*February 1 • *Federal Territory Day* • Public holiday in Kuala Lumpur. Decorations and cultural shows throughout the capital.

February • *Birthday of Tien Kung* • Chinese God of Heaven.

February • *Chap Goh Meh* • 15th day of the Chinese New Year

February • *Birthday of Chor Soo Kong* • Deity of the Snake Temple in Penang.

February • *Tua Pek Kong* • Festival of burning paper money, houses, and cars for deceased relatives. Main celebration at San Ten Temple, Kuching, Sarawak.

February • *Ban Hood Huat Hoay* • Gathering of Ten Thousand Buddhas. Devotees pray for world peace at Kek Lok Si Temple in Penang.

March • *Maha Siva Rathiri* • *Pujas* (ceremonies) performed in Hindu temples through the night. Devotees sing hymns in honor of Lord Siva.

March • *Pangguni Uttiram* • Day of prayers for Hindus that commemorates the marriage of Rama and Sita, hero and heroine of the Ramayana epic.

March • *Kuan Yin* • Day of worship for Chinese Goddess of Mercy, guardian of children.

March 25 • *Police Day* • Recognition of service to the country by the police force.

April • *Good Friday.*

April • *Easter Sunday.*

April • *Cheng Beng* • All Soul's Day. Chinese pay homage to ancestors.

April • *Udhadhi* • New Year for Telegu-speaking Hindus.

April • *Sri Rama Navami* • Marks descent of Lord Rama, seventh Avatar of Vishu Rama and hero of the Ramayana epic. *Pujas* performed by Hindus.

April • *Songkran* • New Year of the Thais. Water Festival.

April/May • *Chitra Pauranami* • Hindus offer *pujas,* carry *kavadis,* and pay homage to Lord Subramaniam in temples throughout the country.

May • *Sipitaxg Tamu Besar* • Blowpipe competitions and ladies' football matches held in Sipitang, a coastal town in Sabah.

May • *Kota Belud Tamu Besar* • A *tamu* (open market) in Kota Belud, Sabah, with cock fighting, native dances, buffaloes for sale, and handicrafts.

May • *Migratory Giant Turtles* • Giant Leathery turtles from South China Sea make annual visits from May to early September to east coast beaches.

*May 1 • *Labor Day.*

*May 7 • *Hari Hol* • Public holiday in Pahang only that marks the anniversary of death of Sultan Abu Bakar.

May • *National Youth Week.*

*May • *Kadazan Harvest Festival* • Traditional thanksgiving by Kadazan farmers only in Sabah.

May • *Hari Pesta Menuai* • Festival for Kadazan farmers to appease rice spirit for good harvest.

May • *Ascension Day.*

May • *Teacher's Day.*

May • *Vesakhi* • Sikhs celebrate New Year.

*May • *Wesak Day* • Commemorates birth, enlightenment, and passing away.

May • *Isra' and Mi'raj* • Isra' is the journey by night of Prophet Muhammad from Al Haram Mosque in Baitul Muqaddis. Mi'raj is the ascent of Prophet Muhammad from Al Aqsa to Heaven to meet Allah. It was on this occasion Prophet Muhammad received orders from Allah to introduce the practice of praying five times daily to Mecca.

June 1–2 • *Gawai Dayak* • Festival celebrates successful *padi* (rice) harvest. Dayaks offer traditional *tunk,* or rice wine, and a bard recites poetry.

*June 2 • *Birthday of Dymn Seri Paduka Baingda Yang Dipertuan Agong* • Thanksgiving prayers offered in mosques, churches, and temples throughout Malaysia.

June 4 • *Martyrdom of Guru Arjan Dev* • Religious ceremonies in all Sikh temples.

June • *Dragon Boat Festival (Tuan Wu Chieh)* • Marks death of a Chinese minister, scholar, and poet, who drowned himself rather than live corruptly like his colleagues.

June • *Nisfu Syaaban* • Moslems perform their religious duties at this time.

June • *St. Peter's Feast* • Celebrated by fishermen at Portuguese settlement in Malacca.

June • *Bird Singing Competition* • Contests held throughout country, but primarily in Kelantan.

July 1 • *International Cooperative Day.*

July • *Awal Ramadhan* • Beginning of month of fasting for Moslems. (Public holiday in Johor.)

July • *St. Anne's Feast Day* • Celebrated by Christians at Bukit Mertajam and Malacca.

July • *Nuzul al Quran* • Holy verses of the Koran were revealed to Prophet Muhammad in Mecca; Moslems celebrate this day by religious gatherings. (Public holiday in Kelantan, Malacca, Perak, Perlis, Selangor, and Trengganu only.)

July • *Heroes's Day* • In remembrance of all Malaysians who fought and died for their country.

July/August • *Hari Raya Puasa* • End of month of fasting for Moslems. Great festivities with prayers, delicacies, and offerings to the poor.

August • *Farmer's Day*.

August • *Festival of Seven Sisters* • A Chinese festival for single girls to pray for a happy marital future.

August • *Hungry Ghosts Festival* • A festival to celebrate the Chinese custom of offering food, *joss* sticks, and paper money to ghosts who apparently come down to earth for a month and mingle with real people.

August • *Sri Krishna Jayanti* • Marks the descent of Sri Krishan as the eighth Avatar of Vishnu and hero of the Mahabharata epic of the Hindus.

August 31 • *National Day* • Parade, cultural performance, and musicals abound; the highlight of the celebration is in Kuala Lumpur.

September • *Moon Cake Festival* • A time of great significance for Buddhists.

September • *Fire Walking Ceremony* • Devotees walk across a pit of glowing embers to fulfill their vows—most apparent at Hindu temple in Gajah Berang, Malacca.

September • *Hari Raya Haji* • Moslem celebration for those who have become *haji* (those who visited the holy city of Mecca).

September • *Vinayaka Chaturti* • A special day for Hindus, when they worship Ganapathy, the elephant-headed god who blesses devotees.

September • *Armed Forces Day*.

October • *Deepavali* • The Hindu festival of lights marks the victory of light over darkness, good over evil, and wisdom over ignorance.

October • *Awal Muharram* • First month in the Hijrah (Islamic) calendar. Marks the journey of Prophet Muhammad from Mecca to Medina.

October • *Universal Children's Day.*

October • *Festival of Loy Krathong* • Buddhist festival of lights. Candles are floated on artificial lotus flowers in memory of Lord Buddha's footprint.

November 1 • *All Saints' Day.*

November • *All Souls' Day.*

November 30 • *Birthday of Guru Nanak* • Founder of Sikhism. Day of prayers, hymns, and religious lectures.

December • *Tung Chih Festival* • Chinese pay homage to ancestors. Marble-sized rice balls (*tung yuan*) are served to symbolize family reunion.

December 25 • *Christmas Day.*

December • *Pesta Pulau Pinang* • Month-long carnival in Penang.

December • *Prophet Mondi's Birthday.*

BACKGROUND MATERIAL

The Jungle Is Neutral by Spencer Chapman (Corgi Books). One of the best on the jungle warfare of World War II.

Great Short Works of Joseph Conrad (Perennial Classic). Many of the stories are taken from Conrad's experiences in this part of the world as a seaman. Read especially *The Lagoon*. His first novel, *Almayer's Folly* (written in 1889) is based on the village of Berau in Borneo.

World Within: A Borneo Story by Tom Harrison (Cresset Press). Very good on Sarawak.

Malayan Safari by Charles Shuttleworth. Tells of the national parks and east-coast islands.

The Cultural Heritage of Malaya by W. J. Ryan. Summarizes this multiracial society.

The Singapore Story by Noel Barber (Fontana paperback). Includes some interesting vignettes on Malaysia and The Emergency.

EAST COAST

___ EAST COAST IN A CAPSULE ___

Peninsular Malaysia's largest tourist region consists of four large states—Johor, Kelantan, Pahang, and Trengganu—plus the islands Tioman and Rawa . . . stretches from the Thai border to the causeway separating Singapore . . . almost 1000 miles of shoreline and beautiful, unspoiled beaches . . . the craft center of the country—batik, silver, kites, weaving, wood carving, and traditional theater . . . turtles, singing birds, and top-spinning contests . . . a 1737-square-mile national park that boasts the peninsula's highest mountain, river trekking, and unexplored jungles . . . it's another world altogether . . . with such expanse of natural beauty and such differing cultures . . . Malaysians insist you have not truly experienced their country until you have seen the East Coast.

WHAT TO SEE AND DO

Johor

Desaru • Village of Casuarinas . . . Johor's newest beach resort is about a 90-minute drive from Johor Bahru . . . situated along 20 km of unspoiled golden beaches at Penawar . . . in southeast corner of peninsula . . . called "last unspoiled corner in Southeast Asia" . . . developed by Kejora (Johor government agency) . . . offers private chalets with Minangkabau roofs . . . verandas overlooking South China Sea . . . Malay restaurant . . . watersports and golf . . . first-class high-rise hotels planned.

Johor Bahru • State capital and city just across the causeway from neighboring Singapore . . . known for **Istana Besar,** palace of the Sultan, which can be visited mornings (except Fri. and holidays) by prior arrangement . . . famous for its gardens, with replica of Japanese teahouse, and adjoining **Johor Zoo** . . . sultan actually lives at Bukit Serene, overlooking the river . . . see also **Abu Bakar Mosque** and pineapple plantations outside the city . . . **Johor Lama** (Old Johor) is located about 18 miles upriver and was the original seat of the sultanate until the Portuguese destroyed the town and fort in 1587 . . . **Air Hitam,** northwest of the capital, is center of Aw pottery works . . . and **Lombong Waterfalls** are popular with tourists.

Kota Tinggi ● Located 56 km east of Johor Bahru (see "Hill Resorts," page 395) . . . noted for waterfalls at foot of Gunung Mountain . . . also for **Kampong Makam,** royal mausoleum for sultans of Johor.

Mersing ● Situated on the mouth of Mersing River . . . known as a quiet fishing port . . . catch the Merlin Hotel launch for **Pulau Tioman,** an idyllic island 2½ hours off the coast or 30 minutes by air . . . another beautiful resort area . . . no automobiles allowed . . . **Pulau Rawa** is smaller and closer to the peninsula . . . known for white coral sand, tall palm trees, and many caves.

Muar ● Peaceful fishing town en route to Malacca . . . known for great restaurants and foodstalls that offer local delicacies for barely a song . . . a traditional Malay village . . . full of *ghazal* music and *Kudang Kepang* dances that are said to induce trances.

Telok Mahkota ● Jason's Bay . . . located just before eastern coastline town of Mersing . . . about 10 more km of sandy beach . . . sheltered from the South China Sea . . . popular with locals as weekend retreat.

Kelantan

Kota Bharu ● Capital of the Land of Pretty Maidens (Kelantan) . . . primarily Malay, Kelantan is also known as the cultural state . . . *Makyong* and *Menora* dance dramas, *Wayang Kulit* (shadow puppetry), traditional Malay music, silverware, *kain songket* and batik, and even *berok* monkeys, who work the coconut palms in tandem with their masters . . . also for kite-flying, top-spinning, and bird-singing competitions . . . Kota Bharu has one of best market squares in Southeast Asia . . . also Old World charm in **Istana Balai Besar,** the Sultan's palace built in 1844 and still used for royal weddings . . . palace also houses a barge called "Flower of the Gods, the Splendor of Kelantan" . . . must be visited.

Kuala Krai • About 64 km from Kota Bharu . . . famous for its fine zoo of local wildlife, including *kijang* (deer) . . . game hunting for wild deer, elephant, and *seladang* (wild buffalo) can be arranged through the State Game Warden here.

Pantai Dasar Sabak • Popular beach lined with casuarina trees . . . located about 13 km from Kota Bharu . . . turtles come ashore here to lay eggs . . . also known because Japanese opened World War II in the Pacific here in December 1941 about 95 minutes before the Pearl Harbor attack began . . . between here and the capital is another beach known romantically as **"Beach of Passionate Love"** . . . other lovely beaches are **Pantai Dalam Rhu** near fishing village of Semerak . . . and **Pantai Irama** near Bachok town.

Pulau Perhentian • Island in South China Sea . . . about 2 hours by boat from Kuala Besut . . . government rest house for those who wish to spend a few quiet days.

Waterfalls • In abundance throughout the state of Kelantan . . . in the district of Pasir Puteh are **Jeram Pasu, Jeram Tapeh, Cherang Tuli,** and **Jeram Lenang** . . . of the lot, Jeram Pasu is the most popular . . . especially at holiday time . . . reach it via an 8-km path through the jungle.

Pahang

Beserah • A fishing village about 10 km north of Kuantan . . . known for its friendly and serene people . . . the village people enjoy visitors and have plenty of souvenirs to offer them . . . giant tops for the local spinning contests . . . carved fishing boats . . . shellcraft items . . . photographers love it here, too!

Cherating • Site of Asia's first **Club Med Holiday Village . . .** Malaysians are proud of this joint venture between TDC and Club Med of Paris . . . biggest tourist complex on the East Coast . . . styled in traditional Malay architecture . . . 2- and 3-story buildings offer accommodations, 2 restaurants, and indoor recreational facilities . . . disco . . . watersports and everything else . . . guests take night tours to Kuantan's famous evening market . . . and can take longer excursions to other East Coast towns . . . local villagers demonstrate art of *pandan* weaving, *congkak,* or offer performances of Wayang Kulit or Rodat, a traditional dance involving elaborate hand movements.

Kuantan • Capital of Pahang, 3rd largest state in Malaysia . . . an important East Coast port . . . noted for its fine beaches . . . **Telok**

Chempedak is just a few kilometers from town center . . . also **Chendor Beach** in the north . . . turtle-watching is a unique pastime here . . . many villages around Kuantan offer cultural traditions . . . kite flying, top spinning, Wayang Kulit, wood carving, batik printing, brocade and pandan weaving . . . **Brocade Weaving Center** features *kain songket* in which intricate designs of gold and silver are added to the silk . . . *bersilat,* Malay art of defense is another tourist attraction . . . demonstrations of all the crafts can be arranged.

Lake Chini • The Loch Ness of Malaysia . . . located 60 km west of Kuantan . . . then left to Lubok Paku and from there by boat . . . mythical monsters reputed to lurk in the mysterious waters . . . also indication that a Khmer city existed near the site . . . interesting sidetrip from the beaches . . . but only for the adventurous . . . it is suggested that both jungle and camping equipment be taken along.

Marathandhavar Temple • Hindu temple along jungle-lined Jerantut/Maran road between Kuantan and Taman Negara . . . devotees flock here in March to celebrate colorful **Panguni Uthiram** Festival.

Pekan • The Royal Town . . . situated near the mouth of peninsular Malaysia's longest river, the Sungei Pahang . . . about 45 km south of Kuantan . . . site of **Istana Abu Bakar,** royal palace of Sultan of Pahang . . . an impressive modern structure that overwhelms the rather quaint little town . . . 4-day cultural and sporting festival held here every year to celebrate sultan's birthday.

Pulau Tioman • Largest of a group of 64 volcanic islands near Malaysia's coastline in South China Sea . . . belongs to the state of Pahang but reachable from Mersing (see page 393) . . . covered with beautiful beaches, jungle, and Gunung Kajan peak of 1037 meters . . . was mythical Bali Hai in movie *South Pacific* . . . coral beds around the island offer superb scuba diving . . . all other watersports available . . . and one or two pleasant hotels.

Taman Negara • National park . . . the oldest tropical rain forest . . . 130 million years old . . . located in north central area of state . . . and covers part of Kelantan and Trengganu as well . . . known for hiking, fishing, swimming, shooting the rapids, mountain climbing . . . a photographer's dream . . . exotic animals to watch . . . journey to Jerantut from Kuantan by train or bus . . . then to Kuala Tembeling by taxi or bus . . . then a 3-hour boat ride upriver to Park Headquarters at Kuala Tahan . . . comfortable lodges, chalets, and government rest houses provide accommodation . . . definitely for the outdoor set.

Trengganu

Kemaman • Small fishing village on Trengganu/Pahang border . . . the beginning of a charming and scenic area along the coastline traveling northward . . . through the villages of **Teluk Mengkuang** and **Kemasik** . . . to **Dungun,** another seaside town . . . from here for 64 km north, the shoreline is a series of peaceful sights . . . small villages, casuarina trees, and beautifully carved *perahus* (boats) . . . well worth a detour to drive along the South China Sea.

Kuala Trengganu • State capital . . . known for its **Central Market** right on the river . . . the sultan's historic palace (across the road from his modern residence) . . . fine wood carvings and intricate patterns with inscriptions from the Koran . . . life is easy here . . . expect to travel slowly around town in a trishaw . . . drink in the local color . . . spend some time in the villages around the capital . . . homes are full of cottage industries and all the crafts are for sale.

Pulau Kapas • Island famous for its coral and seashells . . . located just 6 km offshore from village of Marang, about 10 km south of Kuala Trengganu . . . lovely for swimming and snorkeling . . . but no accommodations yet.

Pulau Perhentian • Considered one of most beautiful islands in the area . . . located about 20 km offshore from village of Kuala Besut . . . in most northern point of Trengganu state . . . fishermen will ferry tourists over and back for a fee . . . take along your refreshments . . . a modest government rest house is available.

Rantau Abang • Turtle-watching village . . . giant leatherneck turtles reputed to be 1000 years old come ashore in this small village to lay their eggs . . . can be seen from May to Sept., best months are July and Aug. . . . star attractions are giant turtles that weigh over 2000 pounds . . . government prohibits collection and sale of eggs to protect species . . . turtle watching is a big hit with East Coast visitors . . . but you must obey the rules.

HOTELS

Johor Bahru (Johor)

★★★**Desaru Merlin Inn** • *P.O. Box 50, Kotatinggi, Tanjung Penawar, Tel: 07–838101* • 100 rooms.

Facilities: Resort on the beach in Johor's newest playground. Malaysian and Western cuisine. Bar. Tennis. Riding. Swimming pool. Golf.
Manager: A. Ghazall. *Reservations:* UTELL.

★★★**Holiday Inn Johor Bahru** • *Jalan Dato Sulai-man Century Gardens, Tel: 323800* • 200 rooms.
Facilities: Meisan Szechuan restaurant. Red Baron Cocktail Lounge. Entertainment. The Boulevard Coffee shop. Satay and seafood terrace. Swimming pool. Movies. The Millennium Disco.
Manager: A. Obrist. *Reservations:* HOLIDEX.

★★★**Merlin Inn Johor Bahru** • *10 Jalan Bukit Meldrum. Tel: 225811. Cable: MERLIN JOHOR BAHRU.* • Futuristic architecture overlooking the Straits . . . 104 rooms.
Facilities: Malay and Continental cuisine. Coffee terrace on seafront. Bar. Conference facilities overlooking the Straits.
Manager: N. Mahendreen. *Reservations:* UTELL.

Mersing (Johor)

★★★**Tioman Island Resort** • *Pulau Tioman Island. Tel: 44544/ 5* • A modern chalet-style hotel on the dramatic island of Pulau Tioman, one of a group of 64 volcanic islands . . . ideal for skin-diving and swimming and getting away from it all . . . boat service from Mersing.

★★**Mersing Merlin Inn** • *1½ Mile, Jalan Endau. Tel: 791312* • 34 rooms.
Facilities: Restaurant/disco with Western and Chinese cuisine. Coffee terrace. Launch for Tioman Island here.
Manager: C. Lai. *Reservations:* UTELL.

Rawa Island Chalets • *Rawa Safaris Tourist Center. Tel: 791204* • 20 bungalows and chalets on Rawa Island.
Facilities: Malay, Chinese, European dining room. Bar.

Kota Bharu (Kelantan)

★★★**Hotel Perdana** • *Jalan Mahmud, P.O. Box 222. Tel: 785000. Cable: HOTDANA Kota Bharu. Telex: MA 53143* • 136 rooms.
Facilities: Golden Jade seafood restaurant. Wayang lounge. Rebana coffee shop. Children's playground. Private beach. Squash and tennis. Bowling alley. Health center. Disco.
Manager: P. Cheng. *Reservations:* Direct.

★★**Resort Pantai Cinta Berahi** • *Kota Bharu, P.O. Box 131, Kota Bharu. Tel: 781307* • 38 rooms and chalets.

Facilities: Dining room. Local entertainment. Boat cruise. Private beach. Watersports. Deep-sea fishing.
Manager: K. Sagadevan. *Reservations:* Direct.

Kuantan (Pahang)

★★★**Club Mediterranee Holiday Village** • *Cherating, near Kuantan, Pahang. Tel: 591131, 591181* • 300 rooms.
Facilities: 250-acre resort. Asian/French restaurant. Bar. Disco. Theater. Library/bridge room. Tennis. Watersports. Basketball, volleyball, calisthenics, yoga, etc. 2 swimming pools. Children's pool and other activities.
Reservations: CLUB MED.

★★★★**Hyatt Kuantan** • *Telok Chempedak. Cable: HYATT KUANTAN. Telex: MA 50252. Tel: 525211* • 185 rooms.
Facilities: 8 acres on sandy beach near mouth of Kuantan River. Kampong Coffee Shop. Hugo's continental restaurant. Chinese restaurant. Sampan Bar. Renang Bar at pool's edge. Disco. Tennis and squash. Health studio. Watersports. Golf course nearby. Swimming pool and kiddie pool. Convention facilities.
Manager: U. Hoppe. *Reservations:* HYATT INT'L.

★★★**Merlin Kuantan** • *Telok Chempedak. Tel: 522388. Cable: MERLINKUANTAN. Telex: MA 50285* • 106 rooms.
Facilities: Next door to Hyatt. All rooms face South China Sea. Chempedak Restaurant. Open-air patio. Magic Circle Bar. Disco. Watersports. Swimming pool. Fishing and golf. Squash courts and health center. Bunga Raya Ballroom.
Manager: S. Taff. *Reservations:* UTELL.

Kuala Trengganu (Trengganu)

★★**Pantai Primula Hotel** • *Jalan Persinggahan, P.O. Box 43. Tel: 622100. Cable: PAN MOTEL. Telex: PANTAI MA 51403* • 260 rooms.
Facilities: Beach location, a mile from town. Rhusila coffeehouse. Local Corner supper spot. 2 cocktail lounges. Swimming pools. Pony riding. Watersports. Children's playground. Supper club, coffeehouse, Bayu bar and Cascade grill, library.
Reservations: TDC Malaysia.

Rantau Abang Visitor Centre • *13th Mile, off Dungun. Phone: 841533. Telex: JARA MA 51449* • 10 chalets . . . operated by TDC.
Facilities: 20-acre site near famous Turtle Beach. Restaurant. Turtle Museum. Turtle Bar. Bazaar.
Reservations: TDC.

★★★**Tanjong Jara Beach Hotel** • *8 miles off Dungun. Tel: 841801. Cable: PEMRESORT. Telex: MA 51449* • 100 rooms . . . operated by TDC.

Facilities: Traditional Malay architecture. Village-style setting reminiscent of sultan's palace of Trengganu. All rooms have view of South China Sea. Danau Chinese/Indian/Western restaurant. Nakhoda Lounge. Disco. Swimming pool and bar. Tennis and squash. Watersports. Fishing. Saunas and gym. Boating.

Reservations: TDC.

HILL RESORTS

___ HILL RESORTS IN A CAPSULE ___

Malaysia has six hill resorts . . . visitors can recharge their energies in cool and invigorating climates found only in the higher altitudes . . . lovely vistas of mountain peaks and tea plantations, peaceful jungle areas . . . active sports like golf, tennis, swimming, and climbing . . . as well as the promise of a log fire every evening . . . most of the areas were discovered and founded by the British, who never could stand the heat and humidity of Asia . . . expect to find colonial overtones in your accommodations and food . . . Foster's Lakehouse and the Tudor-style Ye Olde Smokehouse are examples of the change-of-pace available in the Cameron Highlands . . . golfers will enjoy the many fine and beautiful courses but should avoid the peak months of April, August, and December.

Cameron Highlands • 1524 meters above sea level . . . population of 20,000 . . . linked by winding mountain road to town of Tapah, on the highway between Kuala Lumpur and Ipoh . . . discovered by government surveyor William Cameron in 1885 . . . many tea plantations, vegetable farms, and flower nurseries here . . . also jungle walks and magnificent waterfalls . . . tennis, golf, and swimming . . . accommodations include 65-room **Merlin Hotel** with disco and television; 30-room **Golf Course Inn;** quaint and conservative 20-room **Ye Olde Smokehouse;** smaller hotels and government-sponsored bungalows that rent for a song; and **Strawberry Park** hotel and apartment complex.

Fraser's Hill • 1524 meters above sea level . . . named after Louis James Fraser who built himself a shack up here and traded tin . . . surveyed in 1919 and developed into one of Malaysia's most popular resorts . . . Located north of Kuala Lumpur . . . junction to mountain road is Kuala Kubu Bahru . . . last 5 miles from gap to Fraser's Hill is a long narrow winding road that alternates one-way traffic at posted schedule hours . . . has lovely 9-hole public golf course, tennis, sports complex, swimming beneath **Jeriau Waterfalls** . . . jungle walks and panoramic views of states of Selangor and Pahang as well as Straits of Malacca . . . minizoo and park of some 10 acres . . . and real English gardens everywhere . . . social centers of Fraser's Hill are **The Tavern** and **Hillview** . . . and the local Development Corporation runs bungalows and chalets with full catering facilities for up to 20 people . . . also a 109-room **Merlin Hotel.**

Genting Highlands • 1714 meters above sea level . . . easily accessible from Kuala Lumpur by helicopter (10 minutes) . . . or about one hour by road . . . country's latest and most Las Vegas–style resort . . . opened in 1971 with 5 huge modern hotels, gambling casino, artificial lake, indoor stadium, 18-hole golf course, convention facilities, 1200-seat theater restaurant, cable-car system, and **Chin Swee Cave Temple** (opened Sept. 1979) . . . there are 1116 hotel rooms . . . this is not a true hill resort but a glossy recreation area which can boast the only legitimate gambling casino in the country.

Kota Tinggi • 634 meters above sea level . . . located in the state of Johor and just an hour's drive from Johor Bahru, Malaysia's southernmost town . . . just across the causeway from Singapore . . . popular for cooling off in the many waterfalls and natural pools in the area . . . visitors can also practice a little mountain climbing . . . or carry on down to Teluk Mahkota . . . sandy bay stretches 6 miles and is sheltered from waves of South China Sea . . . accommodations at Kota Tinggi feature seven self-contained chalets . . . a 2-story restaurant and large car park . . . buses run regularly from Johor Bahru.

Maxwell Hill • 1035 meters above sea level . . . also called Bukit Larut . . . known as Malaysia's oldest hill resort . . . just 9 km from Taiping Town in Perak State . . . access by land rover only up winding, hairpin turns . . . only accessible summit is the Cottage . . . at top you can see the coastline from Pangkor Island to Penang on a clear day . . . resort has beautiful semitropical flowers . . . accommodations in fully contained rest houses and bungalows at various levels of the mountain range . . . European and Malaysian food available in rest houses . . . caretaker cooks in the bungalows . . . a most beautiful and unspoiled place for rest and refreshment.

Penang Hill ● 692 meters above sea level . . . situated in the middle of Penang Island . . . accessible by funicular railway . . . there is a 12-room hotel at top of railway station and several small government-run bungalows . . . but most people just prefer to spend a few hours up here . . . having lunch or a drink on the lawn overlooking the city and Kedah Peak.

HOTELS

Cameron Highlands (Pahang)

★★★**Cameron Highlands Merlin** ● *P.O. Box 4, Tanah Rata. Tel: 941205. Cable: Camhotel Cameronhighlands. Telex: MA 30487* ● 60 rooms . . . hill resort 6000 feet up.
Facilities: Malay and western cuisine replaces "Rajah restaurant." Asli bar. Sidewalk cafe. Marquerite lounge. Tennis and badminton. Golf course. Gym. Video movies. Conference room.
Manager: C. Lai. *Reservations:* UTELL.

★★★**Fosters Lakehouse Hotel** ● *Ringlet, Cameron Highlands. Tel: 948680* ● 12 rooms . . . European food . . . forest walks.
Facilities: Dining room. 2 bars. Sports activities.
Manager: S. J. Foster. *Reservations:* Direct.

★★**Golf Course Inn** ● *Tanah Rata, Cameron Highlands. Tel: 941411* ● 30 rooms.
Facilities: Chinese and European restaurants. Coffeehouse. Games room. Bar. Tennis. Golf course.
Manager: M. Bakar. *Reservations:* Direct.

Fraser's Hill (Pahang)

★★**Fraser's Hill Development Corp. Holiday Bungalows** ● *Fraser's Hill. Tel: 382201. Cable: Kebukit Frasershill* ● 69 rooms.
Facilities: Dining room. Bar. Tennis and squash. Golf course. Swimming pool. Pony rides and children's playground. Jungle walks. Mini zoo. Health center. Minitrain and Ferris wheel.
Manager: L. Kamaruddi. *Reservations:* Direct.

★★★**Fraser's Hill Merlin Hotel** ● *Fraser's Hill. Tel: 382247. Telex: MA 30487* ● 109 rooms.
Facilities: Restaurant. Coffeehouse. Bar. Games room. 9-hole golf

course. Riding. Swimming pool and health center. Children's play-ground. Skating rink. Tennis and squash. Minizoo and minitrain. *Manager:* M. Din. *Reservations:* UTELL.

Genting Highlands

★★★**Genting Hotel, Genting Highlands Resort** • *9th Floor, Wisma Genting, Jalan Sultan Ismail, 50250, Kuala Lumpur. Tel: 2613833. Cable: Gentotel K.L. Telex: 32324* • 1070 rooms.

Facilities: Theater restaurant. Western, Malaysian, and Chinese restaurants. Casino. 24-hour coffeehouses. Nightclub. Revolving disco. Bowling. 18-hole golf course. Swimming pool. Tennis. Sauna. Cable car. Boating.

Manager: H.S. Leong. *Reservations:* UTELL.

KUALA LUMPUR

WHAT TO SEE AND DO

Central Market • Huge collection of shops and food stalls adjacent to Putra World Trade Center downtown . . . just across the street from Chinatown . . . wonderful for browsing, souvenirs, snacks, and watching the city's colorful and varied residents.

Chan See Shu Yuan Temple • Built in 1906 . . . features typical Chinese temple . . . open courtyards and symmetrically organized pavilions . . . serves as both religious and political venue.

Chinatown • Home to many of the city's almost half million Chinese residents . . . concentrated in one of the city's busiest areas . . . bounded roughly by Jalan Petaling, Jalan Sultan, and Jalan Bandar . . . everything on sale from dawn to dusk . . . great open-air bazaar, **Pasar Malam** located mid-section on Jalan Petaling at dusk . . . see **Chinese Assembly Hall** at junction of Jalan Foch . . . birdcages on Jalan Sultan . . . visit also **See Yeoh Temple** . . . oldest and most venerated of the city's Chinese shrines.

── KUALA LUMPUR IN A CAPSULE ──

Malay name means "muddy estuary" . . . situated at the confluence of Klang and Gombak rivers . . . city founded around 1858
or so at the beginning of the tin boom . . . made capital of Fed-
erated Malay States in 1895 . . . one of Asia's most beautiful,
green, and tidy places . . . offers a spacious and good life for
over one million inhabitants . . . a multiracial society of Malays,
Chinese, Indians, Arabs, Eurasians, and Europeans . . . was important transportation and administration center during British rule
in Malaya . . . an impressive array of structures in the Islamic,
Gothic, Tudor, and Colonial styles . . . home of country's elegant and modern National Mosque . . . a lovely capital known
affectionately as K.L. by both locals and frequent visitors.

International Buddhist Pagoda • Stands between bodhi tree and
shrine . . . built in 1894 by Sinhala Buddhists . . . pagoda represents
contemporary architectural design of pagodas . . . images and replicas
of pagodas enshrined in octagonal hall at base of pagoda . . . example
of great religious freedom and tolerance of beliefs throughout Malaysia.

Istane Negara • Official residence of their majesties, the elected
rulers . . . set on over 20 acres of beautifully landscaped grounds . . .
originally built in 1928 by a local millionaire . . . occupied by the
sultan elected king for a 5-year term . . . VIPs received in audience in
the west wing . . . state banquets and official functions held in the east
wing . . . their majesties occupy private quarters on the first floor
aboveground.

Jalan Ampang • Ampang Road . . . lovely old mansions and official embassy residences line this street . . . many a bit dilapidated
. . . but some now beautifully restored and ready for business . . .
like the famous **Bok House,** one of the best French restaurants in town
(Le Coq d'Or).

Kampung Bharu • Open-air night bazaar . . . just 10 minutes from
the city center . . . one of the great experiences of K.L. . . . especially interesting on Sat. evenings . . . food and other items to tempt
even the tightest pocketbook!

Karyaneka Handicraft Village • Just behind the Hilton International and near the sprawling race club . . . crafts from various regions
of Malaysia displayed in traditional dwellings in a landscaped park . . .

a crafts museum and the opportunity to buy samples of local handicrafts from the entire country . . . folkloric shows on Saturdays.

Kuala Lumpur Railway Station • Moorish-style structure built by British in 1911 . . . basic design beneath Islamic-influenced exterior, supposed to resemble large glass-and-iron train sheds constructed throughout England at the close of 19th century.

Lake Gardens • Part of K.L.'s "green belt" . . . gardens laid out in 1888 by Englishman named A. R. Venning . . . located in their midst is **Tasik Perdana** or Premier Lake . . . artificial water on which boating is available . . . entire 160-acre parkland open daily to the public.

Malayan Railway Administration Headquarters • Located opposite K.L. Railway Station . . . imposing structure with elements of Islamic design . . . houses offices of country's railway authorities.

Masjid Jame • Old mosque built at confluence of Klang and Gombak rivers . . . close to where first settlers landed . . . mosque nestles within coconut grove . . . 2 minarets rise to the height of the palms . . . prayer hall has 3 domes and opens onto walled courtyard called Sahn.

Masjid Negara (National Mosque) • Pride of Malaysia and one of largest in Southeast Asia . . . center of Islamic activities in the country . . . contemporary structure finished in 1965 . . . on approximately 12 landscaped acres behind the railway station . . . consists of grand prayer hall, mausoleum, library, offices, open courtyard, and 245-foot minaret . . . dome is umbrella-shaped with 18-pointed star to represent the 13 states of Malaysia and 5 pillars of Islam . . . courtyard partly covered by 48 concrete parasols to provide both shade and architectural interest . . . fountains for ablutions located on floor below . . . marble columns placed to signify the many rubber plantations that are so important to country's economy . . . mosque open to public from 8 a.m. to 6 p.m. Sat. through Thur., and after 2 p.m. on Fri. . . . ladies have separate entrance . . . visitor's gallery from which to witness some proceedings.

Merdeka Stadium • Outdoor stadium with capacity for 50,000 . . . the venue where one of Malaysia's most historic events occurred . . . Declaration of Independence (Merdeka) signed here in 1957 . . . sports events and competitions now held here regularly . . . main axis lies north-south so players need not face the evening sun.

National Monument • located in Lake Gardens . . . constructed in 1966 to commemorate Malaysia's national heroes, many of whom died in the cause of freedom and peace . . . seven bronze figures represent triumph of forces of democracy over evil . . . entire monument designed by Felix W. de Weldon, creator of famous Iwo Jima Memorial in Arlington National Cemetery across the Potomac River from Washington, D.C.

National Museum • Muzium Negara . . . completed in 1963 on site of old Selangor Museum which was destroyed during World War II . . . built in old Malay-style architecture with 2 large Italian-mosaic murals by local artist Cheong Lai Tong on front . . . depicts life and customs of Malaysians . . . design of main doors by Kelantanese artist Wan Su Wan Othman . . . carvings by team of local craftsmen under direction of Samsuddin bin Haji Tahir of Trengganu . . . exhibits depict history, culture, arts and crafts, currency, flora and fauna, and major economic activities of country . . . open daily from 9 a.m. to 7 p.m. . . . closed Fri. from noon to 2:30 p.m. . . . admission free.

National Museum of Art • Located in the old Majestic Hotel . . . permanent collection of works by local Malaysian artists . . . plus exhibitions of international nature throughout the year . . . open daily from 10 a.m. to 6 p.m.; closed Fri. from noon to 2:30 p.m. . . . admission free.

Parliament House • Located on elevated grounds in Lake Gardens . . . a contemporary 18-story structure dominates complex . . . includes low building containing House of Representatives, Senate, various offices, library, banquet hall, and committee rooms . . . visitors may enter Parliament House when in session, with prior arrangement . . . formal national dress of Malaysia or Western lounge suit required . . . women must have hemline below the knee.

Royal Selangor Golf Club • Located at junction of Jalan Bukit Bintang and Jalan Pekeliling . . . about 15 minutes from city center . . . oldest golf club in Malaysia and scene of annual Malaysian Golf Tournament . . . elegant club with many fine facilities . . . visitors should inquire about exchange privileges.

Selangor Club • One of the capital's most historic landmarks . . . located opposite Sultan Abdul Samad Building . . . founded in 1884 to provide recreation for British civil servants . . . today stands as a reminder of country's colonial past . . . membership drawn from top strata of K.L. society.

Selangor Turf Club • Racecourse located in Jalan Ampang . . . provides lovely green spot in eastern area . . . site acquired in 1895 when racing allowed for first time in State of Selangor . . . club founded in 1896 and still thriving . . . modern grandstand opened in 1966 . . . best view of area from top of K.L. Hilton.

Sri Mahamariamman Temple • Hindu Temple built in 1873 . . . one of country's largest and most ornate . . . elaborate design incorporates gold, precious stones, Spanish and Italian ceramic tiles . . . located at corner of Jalan Bandar and Jalan Davidson.

Sultan Abdul Samad Building • Formerly known as State Secretariat . . . one of K.L.'s most distinctive and most photographed landmarks . . . opposite Selangor Club . . . built in 1894–7 by the British in Moorish-style architecture . . . clock tower, domes, and curving arches . . . design considered a little ahead of its time by then British-appointed governor of Straits Settlements (what the place was called before turn of century) . . . don't miss the **Dewan Bandaraya** (City Hall), along the same lines . . . an altogether impressive representation of a time gone by.

Wisma Loke • Located in city center at Medan Tuanku . . . one of oldest buildings in the capital . . . fine old mansion with porcelain balustrades from China, Malaccan tiles, and traditional Moongate . . . became first private residence in K.L. to be lit by electricity in 19th century . . . first owned by Cheow Ah Yeok, close ally of Yap Ah Loy (a founder of Kuala Lumpur) . . . later bought by famed millionaire Loke Yew . . . century-old house now renovated into antique shop.

Titiwangsa Gardens • Former mining land . . . landscaped area of about 130 acres . . . lake called **Tasik Titiwangsa** for boating . . . tennis courts and children's playground . . . open daily until 6:30 p.m.

Environs

Batik Factory Selayang • Located north of K.L. . . . demonstrations daily from 8:30 a.m. to 5 p.m. . . . material for sale here . . . no demonstrations from 1 to 2 p.m. . . . special requests honored.

Batu Caves • Sacred place of worship for Hindus . . . great mass of limestone cliffs just north of K.L. . . . largest cavern houses Hindu shrine of Lord Subramaniam . . . climb 272 steps to entrance . . . Hindus make pilgrimage annually during festival of Thaipusam . . . open daily except Wed. and Fri. from noon to 2 p.m.

Mimaland ● 300-acre tourist recreation complex some 30 minutes from K. L. . . . guitar-shaped lake . . . largest natural water swimming pool in Southeast Asia . . . prehistoric center . . . golf course . . . children's playgrounds . . . 24-room motel overlooking lake . . . 10 *bagans* (Malay-style houses) . . . floating restaurant and Western-style restaurant.

National Zoo and Aquarium ● Located in Ulu Klang, just 13 km from K.L. . . . zoo has some 200 species of animals, birds, and reptiles . . . aquarium has 25 species of marine exhibits and 81 species of freshwater fish . . . elephant, boat, and train rides for children . . . open daily from 9 a.m. to 6 p.m. . . . admission charge.

Morib ● Weekend and holiday beach resort some 64 km from K.L. . . . favorite for picnics and family gatherings . . . 20-room government rest house, 9-hole golf course, aviary, and open-air foodstalls.

Pantai Valley ● En route to Petaling Jaya, industrial town . . . location of University of Malaya in rolling green land . . . one of the most beautiful campuses.

Petaling Jaya ● Satellite town some 11 km from Kuala Lumpur . . . covers area of 4000 acres and with population of 200,000 plus over 200 factories . . . Malaysia's industrial showplace.

Port Kelang ● Country's most important seaport . . . located about 40 km from K.L., where original founders of the capital started up river . . . known for excellent seafood restaurants . . . Sultan of Selangor's Palace in Kelang town.

Port Dickson ● A favorite resort area about 1½ hours west of K.L. by car . . . beaches about 18 km long . . . watersports and fishing facilities . . . the Yacht Club has reciprocal arrangements . . . government rest houses and first-class hotels available . . . located about 34 km from Seremban.

Rubber Plantations ● Malaysia is world's largest producer of natural rubber . . . visits arranged by tour operators to view trees being tapped.

Selangor Pewter Factory ● Located at Jalan Pahang on the outskirts of K.L. . . . largest pewter factory in the world . . . can watch demonstrations of the material being made from Malaysian tin, antimony, and copper . . . open from 8:30 a.m. to 4:30 p.m. daily . . . duty-free shopping.

Seremban • Capital of Negri Sembilan . . . Malay word for a federation of 9 states . . . located about 66 km southeast of K.L. . . . commercial and administrative center of Minangkabau state of Negri Sembilan . . . known for distinctive architecture, open-air museum at Lake Gardens, and royal town of Sri Menanti, a few kilometers west . . . this state also traditionally matriarchal . . . women inherit rights over property and land to exclusion of men.

Templer Park • Located near Batu Caves, along same north/south highway just 22 km from K L. . . . beautiful retreat of some 3000 acres of cool and green parkland . . . streams and waterfalls . . . paths through forest . . . home to butterflies, flying lizards, and birds . . . very friendly monkeys . . . named after Sir Gerald Templer, High Commissioner in former Federation of Malaysia.

Tin Mines • Malaysia produces some 40% of the world's tin making it the single largest supplier . . . several large mines can be viewed along Malaysian highways . . . especially in Batu Caves and Templer Park area . . . visits arranged by tour or travel agencies.

Tours

Countryside Tour • 3 hours, daily from Kuala Lumpur . . . visits Batu Caves, rubber plantation, batik demonstration center, Lake Gardens, National Monument, Parliament House, and State Secretariat Building . . . can be combined with K.L. city tour for full day.

Kuala Lumpur City Tour • 3 hours, daily . . . visits National Museum, National Mosque, Parliament House, Railway Station, and other colonial-era buildings.

Kuala Lumpur Night Tour • 3 hours, nightly . . . visits Chinatown plus offers a Malaysian dinner and cultural show.

Kuala Lumpur/Fraser's Hill • 3 nights . . . includes morning tour of K.L. and roundtrip transportation to hill resort.

Kuala Lumpur/Genting Highlands • 2 nights . . . includes return helicopter fare.

Kuala Lumpur/Cameron Highlands/Penang • 5 nights.

Kuala Lumpur/Port Dickson • 8–10 hours, daily.

Kuala Lumpur/Malacca • 8–10 hours, daily.

Kuala Lumpur/Malacca/Singapore • 5 nights.

Kuala Lumpur / Penang / Kota Bharu / Tanjong Jara / Kuantan / Singapore • 10 nights.

HOTELS

★★★★**Equatorial Hotel** • *Jalan Sultan Ismail. Tel: 2422022. Cable: EQUATORIAL. Telex: EQATOR MA 30263* • 300 rooms.
Facilities: Golden Phoenix Chinese, Swiss Chalet, and Japanese Kampachi restaurants. 24-hour coffeehouse. Disco. Swimming pool/health club.
Manager: Jim Kong Yong. *Reservations:* UTELL.

★★**Federal Hotel** • *35 Jalan Bukit Bintang. Tel: 2489166. Cable: FEDEROTEL. Telex: FEDTEL MA 30429* • 450 rooms . . . 20-story, 300-room addition called Imbi Hotel behind existing hotel . . . on Jalan Imbi . . . with 3 bars and restaurants . . . swimming pool and convention center.
Facilities: Mandarin Palace Chinese restaurant. Kon Tiki Room Western restaurant. 5 bars. Federal Club and Sky Room nightclub. 24-hour coffeehouse. Swimming pool and health center.
Manager: N. Hawkes. *Reservations:* UTELL.

★★★**Holiday Inn City Centre** • *Jalan Raja Laut. Tel: 939333* • 200 rooms.
Facilities: Malay and western restaurants with 24-hour coffee shop and cocktail lounge. Swimming pool.
Reservations: Holidex.

★★★★**Hyatt Saujana Hotel and Country Club** • *Subang International Airport Highway. Tel: 746 1188* • 250 rooms . . . Opened in 1987 in the midst of two 18-hole championship golf courses . . . 30 minutes from downtown K.L. and 3 minutes from the airport . . . a variety of restaurants as well as meeting facilities.
Reservations: Hyatt International.

★★★★★**Kuala Lumpur Hilton** • *Jalan Sultan Ismail (P.O. Box 577). Tel: 2422222. Cable: HILTELS KUALA LUMPUR. Telex: MA 30495* • 589 rooms . . . first luxury hotel in town and still holds its own as one of the best . . . located in the heart of the business district . . . has loyal following . . . excellent views right over the Royal Selangor Turf Club.

Facilities: Melaka Grill for businessmen's lunch and nouvelle cuisine. Inn of Happiness Chinese restaurant. Planters' Inn 24-hour coffeehouse. Nirvana Ballroom. The Tin Mine disco. Swimming pool and health club. Tennis and squash courts with full-time coach. Champagne check-in.

Manager: W. Schack. *Reservations:* HILTELS.

★★**Kuala Lumpur Merlin Hotel** • *2 Jalan Sultan Ismail. Tel: 2480033. Cable: MERLIN. Telex: MA 30487* • 687 rooms.

Facilities: Mawar Grill. Dragon Court Chinese restaurant. Harlequin Room. 24-hour coffeehouse. Scots Bar. Japanese lounge. Garden swimming pool.

Manager: S. K. Wong. *Reservations:* UTELL.

★★★**Ming Court** • *Jalan Ampang. Tel: 2619066* • 447 rooms . . . 13-story structure featuring swimming pool, disco, restaurants, and conference seating for 1000 persons . . . owned by Malayan United Industries.

★★★★★**Pan Pacific, Kuala Lumpur** • *Jalan Chow Kitbaru, P.O. Box 11468, Kuala Lumpur. Tel: (03) 4225555. Cable: PANPACKUL. Telex: MA 33706 PPHTKL* • 571 rooms (15 suites). Situated in commercial sector of the capital . . . part of the Putra World Trade Centre . . . Japanese chain.

Facilities: Atrium lobby lounge. Atrium Bar. La Pattisserie. The Continental restaurant. Selera Coffee House. Keyaki Japanese cuisine. Hai-Tien-Lo Chinese restaurant. Pacific Ballroom. Health Club. Tennis and Squash courts. Pacific Executive floors (28th and 29th). No-smoking floors (20th and 21st). The Splash swimming pool.

Manager: H. Hauri. *Reservations:* Pan Pacific.

★★★★**Petaling Jaya Hilton** • *2 Jalan Barat Petaling, Jaya. Tel: 7553533. Cable: JAYAPURI PJ. Telex: MA 37542* • 388 rooms . . . formerly known as Jaya Puri Hotel . . . hotel located between K.L. and airport . . . taken over and refurbished by Hilton . . . counter at Subang Airport to aid guests of both properties.

Facilities: Grill room. Coffeehouse. Nightclub. Chinese restaurant. 2 bars. Disco. Swimming pool and health facilities. Ballroom and theater-style seating for 1300.

Reservations: HILTELS.

★★★★★**Shangri-La Hotel Kuala Lumpur** • *11 Jalan Sultan Ismail, K. L. 04-01. Tel (03) 2322388. Telex: SHNGKL MA30021* • 722 rooms. Newest high-rise deluxe hotel and the showcase of the city . . . welcome to the world of polished marble . . . boasts largest guest rooms

in KL, all with city views . . . combines business with resort hotel
. . . large and well-equipped function rooms for conventions.
Facilities: Swimming pool. Squash and tennis courts. Nadaman
Japanese cuisine. Shang Palace Cantonese restaurant. Restaurant Lafite.
The Coffee Garden. Club Oz. The Pub.
Manager: D. Regazzoni. *Reservations:* Shangri-La Int'l.

Port Dickson

★★★**Ming Court Beach Hotel** ● *Port Dickson, Negri Sembilan.*
Tel: 405244. Cable: MUIPORTSON. Telex: MA 63952 ● 165 rooms . . .
7½ miles from town.
Facilities: Pelangi grill room. Kontiki coffee shop. Coral Reef
lounge/disco. Tiupan lounge. Swimming pool. Private beach. Tennis
and golf on request. Indra Negri banquet hall.
Manager: C. T. Poh. *Reservations:* UTELL.

★★**Si-Rusa Inn** ● *7th mile Coast Rd., P.O. Box 31, Port Dickson,
Negri Sembilan. Tel: 405244. Telex: MA 63865* ● 160 rooms.
Facilities: Dining room. Cocktail lounge. Watersports. Boating and
fishing. Golf on request.
Manager: A. Chelliah. *Reservations:* Direct.

WINING AND DINING

Malaysia's capital offers visitors continual dining experiences—that
range from fun-filled foodstalls full of enticing aromas of local spices
and colorful sights to sophisticated settings and nouvelle cuisine to match
any European restaurant.

The first step to enjoying Kuala Lumpur's eating pleasures is to
immerse yourself in the local cooking, where great pains are taken not
only in the preparation but especially in the presentation of all edibles.
This is the home of *satay,* that succulent dish of skewered meat kebabs
marinated in coconut milk and spices and barbecued over glowing embers. Satay is usually consumed at any number of open-air foodstalls;
dip it in the peanut and chili sauce that tries not to knock your eyes out.

The staple of Malay food is, of course, rice, and it is often eaten
with one's fingers with a variety of curries, *sambals* (a hotter, dry curry),
vegetable dishes, and fried foods. Many local spices and *santan* (coconut cream) give the food an unusual and rich flavor. Specialties range
greatly between the 13 states, and the southern manner of cooking is

quite different from the north. *Nasi dagang* is unique to Kelantan State, while *assam pedas* is a Johor-style fish curry with a tamarind-based sauce. Favorites at open-air foodstalls (*gerai*) are *mee jawa* (boiled noodles) or *mee goreng* (fried noodles) or a variety of rice dishes (*nasi*) with all sorts of accompanying meat, vegetables, and condiments. Chili is a necessary ingredient in Malay cooking, but it is used as much as in neighboring Thai cuisine.

You can feast mightily on Chinese food in the nation's capital and every region is well represented: Cantonese, Pekingese, Szechuanese, Hokkien, Teochew, Hakka, and Hainanese. All differ from one another, and the range of taste treats stretches from *dim sum* (little dumplings) from Canton for breakfast or lunch to Peking duck and steamed pork buns for dinner. The Hokkiens are famous for their noodle dishes (such as fried mee), and Teochew food features porridge and salted side dishes. Hakka offerings include *yong tau fu*, stuffed bean curd and vegetables with a sauce for dipping, while Szechuanese dishes are fiery and use chilis and garlic. Hainanese chicken rice is a bland but popular favorite as a midday repast.

More interesting yet is *Nonya* cuisine, an original and spicy blend of Chinese and Malay cooking. Nonya is the local term for a Straitsborn Chinese woman (*Baba* is the male equivalent). Although Nonyas are notorious for jealously guarding their family recipes from generation to generation, there are some modest restaurants in K.L. now serving authentic Nonya dishes. Most of the recipes begin with a generous helping of *rempah* (mixture of ground spices), which are considered a matter of *agak* (estimation) by the cook at hand. Some of the more recognized dishes are curry *kapitan*, an unusual chicken curry; *otak otak*, a sort of fish pate flavored with spice and coconut cream and wrapped in leaves and grilled; *inche kabin*, a spicy deep-fried chicken; and *poh piah*, a savory stuffed pancake.

Indian food available in Kuala Lumpur represents both northern and southern traditions. Northern cuisine is rather more fitting to the Western palate; it tends to be less hot and pungent. *Tandoori* chicken and *nan*, a flat bread baked in a round clay oven, are world-renowned dishes. There are plenty of Moghul-inspired curries available as well as the other breads (*chappatis* and *puris*) to go with them. Southern Indian cooking is more available in K.L., and many local coffee shops offer rice with hot curries served on banana leaves (consumed without utensils). For breakfast, try *dosal*, a pancake served with coconut chutney, or one of the many vegetarian dishes always on the menu. Aficionados of Indian Muslim food should not miss the many restaurants along Jalan Tuanku Abdul Rahman in the capital.

There are many elegant European-style restaurants, a few with real U.S.-bred steaks, a growing number of Thai and Japanese eateries, and the inevitable fast-food chains that are slowly overtaking the good taste of the world. Hamburger, french fries, and a milk shake anyone?

MALAY RESTAURANTS

Budaya Restaurant and Snack Bar • *Lorong Medan Tuanku Satu, Jalan Tuanku Abdul Rahman. Tel: 2921381.*

The Hut • *Shah's Village, Lorong Sultan, Petaling Jaya. Tel: 569322.*

Indahku • *3rd Floor, Kuwasa Building, Jalan Raja Laut. Tel: 2931372.*

Rasa Utara • *Bukit Bintang Plaza, Jalan Bukit Bintang. Tel: 2438324.*

Satay Aneka • *Bukit Bintang Plaza, Jalan Bukit Bintang. Tel: 2483113.*

Satay 'n' Steak House • *Ground Floor, Wisma Central. Tel: 420570.*

Satay Ria • *9 Jalan Tuanku Abdul Rahman, Kuala Lumpur.*

Yazmin Restaurant • *Ampang Park Shopping Complex. Jalan Ampang. Tel: 2487490.* • One of the best in town.

Warong Rasa Sayang • *Jalan Raja Muda Musa. Tel: 2923009.*

CHINESE RESTAURANTS

Dragon Court • *Hotel Merlin, Jalan Sultan Ismail. Tel: 480033.*

Fatt Yow Yuen • *Jalan Balai Polis. Tel: 80491* • Vegetarian.

Golden Phoenix • *Hotel Equatorial, Jalan Sultan Ismail. Tel: 422022.*

Inn of Happiness • *Kuala Lumpur Hilton, Jalan Sultan Ismail. Tel: 422122.*

Imperial Room • *Malaysia Hotel, Jalan Bukit Bintang. Tel: 427862.*

Kuala Lumpur Restaurant • *Hotel Malaya, Jalan Cecil. Tel: 27721.*

Kum Leng • *119 Jalan Pudu. Tel: 83637.*

Mandarin Palace • *Federal Hotel, Jalan Bukit Bintang. Tel: 27701.*

Marco Polo Restaurant • *1st Floor, Wisma Lim Foo Yong Jalan Raja Chulan. Tel: 2425595.*

Metro Restaurant • *3rd Floor, Wisma MPI Jalan Raja Chulan. Tel: 2424505.*

Ming Court • *Town House Hotel, Jalan Tong Shin. Tel: 424273.*

Rasa Sayang Seafood • *Jalan Imbi. Tel: 2439890* • Outdoor dining in relaxed ambience.

The Pines • *297 Jalan Brickfields. Tel: 2741194.*

The Plaza Court Chinese Restaurant • *Plaza Hotel, Jalan Raja Laut. Tel: 920535.*

INDIAN RESTAURANTS

Akbar • *Medan Tuanku, Jalan Tuanku Bdul Rahman. Tel: 2920366.*

The Bangles • *Jalan Tuanku Abdul Rahman. Tel: 2983780.*

Bilal • *33 Jalan Ampang. Tel: 2320804.*

Ceylon Restaurant • *Malay Street. Tel: 2924708.*

Devi Restaurant • *Jalan Brickfields. Tel: 85505.*

Kassim • *53 Jalan Tuanku Abdul Rahman. Tel: 2928240.*

New Madras Cafe • *Japan Ipoh.*

Shiraz • *Medan Tuanku Abdul Rahman 7. Tel: 2910035.*

Simla Restaurant • *95, Jalan Ampang. Tel: 2328539.*

Vazeer Restaurant • *147A, Jalan Imbi. Tel: 2840744.*

WESTERN RESTAURANTS

Castell Pub & Grill ● *81 Jalan Bukit Bintang. Tel: 428328* ● One of the big favorites among the expatriate and visiting foreigners.

Chalet Restaurant ● *Hotel Equatorial, Jalan Sultan Ismail. Tel: 422022* ● Swiss cuisine.

Cock & Bull Steak House ● *Jalan Bukit Biatang. Tel: 422855.*

Esquire Kitchen ● *Sungei Wang Plaza, Jalan Sultan Ismail.*

Hacienda Grill ● *Hotel Fortuna, Jalan Berangan. Tel: 419111.*

Kontiki Room ● *Merlin Hotel, Jalan Sultan Ismail. Tel: 489166.*

Le Coq d'Or ● *121 Jalan Ampang. Tel: 429732* ● A good choice for quaint atmosphere and delicious, Continental cooking.

L'Espresso ● *G22 Wisma Stephens, Jalan Raja Chulan. Tel: 2413669.*

Melaka Grill ● *Kuala Lumpur Hilton, Jalan Sultan Ismail. Tel: 422122* ● May be the best restaurant in K.L., complete with gorgeous surroundings.

The Ship ● *10–1 Jalan Sultan Ismail. Tel: 2418805.*

NIGHTCLUBS AND DISCOS

Campbell Nightclub and Music Hall ● *Jalan Campbell. Tel: 2929655.*

Epitome ● *Petaling Jaya Hilton, Petaling Jaya. Tel: 553533.*

Federal Club ● *Federal Hotel, Jalan Bukit Bintang. Tel: 2489166.*

High Voltage ● *Massdisco LB29, Lower Basement 2, Sungei Wang Plaza. Tel: 2421220.*

Kira's Nite Club ● *Bangunan Angkasaraya. Tel: 2420556.*

Pertama Cabaret ● *Pertama Complex, Jln. Tuanku Abdul Rahman. Tel: 2982533.*

Pink Coconut • *Hotel Malaya, Jalan Cecil. Tel: 232772.*

Pyramid Club • *3rd Floor, Wilayah Shopping Complex, Jalan Munshi Abdullah. Tel: 2923092.*

Sapphire • *Plaza Yow Chuan, Jalan Tun Abdul Razak. Tel: 2430043.*

Shangri-La Night Club • *Bangunan Hentian Puduraya. Tel: 2321174.*

Sky Swan Nightclub • *22, Jalan Tong Shin. Tel: 2420233.*

Starship Disco • *Wisma Central, Jalan Ampang. Tel: 2427581.*

The Cave • *Jalan Ampang. Tel: 2481589.*

Tin Mine • *Kuala Lumpur Hilton, Jalan Sultan Ismail. Tel: 2422222.*

Toppan Club • *Wisma Stephens, Jalan Raja Chulan. Tel: 2489304.*

Traqs • *Wisma Central, Jalan Ampang. Tel: 2426529.*

MALACCA

WHAT TO SEE AND DO

Baba Nyonya Heritage • Lovely old home at 50 Jalan Tun Tan Cheng Lock . . . museum of artifacts and lifestyle to preserve diminishing community of Babas and Nyonas . . . Chinese men and women born in the Straits . . . full of 19th-century Nonya wares and furniture of blackwood or namwood inlaid with mother of pearl, or embroidery designed backs . . . also carved floral and pictorial motifs . . . ask for Mr. Chan . . . great-grandson of original owner . . . to guide you

MALACCA IN A CAPSULE

City of Living History . . . 125 miles northwest of Singapore . . . 2- to 3-hour's drive from Kuala Lumpur . . . founded in 1403 by a fugitive prince and named after Malacca tree . . . seat of a Malay kingdom . . . Islam entered the peninsula from here . . . Portuguese arrived in 1511 and were supreme for about 130 years . . . Dutch took sovereignty in 1641 and lasted for 150 years . . . British destroyed A Famosa, largest fortress in the East in 1807 . . . won Malacca in Treaty of Holland in 1824 and made it part of their Straits Settlements crown colony in 1867 . . . 100,000 people now inhabit this remarkable, much fought over trading post . . . most of them Straits-born Chinese (Nyonya and Baba) plus large Portuguese Eurasian settlement who speak Cristao, a medieval dialect from the 16th century.

. . . tours at 10 a.m., 11:30 a.m., 2 p.m. and 3:30 p.m. . . . small admission fee . . . Tel: 06–2222065.

Bukit China • China Hill . . . site of first Chinese community in Malacca . . . hill is a gift from Sultan Mansur Shah (c. 1460) to his Chinese princess and her 500 ladies-in-waiting . . . some of oldest Chinese relics in Malaysia are here . . . with **Bukit Gedong** and **Bukit Tempurong** it forms the largest Chinese cemetery outside the mainland . . . more than 106 acres . . . **Perigi Raja,** or Sultan's Well, at foot of Bukit China is said to possess an extraordinary purity . . . person who drinks from it will return to Malacca . . . you may also throw a coin.

Cheng Hoon Teng Temple • Oldest Chinese temple in Malaysia . . . plaque commemorates A.D. 1406 visit of Admiral Cheng Ho, envoy of Ming Emperor . . . one of the most traveled and celebrated figures in Chinese history of the time . . . gables and eaves richly decorated with figures from Chinese mythology . . . porcelain and glass carvings inside welcome visitors.

Christ Church • Built in 1752 . . . one of the town's many unusual salmon-colored buildings dating from the Dutch era . . . built of bricks from Middleburg, Zeeland, and covered with red laterite . . . features louvered windows topped with fan-shaped decorations . . . heavy wooden doors and tiled roof . . . interior most interesting . . . antique silver vessels bear Dutch coat of arms . . . today the church is Anglican.

Church of St. Peter • Built in 1710 . . . known for its unusual facade that mixes Oriental and Occidental architecture . . . testimony to numerous cultures in Malacca during her heyday . . . stained-glass windows of note and ancient tombstones within.

Church of St. Paul's • Atop Residency Hill, overlooking famous Straits of Malacca . . . built in 16th century . . . apparently used by St. Francis Xavier during his visit to Malacca . . . considered another relic of early Portuguese era . . . although the Dutch gave it its present name . . . only the walls remain, along with memorials and tombs of Dutch notables . . . lovely spot to just rest and contemplate after the hefty climb!

Jalan Gelenggang • Formerly called Jonker Street . . . narrow, one-way street full of trishaws and bicycles . . . known world-over for antique shops and dilapidated shops featuring **Peranakan** architecture (symbolic of earliest Chinese settlers in Malaya) . . . lots of junk stores here, too . . . but if you know your stuff . . . you must obtain an export permit from the Director-General of the National Museum in Kuala Lumpur.

Malacca River • A mere shadow of its former self . . . it must have been quite strong and wide during the 17th century to have brought so many traders to the port . . . walk across the bridge at Jalan Gelanggang and use your imagination to recapture the romance and adventure that took place here centuries ago.

Porta de Santiago • Gateway to **A Formosa** . . . greatest Portuguese fortress built in the East in the 16th century . . . fell to the Dutch in 1641 and almost totally devastated by British in 1807 . . . only this gateway stands . . . the Dutch East India Company's coat of arms still intact.

Stadthuys • Oldest building of Dutch origin in the East . . . salmon-colored City Hall built between 1641 and 1660 . . . thick masonry walls and heavy hardwood doors . . . windows with wrought-iron hinges have stood test of time . . . dominates main square just as it has for almost 3¼ centuries . . . one of Malacca's most photographed landmarks . . . everyone must witness the clock tower at noon . . . also houses the **Malacca Museum** . . . a gentle view of the past and some artifacts from the ancient Malays and Chinese as well as the intruders— Portuguese, Dutch, and British . . . open daily . . . admission charge.

Straits of Malacca • Narrow channel of water between Malay Peninsula and Sumatra . . . on the route from Indian Ocean to South

China Sea . . . monsoon winds meet at the mouth of the Malacca River . . . most favorable spot for ships from East and Middle East to meet and exchange goods . . . Joseph Conrad sailed through these straits at age 25 just before his ship blew up off Bangka Island, Sumatra . . . led him to write "the East of the ancient navigators, so old, so mysterious, resplendent and somber . . . living and unchanged, full of danger and promise."

Tranquerah Mosque • Built about 150 years ago . . . of Sumatran design . . . provides a link to British colonial era in Malacca . . . within mosque lies tomb of Sultan of Johor . . . who signed cession of Singapore to Sir Thomas Stamford Raffles in 1819.

HOTELS

★★**Malacca Straits Inn** • *37A Jalan Bandar Hilir. Tel: 21101* • 45 rooms. Shangri-la adding tower . . . convenient to town attractions.
Facilities: La Formosa grill room. Traveller coffee shop. Straits Club disco. Beer garden. Pastry corner.
Reservations: Golden Tulip.

★★★**Malacca Village Resort** • *Ayer Keroh. Tel: 313600. Telex: MA 62854* • 147 rooms . . . opened in 1983.
Facilities: Malacca dining room. Japanese restaurant. 2 bars. Swimming pool. Tennis, squash, and health club. The Club. Businessman's center.
Manager: D. Shakeshaft. *Reservations:* Beaufort Int'l, Singapore.

★★★★**Ramada Renaissance Hotel Malaka** • *Japan Bendahara, P.O. Box 105. Tel: (06) 248888. Telex: RAMADA MA 62966. Cable. RAMADARENA* • 295 rooms. New 24-story high-rise in heart of Malacca . . . only luxury hotel in town until Shangri-La opens . . . special Renaissance Floor (23rd) with club room, lounge, continental breakfast, etc.
Facilities: Taming Sari Grill. Famosa Lounge. Long Feng Cantonese restaurant. Summerfield's Coffee Shop. Stardust Disco. Health Center. Squash courts. Business center. Malacca Garden swimming pool, bar and restaurant. Bunga Raya ballroom.
Manager: W. Schmidt. *Reservations:* Ramada Intl.

★★**Shah's Beach Motel** • *6th mile Tanjong Keling. Tel: 26222. Cable: SHAH'S. Telex: HMSHAH MA 62808* • 50 chalets . . . very restful.

Facilities: Open-air dining room. Bar. Swimming pool. Lovely private beach. Boating and watersports. Out-of-town location.

Manager: D. V. S. Shah. *Reservations:* Direct.

PENANG

PENANG IN A CAPSULE

Pulau Pinang, or Island of the Betel Nut . . . one of Malaysia's 13 states . . . situated just 3 to 13 km off mainland from Butterworth . . . once an uninhabited hideout for pirates plundering ships leaving Malacca . . . natural harbor attracted British captain, Francis Light . . . negotiated lease of island from Sultan Abdullah of Kedah in 1786 . . . Light built Fort Cornwallis and named capital Georgetown after King George III . . . Penang became first British settlement in Straits of Malacca . . . and first member of crown colony . . . British left their colonial architecture but Chinese, Indians, Arabs, and indigenous Malays have contributed their own flavor and culture to the island . . . today it is one vast melting pot of Asia with 500,000 inhabitants . . . one of most popular resorts in the Far East . . . cruise ships disgorge wide-eyed passengers on global voyages . . . other visitors fly or ferry in from the peninsula . . . beautiful beaches . . . interesting sights . . . friendly, no-hurry people . . . calls itself Pearl of the Orient.

WHAT TO SEE AND DO

Batu Ferringhi Beach ● Foreigner's Rock . . . the draw for most visitors . . . a most beautiful silver beach along the island's northern coastline . . . many luxury hotels . . . sumptuous food at open-air restaurants . . . watersports . . . artists and galleries . . . sunseekers from all over the world . . . Europeans during the winter months . . . Australians during the summer . . . Americans from the oil fields of

Indonesia year-round . . . great for a few days at a time . . . a regular call for many luxury cruise ships.

Batu Maung • Shrine dedicated to Admiral Cheng Ho . . . famous envoy of Ming Emperor whom overseas Chinese later deified and gave the religious name of Sam Po . . . although history says he was just a bejeweled eunuch of the Ming Court who spent far too much time traveling . . . located at southern tip of Penang . . . about 3 km from Bayan Lepas Airport . . . near small fishing village of Batu Maung . . . early inhabitants believed Admiral Ho left his footprint here . . . another footprint can be found on Langkawi Island to the north . . . both are supposed to bring good luck to those who light joss sticks.

Botanical Gardens • Considered among the finest in Malaysia . . . located about 8 km from center of Georgetown in lovely 75-acre valley surrounded by jungled hills . . . green rolling lawns, secluded lily ponds, ornamental pools . . . tropical flowering plants of every variety . . . children love to feed the friendly monkeys that roam around.

Clock Tower • A relic of the colonial period . . . located next to Fort Cornwallis, the tower was presented to Penang by Cheah Chin Gok . . . to commemorate the diamond jubilee of Queen Victoria . . . also known as Empress of all Eastern colonies.

Fort Cornwallis • Originally built of wood by Captain Light . . . rebuilt between 1808 and 1810 of convict labor . . . pretty much as it stands today . . . although local children play on the ramparts . . . includes cannon called Meriam Timbul . . . presented to the Dutch by Sultan of Johor in 1606 . . . later captured by Portuguese . . . spent some time in Java . . . then captured by pirates and thrown into Straits of Malacca . . . brought up from the bottom in 1880 and taken to Selangor . . . eventually found its way to Penang . . . Malaysians call it the "traveling cannon."

Guillemard Reservoir • Located on Mount Erskine . . . a lovely spot and often viewed first by passengers flying into Bayan Lepas Airport . . . reservoir surrounded by casuarina trees . . . artfully planted.

Kapitan Kling Temple • Pitt Street . . . built around 1800 by Indian Moslem merchant, Cauder Mohudeen, also known as Kling Kapitan (headman) . . . occupies site of first mosque in Penang . . . dome-shaped minaret reflects Islamic architecture of Moorish influence.

Kek Lok Si Temple • Finest and largest in Southeast Asia . . . entire complex known as "Monastery of the Western Paradise of the

Pure Land Sect of Buddhism'' . . . built from 1890 to 1910 . . . actually a series of altars built along the hillslopes of Ayer Itam . . . midway between the village and the dam of the same name . . . complex dominated by **Ban Hood Pagoda . . .** also known as ''10,000 Precious Buddhas Pagoda'' . . . 7-stories high and filled with images of Lord Buddha from various parts of the world . . . building itself is influenced by Thai, Burmese, and Chinese architecture . . . a complicated and interesting place . . . great tourist attraction . . . crowded with devoted Chinese on weekends and holidays.

Khoo Kongsi • Khoo clan house located near Cannon Square in Georgetown . . . *kongsis* or clan houses originated in China centuries ago . . . were associations for people with same surname . . . **Leong San Tong** (Dragon Mountain Hall) of this structure is considered most elaborate and elegant of its kind in Malaysia . . . rich carvings and decorations and architecture reflect influence of ancient China . . . 200 members of Khoo clan began construction on the house around 1835, and it went through a series of designs . . . the first considered far too ostentatious for mere mortals . . . took 8 years to complete . . . Khoos came from China to Penang around the turn of 19th century.

Kuan Yin Ting • Goddess of Mercy Temple . . . on Pitt Street . . . Penang's oldest Chinese temple . . . one of its most humble . . . attracts working-class devotees . . . built in 1800 by the first Chinese settlers . . . dedicated to the most popular of Chinese gods who is revered by Buddhists, Taoists, and Confucianists at the same time . . . also houses the God of Prosperity . . . very popular at holiday time when joss sticks are lit to tempt good luck through coming year . . . lots of festivities around Kuan Yin's birthday on March 17.

Malay Mosque • On Acheen Street . . . known for finely balanced minaret . . . reminiscent of Egyptian architecture . . . quite a departure from Moorish influences brought by Indians to Penang.

Nattukkotai Temple • On Waterfall Road . . . largest Hindu temple in Penang . . . dedicated to Bala Subramaniam . . . in front of the shrine is a peacock given to Subramaniam by mother Parvathi . . . important rites and ceremonies here during Thaipusam festival.

Peng Buddhist Association • Modern-looking structure on Anson Road built in 1929 . . . considered Buddhism's most serene shrine in Penang . . . 7-tiered pagoda at entrance . . . shrine hall is filled with devotees reciting prayers to 6 huge Carrara-marble statues of Lord Buddha and his disciples . . . under glass chandeliers from Czechoslovakia . . . teak tables inlaid with mother-of-pearl from China hold offerings.

Penang-Butterworth Ferry • A 24-hour ferry service operates between Weld Quay in Georgetown and Butterworth . . . the 4-km ride is free from the mainland to Pulau Pinang (island of Betelnut Palms) and costs just a few pennies on the return to the mainland . . . ferry also transports bicycles, motorcycles, cars, and commercial vehicles.

Penang Hill • Rises some 830 meters in the middle of the island . . . considered one of Malaysia's 6 hill resorts . . . but I think more suitable as a day trip . . . take the 30-minute funicular railway journey from 6:30 a.m. to 9:30 p.m. . . . for a cool and refreshing change . . . temperature drops to at least 65 degrees during the day . . . lovely place to view the city of Georgetown and have a pleasant meal or drink . . . service on the funicular extended until midnight on Wed. and Sat. nights.

Penang Museum and Art Gallery • Located in interesting colonial structure on Farquar Street . . . fine collection of historical documents . . . including the will of Captain Francis Light . . . Chinese carvings and furniture . . . Chinese room, bridal chamber, island room, Tunku Abdul Rahman room . . . art gallery on first floor has batiks, oils, lithographs, and Chinese ink drawings plus exhibitions by Malay artists throughout year . . . open 9 a.m. to 5 p.m. daily (except Sun.) . . . free admission.

Snake Temple • Also known as Temple of the Azure Cloud . . . located about 5 km north of Bayan Lepas Airport . . . dedicated to deity Chor Soo Kong . . . contains poisonous snakes who are not supposed to bite . . . Buddhist devotees pet and coddle them . . . are even photographed with them . . . snakes allegedly made drowsy during the day due to incense fumes . . . become themselves at night . . . temple very busy and colorful during Chinese New Year festivities.

Siva Mariamman Temple • On Dato Keramat Road . . . dedicated to the third God of Hindu Trinity . . . worshiped as a preserver, destroyer, and creator all at once . . . priests chant their prayers at sunset to beat of drums and pipes.

Sri Mariamman Temple • On Queen Street . . . dedicated to the Hindu goddess of Mariamman . . . she is bedecked with gold and silver, not to mention precious stones of diamonds and emeralds . . . quite a sight.

St. George's Church • Located on Farquhar Street . . . built in 1818 . . . considered the oldest Anglican church in Southeast Asia . . . architect was Captain R. Smith . . . British colonial officer whose etchings of early life in Penang can be seen at the museum . . . built by convict labor . . . memorial canopy to Captain Francis Light on front porch . . . see also double-spired Cathedral of the Assumption and Christian Cemetery along the same street.

Telok Bahang Forest Recreation Park • About 22 km from Georgetown . . . about 250 acres of park surrounded by jungle . . . designed for people's recreation as well as to preserve trees . . . also a center for botany and zoology . . . has arboretum and forest museum . . . freshwater pools, footpaths, Malaysian-style rest huts, and children's playground . . . open from 8 a.m. to 6 p.m. daily . . . free admission.

Wat Chayamangkalaram • Thai Buddhist Temple . . . houses third largest reclining Buddha in the world (108 feet) . . . behind statue are niches where ashes of devotees are stored . . . photography not allowed inside temple . . . interesting Thai architecture.

Environs

Alor Star • Capital of the state of Kedah . . . also known as Malaysia's rice bowl . . . visit **Balai Besar,** great Hall where the sultan of Kedah still holds ceremonial functions . . . the Padang, green square in middle of town . . . **Zahir Mosque,** considered one of most beautiful in country . . . interesting old and new architecture here.

Gunong Jerai • Kedah Peak . . . highest mountain in the northwest . . . 1202 meters . . . welcomes climbers and adventurers . . . also amateur or professional archaeologists . . . more than 40 archaeological sites have been discovered on its slopes . . . studies include the migrations of Hindus from India to this peninsula.

Pulau Langkawi • 99 islands lying off the northwest coast of peninsular Malaysia . . . offers some of most beautiful scenery in the entire country . . . quiet and secluded . . . called Land of Legends . . . visit **Tasek Dayang Bunting** (Lake of Pregnant Maiden) . . . freshwater lake on Dayang Bunting, second largest in the group . . . **Tomb of Mahsuri, Gua Cherita** (cave of stories), **Seven Pools,** and **Gua Langsir** (cave of marble-shaped pebbles) . . . largest island is Langkawi and its people have both Thai and Malay origins . . . a 40-minute air ride from Penang . . . great beaches, fishing, and watersports . . . also the **Langkawi Country Club** operated by TDC which has 100 rooms on 100 acres . . . tennis, golf, and riding . . . first-class international resort.

Pulau Pangkor • Pangkor Island . . . a peaceful and lovely bit of land off the southern coast of Perak State . . . another former pirate hangout . . . ceded to Britain by the sultan of Perak in 1876 . . . now just a cluster of charming villages that rely on fishing . . . few international tourists . . . not known for a "swinging" reputation . . . reachable from peninsula from Lumut . . . a ferry runs the 35-minute voyage several times daily . . . a few interesting accommodations . . . Seaview Hotel at Pasir Bogak . . . Princess Hotel on Oyster Bay . . . Pangkor Laut Resort . . . also a somewhat dilapidated government rest house . . . mainly a weekend outing for local university students.

HOTELS

★★**Bayview Beach Hotel** • *Batu Ferringhi. Tel: 811311. Cable: BAYBEACH, PENANG. Telex: MA 40004* • 74 rooms.
Facilities: Dining room. Bar. Freshwater swimming pool with sunken bar. Private beach. Tennis and badminton.
Manager: C. C. Wang. *Reservations:* Utell.

★★★**Casuarina Beach Hotel** • *Batu Ferringhi. Tel: 811711. Cable: CASUARINA PENANG. Telex: MOON MA 40137* • 175 rooms.
Facilities: Dining room. Coffeehouse. Swimming pool. Tennis and badminton. Children's playground. Private beach and watersports.
Manager: U. H. Kunzmann. *Reservations:* Utell.

★★**Eastern & Oriental Hotel** • *10 Farquhar Street. Tel: 375322. Cable: HOTELEANDO. Telex: MA 40270* • 100 rooms . . . view of the bay . . . central Georgetown location . . . very Old World atmosphere.
Facilities: Two restaurants. Cocktail lounge. 2 bars. Swimming pool.
Manager: D. H. B. Chan. *Reservations:* MAS.

★★★**Hotel Equatorial** • *1, Jalan Bukit Jambul, 11900. Tel: 838000/838111* • 415 rooms . . . One of the new hotels built for Penang's busy convention trade . . not on the beach but adjoining an 18-hole golf course . . . Japanese, French, and Chinese restaurants plus a 24-hour coffee shop . . . tennis and squash courts with a health club.

★★★**Ferringhi Beach Hotel** • *Batu Ferringhi Rd., 11100 Batu Ferringhi. Tel: 805999. Cable: FERTEL. Telex: MA 40634* • 350 rooms . . . One of the newer hotels on Penang's most popular beaches . . .

sits on a hill overlooking the water . . . there is a pool, health spa, and disco, as well as Continental and local cuisines.

★★★★**Golden Sands Hotel** • *Batu Ferringhi Beach, P.O. Box 222, Penang. Tel: (04) 811911. Cable: GOLDSANDS PENANG. Telex: MA 40627* • 310 rooms. Situated on the island's best stretch of beach . . . all rooms with balconies . . . lovely landscaped gardens . . . many social activities and special events in the evening . . . barbecues, steamboat dinners, Chinese buffet and Malam Pulau Pinang—local cuisine plus music and dance.
Facilities: Bunga Raya restaurant for Chinese/Malay/Indian food. The Grill continental menu. Coffee House Terrace. Kuda Laut bar by free-form swimming pool. Sunset Lounge. Watersports.
Manager: N. Grocock. *Reservations:* Shangri-La Int'l.

★★**Holiday Inn Penang** • *Batu Ferringhi Beach, Penang. Tel: (04) 811601. Telex: MA 40281 HOLINN* • 165 rooms.
Facilities: Baron's Table German gourmet restaurant. Rock Garden cocktail lounge. Matahari seafood terrace. Mutiara coffee house/sidewalk cafe. Bayan Bar. Pool Deck. Penthouse Garden suites. Watersports.
Manager: D. Nordmann. *Reservations:* HOLIDEX.

★★★**Orchard Sun Penang** • *Tanjung Bungah, Penang. Tel: (04) 891111. Telex: MA 33139 SUNTEL* • 323 rooms (14 suites). 19-story resort at Tanjung Bungah, overlooking own bay . . . all rooms with balconies . . . combination resort and convention hotel . . . associated with Singapore Orchard Hotel.
Facilities: Lobby bar. Squash courts. Cinnamon Tree disco. Vanda Coffee House. Captain's Deck piano bar. Barbecues on pool deck. Swimming pool. Jacuzzi. Tennis courts. Hawker's terrace. The Captain's Table gourmet restaurant. Largest ballroom in Penang. Business Center. Health club.
Manager: P. Cheung. *Reservations:* Direct.

★★**Palm Beach Hotel** • *Batu Ferringhi Beach, Penang. Tel: (04) 811621. Telex: MA 40404. Cable: PLAMHOTEL* • 145 rooms. Located on beach between Rasa Sayang and Golden Sands . . . under same management . . . considered their budget hotel.
Facilities: Watersports. Beach Terrace. Swimming pools/tennis, etc., next door. Special food festivals in evening. Meeting facilities.
Manager: R. Staudinger. *Reservations:* Shangri-La Int'l.

★**Penang Merlin** • *Bukit Burmah Rd., off Larut Rd., Penang. Tel: 23301. Cable: MERLIN PENANG. Telex: MA 40632* • 295 rooms.

Facilities: Zodiac revolving restaurant. Edinburgh European and Chinese restaurants. 5 bars. Nightclubs. Suria coffee shop. Swimming pool. Club Tomorrow disco.
Manager: G. Loong. Reservations: UTELL.

★★★★**Rasa Sayang Hotel** ● *Batu Ferringhi Beach, P.O. Box 735, Penang. Tel: (04) 811811. Cable: RASAYANG PENANG. Telex: MA 40065* ● 305 rooms (13 suites).
Facilities: Feringhi Grill. Furusato Japanese restuarant. Coffee Garden. Tepi Laut bar. Cinta, a Juliana's of London disco. Meeting rooms. Executive Center. Swimming pool and all watersports.
Manager: B. Hladnik. Reservations: Shangri-La Int'l.

★★★★**Shangri-la Inn** ● *Victoria St., Georgetown, Penang. Tel: (04) 612148. Telex: MA 40878* ● 452 rooms (16 suites). 18-story hotel located in heart of Penang's shopping district . . . spacious lobby faces Magazine Road.
Facilities: Chinese restaurant. Coffee House. Lobby Lounge. Swimming pool and poolside bar. Health Center. Business Center. Ballroom and meeting rooms.
Manager: F. Neumann. Reservations: Shangri-La Int'l.

WINING AND DINING

Penang's multiracial population offers the adventurous eater a vast array of tastes and native specialties. Because it is an island, you can dream of the succulence that comes from the sea; there are many casual seafood restaurants along the beaches at **Tanjong Tokong** that feature crab, prawns, and several varieties of freshly caught grilled fish.

In the evening, mobile foodstalls crowd **Padang Brown, Gelugor Road, Gurney Drive,** or along the **Esplanade** in Georgetown. Their tempting aromas indicate that the national pleasure—*satay*—is in the vicinity. These tender bits of chicken or beef are skewered and barbecued, then dipped into a spicy peanut and chili sauce. You should also try *kari kapitan*—tender pieces of chicken cooked with coconut milk, sugar, oil, and lemon juice and served with the ever-present staple, rice. Anyone interested in beef noodles in a delicious broth and topped with bits and pieces of things should venture over to Victoria Street and demand *goo bak kway teow.*

Nonya-type food (belonging to the Straits-born Chinese) is a frequent specialty throughout the island of Penang; no dish is more popular than *laksa assam,* a creation of rice noodles in a sourish fish-based soup. Tamarind, onions, chilis, shrimp paste, and mint leaves are added to the broth—which is then poured over a bowl of special white laksa noodles. Shredded cucumber and slices of an edible, fragrant, pink flower known as *bunga kantan* are sprinkled on top while the concoction is very hot.

Laksa lemak—originally a Thai dish—is slightly milder in taste than laksa assam, because coconut milk is used instead of tamarind. However, the ingredients are basically the same.

Nasi kandar is what the Malaysians call a meal-on-a-plate; it's quite special to Penang. Available at open-air stalls or local coffee shops, it is a plate of steaming white rice on which as many beef, chicken, fish, shellfish, and vegetable curries as you choose have been added—a nutritious, filling, and inexpensive meal.

Visitors may also be interested in the local pizza, called *murtabak*. It is the Indian-style flatbread filled with mutton and onions and usually served with *dhal,* a mild curry cooked with *brinjals* (white beans). Another fun dish (and great ice-breaker) is steamboat, the Malaysian equivalent of a fondue. A pot of boiling water is placed in the center of the table and guests cook their own assortment of meat, seafood, and vegetables as they wish. Later, the broth from the cooking pot is served as a soup to aid the digestion.

Western food is readily available at the major hotels, like the **E & O, Merlin, Holiday Inn, Golden Sands,** and **Rasa Sayang** out at Batu Ferringhi; but Penang is a town where you should strike out and enjoy the local foodstalls and small hideaways that line the streets. I still remember some fabulous tandoori chicken and nan from a small place across from Fort Cornwallis. (Wish I were there now!)

In the evening, there is plenty of action at hotels in Georgetown or down at the beach, where plenty of visitors from the Western world come to have a good time. At the **Eden Restaurant** you can catch cultural shows daily.

SABAH

SABAH IN A CAPSULE

Land Below the Wind . . . so-called by early Sulu pirates because the area is south of the typhoon belt . . . British Crown Colony of North Borneo until 1963 . . . became part of Malaysia . . . capital called Kota Kinabalu (K.K.), formerly known as Jesseltown . . . devastation during World War II . . . thoroughly modern city . . . Sabah known for Mt. Kinabalu (13,450 feet) . . . highest peak in Southeast Asia . . . beautiful national parks . . . Gomantong Caves for edible birds' nests . . . Sepilok Orangutan Sanctuary . . . coral beaches and offshore islands . . . Bajau sea gypsies, Illanun pirates, Kadazan farmers, Murat blowpipe hunters, Rungu villages with stilt houses, Muruts who live in longhouses, etc. . . . plus mix of Malay, Chinese, and Hindus . . . colorful and interesting spot to visit . . . reachable by air from peninsular Malaysia and other Southeast Asian cities . . . also steamer service from Singapore.

WHAT TO SEE AND DO

Kinabalu National Park • Site of Mount Kinabalu . . . called **Akin Nabalu** . . . home of the spirits of the departed . . . by Kadazans who still hold the mountain sacred . . . popular peak for climbers . . . huts line the slopes and summit should be ascended in early morning . . . park itself boasts some 800 varieties of orchids . . . 500 species of birds . . . mousedeer, tree shrews, and red leaf monkeys . . . tour through park takes about 2 hours by Landrover . . . drive through jungle tracks and mountain streams . . . worth it for the scenery and panorama of the countryside . . . and what adventure!

Kota Belud • Small Bajau town about 77 km from Kota Kinabalu . . . known for its Sunday morning market . . . biggest and most colorful *tamu* in the state . . . local products for sale by Bajaus and Kadazans . . . fruits and vegetables as well as handicrafts.

Kota Kinabalu ● Sabah's capital . . . population about 130,000 . . . proud of its modern structures and atmosphere . . . city lines the sea under beautiful skies . . . visit gold-domed **State Mosque** . . . impressive contemporary Islamic architecture . . . and **Sabah Museum** for exhibits of tribal artifacts . . . walk the crowded Chinese section . . . in contrast to the Western-style high rises . . . journey out to **Kampung Ayer** or Water Village . . . to see houses and sidewalks on stilts.

Kudat ● Home of Rungus people . . . located about 4 hours' drive from Kota Kinabalu . . . live in long houses . . . women wear black ankle-length *sarungs* (sarongs) . . . weave baskets and hats . . . make beaded adornments and metal jewelry.

Penampang Village ● 13 km from Kota Kinabalu . . . popular with tourists for quick view of the Kadazan tribe at work . . . traditional structures, activities, and handicrafts.

Sandakan ● Former capital of North Borneo . . . lies on the east coast about 180 degrees from Kota Kinabalu . . . modern city at edge of sea . . . known for **Sandakan Orchid House** with exhibits and collection of rare orchids . . . **Forestry Exhibition** for displays of local handicrafts and tribal hunting weapons . . . **Sepilok Sanctuary** some 24 km from town center . . . largest Orangutan park for "wild men of Borneo" to live in protection . . . also **Gomantong Caves** . . . 32 km across the bay edible birds' nests can be collected with bamboo poles . . . **Turtle Islands** just offshore . . . 100-year-old green turtles live here . . . also **Berhala Island** in Sulu Sea for swimming and picnics and view from lighthouse.

Tanjong Aru ● Capital's seaside resort . . . beautiful beaches . . . **Prince Philip Park** and recreation center . . . located just 5 km south of Kota Kinabalu International Airport . . . lovely spot to enjoy the sunset.

Tawau ● Famous hot spring in southeastern part of Sabah.

Tenom ● Home of the Muruts . . . reachable by Sabah's only railway, very quaint . . . from Tanjong Aru . . . 154-km journey takes you through towns of Papar, Sipitang, and Beaufort . . . crosses Crocker Range and skirts banks of Padas River . . . transits Padas Gorge . . . a memorable journey . . . Murats are "men of the hills" and still live in traditional long houses . . . work at hunting and agriculture . . . love song and dance . . . hospitable to *orang puteh* (white man).

Tuaran • Popular tourist area about a 30-minute drive from Kota Kinabalu . . . interesting visits to the agricultural station . . . *tamu* on market day . . . **Mengkabong Bajau** village built over water . . . **Tamparuli** for handicrafts, local specialties . . . stroll across Sabah's longest suspension bridge.

Tunku Abdul Rahman National Park • Encompasses islands just offshore of Kota Kinabalu . . . sanctuary for beautiful coral and many varieties of fish . . . uncrowded beaches and superb snorkeling . . . popular for weekend picnics . . . boat trips arranged with local fishermen . . . islands are Pulau Gaya, Pulau Sapi, and Pulau Manukan.

Tours

City and Countryside Tour • 4 hours, daily . . . combines Kota Kinabalu with Menkabong fishing village and view of Mt. Kinabalu.

Kampong Scenic Tour • 4 hours, daily.

Kinabalu National Park • Full day to several days . . . can include ascent of Mt. Kinabalu and visits to Ranau as well as the Australian war memorial.

Kota Belud Tamu • 6–8 hours, weekly . . . visits the most colorful and exciting market in Malaysia.

Kota Kinabalu City and Suburb Tour • 2–3 hours, daily . . . visits State Mosque, Tanjong Aru, coastal highway, Signal Hill, Sembulan water village, and Sabah Museum.

Kota Kinabalu Penampang Tour • 4 hours, daily . . . capital sightseeing and Kadazan village.

Labuan Island • All day, daily . . . visits war memorial and site of Japanese surrender . . . only duty-free port in Malaysia.

Penampang Papar Tour • 5 hours, daily . . . river cruise to Kadazan village and Pantai Manis beach.

Rungus Long House • 12 hours, daily.

Rungus Long House • 2 days . . . with accommodations.

Sabah Interior Tour • 2 days . . . by road and rail to Tambunan, Keningau, and Tenom.

Sandakan and Orangutan Sanctuary • Full day, daily.

Tunku Abdul Rahman National Park Tour • All day excursion to one of the offshore islands.

HOTELS

Kota Kinabalu (Jesselton)

★★**Hotel Capital** • *P.O. Box 23, Jalan Haji Saman. Tel: 53433. Cable: CAPITAL* • 102 rooms.
Facilities: Dining room serving Western/Chinese cuisine. Cocktail lounge. Nightclub. Watersports and boating. 20 feet from ocean.
Manager: P. C. V. On. *Reservations:* Direct.

★★★**Hyatt Kinabalu International** • *Tel: 219888. Cable: HY-ATTKI. Telex: KITA MA 80036* • 345 rooms.
Facilities: Chinese and Malaysian restaurants. Hugo's grillroom. 24-hour cafe. 2 bars. Cocktail lounge. Entertainment. Swimming pool. Health center. Regency Club. Businessman's center.
Manager: K. W. Diefenbach. *Reservations:* HYATT INT'L.

★★★★**Hotel Shangrila** • *P.O. Box 1718, Bandaran Berjaya. Tel: 56100. Cable: SHANGRILA. Telex: HOSHAN MA 80001* • 120 rooms.
Facilities: Restaurant. Nightclub. Coffeehouse.
Manager: D. U. K. Fai. *Reservations:* Direct.

SARAWAK

SARAWAK IN A CAPSULE

Land of the Hornbills . . . formerly known as the Land of the Headhunters . . . Malaysia's largest state . . . peninsula lies southwest of Sabah . . . on northwest coast of Borneo . . . originally under sultanate of Brunei . . . placed under administration of British adventurer James Brooke when he quelled a rebellion . . . became part of the Malaysian federation in 1963 . . . present population estimated over 1 million . . . rich in natural resources but many are unexplored . . . many jungles, mountains, rain forests, swamplands, and rivers . . . Kuching, on the banks of Sarawak River, is the state capital . . . accessible from Southeast Asia by air.

WHAT TO SEE AND DO

Bako National Park • Primary forest about 2 hours by speedboat upriver from Kuching . . . full of fascinating flora including carnivorous pitcher plant . . . hiking paths and government rest houses . . . special laboratory for scientists . . . good swimming in little bays . . . with beautiful rock formations above.

Kuching • Riverine capital of Sarawak . . . name means cat in Malay . . . population about 70,000 . . . river bisects city . . . most people prefer to travel back and forth by boat . . . city under White Rajah rule until 1941 when Japanese invaded . . . became part of British crown colony of Sarawak in 1946 . . . a state of Malaysia in 1963 . . . **Sarawak Museum,** built in 1891 by Sir Charles Brooke, houses wonderful tribal artifacts . . . **Istana** (palace) is now the residence of Sarawak's governor . . . **Fort Margherita** (named after Brooke's wife) is now a police museum but is still considered among the best colonial architecture left in Southeast Asia . . . **Masjid Besar** (Main Mosque) famous for impressive contemporary architecture . . . completed in 1968 and incorporates some of first building on site from 1852 . . . many impressive Chinese temples . . . **Tua Pek Kong** (1876) . . . **Hian Tien Shian** (1877) dedicated to god of heaven . . . **Temple of Kuan Yin** (Chinese god of mercy) dates from 1908 . . . and Tien Hou (goddess of seamen) built in 1927 . . . upriver are traditional villages . . . accessible by small craft.

Niah National Park • Archaeologists have found evidence of human habitation as early as 40,000 years ago . . . by air to Miri, Sarawak's main oil town . . . then by road and a 15-minute boat ride . . . park covers over 8000 acres . . . includes famous **Niah Caves** . . . where you can see prehistoric wall paintings and observe collection of birds' nests . . . worth witnessing in Jan. and June . . . nests hang from roofs of caves and collectors bring them down by long bamboo poles equipped with scrapers . . . only for the very adventurous . . . eating them is another matter!

Santubong Resort • Seaside resort about 32 km from Kuching . . . an important trading center during Tang and Sung dynasties from 7th to 13th centuries A.D. . . . ancient rock carvings found at **Sungai Jaong** . . . just upriver from the village . . . but today just a popular place for swimming and fishing . . . government chalets may be booked through District Office in Kuching.

Sibu and Rejang River • Rejang is Sarawak's greatest waterway . . . said to be longest river in Malaysia . . . reachable by air from Kuching to Sibu, a rich timber, rubber, and pepper town . . . take a motorized boat upriver to Kapit . . . a small town in heart of Iban country.

Skrang • River safari . . . a 4-hour drive from Kuching to Skrang River . . . hour-long boat ride along river to Iban villages where people live in traditional long houses . . . guests invited to drink *tuak* (local rice wine) or even spend the night . . . although this long house has modern facilities!

Tours

Bako National Park • 8 hours, daily.

Kuching City • 3 hours, daily . . . visits Sarawak Museum, State Mosque, Malaysian market, Istana, Fort Margherita, and Hong San Temple.

Kuching Long House Tour • 5 days . . . visits Kuching city plus sea and land Dyaks by bus and motorized longboat.

Land Dyak Long House • 3 to 4 hours, daily . . . visit to Iban long house and native lunch.

Niah Caves • Full day to 2 nights . . . includes longboat trip and visits to caves . . . longer versions visit Miri city, oil palm and cocoa plantations.

Sea Dyak Long House • Full day, daily . . . visits Iban long house with native lunch.

Skrang River Safari • 2 days . . . land and longboat transportation to longhouse accommodation and pepper plantation visit.

Skrang River Ulu Long House • 2 days . . . all of the above but more native food and accommodations.

HOTELS

Kuching

★★★**Aurora Beach Hotel** • *Jalan Tanjong Batu, Bintulu. Tel: 20281. Cable: AURORA BINTULU. Telex: MA 73150* • 108 rooms.
Facilities: Continental cuisine. Coffeehouse. Swimming pool. Watersports. Tennis and squash. Garden restaurant.
Manager: C. J. Hunter. *Reservations:* Direct.

★★★**Holiday Inn Kuching** • *Jalan Tunku Abdul Rahman, Kuching. Tel: 23111. Cable: HOLIDAY INN. Telex: MA 70086* • 165 rooms.
Facilities: Serapi restaurant and terrace. Banquet rooms. Rajang Bar. Coffeehouse. Chinese restaurant. Disco. Swimming pool. Tennis. Health club. Minigolf.
Manager: P. E. Mueller. *Reservations:* HOLIDEX.

★**Hotel Long House** • *Abell Rd., Kuching. Tel: 55333. Cable: LONGHOUSE. Telex: MA 70039* • 50 rooms.
Facilities: Dining room. Coffee shop. Snack bar.
Manager: P. Cheng. *Reservations:* Direct.

SHOPPING

The joy of shopping for souvenirs from Malaysia will vary from state to state, as many of the traditional handicrafts are regional. The wonderful batiks from the East Coast are familiar to collectors all over the world, and Selangor pewter is highly prized for its fine workmanship. However, visitors should be prepared for such temptations as Aw pottery from Johor; Sarawak vases; Labu pottery from Perak state; wood carvings typical of Kelantan, Trengganu, Malacca, Kedah, and Negri Sembilan; silverware from Kelantan; Songket weaving from the East Coast region; rattan from Kuantan to Kuala Trengganu; Padan weaving from the state of Trengganu; kites from Kelantan; and birds' nests (yes, for soup) from the caves of Sabah and Sarawak.

Batik is everyone's favorite purchase, as the lovely materials can be used for many things and for all occasions. Clothing is the most popular usage, and Malaysians themselves dress both formally and casually in their batik. You can also find such items as tissue box covers, hats and bags, cushion covers, bedspreads, curtains, and table mats or napkin sets. The batik industry is concentrated in the East Coast, and visitors may have the opportunity to visit factories to observe the production firsthand and make their purchases on the spot.

Songket is another indigenous fabric and the pride of Malaysia. It is a fabric much entwined with the country's history and culture; it has long been worn by royalty and used by the courts for ceremonial occasions. It has also been successfully adapted for Western evening wear. Songket is woven with the finest silk available, and the gold-threaded patterns are reproduced from ancient designs (and often a secret passed from generation to generation). The art of weaving songket dates from as early as the 15th century, and it is said that no two pieces of the cloth have ever been alike. Even the design of the loom has not changed with time, and many weavers now employ valuable antiques in their making of the cloth. Naturally, a piece of songket (1.8 m. in length) is expensive in comparison to other Malaysian traditional crafts, but anyone able to purchase one will never fail to enjoy its exquisite beauty.

Batik painting has become, in recent years, another of Malaysia's contribution to the world of art. The batik artist needs the same skill, draftsmanship, and patience necessary in the making of batik. The only difference is that the patterns may be bolder, because the cloth is sized and framed and not worn on the body or used as household accessories. Batik paintings make excellent souvenirs because they can be framed later (they take up little room in a suitcase).

The Malay is known for his fine wood-carving abilities, as evident from the shutters and railings found on the stilt houses in Penang, Negri Sembilan, Malacca, and the environs of Kuala Lumpur. Carving is a very old craft on the Malay Peninsula, and the timber resources have provided a variety of woods. Visitors are always impressed by the decorative carvings found throughout the country, especially in the Istana Balai Besar built in 1840 for the Sultan of Kelantan or the Istana Lama Sri Menanti built at the turn of the century for the Sultan of Negri Sembilan. Both wooden palaces are still used for ceremonial occasions. Visitors interested in traditional carvings are encouraged to haunt the antique shops, or contact the National Museum in Kuala Lumpur for a list of modern wood carvers. There are also some interesting wood sculptures available, namely from the Mah-Meri and the Jah-Hut groups. The former offers more sophisticated works, while the latter live a rural life in Pahang (where the jungle and mountains are the inspiration for their art). The Mah-Meri wood sculptures are best known in the Kuala Lumpur area.

Pewter is synonymous with Malaysia and one of the world's oldest crafts. Pewter drinking vessels were thought to enhance the flavor of wine in first century Rome. The craft was introduced to Malaya in 1885 by Yoon Koon, who emigrated from the Chinese pewter province of Swatow. He founded **Selangor Pewter** and has been named "Father of Malaysian Pewter." The factory, just outside Kuala Lumpur, produces every item you might desire in this alloy of tin, copper, and antimony, that is cooled and then highly polished. A pewter article takes about three weeks to be produced, and personal engraving can be ordered. Visitors are welcome at the Selangor pewter factory and, of course, there is a retail shop attached—for everyone's convenience.

Silver items made in Malaysia come from the East Coast state of Kelantan, where silversmiths work in the old-fashioned way to craft bowls, trays, salad spoons, and tea sets. Filigree work is still a long process, although machines are now used to make the silver sheets into wire. It is a cottage industry that has not changed much, and many of the designs even show a Hindu influence that dates back approximately 600 years ago.

Locally made **pottery** is also a strong candidate for souvenirs. **Aw pottery** is made at Air Hitam (about 80 miles north of Johor Bahru) by Aw Eng Kwang and his family, five generations in the craft. Aw's pottery follows the Chinese method of making ceramics, and his products range from vases and lampstands in earth tones of amber and burnt sienna to more delicate tea sets and figurines. His kiln is considered the largest outside China.

The colorful vases of Sarawak come from the capital, Kuching, where Chinese from Kwantung province brought their skill. The vases are quite unusual, however, because the hand-applied designs feature local folklore. You can appreciate figures of Iban hunters, Murut men in traditional dress, or the stylized dragon from Bidayuh, Kayan, and Kenyah tribes.

A more primitive type of pottery is made by the Labu people, whose Malay villages are found on the banks of the Perak River in Perak state. The charm of their pottery lies in the ancient craft by which it is made, uninfluenced by modern techniques. The tools employed to work the clay consist of bamboo strips for cutting, a smooth stone for polishing, and small wooden rods for stamping designs. The Labus can be found at Lenggong in Upper Perak, Sayong (near Kuala Kangsar), and Pulau Tiga in Lower Perak.

Pandan weaving is another cottage industry from the East Coast state of Trengganu. The short pandan, or screw-pine, leaves are used to make narrow sleeping mats, fans, baskets, tobacco pouches, slippers, purses, and colorful table mats. The longer *mengkuang* leaves are used for floor mats. Visitors who wish to see this interesting weaving process may visit several village houses, open daily, from Kuantan to Kuala Trengganu. Primarily a women's vocation, the process includes a great sense of camaraderie as the women chat and laugh together while they work. Though the craft looks simple, even a small purse may take an entire day to complete. Considered an East Coast tradition, the weaving is also popular among the women of Malacca, Selangor, and Negri Sembilan.

Rattan, or *rotan* in Malay, is abundant in this country because it is a jungle vine that thrives in dense, tropical rain forests. The furniture made from this vine is inexpensive, attractive, and extremely durable. Basketware is also popular. Although a bit difficult to transport in a suitcase, rattan can be viewed at handicraft centers throughout Malaysia.

Kites are very important to local culture and many ceremonial occasions are preceded by the flying of kites. Children are taught kite legends all their life, and they fly *layang-layang* during the windy season. Adults have their own kite, called *wau* and it requires some skill, discipline, and stamina to maneuver. The wau is so important to one's well being, that even the national carrier MAS uses the wau as its logo. Needless to say, kite fanciers the world over will always appreciate a fine specimen from Malaysia.

Finally, the "caviar of the East" is said to be **birds' nests** found in the Niah caves and Baram in Sarawak, the Gomantong caves and Madai in Sabah. The Chinese insist that birds' nests not only are tasty and nourishing, but also have aphrodisiacal powers. If you don't have the time or interest to collect your own, good quality nests are available from medicine shops (expensive) or packed in plastic bags at supermarkets. But before you tell all your friends with a wok what to expect, check with the U.S. Department of Agriculture. Birds' nests may be classified as plants and not allowed to be imported individually.

Malaysian handicrafts are readily available at the government-sponsored handicraft centers in major cities as well as the duty-free shops in Kuala Lumpur and Penang. However, the best and most enjoyable way to purchase your souvenirs is at the local markets. The famous Sunday night market in Kuala Lumpur (actually held on Sat. night) is located in Kampung Baharu, the exclusively Malay section of the capital. It is a wonderful place to eat and shop on a Saturday night, and the handicraft stalls are overwhelming.

The **Pasar Malam,** or night market, in Penang is another emporium not to miss so inquire about its current location as soon as you arrive. Penang also has some exciting shopping streets, like Jalan Pinang for imported items, Jalan Campbell for Chinese goods, and Rope Walk for antique or junk shops. Chinese opium beds were the rage when I lived in the Far East, but they cost a fortune to be shipped—and then fixed when they arrive in pieces! It is far more sensible to stay with the local fabrics and crafts that can be carried home and enjoyed immediately.

PHILIPPINES

HISTORY

With an archipelago some 7000 islands strong and a shoreline twice that of the United States, it is not surprising that the Philippines plays host to over 100 different ethnic groups—who speak at least 80 separate language and dialects. This country is a contradiction in itself, an anomaly in the midst of Southeast Asia. It is the most "western" of all its neighbors and, after Spanish domination for over three centuries, primarily Christian. Its people range from the fairest of fair, who only follow European trends, to the fiercest and darkest of hill tribes, who rarely see light of day. The Philippines also has the distinction of being the site of the defeat of two men that history books never fail to mention: Ferdinand Magellan, who was stabbed to death on Mactan Island in 1521; and General Douglas MacArthur (USA), who was airlifted off Corregidor Island in 1942 and made good his famous promise . . . "I shall return."

When Magellan and his pals stopped by on their circumnavigation of the world, they found an already viable commercial area, since traders from India, Arabia, and China had exchanged their wares and infiltrated the local culture since the 10th century. Along with spices, silks, and porcelains, they had also brought Islam. To this day, the majority of Mindanao Island is Moslem. Magellan himself is said to have planted the first Christian seed, so offending a local chieftain named Lapulapu that the Spanish explorer never made it to the next port. (A piece of cross he planted still exists and is one of Cebu City's most historic monuments).

Spanish expeditions to the islands continued, and by 1565 the archipelago had been named "Felipinas" in honor of Spanish King Felipe the Second. A treaty was maneuvered and Miguel Lopez de Legazpi installed himself as the first governor-general, and Manila was established as the capital of Spain's new colony. Legazpi defeated the Moslems throughout Luzon Island, and Christianity became the official religion. Baroque churches were built for centuries after, and Spanish culture influenced the architecture, cuisine, and education of the people.

Trade strengthened with other Spanish-dominated countries, namely Mexico, which exported silver from its plentiful mines.

Toward the end of the 19th century, Filipino leaders began to demand a stronger role in their own country. People like physician, poet, and patriot Jose Rizal fanned the flame, and his writings eventually made him a martyr. He was executed by the Spanish in 1896 at a site immortalized by Rizal Monument in the Luneta. With the monument, he was born again as "father of his country." By the end of the century, the Philippine Republic was declared and its first president inaugurated.

But independence was short lived; as a result of the Spanish-American War, Puerto Rico, Guam, and the Philippines were ceded to the United States for $20 million. After decades of more wrangling, the Philippines became a Commonwealth in 1935, with Manuel Quezon its first president. It became a fully independent nation on July 4, 1945. The dream was only delayed a year (1946), for the Japanese invaded the islands just two days after Pearl Harbor in 1941 and stayed for four disastrous years.

The war was not kind to the Philippine Islands. The fall of Corregidor and Bataan and the retaking of Manila are still vivid to those who were there. The infamous "Death March" to Capas cost thousands of lives, and the route is still remembered. This was also the only country in Southeast Asia where the Japanese occupation impeded independence rather than enhanced it. But the glorious day finally arrived, and the Republic of the Philippines was declared on July 4, 1946, with Manuel Roxas the first president. Defense Secretary Ramon Magsaysay, who successfully quelled Communist-inspired internal problems, in the early '50s, became the country's third and (to date) most popular president and served his people well until his tragic death in 1957 in an airplane crash. He was succeeded by Carlos P. Garcia, Diosdado Macapagal, and a lawyer/war hero named Ferdinand Marcos.

For over 20 years, President Marcos was chief of state, with an authority that became more absolute and corrupt. The president and his first lady ruled the country as well as most of the industry, banks and media. In September 1972, Marcos declared marital law, which suppressed the opposition and totally crippled any semblance of a free society. Many fine Filipinos fled the country, taking refuge in the United States, including Mr. and Mrs. Benigno Aquino.

The assassination of Benigno Aquino, one of Marcos's strongest opponents, upon his return from exile in 1983 began the finale for Marcos. In early 1986, Aquino's widow Cory ran against Marcos in an election that was rife with fraud and cheating. Marcos proclaimed himself the winner and had himself re-inaugurated, but hours later was forced to flee the country with his family and an entourage of some 60 fellow corruptors.

Mrs. Aquino was immediately recognized to assume the presidency the world believed was rightfully hers. It was an impressive and peaceful transition led by "rebels" General Ramos, Defense Minister Enrile, and thousands of concerned citizens. It was a wonderful show to the world that democracy is a much wanted and viable instrument in this country, and Filipinos can be proud of their unity and behavior in a tense situation that led to the end of the Marcos regime. Mrs. Aquino has tremendous popular support and has been transformed astonishingly from a simple housewife to a self-assured and sympathetic leader determined to put her beautiful country back on its feet and into the world stream, politically, socially and economically.

So like us and yet so different, the Philippines is a fascinating combination of people and cultures and experiences. With a Mexican-like devotion to the Virgin Mary, it is a country full of colorful religious holidays and communal festivities. On Good Friday each year, young men volunteer themselves for the honor of being "crucified" just as it was done centuries ago, and "flagellants" take to the streets to beat themselves bloody. Even the public transport vehicles—those unavoidable "jeepneys"—are full of Christian images, symbols, and offerings of devotees.

Despite an uneven distribution of the riches and a lack of opportunity for betterment in many areas, Filipinos are a happy and spirited people with a sincere hospitality. Language is rarely a problem here since Tagalog and English are often spoken simultaneously, even outside metropolitan regions. There is plenty to see and do throughout the islands and music everywhere! No one who has ever heard a Philippine band can resist the temptation to have the ensemble "play it again." This inherent talent is amazing and Philippine bands play in every major Southeast Asian nightspot. In the arts, Filipino works and crafts display the original Malay culture as well as European/American influences, and many young painters and sculptors are receiving serious attention from abroad.

Manila is *not* the Philippines, but it certainly reflects all that the 7000 islands have to offer. It is a typical, overcrowded, and quite exasperating Southeast Asian capital, but it also has great beauty, charm, and sophistication. The restoration of the elegant Manila Hotel was one of Mme. Marcos's finer moments. Manila is yet another "hotel town" and, if you can stand the overused air conditioning everywhere, hotel-hopping is the best way to watch how the elite of Manila live. But you should also take the time to walk around Intramuros, the original walled city built by the Spanish, or delve into bustling Chinatown in the district of Binondo. I also suggest a courtesy call at the Rizal Monument in the Luneta, the large and most popular public park fronted by the sea. Save a moment, too, to enjoy the sunset over Manila Bay. It is one of the great sights in the Far East and never fails to provoke thoughts of history, adventure, romance, and intrigue.

PHILIPPINES IN A CAPSULE

7000-odd archipelago on the edge of the South China Sea . . . land mass slightly smaller than Japan but coastline twice that of United States . . . only 10% inhabited . . . largest islands—Luzon and Mindanao—represent 65% of the total land area . . . discovered by Spanish traders in 1521 . . . Malays arrived as early as 700 B.C. from Indonesia . . . islands came under U.S. administration in 1898 following Spanish-American war . . . fully independent on July 4, 1946. . . . Since February 1986 and the election of Mrs. Corazon Aquino, the Philippines is undergoing a "rebirth" . . . almost 50 million Filipinos . . . national languages are English and Pilipino (Tagalog) . . . over 90% Catholic but strong Moslem influence in Mindanao and the Sulu Archipelago . . . tropical climate . . . beautiful beaches and mountain vistas . . . bountiful fruits . . . rice and fish . . . spirited people.

PLANNING AHEAD

THE PHILIPPINE TOURIST INFORMATION CENTERS are located at Ninoy Aquino International Airport (Tel: 828–4791/828–1511), Nayong Pilipino Complex, Airport Road (Tel: 828–2219) and on the ground floor, Philippine Ministry of Tourism building near Rizal Park in Metro Manila (Tel: 501–703). Field offices are situated in Pampanga, Baguio, Legazpi, La Union, Bacolod, Cebu, Iloilo, Tacloban, Cagayan de Oro City Davao, Marawi and Zamboanga.

In North America, the Philippine Tourist Office is located in Philippine Center, 556 Fifth Ave., New York, NY 10036 (Tel: 212–575–7915); Suite 1212, 3460 Wilshire Blvd., Los Angeles, CA 90010 (Tel: 213–487–4525); Suite 1111, 30 North Michigan Ave., Chicago, IL 60602 (Tel: 312–782–1707).

VISAS are not required of travelers holding valid U.S. passports, provided they possess tickets for onward or return journey. Visitors wishing to extend their stay may apply to the Commission of Immigration and Deportation.

INOCULATIONS for smallpox and cholera are not required for entry, but cholera shots are suggested when the Philippines appears on a weekly summary of areas infected (according to the World Health Organization). Yellow fever vaccinations are required of all travelers arriving from infected areas.

ENTRY BY AIR into the Philippine Islands from abroad is primarily through **Ninoy Aquino International Airport,** a modern facility with 14 jetways. Located in nearby Pasay City, the airport is less than 30 minutes away by car to any major hotel and services an average of 170 international flights weekly. Manila is just over an hour by air from Hong Kong, 3 hours from Singapore, 5 from Tokyo, 17 hours from San Francisco, and 22 hours from New York.

Several Southeast Asian regional carriers have direct flights into Zamboanga, Mindanao, and proposed international airports are due for Cebu City and Zamboanga. Domestic flights connect Manila daily with about 50 other towns, cities, and rural areas. Where scheduled flights do not serve, there are aircraft for charter. Local service is bare-bones basic, with nothing but a plastic cup of water available. Allow plenty of time before departure for security inspection.

BY SEA around this archipelago there are interisland vessels with first-class accommodations that sail between several different ports daily. There have been some luxury-liner calls in the past, and interest is picking up, again.

DEPARTURE BY AIR from Ninoy Aquino International or Domestic Airport can be a drudge because of the tight security and zealous inspections. The airport taxes are ₱200 for international flights and ₱25 for domestic flights.

DUTY-FREE items' allowances for incoming visitors (bona fide tourists) are 200 cigarettes or 50 cigars or 250 grams of pipe tobacco (or an assortment of the above), two bottles of alcohol, and as many personal effects as necessary and appropriate for use. These personal items include jewelry, toilet water, camera equipment, portable radios and typewriters, tape recorders, and sports equipment as well as tools of the trade.

Bona fide tourists are not required to complete a customs declaration, and their luggage is generally exempt from inspection. However, travelers with a scruffy appearance may very well be stopped and searched.

Visitors may not import into the Philippines any seditious or subversive materials, pornographic materials, ammunition or weapons of war, gambling equipment or contrivances, and articles of precious metals that are not imprinted with the international code of quality.

THE CURRENCY of the Philippines is the peso (₱), which is divided into 100 centavos. Approximately ₱21.00 equals U.S.$1, although the exact exchange rates fluctuate daily. Coins are in 1, 5, 10, 25, 50 centavo and 1 peso denominations. Five-peso coins are also available. Bills are in 2, 5, 10, 20, 50, and 100 peso denominations.

Hard foreign currency and traveler's checks are easily convertible throughout the Philippines at banks, hotels, and authorized money changers. Always demand a Central Bank receipt, however, as it is necessary to show it in duty-free shops. Credit cards are also widely accepted in shops, restaurants, and hotels. Some international hotel chains now offer their own credit-card systems as well.

LOCAL TIME in the Philippines is Greenwich Mean Time plus 8 hours, i.e., exactly 13 hours ahead of Eastern Standard Time, 14 hours in advance of Eastern Daylight Time. Add another hour for each mainland U.S. time zone (add 5 for Hawaii). Manila is in the same time zone as Beijing, Taipei, Macau, Kuala Lumpur, Singapore, and Hong Kong, but 1 hour ahead of Seoul and Tokyo. It is 1 hour ahead of Bangkok, Ja-karta; and 1½ hours ahead of Rangoon!

LOCAL CURRENT is 220 volts/50 cycles, but don't expect power all the time when out in the provinces. Electric razors can be used in major hotel multifitting bathroom plugs, but most hair dryers will need converters.

LOCAL WATER is generally potable, except for remote rural areas. Those with squeamish stomachs should stick with bottled water at all times, not use any ice, and avoid all fresh, raw vegetables. Fruits that you peel yourself are always considered safe. Drink only bottled beverages that are opened in your presence.

OFFICIAL LANGUAGES in the Philippines are English, Tagalog, and Spanish. The national language is actually called Pilipino, of which Tagalog is one of its 87 dialects, but Tagalog is the tongue most tourists encounter. English is widely spoken and understood throughout the country, and few visitors have any communication problems.

The Philippines are a media man's dreamland, with four major English morning newspapers and two evening papers in Metro Manila (quite heavily censored in the past), plus a host of provincial and local dailies and weeklies in both English and Pilipino.

Filipinos love their radios and television; there are five major channels in the Metro Manila area as well as over 250 radio stations throughout the country. *What's On in Manila* and other visitor-aimed magazines discuss what local entertainers are "hot" at the moment, and how to enjoy their music or songs.

BUSINESS HOURS in the Philippines are from 8 a.m. to 5 p.m. Monday through Friday, with most offices closed from noon to 1 p.m. or so. Banks open from 9 a.m. to 4 p.m. Monday through Friday. Shops in major tourist centers open at 9 or 10 a.m. until at least 7 p.m. daily. The smaller, family-owned shops outside Metro Manila are open whenever and for as long as the spirit prevails.

Metro Manila (the city proper plus environs) is quite a Far East business center, both on the reclaimed land along Roxas Boulevard and in Makati. The **Asian Development Bank** is headquartered here, and there are over 80 other banks with offices in Manila. There are also three stock exchanges (Manila, Makati, Metropolitan) that trade in the Philippine market from 9:30 a.m.–1:30 p.m. Monday through Friday. There are several local professional clubs and organizations in Metro Manila, including Kiwanis and three branches of Rotary. The **Manila Overseas Press Club** is located at Orense in Makati (Tel: 855–981). The **United States Embassy** is situated in a beautiful building near the Manila Hotel, on Roxas Boulevard (Tel: 598–011). The **Canadian Consulate** is located on the fourth floor of the Philippine Air Lines Building, Ayala Avenue in Makati (Tel: 876–536).

TIPPING in the Philippines is not a problem. A service charge of 10% (15% in the top-class establishments) will be included in hotel and restaurant bills. Additional tipping is optional. Taxi drivers are not tipped, unless special service has been rendered. Porters, barbers, and w.c. attendants get a peso or two, and the rate per suitcase at the airport is clearly marked ₱10. If you do not have any pesos, a dollar bill per couple's luggage will bring smiles.

TELEPHONE AND TELEX service in the Philippines is good, although communication with the outside world is slightly less fast than you'll find in other parts of the Far East. Overseas calls take from 30 minutes to an hour to put through, as there is no direct dialing in most hotels. Overseas calls can be costly and frustrating from this country because hotels add a 20% or more surcharge, and you must pay even though no connection was made.

Telex services are available at all major hotels on a 24-hour basis, usually in the Businessmen's Center (now an important part of many travelers' existence). Bilingual secretarial services, current publications, complimentary coffee, and a conference area are also available here.

Local calls are about ₱5 for three minutes from your hotel room, about ₱10 from a red public phone. However, connections are not al-

ways clear, and phone lines have a habit of breaking down. Patience is
the key word here!

WHAT TO WEAR   in the Philippines is what you would wear in any
hot, humid tropical climate. Although synthetics pack well, cottons wear
better in humid climes. Sweaters are necessary in the mountain areas.
Discreet cover-up clothing for both men and women (this is a predom-
inantly Catholic country) are appropriate by day. At night, life is quite
formal in the fine restaurants and nightclubs of Manila, much much less
so in the other cities. Local women wear the *terno,* or butterfly sleeve,
long gown for formal occasions, while the men all don the *barong tagalog,* or Tagalog shirt. The barong is a transparent, embroidered over-
shirt (T-shirts are in order underneath) that makes a fine gift for informal
occasions at home. The shirt dates from the 19th century and was a
symbol of Filipino patriotism.

December to May is the drier and cooler season in the Philippines
and, indeed, the locals may be shivering! Remember that mountain resorts like the popular Baguio is at least 20 degrees cooler than the plains,
and visitors can be quite chilly here if not dressed properly. Expect wet
and warm weather from June to November, with high humidity and a
never-ending procession of tropical storms.

LOCAL TRANSPORATION   in the Philippines consists of a national
railway that serves the island of Luzon, from Legaspi in the south to
San Fernando, La Union in the north. **Buses** also connect major tourist
areas, and both chauffeured and self-drive **automobiles** are for hire.
Traffic does move along the right-hand side, but similarities in driving
styles stop there. Watch out if you intend to drive yourself! Actually,
the colorful and cheap **jeepneys,** colorfully decorated former U.S. military vehicles that carry about 12 passengers each, are the fastest and
most entertaining way to get through the clogged byways. Just hop on,
tell the driver your destination, and he or she will inform you of the
fare. Metro Manila also has a series of **Love Buses,** fast and clean and
with a fixed rate between stops throughout the city. All major cities also
have a large fleet of licensed **taxis,** some more decrepit than others, that
are amazingly inexpensive provided both you and the driver know where
to go!

FESTIVALS   are sustenance to the Filipinos, who will use any excuse
to celebrate patron saints days, mythical figures, or historic events. Festivals throughout the Philippines, whether local or national, are colorful
and fun. Try not to miss one if you happen to be in the neighborhood.
The "fiesta" spirit is quite catching, but don't expect to get much business accomplished during this time.

Public holidays for 1983 are marked with an asterisk (*).

*January 1 • *New Year's Day* • Begins with early morning Mass. The evening before is a family gathering with fireworks, merry making, and a midnight repast.

January 6 • *Feast of Three Kings* • Pageants in Santa Cruz, Gasan, and Marinduque.

January 9 • *Feast of the Black Nazarene* • Traditional procession in Quiapo, Metro Manila.

January 10 • *Fiesta de Santo Nino* • Feast of the Holy Child celebration all week in Cebu City.

January • *Pipigan* • Preparation of native delicacy in Noval-iches, Rizal. Toasted *malagkit* rice is pounded into pinipig to tune of guitars.

January • *Appey* • Three-day thanksgiving rites for a bountiful harvest. Celebrated in Bontoc, Mt. Province.

January • *Mannerway* • Exotic dance festival to awaken the Bontoc rain gods. Bontoc, Mt. Province.

January • *Ati-Atihan* • Rowdy Mardi-Gras-style fiesta involving Kalibo townsfolk dressed as either aboriginal Atis or sea-faring Borneans for three days of dancing and carousing in the streets. Watch for the festivities in Kalibo, Aklan.

January • *Constitution Day* • National celebration during third weekend to commemorate amended Philippine Constitution.

February • *Hari Raya Hadji* • Celebrated throughout the Moslem provinces to commemorate devotees annual pilgrimage to Mecca.

February • *Chinese New Year* • Dragon dances, opera, and plays on streets of Chinatown.

February 2 • *Feast of Our Lady of Candelaria* • Fiesta for patron saint of Jaro, Iloilo.

February 11 • *Tinagba* • Harvest festival and parade in Iriga City.

February 11 • *Feast of Our Lady of Lourdes* • Processions and masses held at the Shrine of the Virgin in Quezon City and the Grotto in Novaliches, Rizal.

February 14 • *Valentine's Day* • Celebrated nationally.

February 22–25 • People Power Anniversary.

February 24–25 • *Bale Zamboanga Festival* • Cultural shows, fairs, regattas, and religious services for both Christians and Moslems in Zamboanga City.

March • *Saranggolahan* • Regional kite-flying contests as prelude to summer season.

March • *Baguio Festival* • Week of culture and celebration in Philippines' summer capital, Baguio City.

March • *Iloilo Regatta* • Sea becomes dotted with racing *paraws* (native sailboats) in Iloilo City's bay.

March 10–16 • *Araw Ng Dabaw* • Religious processions, military parades, cultural fairs, and carnivals to mark founding of Davao City.

March 25 • *Sinulog* • Exotic tribal dance of religion and folklore preserved by Mundos tribe at Ilog, Negros Occidental.

Lenten Week • *Palm Sunday* • National holiday that ushers in the Holy Week.

Lenten Week • *Moriones Festival* • Marinduque townspeople hold spectacular Holy Week street pageant recalling the passion and the legend of Roman centurion named Longinus. Climax is the beheading of Longinus.

Lenten Week • *Holy Week* • Celebrated nationwide. The most solemn of all Philippine religious festivals. Good Friday is a public holiday.

*April 9 • *Bataan Day* • Tribute to the bravery of the defenders of Bataan Island during World War II. Filipinos and foreigners visit Ang Dambana ng Kagitingan, the Mt. Samat Shrine.

April 24 • *Magellan's Landing in Cebu City* • Local festival commemorates Ferdinand Magellan's historic landing in 1521 to "discover" the Philippine Archipelago for the Western World. Celebration takes place in Cebu City.

April • *Handugan* • Landing of ten Bornean *datus* on Panay Island. Celebrated during fourth week of April in San Jose, Antique.

April • *Feast of Virgen de Turumba* • Devotees jump, fall, leap, or dance while following image of Our Lady of Sorrows in procession. Pakil, Laguna.

*May 1 • *Labor Day* • National holiday to honor Filipino work force.

May 1–30 • *Santacruzan* • Cherished nationwide Filipino tradition of month-long Maytime festival. Procession-pageant recalls the quest of Queen Helena and Prince Constantine for the Holy Cross.

May 1–30 • *Flores de Mayo* • Evening processions and floral offerings nationwide to honor the Blessed Virgin.

May 1–30 • *Feast of Our Lady of Peace and Voyage* • Month-long pilgrimages to the shrine of travelers' miraculous patroness, Nuestra Sra. de la Paz y Buen Viaje in Antipolo, Rizal.

May 6 • *Fall of Corregidor* • Ceremonies in Corregidor commemorate the Battle of Corregidor in 1942.

May 7–8 • *International Sea Fair* • Annual international aquatic sportsfest in Balangit, Bataan.

May 14–15 • *Carabao Festival* • Farmers in *carabaos* pay respects to their patron saint, San Isidro Labrador, prior to games, contests, and merriment. Major festivities in Pulilan, Bulacan; Nueva Ecija; Angono, Rizal.

May 15 • *Harvest Festival "Pahiyas"* • This is another colorful celebration that honors San Isidro, in Lucban and Sariaya Quezon.

May 17–19 • *Fertility Rites* • Triple religious fete to honor San Pascual Baylon, Santa Clara, and Virgen de Salambao. Childless couples who participate in the fertility dance, it is said, will become parents. Obando, Bulacan, hosts the festivities.

June • *Pista Ng Krus* • Bountiful harvest procession. Obando, Bulacan.

June 12 • *Philippine Independence Day* • Nationwide celebrations. Most impressive is the military parade at Rizal Park.

June 24 • *Halaran Festival* • Re-enactment of the purchase of Panay Island by Bornean datus. Riotous tribal-type parades in Roxas City, Capiz.

June 24 • *Feast of St. John the Baptist* • Celebration of the baptism of Christ, in San Juan, Rizal.

June 24 • *Lechon Parade* • A procession that includes a crispy roast pig parade honors St. John the Baptist, in Balayan, Batangas.

June 27 • *Our Lady of Perpetual Help* • Major religious procession at Baclaran church in Rizal.

June 28–30 • *Saint Peter and Paul* • Celebrations highlighted by a procession of images along the Apalit River in Apalit, Pampanga.

June 29 • *Feast of San Pedro* • Elegant fair in honor of Davao City's patron saint.

July 1–30 • *Harvest Festival* • Tengao Fagfagto is a combination of Pagan and Christian rituals for a good harvest. The celebrations to see are in Mountain Province.

July 4 • *Filipino-American Friendship Day* • Public holiday throughout the islands.

July • *Bocaue River Festival* • Colorful barge procession the first Sunday in July, in Bocaue, Bulacan.

July 29 • *St. Martha River Festival* • This barge procession is held in Pateros, Rizal.

August 1–7 • *Dance of the Aetas* • Exotic tribal dances and songs at Bayombong, Nueva Ecija.

August 26 • *Cry of Balintawak* • National celebration commemorates the commencement of Filipino revolution against Spain.

August 28 • *Cagayan de Oro City Festival* • Colorful, rowdy pageants, parades, etc. in Cagayan de Oro City.

September • *Sunduan* • Traditional ritual when young men with parasols fetch young girls from their homes in La Huerta, Paranaque.

September • *Penafrancia Festival* • Image of the Blessed Virgin is returned to its home shrine via the Naga River in a spectacular boat procession. Held during the third week in Naga City, Camarines Sur.

*****September 21** • *National Day* • Public holiday commemorates the proclamation of Philippines' New Society by President Ferdinand Marcos in 1972.

October • *Davao Tribal Festival* • Highlanders perform tribal dances, songs, and traditional rituals. Held during the first week of October in Davao City.

October • *La Naval de Manila* • Night procession in honor of the Lady of the Holy Rosary to commemorate Filipino-Spanish victory over Dutch marauders in 1646. Held during the second Sunday in October at Santo Domingo Church, Quezon City.

October 3 • *Our Lady of Solitude* • Feast of the Blessed Virgin whose image was said to have been found in the sea. Festivities take place in Porta Vega, Cavite.

October 12 • *Feast of Our Lady of the Pillar* • Commemorates an apparition at Fort Pilar. Celebrated in Zamboanga City.

October 20 • *Landing of the Liberation Allied Forces* • Commemorates the World War II landing on Red Beach, Palo, Leyte.

October 21–24 • *Great Sibidan Race* • Native canoes race in Legaspi City.

October • *Pista Ng Apo* • Religious procession in honor of Jesus Christ and the Virgin Mary is held on the last Friday of October with sumptuous meals in Angeles City, Pampanga.

October • *Feast of Christ the King* • National all-male processions held throughout the country on last Sunday in October.

*****November 1** • *All Saints Day* • National holiday to pay homage to memories of the departed. Filipinos have their own versions of happenings on Halloween, the evening before.

November 2 • *All Souls Day* • Catholics throughout the country pray for souls of the dead.

November • *Hari Raya Poasa* • Moslem festival marks the end of Ramadan, the 30-day fasting period.

November 23 • *Feast of San Clemente* • Viva San Clemente parade in Angono, Rizal.

November 15–30 • *Yakan Harvest Festival* • Celebrated in Basilan, Zamboanga.

November 18–20 • *Kaamulan* • Tribal dances and rituals in Malaybalay, Bukidnon.

***November 30** • *National Heroes' Day* • Celebrants pay homage to the country's heroes.

December 8 • *Feast of Our Lady of the Immaculate Conception* □ Evening processions, cultural presentations, pageants, etc. in Roxas City, Capiz; Vigan, Ilocos Sur; Pasig, Metro Manila.

December 8 • *Malabon Fluvial Parade* • Procession in Malabon, Rizal.

December 8–9 • *Taal Fluvial Festival* • Rustic river procession is set against the country's twin volcanoes in Taal, Batangas.

December 12 • *Pagsanjan Town Fiesta* • Bamboo arches are set up in this town, famous for its gorge and rapids.

December 16–25 • *Simbang Gabi* • Longest Christmas in the world is ushered in by a nine-day novena in pre-dawn masses throughout the country.

December 24 • *Panunuluyan* • Regional Christmas Eve pageants.

December 24 • *Lantern Festival* • Christmas Eve parade of "paroles" in San Fernando, Pampanga.

***December 25** • *Christmas Day* • Most joyous occasion in every Christian Filipino home.

December 26 • *Bota de Flores* • Floral offerings to the Neustra Sra. de Guia at the Ermita Church, Metro Manila.

December 28 • *Holy Innocents' Day* • Filipino version of April Fool's Day throughout the country.

***December 30** • *Rizal Day* • National celebration to honor Dr. Jose Rizal, greatest of Filipino heroes.

BACKGROUND MATERIAL:

Philippines (apa productions). Excellent photos and text.
Readings in Philippine History by Father Horatio de la Costa.
Traditional Handicraft of the Philippines by Roberto de los Reyes.
The Culinary Culture of the Philippines by Gilda C. Fernando.
A Question of Identity by Carmen Guerrero.

THINGS FILIPINO   means that this fun-loving country of people is most hospitable to visitors. Filipinos enter right into the spirit of whatever is happening, wherever they are, and expect you to do the same. Return the smile, and you will be returning a favor. The following are a few things that may not be particularly useful in your travels around this archipelago, but they are certainly of interest.

Lambanog • A potent alcoholic drink, especially popular in the provinces . . . natives of Samar are said to have offered it to Magellan.

Bagoong • Popular condiment often called the poor man's caviar . . . fermented mixture of fresh anchovies and salt . . . used to flavor vegetable dishes.

Bayanihan • Embodiment of closeness that Filipinos feel for one another . . . Pilipino term for "old team spirit."

Canao • Religious rite performed by mountain provinces natives . . . sacrificial pig is roasted . . . much native wine drunk . . . dancing lasts for several days.

Harana • Shy swains sing love songs on moonlit nights . . . still popular in the provinces . . . although songs have changed somewhat.

Ulog • Communal courting place for young people of the northern mountains . . . test their compatibility here . . . mountain marriages very stable.

Yo-yo • The world's favorite toy is said to have its origins in the Philippines . . . once used as missile weapon . . . skillful Filipinos can do amazing tricks.

MANILA

MANILA IN A CAPSULE

4 million plus people in the metropolitan area . . . originally a small Moslem settlement . . . old city founded in 1571 by Spanish conquistadors . . . encompasses Intramuros as well as Ermita, Pasay City, Baclaran, Makati commercial district, and Quezon City . . . Cultural Center of the Philippines, built on land reclaimed from Manila Bay, was the pride of Mme. Marcos . . . 90-acre Nayong Philipino (Philippine Village) located near international airport offers touristic view of entire country . . . Roxas Boulevard follows Manila Bay and has become the hotel and entertainment center of city . . . one of most colorful, vibrant, and sophisticated areas in entire Far East . . . complete contraposition to rest of archipelago.

WHAT TO SEE AND DO

Metro Manila

Chinatown • Older than city itself . . . center of a flourishing trade in the 12th century . . . considered primary ghetto for over one million Filipino-Chinese . . . enter by foot or *calesa* (horse-drawn rig) at corner of Rizal and Recto streets . . . sidestep touts . . . local restaurants and herbal shops excellent . . . also handmade jewelry . . . Plaza Santa Cruz on Calle Florentino Torres fronts church built by Jesuits in 1608 for Chinese converts . . . taxi to **Chinese Cemetery,** garish blend of Catholic and Buddhist mausoleums with two dragon-temples in the center.

Cultural Center • Pride of the former first lady and governor of Metro Manila, Imelda Marcos . . . built on 1700 acres of land reclaimed from Manila Bay . . . cost untold millions and millions . . . primarily designed by Leandro ''Lucky'' Locsin, the country's favorite local architect . . . complex contains design and exhibition halls, performing arts centers, libraries, museums, and studios . . . impressive convention complex includes Philippine Plaza Hotel . . . 90-day wonder **Folk Arts Theatre** was hastily constructed for the 1974 Miss Universe Pageant . . . watch for more and more . . . reclamation continues as the complex threatens to become a new and self-contained city . . . don't miss **Tourism Pavilion, Manila Film Centre,** and **Design Centre of the Philippines.**

Ermita • Section of Metro Manila known as the "tourist strip" . . . foreigners frequent bars, restaurants, and shops . . . fraternize with local bohemians of artistic nature . . . popular now with busloads of Japanese.

Escolta • Old shopping center . . . originally the commercial center of Manila . . . reachable by MacArthur Bridge across Pasig River . . . part of avenue leading to Binondo is still cobblestoned . . . proud old buildings still standing, though less fashionable now . . . area also leads to Plaza Santa Cruz.

Fort Santiago • Located along old Aduana St. . . . took 149 years for Spanish to complete this bastion on the site of Raja Sulayman's (Manila's defeated ruler) original bamboo stockade . . . former military headquarters of occupying forces . . . now popular tourist site . . . contains Rajah Sulayman open-air theater and museum honoring national patriot Dr. Jose Rizal . . . nice walks among preserved ruins.

Intramuros • Walled city of Manila . . . glimpse of colonial past . . . portions of walls, gates, and ramparts restored . . . originally built by Spanish in early 16th century . . . attacked by Chinese warlord Lim Ah-hong in 1574 . . . gutted by fire in 1583 and rebuilt in 1590 . . . moat added in 1603 when all entrances to city closed at night . . . moat filled during American administration to combat disease . . . old city remained intact until bombing raids and fires at end of World War II . . . a sense of history still stands.

Makati • Former airstrip . . . now plush commercial section of city . . . modern high rises and hotels, shopping malls, and parks . . . edged by Santa Ana Race Track and fabulous Forbes Park where the elite all live behind high walls topped with broken glass . . . **Ayala Aviary** at Greenbelt . . . **Ayala Museum** depicts Philippine culture and history through dioramas . . . visit also **Libingan Ng Mga Bayani** (Graveyard of the Heroes) American Memorial Cemetery where 1700 allied are buried . . . largest U.S. military cemetery in another land.

Las Pinas Church • Built in 1794 by Spanish friar Diego Ceva
. . . best known for its famous **Bamboo Organ** . . . constructed in
the early 19th century of 950 bamboo pipes . . . church damaged in
1850 and organ lay undiscovered until 1972 . . . organ shipped to Germany for restoration . . . has been in service regularly since 1975 . . .
church located just past Paranaque section on way out of city.

Malacanang Palace • Official residence of Philippine heads of state
. . . name means "A noble lives in that place" . . . large complex of
elegant state apartments and guest houses . . . luxurious gardens . . .
fine collections of Chinese trade porcelains, Filipino paintings, Asian
and European treasures . . . an important tourist attraction . . . located
in San Miguel section between J. P. Laurel Street and Pasig River . . .
gardens occasionally accessible. Mrs. Aquino does not live here . . .
she declared upon assuming office "It is not fitting for the leader of an
impoverished nation to live in extravagance" . . . but Mme. Marcos'
shoe collection can be viewed as the palace is now open to the public.

Manila Cathedral • Across from Fort Santiago . . . original church
on this site built in 1571 of *nipa* (Philippine palm) . . . natural disasters
and fire caused four additional cathedrals to be constructed here . . .
latest devastation took place during bloody Battle of Manila at end of
World War II . . . present structure dates from modern times . . .
Italian sculptors are responsible for frontal statues and bronze doors . . .
Plaza Roma facing Cathedral is sister to Piazzale Manila in Rome.

Manila Hotel • A national landmark overlooking the bay at end of
Roxas Blvd. . . . commissioned by American governor-general William Howard Taft in 1908 . . . designed by New York architect William Parsons in California mission-style . . . opened for business 1912
and immediate watering hole for city's elite set . . . 5th floor penthouse
added in late '30s when "American Caesar," General Douglas Mac-
Arthur insisted upon accommodations equal in luxury to Malacanang
Palace . . . headquarters for Japanese during World War II, who shot
up interior before retreating . . . a fine monument to Philippine history
and culture . . . not to be missed . . . MacArthur Suite renovated and
filled with memorabilia of the general, including numerous photographs
and some of his medals.

Nayong Pilipino • Located in Pasay City adjacent to International
Airport . . . a 90-acre tourist attraction showcasing Filipino traditions
and cultures among the multi-island ethnic groups . . . village minia-
tures from different regions . . . typical architectural styles, products
and cottage industries from throughout archipelago . . . plus replicas

of famous tourist attractions . . . handicrafts available in small "authentic" shops and main administrative building . . . open daily with small admission charge . . . another pet project of Mme. Marcos.

Quezon City • Part of Metro Manila . . . antithesis of Makati and Roxas Blvd. areas . . . center of University of the Philippines as well as government service buildings . . . rather sprawling and ugly area . . . overpopulated . . . overcongested with automobiles.

Quiapo • District in heart of Manila famous for church with **Shrine of the Black Nazarene** . . . life-size image in black wood carved by Mexican Indians in 17th century . . . brought to Manila by a Spanish galleon . . . feast of the Black Nazarene celebrated by mammoth January afternoon procession . . . barefooted devotees carry image through local streets . . . church fronts on historic Plaza Miranda . . . colorful area full of itinerant vendors . . . good for photographs and curio seekers.

Rizal Park • Named in honor of Filipino martyr and national hero . . . Dr. Jose P. Rizal . . . monument stands on exact spot where he was executed in 1896 . . . an oasis at the end of Roxas Blvd. . . . Chinese and Japanese gardens . . . topographical map of the Philippines . . . lighted pools . . . multi-colored **Agrifina Circle Fountain** . . . ideal for skating . . . band offers open-air concerts late afternoons . . . visit also **planetarium** with 16-meter dome . . . accommodates 300 viewers.

Roxas Boulevard • One of finest boulevards in the Far East . . . extends along Manila Bay from the airport to the old city . . . lined with deluxe hotels, shops, restaurants . . . dominated by new Cultural Center complex and office towers . . . Manila Yacht Club . . . U.S. Embassy . . . Army and Navy Club . . . **Museum of Philippine Arts** . . . all located on bayside of the boulevard . . . quite an experience . . . quite a sight.

San Augustin Church • Originally built of *nipa* in 1571 . . . present structure dates from 1599–1606 and considered oldest stone church in country . . . miraculously spared during 1945 World War II bombings of Intramuros . . . church located near intersection of General Luna and Calle Real streets . . . guarded by Chinese stone lions . . . interior decorated by Italian painters . . . chandeliers from France . . . hand-carved Philippine wood choir-loft . . . cloister and gardens beautiful . . . monastery-museum houses extensive collection of religious art . . . valuable manuscripts . . . artifacts of note.

University of Santo Tomas • Founded in 1611 . . . oldest university in the Far East . . . beats Harvard by 25 years . . . known affectionately as U.S.T. by Filipinos . . . source of great pride to the country . . . university press housed in small building on campus . . . founded in 1̃592 . . . university also has first-rate museum . . . rare manuscript collection of some 12,000 volumes . . . campus located at Mendoza and Espana avenues . . . short taxi ride from Malacanang Palace.

Luzon Islands

Baguio • Only heaven could be more refreshing . . . resort town and cultural center nestled some 5000 feet high in Cordillera Mountains . . . year-round temperatures average 65° F . . . developed by colonial rulers as a summer retreat from the heat of the lowlands . . . several universities here bring in many interesting youth who stay on . . . cool and invigorating pine-scented air . . . bountiful flowers and vegetables in public market daily . . . beautiful vistas . . . comfortable accommodations and recreation available . . . plenty to visit . . . **Rizal Park** with Tower of Peace and Filipino-Chinese Friendship garden, **Burnham Park, Mines View Park** . . . silversmiths making items at St. Louis University . . . Easter school with Igorot hand looms . . . **Mansion House** was official summer residence of the former first family . . . Camp John Hay U.S. Air Force recreation center . . . 900-plus **Philippine Military Academy . . . Mirador Hill** with unobstructed view (beneath power lines) of Lingayen Gulf, Ilocos coastline, and South China Sea . . . about 5 hours' hard drive from Manila . . . less than an hour by scheduled flights . . . watch the runway.

Banaue Rice Terraces • Monument to skill and patience of Ifugaos tribal artisans some 2000 years ago . . . considered "eighth wonder of the world" by locals . . . terraces rise like giant stairway to the sky for almost 2 miles . . . placed end to end, would be 10 times longer than the Great Wall of China . . . irrigated from the top by manmade waterfalls cascading down through walls to valley below . . . photographer's paradise . . . Ifugaos still inhabit countryside . . . area is several hours' drive from Baguio . . . helicopter tours available. Some of best rice terraces found outside Banaue . . . like Batad, Banga-an, Duclingan, and Mayoyao . . . April to July best months . . . visit also small villages along the way.

Batangas • Historic province southwest of Manila and accessible by land, air, and sea. Known as birthplace of Philippine heroes and statesmen, i.e., Apolinario Mabini and Jose Laurel . . . originally called Bonbon or Balayan . . . rich soil formed from eruptions of Taal Volcano . . . many tourist attractions such as **Matabungkay Beach** situated on China Sea . . . **Taal Volcano,** reputed to be smallest in the world . . . **Lobo Submarine Garden . . . Submarine Caves** beneath the slopes of Mounts Pulangsaya and Kamantigue in San Juan town . . . **Taal Church,** reputed to be largest in Far East, was constructed in 1858 . . . its facade, which resembles St. Peter's Basilica in Rome, can be seen for miles . . . **Mabini Shrine and Mausoleum** contains relics of Filipino patriot in Bo Talaga . . . and **Isla Verde,** resort island with white sand beaches.

Corregidor • The Rock at the entrance of Manila Bay . . . here Filipino and American forces held last stand during Japanese invasion . . . mile-long barracks and anti-aircraft guns on this rocky fortress immortalize this famous battle of 1942 . . . means "to correct" in Spanish, named so because all ships entering Manila Bay stopped here for documentation checks . . . island now reachable from the city by a 50-minute hydrofoil ride . . . plans and funds by both U.S. and Filipino congressmen to restore the island . . . even create overnight facilities for visitors.

Ilocos • North of Luzon . . . best reachable by air . . . region has romantic past with many baroque churches . . . **Paoay Lake** said to contain remains of town that sank due to a curse . . . **Paoay Church** built in 1699 is famous for mixture of Gothic, baroque, and Oriental architecture . . . Vigan is a virtual museum town . . . known as Intramuros of the north . . . portrait of Spanish colonial town . . . **St. Paul Metropolitan Church** built three centuries ago . . . lavishly adorned gold altar.

Legaspi • Southern Luzon . . . best reached by air . . . spectacular attraction here is 8000-foot **Mayon Volcano . . .** semiactive and conal shape said to be one of most perfect in world . . . erupts about every decade . . . visit also ruins of **Cagsawa** . . . only the church steeple and a few walls remain from the once busy town buried by lava and mud flows.

Los Banos • Nestled at foot of mystical **Mt. Makiling** . . . town famous for its thermal springs . . . health-restoring properties in the waters . . . University of Philippines Agricultural College located here . . . lovely green setting . . . excellent environment for learning.

Pagsanjan • Rather quaint Laguna town with Spanish look . . . most famous for its waterfalls . . . shooting the rapids in a *banca* (dugout canoe) through churning currents is not for the meek . . . although expert boatmen steer, the craft shoots between boulders at top speed.

Tagaytay • Resort some 2250 feet above sea level . . . perched on a ridge overlooking Lake Taal and the lowest volcano in the world

. . . Lake Taal boasts the only volcano with a crater rising out of the lake of its original crater . . . new crater has its own lake and island . . . interesting to see . . . situated about a 1½-hour drive south of Manila.

La Union • Located about a 1½-hour drive southeast of Baguio . . . towns of **San Fernando** (founded in 1850 in honor of King Ferdinand of Spain), **Agoo** (founded in 1578 by Friar John Baptist of Pisaro), and **Bauang** (dates from 1815 and word means "garlic" in Ilocano) are primary tourist destinations . . . Bauang actually "beach resort capital" of the country . . . many small resort hotels available here . . . good base for watersports and exploring.

Tours

Manila and Suburbs • 3 hours, daily . . . begins at the Cultural Center and goes along Roxas Blvd. to Rizal Park, Intramuros, Church of San Augustin, Manila Cathedral, Fort Santiago, Pasig River . . . to the University of Santo Tomas, Makati, Forbes Park, Manila American Cemetery Memorial.

Manila Bay Sunset Cruise • 2 hours, daily . . . comfortable cruiser departs Manila Yacht Club to sail along the edge of one of the world's finest natural harbors . . . city lights sparkle from afar . . drinks available at the cash bar . . . romantic guitar music highlights the mood.

Nayong Pilipino (Philippine Village) • 3 hours, daily . . . situated near Manila International Airport . . . 90-acre site represents 6 major regions of the Philippines—Moslem, Visayas, Mountain Provinces, Ilocos, Southern Tagalog, Bicol . . . transportation around grounds by motorcoach, jeepney, or on foot . . . Museum of Philippine Traditional Cultures has life-size models and rare artifacts from different ethnic groups . . . visit cave-dwelling Tasadays or seafaring Badjaos . . . tour also includes Manila American Cemetery and Memorial in Fort Bonifacio.

Manila by Night • 3 hours, daily . . . begins at jai alai fronton where Spanish and Filipino *pelotaris* vie . . . dinner and show at elegant supper club . . . popular nightclub for dancing.

Museum Tour • 3 hours, daily . . . begins at Cultural Center of the Philippines . . . view Filipino paintings in main gallery . . . collection of porcelains, antique jewelry, Moslem artifacts, and ethnic musical instruments . . . National Museum at Rizal Park to view permanent collection . . . Intramuros and San Augustin Church to visit museums there . . . ends at Ayala Museums in Makati . . . dioramas of historic events . . . Filipino costumes . . . models of ships and boats used by early inhabitants.

Corregidor Tour • 4–6 hours, daily . . . hovercraft across Manila Bay to The Rock . . . last Filipino-American fortress to fall during Japanese invasion . . . allied troops on Corregidor held enemy at bay for 5 months . . . will always be honored for their perseverance and bravery . . . considered one of the bitterest episodes of World War II . . . many veterans who survived the Bataan Death March make a pilgrimage here . . . The Rock was recaptured by American parachute troops in early 1945 . . . the suffering here cannot be described . . . among the historic sites visited are Malinta Tunnel . . . General Douglas MacArthur's headquarters, field hospital, and supply depot during siege . . . Pacific War Memorial and eternal Flame of Freedom . . . silent plain at Bottomside where gallant Filipino-American garrison, some 10,000 men strong, finally surrendered.

Tagaytay • 4 hours, daily . . . features drive to Tagaytay ridge to view Taal volcano . . . visit to Church of Las Pinas to see world's only bamboo organ . . . tour of a local jeepney factory.

Pagsanjan • 8 hours, daily . . . colorful country scenery, volcanoes, Laguna de Bay (country's largest lake), native villages . . . highlight is "shooting the rapids" in *banca* through waterfalls from 300-foot cliffs . . . take your bathing suit and a plastic bag for your camera . . . tour may also include a drive through Lake Caliraya and brief stop at International Rice and Research Institute in Los Banos where "miracle rice" was developed.

HOTELS

Metro Manila

★★★**Century Park Sheraton** • *corner of Vito Cruz and M. Adriatico avenues. Tel: 50–60–41. Cable: CENPARK MANILA. Telex: CPH 27791* • 510 rooms . . . all accommodations with private balcony . . . 20-story high rise 2 blocks from Roxas Bld. and Convention Center . . . 6-story high atrium lobby . . . rare tropical birds in huge cages . . . adjacent to Harrison Plaza, one of largest shopping complexes in Philippines.
Facilities: Top of the Century cocktail lounge with buffet lunches

and dinners on 19th floor. Badjao Filipino restaurant serves American breakfast buffet from 7–9 a.m. AOI Japanese restaurant. Peacock Chinese restaurant. Cafe in the Park for coffee and pastries on lobby floor. Iberia grill. Kachina Lounge for nightclub entertainment. Cellar disco. Half-acre swimming pool and health center. Convention facilities and businessmen's area. Medical, travel, airline offices in-house.

Manager: P. Stevens. *Reservations:* SHERATON INT'L.

★★**Holiday Inn** • *3001 Roxas Blvd. Tel: 59–79–61. Cable: HOLIDAY INN MANILA. Telex: 63487* • 370 rooms . . . another high rise . . . directly across from Cultural Center . . . nice views of Manila Bay from all rooms . . . typical Holiday Inn style and atmosphere.

Facilities: Baron's Table continental restaurant. Baron's Bar. Cafe Vienna coffee shop. El Camarote bar with live entertainment. Delicatessen corner. Tsismisan Lounge in lobby. Paseo del Sol poolside snack bar. Outdoor swimming pool. Embassy Ballroom. Business Center.

Reservations: HOLIDEX.

★★★**Hyatt Regency Manila** • *2702 Roxas Blvd. Tel: 80–26– 11. Cable: HYATT MANILA. Telex: PN 3344* • 265 rooms (31 suites) . . . flagship of the Hyatt chain in the Philippines . . . designed by Filipino architect Leandro Locsin . . . plush appointments by Dale Keller Associates . . . 9 guest room floors . . . all accommodations with private balconies and fine views over Manila Bay and Cultural Center . . . 8th floor Regency Club.

Facilities: La Hacienda 24-hour coffee shop. Mandarin Room Chinese and Tempura-Misono Japanese restaurants. Calesa bar. Hugo's gourmet restaurant. The Gallery for local art exhibitions. Crystal Ballroom. Outdoor swimming pool with cascade waterfall and bar. Medical/dental clinic. Businessmen's Centre.

Manager: F. P. Quicho. *Reservations:* HYATT INT'L.

★★★**Manila Pavilion** • *United Nations Ave., Ermita. Tel: 57–37– 11. Telex: 722–3387* • 416 rooms (23 suites). A 22-story tower . . . one of city's tallest buildings . . . terrific views from top . . . non-smoking rooms on the 15th floor . . . Executive 19th floor . . . 2 rooms for handicapped guests . . . hotel loaded with activity and entertainment . . . considered one of the ''older'' and more established hostelries in town. Hilton has relinquished its operating contract with this hotel . . . has been sold to Australian investment group.

Facilities: Ecumenical Chapel on 5th floor for daily masses, weddings, etc. Top of the Hilton luncheon buffets with fashion shows, later Supper Club with Karilagan Dance Group. Rotisserie Grillroom. Cafe Coquilla (coffee shop). Toh Yuen Chinese provincial cuisine. Swimming pool with terrace on 5th floor and health club. Sultana lobby piano bar. The Music Room cocktail lounge with local musical entertainment. Coral Ballroom.

★★★★★**Manila Hotel** • *Rizal Park. Tel: 47–00–11. Cable: MANILHOTEL. Telex: 3496* • 570 rooms . . . owned by Philippine government . . . one of the former first lady's pet projects . . . a national landmark . . . originally built in 1908 . . . fully renovated in 1976 by the team of architect Leandro Locsin and interior designer Dale Keller . . . one of the most historic and renowned hotels in the Far East . . . lousy manana-type service when I was there . . . guest book reads like an international *Who's Who* since 1912 . . . barring war and local disasters, hotel has been in service for 75 years . . . MacArthur Suite in original building still a draw . . . sells for over $1000 per day . . . Penthouse Suite in new 18-story tower overlooking Manila Bay is over $1500 per day.

Facilities: Lovely old-world lobby with adjacent lounge/bar. Tap Room Bar with local entertainment. Apres Disco. Sea Breeze Grill (outdoor barbecues). Champagne Room with 1890s atmosphere and Manila Symphony violinists. Maynila Filipino cuisine and entertainment restaurant. Cowrie Grill for steaks and seafood. Rome Ristorante Italiano. Cafe Ilang-Ilang coffee shop. Bay Club sports center, with swimming pool, tennis courts, sauna. Executive Services Center.

Manager: M. G. Cerqueda. *Reservations:* DISTINGUISHED HOTELS.

★★★★★**Manila Inter-Continental** • *Ayala Ave., Makati Commercial Center. Tel: 89–40–11. Cable: INHOTELCOR. Telex: RCA 7222212* • 420 rooms . . . Pioneer luxury hotel in Makati . . . splendid long-time reputation . . . a favorite with business executives . . . large acreage amid the commercial center . . . overlooks fabulous Forbes Park . . . also known as millionaire's row . . . accommodations not so splashy and plush as some newer hostelries in town . . . but always under impeccable management.

Facilities: La Terrasse for light snacks off lobby. Gambrinus businessmen's club—women welcome after 5 p.m.! Le Boulevadier cocktail lounge. Romantic Prince Albert Rotisserie. Bahia seafood restaurant on rooftop, with elegant buffets. Colorful and fun Jeepney coffee shop. Large swimming pool in shape of female figure with tennis club and Bermuda-grass grounds. Jogging map in every room takes executives through paved section of Forbes Park. Sol y Sombra poolside snack bar. Where Else disco. Meeting facilities. Adjacent to Makati Commercial Center.

Manager: D. Garrido. *Reservations:* IHC.

★★★★**Mandarin Oriental Manila** • *corner Makati Ave. and Paseo de Roxas. Tel: 816–3601. Cable: MANDAHOTEL MANILA. Telex: 63756 MANDA PN* • 470 rooms (20 suites) . . . member of prestigious Mandarin chain . . . offers fleet of white Mercedes Benz 200s . . . circular lobby . . . overly air-conditioned high rise designed by Filipino architect Leandro Locsin . . . interiors by British consultant Don Ashton have just received $11.5 million refurbishment throughout . . . 18th floor has Mandarin Suite with own private outdoor swimming pool . . . plus 5 other special suites (Persian, Georgian, Hong Kong, Philippine, Oriental) . . . artwork and ambiance a blend of European and native works . . . convenient to Makati commercial buildings . . . very tedious and over-trafficked ride to downtown Manila.

Facilities: Carousel Bar off 2-story lobby. Clipper Lounge overlooking lobby. Tivoli restaurant. New Cantonese-style restaurant. L'Hirondelle French restaurant. Marquee coffee shop. Large swimming pool with bar, and Barrio Fiesta buffets on Sunday evenings. Nash Room for private functions. Business Center with IBM PC.

Manager: D. Pauwaert. *Reservations:* LHW.

★★★★**Manila Peninsula** • *Ayala and Makati avenues. Tel: 85–77–11. Cable: PENHOT MANILA. Telex: 22507 PEN PH* • 537 rooms (21 suites) . . . member of the famed Peninsula Group . . . opposite Makati Commercial Complex . . . terrific 4-story lobby with a 24-hour life . . . most gracious personnel in town . . . 2 high-rise towers of 11 floors each . . . helipad with direct access to Presidential Suite . . . fleet of Ford and Mercedes Benz limousines for guest transportation . . . public relations/social directress (Mila Magsaysay Valenzuela) is the daughter of a beloved former Philippine president . . . a lovely person who adds grace and dignity to the hotel . . . however, still some distance from downtown Manila.

Facilities: Old Manila grillroom. La Chesa Swiss specialty restaurant. La Bodega coffee shop. Tipanan cocktail lounge with nightly entertainment. The 4-story Lobby—a modern edition of the famed lobby in The Pen (Hong Kong). Rigodon Ballroom. Business Centre. The Cake Shop. Swimming pool and snack bar. Hatch & Reed fitness center. The Valet Shop. 3000-square-foot Presidential Suite with accommodations for guard plus valet, and easy access to helipad.

Reservations: SRS.

★★★★**Philippine Plaza** • *Cultural Center complex, Roxas Blvd. Tel: 832–0701. Cable: PHILPLAZA MLA. Telex: 742–0443* • 676 rooms (62 suites) . . . owned by the Cultural Center . . . chairman and founder was former first lady Imelda Marcos who maintained the Royal Suite for private parties and friends . . . designed inside and out by Leandro Locsin . . . located within Cultural Center complex . . . dramatic lobby area . . . large adjacent convention facilities . . . spectacular outdoor pool and gardens on edge of Manila Bay . . . built entirely on reclaimed land . . . hotel managed by Westin International . . . vies with Manila Hotel for title of nation's guest house . . . definitely worth a visit just to admire interior if nothing else.

Facilities: Most spectacular outdoor pool in Asia, with Treasure Island bar in middle. *Pistahan* cultural show and buffet dinners at poolside. Plazaspa resort/health club with 4 tennis courts. Abelardo's Continental Restaurant with serenades. Pier 7 Steak and Seafood. The Galley bar/pub. Cafe Fiesta coffee shop. Siete Pecados cocktail/entertainment lounge. Lost Horizon disco. Lobby Court cocktail lounge. Executive Center. Fleet of Mercedes-Benz and complimentary shuttle service to Makati commercial area.

Reservations: WESTIN HOTELS.

★★**Silahis International Hotel** • *1990 Roxas Blvd. Tel: 57–38–11. Cable: SILATEL MANILA. Telex: 63163 SILTEL PN* • 600 rooms . . . flagship of Sulo Group hotels . . . Philippine owned and managed . . . famous as home of the Playboy Club of Manila . . . Silahis means "rays of the sun" . . . excellent location between Cultural Center complex and Rizal Park . . . unimpressive structure and decor.

Facilities: Playboy Club of Manila on 3rd floor, with game/library/conference rooms, VIP Grill, Playmate and Bunny bars and health club. Sunburst coffee shop. Bienvenida piano bar. Capriccio Italian cuisine restaurant. New Stargazer Lounge on 19th floor, with glass elevator. Los Mares Ballroom.

Reservations: UTELL.

Manila Environs

Banaue Hotel and Youth Hostel • *Banaue, Ifugao* • 20 rooms in hotel/30 beds in dormitory . . . perched on mountainside . . . overlooking Poitan Rice Terraces . . . all hotel rooms have balconies with panoramic views . . . about 240 steps to a typical Ifugao village . . . famous Banaue viewpoint about a 20-minute drive from the hotel . . . new Trade Center full of local souvenirs about a 29-minute hike . . . best accommodations in area . . . owned and operated by Tourism Ministry.

Facilities: Fabulous vistas from both hotel and hostel. Outdoor swimming pool. Filipino/Continental restaurant and bar.

Manager: G. Macagba. *Reservations:* Philippine Tourism Authority.

Baguio Park Hotel • *Harrison Rd./P. Claudio St., Baguio City. Tel: 56–26. Telex: 7420329 Rajah PM* • 65 rooms . . . Rajtour . . .

located in front of Baguio's famous Burnham Park . . . easily accessible to middle of town . . . not up to Hyatt standards but better than most of the others.

Facilities: Cafe by the Park. Beer patio. Liu Fu Chinese restaurant.
Reservations: Rajah Tours/Philippines, Inc.

Cresta Ola Beach Resort Hotel • *Bauang, La Union. Tel: 09–2983* • 20 rooms . . . also owned and operated by Tourism Authority . . . situated on Lingayen Gulf . . . swimming pool . . . air-conditioned rooms . . . Filipino/continental restaurant . . . good watersports.

Manager: R. Sanchez. *Reservations:* Philippine Tourism Authority.

★★★**Hyatt Terraces Baguio** • *South Drive, Baguio City. Tel: 56–70/57–80. Cable: HYATT MANILA. Telex: 2920 TERRACES PU* • 303 rooms (49 suites) . . . the only deluxe establishment in town . . . interesting design . . . unusual interior . . . similar to Hyatt Regency's in U.S. . . . all rooms with balconies and views . . . but I'd check out amenities (showers, plugs) before unpacking . . . property adjacent to Camp John Hay's extensive sports facilities (golf, tennis) . . . 4 duplex penthouse suites available.

Facilities: Copper Grill gourmet restaurant. Hanazono Japanese restaurant. Kaili coffee shop. Hunter's Pub for mood music. Gold Mine disco. Indoor heated pool. Conference/banquet rooms.
Manager: H. Maulbecker. *Reservations:* HYATT INT'L.

International Spiritual Center and Resorts (ISCR) • *Lucnab, Baguio City. Tel: 69–06. Telex: 27955 ISCR PH* • 55-plus rooms . . . offers seminars in spiritualism and psychic knowledge . . . 16-acre property . . . main lodge plus cottages . . . hotellike rooms.

Facilities: Japanese gardens and teahouse. Interfaith chapel. Fish pond. Swimming pool. Shuttle service to city center. Restaurant. 100-room beach resort in San Fernando, La Union also in progress.
Reservations: ISCR.

Pagsanjan Falls Lodge and Summer Resort • *Pagsanjan. Tel: 645–1251* • 28 rooms in cottages and houseboats . . . nothing fancy . . . but if you want to shoot the rapids more than once. . . .
Reservations: Direct.

Pagsanjan Rapids Hotel • *Pagsanjan. Tel: 645–1258* • 38 rooms. Take your pick . . . but only if you enjoy rusticity.
Reservations: Direct.

Mt. Data Lodge • *Mt. Data (100 km) Mountain Province* • 8 rooms
. . . located halfway between Baguio and Banaue . . . 8-room lodge
owned and operated by Tourism Ministry . . . nestled in mountains
some 7200 feet above sea level . . . very quiet . . . recommended
highly for honeymooners or mountain climbers.
Reservations: Philippine Tourism Authority.

★★★★**Puerto Azul Beach and Country Club** • *Ternate, Cavite.*
Cable: TERNATEL MANILA. Telex: 64546 Azutel, PN • 350 rooms . . .
located at Puerto Azul beach . . . about a 75-minute drive from Philippine Village Hotel in Manila . . . operated by same Sulo Group . . .
buses run 3 times daily between 2 properties . . . accommodations in
cluster of cottages . . . rooms all have balconies and deluxe amenities . . .
Facilities: Wide variety of watersports. Horseback riding. Outdoor
swimming pool, jacuzzi, and health spa. Game rooms. 27-hole golf
course. Sports village with 12 tennis courts, squash courts, pelota/ badminton courts, bowling, etc. Meeting and convention areas. 6 separate
dining/entertainment areas.
Reservations: UTELL.

Ruff Inn • *1 Maryhills, Loakan Airport, Baguio City. Tel: 22–18*
• 30 rooms . . . rustic lodge located near airstrip . . . in a former
Benguet village . . . family-run inn . . . friendly atmosphere . . . simple
ambiance in accommodations . . . some attic apartments with fire-
places for family groups.
Facilities: Home-style dining room. Conference facilities. Hotel-
organized tours.
Manager: J. Ruff. Reservations: Direct.

★★★**Taal Vista Lodge** • *Tagaytay City (c/o Resort Hotels Corp.,*
Alco Bldg., 391 Buendia Ave. Manila. Tel: 818–0811 or 88–23–82) •
Situated some 2500 feet above sea level . . . overlooks Taal volcano
and lake . . . 25 deluxe rooms with private patio . . . great views
everywhere . . . hotel tourist bus daily to and from Manila . . . about
one hour by road . . . good place to relax after shooting the rapids at
Pagsanjan Falls . . . first ladies of the world met here during the 1960s.
Facilities: Restaurant, bar, disco. Conference facilities. Camping
grounds adjacent. Some sports.
Manager: M. T. Castro. *Reservations:* Resort Hotels Corp.

MINDANAO ISLANDS

MINDANAO IN A CAPSULE

Second only to Luzon in size . . . southernmost of the Philippine archipelago's 11 largest islands . . . varied in shape and topography . . . dramatic and beautiful . . . abundant in natural resources . . . minerals, iron, nickel, wood, copper, silver, gold, and perhaps oil . . . agriculturally important with pineapple, corn, coffee, cacao, etc. . . . home of the Moro (Moslem) who have now become a minority in their own land . . . hence, considerable unrest here between the traditional population and the newly arrived Christians from neighboring Visayas . . . also home of one of the world's most obscure tribes, the Tasaday . . . unfortunately impossible to see . . . island less than 2 hours from Manila by jet.

WHAT TO SEE AND DO

Anguinaldo Pearl Farm • Situated on Samal Island . . . an hour from Davao City across the gulf . . . more attractive for pleasant resort with beach and paddleboats . . . nonfunctioning pearl farm . . . excellent also for swimming and scuba diving.

Barter Market • Tax-free items from neighboring countries . . . don't expect more than sandalwood soap, some tape recorders, and the local noodles, *sotanghon* . . . Chinese porcelains . . . Moslem brass and handwoven tribal cloths are good buys . . . but remember to play the game and bargain!

Buddhist Temple • Located on Leon Garcia St. in city center . . . Davao has largest Chinese population in Mindanao . . . also known as Little Japan, and plenty of kilawin or sashimi is available in local restaurants.

Cagayan De Oro • City of Golden Friendship . . . lies on a plain in the midst of the north coast . . . surrounded by lush and rolling hills . . . astride the Philippine-Japanese Friendship Highway . . . gateway to Del Monte Pineapple Plantation . . . excellent harbor . . . many government offices and banks.

Cagayan River • Flows through the middle of the sprawling city . . . visit Gaston Park on the west bank . . . San Augustin Cathedral . . . Lourdes College . . . Xavier University has interesting museums . . . Huluga Caves an exciting excursion from the city center . . . Machambus Caves also popular with visitors . . . especially for view overlooking river.

Camiguin Island • Reachable by ferry or small aircraft . . . dominated by Hibok-Hibok . . . one of seven volcanoes on the island . . . information available from Volcanology Station . . . Mambajao capital and sleepy, Spanish-style town . . . Bonbon is original capital but covered by lava flow in late 19th century . . . 64-kilometer road circumnavigates the island.

Camp Philips • Headquarters of Philippine Packing Corporation . . . said to be the largest pineapple plantation in the world . . . General Douglas MacArthur flew from this airstrip to Australia . . . after the fall of Corregidor . . . beautiful estate . . . but visitors may be preferred at nearby Bugo where guided tours take visitors through the canning factory.

Davao • Boom town . . . second largest city in terms of land area the world over . . . mostly unspoiled countryside . . . center for Durians . . . also center for lanzones, mangosteens, oranges, pomelos . . . fruit from fruit stalls, candied or preserved . . . relaxing and resortlike atmosphere here . . . 1½ hours from Manila by jet.

Fort Pilar • 300-plus-year-old fortress . . . now moss-covered . . . has survived attacks by Moslems, Dutch, and British as well as Portugese through the centuries . . . Lady of Del Pilar, patron saint of Zamboanga is enshrined here . . . pilgrims flock here with candles on the weekends . . . fort is located near Lantaka Hotel.

Iligan • Drab, industrial city where steel, fertilizer, cement, pulp, and paper mills abound . . . best known for Maria Cristina Falls about 9 km south . . . supposed to be the most beautiful waterfall in the country . . . also the largest at 58 meters high . . . permission to visit must be obtained from Philippine Constabulary in Iligan for travelers on their own . . . good observation platform at the hydroelectric station.

Menzi Citrus Plantation • The agricultural plantation of the South . . . vineyards, mango orchards, and modern citrus processing plant.

Mount Apo • Highest mountain in the Philippines . . . dominates landscape of Davao . . . home to monkey-eating eagle, world's largest and only example of the species . . . Mt. Apo is a dormant volcano some 3000 meters high . . . considered sacred abode of local gods . . . a fine peak for climbing, especially during April and May . . . most enthusiasts plan a 4-day safari up and back . . . guides available in Kidapawan, about a 2-hour ride from Davao . . . starting point of climb is Ilomavis, and first portion through gentle landscapes . . . Agko Blue Lake is located at 1200 meters . . . Marbel River at 1800 meters . . . Lake Venado at 2400 meters . . . from here it's a rocky climb to the summit . . . worth it for the extensive panoramas from the peak.

Pasonanca Park • Just 7 km north of Zamboanga . . . recreational facilities plus treehouse for overnight guests . . . lovely flowers bloom year-round . . . swimming pools fed by mountain springs . . . view spectacular brass objects in Salakot House opposite . . . deluxe Zamboanga Plaza Hotel also nearby . . . offers memorable sunsets over the bay.

Plaza Pershing • Named in honor of the American general who was also the first American governor of the area . . . located in center of town . . . behind wharf and near city hall . . . not far from old-world Lantaka Hotel by the sea . . . tourism offices located here . . . terrific views of the local hustle and bustle from the terrace.

Rio Hondo Village • Home of the seafaring Samal tribe . . . fast losing its charm as urban development spreads . . . a few houses still on stilts like the old days . . . brightly colored sails still hoisted over the local *vintas,* or small boats . . . small children in their birthday suits still play in the waters where the bridge joins the village proper.

Santa Cruz Island • 30 minutes by motorboat from Zamboanga City . . . noted for its pink and white beaches as well as its colorful coral reefs . . . perfect place for swimming, waterskiing, and coral diving . . . the ride over and back is wet . . . no facilities on the island of great comfort.

Talomo Beach • Site of landings of Japanese army in 1942, Americans and allies in 1945 . . . one of many lovely beaches outside Davao

City . . . if you like black sand . . . excellent for fishing, snorkeling, and scuba diving.

Taluksangay Village • 19 km from the city but well worth the visit . . . houses on stilts . . . dramatic mosque with towering silver-domed minarets . . . cultured pearls of good texture are produced here . . . another Samal village.

Zamboanga • Considered the traveler's prize catch in Mindanao . . . melting pot of Christian and Moslem cultures . . . city full of tradition and some charm . . . Castilian heritage apparent in local dialect . . . colorful, still slightly exotic city . . . many flowers and fruits . . . native handicrafts on every corner . . . houses built on stilts . . . cargo center between southern islands and Borneo/Malaysia.

HOTELS

Cagayan De Oro

★★**Alta Tierra Hotel** • *Carmen St., Cagayan de Oro City. Tel: 36–61; 36–62* • 32 rooms.
Facilities: Western/Asian restaurant. Bar. Pelota court. Conference room. Swimming pool.
Manager: D. P. Sarraga. *Reservations:* Direct.

★★**Caprice Hotel by the Sea** • *Lapasan St., Cagayan de Oro City. Tel: 48–80* • 23 rooms.
Facilities: Restaurant. Bar. Swimming pool. Conference room. Car service between hotel/port and airport. Room service.
Manager: A. Sebastian. *Reservations:* Direct.

★★**Mindanao Hotel** • *corner Chavez and Corrales streets, Cagayan de Oro City. Tel: 30–10; 35–51* • 53 rooms . . . newish hotel.
Facilities: Same as Alta Tierra but bigger and slightly more plush. Disco. Executive health center. Sports.
Manager: I. Asuncion. *Reservations:* Resort Hotels Corp.

Davao

Apo View Hotel • *J. Camus St., Davao City. Tel: 7–48–61* • 86 rooms.

Facilities: Swimming pool. Coffee shop. Function rooms. Transport service. Tour office. Car rental. Seafood/barbecue mall.
Manager: M. S. Pamintuan. *Reservations:* Direct.

★★★★**Davao Insular Inter-Continental Inn** • *Lanang (P.O. Box 144), Davao City D9501. Tel: (35) 7–60–61. Cable: DAVINS. Telex: ITT 48209* • 153 rooms . . . a member of the Inter-Continental group . . . true resort with a beach setting.
Facilities: Beautiful facilities. Swimming pool. Bilaan Coffee Shop. La Parilla Grill. Vinta Bar. Maranaw dining room. Badjao pool bar. Function rooms. Transport service. Pelota, basketball, and tennis courts. Minigolf course. Car rental. Worldwide reservation network.
Manager: E. A. Wassey. *Reservations:* IHC.

Imperial Hotel • *Claro M. Recto Ave., Davao City. Tel: 7–84–81. Cable: DAVAO IMPERIAL HOTEL* • 52 rooms.
Facilities: Coffee shop. Ballroom and convention room. Supper club. Gift shop. Pelota court. Car service. Swimming pool.

Zamboanga

★★**Lantaka by the Sea** • *Mayor Valderosa St., Zamboanga City. Tel: 39–31* • 132 rooms . . . historic hotel . . . located near harbor . . . lovely views from the verandah.
Facilities: Restaurant and coffee shop. Talisay bar. Swimming pool. Kombi for guests. Scuba diving gear. Room service. Conveniently located in town.
Manager: Mrs. H. Walstrom. *Reservations:* Direct.

★★★**Zamboanga Plaza Hotel** • *Pasonanca Park. Tel: 20–51* • 210 rooms . . . deluxe hotel right in the park.
Facilities: Restaurant and dining room. Bars. Coffee shop. Swimming pool. Convention facilities. Tennis and pelota courts. Orchidarium. Shops and all services available here. Resort hotel located away from town.

THE VISAYAS

THE VISAYAS IN A CAPSULE

6 major and several lesser islands southernmost in the Philippine archipelago . . . home of ⅕ of the country's total population . . . Magellan landed here in 1521 . . . lost his life to a local chieftain from Mactan . . . Cebu is capital of Central Visayas and the oldest city in the Philippines . . . original settlement of Zubu an important trading center long before arrival of the Spanish . . . still known as Queen City of the South . . . other islands of interest are Samar . . . Leyte, where General Douglas MacArthur landed in 1945 and said, "I have returned" . . . Bohol, with its chocolate hills . . . Negros Oriental and Occidental . . . and Iloilo, famous for its 17th- to-19th-century architecture . . . most areas in the Visayas are just an hour's flight from Manila.

WHAT TO SEE AND DO

Anhawan Beach Resort • Some 12 km from the city . . . offers cottages, good seafood restaurant, lagoon, convention pavilions, seashell collection, and handicraft store . . . excellent for swimming, sunbathing, fishing for the day.

Arevalo • Flower village some 6 km from Iloilo City . . . all sorts of arrangements are produced here . . . Dutch and British attacked the town in the late 16th century . . . Spanish finally built Fort San Pedro in 1617 and kept the others out.

Bacolod • Sugar capital of the Philippines . . . 1 hour by jet from Manila . . . offers old-world charm . . . natural beauties.

Basilica Minore Del Santo Nino • Built in 1565 by Legazpi (who colonized the islands for Spain and established Cebu as the capital) . . . built to house country's oldest religious relic . . . image of Senor Santo

Nino de Cebu . . . much venerated by Cebuanos . . . establishes this city as the center for Christianity in the Far East . . . located on Juan Luna Street in old section of town.

Bohol Chocolate Hills • Major attraction . . . located about 60 km from Tagbilaran City, capital of Bohol Island . . . chocolate hills are actually hundreds of oval limestone mounds . . . they change color from green to brown during summer season . . . recreational facilities located on two of the highest hills . . . but whole chain best seen from the air.

Bohol Island • Small but industrious . . . largest coconut area in the Philippines . . . local weavers make thriving cottage industries and sell handicrafts in Manila markets.

Cebu Island • Most important island in the Visayas . . . Cebu City is the oldest in the Philippines . . . industrial capital of the south . . . second only to Manila in commerce and history . . . Ferdinand Magellan considered first tourist here in 1521 . . . and lost his life in a battle with a local chieftain . . . many Spanish monuments and relics here . . . as well as some of the best rattan furniture factories in the world . . . and finely tuned guitars and ukuleles . . . an hour by jet from Manila.

Chapel of St. Joseph the Worker • Colorful altar mural made from soda bottles in psychedelic design . . . depicts Christ with dark-skinned saints in native dress . . . on grounds of Victorias Milling Company . . . claimed to be largest mill and sugar refinery in the world.

Cockfight Galleries • Not for the fainthearted . . . a Sunday passion with the people of Iloilo . . . galleries include Molo Gamecock Jungle, Gallera de jaro, Gallera de la Paz, Jaro Square Garden, and Gallera de Arevalo.

Colon Street • Oldest thoroughfare in the Philippines . . . laid down by the Spaniards who landed in Cebu in 1565 under Legazpi.

Fort San Pedro • Also begun by Legazpi in 1565 . . . not completed until 1738 . . . a triangular-shaped fort built on a spit of land near the then seashore . . . one of oldest Spanish structures in the Philippines . . . now undergoing reconstruction . . . houses the local tourist office . . . property has been in continual use since 16th century.

Iloilo • The most colorful city in the Visayas . . . a 2-hour boat ride from Bacolod . . . one hour by jet from Manila . . some Gothic architecture still standing . . . and a collection of churches founded by the Spanish . . . still retains much of its colonial character.

Kanlaon Volcano • Twin craters rising some 2500 meters above sea level . . . one extinct, the other active . . . popular with mountaineers, especially during Holy Week . . . serious climbers never miss the chance to peer down both craters.

Mactan Island • Home of the Magellan monument . . . erected in 1886 in memory of Magellan's slaying by the local chieftain Lapu-Lapu . . . a mural beside the monument depicts the historic event . . . Lapu-Lapu has his own monument nearby . . . considered a national hero . . . Cebu International Airport is also located on Mactan Island . . . Maribago is here too, famous for its guitars and ukuleles . . . visitors can watch the instruments being made by hand and listen to an impromptu musicale . . . sales are not discouraged.

Magellan's Cross • Most famous landmark in Cebu City . . . located in a kiosk on upper Magellanes Street . . . the cross was apparently left by Magellan in 1521 . . . he is considered the first foreign tourist to the Philippines—as well as a marauder.

Mambucal Summer Resort • Located on the slopes of Mt. Kanlaon . . . about 45 minutes from Bacolod City . . . drive through lush landscapes rising 400 meters . . . cool and refreshing climate year-round . . . at least a dozen waterfalls . . . hiking trails . . . curative hot springs . . . hotel and cottage colonies . . . swimming pools and other recreational facilities.

Samodal Flowers • A major cottage-industry attraction in Bacolod . . . colorful flowers made from dyed wood shavings are displayed and sold in many houses throughout the city.

Suarez Orchid Collection • More than 100 different varieties of rare orchids: cattleyas, green giants, leilanis, etc. . . . several greenhouses . . . seedlings and cuttings for sale.

Taoist Temple • A monstrous new structure atop Beverly Hills . . . Cebu City's fanciest residential area . . . considered an architectural landmark . . . attracts many visitors (most of whom have little choice), and Taoist ceremonies are held on Wed. and Sun. . . . nonbelievers can still light *joss* sticks and have their fortunes read . . . farther north by car is the Chapel of the Last Supper in Mandaue City . . . life-size statues of Christ and the apostles carved during Spanish occupation . . . if you can stand it.

University of San Carlos ● Founded in 1596 . . . one of the most important cultural centers in the Philippines . . . houses a museum of mosaic prints made from butterfly wings . . . antique collections of jars, jewelry, porcelains, and weaponry.

Fort San Pedro ● Built at the mouth of the Iloilo River by the Spanish in the 17th century . . . as defense against British, French, and Moslems.

Guimaras Island ● A 15-minute ride by motorboat from Iloilo . . . a favorite for picnics since Rizal's time . . . lovely beaches, falls, springs, and Roca Encanta (the enchanted rock).

Iloilo Museo ● Showcase of pre-Hispanic art and culture in the Visayas . . . museum houses collections of fossil shells, pre-Spanish burial coffins, relics from a 19th-century shipwreck, Victorian china, flake tools of early man, and elephant fossils . . . located on Bonifacio Drive.

Jaro ● Religious center of Western Visayas . . . a district just 3 km from the city . . . has romantic and colonial air . . . Antillan houses lining its streets . . . private collections of colonial art and relics . . . Gothic-fronted cathedral . . . center also for weaving . . . hand embroidery of native *pina* and *jusi* . . . traditional fabrics for the *barong tagalog.*

Miagao Church ● Fortress church located about 40 km southeast of Iloilo City . . . yellow sandstone in baroque style . . . facade bears relief carving of St. Christopher amid native papayas, coconuts, and shrubs . . . structure built in colonial era for protection from pirates.

Molo Church ● A Gothic-Renaissance monument in Molo district . . . about 3 km from city . . . completed in the early 19th century . . . district also known for fine *tiongco* antique collections and local Chinese noodle dishes.

San Joaquin Church ● One of the most beautiful in the area . . . 53 km from Iloilo City . . . dates from 1869 . . . built of gleaming white coral . . . facade depicts historic battle of Tetuan in Morocco . . . high-relief style . . . sculpture even depicts pained expression of wounded soldiers.

HOTELS

Cebu

★★★★**Argao Beach Club** • *Casay, Dalaguete, Cebu Island. Cable: BAYVIEW MANILA. Telex: 22482 PTI PH* • 77 rooms . . . lovely beach resort . . . 2 km of coastline in town of Dalaguete . . . 3 coves and coconut groves . . . 2 hours by boat from Tambuli Beach Resort . . . much longer from Cebu City over dusty, bumpy roads . . . be prepared to stay awhile . . . great wind surfing and scuba diving . . . also glass-bottom boat for viewing marine life and coral formations . . . great for honeymoons . . . very quiet.

Facilities: Tan Awan native seafood and international cuisine restaurant with Casay Bar. Swimming pool. Tennis courts. Gift and pro shop. Duwaan game room.

Manager: S. C. Fonacier. *Reservations:* Direct.

★★★**Cebu Plaza** • *Barrio Nivel, Lahug, Cebu City. Tel: 611–29. Cable: BAYVIEW MANILA. Telex: 24861 CEPLA PH* • 450 rooms . . . a low-rise building . . . with new 300-room tower . . . overlooking city and Mactan Island. Under new ownershp and management.

Facilities: Cafe del Monte coffee shop. Lantau native seafood restaurant. 2 swimming pools. Garden setting. Tennis court. All services in new tower.

★★★**Magellan International Hotel** • *Gorordo Ave., Cebu City. Tel 7–46–11. Cable: MAGELLAN CEBU. Telex: 24729 MIH PH* • 200 rooms . . . most attractive place . . . tropical building . . . plenty of grounds . . . lush planting.

Facilities: Swimming pool. 18-hole golf course. Plenty of services. Zugbu Coffee Shop with old plantation atmosphere. Sigay cocktail lounge named after a colorful Philippine sea shell. El Balconaje Lounge for sunrise and sunset refreshments. Puerto Galera restaurant. Camarin Filipino restaurant, highly recommended and closer to town.

Manager: M. Zamora. *Reservations:* Global Service Inc.

★★**Montebello Resort Hotel** • *Banilad, Cebu City. Tel: 7– 76–81/3. Telex: 6232 MONTE PU* • 142 rooms . . . Spanish-style hacienda on 12 acres of beautiful grounds . . . an oasis in the midst of a bustling city . . . comfortable rooms.

Facilities: Swimming pools. Conference facilities. Restaurants and bars. Pelota Court. Services and disco.

Manager: Z. N. Borromeo. *Reservations:* Direct.

★**Tambuli Beach Resort** • *Buyong Beach, Mactan Island, Cebu City. Tel: 7–00–52* • 52 rooms . . . an overcrowded resort out near the airport . . . watch out for the day transients . . . especially those who wash their hair in the shower by the pool . . . dirty when I was there . . . tacky . . . I'd avoid it.
Manager: S. C. Fonacier. *Reservations:* Direct.

Iloilo City

★**Hotel Del Rio** • *M. H. del Pilar, Molo Iloilo City. Tel: 7–55–85* • 57 rooms . . . the least of all evils . . . convention facilities . . . bar and dining room . . . swimming pool . . coffee shop . . . room service and that exquisite modern invention—piped-in music!
Manager: M. Loring. *Reservations:* Direct.

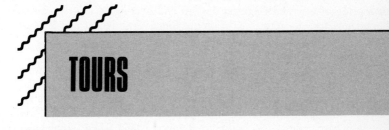

TOURS

Manila/Cebu/Manila • 3 days and 2 nights . . . by air to Cebu City . . . sightseeing in second largest metropolis in the Philippines . . . Magellan's Cross . . . Basilica San Minore del Sto. Nino . . . Fort San Pedro . . . University of San Carlos . . . old Colon Street . . . Taoist Temple . . . cruise along coast of Cebu and Mactan . . . time for skin diving and swimming . . . return to Manila on 3rd day.

Manila/Bacolod/Ilolio/Guimaras/Manila • 3 days and 2 nights . . . by air to Bacolod City . . . capital of Negros Occidental and home of "sugar barons" . . . tours of Victorias Milling Company . . . St. Joseph the Worker Chapel . . . Iloilo City . . . museum and markets . . . Anhawan Beach resort for Filipino seafood specialties . . . Guimaras Island hideaway . . . motorized outrigger to other small islands surrounding Guimaras . . . MacArthur built present wharf at Buenavista . . . return to Manila by air from Iloilo City.

Manila/Davao/Cagayan de Oro/Manila • 4 days and 3 nights . . . by air to Davao . . . city tour of waterfront, suburbs, and Alde-vinco Commercial Center for handcrafts, brassware, and shell products . . . full-day visit to Samal Island . . . depart by air for Cagayan de Oro to visit Del Monte pineapple plantation in Bukidnon . . . one of largest in the world . . . overnight and morning tour before return flight to Manila.

Manila/Zamboanga/Manila • 3 days and 2 nights . . . by air to Zamboanga . . . city of flowers . . . melting pot of Christian and Moslem cultures in the Philippines . . . 17th-century moss-covered Fort Pilar . . . old Zamboanga City Hall once General Pershing's headquarters . . . Rio Hondo Moslem village with houses on stilts over the water . . . Cawa Cawa Blvd. . . . Pasonanca Park . . . Zamboanga market for brassware, antiques, batik, and native woven cloths . . . motorized vinta ride to Santa Cruz Island . . . return by air to Manila.

Manila/Cebu/Davao/Zamboanga/Manila • 6 days and 5 nights . . . most comprehensive tour of the southern Philippine archipelago . . . by air to Cebu City for touring and overnight . . . by air to Davao for touring of city and Cagayan de Oro and overnights . . . by air to Zamboanga for city tour . . . a day at Santa Cruz Island and 2 overnights . . . return to Manila by air.

Visayas Aquasports Tour • 4 days and 3 nights . . . by air from Manila to Cebu . . . transfer for flight to Dumaguete City . . . cruise to Sumilon Island for diving at Silliman University Marine Reservation . . . day at Apo Island to see coral formations, mackerels, jacks, and prowling barracudas . . . cruise to Siquijor Island where coral ledge extends full length . . . also snappers, Napoleon wrasses, and giant pumphead parrots along the reef . . . overnights in Dumaguete City . . . return by air to Manila.

WINING/DINING/ ENTERTAINMENT

Food—glorious food—is abundant throughout the Philippines, where rice is the staple and there are almost as many varieties of fruit as there are islands in the archipelago—7000. However, true Filipino food is the culmination of several overlapping cultures and influences—Spanish, American, Malay, and Chinese—which tends to allow for a pretty fair blending of East and West every time the table is set. And it goes without saying that the Filipinos love to eat—whether a gift of nature straight from the vine, at one of the many *turo turo* fast-food centers in major towns, at home with family, or in a formal restaurant where the *barong tagalog* substitutes for Western jacket and tie. Casual about their dining habits (you use your fingers for most dishes) and superbly hospitable, the Filipinos pay special attention to enjoying every morsel in sight and having a wonderful time doing so!

Even world explorer Ferdinand Magellan was pleased with the many new types of fruits he encountered in these islands, and later visitors wrote favorable reports on the abundance of thirst-quenching edibles bestowed by nature. One of the oldest fruits cultivated by man is the **mango,** reputed to be known for over 4000 years. From its origin in India, the mango found its way to the Philippines in the early 1600s; today there are some 41 varieties available. The two most important types are the **carabao** (named after the Asian buffalo) and the **pico,** both of which make excellent appetizers, desserts, candies, and jellies. The mango has also found favor recently in nouvelle cuisine and is delicious served with seafood in a light curry sauce.

The **watermelon** is no stranger to the Philippine palate; it is known locally as the **pakwan.** Its first cousin the **canteloupe,** brought to the islands by the Spanish, is also abundant. The **avocado** was introduced around the turn of this century and grows in many shapes. It is eaten as is, with salt and salad dressing, or mashed with sugar and milk. The offensive-smelling **durian** is an acquired taste and travelers are requested not to bring the fruit aboard Philippine Airline flights, because fellow passengers do complain about the odor. A favorite of the tropics for many visitors is the **guava,** especially when used in jelly and spread on breakfast toast.

The **papaya** is one of the mainstays of the Filipino fruit diet and a delicious way to begin each day. **Bananas,** whose origins lie in India and southern China, are memorable in these islands and their sweetness extends to some 277 varieties. Most unusual are the clusters of "finger" bananas which grow wild along the roadside. **Jackfruit, pineapple, mangosteen** from Malaysia, **santol, tamarind,** and **rambutan** are among other local fruits. The **pomelo,** resembling a grapefruit, is sold from street stands throughout the Philippines but has very little taste and less juice. Most popular drinks are sugar-cane juice, sometimes called **halo halo** when mixed with other fruits or ice cream, and **buko,** or the juice made from young coconuts (the fleshy white meat is used for salads). Aficionados of the pina colada will often taste fresh coconut and pineapple juices mixed with their tot of rum.

Some typical Filipino dishes feature **adobo,** chicken and/or pork stewed in soy sauce, vinegar, garlic, peppercorn, and other spices, or **arroz valenciana,** a local version of paella without the squid and various other trimmings. A specialty like **balut** is only for the very brave, as it consists of a duck's egg with a half-formed chicken inside; it's considered an aphrodisiac. **Pata** is a pig's thigh deep fried to a crisp and dipped in vinegar seasoned with garlic and chili. **Dinuguan** is pork innards stewed in fresh pig's blood and served with chili, **pan de sal** (small buns) or **puto** (rice cakes). **Inihaw** is anything grilled (chicken, pork, fish, shrimp) and dipped in a dish of vinegar with crushed garlic and hot chili.

Lechon, suckling pig roasted whole over an open fire and brushed with spices, is the highlight of any barrio festival. By tradition, its crisp slices of meat are then dipped into a liver sauce. **Kare kare** is oxtail or knuckles stewed in a thick peanut sauce, in which rice and other vegetables are thrown. It is served in an earthen pot and accompanied by **bagoon,** a paste made from tiny shrimp and similar in taste to anchovies. **Alimango** is a large crab whose grilled meat is dipped in the popular vinegar sauce. **Achara** is a native relish of unripe papaya, carrots, peppers, and onions carved into a flowered design and served with grilled specialties. **Banana-cue,** a popular snack, consists of bananas on a stick dipped in brown sugar and deep fried. **Champurrado** is glutinous rice prepared with thick chocolate and served with beef tapa (dried beef), tenderloin tips, or for breakfast.

Filipino soups are simply made by simmering food in plain water and adding a dash of salt. Some of the more popular soups are **tinolang manok,** chicken with green papaya, garlic, onion, and pepper leaves; **sinigang na baboy,** a pork stew with a slightly sour taste; and **batsoy,** a thick and tasty soup of pork meat as well as the liver, heart, and kidneys.

Seafood from the waters surrounding these 7000-plus islands is abundant, inexpensive, and truly delicious! Oysters are quite often served fresh from the sea as appetizers. Large crabs are steamed or grilled, torn apart with one's hands and dipped into that popular vinegar sauce. **Lapu lapu,** known as the king of the Philippine fish species, is named after the famous native chieftain encountered by Ferdinand Magellan. It is actually a large-mouthed grouper that can be prepared in any number of ways. Local shrimps and prawns are often found in **sinigang na hipon,** the Philippine version of bouillabaisse, or as a snack with noodles and condiments.

The Filipinos love to eat out, frequently with the entire family, and prices are always reasonable (except in some of the top hotel specialty restaurants). San Miguel beer and sodas are plentiful and cheap, but imported wines and spirits are not. Those with tender stomachs should drink only bottled water, avoid raw vegetables, and eat only fruit that you peel yourself. Patronizing roadside snack stands in any country is asking for trouble—so, why tempt fate? The wise traveler chooses his food carefully and enjoys every meal no matter how simple or fancy.

However, good Filipino restaurants can be found on every main boulevard both in Metro Manila and throughout the country. Below are some of the best known.

FILIPINO RESTAURANTS

Aristocart • *Roxas Bvd., Metro Manila* • *Tel: 502621* • Cozy and informal . . . specialties are chicken barbecued or baked in honey . . . try also *alimango* (crabs wrapped in banana leaves).

Badjao • *Century Park Sheraton, Roxas Blvd., Metro Manila* • *Tel: 506041, ext. 736* • Specialties are kare kare . . . inihaw or anything grilled . . . beefsteak Pilipino . . . folk dances.

Barrio Fiesta • *Buendia Ave., Makati* • *Tel: 874728* • Try crispy pata and sinigang here.

Bulakena • *2102 Roxas Blvd., Metro Manila* • This is a *salu-salo,* or eating together Filipino-style, restaurant . . . specialties are *kilawin* (oysters marinated in vinegar, onion, and garlic) . . . *paksiw* fish . . . rellenong bangus (stuffed milk fish) . . . crispy pata.

Cafe Ilang Ilang • *Manila Hotel, Metro Manila* • *Tel: 470011* • A coffee-shop atmosphere . . . try lapu lapu broiled in banana leaves.

Evelyn's • *corner Roxas Blvd. and Concepcion St., Metro Manila* • *Tel: 505130* • Local lobsters and prawns . . . regional dishes . . . very reasonable.

Fisherman's Hut • *Makati Ave. and Durban St., Makati* • *Tel: 8189458* • Specialties include kare kare, *bulalo,* all kinds of sinigang . . . also many types of adobo, inihaw meats, and *kinilaw* (seafood).

Grove • *7850–C Makati Ave., Makati* • *Tel: 898383* • Specialties are kuhol (local escargot cooked in coconut milk) . . . laing (vegetables cooked in same).

Kamayan • *Pasay Rd. and Santillan, Makati* • *Tel: 883604* • Eating is by hand here . . . crabs, lobsters, and shrimp right from the sea.

Maynila • *The Manila Hotel, Rizal Park, Metro Manila* • *Tel: 470011* • Expensive but includes show of traditional dances and songs . . . *halabos na banagan* (steamed lobster) and chicken *pakan na manok* (cooked in a young coconut shell) are specialties.

Via Mare • *La Tasca Bldg., Legaspi Village, Makati* • *Tel: 852306* • Lobster . . . grilled lapu lapu, Pampano, and *maliputo* (freshwater fish from Lake Taal).

Zamboanga Restaurant • *8739 Makati Ave., Makati* • *Tel: 894932* • Grilled lobster, prawn, crab, and fish . . . entertainment nightly with Filipino folk dances.

CHINESE RESTAURANTS

The Philippines also boasts excellent Chinese cuisine and the restaurants range from family-style to very fancy, indeed. You can opt for a several course banquet or stop in for some local noodles with bits of this and that on top.

Aberdeen Court • *7842 Makati Ave., Makati* • *Tel: 899372* • Peking duck . . . seafood.

Cathay House • *PV Kalaw Bldg., Metro Manila* • *Tel: 497821* • 6-course banquets . . . shark-fin soup . . . abalone with mushroom sauce.

Green Patio • *1014 Pasay Rd., Makati* • *Tel: 878215* • Considered one of the best in town . . . small . . . lemon chicken . . . Taiwanese noodles . . . shrimp . . .Green Patio maki noodles.

Mandarin Room • *Hyatt Regency Hotel, Metro Manila* • *Tel: 802611* • Expensive . . . lavish service . . . presents special festivals of food.

Marco Polo Restaurant • *750 Shaw Blvd. Metro Manila* • *Tel: 709077* • *also 7872 Makati Ave., Makati* • *Tel: 8189446* • Peking chicken.

Peacock • *Century Park Sheraton, Metro Manila* • *Tel: 506041, ext. 1838* • Cantonese-style . . . boasting Hong Kong chefs.

Tai Hang Lau • *816 Pasay Rd., Makati* • *Tel: 886793* • Specialties include bird's nest with coconut milk . . . abalone in oyster sauce . . . roast pigeon . . . minced beef soup.

WESTERN RESTAURANTS

There is no dirth of impressive Continental or European/American restaurants in the Metro Manila area. In fact, there are many more than you can possibly sample in a few days' visit. The better restaurants are located in the deluxe hotels that line Roxas Boulevard and Makati Avenue, and each one has its own personality and ambiance.

Abelardos • *Philippine Plaza Hotel, Cultural Center Complex, Metro Manila* • *Tel: 8320701* • Elegance plus . . . serenaders accompany menu of imported items . . . worth a visit.

Au Bon Vivant • *1133 L Guerrero St., Ermita; and Makati Commercial Center, Makati* • *Tel: 875950/875802* • An old favorite among the locals . . . 5 private dining rooms . . . specialties include tournedos perigourinde . . . chateaubriand with sauce bernaise . . . steak au poivre.

Baron's Table • *Holiday Inn, Roxas Blvd., Metro Manila* • *Tel: 597961* • Continental cuisine . . . dark, Germanic atmosphere.

Champagne Room • *Manila Hotel, Rizal Park, Metro Manila* • *Tel: 470011* • A lovely dining experience . . . romantic ambiance . . . beautiful setting . . . French cuisine with music . . . best service in hotel.

Chesa • *Manila Peninsula Hotel, Makati* • *Tel: 857711* • Swiss specialties in chaletlike setting . . . a regular in Peninsula hotels.

Cowrie Grill • *Manila Hotel, Rizal Park, Metro Manila* • *Tel: 470011* • Steaks and seafood in pleasant surroundings.

Guernica's • *1326 MH del Pilar, Ermita* • *Tel: 500936* • Old Spanish tavern atmosphere . . . try paella here . . . also lengua and steaks.

Hugo's • *Hyatt Regency Manila, 2702 Roxas Blvd., Metro Manila* • *Tel: 802611* • The chain's gourmet restaurant throughout the Far East . . . Continental specialties . . . good wine list.

L'Hirondelle • *Manila Mandarin, Makati* • *Tel: 857811* • French restaurant . . . interiors by Don Ashton . . . very expensive.

Iberia Grill • *Century Park Sheraton, Roxas Blvd., Metro Manila* • *Tel: 506041, ext. 534* • Roast beef on the cart . . . grill items . . . wine list . . . businessman's 3-course luncheon offered weekdays.

Old Manila • *Manila Peninsula, Makati* • *Tel: 857711* • Beautifully decorated grillroom . . . off lobby level . . . lovely atmosphere.

Pier 7 • *Philippine Plaza Hotel, Cultural Center Complex, Metro Manila* • *Tel: 8320701* • Seafood and steaks in pleasant atmosphere.

The Steak Town • *1840 Makati Ave., Makati* • *Tel: 866267* • Old West atmosphere . . . steak and lobster specialties.

The Filipinos are also fond of buffets, often when all you can eat is combined with song and dance or a fashion show. The major hotels are very busy during the lunch hour, and some offer buffets in various restaurants three times daily. For example, the Manila Hotel offers buffet breakfast in the Lobby Lounge, buffet lunch in both Maynila and Champagne Room, and buffet snacks in Cafe Ilang Ilang. The Hotel Inter-Continental has an international buffet daily in the Bahia, while the Century Park Sheraton utilizes both the Iberia Grill and Cafe in the Park. The Philippine Plaza offers a breakfast buffet in Cafe Fiesta, luncheon buffet in Pier 7 and a native dinner buffet in Pergola with folk dances. Look also for Barrio Fiesta evenings at poolside in most hotels.

ENTERTAINMENT

The Filipinos are music mad, and their bands are the best in the Far East. So, it is no coincidence that the sounds of the cities are to the latest beat. Popular singers and musicians are abundant here and the "stars" make albums, have their photos splashed in the media, are called the "Frank Sinatra of the Philippines" or the "Diana Ross" and drive around town in the back of limousines. Who's Who and Who's In throughout the entertainment field is very important and seems to be the No. 1 diversion of most young people. While most visitors can probably take or leave the evening hours, the local scene is worth some attendance because it is so much of the current culture.

Discos and Watering Holes

Apres • *Manila Hotel* • Live music and disco records until 1 a.m.

Another World • *Greenbelt Park, Makati* • Disco dancing until 2 a.m.

Birds of a Feather • *802 Tomas Morato St.,Quezon City* • Jazz pub.

Cellar Disco • *Century Park Sheraton* • Minimum charge.

Circuit • *Hyatt Regency Manila* • Disco with minimum charge.

Coco Banana • *610 Remedios St., Malate, Metro Manila* • Gay bar. Entrance fee.

Grape Escape • *1038 A. Mabini St., Ermita* • House band. No cover.

Hobbit House • *1801 A. Mabini St., Ermita* • Various folk singers.

Lost Horizon • *Philippine Plaza Hotel* • Showband alternates with disco records. Open until 3 a.m.

Playboy Club of Manila • *Silahis International Hotel* • Members and guests free of charge. Considered very plush. Good drinks.

Stargazer • *Silahis International* • Lavish atmosphere. Drinks and dancing. Cover charge of about $10 a person.

Tipanan • *Manila Peninsula Hotel, Makati* • Live music until midnight.

Where Else • *Hotel Intercontinental, Makati* • Cover charge.

Hotel Music and Entertainment

Century Park Sheraton • Atrium Lobby from 4:30 to 8:30 p.m. Kachina Lounge from 7 to 11:30 p.m. Top of the Century until 1 a.m.

Holiday Inn • Braukeller from 9:30 p.m. Cafe Vienna from 7:30 p.m. Baron's Table from 8 p.m.

Hotel Inter-continental • Bahia lounge and restaurant until 11 p.m. Le Boulevardier until 1 a.m. Prince Albert Rotisserie until 11 p.m. La Terasse at noontime and Gambrinus until 10 p.m.

Hyatt Regency Manila • Calesa Bar until 1:45 a.m.

Manila Hotel • Champagne Room with 11-man string ensemble until 11:30 p.m. Tap Room Bar until 1 a.m. Lobby Lounge with piano cocktail music. Fiesta Pavillion special shows. Maynila Room dinner shows.

Manila Mandarin • Carousel Bar from 8:30 p.m. L'Hirondelle until 11 p.m.

Manila Peninsula • Tipanan nightly performances from 6 to 9 p.m.

Philippine Plaza Hotel • Abelardo at lunch and dinner. Lobby Court pianist in the afternoon. Pier 7 Filipino entertainment. Siete Pecados until 1:30 a.m.

Silahis International Hotel • Bienvenida Bar and music until 12:30 a.m.

SHOPPING

The Philippine archipelago is often called a "giant bazaar" of local handicrafts, which tells tale of the many influences that these people have come under. Serious shoppers can fill their suitcases with a wide range of mementoes and gifts found in both the bountiful native markets (where bargaining is definitely part of the game) and the modern commercial centers full of sophisticated specialty stores. Boutiques along the public areas of major hotels are just teasers for what lies beyond, once you begin to explore the great outside. And enthusiasm for more shopping builds as discoveries include santos, the comfortable barong tagalog, handwoven baskets and cloth from the mountain provinces, finely crafted guitars, local cigars and rum, San Miguel beer as it never tasted before, custom-made shoes and handbags, Kapiz jewelry and novelties, brass and bronzeware, fine embroideries, and high-quality bamboo/rattan/wicker furniture that can enhance the most splendid of decors.

Some of the most popular shops for tourists these days feature **"antiques,"** and seem to concentrate on three specific types: porcelains, Santos, and furniture. An abundance of Chinese-style porcelains have allegedly been found recently in excavations of early grave sites throughout the country and are claimed to be of the T'ang and Sun periods. Among the most prevalent of these so-called early Chinese porcelains, obtained during trade and buried with the dead, are the early brown and white, the red and white, the early blue and white, and the celadon. But buyers must be aware that reproductions are not uncommon, even among the most reputable and expensive dealers.

Only slightly less suspect are the shelves and shelves of carved **santos,** or statues of favorite saints. The early Spanish friars always encouraged their Filipino flock to consider these statues necessary to home devotion, and the more affluent boasted up to a dozen fine pieces that were imported from Mexico or Spain. The average folk were content with more primitive carvings of their patron saints, but both types of religious artifacts seem to have found their way into the antique shops. Again, be cautious and purchase only what pleases you (despite the claims of dealers). There are many worthy reproductions around, carved yesterday from old wood. A favorite trick is to chip off the aquiline nose of the Santos, because Filipino revolutionists in former days would associate the statues' profile with that of Spanish tyrants and desecrate the faces.

Hardly suitable for your suitcase but nonetheless a worthy purchase for antique aficionados is early Filipino **furniture,** ornately carved and heavily influenced by Spanish tradition. Most interesting are the *gallineras,* or long wooden benches that have an undercage for prized cocks. Also unusual are the *amarios,* or low canopied cupboards for the storage of sleeping paraphernalia. However, the Filipinos show their superb craftsmanship in the top-of-the-line furniture made from bamboo, rattan, or wicker that is produced daily in local factories. Hand-bent bamboo frames that take many intricate steps to accomplish are shipped to our West Coast where they are refinished and upholstered for U.S. tastes and then sold through exclusive interior designers. Check the mouthwatering advertisements of McGuire and Company in your favorite magazine for just such products.

Perhaps the most widely recognized Philippine handicraft is the **barong tagalog,** the national dress shirt that is both comfortable and cool. The garment was originally made of woven pina cloth or pineapple fiber, and derives its name from the Tagalog Province where fine needlework is a tradition. Unfortunately, most of the ready-to-wear racks of barong tagalogs today are made from synthetic materials, and the embroidery is obviously by machine. However, the popularity of this garment among Western men never wanes as it is a cool alternative to a coat and tie at any formal gathering in this warm climate. (The shirts are transparent, so it is customary to wear a T-shirt underneath for modesty's sake). Neither has this traditional costume bypassed ladies' wear; both dresses and pantsuits are available. Name designers have added high fashion to the garment for men and women, and a popular version now is the Mandarin collar, which President Marcos wore on many occasions. Both **Tesoro's** and **Rustans** are popular stores for the barong tagalogs and both have many branches throughout Metro Manila. If you don't mind paying a high premium, the natural fibers of ramie (China grass), jusi (banana silk), and pina, with hand embroidery, are beautiful for evening clothes and table linens.

Other natural fibers—rattan, bamboo, nipa, and various palms are used to make decorative **baskets** in various sizes and for many different purposes. Smoked, old-age-type baskets from northern Luzon are considered worthy of collecting and eventually can become heirlooms. **Mats** made from the same products are plentiful in the markets, and their uses range from beach mats to wall hangings. Brightly colored mats with floral designs come from the Visayas, while more exotic geometrics can be found in Mindanao. The Moslems in Mindanao also make lovely **brassware,** such as jugs and urns and trays etched with intricate geometric designs. Among the favorite pieces available as souvenirs are *sarimanok,* or Moslem teapots, and *kulintang,* a Moslem xylophone.

The **hardwood** of the Philippines also makes fine, carved objects, especially when crafted by Igorot tribesmen. Statues, salad bowl sets, curios, kitchen equipment, and a variety of containers are plentiful. Paete wood carvings from the town of Paete in Laguna are popular tourist items for their elaborate floral and foliage designs. Furniture, wall panels, and dividers are also available. But **kapiz** is the most frequently associated product in the world of Philippine handicrafts. Kapiz shells, plain or pearlized, are made into a variety of novelties such as coasters and table mats, lamp shades, chimes, etc. Mother-of-pearl shells are used for buttons, brooches, ashtrays, and jewelry, while other shells that are called "cat's eyes" are set with silver or gold-plated filigree and sold as more expensive adornments. The ornamental hairpieces made by tribal craftsmen are especially interesting and can be found in both native markets as well as Metro Manila boutiques. Look also for coral or tortoise-shell jewelry.

The mountain tribes of northern Luzon also make fine handwoven **cloth,** for use as place mats and napkins, blankets or beach bags, and even as draperies and upholstery materials. You can find exquisite hand embroideries or evening bags, blouses, and other garments, table sets, etc. A visit to local centers, such as in Baguio, will yield not only a feast for one's eyes but also some good bargains. Handmade silver flatware from Baguio is also a good buy as it is sold by weight (visit the silvershop at St. Louis University).

The distinctly flavored Philippine **cigars** are said to be among the best in the world, and their prices are certainly reasonable. Among the best known brands are *Tabacalera* and *Alhambra* and the attractively boxed items make fine gifts (as long as they are smoked far, far away). *San Miguel* **beer** is no stranger to most American visitors either, although I hear that its taste is quite different in the Philippines than it is abroad. **Rum,** another local beverage, comes in four different types: light, pale, dark, and special five-year-old. Most of the **rum** available is manufactured by three firms—*Manila Rhum, Anejo Rhum,* and *La Tondena* distilleries. They all claim to have captured international rum competitions.

Local **tailoring** in the Philippines is excellent should you wish to have something whipped together for a special occasion. Custom-made **shoes** are also a bargain and the beaded sandals for evening wear are a steal (if you don't expect them to last forever). Another female temptation is the *kimona,* the loose-fitting embroidered or beaded blouse worn over a long skirt for formal occasions.

For tourists who wish to supplement their purchases with imported goods, there are many tourist duty-free shops available where tax-free privileges are rendered upon presentation of passport and confirmed flight departure. You can walk out with two bottles of liquor, two cartons of cigarettes, two ounces of perfume, four ounces of toilet water, three pieces of soap, and one of any other kind of merchandise (designer scarves, handbags, briefcases, pens, etc.) for personal use. Additional items may be purchased but only collected at the Manila International Airport pre-departure area. In addition to the airport, duty-free shops can be found at the Makati Commercial Center, the Philippine Plaza Hotel and Convention Center, the Manila Hotel, Manila Hilton Hotel, Hyatt Regency shopping arcade, in Cebu City, and at Zamboanga International Airport. The shops are truly a godsend, but don't get caught buying for anyone else but yourself!

The exportation of National Cultural Treasures (rare and unique cultural properties) is prohibited unless authorized in writing by the director of the National Museum, and only for the purpose of exchange programs or for scientific scrutiny, and shall be returned promptly following the exhibition or study. Travelers are warned that when buying antiques, only the stamp of the National Museum attests that a particular piece has been authenticated. (The word is: Buyer beware.)

SINGAPORE

HISTORY

It will always be somewhat of a mystery to me why the name *Singapura*—Sanskrit for "lion city"—was bestowed upon this island settlement situated just below the Straits of Malacca. The existence of lions has never been verified, although tigers and an abundance of rather nasty crocodiles in the surrounding swamplands have been well recorded. Nonetheless, the name has withstood both time and several upheavals, mainly because founding father Sir Thomas Stamford Raffles accepted it readily as he stepped ashore on January 29, 1819.

That Sir Raffles is synonymous with the success of Singapore is no mean happening. This self-made English fellow (a scholar/historian/politician/businessman), who snuck around the Dutch to claim this place for his countryland, always considered Singapore his own child. Although he spent no more than the total of one full year here (on three separate occasions), he laid the cornerstone for present-day Singapore. Until the Japanese occupation, his laws banned slavery, cockfighting, brothels, and other nuisances. As a final official act before his departure in 1823, he established Raffles College which has educated a number of noteworthy Singaporeans (among them, Prime Minister Lee Kuan Yew).

Raffles insisted that this island settlement, caught as it was amid the sea-lanes between the East and Middle East, become a free trading port under the aegis of England. His grand scheme showed fast results, for not three years after the Union Jack was first raised the number of ships in harbor and the total trade figures were quite astounding. Population figures boomed along with business and by 1867 (a year after Raffles' death), Singapore became a British Crown Colony. Two years later the Suez Canal opened and ships came through in half the time.

Life was very pleasant and very colonial, especially for "white Singapore," whose members had big houses with full domestic staff, parties, and teas; Sunday *tiffin* at what was to become Raffles Hotel; the Singapore Cricket Club at one end of the *padang* (playing field) and the Eurasian Sporting Club at the other. Life was also rather inexpensive (being duty free, as it was) and residents drank a lot of tax-free gin and whiskey—either as *pahit* (a short drink) or the famous stengah (half liquor/half water). There was entertainment galore and plenty of companionship for the English bachelors, and daily business was mainly conducted on credit. Although people had plenty of money, they didn't like to carry it about because of the heat and humidity!

The fun and frolic lasted until Monday, December 8, 1941, when the Japanese attacked (among other places) the east coast of Malaya. Two months and one week later, the government of Singapore surrendered to the Japanese invaders. It was hardly one of England's finest hours and paved the way for the end of colonial rule in Singapore. Now, in hindsight, historians agree that Japanese battle victories in the early part of World War II destroyed (more than anything else) white supremacy in Asia. However, the local populace first had to deal with the captors who changed the name of Singapore to Shonan (it didn't stick) and generally ruled with malice. Their one contribution to mankind's progress was the introduction of trishaws (three-wheeled pedicabs) versus the traditional rickshaws (pulled by single runners), because the latter were considered inhumane.

The British reassumed control of Singapore when the war ended (many of them straight from the famous Changi prison), and the statue of Raffles was reinstated beside the river but (as one writer put it) "people looked at him a little differently." The yellow brick road to independence was being laid, held back briefly by the 1950s Emergency (Communist rebels) that struck the Malay peninsula. Finally in June 1959, a 36-year old Cambridge-educated *Baba* (local name for Straits-born Chinese male) won election as the first Prime Minister of the independent state of Singapore. His name was Lee Kuan Yew and he long ago earned his place in history books right next to that of the Founding Father.

For 30 years Prime Minister Lee has dedicated himself to making miracles happen and disproving that well-known "white" epitaph, "Here Lies a Man Who Tried to Hurry the East." Through a combination of strategy, cunning, imagination, and very, very hard work (some say Calvinism), Lee Kuan Yew has transformed this island republic into the most modern Asian nation possible. He has been ruthless at every step (all white clubs that did not open their doors to "others" would be closed forever), but is frequently touted as the only incorruptible politician in all of Asia (perhaps the world). He lives for work and dislikes cigarettes, litter, long hair and the hippie look, drugs, rush-hour traffic, and overweight people (among other things). He does not "drink" and eats very little (no rice). His only passion (if he has any) is golf, and it is not difficult to note the many fine golf courses scattered around Singapore and Sentosa.

Lee believes in order and structure, and in keeping the body and mind fit. Jogging is now encouraged (even among visitors) within the city's many lovely public gardens and parks. Young people are told that it is their responsibility to do well in government-sponsored schools, and everyone who is eligible must vote. Working singles have a percentage deducted from their weekly salary, redeemable only upon marriage and as a down-payment for a house or flat. The elderly, many of whom lived in hovels or small boats, now find themselves in frighteningly strange high rises that are far away from familiar neighborhoods.

After reclaiming land at an alarming speed (making maps obsolete) for more high-rise housing projects, more golf courses and parks, more factories, and entertainment facilities, Singapore has responded to negative reactions by visitors and slowed development, even recreating sections of Old Singapore that had been domolished in the name of progress. And when early morning traffic in the city center threatens paradise with its fumes and congestion, barriers are erected to keep cars out, despite the inconvenience. Yet Singaporeans continue to celebrate an annual tree-planting Sunday that keeps theirs a "garden city." An amazing number of festivals and public holidays celebrate the traditions and religions of all four cultures that live together so peacefully on this island.

Lee Kuan Yew has proved that the good old Protestant work ethic will produce success every time (he is often said to have manners "more English than the English"). The Singapore he has shaped is booming in trade, local industries, banking, and finance; and the number of annual visitors (for business or pleasure) has surpassed the total local population. He has also created one of the most literate of Asian societies, although the media are strictly controlled and "bad" outside influences are not to be tolerated.

Although most Americans would consider Singapore dull to live in (even though some 7000 do), it is pure heaven to visit. Nowhere in the world are the gardens so lovingly cared for and enjoyed. Nowhere are the streets so clean, the laws so well obeyed, the food so abundant and enticing. With four cultures intermingling peacefully, nowhere can you catch such a perfect glimpse of Instant Asia!

PLANNING AHEAD

SINGAPORE TOURIST PROMOTION BOARD (STPB) is efficient. It is located at Raffles City Tower, #36–04, 250 North Bridge Rd., Singapore 0617. Tel: 339–6622, and hours are 8 a.m.–5 p.m. daily, except Sun. and public holidays. Receptionists assist visitors with information and complimentary maps and publications. They will also

———— SINGAPORE IN A CAPSULE ————

Island Republic of approximately 226 square miles . . . completely surrounded by sea and separated from the tip of Malaysia by causeway . . . about same land mass as Isle of Man . . . closest metropolis to the Equator (60 miles north) . . . annual rainfall almost 100 inches . . . average daily temperature 80°F . . . present city founded in 1819 by Sir Thomas Stamford Raffles as a free port . . . present population about 2.6 million, half of them under the age of 20 . . . population mix is 76% Chinese (majority Hokkien origin), 15% Malay (original inhabitants), 7% Indian, 2% others (Caucasian and Eurasian) . . . official national language is Malay . . . median salary (U.S.$2,000) is second only to Japan in Far East . . . 80% of the population will live in government housing by the 1990s . . . all 18-year-old males must enlist in the National Service for 2 years . . . all persons 21 years and over must vote, by law . . . government is a tight democracy under the leadership of Prime Minister Lee Kuan Yew since June 3, 1959.

arrange for the (paid) services of an official tourist guide, if you like. Brochures are also available at the STPB Information Center in the arrival hall of Changi Airport from 6 a.m.–10 p.m. daily.

The STPB has four regional offices in North America: 590 Fifth Ave., New York, NY 10036 (Tel: 212–302–4861); 8484 Wilshire Blvd., Suite 510, Beverly Hills, CA 90211 (Tel: 213–852–1901); 333 N. Michigan Ave., Suite 818, Chicago, IL 60601 (Tel: 312–704–4200); The guardian Tower, Suite 1202, 181 University Ave., Toronto, Ont. M5H 3M7 (Tel: 416–867–1050).

VISAS are not required of travelers holding valid U.S. or Canadian passports, for a stay for purpose other than employment or residence. All persons entering Singapore must be in possession of valid passports or internationally recognized travel documents.

INOCULATIONS for smallpox or yellow fever are required only if travelers have arrived from an infected area within the preceding 14 days.

ENTRY BY AIR is at Singapore's impressive new **International Airport** at Changi, now several miles from city center. Taxi service from the airport is about S$15 to the Orchard Rd. hotels, plus surcharges for baggage and more than two passengers. Deluxe hotels have limousine service available. Changi Airport has left luggage facilities, restaurants, bars, VIP Rooms, and duty-free shopping.

Departure tax is S$12 for all international flights, S$5 to Malaysia destinations and Brunei.

ARRIVAL BY SEA in the world's second busiest harbor can be aboard any number of passenger vessels, ranging from the *Queen Elizabeth 2* to Royal Viking Line, and Royal and Pearl Cruises. Singapore is a favorite port on around-the-world cruises as well as the many ships departing from Australia on year-round sailings. Entry formalities and port taxes are the responsibility of the individual shipline, and the Singapore Tourist Promotion Board is on hand with a mobile information service to greet all passengers stepping ashore from **Keppel Harbor.**

RAILWAY is yet another alternative transportation to and from Singapore. The Express Rakyat takes exactly 24 hours to Bangkok, with stops at Kuala Lumpur and Butterworth (for Penang Island). There are air-conditioned coaches and berths as well as dining car. Tickets can be purchased three days in advance from the railway station on Keppel Rd. (Tel: 2225165).

BUSES to and from Malaysia run daily. Departures are every 10 minutes via the Causeway to Johor Bahru from Rochor Rd. Terminus and every 15 minutes from Queen St. or Bukit Timah Rd. Malacca buses leave from the Beach Rd. Terminus six times daily; while Kuala Lumpur, Penang, Butterworth, Mersing, and Kuantan buses all depart from the New Bridge Rd. Fringe Car Park Terminus.

DUTY-FREE is the case for most items in Singapore. There are no currency restrictions on the amount allowed imported or exported in either local or foreign notes. Incoming travelers are allowed (except when coming from Malaysia) duty free one bottle of spirits; one bottle wine; one bottle beer, ale or stout; 200 cigarettes, 50 cigars, or 250 grams of tobacco. All can be purchased at the **Duty-free Emporium** at the Airport Arrival Hall. Dangerous weapons are prohibited, and household pets from other than the U.K., Ireland, Australia, or New Zealand are subject to quarantine at owner's expense for at least 30 days.

Teenagers of all ages should take note that the "hippie look" is not tolerated in Singapore, and possessing or trafficking any kind of drug or narcotic is a severe offense and punishable by jail, fine, or death. Drug abuse in this Republic is not to be taken lightly.

CURRENCY of Singapore is the dollar (S$). Each Singapore dollar is worth just under US$.50 (2 to 1) although the exact exchange rate fluctuates daily. Notes are used in the denominations of S$1, S$5, S$10,

S$20, S$50, S$100, S$500, S$1,000, S$10,000. There are 100 cents to each dollar and coins can be found in 1 cents, 5 cents, 10 cents, 20 cents, and 50 cents.

Like Hong Kong, Singapore is an important Far East financial capital and there are more than 80 banks and some 75 insurance companies doing big business here. Banking hours are 10 a.m.–3 p.m. Mon. through Fri. and 9:30 a.m.–11:30 a.m. on Sat. Branches of the Development Bank of Singapore remain open until 3 p.m. on Sat. However, licensed moneychangers often give the best rates and don't deduct a surcharge when converting foreign currency for tourist purchases. Look for them at shopping complexes and in Change Alley. Exchange rates at hotel desks are always too low.

LOCAL TIME in Singapore is Greenwich Mean Time plus 8 hours. When it is noon Sun. in Singapore, the local time on the west coast is 8 p.m. Sat. and on the east coast 12 a.m. Sun. morning. Singapore time is the same as Hong Kong, Taipei, Manila, and the entire Malay peninsula. It is one hour in advance of Jakarta and Bangkok.

LOCAL CURRENT is 220-240 volts AC, 50 cycles. Most hotels have a transformer to reduce the voltage to 110-120 volts, 60 cycles, if necessary for electric shavers, hair dryers, etc.

LOCAL WATER is pure and potable. Tap water is safe to drink anywhere, and it is wise to drink at least six glasses daily while adapting to this tropical and somewhat debilitating climate. There is no water shortage in Singapore, but you still must take care not to waste any water.

OFFICIAL LANGUAGES in Singapore are English, Mandarin, Malay, and Tamil. English is the language of business, administration, and tourism. Most Singaporeans are tri-lingual (at least). Schools are required to educate children in their mother tongue as well as English.

One English-language newspaper is published daily, the *Straits Times* (morning). For outside news, look for the *International Herald Tribune* and the *Asian Wall Street Journal* in addition to the weekly news magazines. English radio service airs from 6 a.m. to midnight daily, FM stereo from 6 a.m.–11 p.m. Color television programs are broadcast in all four languages on Channel 5 (3 p.m. to midnight) and Channel 8 (6 p.m.–11 p.m.). Two stations from Malaysia can also be received.

Singapore is also a publishing capital and there are any number of excellent books available, so don't pass by the local stores too fast.

BUSINESS HOURS in Singapore range from 8 a.m.–5 or 6 p.m. Singaporeans are industrious and serious in their work, and they follow the example of Prime Minister Lee Kuan Yew, who arrives at his office very early and leaves late. Shops may stay open until 7 p.m. and the Chinese Emporiums until 10 p.m. Stores are open in the large centers on Sun.

TIPPING is not supposed to be a way of life in Singapore. It is prohibited at the airport, in hotels and restaurants that add a 10% service charge, and in restrooms. Taxi drivers do not expect much, but it is nice to offer small change. Bellboys should be tipped for services rendered. Away from the tourist centers, a smile suffices.

TELEPHONE AND TELEX services in Singapore are excellent. Local phone calls (except in public booths) are free of charge. The telephone system is extensive throughout the city, and it is even possible to speak with a vessel in Keppel Harbor (dial 105 for operator) or a ship at sea (dial 907). The city also has IDD (International Direct Dialing).

Telex and cable services are available 24 hours a day at your hotel, or from the General Post Office, Fullerton Building (Tel: 983111). You can mail cards and letters at the front desk of your hotel or with the concierge. In addition, the Post Office at Changi Airport and at Killiney Rd. are both open from 8 a.m.–9 p.m. daily. Postcards to other parts of the Far East are S$.20, to the U.S. about S$.55. Airletters to anywhere in the world are S$.35.

WHAT TO WEAR is what makes you comfortable in this hot and humid climate. Casual cotton clothing (skirts, short-sleeve blouses for women and slacks and shirts for men) is best for daytime wear, with something more formal for the evening. Singapore is actually a very casual city (open shirts or safari suits for men), unless you plan to attend business meetings daily and to dine in a premier hotel restaurant every evening. Coat and tie are required in many restaurants and clubs; forget them if you're wandering out for some satay or to your favorite curry place. But blue jeans and T-shirts are frowned upon, even at some of the better discos where they are considered unacceptable. And if your visit is scheduled during the rainy season (Oct. through Jan.), expect to be drenched from time to time in heavy downpours. An umbrella, light slicker, and rainhat are necessities during these winter months. And at any time of the year, pack enough wraps for evening to protect yourself against too-cold air conditioning after a day in tropical heat.

LOCAL TRANSPORTATION is clean and efficient in Singapore. There are more than 10,000 metered **taxis,** with a maximum allowance of four passengers each. Fares begin at S$1.60 for the first 1.5 km, plus S$.20 for each subsequent 300 meters and for each 45 seconds waiting time. Add a surcharge of S$.50 for each third or fourth passenger, and each piece of luggage is an additional S$1. In addition, there is a 50% surcharge for service between the hours of midnight and 6 a.m.

If your hotel or morning destination is located within the Central business district, you may experience some difficulty arriving and departing between the hours of 7:30 a.m. and 10:15 a.m. Mon. to Sat. (except public holidays). A "restricted zone" in the city center has been designated to alleviate traffic congestion in the morning hours. Unless you are in a vehicle carrying at least four persons, you can not enter this zone without a permit or Area License. It's all rather complicated and totally annoying if you have to be somewhere within this zone in the early morning. The best advice I can give is to have the taxi driver drop you as close as possible to your destination, then WALK!! (Finding a driver who speaks English well enough to understand all this is another challenge.)

If you have any **taxi complaints,** do not hesitate to direct them to Registry of Vehicles, Sin Ming Dr., Sing. 2057 or the STPB at its headquarters.

A **dial-a-taxi service** is available 24-hours daily. Contact by telephoning: 363636, 36333, 2933111, or 2932057.

City **buses** run from 6 a.m.–11:30 p.m. Fares are computed by distance, in stages that average about four-fifths of a kilometer in length. The fares range from S$.40 to S$.80, and exact change is required. Bus guides and routes are available for about S$.50 at local hotel shops and bookstores. The Singapore Explorer ticket allows holders unlimited use of the local bus service for one or three days (S$5, S$12).

Trishaws are still "in" and an interesting way to explore the back alleys of the older sections of the city. Find out the going rate from someone in your hotel or at the STPB, and then settle the amount before you enter the "cab." And be a little sensitive about the differences in size between East and Western bodies. Should a 60-pound trishawist, who lives on a few bowls of rice, cart around a 200-lb steak-and-potatoes American? Many cyclists will say NO—for any price.

Singapore's new, gleaming, air-conditioned subway system is an inexpensive, very comfortable (particularly in hot weather) way to get around. Stops are conveniently located at major shopping, business, and sightseeing points.

In the early morning or the cool of the evening, Singapore is a **walking** city, and you will find the streets much more revealing after dark than at anytime during the day. The sidewalks of Chinatown become one great open-air cafe, with odors of regional specialties mingling together to tempt bypassers. Local street operas, mini-festivals and block bazaars only occur when the sun has gone to rest and the workday stops. Have a taxi driver aim you in the right direction, then get out to walk, eat, watch and ENJOY!

Whether by night or day, **jaywalking** is a severe offense in Singapore, punishable by a S$50 fine. Cross streets at traffic lights only (especially as you may not be accustomed to left-hand drive), and if there is an overhead bridge or underpass for pedestrians, use it.

NOTE · · · Littering is also a grave offense against the city, and even a cigarette butt dropped is risking a S$500 fine. In fact, smoking in general is discouraged by the government and absolutely forbidden in some taxis, all public buses, elevators, theaters and cinemas, and government offices.

Seeing Singapore by water is a delight, but BE FOREWARNED that the "**bumboats**" for hire off Clifford Pier are not totally seaworthy. Further, we have discovered that the boatman we used did not deal well with the unexpected and could not swim. On a recent trip, our boat was almost swamped by a police launch that passed by portside too fast and too close. The resulting wake drenched our sensitive and expensive photographic equipment (two cameras with motor drives, six lenses, and several filters). Serious photographers understand the consequences of seawater, and we almost lost everything. (However, a Mr. Tang of the Nikon outlet on Orchard Rd. saved the equipment and made available camera loans during the interim.)

Otherwise, Singapore is reputed to be one of the safest cities in the Far East, and travelers find little difficulty in getting about on their own. There are a great many rules and regulations in this city, and it's best to obey them while you are a paying guest. Apart from charity draws, certain lotteries, and betting through the Singapore Turf Club, gambling is illegal. Always deal with a licensed money changer and NEVER get into a discussion or promotion of drugs with ANYONE.

HOLIDAYS AND FESTIVALS permeate life in Singapore; the holidays of four different religions are celebrated with equal fervor. The Chinese celebrate feasts in honor of hungry ghosts, monkey gods, Confucius, moon cakes, and dragon boats, as well as the birthday of Buddha. The Moslems observe Ramadan without fail, and Hari Raya Puasa at the finale is a time of much feasting. The Hindu population has Thimithi, its fire-walking festival, and the Taoists honor the birthday of the Third Prince with a street procession. Christians deck the hall with bows of beautiful poinsettias at Christmastime and with abundant wild orchids at Easter. And visitors are always warmly invited to all the festivities.

The following are holidays scheduled for Singapore each year. Only those marked with an asterisk (*) are public holidays.

 *January 1 • *New Year's Day.*

 January • *Ponggol or Harvest Festival* • A four-day festival from Southern India in which Tamils honor the Sun God with prayers of thanksgiving and offerings of rice, sugar cane, spices, and vegetable curry. The *prasadam* (sacred food) is then distributed . . . visit the Perumal Temple on Serangoon Rd.

January • *Maulidin Nabi or Hymns for the Prophet Mohammed* • Devotees gather in mosques to chant Murhaban hymns of praise and recite the Berjanzi, book on the life of Mohammed. Visit Sultan Mosqueoon North Bridge Rd. for biggest celebrations. (Women are not permitted in certain parts of the building.)

January • *Thaipusam or Celebration of Lord Subramaniam's victory over demon Idumban* • A two-day festival in two parts, with a Kavadi procession from the Perumal Temple in Serangoon Rd. to the Chettiar Temple in Tank Rd.

*February • *Chinese New Year* • The most important festival in the Chinese lunar calendar. Two days of *Kung Hei Fat Choy*—feasting and visiting in new clothes, good will and merrymaking all around. Most businesses open the third day but the holiday continues until the 15th day.

*February • *Chingay Procession* • Decorated floats held on the first weekend of the Chinese New Year along a predetermined route. Lion dances, drums, martial artists, stiltwalkers, swordsmen, beautiful young ladies, etc.

February • *Birthday of Monkey God* • A colorful festival in honor of T'se Tien Tai Seng Yeh, celebrated lavishly twice annually in several Chinese temples around the city. *Wayang* (Chinese street opera) and puppet shows are performed in temple court yards and processions are held at temples on Eng Hoon St. and Cumming St.

April • *Birthday of the Saint of the Poor* • Image of Kong Teck Choon Ong is carried in a palanquin by worshipers and spirit mediums from White Cloud Temple on Ganges Ave. on a tour of the neighborhood.

April • *Ching Ming Festival or Remembrance of Ancestors Day* • A tradition since the Han Dynasty, Chinese families clean and freshen ancestors' graves and then have a picnic on the site. A splendid outing.

April • *Songkran Festival* • A Thai Buddhist festival celebrated with throwing holy water at believers. Signifies start of year's solar cycle, when sun returns to first position in the zodiac. Visit Ananda Metyrama

Thai Buddhist Temple at Silat Rd. or Sapthapuchaniyaram Temple in Holland Rd. but be prepared for a drenching!

*Lenten Week • *Good Friday* • Solemn services held at all Christian churches, plus a candlelight procession in the grounds of St. Joseph (Catholic) Church in Victoria St.

End of Lent • *Easter Sunday* • Hotels and restaurants have special menus, with gifts for the children.

May • *Birthday of the Third Prince of the Lotus* • A temple in his honor is located at Clarke St./North Boat Quay near Chinatown. Here on the day of celebration are pantomimes, Chinese wayangs, mediums in a trance, and charms written in blood. Go if you must.

May • *Vesak Day* • In honor of the Lord Buddha's birth, death and enlightenment. Free meals are offered to the poor, birds are released from their cages, and devotees go vegetarian or fast altogether. The Temple of 1000 Lights (Sakya Muni Gaya Temple) on Race Course Rd. and Pher Kark See Temple on Bright Hill Dr. are centers for this celebration.

June • *Dragon Boat Festival* • One of the most colorful and fun of the entire calendar, this festival commemorates the ancient Chinese poet Ch'u Yuan, who drowned himself in protest against injustice and corruption. International dragon boat races highlight the festival as well as the consumption of *chang* (glutinous rice dumplings) that legend says fishermen threw into the water to sustain the drowning hero.

June 1 • *Commencement of Ramadan* • The first day of the ninth month of the Moslem calendar, when devotees observe daylight fasting until the next new moon. Stalls behind Sultan Mosque sell colorful cakes for evening, when the fast is broken, and Arab St. livens up after sundown.

*June 30 • *Hari Raya Puasa* • The end of Ramadan arrives with the sighting of a new moon and the beginning of the tenth month in the Moslem calendar. The holiday means much feasting, visiting, and weaving new fabrics.

July • *Market Festival* • A month-long festival held in conjunction with Feast of the Hungry Ghosts and celebrated lavishly by stallholders. Street operas are popular to entertain the spirits, especially throughout Chinatown. Visit also the Cuppage Rd. Hawkers' Center off Orchard Rd.

August • *Festival of Seven Sisters* • Dedicated to young lovers and celebrated since the 8th century B.C., this festival signifies the meeting of a cowherd and a spinning maid every year on the 7th day of the 7th moon (in the lunar calendar).

*August 9 • *National Day* • Displays by Singapore's cultural mix and a huge parade that ends in the National Stadium at Kallang to celebrate the formation of an independent Republic in 1965.

August • *Feast of the Hungry Ghosts* • A Chinese tradition since the 6th century during the month of the 7th moon. Celebrations held on a grand scale at temples, market places and even neighborhood street corners. The Chinese stay home on the last night, lest their spirit get carried away by a ghost returning to the underworld.

September • *Mooncake Festival* • Another Chinese legend about a lovely young lady in the heavens, but the more practical prefer the story about the patriots who communicated through messages hidden in cakes while attempting to overthrow the Mongols. To commemorate liberation from foreign domination, Chinese traditionally eat mooncakes and light lanterns on the 15th night of the 8th moon. The cakes are filled with bean paste, lotus seeds, orange peel, egg yolks, etc. There are also lantern processions, lion dances, concerts, and competitions with children in ancient costumes.

September • *Kusu Pilgrimage* • Every day for a month or so, Taoist devotees flock to the turtle-shaped island of Kusu to pray for prosperity, fertility, and good luck at the Chinese temple of Tau Pek Kong, or a Malay Kramat (shrine). Better to avoid this islet during pilgrimage time.

September–October • *Emperor Gods and Double Ninth* • From the first to the 9th day of the 9th moon, nine Chinese Emperor Gods are venerated with street operas and float processions. Their spirits cure ailments, bring luck, wealth, and longevity, and are said to possess their images in sedan chairs, etc. On the 9th day, whole families take to the hills for a picnic or visit Kusu Island on pilgrimage.

September • *Hari Raya Haji* • A Moslem festival of pilgrimage with praises to Allah, alms for the poor, and the forgetting of old quarrels. Celebrations at all mosques in Singapore, especially Sultan Mosque on North Bridge Rd.

October • *Thimithi Festival or Fire Walking* • Held to honor the purity of Hindu Goddess Durobatha. Supplicants pray to the goddess and then walk across burning coals to pay a debt for wishes granted. If you can stand it, visit Sri Mariamman Temple on South Bridge Rd.

October • *Navarathi Festival* • A 10-day homage to the consorts of the three gods of the Hindu trinity. The first week is spent in worship; the last days are for feasting and merrymaking. Goddess Durga, also known as Parvathi, consort of Lord Siva the Destroyer, commands the attention of the devotees during the first three days of the festival; the next three are for Lakshmi, Goddess of Wealth and consort of Lord Vishnu the Protector; and the final three belong to Saraswathi, Goddess of Education/Literature/Music/Eloquence and consort of Lord Brahma the Creator. On all nine evenings of the festival, classical Indian musical shows from 7 p.m.–10 p.m. are staged at the Chettiar Temple on Tank Rd. On the 10th day, traditional Hindu families teach their young how to write *om,* the universal word, and Hari (Vishnu). The festival closes with a grand procession from Chettiar Temple through the nearby streets.

*October • *Hari Raya Haji* • The 10th day of the 12th month of the Moslem calendar has special significance for all who have completed their pilgrimage to Mecca. (They wear white caps, and the men are addressed as Haji, women as Hajjah.) This day is observed at most mosques with prayers from 8 a.m.; goats are sacrificed to Allah in remembrance of the prophet Ibrahim's sacrifice of his son.

*October or November • *Deepavali* • Festival of Lights, a traditional Hindu celebration centuries old. Legends disagree exactly why this festival is celebrated—either the triumph of Lord Krishna over the demon king Nasakasura or the one day of the year when Lakshmi returns to earth. Hindu temples are colorful sights on this day, especially Perumal Temple on Serangoon Rd.

*December 25 • *Christmas Day* • If you happen to be in town, you will find everything here but the snow!

BACKGROUND MATERIAL *The Singapore Story* by Noel Barber is the very best and most readable history of Singapore (from Raffles to Lee Kuan Yew). It is available in Fontana paperback at hotel bookshops throughout Singapore, for about U.S.$4. The British Barber, a former foreign correspondent, is author of some 27 books. Others of interest and also in paperback are *Sinister Twilight* (the fall of Singapore and Japanese occupation) and *The War of the Running Dogs* (the Emergency years after the war).

King Rat by James Clavell is a fictionalized account of life in Changi prison during the Japanese occupation. The book rings very true (because Clavell was, indeed, interned there) and is one of his best.

Raffles Hotel by Ilsa Maria Sharp is the first book by this local resident. It's a history of Singapore's most famous hostelry. It should be a fascinating account of the years from 1887 to present and who did what, when. Especially, if you stay at Raffles.

Lord Jim, The Nigger of the Narcissus, Almayer's Folley, The Shadow Line by Joseph Conrad are all products of his visits to Singapore several times as a seaman. It is still possible to see something of Conrad's Singapore along the river—Cavenaugh Bridge (oldest bridge still in use), the godowns where goods are still unloaded and stored, the Old Ice House (now occupied by the TaiThong Rubber Works).

Singapore (apa productions) is also highly recommended.

WHAT TO SEE AND DO

Arab Street • Between Singapore River and Rochor Canal . . . Muslim Malay quarter . . . dominated by **Sultan Mosque** . . . herbs and spices from Moluccus islands permeate the air here . . . good buys also in Middle Eastern materials, rugs, baskets, and jewelry.

Botanic Gardens • Cluny and Holland Rds. . . . if you can only visit one of the city's lovely green spots, pick this . . . close to hotelland . . . Malaysia's thriving rubber industry began here when Henry Nicholas Ridley experimented with hevea seeds and gave them to planters across the causeway . . . the gardens are now a well-planned oasis with lily ponds, happy swans, orchid pavilions, herbarium . . . one of the most popular spots in town . . . 80 lush acres and paths for joggers . . . Tai Chi followers . . . lovers (newlyweds come here for photographs after the big event) . . . and whole families on picnic . . . open weekdays from 5 a.m.–11 p.m. weekdays, to midnight on weekends and holidays . . . admission free.

Bukit Timah Nature Reserve • Upper Bukit Timah Rd. . . . more for residents who must escape the city steam than for visitors . . . nonetheless, a well-kept 185-acre retreat with footpaths, jungle atmosphere, shelter huts, and views . . . walkers can take the road to summit (no vehicles allowed) . . . plan a half-day for communing with nature.

Cenotaph • Connaught Dr. . . . towering landmark dedicated to dead of two world wars . . . unveiled by the late Duke of Windsor (then Prince of Wales) in 1922.

Central Park • Clemenceau Ave. . . . 100 acres in former Fort Canning . . . historic cemetery . . . floral clock . . . national theater . . . **Van Kleef Aquarium** . . . hilltop view of city . . . plus restaurant, roller-skating rink, and children's playground . . . thought to be where Malay Sultanate governed Temasek (Singapore) . . . the British built their garrison here in 1857–58 . . . lights switch off at 11 p.m.

Chinatown • Bounded by New Bridge Rd. and South Bridge Rd. . . . some scenes unchanged for more than 100 years . . . you cannot visit Singapore without spending some time here . . . constant hubbub of activity from dawn until after midnight . . . over 100,000 people occupy one square mile and wouldn't dream of moving . . . trades thousands of years old carried on daily . . . walk through slowly to do it justice . . . a surprise and new sensation at every turn.

East Coast Park • East Coast Parkway . . . 865 acres of seaside recreational facilities off the highway between Changi Airport and the city proper . . . swimming, jogging, tennis, golf, barbecues, squash, etc. . . . plus a Crocodilarium with more than 1000 crocodiles and a man-made lagoon for 6000 bathers . . . if you like crowds . . . also windsurfing lessons and boards for rent.

Elizabeth Walk • At the other end of Merlion Park . . . sit on the rustic benches and imagine what colonial Singapore was like . . . look across the road at the **Padang,** the famous green of the Cricket Club where so many good times take place (and some bad times have occurred) . . . best known in the evening, when the Satay Club begins . . . with skewers of meat barbecued and consumed in the open air.

Hajjah Fatimah Mosque • Beach Rd. . . . built in 1845–46 in honor of a Malay woman from Malaca . . . stands in a grove of glam trees which provided medicinal oil to the Malays and bark for their boats . . . daughter and son-in-law of Hajjah Fatimah buried in backyard . . . inspiring and charming small mosque . . . open daily.

House of Tan Yeok Nee • Junction of Clemenceau Ave. and Somerset Rd. (opposite Singapore Shopping Centre) . . . built in 1885 of carvings and granite pillars imported from China . . . for prominent Teochew Chinese gambler and pepper merchant . . . now Salvation Army headquarters and preserved by National Monuments Board.

Instant Asia Show • Pajir Panjang . . . Three Asian cultures (Chinese/Malay/Indian) mix through song and dance in a 45-minute spectacle . . . entertains and offers insight on this unique city/republic

. . . daily (without fail) at 9:45 a.m. for S$5 adults, S$3 children . . . good place to start any tour.

Jurong Bird Park • Jalan Ahmad Ibrahim, Jurong . . . 50 acres in the heart of Jurong industrial town . . . 7000 birds from all over the world . . . some 350 species . . . 5-acre walk-in aviary where more than 3000 birds (65 varieties) fly free . . . park open from 9 a.m.–6 p.m. weekdays, to 7 p.m. weekends and holidays . . . admission is S$3.50 for adults, S$1.50 for children . . . tram and camera surcharges.

Kuan Yin Temple • Waterloo St. . . . dedicated to Goddess of Mercy, who devoted her life to helping mankind . . . humble temple with few adornments . . . one lustrous image of the goddess, adorned in silk vestments . . . temple jammed at New Year's time as supplicants flock to seek favors for the coming year.

Little India • Serangoon Rd. . . . a stretch along **Kandang Kerbau** populated by Singapore ethnic Indians . . . visit from 8 a.m.–9 p.m. any day . . . jasmine garlands sweeten the air . . . barrels of spices mingle in the air too . . . gold bangles are heard even before they're seen on sari-clad women . . . Sikhs fill the streets . . . vegetarian restaurants abound . . . good bargains if you know where to look.

Merlion • Symbol of Singapore . . . a 26-foot statue with a lion's head (Singapura means lion city) and the body of a fish (*Tumasek* is Javanese for sea) that guards the harbor . . . situated at the mouth of Singapore River . . . spews a constant flow of water . . . often forms a rainbow on the horizon because of this tropical climate . . . can't miss this fellow . . . one of the city's most popular camera subjects . . . also commands **Merlion Park,** a small green area fronting the sea.

Mt. Faber • Off Kampong Bahru Rd. . . . 385-foot hill view of city and harbor . . . reachable by cable car from Jardine Steps or from Sentosa Island station . . . art gallery and restaurant on top . . . last cable car departs top of the hill at 6:30 p.m.

National Museum and Art Gallery • Stamford Rd. . . . an idea Sir Stamford Raffles talked about in 1823 . . . actually begun in 1849 and moved to present building in 1887 . . . collection includes archaeological artifacts, Chinese bronzes and porcelains, Nonya fabrics (Chinese/ Malay design), costumes and furniture, maps and paintings of old Singapore, contemporary artworks, plus Haw Par 385-piece priceless jade collection, largest of its kind in the world . . . free admission . . . open weekdays from 9 a.m.–5 p.m., to 7 p.m. on weekends . . . Art in Action for young Singaporeans to display creative talent on first weekend of each month.

Orchid Gardens • Mandai Lake Rd. . . . 10 acres of orchids to feast the eyes . . . all varieties and all colors . . . an entire hillside covered with wild orchids . . . including Singapore's national flower, the Vanda Miss Joaquin . . . two hundred hybrids here . . . open daily from 9 a.m.–6 p.m. with S$1 admission for adults, S$.50 for children (refundable against purchases at garden shop).

Pasar Malam (Night Market) • newly created weekly tourist attraction . . . takes place daily from 6 to 10 p.m. . . . 4 to 10 p.m. on weekends . . . specializes in handicrafts.

Raffles City • Corner North Bridge and Stamford Rds. . . . huge "city within a city" to be finished by 1986 . . . 3500 seat Convention City . . . luxury 30-twin-story hotel with 800 rooms . . . less luxurious 72-story tower hotel with 1200 rooms . . . 44-story office tower . . . atrium and public concourse with shops, restaurants, roof garden . . . Westin manages both hotels.

Raffles Hotel • Beach Rd. . . . more than just a hotel . . . a world-renowned institution . . . "stands for all the fables of the exotic East" wrote Somerset Maugham . . . originally a tiffin house but turned into a luxury hostelry by the Sarkie brothers in 1886 . . . became a Far Eastern stopover for many accalimed authors . . . Maugham, Coward, Conrad, and Kipling . . . home of the Singapore Sling . . . have one at the Long Bar, although they're not what they used to be. Raffles is closed until 1991 while it undergoes a complete, historically accurate renovation.

Seiwaen Japanese Garden of Tranquillity • Off Yuan Ching Rd., Jurong . . . 32½ acres . . . largest of its kind outside Japan . . . in traditional *Kaiyu-chikuyomarinsen* style . . . carefully manicured . . . ponds, bridges, a waterfall, quietude . . . open daily 9 a.m. to 6 p.m. with S$1.00 admission for adults, S$.50 for children . . . admission to both Chinese and Japanese gardens: S$2.50 for adults, S$1.20 for children.

Singapore Cricket Club • Stamford Rd. and Connaught Dr. . . . one of the oldest institutions in the city . . . on the site of the home of Singapore's first resident . . . facing the famous Padang or playing field . . . where once "white" Singapore frolicked . . . now 4 cultures compete on good terms.

Singapore Science Centre ● Off Jurong Town Hall Rd. . . . opened 1977 . . . 4 galleries and over 300 exhibits . . . great for children . . . theater and multi-screen audio-visual show "Flight: The Myth, the Dream and the Reality" . . . open Tues. through Sun. from 10 a.m.– 6 p.m. with S$1 admission for adults and S$.50 for children.

Siong Lim See Monastery ● Jalan Toa Payoh . . . also known as Twin Grove of the Lotus Mountain Buddhist Temple . . . set in a bamboo grove off the Pan Island Expressway . . . it is guarded by **Four Kings of Heaven** in full military regalia . . . statues of **Gautama Buddha** and Goddess of Mercy, **Kuan Yin** . . . murals depicting adventures of the Patriarch, the Monkey God, and "Piggy" on a mission for the Jade Emperor.

Sir Thomas Stamford Raffles ● Founder of Singapore . . . bronze lifesize statue sculpted by Thomas Woolner . . . in Empress Place . . . his eyes cast toward Singapore River, the spot where he landed on Jan. 29, 1819 . . . Japanese considered melting him down after the war . . . fortunately, they never got the chance.

Sir Stamford Raffles Landing Site ● Singapore River . . . another statue of the city's founder . . . placed on the east bank of the river to mark his historic arrival in 1819 . . . pass it on the way upriver for added drama.

St. Andrew's Cathedral ● Coleman St. . . . between the Padang and Raffles City . . . another fragile relic of the past . . . foundation stone laid 1853 . . . built by Indian convicts . . . one of the stained glass windows dedicated to Sir Stamford Raffles himself . . . a designated national monument . . . open from 7 a.m.–6 p.m. daily.

Sri Mariamman Temple ● South Bridge Rd. . . . Singapore's most photographed temple . . . located on the fringe of Chinatown . . . on land donated by a Tamil Hindu from Penang who arrived in Singapore with Sir Stamford Raffles . . . temple decorated by Indian artisans . . . prayers offered for the price of a banana or coconut . . . open daily from 6 a.m.–noon and from 4:30–8:30 p.m.

Sultan Mosque ● North Bridge Rd. . . . the city's biggest Moslem structure . . . Muezzin broadcast daily at 5:30 a.m. from tallest minaret . . . filled with worshipers every evening and Fri. noon . . . built over a century ago with money donated by Sir Stamford Raffles

. . . open from 8 a.m.–5:30 p.m. daily . . . remove shoes and wash feet before entering.

Supreme Court and City Hall • St. Andrew's Rd. . . . neo-classical structures built between 1929 and 1939 . . . Japanese surrender in 1945 and declaration of the Republic in 1965 took place in City Hall . . . worth a look as you drive past.

Telok Ayer Market • Raffles Quay . . . first built in 1825 and rebuilt in 1894, octagonal **Lau Pa Sat** (old market) stands proudly beside high rises . . . prefabricated cast iron building believed made in Europe and shipped here . . . now a giant cafeteria filled with foodstalls . . . great for lunch but get there early.

Telok Ayer Street • Three national monuments here . . . all within walking distance . . . **Thian Hock Keng Temple** dedicated to Ma Chu Poh, Queen of Heaven and patron of sailors . . . **Al-Abrar Mosque** at No. 192 . . . built in 1850–55 from a humble shack and now a holy place for Singapore's Moslems . . . **Nagore Durgha Shrine** at No. 140 . . . actually another mosque but erected by southern Indian Moslems in 1829–30 . . . mixture of Eastern and Western architecture.

Temple of 1000 Lights • Race Course Rd. . . . a 50-foot statue of Lord Buddha . . . framed by hundreds of lights . . . temple built by a Thai monk named Vutthisasara . . . relics include replica of Buddha's footprint and piece of bark from the bohdi tree . . . open from 9 a.m. until after 4:30 p.m. . . . prayers daily.

Thian Hock Keng • Temple of Heavenly Happiness . . . Telok Ayer St. . . . oldest Chinese temple in Singapore . . . built in 1840 by Chinese immigrants in honor of Ma Chu Poh (Queen of Heaven) . . . believed her blessings got them to safety in Singapore . . . hence her birthday celebrated here with great gusto . . . temple throughout embellished with intricate pillars and stone carvings imported from China.

Thong Chai Medical Institution Building • 3 Wayang St. . . . ornate building in heart of Chinatown . . . began as hospital around 1830 . . . now a showplace of Chinese architecture and curios . . . fascinating, well-preserved monument . . . worth a stop.

Tiger Balm Garden • Pasir Panjang Rd. . . . Chinese Disneyland without any humor . . . built by the Aw family whose fortune was made in Tiger Balm medicines . . . full of what I thought were badly sculpted tableaux with morals to preach . . . how the Chinese see life now and during Salvation . . . my advice is to avoid it if you can . . . free admission . . . open daily from 8 a.m.–6 p.m.

Victoria Theatre and Memorial Hall • One of the few colonial structures still standing . . . built in 1906 . . . topped by its own version of Big Ben which has stopped only on 3 occasions . . . the last time during the fall of Singapore in 1942 . . . lovely theater and hall used for symphony concerts and professional dramas.

War Memorial • Beach Rd. Memorial Park Land . . . commemorates thousands of civilians who died during Japanese occupation of World War II . . . four tapering white columns representing four cultures of Singapore erected on site where Japanese said to have murdered so many . . . memorial ceremony held here every Feb. 15.

Yu Hwa Yuan Chinese Garden • Off Yuan Ching Rd., Jurong . . . something new based on Peking's famous Summer Palace gardens with some architectural traditions of the Sung Dynasty . . . 32½ acres of bridges, pagodas, stone lions, lotus ponds, and bamboo groves . . . a favorite with families in neighboring **Jurong Town,** which houses workers from 600 factories . . . also popular with newlyweds for that "first" photo . . . how about the White Rainbow Bridge or the Cloud-piercing Pagoda? . . . Open daily from 8 a.m.–6 p.m. with S$2 admission for adults, S$1.00 for children.

Zoological Gardens • Mandai Lake Rd. . . . over 1300 animals involving some 140 different species roam around an open zoo . . . 70 acres of landscaped park . . . one of world's largest collections of orangutans . . . animal showtime with elephants and sea lions entertaining . . . open 8:30 a.m.–6 p.m. daily . . . showtimes at 3:30 p.m. weekdays, with additional 11 a.m. show on Sun. and holidays . . . admission is S$3.50 adults, S$1.50 children . . . tram and photograph surcharges.

Sentosa and the Southern Islands

Buran Darat • Next door to Sentosa . . . some 37½ acres with lovely swimming lagoon . . . being developed into a marina . . . bridge to Sentosa also under consideration.

Kusu • Tortoise Island . . . the most popular of the 42 islands in the so-called southern chain . . . only 3½ miles from Singapore . . . land recently reclaimed and enlarged to 21 acres with 3000-plus foot beach . . . **Tua Pek Kong,** a Chinese Taoist temple juts into lagoon

. . . also Malay *kramat* . . . both visited by devotees . . . also tortoise sanctuary, swimming lagoons, changing huts . . . ferries depart World Trade Centre pier from 9 a.m.–6:20 p.m. daily . . . return fare is about S$3 adults, S$1.50 children.

Lazarus • Pulau Sekijang Pelepah in Malay . . . some 81 acres of island between Kusu and St. John's . . . no regular ferry service . . . must hire own boat.

Pulau Hantu • Ghost Island . . . about 4 miles from mainland and popular with swimmers . . . 1½ miles of sandy beach on 32 acres of land . . . 3 lovely lagoons . . . busy on weekends.

Pulau Renggit • 3 miles from mainland . . . lies near St. John's and Lazarus islands . . . reclaimed to 30 acres now.

Sentosa • Isle of Peace and Tranquillity . . . new name by contest for an island previously used as a military base and called Pulau Blakang Mati (island of leaving death behind) . . . almost 1000 acres just ⅓ mile from shore . . . much promoted by STPB as resort area . . . swimming, boating, jogging, roller-skating, tennis, squash, you name it . . . **Maritime Museum** . . . **Coralarium** . . . two 18-hole golf courses . . . **Art Centre** . . . **Surrender Chamber** (reenactment of Japanese surrender in 1945 at City Hall) . . . **Fort Siloso** and **Siloso Beach** . . . 10-acre Apollo Hotel resort complex with 165 rooms and chalets and conference hall for 1000-plus swimming pool and tennis courts, etc. . . . Swiss-designed monorail around the island . . . Musical Fountain a la Disneyworld for evening entertainment . . . restaurants and snack bars . . . all accessible by cable car from Jardine Steps between 10 a.m. and 6:30 p.m. weekdays, from 9 a.m. Sun. and holidays (S$6 roundtrip for adults, S$3 for children) . . . or by ferry from World Trade Centre Ferry Terminal between 7:30 a.m. and 11 p.m. daily (fares included in Sentosa ticket) . . . admission to Sentosa, including transportation and all attractions, soft drink, and brochure is S$4.50 for adults and S$2.50 for children.

St. John's • Former leprosarium . . . 4 miles from mainland . . . 93 acres of gentle hills and shade trees . . . a mile-long beach made for the picnic crowd . . . holiday camps and bungalows for government workers . . . many facilities programmed here . . . ferry same as for Sentosa.

Subar Laut/Subar Darat • Sisters' Islands . . . reclaimed to a total of 13½ acres . . . 5½ miles from Singapore . . . sandy beaches and overnight camping allowed.

Terembu Retan Laut • 30-minute ride from Jardine Steps . . . 37 acres sheltered beautifully . . . Singapore Yacht Club leases western part of island for mooring facilities.

Tours

Arts and Crafts of Singapore • 3 hours . . . Instant Asia cultural show, Singapore Handicraft Centre, crocodile farm, batik factory, pewter factory, gem-cutting factory.

Changi and East Coast Tour • 3–6 hours, by arrangement only . . . batik factory, Changi Prison (chapel and roof garden), Selarang barracks, Changi murals, Changi Village, East Coast Park, Singapore Handicraft Centre.

City Tour • 3½ hours, daily . . . Elizabeth Walk, Merlion Park, Supreme Court and City Hall views, Singapore River, Chinatown, Sri Mariamman Hindu Temple, Mt. Faber, Instant Asia cultural show, Tiger Balm Gardens, Queenstown Housing estate, Orchid Pavilion at Botanic Gardens, National Museum, and sometimes Singapore Handicraft Centre.

East Coast Tour • 3½ hours, daily . . . Merdeka Bridge, National Stadium, East Coast Park, villages and fishing ponds, rubber and coconut plantations, crocodile farm, Siong Lim Temple and garden, Temple of 1000 Lights.

Flora and Fauna • 3–5 hours, by arrangement only . . . Mandai Orchid Garden and Zoological Gardens.

Genting Highlands Tour • 2 days . . . by coach to Kuala Lumpur via Ayer Itam, Yong Peng, Segamat Seremban, and Kajang . . . on to Genting Highlands and casino . . . pass through Malacca on return.

Harbour Tour • 2½ hours from 10 a.m. and 1:30 p.m. weekdays . . . harbor, islands, and 20-minute stopover at Kusu Island.

Johor Bahru Tour • 3½ hours, daily . . . Sultan's old palace, Bukit Serene (new palace), Sultan Abu Bakar Mosque, sarong weaving factory, rubber plantation.

Junk Cruise • 2½ hours from 10:30 a.m., 3 p.m., and 4 p.m. daily.

Jurong Tour • 3½ hours, daily . . . Jurong Bird Park, Jurong Town, and Chinese Garden.

Malacca Tour • 8–12 hours, by arrangement only . . . Johor Bahru, drive past rubber and pineapple estates, past fields and villages, Malacca, Dutch churches, Portuguese fortress, Malaysia's oldest Moslem mosque, and first Chinese temple.

Our People, Our Heritage • 3 hours . . . Thian Hock Keng Temple, Chinatown, Little India on Serangoon Rd., Sri Srinivasa Perumal Temple, Sultan Mosque on North Bridge Rd., Arab St.

Pulau Tioman Tour • 3 days . . . by coach to Mersing, by launch to Tioman, tour of village, swimming, water skiing, scuba diving, and fishing.

Sentosa, Southern Island and Cable Car Tour • 3 hours from 9:30 a.m. and 3:30 p.m. weekdays . . . tour of harbor, stop at Sentosa to visit attractions, cable car return to Singapore.

Sunset Cruise • 1½ hours, daily at 7:15 p.m. . . . a cruise around harbor plus Kusu and St. John's islands.

Temple Tour • 3½ hours, by arrangement only . . . Siong Lim Buddhist Temple, Sultan Mosque, Sri Mariamman Hindu Temple, Buddhist Temple of 1000 Lights.

Trishaw Tour • 1–3 hours, by arrangement only . . . start from Raffles Hotel to seafront, through Chinatown.

Ulu Tiram Tour • 6–7 hours, Wed. and Sat. . . . Johor Bahru, Sultan Abu Bakar Mosque, Ulu Tiram Estate (oil palm, toddy, rubber taping, rubber factory).

West Malaysia Tour • 7 days, by arrangement only . . . Malacca, Kuala Lumpur, Penang, Cameron Highlands, Genting Highlands.

HOTELS

★★★**Century Park Sheraton** • *16 Nassim Hill, Singapore 1025.*
Tel: 732–1222. Cable: CENPARK Singapore. Telex: CPHSIN
RS21817 • 462 rooms (17 suites) . . . quiet location a few minutes from
Orchard Rd. . . . cabana rooms with terraces by 2nd-floor pool . . .
superb views from other accommodations . . . pleasant atmosphere with
paneled lobby and bar . . . owned by All Nippon Airways . . . one of
the better Sheratons in Asia . . . if you avoid the Japanese groups.

Facilities: Hubertus Grill, Fountain Lounge and Cafe in the Park
coffee shop on ground level. Ridley's Has the Rubber (one of the hottest discos in town) on mezzanine. Unkai attractive Japanese restaurant
on 1st floor. Secretarial services. Steambath, sauna, and swimming pool.

Manager: G. Jonas. *Reservations:* Sheraton Worldwide.

★★★★**Crown Prince Hotel** • *270 Orchard Rd., Singapore 0923.*
Tel: 732111. Telex: RS 22819 HCROWN • 303 rooms. Managed by Prince
Hotels of Japan . . . expect to find little touches like bedroom slippers
. . . attractive structure with spacious atrium lobby.

Facilities: Fen Cheng Lou Teochew Chinese cuisine. Cafe de Prince.
Sushi Kaiseki Nogawa. The Lounge. Swimming pool. Business Center.
Presidential and Corner Executives suites with steam and whirlpool baths.
Meeting rooms.

Manager: Y. Yamada. *Reservations:* UTELL.

★★★★**The Dynasty** • *320 Orchard Rd., Singapore 0923. Tel:*
7349900. Cable: DYNASTY Singapore. Telex: RS 36633 • 400 rooms
(72 suites) . . . dramatic structure on the Singapore skyline . . . 33-
story pagoda-style hotel linked to C.K. Tang's new department store
. . . roof tiles from China . . . dramatic 3-story lobby . . . interiors
by Don Ashton . . . energy-saving exteriors and the latest in guest-
room locks . . . unusual concept here.

Facilities: Bill Bailey's bar, Golden Dew coffeehouse, and sidewalk cafe on ground floor. La Vendome restaurant on 2nd floor. Tang
Court Chinese restaurant on 3rd floor. The Executive Club in lower
basement. 5th-floor Chinese garden, pavilions, and swimming pool. Pedestrian walkways to Orchard and Scotts roads. Executive services. IDD.

Manager: R. Oon. *Reservations:* Distinguished Hotels.

★★★**The Glass Hotel** • *317 Outram Rd., Singapore 0316. Tel: 733 0188. Telex: 50141* • 509 rooms. One of the city's unheralded glamorous hotels . . . spectacular atriuim with restaurants (Italian, Chinese, Continental, coffee shop/buffet) . . . noted for its luncheon buffets . . . 5 minutes from downtown.
Facilities: tennis courts, swimming pool, 24-hour room service.
Manager: C. Ricca.

★★★★**Goodwood Park Hotel** • *22 Scotts Rd., Singapore 0922. Tel: 7377411. Cable: GOODWOOD Telex: RS 24377* • 235 rooms (81 suites) . . . original tower built in 1900 as Teutonia Club . . . 15 acres of grounds . . . fantastic Brunei suite with private lift, dining room with roof garden, and octagon-shaped lounge area . . . 64 Parklane suites with balcony in separate wing . . . 2 swimming pools . . . 7000-plant nursery . . . old-world charm and Commonwealth clientele . . . watch out for visiting "royalty."
Facilities: L'Espresso indoor-outdoor terrace cafe, coffee lounge, Highland Bar and Gordon Grill on lobby level. Former West End Club closed. Shima Japanese restaurant. Carlton bar. Gourmet market on lower ground level for suite kitchenettes. York Hotel next door (same ownership) offers another swimming pool, squash courts, Mario's Italian restaurant, and Bamboo Court for Chinese cuisine. Goodwood Park group also owner/manager of Ladyhill and Malaysia hotels, manager of Ming Court Hotel.
Manager: Christine Cheng. *Reservations:* SRS.

★★★★**Hilton International Singapore** • *581 Orchard Rd., Singapore 0923. Tel: 7372233. Cable: HILTELS. Telex: RS 21491* • 435 rooms (43 suites) . . . a longtime favorite with businessmen . . . dependable and efficient . . . opened 1970 and constantly refurbished . . . exclusive 21st floor of suites designed by French couturier Hubert de Givenchy, with private balcony, whirlpool bath, crystal decanters of liquors, butler/maid service, complimentary laundry/valet, etc. . . . try the "Suite Life."
Facilities: Rooftop garden with swimming pool (23rd floor) and health club (22nd floor). Tradewinds foodstalls featuring local ethnic snacks and feature films on Sun. (23rd floor). Inn of Happiness Cantonese and Szechuan restaurant (23rd floor). Harbour Grill (2nd floor). Orchard Cafe coffee shop (ground floor). The Music Room (2nd floor) for afternoon teas, drinks, and music. Lobby bar (ground floor). Executive business centre with worldwide courier service, word processing service, electronic pagers, and overnight film developing service.
Manager: V. Wee. *Reservations:* HRS.

★★★**Holiday Inn Park View** • *11 Cavenagh Rd., Singapore 0922. Tel: 733 8333* • 320 rooms. Strategically located for shopping just off

Orchard Rd., this is a lovely, unpretentious hotel with a friendly feel to it.

Facilities: New Orleans Restaurant and Bar, Fragrant Blossom Restaurant for Chinese food, The Tandoor for Indian, a coffee shop and Clemenceau's for cocktails . . . an excutive lounge and executive floor.

Manager: R. Van. *Reservations:* HOLIDEX.

★★★**Holiday Inn Hotel** ● *25 Scotts Rd., Singapore 0922. Tel: 7377966. Cable: HOLIDAYINN. Telex: RS 21818* ● 600 rooms . . . a cut above your average Holiday Inn . . . especially for travelers who like sea-green interiors . . . convenient location . . . near Shaw Centre . . . across from Hyatt Hotel and Far East Plaza.

Facilities: Department store and nightclub next door. Winter Garden lobby bar and Cafe Vienna 24-hour coffeehouse with live music in evenings. Baron's Tavern/Baron's Table (German provincial) restaurant. Treetops Bar. Meisan Szechuan Restaurant. Rooftop swimming pool, mini-golf course. Health center. Business Center.

Manager: SK Boon. *Reservations:* HOLIDEX.

★★★★**Hyatt Regency Singapore** ● *10-12 Scotts Rd., Singapore 0922. Tel: 7331188. Cable: HYATT SINGAPORE. Telex: RS 24415* ● 1174 rooms . . . an excellent hotel . . . reputed to have very good *feng shui* . . . well managed and quite capable of holding its own against the competition . . . walking distance to Orchard Rd. activities . . . fine shopping in Serendipity Row off the lobby . . . a leading businessman and convention hotel . . . can't beat the pampering of the Regency Club. Don't miss Malam Singapura cultural show and splendid barbecue three times a week.

Facilities: Gallery 10–12 for European/Asian artist showings and sale on mezzanine. Regency Club for guests on 19th, 20th, and 21st floors with own concierge, butler station, complimentary continental breakfast and cocktail hour, personalized stationery, etc. Nutmegs Art Deco specialty restaurant on mezzanine. Hugo's gourmet restaurant with French provincial decor and dishes on mezzanine level. Scott's Bar off lobby. Chinoiserie membership club/disco on mezzanine. Pete's Place pizza and Italian menu restaurant on lower level. Swimming pool with daily buffets/barbecues and health center on 4th floor. Businessman's Centre with full services and IDD telephones. Elegant, new 350-room extension, Regency Terrace, with tennis and squash courts, Fitness Center, and landscaped pool with 4-story waterfall!

Manager: A. Holliger. *Reservations:* Hyatt Hotels.

★★★★**The Mandarin Singapore** ● *333 Orchard Rd., Singapore 0923. Tel: 7374411. Cable: MANRINOTEL. Telex: RS 21528 Manotel* ● 1200 rooms (75 suites) . . . the largest hotel (two 40-story towers) in

Singapore thus far . . . lavish public areas . . . impossible to find one's way about without effort . . . enormous lobby in Venetian/Tang Dynasty style . . . guest-oriented energy-saving systems in rooms . . . all with excellent views . . . well-appointed bathrooms . . . 6 restaurants . . . 5 cocktail lounges . . . 2-tiered sundeck . . . good conference hotel . . . Kuan Dai (means hospitality in Mandarin) service arranged by Leading Hotels of the World . . . includes airport greeting, complimentary cocktail, fruit basket, express check-out.

Facilities: Full banking facilities on the property. 24-hour call medical clinic. 3-story shopping arcade. Recreation and health center with mini-golf course, tennis and squash courts, saunda, hydropool, and gym on 38th floor. Outdoor swimming pool with sundeck and snack bar on 5th floor. Belvedere gourmet restaurant on 5th floor. Chatterbox coffeehouse on ground floor South Wing. New Tsuru-No-Ya Japanese restaurant on 3rd floor. Pine Court Peking restaurant on 36th floor. Top of The M revolving restaurant on 40th floor. The Stables grillroom on 5th floor. (Mandarin also manages Neptune theater-restaurant on Collyer Quay.) Act I bar adjacent to lobby. Clipper bar and Mezzanine Lounge on mezzanine floor. Observation lounge on 39th floor. 3 airline offices in hotel. Kasbah nightclub on 36th floor. The Library club/disco for members only. Mandarin Executive Service (secretarial, etc.) on mezzanine.

Manager: T. W. Lien. *Reservation:* LHW.

★★★★★**Marina Mandarin Singapore** • *6 Raffles Blvd. #01–100, Singapore 0103. Tel: 338–3388. Telex: RS22299* • 640 rooms (48 suites). Located in heart of town at Marina Square . . . largest atrium in Asia . . . scenic views of Marina Bay and city . . . brand-new and exciting hotel . . . part of Mandarin Singapore Int'l Hotels. John Portman exteriors . . . Don Ashton interiors . . . fabulous!

Facilities: Swimming pool. Squash and tennis courts. Health center. 250 shops. Les Oiseaux French restaurant with dinner music. Ristorante Bologna Italian specialties. The Cricketer Pub. House of Blossoms, Teochew Chinese cuisine. Brasserie Tatler (coffee shop). Reading Room disco. Video recorder rentals. Banquet and meeting rooms. Poolside restaurant/bar.

Manager: A. Ihlenfeld. *Reservations:* LHW.

★★★★**The Marco Polo Singapore** • *Tanglin Rd., Singapore 1024. Tel: 4747141. Cable: HOMARCPOLO. Telex: RS 21476* • 603 rooms (30 suites) . . . lovely 4-acre setting with landscaped gardens . . . well managed with small hotel friendliness . . . excellent accommodations in the better rooms . . . minutes from Botanic Gardens . . . a step away from Handicraft Centre and Rasa Singapura . . . impressive service except in early a.m. checkout . . . complete 9th floor for non-smokers . . . pool-side terrace rooms for fresh air fiends.

Facilities: Full Business Center (off lobby) and IDD service in guest rooms. Clark Hatch Physical Fitness Centre (men only). Beautiful swimming pool and gardens on 2nd floor. Marco Polo Lounge for meetings and cocktails. Marco Polo steak house, San Marco gourmet restaurant, Brasserie la Rotonde, La Pinata coffee shop, and El Patio all on ground level. Marco Polo cake shop in shopping arcade, and The Club disco in basement.

Manager: H. Oldenburger. *Reservations:* SRS.

★★★★**The Meridien Singapore** • *100 Orchard Rd., Singapore 0923. Tel: 7338855. Telex: RS 50163 Homeri* • 414 rooms (33 suites). 6-story hotel managed by Air France subsidiary . . . in heart of business district.

Facilities: La Brasserie French restaurant. La Terrassee coffee shop. Le Rendezvous lobby bar. Swimming pool and La Veranda bar. Meeting rooms. Commercial Center.

Manager: J-C Bailly. *Reservations:* Meridien Int'l.

★★★★**Hotel Meridien Changi-Singapore** • *1 Netheravon Rd., Upper Changi Rd., Singapore 1750. Tel: 5427700. Telex: RS 36042 HOMRA* • 276 rooms. Situated in a garden setting near Changi International Airport . . . just a few minutes from the beach . . . guests have plenty of watersports opportunities as well as access to golf and tennis nearby. Offshore island tours and junk cruises.

Facilities: La Veranda restaurant. Changi Cafe. Lotus bar. Lobby Bar. Swimming pool. Meeting rooms. Business Center.

Manager: R. J. Andre. *Reservations:* Meridien Int'l.

★★★★★**The Oriental** • *6 Raffles Blvd., Singapore 0103. Tel: 3380066. Telex: RS 29117 ORSIN* • 402 rooms (62 suites). Operated by the Hong Kong-based Mandarin Oriental Hotel Group . . . brand-new beautiful hotel in Marina Square complex designed by John Portman . . . distinctive 21-story triangular-shaped structure . . . luxurious accommodations overlooking harbor and city . . . 7th hotel in Mandarin Oriental's portfolio . . . all top-rated . . . interiors by Don Ashton.

Facilities: Fourchettes continental restaurant. The Gallery for coffee, tea, and cocktails. Captain's Bar. Cafe Palm brasserie. Cherry Garden Chinese restaurant. L'Aperitif Bar. Taeping and Ariel suites for private parties. Atrium Lounge. Swimming pools with Marina Bar and Barbecue. Health Center. Air-conditioned squash courts. Executive Center. 240 shops. Oriental Ballroom.

Manager: J. Toh. *Reservations:* LHW.

★★★★★**Pan Pacific Hotel** • *7 Raffles Blvd., Singapore 0103. Tel: 336–8111. Telex: RS38821* • 800 rooms. The third of Singapore's newest hotels in Marina Square . . . with its sisters, a statement about the latest in hotel design and construction . . . convenient to the business district, Raffles City, and sightseeing attractions, and adjacent to subway stop for shopping areas . . . glass bubble elevators, atrium, and the largest shopping complex in Southeast Asia.

Facilities: 10 restaurants and bars serving every kind of food imaginable . . . fully equipped health spa and gym, 24-hour business center, breathtaking views from every room.

Manager: J. Wasser.

★★★★★**The Regent of Singapore** • *No. 1 Cuscaden Rd., Singapore 1024. Tel: 7338888. Cable: INHOTELCOR. Telex: RS 37248* • 443 rooms (44 suites) . . . 3-acre site across the road from Marco Polo Hotel . . . adjacent to Handicraft Centre and Rasa Singapura . . . interesting design by Atlanta-based architect John Portman . . . guest rooms and public areas spaced around sky-lit 12-story interior atrium . . . east and west accommodations have large balcony areas . . . Opened in 1988, Regent is in the process of putting its highly distinctive touch on the hotel and has already created the most elegant property in Singapore.

Facilities: Maxim's de Paris (since 1893) is exact replica on 2nd floor . . . Summer Palace Cantonese restaurant on 2nd floor. Tea Garden coffee shop on 1st floor. 2 atrium lobby bars. Swimming pool and health center on ground level. Lobby filled with 40,000 yellow chrysanthemums. Business Centre.

Manager: Ms. F. Cheong. *Reservations:* IHC.

★★★★★**Shangri-la Singapore** • *22 Orange Grove Rd., Singapore 1025. Tel: 7373644. Cable: SHANGRI LA. Telex: RS 21505* • 809 rooms . . . located on 12½ acres in a lovely residential area . . . 24-story main tower plus Garden and Valley wings . . . rated 4th in Institutional Investor's assessment of world's best hotels (for what it's worth) . . . spacious and soothing accommodations . . . nice views . . . excellent service and restaurants . . . beautiful grounds . . . waterfall connects 2 buildings . . . absolutely one of the top hotels in Singapore.

Facilities: Recreation facilities with swimming, squash, tennis, golf, and health club. La Tiara rooftop supper club with international cabaret. Spacious lobby bar (where much business is conducted over drinks). Golden Peacock continental restaurant and Peacock Bar with country-and-western music (a favorite with the oil crowd) off lobby. Shang Palace Cantonese restaurant on upper level. Waterfall Cafe on ground level of Garden Wing. 24-hour coffee garden on lower level. Full Business Center.

Manager: R. Guthrie. *Reservations:* Shangri-la Int'l.

★★★★**Sheraton Towers Singapore** • *39 Scotts Rd., Singapore 0922. Tel: 737–6888. Telex: 37750 SHNSIN* • 406 rooms. A new Sheraton concept . . . to appeal to a more discerning segment of the travel market . . . 21-story tower featuring many elegant touches for guests . . . butler service on every floor . . . 24-hour pressing service . . . complimentary coffee and tea in rooms . . . complimentary continental breakfast . . . and hors d'oeuvres . . . terry bathrobes . . . special personal care amenities.

Facilities: Domus continental cuisine. Li Bai Chinese restaurant. Terazza coffee shop. Health Club. Swimming pool. Business Center. Disco.

Manager: C. Nicholas. *Reservations:* Sheraton.

★★★★★**The Westin Plaza** • *2 Stamford Rd., Singapore 0617. Tel: 338–8585. Telex: RS 22206 RCHTLS* • 796 rooms (47 suites). Located in new Raffles City complex . . . 2 29-story towers connected to sister-hotel Westin Stamford by air-conditioned multitiered complex of shops, meetings rooms, restaurants, lounges, and atria.

Facilities: 5 restaurants. 2 cocktail lounges. Disco. 4 air-conditioned squash courts. 6 tennis courts. 2 swimming pools with snack bar. Health food shop and bar. Executive Busines Center. In-house fitness expert.

Manager: W. Godfrey. *Reservations:* Westin.

The Westin Stamford • *2 Stamford Rd., Singapore 0617. Tel: 338–8585. Telex: RS 22206 RCHTLS* • 1257 rooms (80 suites). Billed as the world's tallest hotel . . . guests can enjoy spectacular views of neighboring Malaysia and Indonesia (so they say) . . . from their private balconies . . . quite a sight if you don't mind the height.

Facilities: Palm Grill. Canton Garden. Szechuan Court. Somerset's Bar. Inagiku Japanese restaurant. The Terrace Lounge. Prego. L'Express. The Raffles Deli. Scribbles. The Compass Rose. Health club shared with Westin Plaza. Executive business center. Convention center.

Manager: W. McCreary. *Reservations:* Westin.

NEW ATTRACTIONS

Empress Place • A new museum created from one of the old British colonial office buildings within walking distance of Raffles City and the Cathedral . . . captures much of Singapore's history in the building

itself, with exhibits devoted to the country's various historical traditions
. . . the opening exhibit featured the personal effects of the last emperor of China.

Marina Square • Designed by American architect John Portman
on reclaimed land . . . the new square is accessible from Nicoll Highway, Bras Basah Road, and East Coast Parkway . . . an enormous
complex of 3 large hotels, landscaped gardens, 4 department stores,
some 240 retail outlets, entertainment and sport facilities and parking
for 2300 cars . . . the hotels are the top-rated Oriental and Marina
Mandarin . . . as well as the Pan Pacific—a division of Tokyu International Hotels that will appeal to the Asian trade . . . of the three,
The Oriental boasts the distinctive Portman atrium concept.

Raffles City • This modern complex of a city within a city has
been conceived and designed by Chinese-American architect I. M. Pei
. . . occupies 8 acres in heart of downtown Singapore . . . features 4
separate towers including a 42-story tower connected by a 7-story enclosed space . . . truly a 21st-century version of the town square . . .
71-story Westin Stamford and twin-core 28-story towers of Westin Plaza
offer some 2000 accommodations, 18 restaurants and lounges . . . and
the ultimate in meeting and exhibit facilities . . . Raffles City promises
the utmost in technology . . . convenience . . . comfort . . . largest
convention and meeting center in Far East.

DINING

To say that Singaporeans *love* to eat is an understatement—they
live for their food. And they do so in four major cultures, with another
dozen or so cuisines ready on the back burners. Dining in this city is a
continual taste treat, and not so much a planned event but a spontaneous
happening. As a visitor, you will probably become so tantalized by the
mixture of cooking odors from shops and sidewalk foodstalls that sud-
den hunger will demand a nibble here and another there. Voila! You
have just consumed a spectacular meal of satay, kai fan, and mee goreng, and a bottle of local beer for just a few dollars—totally unplanned
and more enjoyable than you ever imagined. Here, more than any other
city in the Far East, you can be adventurous and daring, for the food is
fresh, delicious, and completely safe.

The majority of dishes found in Singapore are Chinese to satisfy
that 75% of the population, but Indian, Malay, and Indonesian cuisines
also prevail. There is also Nonya food, a combination of the most del-

icate of Chinese and Malay. Western cuisine here is comparable to anywhere in the world, and if you must have your American steaks and hamburgers or pasta or Swiss fondue—none is difficult to find. Most of the restaurants, and especially the foodstall complexes, require only the most casual of attire and manners. Do not be put off by the lack of utensils offered—Chinese dishes are eaten with chopsticks (known as fai tse or nimble brothers to Singaporeans), but both Malay and Indian food is often consumed with either a spoon or your fingers. Only in hotel restaurants and the better independent places will you find the table fully laid with the gamut of silver flatware and dressed with starched cloth and napkins. Of course, at these places you are expected to dress accordingly (and leave fingers in your lap). Otherwise, open shirts and cool slacks are the norm for gentlemen—something equally informal for women.

CHINESE FOOD

Cantonese cuisine, with its emphasis upon freshness and retention of the taste of the original ingredients is still the most prevalent of all Chinese cooking in Singapore. And you can count upon an endless array of dim sum (which is called tim sum here) for breakfast or lunch. But most Singaporeans are descended from Fukien province families, and Hokkien cooking features fresh seafood dishes, stews, and the best soya sauce in all of China. *Hokkien mee* (wheat-flour noodles in a soup with bits of shrimp and other seafoods) is a favorite of food carts, along with *poh piah* (spring rolls of the thinnest rice-flour pancake filled with shrimps and egg, beansprouts and dried squid, vegetables and chili).

It's interesting that in such a tropical climate, something known as Steamboat is on most menus. This is a chafing-dish meal that comes from the Teochew district of Kwantung province and resembles the Mongolian Hot Pot popular in Hong Kong during the winter months. Steamboat features plates of thinly sliced fish, meat, and just-picked vegetables, cooked individually in a broth (that is then consumed at the end of the meal). It is meant to bring a group of diners together, much as Westerners treat cheese or beef fondues.

Other Teochew dishes to savor are roast suckling pig, roast goose, and *orr chian* (tiny oysters cooked into an omelet). From the island of Hainan comes chicken rice, flavored with ginger and chilis. Neither can you miss the chilis and fire in Hunan and Szechuan (Sichuan) dishes, which are guaranteed to keep you warm inside and out (order extra bottles of beer)! If you are a Peking duck aficionado, there is plenty to behold, as well as Shanghainese beggar's chicken and bird's nest soup. Taiwanese food is also represented here, with a porridge surrounded by foods such as oysters, mussels, and pork stewed in a rich, black sauce.

CHINESE RESTAURANTS

Many of these eating places are simply "walk in off the street," and there is little need for reservations except in the top hotels which might have a full house. Try both the plain and the fancy establishments. However, there is a local superstition that the less rich the decor, the more appetizing the meal (because that's where the owner puts his money). However, suit yourself and loosen that belt!

Huan Long Court • *Apollo Hotel, Havelock Rd.* • Hunan-style with minced pigeon in bamboo cup, spicy honey ham, deep-fried scallops.

Chiu Wah Lin • *Mosque St., Chinatown* • Teochew roast suckling pig and roast goose.

Imperial Herbal Restaurant • *Metropole Hotel, Seah St.* • A Hakka restaurant featuring fried bean curd stuffed with pork and vegetables (*yong tau foo*), fish in rice wine (*ng teow chou sui tong*), and fried intestines of pig with vegetables . . . definitely for the most adventurous.

Canton Garden • *Westin Plaza Hotel* • A gracious setting for China's most popular regional cuisine . . . located in the Westin complex that includes a dozen restaurants, shops, and two hotels.

Golden Phoenix • *Hotel Equatorial, Bukit Timah Rd.* • Glamorous surroundings for spicy Szechuan dishes with chilis and smoked duck.

Great Shanghai • *Armenian St.* • Crab meat and sweet corn soup, braised fish heads, fried eels.

Hillman Restaurant • *Cantonment Rd., Manhill, Pasir Panjang Rd.* • Nothing elaborate, but terrific for "clay pot" dishes like chicken, prawns, and fish heads.

Hung Kang • *North Canal Rd.* • Popular for Teochew Steamboat.

Inn of Happiness • *Hilton International Singapore. Tel: 7372233* • Cantonese/Szechuan . . . chili prawns, abalone with broccoli, three mushrooms.

Min Jiang • *Goodwood Park Hotel* • The interesting blend of excellent Chinese cuisine in a quiet, colonial hotel setting.

Ming Palace • *Ming Court Hotel* • Excellent and very popular dim sum lunches . . . take the mooncakes home and compare, as one friend did.

Omei • *Hotel Grand Central, Orchard/Cavenagh Rds.* • Szechuan smoked duck, chicken with dry chilis, braised beef on fire pot.

Peking Restaurant • *International Building, Orchard Rd.* • Also **Eastern Palace** • *Supreme House, Penang Rd.* • Specialties are Peking duck with all the trimmings (skin, succulent meat, soup from the carcass), shark's fin, prawn ball soup, and beggar's chicken.

Pine Court • *Mandarin Hotel* • Reputed Peking duck, baked tench, shark's fin, and marinated lamb on the 36th floor . . . weekend dim sum buffet lunches, with northern Chinese specialties.

RuYi • *Hyatt Regency* • Probably the most elegant Chinese restaurant in Singapore, with food to match.

Shang Palace • *Shangri-La Hotel. Tel: 7373644* • Considered one of the best and very posh . . . Dim Sum for lunch and Cantonese specialties for dinner . . . try crystal prawn ball and abalone with kailand.

Swee Kee • *Middle Rd.* • Hainanese chicken rice a specialty.

Tai Tong • *Mosque St., Chinatown* • Popular among locals for dim sum breakfasts . . . reputed to have the best mooncakes in Singapore.

INDIAN FOOD

You may think that a curry is a curry is a curry, but some of them are blends of over 20 different spices. And not all are HOT. India boasts over 15 centuries-old cuisines, evenly divided (if you can) between north and south. The northern dishes are milder, with flavors added to meats and vegetables that are considered more subtle and somewhat less stomach-clutching. One of the most well known of all northern Indian delicacies is tandoori chicken, in which the skinned fowl is halved and marinated in yogurt and spices and then grilled in an amphoralike clay oven. This dish is accompanied with grilled onions, mango chutney, and *naan* (unleavened bread baked on the side of the tandoor oven). The result is absolute heaven! Chicken tikka, kebobs of mutton and chicken, and subtle but aromatic curries can also be found on the menu.

Southern Indian food is as hot as you like, to be diluted with saffron rice, chappati bread or *puri* (a deep-fried pancake), and plenty of beer or tea. Some favorites among the hot dishes are chicken beryani, mutton Mysore, and prawn curry. You can also attempt several variations of vegetarian curries with boiled white rice, a glass of yogurt, or pepper water. A tray of condiments may include several types of chutney, fresh onions, cucumbers, yogurt, and cottage cheese.

INDIAN RESTAURANTS

Banana Leaf Apollo • *Racecourse Rd.* • If you must, they will give you a spoon but mostly it's with the fingers . . . chili prawns and other hot dishes.

Jubilee Cafe and **Islamic Restaurant** • *North Bridge Rd.* • Two eating places side by side . . . don't go by the decor . . . chicken madras curry and mutton bombay . . . it's hot here, so come prepared to suffer.

Moti Mahal • *Food Alley on Murray St.* • Specializes in Kashmiri and Punjabi dishes . . . forget the decor, concentrate on the food.

Omar Khayyam • *Hill St.* • Northern Indian (Mogul) and one of the most chic . . . house specialty is tandoori chicken . . . mild curries . . . make an evening of this one.

Rang Mahal • *Oberoi Imperial Hotel, Jalan Rumbia* • Northern Indian and bound to be excellent . . . featured dining spot in an Indian hotel chain.

MALAY FOOD

There are curries blended with rich coconut milk, and there are the exquisite satay sticks. The curries are of beef, fish, prawns, and vegetables and eaten with white rice, *sambals* (chili, onion, and tamarind), and *ikan bilis* (tiny anchovy-like fish). The satay is something very special in the Far Eastern diet. These are tiny pieces of beef, mutton, or chicken marinated in crushed spices, skewered and grilled over charcoal. Although the magic is in the grilling, they say, these tasty morsels of meat are not complete until dipped into a sauce of ground peanuts, coconut milk, and other spices. You then alternate eating a stick of meat (with bits of raw onion and cucumber) with cubes of glutinous rice steamed in banana-leaf wrappings. Satay tastes best at the open-air foodstalls for which Singapore is justly famous.

MALAY RESTAURANTS

Aziza • *Emerald Hill Rd.* • Serves Malay dishes in Western surroundings . . . the restaurant most recommended for visitors.

Rasa Singapura • *Behind Handicraft Centre on Tanglin Rd.* • By popular local vote, the best of all the foodstalls in Singapore were brought here . . . try the satay, plus *mee Siam* (noodles Malay style), Chinese and Indian specialties, and *chye tow kway* (carrot cake). Other foodstalls not to miss are in **People's Park, Bridge Road, Cuppage Centre,** and **Chinatown.**

Satay Club • *Elizabeth Walk* • Not so much a ''club'' as a nightly happening, with dozens of stalls grilling satay before your eyes and offering other Malay dishes.

Tradewinds Foodstalls • *Poolside at Singapore Hilton, Orchard Rd.* • A delightful way to relax in comfort and taste all the local offerings.

OTHER ASIAN FOODS

Indonesian cuisine is similar to Malay, with rice (*nasi*) as the main staple, accompanied by a variety of spicy dishes, coconut milk, and peanuts. Popular dishes available in Singapore are beef rendang, chicken curry, *udang sambal* (prawns), and the famous *gado gado* (salad with spicy peanut dressing). A good way to enjoy what this cuisine offers the palate is the *rijstaeffel,* or rice table, a Sunday buffet the Dutch seem to have invented. **Nonya** food is a fragrant blend of Chinese and Malay and owes its descent to the fact that so many Malay and Chinese have intermarried. There is generous use of ginger, scented laos root, lemongrass, and dried shrimp paste (*blachan*) in many Nonya dishes. Singaporeans prefer to frequent foodstalls for their Nonya specialties, especially *laksa* (noodles in spicy coconut and herb broth). Piquant **Thai** dishes and seafood are also well represented in Singapore as well as **Korean** bulgogi (thin slices of beef marinated in soya, sesame, and garlic and grilled) and the entire gamut of delicate **Japanese** cuisine.

ASIAN RESTAURANTS

Korean Restaurant • *Specialists' Centre, Orchard Rd.* • For your kimchee, origuljot (oysters), and bulgogi.

Luna Coffee House • *Apollo Hotel, Havelock Rd.* • Noted for Nonya dishes, especially satay babi (pork), tangy broths, and laksa.

Rendezvous • *Bras Basah Rd.* • Nothing fancy, but everyone loves the place across the street from the Cathay Building . . . if you don't know what the dishes are, just point to the display case and be pleasantly surprised . . . best Indonesian food in town, they say.

Shima Restaurant • *Goodwood Park Hotel, Scotts Rd.* • Specializes in prime beef for teppanyaki, sukiyaki, yakiniku, and shabu shabu.

Thai Seafood Restaurant • *Cockpit Hotel, Oxley Rise* • Well known for seafood dishes as well as popular Indonesian *rijstaeffel* on both Sat. and Sun. lunchtimes.

The New Tsurunoya • *Mandarin Hotel, Orchard Rd.* • Elegant Japanese restaurant with sushi flown in daily from Tokyo and Osaka.

Unkai Restaurant • *Century Park Sheraton, Nassim Hill* • One of the most attractive Japanese restaurants in Singapore . . . special sushi and tempura sections, private rooms for parties.

Inagiku • *Westin Plaza* • Traditional Japanese cuisine in a contemporary setting . . . one of a chain of restaurants founded in 1905 . . . separate dining areas for tempura, sushi, and teppanyaki.

WESTERN FOOD

If you must, there is a Kentucky Fried Chicken and a McDonald's on Orchard Rd. For more genteel dining, there are several fine grill rooms (English, Scottish, Continental) in the top hotels as well as French, Italian, Swiss, Russian, German, Spanish, and Mexican specialty restaurants. Prices tend to be higher, the atmosphere more gracious, and dress codes more formal at these Western establishments. Reservations are recommended and major credit cards are accepted.

WESTERN RESTAURANTS

Baron's Table • *Holiday Inn, Scotts Rd. Tel: 7377966* • German groaning board, if you can take it in this climate.

Compass Rose • *Westin Stamford* • A blend of east and west on top of the tallest hotel in the world . . . elegant dining with French dishes presented Japanese style, using seasonings and condiments inspired by Eastern cultures.

Elizabethan Grill • *Raffles Hotel, Beach Rd. Tel: 3378041* • *Very* old-world atmosphere, with food and service to match.

Gordon Grill • *Goodwood Park Hotel, Scotts Rd. Tel: 7377411* • Noted for Scottish fare and good steaks . . . stop first in the Highland Bar.

Harbour Grill • *Singapore Hilton, Orchard Rd. Tel: 7372233* • Award-winning nouvelle cuisine and Continental menu . . . 5-course Chef's Surprise gourmet menu nightly.

Hubertus Grill • *Century Park Sheraton, Nassim Hill Tel: 7379677* • Another Continental-style grill room with decent food, but a sour-faced maitre d'hotel (when I was there).

Hugo's • *Hyatt Regency, Scotts Rd. Tel: 7375511* • French provincial decor with special Captain's Table for 10 diners . . . set menu and a la carte . . . exclusive wine cellar.

La Rotonde Brasserie • *Marco Polo Hotel, Tanglin Rd. Tel: 647141* • The most charming French-style bistro outside of Paris . . . a definite favorite . . . choose chef's specialties chalked on The Mirror.

La Vendome • *The Dynasty Hotel, Orchard Rd. Tel: 2354188* • French cuisine in the spectacular new pagoda-style hotel . . . not seen.

Le Chalet • *Ladyhill Hotel, Ladyhill Rd. Tel: 7372111* • Swiss fondues, raclette, etc. in chic atmosphere . . . quiet and comfortable.

Palm Grill • *Westin Plaza Hotel* • A luxurious bit of Olde England in the Far East, complete with Chippendale furniture, an international cuisine, and extensive wine list.

Marco Polo Restaurant • *Marco Polo Hotel, Tanglin Rd. Tel: 647141* • Gracious setting with scenes from old Singapore . . . recently redesigned as a steak/grill room.

Maxim's De Paris • *Regent of Singapore, Tomlinson Rd. Tel: 913211* • A replica of the original on Rue Royale since 1893, with staff trained by Parisian personnel . . . sounds intriguing and expensive.

Nutmeg's • *Hyatt Regency, Scotts Rd. Tel: 7375511* • The former Islander now in Art Deco and most attractive . . . seafood in tanks

. . . homemade ice cream and cheesecake . . . fashion shows Tues. lunch.

Pete's Place • *Hyatt Regnecy, Scotts Rd. Tel: 7375511* • Don't know who Pete is, but this is one of the most swinging places in town . . . live music in evening . . . pizzas, pastas, carafe wines, great desserts.

San Marco • *Marco Polo Hotel, Tanglin Rd. Tel: 647141* • A recent addition to the Italian restaurant scene, and pride of general manager Dario Regazzoni . . . bound to be a success.

Tangle Inn • *Tanglin Rd.* • Local favorite with colonial atmosphere and traditional English fare.

The Stables • *Mandarin Singapore, Orchard Rd. Tel: 7374411* • English-inn theme with gaslight and brass . . . rustic charm and steak/kidney pies, oxtail stew, daily roasts, sherries, and wines.

Top of the M • *Mandarin Singapore, Orchard Rd. Tel: 7374411* • Revolving restaurant on 40th floor . . . salad bar and East/West menu . . . go for the superb view both day and night.

SEAFOOD

In a city completely surrounded by the sea, it is natural that the *fruits de mer* will be succulent. All the more formal restaurants above serve delicious seafood, but the local populace prefers to consume such delicacies as crab, jumbo prawns, cockles, and mussels in a casual manner . . . with fingers. Much of the seafood offered is cooked quickly in a succulent chili sauce (not hot) or as for prawns, in a sweetish, black sauce. Try the foodstalls at Albert St. if you are in town, or drive out to the **Seaview** or **Palm Beach** restaurants at East Coast Park. Here, you sit on tiny stools at make-shift tables in what looks like the back of a garage. But the chili crab, steamed prawns (jumbo and you peel your own), fried squid, mussels in soya bean sauce, and huge bottles of beer transform the place into a palace. Hot towels and finger bowls arrive to clean your hands. Great fun and dress accordingly. For perhaps the best seafood of all, try Ponggol Village at the northern tip of Singapore (40 minutes by car). What's lacking in elegance is more than made up for in abundance of dishes featuring every kind of fish, mullusk, and shellfish imaginable. A favorite with the locals.

FRUITS

It is impossible to discuss the abundance of food in Singapore without mentioning the many unusual tropical fruits available. In addition to the familiar coconuts, pineapples, bananas, watermelons, and limes, you can also indulge in long, skinny papaya—the juiciest papayas ever! Why not also try the hybrid mangosteen or the smelly durian, which Singaporeans are fond of calling the "king of all fruits" (do not take one into your hotel room because of the odor). Then, there is the jambu ayer, to be cut and dipped into a mixture of soya sauce, sugar, and chilis, or the *jambu batu* (also known as guava). Ranbutan is a weird-looking fruit, but starfruit looks like a star when cut cross-wise; it's a good thirst quencher. Other thirst quenchers seen in marketplaces in huge plastic containers are *kam chia chui* (sugar cane water) and *ya chui* (coconut water).

If you feel like a little pick-me-up in the warm weather, buy some pieces of fruit from one of the street vendors with iced carts. It's perfectly safe and so refreshing.

NIGHTLIFE

Chinatown • Spend several hours here at nighttime and see a different side . . . fortune tellers, letter writers, Sago Lane (the funeral parlor road), block parties, local entertainers, and ever-present food-stalls . . . it's all here . . . enjoy before this historic section becomes a massive high rise . . . get a guide from STPB if you feel timid, and remember not to photograph the superstitious old folk.

Cinemas/Theater/TV • There are over 50 air-conditioned cinemas in the city, many of them with Western films . . . there is a national theater with first-run dramas . . . and a symphony orchestra with its own hall . . . television is terrible (as everywhere) but some hotels (like Pavilion Inter-Continental) are now offering in-house movies.

Cultural Shows • Check with hotel concierge.

Discos • Still going strong in Singapore . . . **Kasbah** in Arabian nights style at the Mandarin Hotel . . . **El Morroco** at the Oberoi Imperial . . . **Black Velvet** at the Century Park Sheraton . . . **The Library** at the Mandarin (for members and hotel guests only) . . . **The Club** at the Marco Polo (members and hotels guests only; no T-shirts or blue jeans) . . . **Chinoiserie** is tres chic at the Hyatt Regency . . . **The Music Room** at the Hilton.

Night Tours • There are a few organized evening tours, with one drink here and another there, but you're much better off on your own . . . Singapore is a safe and clean city, so enjoy the cooler hours!

Supper Clubs • The posh **Belvedere** with live music at the Mandarin . . . *La Tiara* on the rooftop of the Shangri-La Hotel, with international cabaret . . . **Neptune Theatre Restaurant** with Cantonese cuisine and lavish revues . . . **Grand Restaurant and Niteclub** (Chinese) in Shaw Towers . . . **Tropicana Theatre Restaurant** in Tropicana Building on Orchard Rd., with Chinese dinner and international shows.

Trishaw Tours • Not a bad way to spend an hour or so being cycled through Chinatown.

Wayang • Chinese street opera with grand performances on festive dates and holidays, especially during Feast of Hungry Ghosts in Aug./ Sept. . . . the best place in the Far East to enjoy this ancient entertainment . . . special platforms erected in heart of Chinatown . . . watch for them . . . also held in housing estates and parks.

SHOPPING

Singapore can certainly be considered a "shopper's paradise" but I would hardly call it the "bargain basement of Asia" as local promotions claim (because there is no such creature). However, shopping here is on a par with Hong Kong, as all tourist-interest goods sold are duty free and often at prices below retail cost in country of origin. These include the inevitable photographic and stereo equipment, watches, and jewelry in 18K gold, electric shavers, silk, and leather goods (excluding ready-made clothing), pearls and precious stones, ivory and antiquities, luxury smoking paraphernalia, calculators, perfumes, and imported apparel from Europe. People used to think that prices in Singapore were slightly higher than in Hong Kong (mainly because the stacks were more orderly), but that doesn't mesh anymore, and studies have shown that most items are competitive.

As in Hong Kong, just about everything you would ever want but don't need is available in Singapore either today or early tomorrow. And the young Singaporeans are buying everything they can! The shops are loaded with electrical gadgetry, computer-age games, elegant fashions from all over the world, gold Swiss watches plus counters and counters of the less expensive Japanese brands, locally made leather goods and pewter, imported goods from mainland China, accessories, and furnishings from all over Asia. If you want something copied or tailored, there is a shop around the corner (or your hotel concierge will call a friend).

However, the Singapore Tourist Promotion Board suggests that you seriously compare prices before buying, avoid touts, insist upon official records of purchase and world warranty (if available), and shop at approved STPB stores. Shopping hours are approximately 10 a.m. to 6 p.m. including Sun., with the most crowds predicted from noon to 2 p.m. (lunch-hour browsers). Credit cards are widely accepted, but the shops may add a surcharge (which is highly illegal but common). It is also suggested that you clarify customs regulations for the U.S. and Canada if you plan on purchasing extraordinary items, i.e. ivory and other wildlife products.

With the exception of the many new department stores and the elegant, European-style boutiques, definitely bargain. Test the water a bit first if you happen to be patronizing a large appliance store. However, if it's the **Thieve's Market** or **Change Alley**—well, merchants would think you were crazy if you didn't make a counter offer! And always remember, you get what you pay for, and you will be happy with your purchases.

One of the more rewarding aspects of shopping in Singapore is in discovering the abundance of so many handicrafts and arts from neighboring countries. For a capsule of what is available here, walk over to the Singapore Handicraft Centre on Tanglin Rd., directly fronting Rasa Singapura. This well-planned complex of shops does not intimidate the casual browser and offers arts and crafts from all over Asia—from China to Sri Lanka. There is everything on display and sale from costume jewelry to batik shirts and dresses to rugs from India and furniture made from Thailand teak. If you have your heart set on a sari, look here first before canvassing the scented shops of Serangoon Rd. Chinese carpets, batiks, brass, and pewter are all well displayed at the Handicraft Centre.

Antiques • are sought after the world over and it is not impossible to find some lovely items in Singapore—if you know what you are buying. Chinese porcelains, Malaccan chests, opium beds, Victoriana, Indonesian carvings, Burmese buddhas, etc. are all here, but it is wise to frequent the better shops if you plan to spend good money (as opposed to a few dollars). Orchard Rd. has always been known for fine antique shops and many have moved into the new shopping plazas. If you prefer out-of-the-way places, try the **Changi Junk Store** on Changi Rd. or **Katong Antique House** on East Coast Rd. Items over 100 years old can be imported to the U.S. duty free, but unless they are packable (or you hand carry them on the plane), the expense of shipping and insurance can be quite a burden.

Arab Street • is frequented by the Moslem community, with its own variety of spices and intriguing smells. Baskets, brassware, Malay and Indonesian *batiks,* Haji hats, dried fruits and woven flowers are just some of the items spilling from the shops that line this street.

Change Alley • has changed little since the good old days when sailors jostled through the narrow tunnel of bizzare fantasies just off the waterfront. That it still exists is somewhat of a miracle, jostled as it is between multimillion dollar high-rise office buildings. For a bit of local color, and perhaps a bargain or two, Change Alley is certainly worth a visit, but take your skepticism along and plan serious shopping else-where.

High Street • is a mere quarter-mile stretch in the middle of town with high quality shops of luxury items: pearls, breathtaking jewelry, gold watches, crystal, and brassware as well as imported dress materials. Prices match value but custom-made jewelry is available here.

Little India • is the nickname of that wonderful area along Serangoon Rd., filled with spices and fragrant garlands and exquisite women in saris with gold bangles up and down both arms. This is also where you can buy your own hand-dyed cottons and silks, colorful pillows and bedcovers, and pounds of curry powder. No special time to shop here, but don't expect to do much business on one of the Hindu holidays.

North Bridge Road • is just a stone's throw from High St., but seething with electrical bargains and some of the less expensive brands of watches. Shop around here because the game is to "sell"—even at a bigger discount than desired.

Orchard Road • has a long history of interesting shopping in Singapore although its face has changed in recent years. Gone are all the quaint single-story buildings, replaced by high-rise hotels and shopping plazas. Still known as "up market," you can enjoy a delightful spree wandering among the elegant boutiques in hotel arcades as well as the variety of shops in such huge complexes as **Far East Shopping Centre,** the **Chinese Emporium** in International Building, **Lucky Plaza** (one of the most popular), **C. K. Tang's** remodeled department store. At the northern end of the thoroughfare, which becomes Tanglin Rd., there are still a few of the old-time antique shops and specialty stores (including 24-hour tailoring).

People's Park ● was once an area of the old Singapore. It is now a showplace of the new Singapore, with clean streets, high rises and organized street bazaar businesses all packaged in a modern high-rise shopping complex.

Raffles Place ● was once the domain of the famous Robinson's Department Store, which supplied the "colonials" with everything from soup to swans. But that was all before the War, Occupation, and Independence, and Robinson's has moved northward to become a less important establishment. The Place is now a garden mall surrounded by high-rise office towers on most sides. If you're lucky, you may still be able to visit a few of the old-time shops on the western edge.

TAIWAN

HISTORY

Christened "Ilha Formosa" or Beautiful Island by 16th-century Portuguese sailors, this lovely leaf-shaped land mass just 90 miles from China's southern coastline has been the pawn of fighting powers for more than four centuries. Formosa is an appropriate name for an island that boasts many noteworthy natural wonders, including the highest mountain in northeast Asia (called Yu Shan or Jade Mountain) that rises to 13,114 feet. Its Chinese name—Taiwan—means terraced bay and refers to the tiers of rice paddies found everywhere. Although two-thirds of the island's 14,000 square miles is mountainous (with more than 60 peaks over 10,000 feet high), the farming of an alluvial plain in the western portion produces enough food to satisfy some 19 million inhabitants plus leaves a surplus for export.

Populated by aborigines in prehistoric times (about 260,000 are still counted), Taiwan was first settled by the Chinese about 1400 years ago. It became a protectorate of the Chinese empire when Genghis Khan founded the Yuan Dynasty in A.D. 1206. However, the Dutch invaded the Tainan area in 1624 (and left some fine fortress relics), while the Spanish claimed primacy in the north in 1626. The Spanish were easily thrown out by the Dutch in 1641, and the Dutch were overthrown by Ming Dynasty patriot and hero Prince Kuo Hsing Yeh (Koxinga) in 1661. In 1684 Taiwan became a prefecture of Fukien province and its own Province of China in 1887 (which it officially remains).

Meanwhile, the French occupied the Keelung port region as well as the Pescadores Islands for a short period in 1884. They were not the final foreign powers to arrive. The Treaty of Shimonoseki ceded Taiwan and the Pescadores to Japan in 1895. The Japanese ruled with a heavy hand until the end of World War II, leaving behind a shattered 1945 economy—although trains still left on time. However, Taiwan's destiny in our lifetime seems to have been set with the fall of the Ching Dynasty in 1911 and the subsequent founding of the Republic of China by Dr. Sun Yat-sen. When Communist forces assumed control of the mainland in 1949, the Nationalist government under the direction of Chiang Kai-shek fled to Taipei. It has remained the seat of Nationalism since, and only tomorrow will tell what is truly manifest. Chiang Kai-shek died in 1975 (during his fifth consecutive term of the presidency), and power was finally passed to his son Chiang Ching-kuo in 1978.

After almost 30 years of devoted support, the United States terminated formal diplomatic relations with Taiwan in December 1978 (due to a belated recognition of mainland China). The political situation, however, has not affected trade or tourism between the U.S. and Taiwan. Indeed, business has never been better! Taiwan's progress has been miraculous, and its billion-dollar exports include machinery and metals, chemicals, fruits and other food products, textiles, and electronic equipment. The tiny country has an enviable trade balance of almost U.S.$80 million annually. Per capita income is targeted to reach about U.S. $6000 by the end of this decade, and the country boasts an almost 100% literacy rate. Visas are easy to obtain (gratis for U.S. citizens), and the fact that you may also plan to visit the PRC (People's Republic of China) is no longer an issue.

Although its populace has lived under a strict militaristic regime for more than three decades, Taiwan has remained a powerful force in traditional Chinese culture and it offers the visitor a delightful venue. There are an estimated 5000 temples and shrines throughout the islands, about one every 2.8 square miles. Artworks and architecture, festivals, and operas are all nurtured here to follow the mainstream of history. Industry, on the other hand, grabs for the novel and manufactures for the moment. As a result, many travelers treat Taiwan with deference, as if it were neither exotic enough nor worthy enough in the worldwide community to be taken seriously.

And then there is the problem of Taipei—capital of the Republic and a drab and polluted city of some 2.2 million inhabitants. Taipei is a man's town: the departure of the American military left a cavity soon filled with Western importers and Japanese businessmen (the latter who come in droves for sports and sex). But once outside of Taipei, the island overflows with beautiful vistas and interesting spots to explore. To the north is the rainy but busy seaport of Keelung, one of the most important harbors in the Far East. To the south is the historic and charming Tainan as well as the industrious and vibrant Kaohsiung. To the east is Hualien and the spectacular 12-mile drive through Toroko Gorge—like no other in Asia. Those rich in time and adventurous spirit should not miss Oluanpi and Kenting Park at the tip of the main island or the offshore islands of Lan Yu or the Pescadores. Unfortunately, Quemoy and Matsu, directly off the coast of Fukien province, are "military frontiers" and are off limits to visitors.

Although Taiwan claims to receive more than 1.75 million visitors annually, most of them are on business and just 12% of the bona fide tourists are Americans. Indeed, Taiwan is being left behind in the tourist trade for several reasons, mainly that one can visit the "real" China so readily. But more important, the Taiwanese are unimaginative and extremely lazy in promoting their island country around the world; the tourist offices are understaffed and certainly do not understand how important visitors are to a controversial country like Taiwan, for they begin to understand a little about the political and cultural aspects. After all, Taiwan has been an important part of American foreign policy since the second world war; even now, one cannot ignore it.

Meanwhile, the Taiwanese are not so warm and friendly as the Thais, nor so charismatic as the Filipinos, nor run a clean and efficient place like Singaporeans. Taiwan is also becoming quite expensive since the Taiwan dollar has appreciated 25% against U.S. currency recently. On the other hand, the food is good; there are fine hotels and interesting sights to see.

TAIWAN IN A CAPSULE

A 14,000-square-mile province of the Republic of China . . . also known as "the other China" . . . lies between Pacific Ocean and Taiwan Strait . . . just 90 miles east of China coastline . . . includes islands of Orchid and Green and the Pescadores . . . subtropical climate with long rainy season and typhoons prevalent June through Sept. . . . humid year-round with summer temperatures above 90°F . . . population of approximately 2 million, with growth rate under 2% . . . official national language is Mandarin . . . population mix is nationalist Chinese from the mainland and descendants, plus native Taiwanese (Hokkien and Fukien ancestry) . . . booming economy with more than U.S. $3000 per capita income and U.S. as Number 1 export customer . . . primary visitors are Overseas Chinese, Japanese, and North American importers.

PLANNING AHEAD

REPUBLIC OF CHINA (TAIWAN) TOURISM BUREAU is located in Taipei at 280 Chunghsiao East Rd., Section 4, 9th floor (Tel: 721–8541 or 751–8445. There are three tourism bureau offices in the U.S.: Suite 1605, 166 Geary St., San Francisco, CA 94108 (Tel: 415–989–8677); Suite 8855, 1 World Trade Center, New York, NY 10048

(Tel: 212–466–0691); and 333 N. Michigan Ave., Suite 339, Chicago, IL 60601 (Tel: 312–346–1037). There is also a good Information Counter in the Arrival Hall of Chiang Kai-shek International Airport in Taoyuan.

VISAS are required of travelers holding valid U.S. and Canadian passports and must be obtained prior to arrival in the Republic of China at Coordination Council for North American Affairs (CCNA) offices in Washington, DC, Atlanta, Boston, Chicago, Honolulu, Houston, Kansas City (MO), Los Angeles, New York, San Francisco, and Seattle. Contact the office nearest to your home. All visas are gratis to U.S. citizens and transit, tourist and commercial visas allow four-year multiple entry. Tourist A visas allow maximum of 60-day stay plus two well-reasoned extensions. Three photos and confirmed travel plans are required.

INTERNATIONAL INOCULATION CERTIFICATES are not normally required unless a traveler arrives from smallpox- or cholera-infected area.

ENTRY BY AIR is through the sleek, new **Chiang Kai-shek International Airport** (CKS) built in the county of Taoyuan, about 25 miles west of Taipei. The airport was not designed to satisfy the needs of today's traveler (you walk up and then down and then up again) so watch your hand luggage. Despite the diplomatic tensions created worldwide in recent years, Taiwan is still served by all the major international carriers that called before, and is just over a two-hour flight from Tokyo, under 1½ hours from Hong Kong. CKS Airport is linked to downtown Taipei by the North-South freeway, about a 45-minute ride by taxi or hotel bus. (Allow plenty of time each way as city traffic can be beastly). A hotel representative in the Arrival Hall will offer assistance in obtaining local transportation, but be sure to compare rates before you decide which way to travel. Taxi rates now begin at NT$35, with each additional 400 meters NT$5, time charged for waiting, and an additional 20% of the fare added between 11 p.m. and 5 a.m. Airport buses serve both the east and west side terminals of Taipei, with standard fare NT$73. Service runs from 7:50 a.m. to 11:30 p.m. outside the arrival lounge.

Domestic air services utilize the "old" Sungshan Airport, just a few minutes from the center of Taipei. Domestic carriers China Airlines (CAL) and Far East Air Transport (FAT) make frequent flights to Hualien (25 min.), Kaohsiung (40 minutes), Tainan (45 minutes), or Taichung (35 min). Taiwan Airlines (TAC) flies to both Orchid and Green islands. Rates are reasonable, but always arrive early to claim your reservation—and carry your passport to confirm status.

DEPARTURE BY AIR is less of a hassle, but remember those absurd sets of stairs you must climb up and then down! Bus service direct from hotel to CKS Airport is easily arranged through your concierge. Allow plenty of time for check-in and then hand-checking of checked baggage. Security officials find themselves very interested in what people are taking OUT of Taiwan.

Departure tax at CKS Airport is NT$300 per person over two years of age.

ARRIVAL BY SEA is through the port of Keelung, about 20 miles north of Taipei and easily accessible by freeway. Thus far, luxury cruise ships do not call here, but the port is considered one of the best in the Far East and freighter services between here and the West Coast are excellent. Contact your favorite cargo line to query whether passengers (maximum 12) are carried among all those Made in Taiwan exports.

DUTY FREE is not the password in this carefully controlled country, although restrictions are not so tight as they once were. Items of a personal nature are always acceptable but it is wise to declare all expensive jewelry, cameras, lenses, and other equipment. A bottle of liquor, a carton of cigarettes, and ½ pound of tobacco (all very costly in Taiwan) are considered personal effects.

CURRENCY of Taiwan is the new Taiwan dollar (NT$). At press time the rate of exchange was approximately NT$28.50 to U.S.$1. Coin denominations are NT$.50, NT$1, NT$5, and NT$10. Bank notes of NT$10, NT$50, NT$100, NT$500, and NT$1000 are in circulation. Unlimited foreign currency may be imported for exchange, but save receipts for reconversion at departure. No more than NT$8000 and 20 coins (in local currency) may be exported.

LOCAL TIME in Taiwan is Greenwich Mean Time plus 8 hours (13 hours in advance of Eastern Standard Time, 12 hours ahead of Eastern Daylight Time). Taiwan is in the same time zone as Peking, Hong Kong, Macau, and Manila, one hour behind Tokyo and Seoul.

LOCAL CURRENT is 110 volts, 60 cycles AC.

LOCAL WATER from the tap should probably not be drunk. Boiled or distilled water is recommended. Top hotels (like the Ritz) have proper drinking water faucets in all bathrooms.

OFFICIAL LANGUAGE in Taiwan is Mandarin Chinese as spoken by Nationalist officials, although many of original island families speak

Hakka and Amoy dialects. Japanese is also spoken by many of the older Taiwanese since it was imposed upon them during the Japanese occupation between 1905 and 1945. English is the business language and spoken in all the top hotels, mainly because the U.S. military had such a visible presence here for 30 years.

Many English-language publications are available as well as tourist-oriented pamphlets and other helpful information. The "pirated" books sold everywhere are mainly American bestsellers.

BUSINESS HOURS in Taiwan are 9 a.m. to 5:30 p.m. weekdays and 9 a.m. to 12 noon on Sat. The Taiwanese are a diligent society and it is possible to find shops open until 9 p.m., even to have your latest garment fitted after a late, sumptuous banquet. Since most visitors to this island combine business with pleasure, your business associates will arrange their schedules to yours.

There are a number of local trade associations helpful to the visiting businessman, among them are the **American Chamber of Commerce,** Room 1012, Chia Hsin Building Annex, 96 Chung Shan North Rd., Section 2 (Tel: 551–2515; 581–7089; 551–5211), the **Taiwan Footwear Exporters Association,** 13th floor, 131 Sungkiang Rd. (Tel: 506–6190) or the **Taiwan Yacht Industry Association,** 14/F-3, 665, Tun Hwa S. Rd., Taipei (Tel: 703–8481). In addition, there is an annual publication of U.S. firms in Taiwan and an extensive Taiwan Yellow Pages available in your hotel room.

TIPPING is not encouraged in Taiwan but the world is changing here too. Current tourist publications suggest NT$20 (about U.S.$1) per bag at airports, bus/train stations, and hotels. A 10% service charge and 5% tax are added to hotel bills and there is an entertainment tax of almost 40% (in addition to service charge).

TELEPHONE AND TELEX services in Taiwan are pretty good, especially if you are dealing with the top hotels. You may encounter somewhat of a language problem (as I did) with hotel operators who don't want to acknowledge registered guests, and overseas calls are billed the standard three minutes even if you hang up immediately.

Dial (02) if you are calling Taipei from CKS Airport in Taoyuan County. English-speaking assistance is available at Tel: 311–6796, English-speaking police at Tel: 311–9940, and overseas calls are 100. If you need more informa-tion, you can call the Communications Company at Tel: (02) 321–2535. There is also a tourist information hotline (02–717–3737) for travel information, emergency assistance, accidents, lost and found, language problems, and complaints!

WHAT TO WEAR in this climate is the eternal question. Taipei is either hot and humid or less hot and humid. It is also one of the most

polluted cities in the world—so bring washables. It is considered subtropical with a mild winter (mid-Dec. to mid-Mar.), and they say that
the skies actually are blue in some parts of the island. In fact, the southern tip does enjoy almost daily sunshine and is warmer than the rest of
the island. Light summer clothing, with a light pullover and raincoat
are fine throughout the year. In the mountain areas, wool slacks and
sweaters might be needed occasionally. Always carry an umbrella and
wear durable shoes. The best advice here is to be practical—not glamorous! Safari-type suits are fine for men year-round (or lightweight business suits). Cotton dresses and pantsuits are best for women. Only in
some of the top hotel restaurants and bars (like the Ritz) would you
dress for the evening. Typhoon season is from June to October, but
that's only what the books say. Be prepared for gray skies around Taipei
most of the year.

LOCAL TRANSPORTATION is crowded, especially in the cities.
Taxis are cheap and rather plentiful, but they are tiny and can be very
dirty. In addition, the drivers do not always understand orders from
hotel doormen, so double check before you proceed into time-consuming, horrendous traffic the wrong direction. Taipei is criss-crossed with
a comprehensive network of public **buses,** but unless your knowledge
of Chinese is considerable, local buses can be difficult to maneuver.
You can, however, take them up to the Martyrs' Shrine and National
Museum if you ask the hotel concierge to explain the route.

The country's version of "Greyhound" is Kuo Kuang (National
Glory Line), which travels smoothly along the North-South freeway
system from Keelung to Kaohsiung. The entire route takes about 4½
hours, half to Taichung, and is a splendid way to see the countryside.
Taiwan highway buses will transport you throughout the island, even to
remote mountain areas, and are far less uncomfortable than the city
taxis.

The **train** system in and out of Taipei is also very good—a legacy
left by the Japanese. Train schedules are available at the Tourism Bureau office in Taipei (see above) and someone here can guide you in
making reservations (Tel:312–2233) and explain how to buy your return
ticket (there is no such thing as "roundtrip"). The Tze Chang express
takes about two hours to Taichung; the Chu Kang express runs just four
hours to Kaohsiung and is a very pleasant ride.

There are also many fine **conducted tours** to Toroko Gorge, Sun
Moon Lake, and other scenic spots. In three full days, you can see
Taipei, Hualien, Toroko Gorge, Taichung, and Sun Moon Lake for less
than U.S.$250 (without meals). Five days includes Changhua, Tainan,
and Kaohsiung as well. Contact Cathay Express Co. (among others) in
Taipei for daily departures.

Taiwan's only passenger ship service is operated by the Japanese flag Arimura Line's *Hiryu 2* and *Hiryu 3*, with weekly sailings from both Keelung (port for Taiwan) and Kaohsiung for Naha, Okinawa, and Japan. Accommodations range from tatami mat dormitories to real cabins, with rates from about U.S.$100 to about U.S.$150 per person for the overnight voyage. Call Mr. Garret (771–5911) or the Tourist Information Hot Line (717–3737) for reservations.

FESTIVALS AND HOLIDAYS in Taiwan combine Nationalist shows with age-old traditions in ''The Other China,'' as this country used to call itself. Visitors are advised that during any type of festival, anniversary or national holiday, taxis will be scarce and prices in restaurants (if you can get a seat) may be greatly increased. Business and banking facilities may be closed, and your local contacts may have left the country for a bit of diversion (i.e. gambling) in other parts of the Far East. The following is a complete list of every occasion recognized in Taiwan. Public holidays are marked with an asterisk (*).

*January 1 • *Founding of Republic of China by Dr. Sun Yat-sen in 1912; New Year's Day (Western style).*

*January 2 • *Continuation of Founding Day.*

February • *Chinese New Year festivities* • Note: Actually 1st day of 1st moon.

February/March • *Lantern Festival* • End of Chinese New Year celebrations. Note: Actually 15th day of 1st moon.

March 12 • *Arbor Day* • Thousands of trees planted in observance of death of Dr. Sun Yat-sen.

March/April • *Birthday of Kuan Yin, Goddess of Mercy* • Celebrated at Taipei Lungshan (Dragon Mountain) Temple. Note: Actually 19th day of 2nd moon.

*March 29 • *Youth Day* • Historic exhibits and parades honor 72 young revolutionary martyrs of the 1911 uprising against the Ching Dynasty.

*April 5 • *Tomb Sweeping Day* • National holiday commemorating death of President Chiang Kai-Shek.

April/May • *Birthday of Matsu, Goddess of the Sea* • Celebrations in all Taiwan's 380 temples dedicated to Matsu, especially at Peikang and Tainan. Note: Actually 23rd day of 3rd moon.

April 29 • *Cheng Cheng Kung Landing* • Commemorates landing of Ming Dynasty loyalist/warrior/statesman who ousted Dutch colonists from the island in 1661. Main festivities at Tainan.

May 11 • *Buddha Bathing Festival* • Images of Lord Buddha sprinkled with water, decorated and paraded in honor of his birth.

* **June** • *Dragon Boat Festival* • Also known as Poet's Day. Boat races to commemorate drowning of poet/statesman Chu Yuen in Milo River in 299 B.C. Note: Actually 5th day of 5th moon.

June • *Birthday of Cheng Huang, City God* • Procession of actors on stilts, dragon, and lion dances. Note: Actually 13th day of 5th moon.

* **September/October** • *Mid-Autumn Festival* • Taiwanese gather to watch the moon, which legend says is most radiant at this time. Note: Actually 15th day of 8th moon.

* **September 28** • *Confucius's Birthday* • Also known as Teacher's Day, in honor of China's greatest philosopher.

* **October 10** • *Double Ten* • National Day to commemorate 1911 revolution and overthrow of Ching Dynasty (leading to establishment of Republic of China in 1912). Lion and dragon dancers, bands, floats, parades past Presidential Building in downtown Taipei.

October 21 • *Overseas Chinese Day* • Chinese living abroad return to Taiwan to visit relatives and enjoy festivities.

* **October 25** • *Taiwan Retrocession Day* • Recognizes formal return of Taiwan to Chinese rule after 50 years of Japanese occupation.

* **October 31** • *Birthday of President Chiang Kai-shek* • Also known as Veterans' Day.

* **November 12** • *Birthday of Dr. Sun Yat-sen, father of the Republic of China.*

* **December 25** • *Constitution Day and Christmas Day.*

WHAT TO SEE AND DO

Greater Taipei

Ch'eng Huang Mial (Temple of the City God) • Ti Hua St. . . . the city god is considered an essential power to protect against enemies and epidemics . . . he has the ability to communicate with the Lord of Heaven . . . temple is as old as the city itself.

Chinankung Taoist Monastery • About 7 miles from the city . . . built at the peak of the Monkey Hill at Musa . . . best to climb up the famous thousand stone steps . . . great exercise.

Chinese Opera • The best place in the world to pursue traditional Chinese opera . . . over 400 works of this 6th-century-old artform are in the repertory of the Taipei Opera company . . . exquisite antique costumes and elaborate makeup part of the spectacle . . . most performers attend local opera schools from early age . . . still a most favored theatrical event . . . performances at 7:30 p.m. daily at the Chinese Armed Forces Culture and Activity Center (69, Chung Hwa Rd., Sec. 1), or on local television . . . watch announcements and try to see at least one!

Chung Cheng Aviation Museum • Located near Taipei's international airport . . . life-size model of Orville and Wilbur Wright's first aircraft . . . 4 exhibition areas devoted to civil aviation, flight technology, history of aviation and space . . . 700 plane models . . . 13 audiovisual screens . . . open daily from 9:30 a.m.–5 p.m. . . . admission about 80¢ for adults, 50¢ for children.

Confucius Temple • Classic Chinese architecture . . . more a memorial hall than a place of worship . . . quiet and peaceful and located on Chiuchuan St., west of the Zoo . . . best time to visit is Confucius's birthday (Sept. 28), also known as Teacher's Day . . . impressive ceremonies with ancient music and dance . . . open daily.

Fort San Domingo (Hung Mao Cheng) • Built in 1628 by the Spanish, the only relic of Western colonialism in northern Taiwan . . . about 11 miles from Taipei in Tamsui . . . grounds closed to public but good views from college below.

Founding Father of the Republic of China's Memorial Hall • A new edifice dedicated to Dr. Sun Yat-sen . . . huge building with

auditorium, library, and exhibition areas in eastern section of city . . .
watch for programs here.

Hsing Tien Temple • Taoist temple dedicated to Kuan Kung, a
legendary hero from the 3rd century A.D. . . . red-faced God of War,
who actually lived as a general during the Three Kingdoms period . . .
centrally located and crowded night and day with pious women . . .
business men love him too . . . located on Ming Chuan East Rd., near
the Ritz Hotel.

Kuan Yin Shan (Goddess of Mercy Mountain) • Situated across
the Tamsui River, the mountain is named after the Goddess of Mercy
because of the resemblance to her head . . . along the path to the
mountain is **Ice Cloud Temple,** which shows Kuan Yin with 24 arms.

Lungshan Temple • Built in 1738 of Chinese classical and very
ornate temple architecture . . . Taipei's oldest and most famous Buddhist structure . . . first temple in Wan Hua district . . . dedicated to
Kuan Yin, Goddess of Mercy, although Taoist deities are also worshiped here . . . full of devotees praying for good fortune and guidance
. . . located on Kwangchow St., west of Botanical Garden . . . also
known as Dragon Mountain Temple.

Municipal Zoological Garden • Located at 66 Chung Shan North
Rd. . . . one of largest zoos in the world, with 204 mammal, 528 bird,
232 reptile, and 728 fish varieties . . . shows on Sun. at 10:30 a.m.
and 3:30 p.m. . . . open daily.

Nanhai Academic Park • National Historical Museum, National
Arts Hall, National Science Hall, National Central Library, and Taiwan
Botanical Garden all located here . . . displays of national and local
historic objects . . . modern plays and Chinese traditional operas . . .
700 species of tropical, subtropical, and temperate trees and shrubs in
garden . . . open daily from 9 a.m.–5:30 p.m.

National Palace Museum • The primary reason for stopping off in
Taipei . . . located 5 miles northwest of the city . . . largest and most
comprehensive collection of Chinese artifacts extant . . . begun by Ching
Dynasty emperor Kao-tsung in mid-18th century . . . passed through
successive Manchu rulers . . . became property of Chinese Republic in
1925 . . . housed first in Peking Palace Museum . . . over 600,000
items packed and hid during Japanese invasion, war, and Communist
takeover . . . finally brought to Taiwan by Nationalist government in
1949 . . . National Palace Museum constructed in neo-Chinese style to
protect collection in late 1960s . . . only 6000 to 9000 items on view

at any time . . . rest stored in caves behind . . . collection features finest porcelains and ceramics, jades and lacquerwares, bronzes and enamels, scroll paintings from 10th to 17th centuries, calligraphy, rare books, and manuscripts . . . truly finest visual history of Chinese culture in the world today . . . center for scholars and art historians . . . receives over one million visitors each year . . . open daily from 9 a.m.–5 p.m. . . . general admission about NT$20, plus surcharge for twice daily guided tours in English . . . located in Wai Shuang Hsi suburb, 20 minutes by taxi from city center, or via buses #213 and #255 . . . Tel: 881–2021.

National Memorial • Dedicated to Chiang Kai-shek . . . massive and monstrous structure in middle of city . . . several blocks with gardens and 230-foot memorial gate . . . exhibits of his life and work . . . library and national theater, national concert hall and recital hall, which offer performances in opera (both Peking and western versions) and hear plenty of local and visiting musicians . . . open daily from 9 a.m. . . . admission free.

New Tanshui Golf Club • At foot of Tatun Mountain, highest peak around Taipei . . . one of best courses in Taiwan . . . open to visitors . . . spectacular scenery.

Peitou Hot Springs • A popular resort town about 12 miles north of Taipei . . . notorious for sin and sex and hot springs . . . U.S. military frequented here during Korean and Vietnam wars . . . now overrun by Japanese tour groups . . . to be avoided (I think) for many reasons!

Postal Museum • In Hsintien near Green Lake . . . established less than 15 years ago . . . interesting summary of Chinese postal history . . . collection of Chinese stamps since 1878.

Presidential Square • Epitome of drab nationalism in the middle of the city . . . political and administrative center of the Republic . . . ceremonies held here on national days, especially the famous "Double 10" with parades, flowers, flags, armaments, etc.

Shuangchi Park (Double Creek Park) • Small artificial park located between Shih Lin area and National Palace Museum . . . designed like classical Chinese park with cobbled paths, lotus ponds with goldfish, roaring waterfalls, and carved pavilions . . . open year-round for walking and solitude.

Suspension Bridge Over Green Lake in Pitan • South of the city and very scenic . . . a chance to escape the smog . . . the lake is named Pitan after the beautiful jade green color of the water . . . visitors may go boating, swimming, and fishing on the lake.

Taipei Martyrs' Shrine • Located in the Chungshan district, just a few minutes' drive from the Grand Hotel . . . dedicated to war heroes from the 1911 revolution to the present . . . neo-Chinese classical structure designed to resemble Beijing's Hall of Supreme Harmony (Tai Ho Tien) . . . changing of the guard on the hour . . . colorful ceremony worth seeing . . . national services held here in May and Sept. . . . open daily.

Taipei New Park • 3-story Chinese pagoda is main attraction . . . visit **Taiwan Provincial Museum,** specializing in indigenous island wildlife and aborigine artifacts . . . plus frequent exhibitions of works by contemporary artists . . . open daily from 9 a.m. except Mon. and Wed., Tel: 361–3925 . . . **Cathay Art Museum** just down the road . . . displays old and contemporary artists . . . Tel: 311–3575.

Taipei World Trade Center • *5 Hsin Yi Rd., Sec. 5* • Trade and exhibition hall . . . hoping to draw more visitors to Taiwan for business and pleasure . . . adjacent to Hyatt Regency Taipei.

Wulai Waterfall • Aboriginal village about an hour south of Taipei . . . not really worth the trip, I'd say . . . very touristy and expensive . . . tribal dancing plus pushcar ride to the waterfall . . . Fairyland Park at Wulai . . . if you must, hire a taxi instead of going by tour bus.

Yangmingshan (Grass Mountain) Park • About 10 miles north of Taipei . . . very beautiful during spring when cherry blossoms and azaleas grace the area . . . recommended for a breath of fresh air now and again.

Northern Taiwan

Keelung • Second largest seaport in Taiwan . . . situated on northern coast overlooking east China Sea . . . colorful history and known as Santissima Trinidad when occupied by Spanish from 1626 to 1641 . . . driven away by the Dutch, who were themselves expelled from Taiwan in 1661 . . . strategically important to country, although it rains here some 214 days annually . . . known for 74-foot high statue of **Kuan Yin,** Goddess of Mercy, that overlooks harbor.

Northcoast Highway • Leads from Keelung along east China Sea then southwest to seaside town of Tamsui, near Taipei. Passes through

Yehliu (Wild Willow) fantastic rock formations . . . **Green Bay** resort. . . **Chinshan** (Golden Mountain) and **Paishawan** (White Sand Bay) beaches and **Tamsui.** A nice excursion with lunch.

Northeast Coast National Scenic Area • Tapped for tourism development. Lovely area on Pacific Ocean. . . perfect for fishing, swimming, and other watersports . . . hiking trails and natural parks . . . tranquil rural towns.

Tamsui • Small town on northwest coast of Taiwan. Known for Fort San Domingo . . . built by the Spanish in 1629 . . . now a historical site.

Window on China • Chinese Lilliputian land at Lungtan, 33 miles southwest of Taipei. Mini-reproductions of life in Taiwan and mainland China cover almost 5 acres . . . privately owned.

Shihmen Dam • Year-round resort and reservoir about 32 miles southwest of Taipei. Dam is magnificent manmade lake and good for jogging and hiking. Nearby are Leofoo Safari Park and Window on China.

Wulai • Mountain resort south of Taipei (less than 20 miles) through rolling hills along the Hsintien River. Noted for aborigines . . . second largest tribe in Taiwan after the Ami . . . now quite commercial with song and dance shows and peddling handicrafts.

Central Taiwan

Alishan Forest Recreation Area • Linked by narrow-gauge railway to Chiayi in Central Taiwan. Alishan House and other hotels in area . . . also **Mt. Chu** (Celebration Mountain) for view of "sea of clouds" that ring **Yushan** (Mt. Jade)—best time for viewing is sunrise. Yushan National Park, partly situated in Central Taiwan, is largest in country.

Chitou (Riverhead) Forest Recreation Area • Situated about 50 miles south of Taichung. Notes for bamboo forest . . . from which are made so many Taiwanese products. A favored spot for honeymooners . . . especially University Pond and sacred cypress tree said to be 2800 years old.

East-West Cross-Island Highway • Passes through Central Taiwan from Toroko to Tungshih. A sinuous mountain road some 120 miles long . . . considered one of the most beautiful in Asia . . . also known as "rainbow of Treasure Island" . . . most traveled section is 12-mile stretch through **Taroko Gorge** . . . a great natural wonder attracting 5000 visitors daily . . . midway is **Lishan** (Pear Mountain) year-round resort . . . took 10,000 laborers 4 years to construct highway . . . completed in 1960.

Formosan Aboriginal Cultural Village • Located near Sun Moon Lake. Consists of dwelling and artifacts representing Taiwan's 9 surviving aboriginal tribes—the Yami, Ami, Atayal, Bunun, Paiwan, Puyuma, Rukai, Saisiyat, and Tsuo.

Hohuanshan • Mountain of Harmonious Happiness. Situated on Tayuling-Wushe branch of East-West Cross-Island Highway . . . skiing in January and February . . . 400-meter lift and Sung Hsueh (Pine Snow) Hostel.

Lukang • Deer Port. Once a historic and thriving seaport, it was closed by the Japanese at the beginning of their 50-year occupation of Taiwan in 1895 . . . still retains evidence of a colorful past . . . in architecture and local crafts and Lukang Folk Arts Museum . . . also known for temples to Kuan Yin, Goddess of Mercy, and Matsu, Goddess of the Sea.

Peikang • Temple dedicated to Matsu, Goddess of the Sea and Empress of Heaven. One of the oldest temples in the country . . . an hour's drive toward the west coast from Chiayi . . . best place in Taiwan to celebrate her birthday, which falls on the 23rd day of the 3rd moon.

Phoenix Valley Bird Park • Home of more than 5000 birds of 300 different species on 74 acres in the Phoenix Valley Scenic Area . . . just north of Chitou.

Sun Moon Lake • Year-round resort in mountains of Central Taiwan. Located 50 miles southeast of Taichung . . . in lovely region of the country . . . known for natural beauty and interesting sites . . . **Husuan Chuang Temple** . . . **Wen Wu** (Literature Warrior) **Temple** dedicated to Confucius (Master of the Pen) and Kuan Ti (Master of the Sword) . . . **Tzu En** (Filial Devotion Pagoda) completed in 1971 is highest (150 feet) in Taiwan.

Taichung • Third largest city in Taiwan after Taipei and Kaohsiung. Economic, cultural, and communications center of Central Taiwan . . . important international seaport . . . southwest of city is giant

Buddha of Changhua . . . also Buddha at Wufeng . . . plus the Happy Buddha of Taichung . . . obviously a goldmine for Buddha fans!

South Taiwan

Coral Lake • Originally known as Wushantou Reservoir. Resort area where boating and hiking and camping area all popular. Reached by highway from Tainan (just over 20 miles).

Kaohsiung • City on southwest coast of Taiwan overlooking the Formosa Strait. Largest international seaport and island's largest ship-building center. International airport also located here . . . impressive city with harbor panorama from **Shou Shan** (Long Life) Mountain . . . Lotus Lake area with modern (1976) Confucian Temple . . . **Hsi Tzu Bay** beach within city limits . . . **Cheng ching** (Crystal Clear) lake resort just a 15-minute drive from city center, adjoined by Grand Hotel and Kaohsiung Golf and Country Club . . . with rolling grounds overlooked by **Chung Hsing Padods** . . . an hour south of the city is **Fo Kuang Shan** (Buddha Torch Mountain), a favorite with pilgrims who come from all over Asia.

Kenting National Park • Southernmost part of Taiwan. Flanked by Formosa Strait, South China Sea, Bashi Channel, and Pacific Ocean. Kenting means "plowman" and originated with farmers from mainland China who settled in Hengchun (Eternal Spring) Peninsula . . . park covers 125 square miles and includes Kenting Forest Recreation Area . . . Kenting Beach . . . Oluanpi Park (145 acres) . . . Chuan Fan Hsih (Sail Rock) in the sea between Kenting Beach and Oluanpi . . . Maopitou (Cat Nose Tip) of the Hengchun Peninsula . . . and Chialoshui (Good Running Water), an area noted for coral limestone formations.

Lanyu (Orchid) Island • Off southeast coast of Taiwan. Home of the Yami, smallest and most primitive tribe of aborigines. Yami live by fishing in beautiful boats . . . practice nature conservation in wild orchids . . . and grow taro—a type of sweet potato.

Penghu (Pescadores) • Fishermen's Isles—an archipelago of 64 islands in the Formosa Strait. Proclaimed a county of Taiwan in 1961 . . . some 21 islands uninhabited . . . bridge to Makung, capital of Penghu, is one of longest inter-island bridges in the Western Pacific Region.

Tainan • Oldest city in Taiwan and its capital from 1684 to 1887. Linked with memory of Cheng Cheng-kung (Koxinga), one of China's greatest national heroes . . . Koxinga was Ming Dynasty commander whose army ended 37-year Dutch occupation of Taiwan that began in 1624 . . . Koxinga believed to be a "chun tzu" or perfect man by Taiwanese . . . he originated island's first cultural renaissance by bringing some 1000 literati and devotees to the arts with him . . . famous shrine to Koxinga in Taiwan . . . a city of 100 temples including the oldest Confucian temple in Taiwan . . . **Yi Tsai** (Eternal) Castle—a fortress built without view of the sea . . . **Lu Erh Men** (Deer's Ear Gate) on the spot Koxinga landed in 1661 . . . **Kaiyuan Temple**—one of the oldest Buddhist structures in Taiwan. . . and the temple dedicated to the five concubines—don't miss!

Tsengwen Reservoir • In western foothills of Central Mountain Range. Completed in 1973 and larger than Coral and Sun Moon lakes. Motorboat hire popular and a fine day excursion from Tainan.

East Taiwan

Chiaohsi • A small town on Taiwan's northeastern coast . . . features one of the finest natural hot spring spas in the country . . . odorless waters . . . good for skin, stomach, and nervous ailments . . . **Five Peak Waterfall** a 7-minute ride from town . . . specialties in the area are candied and preserved plums, kumquats, jujubes, and tiny golden oranges.

Chihpen Hot Springs • Resort about 30 miles south of Taitung . . . carbonate chief ingredient here . . . waterfall to climb plus half-hour walk along riverbank to Buddhist **Chingchueh Temple.**

Hualien • Taiwan's eastern port on Pacific coast . . . ferries travel daily from Keelung . . . **Wan Jon Spa** is 1 of 8 famous local scenes . . . highway links Hualien with Suao and hugs rocky cliffs facing Pacific Ocean along the way . . . thrilling views . . . town is starting point for Taroko Gorge trips.

Taitung Ba Hsien Dong (Eight Fairy Caves) • Found only in 1968 by archaeological expedition from Taiwan University . . . 12 large caves filled with ancient treasures . . . largest is Lin Yen with Buddhist temple, lotus pond, and stone furniture . . . just 220 yards from seashore.

Taroko Gorge • One of the most spectacular sights in the Far East . . . a 12-mile stretch of the East-West Highway is along bottom of gorge . . . breathtaking views through 38 tunnels and sheer drops of 1000 feet . . . several lookout points . . . **Eternal Springs Shrine** . . . **Swallows Grotto** . . . **Tunnel of Nine Turns** . . . **Bridge of**

Motherly Devotion (Tsu Mou) . . . end of the road is Tien Hsiang, where a simple but comfortable lodge offers restful accommodations . . . spend the night and savor the drive back through the gorge.

Islands

Kuei Yu (Tortoise Islet) • Volcanic island located 6 miles east of Tou Cheng Chen . . . looks like giant tortoise swimming up and down . . . listed as 1 of 8 famous Lan Yang scenes.

Lu Tao (Green Islet) • 18 miles from eastern coast . . . reachable by ferry from Taitung . . . island also known as Flaming Islet . . . lovely beach with colorful sea shells.

Lan Yu (Orchid Island) • Famous for butterflies and orchids and unspoiled beauty . . . located about 45 miles off southeastern coast . . . inhabitants are 3000 Yami aborigine tribespeople . . . some in stone houses . . . simple life here with fishing, skin diving, farming millet and yams, taro, and fruit.

Matsu • Off limits.

Penghu • Largest of 64 islands in the Pescadores . . . located about 34 miles off the western coast . . . reached by air or boat from Tainan/ Kaohsiung . . . Makung is capital of island group . . . fishing villages, old temples, beaches, beautiful scenery . . . known for windswept ambience.

Quemoy • Off limits.

Ryukyu Islet • Offshore island just 9 miles southwest of Tung Kang, Kaohsiung . . . more than 30 temples . . . lighthouse on Pou Fu Hill . . . famous for sunrises and sunsets . . . ghost cave and vase rock.

HOTELS

Taipei

Taipei has an abundance of hotels—most of them in the middle class variety—but Americans, especially on business, would feel more comfortable in the familiar international-class names listed below (Hyatt, Hilton, Holiday Inn, Regent, Sheraton). However, the two hotels that make the most splash are the government-operated Grand Hotel and the privately owned Ritz Taipei. Even if you choose one of the more familiar hotels, save time for a peek at the Grand and Ritz—to see what all the shouting is about!

★★★★**Grand Hotel** • *1 Chungshan North Rd., Section 4, Taipei. Tel: 596–5565. Cable: GRANDHTEL. Telex: 11646; 11647* • 530 rooms (84 suites) . . . Madame Chiang Kai-shek's masterpiece . . . claims 20 acres on slope of Yuan Shan (Round Hill) in northern section of city . . . former government guesthouse, original 3 pavilions were designed to resemble Beijing's Imperial Palace . . . now overshadowed by neoclassical, vermillion lacquered "monstrosity" called the Main Building . . . guests have use of adjacent Yuan Shan Club of Taipei . . . whole area considered a showpiece for the country . . . if you must, demand rooms in original structure (Chi-Lin Pavilion) . . . not one of my favorites.

Facilities: Tennis, bowling, swimming at Yuan Shan Recreation Club. Cantonese restaurant, Chinese teahouse, Ming Grill, tiny bar, and shops on ground floor. Western dining room (overlooking city), Gold Coin Bar, and Chinese dining room off main lobby. Coffee shop on upper level. Telex and postage facilities on ground floor. Gardens.

Manager: E. Zee. *Reservations:* Direct.

★★★**Hilton International Taipei** • *38 Chung Siao Rd. West, Section 1, Taipei. Tel: 311–5151. Cable: HILTELS TAIPEI. Telex: 785– 11699* • 527 rooms (32 suites) . . . also known as Taipei Hilton . . . first international-standard hotel in Taipei when it opened in 1973 . . . always successful and well managed but now facing stiff competition from the newcomers in better parts of town . . . undergoing massive, multimillion-dollar renovations . . . 90% of guests American businessmen . . . boasts Taipei's first executive floors—a total of 54 rooms with exclusive check-in desk, private lounge with complimentary breakfast and cocktails, and extra room amenities . . . area around Hilton also being renovated, with showcase Mitsukoshi department store next door.

Facilities: Business Center. Health club. La Pizzeria. Lobby lounge/ bar. Trader's Grill. Coffee Garden and Galleon Pub. Deluxe Hunan restaurant. Tiffany's banquet area. 24-hour room service. Non-smoking floors.

Manager: P. Paxton. *Reservations:* HILTELS.

Howard Plaza Hotel • *160 Jean Ai Rd., Sec. 3 Taipei. Tel: (02) 700–2325. Telex: (785) 10702* • 606 rooms (135 suites). 13-story new rise in fashionable district . . . magnificent lobby with airy atrium . . . nicely appointed rooms . . . 2 royal suites. Keio Plaza associate hotel.

Facilities: Outdoor landscaped swimming pool. Tennis court. Health Center with sauna. Business Center. Shopping mall. Pearl River dim sum restaurant. Yangtse River Shanghainese cuisine. Miyama Japanese delicacies. Le Louvre Grill room. Champs Elysees coffee shop. Club Celebrity disco. Golden Cup bar. Orchid Gazebo bar. Seven Scholars bar. Large banquet rooms. Howard Executive Society membership to guests.

Manager: M. Liao. *Reservations:* Distinguished Hotels.

★★★**Lai Lai Sheraton Hotel** • *12 Chung Hsiao East Rd., Section 1, Taipei. Tel: 321–5511. Cable: SHANGTEL. Telex: 23939* • 705 rooms . . . A big and busy hotel . . . like Taipei indoors. . . has had a series of ups and downs but the plant is there . . . you never have to leave . . . everything is available here and business conferences take place in every corner.

Facilities: Executive Service Salon for businessmen (but I wouldn't count on it). Four Seasons (coffee shop). Cafe on lobby level. Le Bar off lobby. Momoyama restaurant (Japanese), Happy Garden (Chinese), Antoine restaurant (French), and Crystal Palace (Continental) on 2nd floor. Peacock Bar on 2nd floor. Shangri-la Garden restaurant (Shanghai) on basement 2. Jade Garden restaurant (Cantonese) on basement 1. Extensive shopping arcade. Top floor pool and health club. Private club on 17th/18th floors for local business executives which guests can use for a fee.

Manager: C. Tsai. *Reservations:* Sheraton Int'l.

★★★★**Ritz Taipei Hotel** • *155 Min Chuan East Rd., Taipei 104. Tel: 597–1234. Cable: THERITZ, TAIPEI. Telex: 27345 THE RITZ* • 220 rooms (90 suites) . . . French Art Deco 1930s motif throughout . . . an oasis of beauty and calm in the midst of this drab, polluted capital . . . fabulous hotel for those that afford and appreciate the very best . . . offers personalized but most subdued service . . . worth the price and slightly out-of-the-way location . . . dream place to stay!

Facilities: Matisse Suite with Executive Services. Health center and sauna. Same day laundry and complimentary shoeshines. Deluxe limousine transfers. Staff speaks 10 languages. Aldebaran Music Lounge on 2nd floor. Paris 1930 restaurant (French) on 2nd floor. La Brasserie elegant coffee shop off lobby. Le Salon. Les Copains De Chine restaurant (Hunanese) on lower level.

Manager: S. Yen. *Reservations:* LHN.

★★★★**The Regent of Taipei** • *41 Chung Shan North Rd., Sec. 2, Taipei. Tel: (02) 542–1024. Telex: 23466 PRUNDENCO* • 560 rooms (61 suites). The city's newest hotel and done up in the elegant Regent style . . . to which we are all becoming accustomed . . . located in center of major commercial district . . . between Chung Sang Road North and Linsen Road North.

Facilities: Ballroom. Business Center open 24 hours. The Cafe for informal meals. Two Chinese restaurants. Steak House. Atrium Lounge with live music.

Manager: R. Chapman. *Reservations:* REGENT INT'L.

Kaohsiung

★**Ambassador Hotel** ● *202 Minsheng 2nd Rd., Kaohsiung. Tel: (07) 211–5211. Telex: 72105. Cable: AMTELKAO.* ● 457 rooms (18 suites) . . . newest hotel in Taiwan's second largest city . . . 23-story shiny, red-tile building . . . ask for a room with a splendid view of the river . . . tallest building in the city . . . accommodations furnished in "tropical" style . . . 4th-floor roof garden features Executive Club. Member of Nikko Hotels International.

Facilities: French, Japanese, Cantonese, and Szechwanese restaurants. 15 banquet halls with 4-language simultaneous translation equipment. Swimming pool. Nightclub. Shopping arcade and art gallery. Cocktail lounge.

Manager: T. Wang. *Reservations:* Tokyu Hotels.

★★★**Grand Hotel** ● *Cheng Ching Lake 833, Kaohsiung. Tel: (07) 383–5911. Cable: GRAND HOTEL. Telex: 71231* ● 108 rooms (12 suites) . . . six miles from city . . . located on Cheng Ching lake . . . a replica of the new building of Taipei's Grand . . . another of Madame Chiang Kai-shek's projects . . . overwhelming and unpopular structure.

Facilities: Cavernous lobby lounge. Bar. Chinese restaurant. Coffee shop. Swimming pool. Tennis courts. Gymnasium. Gift shop. Sauna.

Manager: N. K. Chung. *Reservations:* Direct.

★★**Holiday Garden of Kaohsiung** ● *279 Liuho 2nd Rd., Kaohsiung. Tel: (07) 241–0121. Cable: GARDEN. Telex: 81948 GARDEN* ● 313 rooms . . . complimentary transportation from airport 20 minutes away . . . Chinese decor with Swiss-management philosophy . . . newish wing . . . considered a good hotel.

Facilities: Swimming pool and garden area. Chinese restaurant. Bar. Western-style coffee shop.

Manager: H. N. Chen. *Reservations:* Direct.

Hualien

★★★**Astar Hotel** ● *Seaview Ave., Mei-Lun, Hualien. Tel: (038) 326–111. Cable: ASTAR. Telex: 11540* ● 170 rooms . . . pleasant location . . . half the rooms overlook the Pacific Ocean . . . the others over pool and grounds . . . interesting lobby area.

Facilities: Swimming pool. Garden and views. Chinese and Western restaurants. Bars. Shopping Arcade. Bowling Alley.

Manager: M. Y. Wu. *Reservations:* Direct.

★★★**China Trust Hualien Hotel** • *2 Yong-Shing Rd., Hualien. Tel: (038–221–171–185). Telex: 11144 CTCOM* • 327 rooms (2 suites). Lovely new tourist hotel overlooking sea.

Facilities: Restaurant and bar. Coffee Shop. Swimming Pool. Ballroom/banquet area. Gift Shop.

Manager: C. H. Lin. *Reservations:* Direct.

★★**Marshal Hotel** • *36 Kungyuan Rd., Hualien. Tel: (038) 326–123. Cable: MARSHALHTL. Telex: 21656* • 350 rooms . . . new and modern and quite comfortable . . . another pleasant location . . . worth a visit.

Facilities: Swimming pool. Bar. Chinese and Continental restaurant. Coffee shop.

Manager: F. H. Chang. *Reservations:* Angel Hotels, Taipei.

Nantou/Sun Moon Lake

★★★**China Trust Sun Moon Lake Hotel** • *23 Chung Cheng Rd., Nantou. Tel: (049) 855–911–5. Cable: SOMOTEL NANTOU. Telex: 11144 CITC TAIPEI* • 116 rooms . . . pagoda-style structure overlooking lake and Wen Wu Temple . . . lovely hillside views . . . a quiet retreat . . . Chinese decor in lobby and new wing . . . friendly atmosphere and service.

Facilities: Boat landing on lake. Swimming pool. Waterskiing. Golf. Chinese restaurant. Bar. Coffee shop.

Manager: S. Shih. *Reservations:* Direct.

Taichung

★★★**Hotel National** • *257 Taichung Kang Rd., Sec. 1, Taichung. Tel: (04) 321–3111. Cable: NATIONALHTLA TAICHUNG. Telex: 51393 NATALHTL* • 404 rooms (13 suites). Modern hotel in the midst of the city.

Facilities: Chinese, Western, and Japanese restaurants. Night Club. Lobby Bar. Sauna/swimming pool.

Manager: H. Chen. *Reservations:* Direct.

★★★**Park Hotel** • *17 Kung Yuan Rd., Taichung 40007. Tel: (04) 220–5181. Cable: PARKHOTEL, Taichung. Telex: 51525 PARKTEL* • 124 rooms (1 suite). Small new modern hotel in town.

Facilities: Szechwan and French cuisine. Coffee Shop. Bar. Cocktail Lounge. Night Club. Convention area.

Manager: C. T. Chen. *Reservations:* Direct.

Tainan

★★**Hotel Tainan** ● *1 Cheng Kung Rd., 70001 Tainan. Tel: (06) 228–9101. Telex: 71365 TANHOTEL* ● 152 rooms (10 suites). Small hotel with decent services.

Facilities: Chinese and Western restaurants. Coffee Shop. Bar. Ballroom. Swimming pool.

Manager: Y. H. Lin Cheng. *Reservations:* Direct.

Pingtung (southernmost tip of Taiwan)

★★★**Caesar Park Hotel-Kenting** ● *6 Kenting Rd., Henchun Town, Ping Tung Hsien, Taiwan. Tel: (08) 889–5222. Telex: 71882 CAESARKT* ● 250 rooms (5 suites). One of the few resort hotels in the ROC. Contemporary rattan throughout . . . each guest room has own balcony . . . half overlooking the sea . . . area offers many outdoor activities as well as watersports.

Facilities: Piano Lobby Bar. Oluanpi music lounge. Paiwan Karaoke Bar. Swimming pool with Tucano pool bar. Discovery Disco. Western, Japanese, and Chinese cuisines. Caesar Leisure and Health Center.

Manager: J. I. C. Chan. *Reservations:* Direct.

DINING

Dining in Taiwan offers yet another exciting opportunity to enjoy total immersion in Chinese cuisine. All the nuances of China's varied provincial cookery are represented here as well as the familiar flavors of Peking, Shanghai, Kwangchow, Szechuan, Hunan, and Shanxi dishes. In addition, there are some interesting specialties of Taiwan itself which rely on a super-abundance of fresh seafood daily. The fish is often served in thickish sauces, but there are also oysters cooked in a variety of ways (stir-fried, in soups or omelets) and excellent tuna (so good, it is flown every day to Japan for use as sashimi). Many of the so-called Taiwanese restaurants boast huge fish tanks, so you can pick your own victim.

Some travelers insist that the Chinese cuisine found in Taipei is better than anywhere else in the Far East. Surely, it's all a matter of personal opinion and palate, but a sumptuous and full meal here will cost less—including local beer, rice wine, and taxes—than in most other places. Expect fairly clean and very casual restaurants. Some are open from 8 a.m.–11 p.m. and serve the local version of dim sum from early morning until about 2:30 p.m. These little snacks or "walking cafeteriae" are generally known as *yam cha* and are terrific if you like a taste of this and that, together with strong tea. As "small chow" is a Cantonese specialty, all the dishes are freshly prepared and either steamed or deep fried.

Another popular meal around Taipei is "Mongolian Barbecue," and one of the biggest eateries that serves this type dish is the Genghis Khan. There are two varieties, one resembling the Japanese sukiyaki (but not drowned in sweet shoyu) and the other similar to an Oriental Sloppy Joe (sesame bun stuffed with grilled meats and vegetables). But, both are fun and tend to serve the same social purpose as beef or cheese fondue (dress casually, for a frolicking good time).

Another traditional dish, especially among the older generation, may not tempt the taste buds of most visitors—snake. The Chinese consider snakes almost mystical and feel that their consumption is beneficial to ailments (even future, yet undefined ills). The special snake restaurants are located in one of Taipei's oldest areas, just below the popular Lungshan (Dragon Mountain) Temple, so the unsuspecting need not enter. But if you are curious and your stomach can stand it, walk through the winding Hwa Hsi Street (also known as Snake Alley) to see quite a spectacle.

As in all other parts of the Far East, street vendors abound throughout Taiwan. However, Taipei especially is not a place you want to stop and snack along the sidewalk. Combine air, water, and noise pollution and you will want to enjoy your meals in safe, clean, and just-as-colorful restaurants. Try any place that exhibits happy and healthy clients, and remember to order bottled drinks or hot tea.

If your palate demands a Western meal now and again, there are some very fine restaurants in Taipei that serve French/Continental cuisine as well as Italian (pizza and pasta), American (coffee shops with hamburgers and french fries) and English (fish and chips) fare. But watch out for the prices—especially for imported meats and all spirits (very costly in Taiwan). There are also a few nightclubs around the town, with meals/drinks/entertainment, but be prepared to pay a 39% government tax (plus service and regular tax) for your frivolous evening.

CANTONESE RESTAURANTS

An Lo Yuan • *232 Tunghwa St., Tel: 772–5929* • Sweet and sour pork very good.

Ruby Restaurant • *135 Chung Shan North Rd., Tel: 571–1157* • Everyone knows it.

Canton • *11 Nanking East Rd., Tel: 541–4964* • A favorite.

Cantonese Restaurant and Chinese Teahouse (Yuan Yuan) • *Ground floor, Grand Hotel* • Yam cha and good dishes.

Jade Garden • *Basement level, Lai Lai Sheraton Hotel* • Pleasant and formal setting . . . yam cha from 7:30 a.m. . . . a la carte for lunch/dinner.

Old Fatty Chou's • *53 Han Chung St., Tel: 331–0085* • Great for Chinese snacks and tea.

HANGZHOU RESTAURANTS

Tien Hsiang Lo • *House of Heavenly Aromas—Ritz Hotel Taipei* • The only restaurant in town devoted to Hangzhou cuisine. Memorable meals in an elegant setting—as befitting the Ritz.

HUNANESE RESTAURANTS

Charming Garden Restaurant • *16 Nanking East Rd., Tel: 521–4131* • Pigeon dumpling soup . . . smoked ham . . . date dumplings for dessert.

The Hunan Restaurant • *Taipei Hilton* • Decorated with antique Chinese robes and furnished with deluxe tableware. Elegant and expensive but popular with locals.

Liu's Palace • *1st floor, Taipei Regency* • Rated one of the very best in town . . . fabulous lunchtime buffet.

Golden China • *3rd floor, Taipei Hilton* • Traditional atmosphere . . . replicas of National Palace Museum treasures around . . . food good, too.

SZECHUAN RESTAURANTS

Rong Shing • *45 Chilin Rd., Tel: 521–5341* • Spicy bean curd, pork with garlic, stewed carp with hot bean paste.

Szechuan Restaurant • *12th floor, Ambassador Hotel, Tel: 551–1111* • Good reputation and loyal following.

Chinese Dining Room • *Lobby level, Grand Hotel, Tel: 596–5565* • Szechuan and Shanghai cooking.

TAIWANESE RESTAURANTS

Happy Garden • *2nd floor, Lai Lai Sheraton Hotel, Tel: 321–5511* • Happy setting . . . fresh, wholesome fare.

Taiwan Shiau Diau • *71 Chuangshan North Rd., Tel: 561–0879* • Good seafood and sauces.

Orchid Isle • *2nd floor, Taipei Regency Tel: 705–9171* • Taiwanese fishing village atmosphere . . . fresh and abundant fish . . . terrific!

Ching Yeh (Green Leaf) Restaurant • *No. 1 Chung Shan North Rd., Tel: 551–9757* • Good reputation.

WESTERN RESTAURANTS

Paris 1930 • *1st floor, Ritz Hotel, Tel: 597–1234* • Tres chic and tres cher . . . elegant French cafe-style with Art Deco atmosphere . . . impeccable service . . . superb food . . . hard to believe this is Taipei!

La Brasserie • *Ground floor, Ritz Hotel, Tel: 597–1234* • Tres Continental . . . popular with foreign businessmen at lunchtime.

The Trader's Grill • *2nd floor, Taipei Hilton, Tel: 311–5151* • The hotel's gourmet restaurant . . . imported beef and other delicacies.

Galleon Pub • *2nd floor, Taipei Hilton, Tel: 311–5151* • Pub lunches and draught beer, etc.

La Pizzeria • *Lower level, Taipei Hilton, Tel: 311–5151* • Red-checked tablecloths, pizza, and all the trimmings.

Western Dining Room • *Main floor, Grand Hotel, Tel: 596–5565* • Used to be considered one of the best . . . now surpassed by new spots in town, in my opinion.

Antoine Restaurant • *2nd floor, Lai Lai Sheraton Hotel, Tel: 321–5511* • Haute cuisine . . . high style in attractive setting.

Amigo • *66 Lane 107, Lin Shen North Rd., Tel: 561–7487* • Spanish cuisine and atmosphere . . . cozy . . . romantic candlelight and music.

Crystal Palace • *2nd floor, Lai Lai Sheraton Hotel, Tel: 321–5511* • Luncheon buffets . . . fashion shows . . . gourmet dinner menu . . . disco.

Les Rotisseurs • *15th floor Taipei Regency, Tel: 705–9161* • Elegant setting and ambiance . . . touted as Taipei's most luxurious restaurant.

MISCELLANEOUS RESTAURANTS

Genghis Khan • *176 Nanking East Rd., Tel: 711–3655* • Touristy but popular for Mongolian barbecues . . . outside grills also.

Great Wall • *No. 1 Linsen South Rd., Tel: 321–4646* • Much cheaper than GK and more familiar to local residents.

Peace Vegetarian Restaurant • *3rd floor, Ho Ping Bldg., No. 177 Ho Ping East Rd., Tel: 393–4044* • Altar of Kuan Yin in corner so devotees can worship and eat . . . Buddhist food, lectures, and literature . . . open 11:30 a.m.–9 p.m.

Momoyama Restaurant • *2nd floor, Lai Lai Sheraton Hotel, Tel: 321–5511* • Kaiseki cooking . . . sushi, sashimi, tempura . . . nice setting . . . but all Japanese food too expensive in Taipei.

ENTERTAINMENT

Hoover Theater Restaurant • *21–23 Fu Shun St., Tel: 596–7171* • Cantonese food and classical floor shows (7:30 and 9:30 p.m. nightly) . . . an NT$300 minimum per person, plus 49% (service and taxes).

Tiffany's Disco • *3rd floor, Taipei Hilton, Tel: 311–5151* • Disco from 8:30 to midnight . . . an NT$390 minimum per person, plus 49%.

Aldebaran Music Lounge • *2nd floor, Ritz Hotel, Tel: 597–1234* • Open from 4 p.m. to midnight for drinks, snacks, and taped music . . . Arabian nights atmosphere.

Crystal Palace • *2nd floor, Lai Lai Sheraton Hotel, Tel: 321–5511* • Becomes dazzling disco from 9 p.m. to midnight . . . Lights, tapes.

Champagne Room • *11th floor, President Hotel, Tel: 595–1251* • Live orchestra and dancing . . . if not dining, NT$250 cover charge plus service and taxes.

International Room • *Ambassador Hotel, Tel: 551–1111* • Largest nightclub in Taipei . . . 14-piece orchestra from 8:30 p.m. to midnight . . . an NT$220 minimum, plus service and taxes.

Piano Bar • *15th floor, Taipei Regency, Tel: 705–9161* • Quiet and subdued . . . popular with locals.

The Horseshoe • *2 Lane 28, Shuang Cheng St., Tel: 591–6856* • English Pub/Restaurant . . . happy hours . . . draught beer . . . live jazz.

Waltzing Matilda Inn • *3 Lane 25, Shuang Cheng St., Tel: 594–3510* • Pub atmosphere, cuisine, entertainment . . . Draught beer . . . Australian.

The Ploughman Pub • *9 Lane 25, Shuang Cheng St., Tel: 594–9648* • Step back into merry olde England here . . . darts . . . draught beer.

Zum Fass (Beer House) • *55 Basement Lane 119, Lin Shen North Rd., Tel: 531–3815* • Swiss/German atmosphere, cuisine, beer.

SHOPPING

Of all the wondrous shopping paradises extant in the Far East, Taiwan is truly the "bargain basement." It seems that just about everything possible is manufactured here and then exported to Number One customer—the United States. Look around any hotel lobby or bar at the groups of Western importers and their local agents deep in conversation over lists. A breeze through the Taiwan version of the Yellow Pages shows thousands of products available, from "abrasives" to "zippers." While the average visitor may not be interested in children's outerwear or a custom-made yacht, there are plenty of other things to catch one's fancy.

Taiwan is well known for its indigenous coral and the lovely jewelry or carved art objects made from it. This is also a center for furniture of teak or rosewood, Chinese carpets, ceramic reproductions of Sung and Ming Dynasty pieces (be wary of antique dealers), souvenirs from local shell or horn, as well as bamboo and 300 different species of butterflies, digital throw-aways (key rings, pens, etc.), local jade and cloisonne, cheap "pirated" books (especially bestsellers), and excellent tailoring.

To appreciate the variety of what is "Made in Taiwan," plan on browsing first in the **Chinese Handicraft Mart,** a multistory, one-stop shopping center sponsored by the government. Among the many, many items on display and sale here are ceramics, cloisonne, brass and bronze, marble products, wood carvings, crystal and glassware, lamps, handbags, dolls, handcrafts, jade, coral and other semiprecious stone jewelry, jade and stone carvings, carpets, furniture and screens, paintings, and scrolls. The Mart is actually four one-price (no haggling) stores in the same building, with money exchange and packing/shipping facilities for patrons. It is located at 1 Hsu Chow Rd., just a few blocks behind the Taipei Hilton and Lai Lai Shangri-La Hotel. Hours daily (including Sun. and holidays) are 9 a.m.–5:30 p.m. There are also the **Taipei Handicraft Trade and Exhibition Center** at 501 Ming Chuan East Rd., and the **Taiwan Arts and Handicraft Center** at 420 Chang Chun Rd.

Books One of the more popular reasons for stopping by Taipei is to pick up a few bestsellers at cheap, cheap prices. Taiwan does not adhere to the international copyright laws (something about its being too expensive for their young people to buy textbooks published abroad) so they print their own editions. If you don't mind bindings that don't last or paragraphs that slope downhill, these editions of everything from bestsellers to encyclopedia are not too bad, considering the cost. Ostensibly, you are not supposed to export these purchases but if you do, tear out the frontispiece and write your name in the edition. It is against the law to bring one or two back into the U.S., and it is strictly illegal to resell them. The biggest and best selection of these "pirated" editions is available at **Caves Books,** 107 Chungshan North Rd. (Tel: 541–4754), open daily (including holidays) from 9 a.m.–10 p.m. Another well-known shop is the **Kou Book, Sound & Gifts** at 54–3 Chung Shan North Rd. (Tel: 591–2900). Pirated cassette tapes are also available at both places.

Antiques and Artifacts Unless you are willing to wait three years (as one friend did) to return her so-called "Tang Dynasty horses" to the dealer for a money-back guarantee of authenticity, be very wary of buying antiques. In a place like Taiwan (where so much is reproduced), only an expert's expert is intuitive enough to feel the difference between real and fake. However slim the chance of discovering a real 14th-century porcelain, you should not be deterred from spending many happy hours along Chungshan North Rd., in the **Curio Market** or **Haggler's**

Alley (Chunghua Rd.) or in **Shih Lin.** Serious collectors congregate at **Kuo Hwa Tang Galleries,** at 108 Hankow Rd. Another reputable and rather expensive shop is **Yang Lun Tien Antique Center,** 609 Sinsen North Rd. (5th floor), across from the Imperial Hotel.

For artifacts in jade, coral, cloisonee, etc., try the **Far East Department Store** on Pao Ching Rd. or Jen-Ai Rd. in Taipei (also in Taichung, Tainan, or Kaohsiung) for fixed prices and courteous service. The coral products are lovely and worth buying. The local jade is nothing when compared with what you can find in the People's Republic of China. And watch out for what passes as gold. Even a certificate of weight is not always a legitimate piece of paper. Hotel arcade shops are filled with interesting items for sale—compare prices and try a little bargaining.

Tailoring   Custom-made clothing is much cheaper in Taipei than in Hong Kong or Singapore, although the selection in fabrics is somewhat limited. Prices vary from shop to shop, but a man's safari suit in lightweight wool runs at about $100, a dress suit between $160 and $180 (depending upon choice of imported fabric). Women can have anything copied in local synthetics or silks, as well as order custom-made shoes and handbags (snakeskin is popular). There are many tailor shops around the Ambassador and President hotels and in any shopping arcade. We have had good luck with **Jonie Cherie Tailor** in the Lai Lai Sheraton Hotel, but it's all a matter of personal preference (and often personalities, too).

Furniture   You'll find many satisfied customers of Taiwan-made furniture. However, there are certain precautions you must take: make sure the woods have been properly kiln-dried (to prevent future cracking in overheated American homes), the designs are refined enough to be enjoyable, the packing is expert and the shipping dependable enough to arrive overseas safely. The Shi Ling area of Taipei is the very best for handcarved furniture, as is Shaneyi, about a two-hour drive south of the capital. There are many furniture showrooms around Taipei, in addition to the floor at the **Taiwan Handicraft Promotion Center.** But for substantial investments in long-lasting pieces, take the advice of friends and acquaintances on where to place your order and what follow-up is necessary.

Carpets   You can expect to find some exquisite handmade Chinese carpets at bargain prices. Both the traditional Tsientsin-design and contemporary carpets are available. There are shops along Chungshan North Rd. (and in hotel arcades). Factories are far out from the capital in Chung Li or Tao Yuan Hsien area.

Scrolls and Prints Decorative silk screens handpainted and often copied from classical masterpieces in the National Palace Museum are a popular and well-priced art here. Pay a visit to the **Chien Ho Arts and Crafts Company,** 275 Wen-lin Rd. in the Shih Lin district of Taipei (Tel: 881–8075) to watch some 40 artists working on over 200 stock designs on 100% silk screens. Custom work is also solicited.

For the latest in what local and living artists are creating, there are many galleries to visit and it is wise to call ahead to see what's hanging on the walls. Try the **Alpha Art Gallery** (Tel: 781–1714), **Avant-Garde Art Gallery** (Tel: 705–4221), **Apollo Gallery** (Tel: 781–9332), **Cathay Art Gallery** (Tel: 311–3575), **Gallery of Spring** (Tel: 781–6596), **Lung Men Art Gallery** (Tel: 781–3979), **Print Makers Art Gallery** (Tel: 707–9424), and the **Taipei Art Guild** (Tel: 882–3374). The Art Guild is a cooperative of very talented new artists, who show their works on rotation. Among these artists is the charming Swallow Lin, whose wood block prints equal the best that is "made in Taiwan."

Chops, or name stamps, are also popular buys in Taipei. For about U.S.$10, you can have your surname translated loosely into Chinese characters and carved into the bottom of a jade or ivory stamp. Together with a box of sticky red ink, you will be saved from the effort of ever scribbling your signature again. Walk along Chungshan North Rd. and pick the shop for your chop—or patronize one of the local places in Hengyang Rd.

Coral and Jade If the shops in your hotel arcade have not already tempted you, plan on spending a few hours along Hengyang Rd., but take along an interpreter. The coral of Taiwan is lovely and comes in many different shades of pink to deep red. As both jewelry and artful carved pieces, the coral is a good buy. The jade is somewhat less good and not recognized worldwide.

THAILAND

HISTORY

The colorful Kingdom of Thailand is the only country in Southeast Asia that never served time as a European colony, although various parts of it have been occupied by not-so-friendly neighbors through the ages. Until 1939 it was called Siam, a Sanskrit word meaning "gold" or "green," but history is unclear which color actually applied. There are a few gold mines in the southern part, but traditionalists say the beautiful green color that covers the mountains and fields and lies along the rivers must have inspired the name. Alas, when the "absolute" monarchy was abolished in the 1930s and a "constitutional" monarchy established, Siam became known to the world as Thailand—land of the free—splendid but less romantic.

The origin of the Thai people is somewhat vague, but scholars believe migrations probably occurred from the Chinese province of Szechuan (Sichuan in Pinyin) around the 1st century A.D. However, discoveries since the Second World War in the caves of Kanchanaburi (near the Burmese border) and the tiny village of Ban Chiang (in the northeast) have led archaeologists to proclaim that a sophisticated culture existed here that predates even the Chinese. Furthermore, it can be documented that a mysterious kingdom of Indian origin was established around the 3rd century B.C. in the Nakhon Pathom area, where the country's largest and most important Buddhist monument now stands. Add to this migrations of the Mons from the West and the Khmers from the East, and that is the make-up of the present Thai people.

Thai history really begins with the founding of the independent kingdom of Sukhothai in A.D. 1238, for it gave the people a distinction and marked a period of great cultural development. The "cradle of Thai civilization" lasted just a century, during which time the tiny kingdom absorbed elements of neighboring cultures. From China came fine potters who established the famous kilns at Sawankhalok, and over the trade route contact was made with India. (The influence of Indian art can be appreciated at the ruins of Sukhothai today.) From Cambodia, the Sukhothai kingdom absorbed elements of administration as well as architecture.

King Ramkamhaeng the Great (1277–1317) is the most famous leader of this era, and best known for creating the Thai alphabet and introducing a uniform system of currency. He also initiated political and cultural relations with China, and opened the door to diplomatic relations with the world outside.

When King Ramathibodi assumed the throne in 1350, he moved his kingdom to Ayuthaya where it flourished for over four centuries in one of the world's most fertile rice bowls. A succession of 33 kings ruled over the capital situated where three great tributaries join to form the mighty Chao Phraya River, at a point just 110 kilometers from the sea. During the first 200 years of the Ayuthaya period, the kingdom prospered and annexed neighboring territories. The Portuguese came to call in 1511 and diplomatic relations were established. However, the Burmese arrived in 1569 and occupied the country until King Naresuan the Great "liberated" Siam in 1584.

During the 17th century, the country opened its door to the West. In 1612 the British were granted permission for a small settlement on the banks of the Chao Phraya River in Ayuthaya. During the next decade, envoys were received from both Denmark and Japan. King Narai the Great was coronated in 1656 and arranged an exchange of ambassadors with the French court of King Louis XIV in 1685. Siam had its place in the world and was known for its fine cloth, spices, metals, and semiprecious stones.

But the Burmese, who had waged war with Siam almost continually since the 15th century, arrived again and completely sacked Ayuthaya in 1767. Phya Tak is credited with driving the aggressors away, and became known as Taksin the Great. He established a new capital at Thonburi, across the river from present day Bangkok. Unfortunately, he was "seized by religious delusion" some 15 years later (he actually went mad). So one of his generals, Chao Phya Chakri, on return from a victorious campaign against Cambodia, proclaimed himself king in 1782. He called himself Rama I, founder of the Chakri Dynasty, and moved his capital to the eastern bank of the Chao Phraya River as a precautionary measure. It was named **Krung Thep,** or Bangkok.

Rama I reigned for some 27 years and successfully kept the Burmese at home. He also set about re-creating the glory that was Ayuthaya in this new "city of angels." He brought the legendary Emerald Buddha (first discovered near Chiang Mai in the 15th century) back from Laos during another victorious military campaign. The small emerald image (in reality, made of jasper) was housed in an elegant new temple, Wat Phra Keo, and given the supreme place of honor it still enjoys in the palace compound (indeed, the kingdom).

Rama IV or King Mongkut (1851–1868) is considered one of the country's enlightened monarchs, for he established modern Thailand. He was known as a scholar, having spent some 27 years as a Buddhist monk before assuming the throne. He was fluent in English, studied Latin, and was knowledgeable in astronomy and astrology as well as Western sciences. He was also the innovator who brought an English governess to his court, resulting in one of the most delightful (but hardly accurate) stories of all time—*Anna and the King of Siam*. During Mongkut's reign, foreign trade flourished and some 200 foreign vessels were calling at the port of Bangkok annually.

The eldest of the alleged 39 sons of King Mongkut ascended the throne in 1869 and became known as Chulalongkorn the Great (Rama V). He ruled for over four decades and was so admired that the people built him a statue—while he was still alive! He abolished slavery, instituted social reforms, public education, and reorganized the courts of law. He brought such stability to the country that it was the only Asian nation able to resist the sweeping European colonization of the late 19th century. (However, that did not prevent him from sending a few offspring to Europe for their education and fresh ideas.) Chulalongkorn is still so beloved that both students and government workers lay wreaths before his statue in front of the National Assembly on October 23, the day he passed away in 1910.

Thailand's present monarch, King Bhumibol Adulyadej (Rama IX) assumed the throne in 1946 upon the mysterious death of his brother in the Grand Palace. He is a thoroughly modern and gentle man, who was born in Cambridge, Massachusetts, in 1927 (where his father Prince Mahidol was attending Harvard University Medical School). Although his present duties are more spiritual and social than anything else, Bhumibol is highly respected by his people. They are proud of his many accomplishments as a sailor, poet, historian, and Buddhist scholar. He plays no less than eight different musical instruments and has appeared with professional jazz musicians throughout the world! He and his beautiful consort, Queen Sirikit, are familiar sights all over Thailand and give their time most generously to all occasions.

Thailand is also the only Asian country that was not devastated by World War II. The government capitulated immediately to Japanese invasion to avoid "unnecessary bloodshed of its people." However, the Thais did not totally ignore the Allies and were very helpful to the POWs building the "Death Railway" over the River Kwai. They have tried to remain neutral since to the warring factions that line their many borders, but that is not an easy task. There have also been internal political difficulties over the past few decades, including bad student riots in 1973 and a coup d'état in 1976. The military runs the country, but they do it with subtlety. You are only aware of their presence because the number of olive-drab uniforms almost matches the number of saffron-robed monks seen everywhere!

Thailand is a wonderful place to visit and must be included on every Far East itinerary. Its people are gentle and warm, smiling and helpful. They are devoted to their land, their Buddhism, and their royal family. Their manners are impeccable, and you can learn much from their respect for life and the living.

THAILAND IN A CAPSULE

518,000 square miles of land with more next-door neighbors than any other Far East country . . . bordering on Burma, Laos, Cambodia, and Malaysia in the extreme south . . . as well as Gulf of Siam and Andaman Sea . . . known as Siam until 1949 . . . population approximately 55 million . . . 80% still agrarian . . . constitutional monarch . . . a long and turbulent political history . . . the result of being situated at the Crossroads of Southeast Asia . . . the only country in the Far East that never succumbed to colonization by the Europeans . . . a proud and independent people whose gentleness is an endearing quality . . . fortunately, "progress" is taking its time in all but the major tourist centers, though the annual growth rate of the Thai economy is among the highest in Asia.

PLANNING AHEAD

TOURISM AUTHORITY OF THAILAND (TAT) works admirably to foster and serve the kingdom's more than two million international annual visitors, who spend well over $1 billion directly related to tourism. TAT has offices around the world and publishes an array of literature describing the delights of Thailand as well as information on special festivals and lavish photographs of the beauty spots. All TAT employees are knowledgeable, courteous, and efficient, and they are fluent in English.

TAT Bangkok headquarters is a building located on Ratchadamnoen Ave. (not far from the Grand Palace), Tel: 2821143–7. Within Thailand, there are TAT offices in Chiang Mai (135 Praisani Rd., Tel: 235334), Kanchanaburi (Saeng Chuto Rd., Tel: 511200), Nakhon Ratchasima (54/1–4 Mukkhamontri Rd., Tel: 243427), Pattaya Beach (Chai Hat Rd., Tel: 418750), Phuket (73–75 Phuket Rd., Tel: 212213), and Hat Yai (1-1 Soi 2 Niphat Uthit 3 Rd., Hat Yai, Songkhla 90110, Tel: 243747).

There are two additional offices in Phitsanulok and Surat Thani, and ten TAT overseas offices, of which two are in the U.S.: at 5 World

Trade Center, Suite 2449, New York, NY 10048 (Tel: 212–432–0433); and 3440 Wilshire Blvd., Suite 1101, Los Angeles, CA 90010 (Tel: 213–382–2353).

VISAS are not required for a stay in Thailand of up to 15 days, provided that travelers are holding valid U.S. passports and have confirmed onward tickets. The same applies to Canadian passport holders.

INOCULATIONS are required only of travelers who have been in a smallpox infected area within 14 days of arrival, or in a yellow fever infected area within six days of arrival in the kingdom.

ENTRY BY AIR is primarily through Bangkok's modern **Don Muang Airport,** about 15 miles from the city center. Bangkok serves as a Southeast Asian junction for over 700 international flights weekly from Europe, the Middle East, South Pacific, and Western Hemisphere. An average of 3500 travelers pass through the airport daily and make use of the local Tourist Authority of Thailand information bureau as well as the reservation service operated by the Thai Hotels Association. Porterage and limousine service are controlled by the airport and travelers are advised to use only authorized baggage handlers and taxis into town, at least until you become a master at the custom of bargaining over the fare. The airport also has restaurants, an inoculation center, banks, and shops.

Thai Airways International (THAI) has contributed to making Bangkok an important hub for air traffic, and instituted the Amber One air route to Hong Kong a few years ago which saves at least an hour's flying time. The Thai Airways Company (TAC), the kingdom's domestic carrier, was among the first to schedule passenger flights to China and to reopen service to Laos, Vietnam, and Cambodia. Bangkok is still the only doorway to Rangoon from the east, to Vientiane from the south, and to Cambodia from the west.

Departure tax is approximately 200 baht, or about US$8.

ARRIVAL BY SEA is likely to be via the Eastern Gulf of Thailand into Pattaya, a popular beach resort some two to three hours by road from Bangkok. Indeed, the great world cruise liners have "discovered" this port of entry versus Sattahip a few miles south, home of the Royal Thai Navy and where most of the country's shipping is handled. Cruise passengers are expected to "tender into shore" (be transported in small craft) for sightseeing excursions in Bangkok or relaxing on the beaches of this Acapulco-like playground.

Cunard Line, Cunard/NAC, Royal Cruise, and Royal Viking Line often schedule port calls in Pattaya, and the average length of stay in the Eastern Gulf is just under 48 hours.

DUTY-FREE allowances for bona fide tourists include 200 cigarettes or 250 grams of smoking tobacco, one quart of wine or liquor, and personal effects. Narcotics, obscene photos or literature, firearms and ammunition, certain types of fruits, vegetables, and plants are all prohibited. The importation of currency is limited to 2000 baht per person or U.S.$2000 per person (unless a higher amount has been declared upon arrival). 500 baht, however, is the limit, per person, on departure.

NOTE · · · Imported goods are heavily taxed in Thailand, so visitors should bring what they will need in cigarettes, spirits, film, cosmetics, etc. (Wine seems to have an especially heavy duty here.)

CURRENCY of Thailand is the baht. Each baht is worth about 4¢ and there are roughly 25 baht to the U.S. dollar. The baht is divided into 100 satangs, just for confusion's sake. Notes are used in denominations of 10 baht (brown), 20 baht (green), 100 baht (red), and 500 baht (purple). Coins come in 25 satang, 50 satang, 1 baht, and 5 baht pieces. Traveler's checks are accepted everywhere but best cashed at authorized money changers, like banks and most hotels or tourist shops. Hotels notoriously offer terrible rates, even though the baht does not tend to fluctuate very much. Since the Vietnam War, American money is quite well recognized and some shops will take it directly.

LOCAL TIME in Thailand is Greenwich Mean Time plus 7 hours. For our purposes, Thailand is exactly 12 hours ahead of Eastern Standard Time (and just about halfway around the world from New York City), 11 hours in advance of Eastern Daylight Time. Add another hour for each mainland U.S. time zone (5 hours for Hawaii). Thailand is in the same time zone as Jakarta and Kuala Lumpur; one hour behind Hong Kong, Manila, and Taipei; 2 hours behind Tokyo and Seoul; 1 hour behind Singapore and ½ hour ahead of Rangoon.

LOCAL CURRENT is 220 volts/50 cycles, with adaptors available in most city and resort hotels.

LOCAL WATER is considered quite safe to drink in the major deluxe hotels, but the cautious should always stick with bottled mineral water and sodas. The Thais are a clean and hygienic people; in fact, their sanitary habits are certainly admirable in a country so hot and humid. Expect ice in major hotels to be potable, but not from street stalls or small shops. Green Spot soda and Thai beer are available ice cold everywhere and are excellent antidotes for the fiery dishes served. Thai beer tends to be rather potent, however, and should be avoided during the heat of the day.

OFFICIAL LANGUAGE in the kingdom is Thai, which has origins in Chinese, Khmer, Sanskrit, and Pali. In the southern region, Malay words are interspersed with the Thai. The written language dates from the late 13th century and is an art unto itself. In a week's visit, it is impossible to conquer more than the polite greeting *Sawadee* (followed by *khrap,* spoken by a man, and *kha,* spoken by a woman). However, visitors can be assured that English is widely used in major hotels, tourist attractions, shops, restaurants, and bars. There are also many Roman-lettered signs around the center of Bangkok, Chiang Mai, Pattaya, and Phuket Island. Thai is a very polite language, which explains much of the behavior of the Thais themselves.

There are two English-language dailies in Bangkok, the morning *Post* and the *Nation.* Do not expect much in the way of enlightening coverage of major events, but they are better than nothing. There are also some tourist newspapers that offer helpful information on sightseeing, food, and entertainment in English, German, and French. Otherwise, the *International Herald Tribune* and the *Asian Wall Street Journal* can be found at the concierge desks in major hotels—and generally as a complimentary bonus with your breakfast tray.

The BBC "World News Tonight" is broadcast on Thai radio via an FM station, and more programs with English subtitles or sound are becoming available in the better Bangkok hotels. And martial arts fans can view any number of the latest films in theaters throughout Thailand.

BUSINESS HOURS in Thailand range from 8 a.m.–9 p.m. Government offices are open from 8:30 a.m.–4:30 p.m., with an hour lunch break at noon (avoid this hour). Private offices have working hours from 8 a.m.–5 p.m. with an hour at noon free. Banks are open from 8:30 a.m.–3:30 p.m. except branches in major hotels and tourist attractions. Major shops are open from 10 a.m.–7 p.m. while family run places set their own hours—long ones! Only the Tourism Authority of Thailand (TAT) is open for service on weekends and holidays, but call ahead to be sure.

Local trade associations and multinational company offices are located easily through the English language telephone directory in your hotel room. The **American Chamber of Commerce** is located at 140 Wireless Rd., Bangkok (Tel: 2511605) and the **Foreign Correspondents Club** is now in the shopping plaza across from the Oriental Hotel. The **U.S. Embassy** can be found at 95 Wireless Rd. in Bangkok (Tel: 2525040–9) and working hours are 7:30 a.m. to noon, 1–4:30 p.m. The **Canadian Embassy** is at 138 Silom Rd., 11th floor, Boonmitr Bldg. (Tel: 2341561–8), with office hours from 8 a.m.–12:30 p.m. and 1:30–4:30 p.m.

TIPPING is strictly optional in Thailand because most people here aim to please, anyway. The visitor who wishes to show his appreciation for good service should follow the European or American standards for tipping, but note that offering 1 baht (about U.S.4¢) is considered an insult—so get the coins organized. Most hotels and better restaurants add a straight 10% to 15% service charge to the bill, so additional tipping is optional. You do not need to tip in taxis or trains unless the service was exceptional. Porters at the airports and railway stations have a set fee and you are required to pay a central cashier before retrieving luggage. Guides will, of course, take anything; their remuneration is up to your conscience. A 10-baht note (40¢) is plenty to tip in both beauty and barber shops.

TELEPHONE AND TELEX services in major hotel chains are fine and many also have Businessman's Centers, where secretarial help and translation can be arranged. Try not to tax your patience and knowledge of the Thai language by trying to telephone outside the hotel, especially without use of a telephone directory in English. Cables can be sent through the Post and Telegraph Department on New Rd., Bangkok, or via your hotel concierge. Don Muang Airport, the Erawan Hotel, and other major hostelries have small post office branches for the purchase of stamps and mailing small items.

WHAT TO WEAR in this hot and humid tropical climate can be a problem because synthetic materials are not comfortable in this weather. March to May is very, very hot and humid; June through October is the official rainy season; and the months from November through February are more pleasant and mild (but still very hot to the unsuspecting). Cottons and seersucker suits are preferable to polyester pants, even though the cotton material tends to wrinkle in the heat. However, life is very casual in Thailand; very few restaurants even require jackets and ties (check in advance). Women should dress modestly at all times because the Thais are offended by too much "skin" in public, and tradition calls for being properly covered (no short shorts) when visiting temples. The evenings are lovely, especially during the winter season, and gentlemen usually wear a short-sleeved shirt while the ladies don colorful long cotton skirts. At all times, you should carry a light sweater or wrap as defense against the air conditioning.

LOCAL TRANSPORTATION in Thailand ranges from good to bad, and can be a bit tricky unless you know the ropes. Taxi drivers have the annoying habit of keeping the meter running continually, so each new passenger must bargain over the fare before the journey even begins. Bangkok especially has a crazy traffic system and you can expect constant noise, fumes, and heat at every curve in the road! The city must have thousands of three-wheeled "tuk-tuks" that also serve as taxis, albeit much cheaper than the others. Many hotels advise their guests to use the hotel taxi system, which is air-conditioned and trustworthy and expensive, but it's not a bad idea for a short visit. Just be certain the vehicle *is* air-conditioned or you will quickly perish from the dreadful fumes. The capital needs considerable help in cleaning up the heavy, putrid air.

There is excellent transportation from Bangkok to other parts of the country, via bus, train, or domestic plane service. **Buses** run regularly from the city to Pattaya (2½ hours) as well as to the north, east, and south. There are three different bus terminals, so be sure you are at the Southern Bus Terminal (Khonsong Sai Tai) to embark on a bus traveling southward! Fares are very reasonable (about 80 baht for a 9-hour journey) and most of the vehicles are "air-conditioned." Carry your own refreshments.

Railway service within Thailand is also excellent, although the trains are not super modern as in Japan. Nonetheless, they are well-run and most often on time. There are three classes of service on lines that run to the north, northeast, east, and south as well as a Malayan Express that can be embarked upon between Butterworth (Penang) and Singapore. (However, it's a 24-hour journey from Bangkok to Butterworth and another 19 hours to Singapore so pack a few cushions!) Trains in Thailand and neighboring Malaysia are an excellent way to see the lush, tropical landscape and the fares couldn't be more reasonable, especially in second class. Example: the 1927-kilometer ride to Singapore from Bangkok is about U.S.$40 one way. The 13-hour overnight trip to Chiang Mai from Bangkok (751 km) is about $15 one way in second class.

Thai Airways, the government owned and operated domestic carrier, is the best in the Far East. There are frequent daily flights between the capital city and the popular tourist areas: Phuket, Songkhla, and Chiang Mai. In contrast to the local service in other Far Eastern countries, Thai Airways offers smiling attendants (cute as a button, too), and such creature comforts as the late edition newspaper, fresh coffee, and a full hot breakfast on the less-than-one-hour early morning flight to Chiang Mai! Sandwiches and drinks were offered on the late afternoon return, a few days later. Seats may be reserved but there is a 25% no-show charge—which applies to EVERYONE.

Rivers and *klongs* (canals) are a vital part of life in Thailand. For over four centuries, the kingdom's former capital of Ayuthaya was situated on an artificial island in the Chao Phraya River and crisscrossed by some 55 kilometers of waterways. A similar intricate network of klongs was devised when the capital was transferred to Bangkok in 1782. Unfortunately, many of these picturesque old klongs have been sacrificed to "progress" and high rises, but the Chao Phraya (River of the Kings) still plays a majestic role in big city life and is an important thoroughfare for the transportation of cargo and food. There are plenty of interesting river trips still available to visitors, mainly from the pier beside the Oriental Hotel. Here, you can find regular ferries that go upriver past Wat Arun (Temple of the Dawn), Wat Po, and the Grand Palace. Or, you can bargain a bit with one of the boatmen and make your own sightseeing tour for just a few dollars. The Oriental Hotel operates the posh *Oriental Queen* riverboat on daily trips to Ayuthaya, and on dinner cruises every evening.

Touring the klongs by *hang yao* or long-tailed motorized boats is one of the highlights of anyone's stay, for here one can view a most lively panorama of typical Thai life. The ramshackle huts beside the water have antennae and large color televisions, but the inhabitants still bathe in the water below. Most colorful are the daily floating markets at which the locals trade wares and offer themselves to amateur photographers. Alas, Bangkok's famous floating market has moved across the river to Thonburi and there is another popular one in Ratchaburi Province. The price of a seat in one of these *hang yao* is only a few baht apiece, or you can charter your own for about 50 baht an hour. Be warned, however, that these craft are not the most seaworthy you have ever encountered so photographic equipment and small children should be safely guarded at all times. (And dress in boat clothes as you are apt to be splashed by muddy water from other drivers in a hurry.)

Water tours outside of Bangkok are also popular but may be slightly dangerous at these times. The State Department advises that travelers do not venture unaccompanied along the waterways of the "Golden Triangle" area, center of the world's opium trade, because local bandits have been known to harrass and rob tourists. The northeast, along the famous Mekong River valley, borders the Khmer Republic (formerly Cambodia) and the natives may not be friendly on the other bank. During the 1960s, it was something of an adventure to take the train to Nong Khai (624 km from Bangkok), cross the Mekong River by boat to the Laotian side, and hop a dilapidated bus into the dusty capital of Vientiane. Alas, these days are over and the adventure now just a happy memory of youth.

If you can't stay away from the sea, there are boats to two islands offshore from Pattaya, called Koh Sak and Koh Larn (also known as "Pattaya 2"). In Southern Thailand, the island of Phuket can be reached from a causeway from Khok Kloi and is a highlight of any visit to "phak tai" as the southern region is known. On the Eastern coast of the Thai isthmus is Ko Samui, the country's largest island, and accessible only by ferries from Ban Don in Surat Thani Province but note that the "express" takes about three hours. Songkhla is another seaside resort on the southeastern coast and famous for an inland lake dotted with islands. It is linked to the Gulf of Siam by only a tiny channel at one end.

CUSTOMS in Thailand are special enough to deserve their own category, and the government advises a few "dos" and "dont's" so that unsuspecting Westerners do not offend their charming and hospitable hosts. The Thai people have a deep reverence for their Royal Family and the National Anthem is played at all public events, with all in attendance standing silently. They are also very serious about their Buddhism and anyone acting in a manner insulting to religious custom will be severely punished. Shoes are never worn inside a chapel where the principal image of Buddha is kept. Buddhist priests are forbidden to touch (or be touched) by a woman, or to accept anything from the hand of one. Buddhist images are regarded as sacred objects and are not to be handled.

In social behavior, Thais do not normally shake hands but greet one another with palms pressed together in a prayerlike gesture. This is known as a *wai* and Thais are very honored when Westerners return the polite gesture. It is considered rude to point your foot at a person, so try to avoid doing so when seated. Thais are also insulted to be touched on the head (so don't ever pat the heads of young ones). In fact, public displays of affection are frowned upon and even holding hands is rarely seen. The people are among the most friendly and polite in the world, and visitors are expected to keep a cool head (especially when angry) and conceal emotions at all times. Finally, don't be surprised if you are always addressed by your first name, as this is the manner in which Thais refer to one another (the plus factor is that Thai surnames are unpronounceable!).

FESTIVALS in Thailand are colorful, slightly exotic, and loads of fun. Most of them relate to monarchial and religious traditions, and floral processions with monks in their saffron robes are the main spectacle. In addition to the main fetes, there are such charming customs as buying the chance to free caged birds and making a wish (which is supposed to be granted). Of course, the birds are quickly recaged and the next innocent falls into the trap, but it's an enjoyable few moments for very little money!

The following are public holidays and festivals throughout Thailand in 1984, when there is great rejoicing and very little business accomplished. Public holidays are marked with an asterisk (*).

*January 1 • *New Year's Day.*

January • *Red Cross Fair* • Held throughout the month in Bangkok under the patronage of Her Majesty Queen Sirikit.

February to April • *Kite flying season* • Contests held at Royal Ground in Grand Palace in Bangkok, weekday afternoons. Fine Arts Department stages dances and concerts every Friday and weekend afternoons in National Museum Compound throughout season.

February • *Flower Carnival in Chiang Mai* • Colorful flower floats and parades, expositions of tropical flowers and orchids, country fair and bazaar, workshops for floral arrangements. Usually held in second week of month.

February 1 • *Phra Buddhabaht Fair* • Buddhist devotees make annual pilgrimage to the Shrine of Holy Footprint near Saraburi (236 km north of Bangkok). Temple fair, country music, plays, and bazaar.

February • *Maka Bucha* • Commemorates preaching of Lord Buddha to 1250 disciples who gathered without summons. Candlelit processions around main temple buildings and full moon throughout kingdom.

February (early) • *Chinese New Year* • Thailand's several million Chinese close their shops, feast with their families, and visit their temples to offer prayers for prosperity in the coming year.

March • *Kite flying season continues* • Official kite-fights on weekday afternoons at Sanam Luang in Bangkok.

*April 6 • *Chakri Day* • Honors King Rama I, first monarch of present Chakri Dynasty who established Bangkok as capital in 1782. Extensive bicentennial celebrations took place in city during 1982.

*April 13–15 • *Songkran (water) Festival* • Traditional Thai New Year's Day marking entrance of Sun into Aries. Folk festival features sprinkling water upon Buddha images, monks, and family elders. Fish and birds set free. Colorful processions in Chiang Mai and Paklat.

*May • *Royal Ploughing Ceremony* • Rice seeds are blessed by Buddhist monks and distributed to farmers for good luck. Graceful Bhraminical processions in white and gold, with soldiers in red, at Royal Grandstand in front of Grand Palace. His Majesty the King presides.

*May 5 • *Coronation Day* • Their majesties, King Bhumibol and Queen Sirikit, proceed to Royal Chapel for ceremony commemorating their coronation in 1946. Government officials in full dress pay respects.

May • *Rocket Festival* • Falls between the harvest and rainy season. Drumming, dancing, singing, and shooting rockets into the sky as a plea for rain. Best celebrated in Yasothorn, northeast of Bangkok. Generally last weekend in May.

*May • *Wishaka Bucha* **•** Commemorates birth, enlightenment, and death of Lord Buddha. Floral arrangements and candlelit processions around main temple buildings with full moon throughout kingdom.

*July • *Asanha Bucha* **•** Commemorates first sermon delivered by Lord Buddha to first five disciples. Candlelit processions around main temple buildings in full moon throughout kingdom.

*July • *Khao Phansa (Buddhist Lent)* **•** Marks the return to the monastery of all monks to resume study and meditation during rainy season. Youths of 20 years of age are ordained during this period. Best celebrated in Ubon with colorful Lenten candle processions in the town streets.

*August 12 • *Queen's Birthday* **•** Queen Sirikit attends religious ceremonies and present offerings to monks at Chitralada Palace as well as other places in Royal Household program.

October • *Boat races at Nan* **•** Celebrates end of Buddhist Lent. Colorful processions along streets and boat races on local rivers. Best celebrations occur in Nan Province, Northern Thailand.

October • *Thot Kathin Ceremony* **•** Lasts a full month to mark end of rainy season and Buddhist Lent. Time of annual offering of new yellow robes and necessary utensils to monks. Colorful processions along streets and rivers of people who sing and dance their way to monasteries with gifts.

October • *Phra Chedi Klang Nam Fair* **•** Colorful processions, boat races, amusing games as part of celebration in worshiping of pagoda at Paknam, south of Bangkok.

*October 23 • *Chulalongkorn Day* **•** Commemorates death of beloved King Chulalongkorn, son of King Mongkut and grandfather of present king, who died in 1910. Floral tributes and incense placed at foot of equestrian statue at end of Ratchadamnoen Avenue in Bangkok.

November • *Golden Mount Fair and Phra Pathom Chedi Fair* **•** Buddhist devotees make pilgrimage to relics at temple of Golden Mount in Bangkok and the Phra Pathom Chedi in Nakhon Pathom.

November • *Loi Krathong Festival (Festival of Light)* **•** Rivers, streams, canals, and ponds throughout kingdom full of tiny flickering flames from thousands of banana leaf and lotus petal cups containing candles and incense. A thanksgiving to Mae Khongkha, goddess of all rivers and waterways, during full moonlight. Best celebrations are in Sukhothai (first capital of Thailand) where Lady Nopphamat invented first flower lantern some 700 years ago. Also grandly celebrated in Bangkok and Chiang Mai.

November • *Elephant Roundup at Surin* • Elephant demonstrations, races, roundup show, soccer match, tug-of-war between 100 men and an elephant. Town streets closed for elephant rides, country fair, and bazaar. Held every third weekend of November.

December 3 • *Trooping of the Colors* • Parade of Royal Guards in honor of His Majesty King Bhumibol's birthday.

*December 5 • *King Bhumibol's Birthday and National Day* • Celebrations throughout kingdom with colorful pageantry. Public buildings and houses decorated with spectacular night illuminations.

*December 31 • *New Year's Eve Celebration.*

BACKGROUND MATERIAL

Anna and the King of Siam by Margaret Landon (adapted from the original *An English Governess in the Court of Siam* by Anna Leonowens) tells the story of a prim Victorian who taught at the court of King Mongkut (Rama IV) during the late 19th century.

Bridge Over the River Kwai by Pierre Boulle. The story of the "Death Railway" built by POWs over what the Thais called the Meklang River, but known to the world as the River Kwai.

The Legendary American by William Warren (Houghton Mifflin). A fascinating account of Jim Thompson, the man who is credited with reintroducing Thailand's silk industry to the world, and the facts of his strange disappearance in 1968.

The House on the Klong by William Warren (Weatherhill, Tokyo). A sketch with photos of Jim Thompson's beautiful teak museum/house in Bangkok.

From the Hands of the Hills by Margaret Campbell. Published locally and researched/written by a Canadian teacher, this beautifully photographed volume describes the customs and crafts of the hill tribes.

Thailand (apa productions). Beautiful photos and text.

BANGKOK

BANGKOK IN A CAPSULE

Established in 1782 on eastern bank of Chao Phraya River by Rama I, founder of present Chakri Dynasty . . . originally called Rattanakosin . . . name changed to Krung Thep by Rama III . . . always known as Bangkok to foreigners . . . means City of Angels . . . 6 million inhabitants live here in chaos . . . with occasional patches of serenity . . . capital is part boomtown, part traditional . . . a hub of traffic between East and West . . . not a place you love at first sight . . . but its dawn to dusk vitality and everchanging face give the city a strong character . . . the unexpected in sight and sound is very much a part of the Bangkok scene.

WHAT TO SEE AND DO

Chao Phraya River • Lifeline of the capital founded by King Rama I 200 years ago . . . original city located between a dramatic, sweeping curve of the river and an elegant *klong* built to meet it . . . here can be viewed **Grand Palace Complex** . . . **Wat Phra Keo** (Temple of the Emerald Buddha) . . . and **Chatuchak Park,** where colorful weekend markets held every Sat.

Grand Palace Complex • Built by King Rama I in 1782 for the Chakri Dynasty . . . interesting potpourri of Eastern and Western architectural styles from Thai to Italian Renaissance . . . used only for state occasions and royal ceremonies . . . visitors may tour formal reception rooms of **Chakri Maha Prasad** (royal residence of Grand Palace) daily . . . dress code stipulates coat and tie for men, no slacks or shorts for women . . . tour very worthwhile and led by knowledgeable guides . . . since the untimely death of present King's brother in 1946, royal family lives down the road not far from the Marble Temple . . . hours: 8:30 a.m. to noon, 1 to 4 p.m. . . . admission 30 baht.

Jim Thompson's House • Located at Soi Kasemsan 2, opposite National Stadium . . . a former architect and military intelligence officer, the late American Jim Thompson adopted Thailand as his permanent residence . . . is credited with contributing substantially to growth of Thai silk industry after World War II . . . combined 6 traditional teak structures to make his house . . . filled it with collection of valuable artifacts . . . even chandeliers come from 18th and 19th century Bangkok palaces . . . opened house to public to aid Thai charities . . . Thompson himself disappeared in 1968 during a visit to the Cameron Highlands, Malaysia . . . no clue to his whereabouts has surfaced in the ensuing years . . . house now belongs to James H. W. Thompson Foundation . . . legacy of his creativity and deep love for all things Thai . . . hours: 9:30 a.m. to 3:30 p.m. weekdays only . . . admission 50 baht for guided tour.

Khao Din Zoo • Located on Rajawiti Rd. . . . name means Mountain of Earth . . . man-made hill in middle for picnics and family outings . . . also known as Dusit Zoo . . . animals from all parts of world as well as domestic ones can be viewed . . . hours: 8 a.m. to 6 p.m. daily . . . admission 10 baht for adults, 5 baht for children; also small charge for cameras.

Lak Muang • City Pillar . . . located at southeast corner of Sanam Luang in Inner City . . . considered foundation stone of the capital . . . visited daily by believers . . . lavishly costumed dancers perform here in honor of spirits . . . paid by those whose wishes have been fulfilled . . . distances throughout city measured from this shrine.

National Assembly Hall • Sri Ayuthaya Rd. . . . the original throne hall . . . constructed of white Italian marble . . . lavish gold leaf interior . . . statue of King Chulalongkorn, grandfather of present king, dominates square in front . . . statue festooned with flowers every Oct. 23, the day of his death in 1910 . . . hours: Mon. through Fri., except Thurs., by prior appointment.

National Museum • Located next to Thammasat University on Naprathat Rd. . . . one of the largest museums in Far East . . . with 26 different low structures and exhibition halls . . . traces history of Thai culture from 5600 B.C. to present Chakri dynasty . . . many Buddha images from Ayuthaya and Sukhothai periods . . . many objects from royal household, including a whole pavilion of funerary coaches and palanquins . . . buildings not air-conditioned so try to visit early in the day . . . extensive walking necessary to see majority of exhibits . . . hours 9 a.m. to noon, 1 p.m. to 4 p.m. Tues. through Thurs. and the same on Sat. and Sun.; closed Mon. and Fri. . . . admission 20 baht, free on Sat. and Sun.; English guidebooks available and docent tours daily—check times through your hotel.

Royal Barges • Klong Bangkok Noi, Thonburi side . . . parked farther upriver from Wat Arun . . . richly carved barges are used in ceremonial processions . . . especially when the King offers gifts and new robes to the monks of Wat Arun . . . most impressive of the boats is the Sri Supannahong, or the Royal Barge . . . where king sits in a golden pavilion and is transported by over 50 oarsmen.

Royal Pantheon • Located in Grand Palace complex . . . contains life-size statues of Chakri Dynasty kings . . . only open to public on Chakri Day (April 6) . . . but don't miss mythological figures that adorn it . . . see detailed model of Angkor Wat nearby . . . built by Rama IV when temple was in Thai territory.

Sanam Luang • Pramane Ground . . . a 32-acre oval expanse in the heart of Inner City . . . has been historic site of royal cremations and annual Ploughing Ceremony since birth of Bangkok . . . kite flying contests here from Feb. to April are an annual tradition.

Siam Society • Located at Soi Asoke and Sukhumvit Rd. . . . founded under royal patronage at the turn of the century . . . to promote study of anthropology as well as history and zoology of Thailand . . . interesting publications available here and good reference library . . . Kamthieng House from Chiang Mai also worth a visit . . . guided tours available . . . hours: 9 a.m. to 5 p.m. weekdays only.

Snake Farm and Pasteur Institute • Corner of Rama IV and Henri Dunant roads. King cobras kept here . . . along with other varmints . . . venom extracted from the snakes for use in serum . . . only the hardy should stop off here . . . hours: daily except holidays; venom extracted at 11 a.m. . . . admission 40 baht.

Suan Pakkad Palace • Sri Ayuthaya Rd. . . . resident of the present king's aunt, Princess Chumbhot . . . the Princess is one of Thailand's leading gardeners and art collectors . . . palace is a series of small structures brought to this site . . . some dating from mid-19th century . . . furnished authentically and filled with fine antiquities . . . land-scaped gardens with flora brought back from all over the world by the Princess . . . plus a lacquer pavilion discovered near Ayuthaya by the late Prince and reassembled here . . . hours: 9 a.m. to 4 p.m. Mon. through Sat. . . . admission 50 baht and well worth it.)

Theves Market • Located in Thevet district of Bangkok . . . not for thieves . . . but for plants . . . thousands of orchids sold here . . .

along with every other tropical species possible . . . a great place to visit for both gardeners and photographers . . . don't miss picturesque bridge across Klong Krung Kasem.

Vimanmek • The world's largest teakwood mansion and one of the country's major new tourist attractions . . . the residence of King Chulalongkorn during the early 1900s, it had been unoccupied since 1910 (but for a few months during 1925) . . . reopened in 1982 by Queen Sirikit as a period museum, its collection includes glassware, porcelain and "collectibles" (all considered treasures) that display the tastes of the court at the turn of the century . . . open Wednesday through Sunday, 9:30 a.m. to 4 p.m.

Yaowaraj • Chinatown . . . a bustling section of the city . . . full of amusing markets . . . Chinese were original traders here . . . now number ⅓ of the population . . . the traditional (birds nests for soup) to the ridiculous can be found here.

Temples

The **wat,** or temple, of Thailand is what makes the skyline so unique. Although similar in style to the structures found throughout the lands of their neighbors (Laos and the Khmer Republic to the east, Burma to the west), the wat of Thailand is more sophisticated and refined in architectural manner and decorative elements. Thai fancy appears in the colorful, multitiered roofs and carved gables juxtaposed upon striking Indian, Khmer (Cambodian), and Chinese influences. The wat found in Bangkok are especially refined and sophisticated because none of them is more than two centuries old. When Rama I founded the city in 1782, he began a palace and temple building program that anyone today would envy!

No less impressive than the outside view of these many temples scattered throughout the capital is the inside view of the **bot,** or main chapel that holds the Buddha image, for many are filled with an awesome display of precious stones and metals. Look also for the brightly painted murals, often scenes from the *Ramakien* or Thai version of the Indian-origin *Ramayana* epic. Devotees arrive at these chapels all day long, bearing gifts of fruit and flowers as well as paper-thin pieces of beaten gold that are pressed to the images in gratitude for favors bestowed.

The Thais are a reverential people with a highly sensitive etiquette toward their religious monuments. In addition to heeding the advice offered in "Customs" (see page 478), visitors should note that no cameras of any type are allowed inside a **bot,** and only still or 8 mm cameras in the compound.

Wat Arun • Temple of the Dawn, Arun Amarin Rd., Thonburi . . . located on the Thonburi side of the Chao Phraya River . . . easily reached by tour boat or water taxi . . . also known as Wat Chang . . . because of an original temple on this spot . . . parts still date from before 1782 . . . tall *prang* (Angkorean spire) much used in travel posters . . . view splendid from central tower . . . across river to **Grand Palace, Wat Phra Keo** and **Wat Po** . . . bot built by King Chulalongkorn . . . some ashes of King Rama II at Wat Arun so present king travels across the river in Royal Barge to bestow gifts at end of rainy season.

Wat Benchamabophit • Marble Temple, Sri Ayuthaya Rd. . . . name actually means Temple of the Fifth King . . . built by King Chulalongkorn and finished just after his death in 1910 . . . but called Marble Temple because main buildings constructed of Carrara marble . . . and 2 huge marble lions guard entrance to bot . . . houses famous collection of Buddhist images . . . don't miss the bodhi tree in rear courtyard . . . 70 years old and supposedly descended from a tree in India where Lord Buddha was born.

Wat Pathum Wan • Lotus Temple, located near Siam Intercontinental Hotel . . . part of former palace area which hotel grounds now occupy . . . temple noted for blossoms in lotus pond behind it . . . also favored by taxi drivers . . . who come to have their vehicles blessed.

Wat Phra Keo • Temple of the Emerald Buddha, located in Grand Palace complex . . . most famous temple in Thailand . . . built by King Rama I in 1782 to house image of **Emerald Buddha** . . . a small image whose origin is lost in legend . . . found at Chiang Rai in northern Thailand in 1434 . . . at beginning of each season (summer, rainy, and winter), King dresses Emerald Buddha in appropriate costume . . . a ritual instigated by King Rama I . . . figure of a single piece of jasper from southern China . . . sits on golden throne flanked by other decorated Buddha images . . . surrounded by offerings from kings, royal princes, and commoners . . . truly the most important Buddha image in Thailand.

Wat Po • Temple of the Reclining Buddha, located on either side of Jetupon Rd. just south of Grand Palace . . . enormous complex covering almost 20 acres . . . also known as "Thailand's first university" because of its educational value . . . first 4 Chakri Dynasty kings favored Wat Po . . . added greatly to its art treasures . . . temple for reclining Buddha just one of many structures here . . . look at the old murals depicting daily Thai life.

Wat Rajabopitr • Located near Klong Lawd and near Ministry of Interior . . . seldom visited by tourists . . . interesting example of

King Chulalongkorn's interest in the West . . . built by the king in 1863 and combines Western and Thai architectural styles . . . European influence also in bas reliefs.

Wat Sraket • Washing the Hair Temple, Boriphat Rd. . . . name derives from legend that Rama I stopped here for a washing . . . while en route to Thonburi to be crowned . . . a Bangkok landmark because of Golden Mount on top . . . gilded chedi containing relics of the Buddha (presented to Rama V by Lord Curzon, then Viceroy of India) . . . Golden Mount begun under Rama III and completed by Chulalongkorn . . . circular stairway of 300-plus steps to the top offers panoramic view of the capital . . . temple most impressive during annual Nov. fair . . . when worshipers make candlelight processional all the way to top of Golden Mount.

Wat Suthat • And the Giant Swing, Dinso Rd. . . . Suthat means "God Indra's heavenly monastery" . . . temple faces Giant Swing or *Sao Ching Cha* . . . actually 2 tall red poles joined at top with carved beam . . . swinging ceremony no longer takes place . . . used to honor Brahman god who came down to earth in Jan. . . . Suthat has tallest chapel in Bangkok . . . 14th-century bronze Buddha image brought from Sukhothai by Rama I.

Wat Traimit • Temple of the Golden Buddha, Yaowarat Rd. . . . Temple built about 1238 . . . 10-foot golden Buddha weighs more than 5 tons . . . found by accident by construction workers . . . covered with stucco which cracked during severe storm . . . revealing pure gold Sukhothai-style image . . . believed to have been covered in 18th century to prevent theft by invading Burmese.

Environs

Ancient City • The country's largest outdoor museum . . . located in Samut Prakan Province . . . some 33 km from Bangkok . . . 200 acres of spectacle . . . 65 of Thailand's most impressive temples and historical monuments reconstructed here . . . many of them full size . . . also restaurants, elephant rides, streams, and waterfalls . . . simulated rural village for wandering . . . hours: open daily from 8 a.m.–7 p.m. . . . admission 150 baht per person . . . further information available from The Ancient City Co., Ratchadamnoen Ave., Bangkok. Admission: 50 baht.

Ayuthaya • Capital of Thailand for a period of 417 years . . . site of magnificent ruins, archaeological excavations and restorations . . .

located about 88 km from Bangkok and reachable by bus, car, train, or boat . . . founded by King U Thong in A.D. 1350 . . . during Ayuthaya period, some 33 kings reigned over territory . . . ancient capital invaded by Burmese in 1767 . . . destroyed beyond repair . . . principal monuments are Chandra Kasem Palace, 13th-century Phra Maha That Temple, Ratchaburana Temple, Na Pramen Temple (also 13th century), Memorial of Queen Si Suriyothai, Temple of Golden Mount Pagoda, Elephant Kraal, 14th-century Chao Phraya Thai Temple just outside the area, and 14th-century Phanan Choeng Temple on the river bank south of the town . . . hours: open daily from dawn to dusk; 2-hour bus ride and 90-minute train trip from Bangkok.

Bang Pa-in • Former country residence of Ayuthaya monarchs . . . also used by Chakri kings Mongkut and Chulalongkorn . . . Royal Summer Palace complex consists of 5 buildings . . . 2 of them in classical Greek style . . . also Gothic church and replica of Beijing Palace along with fine examples of Thai architecture . . . lovely temples skirt a lake . . . hours: Royal Palace open daily except Mon., 8:30 a.m.–3 p.m.; permission to visit necessary but easily granted.

Crocodile Farm • Located in Paknam, some 30 km from Bangkok . . . 10,000 crocodiles on view here . . . best time to visit is 6 p.m. when animals are fed . . . also a demonstration on how to catch a crocodile barehanded . . . hours: 8 a.m.–6 p.m. . . . admission 80 baht.

Floating Markets • To view Venice of the East . . . two of the most popular floating markets for tourists are the **Wat Sai** in Thonburi (just across the Chao Phraya from Bangkok) . . . and the **Damnoen Saduak** in Ratchaburi Province some 104 km from the capital . . . early morning hours are the best . . . men and women hidden by huge straw hats guide their *sampans* (narrow boats) full of rice sacks, mounds of colorful fruits and vegetables, local liquor, whole sides of beef and pork, flowers, and other goods . . . waterways are crowded and air vibrates with hawker calls . . . photographer's dream . . . but please don't drink the water!

Hua Hin • Summer residence of royal family . . . popular resort on West Coast of Gulf of Thailand since King Rama VII built summer palace in 1920 . . . located about 200 km south of Bangkok . . . area has beautiful white sandy beaches . . . good golf course and tennis courts . . . nice surrounding countryside . . . small hotels are available . . . and small shops in town for browsing . . . accessible by car, bus, or train.

Kanchanaburi • The Bridge over the River Kwai . . . one of Thailand's most attractive provinces . . . spectacular waterfalls, wild jungles, rugged terrain . . . but more renowned for the atrocities that occurred here to Allied POWs during World War II. . . . British, Dutch, American, Indian, Australian soldiers lost their lives during construction of famous Death Railway . . . bridge over Kwai River built to link valleys of Kwai Noi with Kwai Yai . . . railway to carry war supplies into Burma . . . visit the sobering cemeteries . . . the JEATH Museum . . . and the Sound and Light program at the River Kwai—the most spectacular ever made!

Khao Yai • National Park and Hill Resort . . . total area consists of 542,000 acres . . . approximately 50,000 acres are rolling hills and gentle slopes . . . average elevation is 2500 feet above sea level but highest peak is Khao Khieo at 5000 feet . . . park is for preservation of wildlife . . . hiking, fishing, 6 waterfalls, open grass and golf provide diversion . . . motor lodge and small bungalows available for accommodations.

Lop Buri • Noted for historical significance during Dvaravati period (6th to 11th century) . . . **Phra Narai Rachanivet Palace** houses ancient artifacts . . . **Prang Sam Yot** (Sacred Three Spired Pagoda) believed to be work of Khmer craftsmen . . . **Wat Phra Si Ratana Maha That** built by Khmers during 12th century . . . Hindu shrine dates from 10th–11th centuries . . . **Phra Kan Shrine** is from the 17th century, during reign of King Narai . . . **Nakhon Kosa monastery** may have been a Khmer Hindu shrine . . . Lop Buri is located about 150 km. north of Bangkok . . . reachable by car, bus, and train . . . simple hotel accommodations available.

Nakhon Pathom • oldest city in Thailand . . . Buddhism was first introduced to the Thais here . . . but city dates from 150 B.C. . . . **Phra Pathom Chedi** is one of largest in the world . . . 3-day fair in Nov. highlight of the year . . . 4 viharas (halls) at 4 points of the compass contain Buddha images . . . the Chedi is an enormous inverted golden bowl of almost 380 feet . . . seen from all over . . . a museum in the courtyard of this great temple complex contains priceless relics . . . east of Phra Pathom Chedi is Nakhon Pathom Palace built by King Mongkut (1861–1868) . . . another palace slightly south is Sanam Chan and built by King Vajiravudh (1910–1925) but now used as government offices and clubs . . . in front of the Mongkhon Asna building is the bronze statue of King Vajiravudh's favorite dog Yaleh.

Pathum Thani • Sanctuary for open-billed storks . . . located about 45 km north of Bangkok . . . reachable by car or boat . . . most famous monument is **Wat Phai Lom.**

Petchaburi • Limestone hills pocketed with Buddhist shrines . . . located about 150 km south of Bangkok . . . Palace of King Mongkut and Khao Luang Cave are 2 main attractions . . . Kaeng Krachan Dam some 60 km from Petchaburi is a scenic man-made lake . . . Cha Am is a popular beach resort among the Thais . . . accommodations are available . . . area reachable by car, bus, or train.

Rose Garden • Suan Sam Phran, located about 32 km southwest of Bangkok (on the way to Nakhon Pathom) . . . a private recreation area of 50 acres . . . landscaped flower gardens . . . 18-hole golf course . . . Thai houses, hotels, and thatched cottages for accommodations . . . 5 restaurants, 2 swimming pools, and large convention rooms . . . highlight is performance of local arts and crafts every afternoon . . . if you have the time . . . otherwise there are much more enriching places to visit . . . hours: daily from 8 a.m.–6 p.m. . . . admission 10 baht plus 140 baht for Thai classical shows.

Sattahip • Biggest commercial port in the country . . . built as part of American war effort in Vietnam . . . now home of Royal Thai Navy . . . about 20 km south of Pattaya . . . also known for large cruise vessels but they now come into Gulf of Siam at Pattaya.

SIGHTSEEING TOURS

Floating Market • 5 hours, daily . . . cruise by motor launch along Chao Phraya River into klongs . . . market itself is on Thonburi side of river . . . stop at Wat Arun (Temple of the Dawn) upon return.

City Tour • 3 hours, daily, at 9 a.m. and 2 p.m. . . . visits to Marble Temple . . . Reclining Buddha and Golden Buddha . . . or Wat Trimitr with its 5½-ton Buddha image of pure gold.

Grand Palace • 3 hours, daily, at 9 a.m.–2 p.m. . . . visits entire royal complex . . . Temple of Emerald Buddha . . . Coronation Hall . . . replica of Angkor Wat of Kampuchea.

Ancient City • 4 hours, daily, at 8:30 a.m.–1:30 p.m. . . . drive to outdoor museum some 30 km from Bangkok . . . parkland features reconstructions of more than 60 of the kingdom's famous temples and monuments.

Rose Garden • 4½ hours, daily, at 1:30 p.m. . . . an hour's drive from Bangkok to this new resort area . . . man-made klongs and gardens . . . hotels and restaurants . . . Thai Village Show allows a taste of the local culture.

Damnoen Saduak Floating Market • 10½ hours, daily, at 7:30 a.m. . . . a 110 km drive to most colorful market in the country . . . followed by a rice barge ride to the Rose Garden . . . attend Thai Village cultural show.

Rice Barge Cruise • 3½ hours, daily, from 3 p.m. . . . A quiet cruise along the klongs of Bangkok . . . visit to riverside house . . . some residential areas . . . rice farms.

Canal Trip by Speed Boat • 3 hours, daily, from 3 p.m. . . . exciting journey along klongs of Bangkok by long-tailed speed boat . . . dress casually and watch camera lens . . . can get splashed easily.

Jim Thompson's Thai House • 2½ hours, Mon. and Fri. only, from 9 a.m.–2 p.m. . . . visit the museum-like house of legendary Jim Thompson . . . the American credited with developing the Thai silk industry after the war . . . an exquisite compound of Thai architecture and oriental antiquities.

Crocodile Farm • 4 hours, daily, from 8:30 a.m.–2 p.m. . . . a drive outside the capital to one of world's largest crocodile farms . . . more than 10,000 species here . . . especially from Siam and Africa . . . watch how beasts are bred, fed, and raised . . . also wrestling match between beast and man . . . may also be combined with tour of Paknam fish market.

National Museum • 3 hours, daily, from 9 a.m.–1:30 p.m. . . . view of the kingdom's many art and historical treasures . . . one of the most enjoyable museums in the Far East . . . and guided by charming and competent docents . . . highly recommended.

Thai Dinner and Dance • 3 hours, daily, from 7:30 p.m. . . . a dinner of Thai delicacies (even for the non-Thai palate) plus performance of classical dances . . . folk dances and demonstrations of Thai martial arts.

River Cruise with Dinner • 3 hours, daily, from 5:30 p.m. and 7:30 p.m. . . . evening cruise on the Chao Phraya River . . . aboard either *Tasanee Nava* rice barge or *Oriental Queen*.

Ayuthaya • 8 hours, daily, from 9 a.m. . . . tour of former ancient capital . . . drive some 90 km north of Bangkok . . . visit ruins with informed guide . . . lunch and visit to Bang Pa-in . . . previous royal summer residence.

Ayuthaya via Oriental Queen • 9½ hours, daily, from 7:30 a.m. . . . cruise one way between Oriental Hotel and the ancient capital . . . other way by bus with a stop at Bang Pa-in . . . buffet lunch served aboard vessel.

Thai Boxing • 4½ hours, daily, from 5 p.m. . . . boxing with fists, feet, elbows, and knees . . . a local tradition . . . not for the timid.

Kanchanaburi and the River Kwai • 1 to 4 days . . . A 130 km drive north from Bangkok to Thailand's most attractive province . . . visit to the famous bridge over the Kwai River . . . remains of the Death Railway in cemeteries and museums . . . lovely waterways and falls . . . adventures by jeep, long-tailed boat, train, and elephant back to visit waterfalls, caves, local villages, and large plantations . . . accommodations at River Kwai Village Hotel.

Pattaya and Coral Islands • 1 to 2 days . . . Pattaya is but a 2½-hour drive from Bangkok . . . a beautiful beach resort . . . offshore islands also filled with coral wonders . . . trip out to them by converted fishing boats.

Phuket • 3-day packages minimum . . . by air from Bangkok to Phuket . . . a tropical island of sweeping bays and uncrowded beaches . . . also see the caves of Phangnga . . . fishing village of Koh Panyee . . . small town of Phuket.

Phimai • 2-day tour . . . the Angkor Wat of Thailand . . . designed by the same architects . . . this area was an important center of the Khmer Empire . . . linked by a road 240 km long to the original Angkor . . . visit includes overnight stay . . . and combined with Khao Yai National Park . . . or in Khorat . . . view of Phimai's ruins and museum . . . on return the famous Wat Phra Buddhabadh.

Chiang Mai • 2 to 3 days . . . by air from Bangkok . . . visit to handicraft villages . . . Doi Suthep and Meo hilltribes . . . also includes visits to temples and local industries . . . umbrella and lacquer and carving.

Chiang Rai • 2 to 3 days as extension to Chiang Mai tour . . . Thailand's northernmost province borders on Burma and Laos . . . with interesting hilltribes like Akhas, Yaos, Lahus . . . still unspoiled but not always safe for tourists . . . drive north to Fang and Thathon via Chiang Dao and a boat journey of 5 hours . . . stopping at hilltribe villages along Kok River . . . drive to Mae Chan to visit Akha and Yao before returning to Chiang Mai.

Old Kingdoms • 3 days . . . visits to Bang Pa-in, Ayuthaya, Phitsanulok, Sukhothai, and Si Satchanalai . . . exploring ruins and old temples . . . 6-day extension available to Nakhon Sawan, Kamphaeng Phet, Lampang, Chiang Mai, and Lamphun.

Trekking in the West • 3 or 7 days . . . shorter tour features night on floating rafts on River Kwai . . . tour by boat and jeep to Three Pagodas Pass near Burmese border . . . visit to Mon hilltribe villages and surrounding jungle . . . longer version includes more hilltribe visits, more bamboo forests and jungles and tin mines . . . new tour.

Trekking in the North • 8 days . . . by air to Chiang Mai for overnight . . . by bus and boat to Ban Mai via Fang . . . overnight in Shan village . . . 2-hour trek on 3rd day to Three Hills . . . overnight at Lisu village . . . trekking every subsequent day through spectacular forests, jungles, and green valleys . . . an off-the-beaten-track sort of tour.

Around Thailand • 7 days . . . several variations possible . . . but most include visits to Khorat and Phimai . . . Khmer temples and overnight at Kaho Yai National Park . . . Lopburi's famous temples . . . Phra Buddhabadh to see shrine with holy footprint of Lord Buddha . . . overnight at Phitsanulok . . . ancient towns of Sukhothai and Si Satchanalai . . . overnight at Bhumibol Dam guesthouse . . . Chiang Mai and Lamphun, Chiang Dao and Fang, Chiang Rai, and Mae Chan . . . return by air to Bangkok.

South Thailand • 7 and 14 days . . . the tour with a "difference" according to past travelers . . . ethnic, cultural, gastronomic, scenic, and relaxing . . . are the bywords . . . unspoilt beaches of Nakhon Si Thammarat . . . spectacular Wat Mahathat . . . provincial scenes of Krabi, Thar Bokkha Thoranee National Park, Phangnga, and Phuket . . . tour begins in Bangkok . . . by train south . . . by air back to the capital.

HOTELS

★★★★**Ambassador Hotel** • *171 Sukhumvit Rd. Tel: 254–0444. Cable: AMTEL Telex: 82910 AMTEL TH* • 942 rooms (many suites) . . . enormous hotel/convention complex . . . rather away from city center . . . guest rooms in tower most attractive . . . nice grounds.

Facilities: Several restaurants include Hong Teh Cantonese, Chiu Chau Chinese, Tokugawa Japanese, Cafe Ambassador open 24 hours, Amigos Grill featuring Spanish and Continental specialties, Dickens Pub, Le Bistro, Garden Cafe (coffee shop) and Ambassador seafood restaurant. Also lobby lounge, garden bar and The Club for non-stop live music. Largest swimming pool in the capital and sun terrace. Post office and secretarial services.

Manager: D. Wiig. *Reservations:* UTELL.

★★★★**Dusit Thani** ● *Rama IV Rd. Tel: 236–0450-9. Cable: DUSITOTEL Telex: TH 81170* ● 525 rooms (18 suites) . . . name means "town in heaven" . . . huge hotel with lobby that is reminiscent of your favorite railway station . . . great hotel for conventions . . . the presentation makes big impact on delegates . . . hotel manager Tony Tuor considered a "showman of first order" . . . centrally located, well-established property.

Facilities: Restaurants: Castillion Garden, 22nd-floor Tiara Buffet, lounge and nightclub, Sukhothai traditional Thai feast and dancing, Shogun Japanese restuarant, Pavilion Cafe (coffee shop). Also Bubbles discotheque and Cookie Corner (for take-away snacks). Swimming pool. Tennis courts. Health club. Shopping Arcade. Executive Center in new 14-story Executive Tower.

Manager: A. C. Tuor. *Reservations:* UTELL.

★★★★★**Hilton International Bangkok** ● *2 Wireless Rd., off Ploenchit Rd. Tel: 253–0123. Cable: HILTELS BKK. Telex: TH 72206 HILBKK TH* ● 389 rooms (43 suites) . . . located in the 8.5-acre Nai Lert Park . . . in midst of Bangkok's diplomatic and business districts . . . all guest rooms have private balconies overlooking lush gardens . . . curved atrium building with Thai motifs throughout . . . low-rise structure with 3 atrium lobbies and thousands of bougainvilleas for effect.

Facilities: Garden restaurant and terrace (Thai/Western specialties). Ma Maison French restaurant. Genji Japanese restaurant. Lobby lounge. Juliana's of London Club. Swimming pool. Health club. Tennis and squash courts. Thai Village handicrafts and folkloric entertainment. Executive service Center.

Manager: P. Mermod. *Reservations:* Hiltels.

★★★**Holiday Inn Bangkok** ● *981 Silom Rd., Bangkok. Tel: 234–1010. Cable: RAMATOW. Telex: 82998* ● 360 rooms. Former Rama Tower . . . upgraded and renamed by Holiday Inn . . . good group hotel.

Facilities: Orchid Terrace coffee house. Chef's Table restaurant.

Tropicana disco. La Rotisserie. Embassy lounge. Swimming pool. Executive business center. Opening December 1989.

Manager: M. Hauck. *Reservations:* HOLIDEX.

★★★★**The Imperial Hotel** • *Wireless Rd., Bangkok 5. Tel: 254–0023. Cable: Imperhotel. Telex: TH2301.* • 400 rooms. Set in 6 acres of garden in Embassy section of town . . . designed for business travelers . . . large convention facilities.

Facilities: Tennis and squash courts. Jimmy's Kitchen Coffee Shop. Tudor Grill. Jarmjuree seafood restaurant. Garden Room for luncheon buffet. Peep Inn nightclub. 2 swimming pools.

General Manager: A. Hoontrakul. *Reservations:* H. Jarvinen & Assoc.

★★★**Indra Regent Hotel** • *Rajprarob Rd. Tel: 251–1111. Cable: INDRAHOTEL. Telex: 82723 INDRA TH* • 500 rooms (24 suites) . . . dark interior lobby . . . commercial atmosphere but some nice amenities . . . centrally located . . . near Prahunam Market.

Facilities: Indra Grill Room. Ming Palace. Garden bar. Pratunam Cafe (coffee shop). Sala Thai, replica of 13th-century aristocratic home for traditional Thai dinners and dances. Indra Sky Room on 18th floor. The Den Night Club. Swimming pool on 4th level and massage parlor. Indra Cinema, only cinerama-equipped theater in Thailand. Convention facilities for up to 1500.

Manager: Dr. P.A. Poon. *Reservations:* UTELL.

★★★★**Mandarin Hotel** • *662 Rama IV Rd., Bangkok 10110. Tel: 233–4980. Telex: 87689. Cable: MANOTEL* • 343 rooms . . . Reputable chain of Asian hotels . . . luxury category.

Facililties: Restaurants, nightclub, coffee shop, swimming pool, conference facilities, and shopping arcade.

★★★ + **The Menam** • *2074 New Rd., Yannawa. Tel: 289–1148. Cable: MENAMHOTEL. Telex: 87423 TH* • 727 rooms. Listed as Bangkok's newest riverside resort hotel . . . finally opened after years of delays . . . 4th hotel on Caho Phya River . . . but not intending to compete with worldwide reputations of The Oriental, The Royal Orchid Sheraton, and the Shangri-La . . . Menam is offering first-class amenities with superior service . . . you be the judge! . . . claims sundecks as big as a beach . . . amidst acres of the landscaped gardens.

Facilities: Jogging tracks. Squash, tennis, health club. Floating seafood restaurants. Thai, Chinese, and French cuisine. Riverside terrace. Cocktail lounge. Disco. Large shopping arcade.

Manager: K. Chaturachinda. *Reservations:* Menam.

★★★★**Montien** • *54 Suriwongse Rd. Tel: 234–8060. Cable: MONTELBKK. Telex: TH 81038* • 600 rooms (20 suites) . . . privately owned and operated by local Thais . . . lovely lobby and gracious atmosphere throughout . . . a nice departure from the big "hotel chain" mentality . . . well located . . . sumptuous furnishings throughout . . . one of the most pleasant hostelries in Bangkok.

Facilities: Le Gourmet Grill with award-winning French chef. Ruenton Coffee Shop. Jade Garden Cantonese restaurant. Montientong cocktail bar with unusual Thai interiors. Casablanca nightclub on lower lobby. Secretarial Service Center. Swimming pool in rooftop garden setting. Post office. Convention facilities for up to 1500.

Manager: P. Eaetwirer. *Reservations:* Alexander Assoc.

★★★**Novotel Bangkok** • *Siam Sq. Soi 6, Bangkok 10500. Tel: 255–2444* • One of the newer hotels in a city of new hotels . . . Novotel is one of the largest European hotel chains, with properties all over Africa and Asia.

Facilities: Restaurant, barber shop, coffee shop, shopping arcade, convention facilities, and swiming pool.

★★★★★+**The Oriental** • *Oriental Ave. Tel: 226–04000. Cable: ORIENHOTEL. Telex: TH 2997* • 402 rooms (21 suites) . . . situated on the banks of the Chao Phraya River . . . romantic views of this muddy water from all guest rooms . . . began as a colonial structure in 1876 . . . modern tower block added in 1958 . . . River Wing in 1976 . . . managed by Mandarin Int'l since 1974 . . . considered the best hotel in Asia by readers of the financial publication *Institutional Investor* . . . a favorite of Somerset Maugham and Noel Coward (I saw the latter there in 1968).

Facilities: Prestigious rooftop Normandie Grill. Verandah Coffeehouse and Riverside Terrace. Bamboo Bar. Lord Jim's seafood restaurant. Author's Lounge. Riverside Cafe for barbecues. 2 swimming pools. River cruises aboard hotel's *Oriental Queen* and *Orchid Queen*. Squash/ tennis courts. Health Centre. Diana's Disco. Ballroom. Sala Rim Naam for Thai buffets and cultural shows—across river from hotel.

Manager: K. Wachtveitl. *Reservations:* LHW.

★★★★★**The Regent of Bangkok** • *155 Rajadamri Rd., Bangkok. Tel: 2516127. Telex: TH 20004. Cable: REGHO* • 424 rooms. The former Peninsula property . . . beautiful structure with masterpiece lobby designed by one of Thailand's most famous artists . . . tropical paradise inside and out . . . rooms overlook Royal Bangkok Sports Club, poolside terrace, or city.

Facilities: Combinations of suites and interconnecting rooms. Lobby

lounge. Spice Market Thai cuisine. La Brasserie. Le Cristal continental restaurant. Garden Terrace. Rommanee Lounge/piano bar. Business Center. Largest hotel pool in Bangkok and Rimsra Terrace. Fitness Center with squash courts, jaccuzzi, massage, health bar, and gymnasium.
Manager: William Black. *Reservations:* Regent Int'l.

★★★★**The Royal Orchid Sheraton** • *Captain Bush Lane, off Siphya Rd., Tel: 234–5599. Cable: RAYORCH-BANGKOK. Telex: 84491* • 698 rooms (78 suites) . . . built on former site of Hong Kong and Shanghai bank . . . just 450 meters upriver from The Oriental . . . all rooms with uninterrupted view of Chao Phraya River from 28-story Y-shaped structure . . . 10 minutes by boat to Grand Palace . . . hotel provides river transportation to Don Muang International airport.
Facilities: The Gazebo Terrace Mediterranean and seafood restaurant. The Bird Cage coffee shop with river view. Bank Vault grillroom. Japanese restaurant with river view. River Wharf Bar off lobby. Giorgio's Grill alfresco on riverside terrace. Silk's Nightclub on 2nd floor. Open air swimming pool. Secretarial services. Tennis court.
Manager: G. Laird. *Reservations:* Sheraton Hotels.

★★★★★**Shangri-la Hotel** • *89 Soi Wat Suan Plu, New Rd., Bangkok 10500. Tel: 235–6310–2. Cable: SHANGRILA BANGKOK. Telex: 84265 SHANGLA TH* • 650 rooms (47 suites). All deluxe accommodations with uninterrupted views of Chao Phraya River . . . palatial lobby looking onto river . . . $100 million structure . . . intent upon attracting convention and incentive groups to Thailand . . . large ballroom with meeting and board rooms . . . 30 stories . . . adjacent to South Sathorn bridge.
Facilities: Executive 21st floor with 24-hour purser. Business Center. Coffee Garden and barbecue Terrace. Poolside Snack Bar. Sala Thai banquet room. Palm Court. French specialty restaurant. Shang Palace Chinese restaurant. Swimming pool. Tennis and squash courts. Health Club.
Manager: J. Hollender. *Reservations:* Shangri-la Intl.

★★★★★**Siam Inter-Continental** • *Srapatum Palace Property, Rama I Rd. Tel: 252–9040. Cable: INHOTELCOR. Telex: TH 81155* • 411 rooms . . . built within 26 acres of tropical gardens and a pond . . . that back up to the Srapatum Palace . . . this hotel presents an oasis of calm in the middle of Bangkok . . . recently extensively refurbished . . . good service and peaceful atmosphere . . . lovely gardens in which to stroll . . . even a mini-zoo . . . 12-room Royal Suite . . . stupendous!
Facilities: Sivalai coffee shop. Talay Thong seafood restaurant. Avenue One European/Oriental gourmet restaurant. Naga Bar. Thai Night

buffet poolside. Business Center. Bank and post office. 2 tennis courts, 2 jogging trails. Croquet.

Manager: D. Desbaillets. *Reservations:* IHC.

★★★**Tawana Ramada** ● *80 Surawongse Rd. Tel: 236–0631. Cable: SHERATON. Telex: TH 81167* ● 265 rooms (7 suites) . . . much needed refurbishing has brought it back to snuff . . . guest rooms completely redone . . . suites sport Thai silk interiors . . . marble lobby.

Facilities: Bon Vivant grillroom overlooks pool and garden. Port of Call lounge. Cavern Bar nightclub/disco. Swimming pool. Massage and steam baths.

Manager: S. Bunnag. *Reservations:* Ramada.

WINING AND DINING

Thai food can best be described as Hot, Hotter, and Hottest since every recipe begins with "take a handful of chilis;" they may be tiny but they pack a mighty wallop in the mouth of unsuspecting visitors. Spicy and fiery are the two adjectives most used in Thai cookery from sweet-and-sour soups to curries and fish dishes. In addition to the basic ingredient of chilis, other frequent seasonings are coriander, garlic, basil, cardamon, and local vegetables. Regular, sticky rice is, of course, the mainstay of every Thai meal and the centerpiece of every family table. It is accompanied by side dishes of curries, meat, fish, and vegetables and soup, the whole eaten with a large spoon. Chopsticks are employed in authentic Chinese restaurants and may turn up elsewhere if noodles are on the menu.

However, there are many excellent Thai restaurants that cater to the foreign palate and temper the degree of garlic and chilis and the Thai Night buffets, such as found around the pool at the Siam Inter-Continental Hotel, have been carefully planned with Western stomachs in mind. A sample menu features *kuay tiaw* (rice noodle soup), *yam koonchiang* (sweet Chinese sausage salad), *kaeng kai noh mai* (chicken curry with bamboo shoots), *hoh mok pla* (fish pudding in banana leaves), *phad priew wan pla* (sweet and sour fish), *poh piah* (spring rolls), *phad Thai* (Thai-style fried noodles) as well as beef, pork and chicken satays, spare ribs, and other barbecue items.

As in all Southeast Asian countries, Thailand can boast a long list of delicious fruits, some of which are quite new to most visitors. Familiar favorites abound, like succulent pineapples *(saparot)* and finger bananas *(klue khai)* that are frequently used in desserts. The mango *(ma-muang)* is probably the most popular and typical of Thai fruits, and incomparably sweet and delicious. Familiar to Westerners but still foreign to Thais is the guava *(farang)*, which is both used in jelly or consumed right from the tree with a little sugar and salt. The longan *(lamyai)* is abundant in northern provinces and, in fact, brings an annual income of about U.S. $4 million to Chiang Mai and is considered quite a delicacy in Bangkok. Other sights in local markets are the langsat *(langsard)*, pale brown berries with sweet flesh, and the mangosteen *(mang-khud)* whose purple rind covers delicious white segments, and the rambutan *(ngo)* with a hairy exterior and translucent interior. The sapodilla *(lamood)* is eaten much like the mango and has an equally luscious pulp. The apple family is no stranger in Thailand, for there are plenty of crabapples *(pood-sa)* the size of a small plum, custard apples *(noi-na)* that must be eaten with a squeeze and a spoon for it is difficult to separate the seeds from the flesh, and roseapples *(chompoo)* that are shaped like a miniature pear and have a pink waxy surface. This fruit has a subtle sweetness and is usually preferred with a dash of salt.

Thai desserts are sweet and sticky, often combining rice with syrups and fruits and served in the leaves of local plants. You can taste sticky rice baked in bamboo *(kow laam)*, bananas in sweet coconut milk *(gluay buad chee)*, or that old favorite egg custard *(maw gang)*. Drinks available include bottled sodas, tea and coffee in all guises, lemonade with or without salt, bottled fresh, or soybean milk, juices, and beer. Wines and hard liquor are very, very, very expensive in Thailand, so pay close attention to the bar bill. Frankly, the local beer is potent enough and should be consumed very slowly.

ASIAN AND THAI

Akbar • *¼ Soi 3 Sukhumvit* • Indian/Moslem dishes.

Bakee Pochana • *1784–8 Corner Soi Pae Sa* • Hunanese Chinese.

Chanphen Restaurant • *1031/1 Rama IV Rd.* • Thai specialties.

Charmchuree Restaurant • *287 Bangkok Bazaar* • Cantonese.

Chit Pochana • *1082 Phaholyothin Rd. and Sukhumvit Soi 20* • Most comprehensive Thai menu in town.

Chiu Chau Chinese Restaurant • *Ambassador Hotel* • Chiu Chau dishes.

Daikoku Restaurant • *960/1 Rama IV Rd.* • Japanese food.

Dragon Gate • *894/1-3 Rama IV Rd.* • Taechew Chinese.

Fu Lu Su Restaurant • *23–27 Raiprasong Rd.* • Hakka Chinese style.

Himali Cha Cha • *1229/11 New Rd.* • Indian/Moslem tandoor, kebabs, and vegetarian dishes.

Intown • *66–70 Soi Tontan, Rama IV Rd.* • Chinese fish restaurant.

Jade Garden • *Montien Hotel* • Cantonese cuisine in elegant setting.

Ming Palace • *Indra Regent Hotel* • Cantonese dishes prepared by Hong Kong chefs . . . lavish decor . . . Chinese music and entertainment.

Moghul Room • *1/16 Soi 11, Sukhumvit Rd.* • Indian/Moslem menu.

Moti Mahal • *18–20 Old Chartered Bank Lane* • Indian/Moslem menu.

Nang Phya • *38/16–17 Soi Pratuchai, Suriwong Rd.* • Also Indian/Moslem dishes . . . tandoori and kebabs.

Omar Khayyam • *2/7–8 Soi 3 Sukhumvit Rd.* • Arabic, Indian, Iranian, and Pakistani dishes . . . extensive menu.

Peking Restaurant • *187/1 Rajdamri Rd.* • Shanghai-style food, believe it or not.

Rochana • *Regent Hotel* • Thai food.

Salanorasingh • *20 Sukhumvit Soi 6* • Thai-style cuisine.

Shalimar • *opposite Ambassador Hotel* • Indian/Moslem menu.

Shangrila • *154/4–5 Silom Rd.* • Shanghai-style Chinese cuisine.

Sheesh Mahal • *1/22 Nana Nua Sukhumvit Soi 3* • Indian/Moslem menu.

Shogun • *Dusit Thani Hotel* • Japanese, of course.

Shu Shi Kin • *9/23–24 Thaniya Rd.* • Japanese noodles and such.

Siriwan • *Siam Square Soi 2* • Thai soups, curries, and spicy dishes.

Sorn Daeng • *near Democracy Monument* • Good menu and plenty of less fiery Thai dishes . . . tempered to visitors.

Talay Thong • *Siam Inter-Continental Hotel* • Excellent seafood restaurant . . . fixed Thai style.

Teppanyaki Steak House • *Ambassador Hotel* • Meats and seafood grilled before your eyes.

The Spice Market • *Regent Hotel* • Superlative Thai food, prepared with a sensitivity to visitors' tolerance of spicy food . . . in a cool, elegant setting that recreates an authentic spice market . . . spices, etc., can be purchased to take home.

The Whole Earth • *93/3 Soi Lang Suan, Ploenchit Rd.* • Thai menu.

Tokugawa Japanese Restaurant • *Ambassador Hotel* • Au-thentic setting.

U Fu Lao • *442/1–3 Rama IV Rd.* • Cantonese Chinese . . . good.

Vietnam Restaurant • *82–84 Silom Rd.* • You guessed it!
Bangkok is an exceptionally sophisticated dining city and can boast many fine international-style restaurants. There are fine French, German, Italian, Hungarian, Swiss, and Scandinavian establishments as well as several grillrooms featuring beef from the U.S. and succulent lamb from New Zealand. And because the Gulf of Siam is just a few hours distant, fresh seafood is a daily treat whether grilled under the stars or consumed in air-conditioned comfort. You can also dine by candlelight while cruising along the Chao Phraya River or eat in a splendid Thai teak pavilion while classical dancers and musicians entertain you. Because of the climate, most restaurants do not require coat and tie for the men but certainly do expect all their patrons to be properly dressed. If dining inside, ladies will want to carry a shawl or sweater in case blasts of cool air are aimed directly at their table.

EUROPEAN AND AMERICAN

Alleycat • *116 Silom Rd.* • English and inexpensive . . . steak and kidney pie, pork pie, etc. . . . open from 11 a.m. daily.

Amigo's Grill • *Ambassador Hotel* • Spanish decor and menu . . . a total contrast to the world outside.

Bank Vault • *Royal Orchid Hotel* • Grillroom so named because new hotel stands on site of former Hong Kong and Shanghai bank.

Bobby's Arms • *Soi Charuwan* • Popular English-style pub.

La Brasserie • *Regent Hotel* • This is the Regent's bistro, with a dining room and indoor fountain/courtyard seating areas . . . service is superb, food is excellent (Continental, Chinese, you name it) and remarkably reasonably priced . . . one of Bangkok's best values.

Castillion • *Dusit Thani Hotel* • French cuisine despite its name.

Cedar • *54 Soi Lang Suan, Ploenchit Rd.* • Lebanese dishes.

Charly's • *66 North Sathorn Rd.* • Restored villa with fondue restaurant featuring Swiss favorites . . . and international grillroom for steaks . . . extensive and attractive grounds.

Le Cristal • *Regent Hotel* • The finest European dining in Thailand may not be an exaggeration . . . a charming blend of the Continent and Thai styles, with service Regent is renowned for throughout Asia.

Fireplace Grill • *Regent Hotel* • Charming and intimate . . . downstairs . . . continental menu.

Fondue House • *28 Soi Somkhit, Ploenchit Rd.* • Beef fondue and other Swiss dishes in pleasant setting.

Gazebo Terrace • *Royal Orchid Hotel* • Mediterranean and seafood specialties on an edge of Chao Phraya River.

George and Dragon • *Soi 23 Sukhumvit* • Another English-style pub.

Giorgio's • *Royal Orchid Hotel* • Grills alfresco on riverside terrace.

Indra Grill • *Indra Regent Hotel* • Steaks from the U.S. and continental dishes grilled Turkish-style.

Italian Pavilion • *19 Soi 4 Sukhumvit Rd.* • Italian specialties.

Kanit • *Soi Charuwan* • Spanish decor and menu.

Le Gourmet Grill • *Montien Hotel* • Pressed duckling and other French creations . . . award-winning chef Michel Binaux.

Le Petit Moulin • *2/33 Soi 22 Sukhumvit* • More French cuisine.

Lord Jim Restaurant • *Oriental Hotel* • Very popular seafood spot.

Molo Kai • *35 Soi Pipat 2 Convent Rd.* • Steaks and lobster French style.

Nana Fondue • *4/3 Soi 3 Sukhumvit Rd.* • Fondues the French way.

Norden • *5 Soi 20 Sukhumvit Rd.* • Scandinavian smorgasbord daily.

Normandie Grill • *Oriental Hotel* • The best in town for French food and atmosphere . . . nice views . . . tres elegant.

Pornphet Seafood • *2662 New Petchaburi Rd.* • Phuket lobster and other sumptuous fruits of the sea.

Riverside Terrace • *Oriental Hotel* • Casual ambiance by the Chao Phraya . . . family barbecue dinner on Tuesday, Thursday, and Sunday . . . Thai buffets on Monday and Friday evening . . . romantic.

Ro De Orm • *440/2 Suriwong Rd.* • Danish open sandwiches and other Scandinavian specialties.

Avenue One • *Siam Inter-Continental Hotel* • Excellent grillroom with French haute cuisine . . . established reputation.

Tara • *Siam Square Soi 9* • American steak house.

The Bachelors • *593 Sukumvit Rd.* • Lobsters as you like them!

Tramps • *95/4–5 Rajdamri Rd.* • Seafood and imported meats.

Trattoria Da Roberto • *Patpong II* • Italian cuisine.

Zur Taverne • *1/11 Soi 3, Sukhumvit* • German dishes and pizza.

NIGHTLIFE

During the Vietnam war years, Bangkok boomed as the GI's favorite R & R (rest and recreation) town, and the Patpong area of the city would have made Suzie Wong very proud. Bars, massage parlors, go-go girls, disco clubs, key clubs sprang up and set up their neon signs. For years, the Thais blamed this "nasty" area on the Americans but what happened when the military left? It expanded into Patpong II, III, and even IV because the void was quickly filled with Japanese and European tour groups who descend upon Bangkok not only for their own R & R but also for some well-planned S & S (sun and sex). In fact, few other metropoli today offer the variety, profligacy, and non-stop activity that one can find at any moment of the day in Bangkok. Those who indulge in this sort of thing say that only one's quest for passion and the size of one's wallet are deterrents to the experiences available.

However, those wishing to indulge in such pleasures are forced to profit from their own research (at least, in this book) as I am quite certain that my editor would not approve of using precious space to discuss some of the major suppliers of amusements after dark. But, if you just wish to browse and gawk and not commit yourself, head straight for **The Bookseller Company** at 81 Patpong Rd.—a terrific excuse for getting a good book or magazine (in any language) and testing the water at the same time.

Other nighttime activities include Thai-style boxing, which can be at either **Rajdamnern** or **Lumpini** stadiums at 6 p.m. (also 1 p.m. on weekends). As in all boxing, this sport is not for the timid but can be interesting because of the ritual that precedes each bout, the music, and the manner in which the barefooted combatants attack each other. This is not simply a match of gloves but of fists, elbows, knees, bare feet, and body rushes while the crowd roars and jeers. On-the-spot gambling is also a major activity at these matches.

At least one evening in Bangkok should be spent at a typical Thai dinner, planned with your Western palate in mind, and accompanied by classical dances and songs, a bit of sword fighting, and some fairy tales. There are many excellent opportunities available: the **Sukhothai Restaurant** at the Dusit Thani Hotel, the **Thai Night buffet** and dancing under the stars at the Siam Inter-continental Hotel, the **Salanorasingh Restaurant,** 20 Sukhumvit Soi 6 (opposite Rajah Hotel), **Riverside Terrace** on Monday and Friday at the Oriental Hotel, **Maneeya Lotus** in Ploenchit Rd., and the **Thai-Mon Twilight cultural tour** of Koh Kred. This begins at 3 p.m. and lasts five hours, featuring a riverboat cruise, dinner, sightseeing, and classical show. A **candlelight dinner**

cruise is also available aboard the *Oriental Queen,* on a charter basis. Check with the Oriental Hotel for details.

There are many legitimate **nightclubs** and **discos** in Bangkok, especially among the better hotels, that are worth visiting for a little diversion and local music:

Bubbles • *Dusit Thani Hotel* • Disco open from 9:30 p.m. to midnight.

Casablanca • *Montien Hotel* • Upbeat nightclub . . . live music from 9 p.m.

Cat's Eye • *President of Bangkok* • Musical groups nightly.

Juliana's of London • *Bangkok Hilton* • Features one of the *in* groups in town.

The Club • *Ambassador Hotel* • Live nightclub from 8 p.m.–1 a.m.

The Den • *Indra Regent Hotel* • Imported musical groups from 9 p.m. nightly.

Tiara • *Dusit Thani Hotel* • Supper club with panoramic view of capital . . . international entertainment and house band for dancing . . . open from 7 p.m. to midnight weekdays, until 1 a.m. on weekends/holidays.

Tropicana • *Rama Tower* • Disco from 8 p.m. nightly.

SHOPPING

Absolutely the most sensible way to survive the "elements" of Bangkok—traffic noises and fumes, enervating heat, and humidity—is to plan plenty of time for browsing through the many colorful shops full of Thai silks and cottons, semiprecious and precious stones for jewelry, bronze ware and celadon, and delightful handicrafts. Shopping in Bangkok is truly a feast for one's eyes, and the prices are not so bad that the pocketbook doesn't suffer too much, either. Check the cost of a Thai silk gown or complete place-settings for 12 in bronze flatware at any North American department store, then shop around in Bangkok and realize savings of up to 400%.

The Tourism Authority of Thailand publishes a shopping booklet with a list of recommended specialty stores that are members of TAT, and where visitors can expect English to be spoken, credit cards to be accepted, and general quality of goods to be insured. TAT also suggests that you avoid touts (strangers who approach you with a "deal") and sidewalk vendors—unless you just wish to practice the well-known Asian art of bargaining. It is wise always to demand a receipt for any goods purchased as well as a certificate of guarantee for jewelry and gems. Antiques and genuine works of art should only be considered in the most reliable of shops, and export documents are often necessary upon departure. As mentioned before, Buddha images are forbidden to leave the county under any circumstances and ignorance of the law still constitutes a crime.

Most of the TAT-member shops will also arrange for shipping and insurance, but remember to safeguard receipts in case of loss or theft. For major complaints, TAT suggests that you write to them directly and someone in the Tourist Service Improvement Division will investigate the problem and keep you informed of any progress in the matter.

Thai Silk   The American Jim Thompson is irrevocably tied to the present success of the Thai silk industry, for he is generally credited with reviving this ancient art after World War II and with promoting its value and variety in the best fashion houses and boudoirs around the world. Thompson was a 40-year-old former O.S.S. agent in Bangkok at the end of the war, and he fell in love with Thailand and considered it home from then until his mysterious disappearance in the Malaysian jungle in 1968. (The biographer William Warren believes Thompson simply got lost deep in the underbush, walked away from the search party, and finally succumbed). An architect by training, Thompson started the Thai Silk Company with a few weavers and gradually upgraded the quality of the material by using color-fast dyes and broader looms to meet the specifications of decorators and designers in Europe and the U.S.

Making silk has always been a home industry for the Thai people, and lovely maidens were expected to rear their own silk worms, produce the yarn, and weave all the fabric for their family life. By tradition, every maiden would create a masterpiece once in her lifetime—a wedding costume. Today's Thai silk is one of the most sumptuous fabrics available, with colors and patterns that knock your eyes out. Choosing some dress lengths from among a variety of bolts is like being in an ice cream emporium—there are too many tempting flavors. True Thai silk is made in 40-inch widths and can be used for evening gowns, dresses and suits, men's shirts, any kind of accessory for both sexes, and home furnishings. Good Thai silk is 100% pure, heavier, and more expensive than lesser quality (or silk and synthetic mixtures), and must be properly cared for with professional dry cleaning and pressing. However, it is worth the expense and will last a lifetime if treated with kindness.

Her Majesty Queen Sirikit rarely appears publicly without wearing some type of Thai silk fabric, and she is especially fond of *Mut-Mee,* which is a particular tie-dye process that is said to date from prehistoric times. Mut-Mee silk is peculiar to the northeastern part of Thailand; the designs on the material are usually taken from nature. Most popular are animal designs, trees and flowers, waves and watermelon. Even King Bhumibol is interested in supporting the making of this unique material, and has suggested that a national attire of Mut-Mee silk would be far more comfortable for men in this tropical climate. Already, Mut-Mee silk shirts are replacing formal wear for men in the evening.

There are many excellent shops selling Thai silk throughout Bangkok. **Jim Thompson's Thai Silk Company** on Surawong Rd. is one of the best, although the clerks when I've been there have been particularly snotty. Try **Star of Siam** on Ratchadamri Rd. for a more gracious experience. And if you prefer lesser quality silk and a synthetic mix, there are material shops around every corner and 24-hour tailors to boot. Many of the beautiful costumes worn by hotel and restaurant staff are a synthetic mix and nothing is lost in the process. Thai cottons are also wonderful and inexpensive, with equally vibrant colors and patterns, and very cool for both men and women in this heat and humidity.

Handicrafts The Thais are imaginative carvers, beaters, molders, and painters, and there are plenty of interesting handicrafts to buy as gifts and souvenirs. Carvings of teak, lacquerware, macrame jute plant hangers, celadon bowls and antique animal reproductions, papier mache mobiles, prints of temple rubbings, stuffed cotton animals and exquisite dolls, pounded silver items, and nielloware. One of the most popular items is the 100-and-some piece set of bronze flatware, manufactured now with a nontarnish finish, that services up to a dozen diners and several courses. Other bronze items include candlesticks, bowls, ashtrays, punch bowl sets, large and small knickknacks. Teak and rattan furniture are also plentiful, but one never knows how it all will wear in another climate.

There are numerous handicraft shops in Bangkok but perhaps one of the most interesting is the **Silom Village Trade Center,** which offers exhibitions of silk weaving and printing, silversmithing, celadon pottery, bronzeware, lacquerware, umbrella making, teak wood carving, and more. There are also some very touristy, but nonetheless colorful, shows of classical dance, swordfighting, and boxing as well as three different eating places.

Jewelry Semiprecious and precious stones are wonderful buys in Bangkok, especially if you know your gems and their relative value in the marketplace today. Both mounted or free stones of diamonds, rubies, emeralds, topaz, sapphires, garnets, moonstones, zircons, and cat's eyes are on display wherever you cast your eyes. One of the most popular items available is the Princess Ring, set with a series of jeweled tiers graduating to a single stone at the peak. Another is the Nine-stone Ring, a narrow gold band set with a diamond, ruby, emerald, topaz, garnet, sapphire, moonstone, zircon, and cat's eye, in that order. However, unless you plan to spend more than a few hundred dollars on some pleasing bauble, be very, very careful. Even top jewelers have a difficult time determining the authentic from the fake, today. Make large purchases from a reputable, TAT-member store and insist upon a Certificate of Authenticity. No matter how attractive or tempting a piece of jewelry might be, keep in mind that it's practically impossible to demand a refund from 12,000 miles away in the Western Hemisphere.

Hotel Shops and Arcades: Bangkok's top hotels all have large shopping arcades for browsing and price comparison (remember the high rents they must be paying). There are also plenty of shops in the Patpong-Surawongse-Silom area (near the Montien, Sheraton, Dusit Thani hotels) as well as a **Central Department Store** and a large Thai handicrafts shop on Oriental Avenue. Guests at the Oriental Hotel are next door to many fashionable boutiques, Thai handicrafts, and jewelers in the **Oriental Plaza** shopping center. **Siam Centre** is next to the Siam Inter-Continental, with a variety of shops selling women's fashions and jewelry as well as two foreign exchange facilities. Guests at the Erawan and Regent of Bangkok are close to the **Rajprasong Shopping Centre** as well as the two-story **Star of Siam** and other fine stores. And arcade fanciers will find that the **Indra Hotel** has the largest variety of shops in town.

Markets: No shopping spree in Bangkok is complete, however, without a tour of the markets that offer a whole new world of exotica as well as plenty of local color! Every Friday evening, hundreds of sellers begin setting up their wares in the Chatuchak Park by the northern bus terminal. This is the **Weekend Market,** which swings from Saturday morning until dusk on Sunday and is especially appealing to those who love a carnival atmosphere. Everything possible is available here, from dyed mice (live) to hot chilis. Plan to spend a few hours wandering among the stalls, but watch your handbags and camera cases because— well, nobody's perfect and pickpockets love crowded places.

There are also two Thieves' Markets in town, one full of antiques and porcelain (**Verng Nakorn Kasem**), situated between New and Yawaraj roads near the Sang Burapa shopping complex. The other (**Hlung Ga-Suang**) is east of the Pramane Ground on Atsadang Rd. (along Klong Lawd) and offers everything but antiques. Both are open daily. Spices and saris can be found in the Indian district on Pahurat Rd. and the Chinese district on Sampeng Lane is crowded, noisy, and full of intrigue.

CHIANG MAI

Cultural capital of the north . . . City of Roses . . . 500 miles northwest of Bangkok . . . reachable by plane, train, or bus daily . . . known for beautiful women and charming people . . . once an independent state . . . founded by King Mengrai in A.D. 1298 in fertile flatland of Ping River . . . 1000 feet above sea level . . . uncrowded and unhurried . . . Buddhism reached highest peak here around 1450 . . . more than 100 ancient temples still exist within 1 square city mile . . . population around 200,000 . . . lovely mountain vistas . . . colorful hilltribes . . . local crafts and cottage industries . . . dry and cool climate . . . a popular hill station during the winter months . . . especially with royal family . . . the favored city with most travelers.

WHAT TO SEE AND DO

Bhubing Palace • Summer home of royal family . . . about 5 km from Wat Prathat . . . some 1300 meters high . . . beautiful mountain views and flowers . . . grounds open to public on weekends and holidays.

Chiang Mai National Museum • Near Wat Jed Yot . . . ancient statues of Buddha . . . collection of old weapons . . . open 9 a.m.–noon, 1–4 p.m., closed Mon. and Tues. . . . admission 2 baht on weekends only.

Chiang Mai University • Opened 1965 . . . located about 5 km from town . . . on approximately 500 acres . . . visit Tribal Research Center on weekdays . . . also Arboretum and Zoo nearby.

Huay Kaew Falls • Near Chiang Mae Zoo . . . located only about 7 km from town . . . also lovely spot for picnics . . . very popular.

Kruba Srivichai Monument • Near Huay Kaew Falls . . . shrine honors venerable old monk . . . who initiated road up to monastery on Suthep Mountain.

Meo Village • Located near Bhubing Palace . . . nearest hilltribe of interest . . . reachable by jeep and foot . . . friendly people and children . . . accustomed to Western visitors . . . have interesting handicrafts for sale.

Wat Chiang Man • Former residence of King Mengrai, founder of Chiang Mai . . . first temple built . . . dates from 1300 . . . elephant statues are Ceylonese-style . . . also 2 famous Buddha statues here.

Wat Jed Yod • Located near National Museum . . . contains ashes of King Tilokaraj in stupa . . . the king sent his architects to Burma . . . designed this copy of Buddha Gaya in 1447 . . . chedi has 7 spires . . . but suffered damage during Burmese invasion of 1566.

Wat Jedi Luang • Built in 1411 . . . large chedi damaged by earthquake in 1545 and never repaired . . . Emerald Buddha said to have resided here in great pagoda for over 80 years . . . King Mengrai said to have been killed by lightning on the grounds . . . **Indakin** or City Pillar near entrance of this Wat.

Wat Ku Tao • Built in 1613 . . . built in shape of 5 gourds of various sizes . . . beautifully decorated with colored porcelain . . . said to represent 5 Lord Buddhas.

Wat Pra Singh • Built in 1345 . . . one of Chiang Mai's oldest and biggest temples . . . built to house **Pra Singh** . . . most venerated statue in the north . . . important to Songkran Festival mid-April.

Wat Prathat • Located on top of Suthep Mountain . . . the city's landmark . . . reachable by 290 naga-lined steps . . . 3520 feet above sea level . . . built in 1383 by King Guena . . . large chedi in center of temple contains part of holy relics of Lord Buddha . . . visited each year by Buddhist pilgrims from throughout the land . . . tempting little stalls run by local Meo people . . . all the way up.

Wat Suan Dork • Built around 1383 . . . contains ashes of Chiang Mai's royal family . . . 500-year old bronze image said to be one of largest and most beautiful in Thailand.

ENVIRONS

Doi Indhanon National Park

About 100 km from Chiang Mai . . . Thailand's most famous park area . . . 1005 square km of space in 3 provinces . . . very impressive scenery and wildlife . . . includes country's highest mountain . . . visit also Vachiratarn and Siriphum waterfalls and Borijinda Cave . . . all great for picnics and the most adventurous of travelers.

Hot Springs • About 165 km north of Chiang Mai . . . near Fang and in Ban Pa-in area . . . about 50 hot springs in a 10-acre clearing in forest . . . 3 bubbling continuously . . . avoid it if you can't stand the smell of sulfurous gases.

Lamphun • Quaint small town some 26 km south of Chiang Mai . . . pleasant trip . . . along winding road lined with elegant trees . . . 2 interesting temples and a silk brocade factory here.

Mae Klang Falls • Located along Chiang Mai-Hod Rd. . . . about 70 km from the city . . . huge waterfalls and scenic spot for picnics.

Mae Sa Falls • About 25 km from city . . . known as the cascade because one part is broken into sections.

Mae Sa Mai • About 30 km from Chiang Mai . . . known for the possibility of watching elephants at work in the forest . . . daily demonstration from 9:30 a.m.–11 a.m. . . . 40 baht admission fee.

Ob Luang • Famous gorge about 105 km from city . . . located on Chiang Mai-Mae Sarieng Rd. . . . lovely view of deep valley . . . scenic mountains and teak forest.

Wat Chedi Liem • Located at Sarapee, about 15 km south of city . . . name denotes squared-shape of chedi . . . copy of chedi at Wat Ku Kut at Lamphun.

Wat Ku Kut • Lamphun, about 26 km from Chiang Mai . . . built during reign of Queen Chammadhevi . . . legendary monarch . . . about 60 ancient Buddhas gaze upon you here.

Wat Phra Baht • Pasang, about 44 km from Chiang Mai . . . legend says that Lord Buddha and His Disciples rested here . . . dried his robes on some stones . . . which now have mystical quality . . . in the monastery is Buddha's footprint . . . although not considered so sacred as the Shrine of Holy Footprint near Saraburi, 136 km north of Bangkok . . . village of Pasang also famous for handwoven cottons and batiks.

Wat Prathat Chom Thong • About 58 km from city along Chiang Mai-Hod Rd. . . . located near Mae Klang Falls and Doi Indhanon National Park . . . Burmese-style temple built around 1451 . . . houses notable collection of bronze Buddha statues.

Wat Prathat Haripoonchai • Located at Lamphun, some 26 km from Chiang Mai . . . temple built in 1157 . . . along banks of Kuang River . . . not far from Wat Ku Kut . . . large chedi here houses holy relic called **Prathat Haripoonchai** . . . considered one of most sacred monuments in the north.

Chiang Rai

Considered "upcountry" and linked to Bangkok (950 km south) and Chiang Mai by air and road . . . founded by King Mengrai in 1262 . . . whose statue stands along road to Mae Chan . . . 2 famous temples in Chiang Rai . . . **Wat Pra Singh** and **Wat Phra Keo** . . . latter said to be original residence of Emerald Buddha . . . which now sits in temple of same name on royal palace grounds.

Hilltribes

One of the great attractions of visiting the north of Thailand . . . there are about 7 tribes around the Chiang Mai area . . . Meo, Red and White Karen, Lisu, Lahu, Yao, and Akha . . . sometimes outnumbering indigenous Thais in small villages . . . Chiang Rai province boasts its own large group . . . Akha, Yao, Blue and White Meo, Lisu, Lahu, and Skaw . . . Karen are most nomadic and clusters range from Burmese border down . . . most of the tribes in Thailand only appeared within last century . . . most are Chinese/Burmese/Laotian in origin . . . many villages can be visited quite safely . . . especially if you carry small gifts of cigarettes and pens . . . and plenty of money to buy locally made handicrafts.

Golden Triangle

Constitutes northernmost part of Thailand as well as neighboring areas of Burma and Laos . . . known as the smuggling capital of the Far East . . . especially in the trade of opium . . . not always safe to visit here . . . bandits are prevalent and foreigners should be accompanied by armed protection . . . it's an adventure, especially from Chiang Saen to Chiang Rai in boats down the notorious Mekong River . . . through exciting jungle on both sides . . . the Laotian town of Ban Houei Sai . . . none of this for the faint-hearted.

Tours

Bhubing Palace and Wat Prathat • 3½ hours, Fri., Sat., and government holidays only . . . 8:30 a.m. and 1:30 p.m. . . . visit to their Majesties' palace . . . and most famous temple in Chiang Mai . . . contains holy relic of Lord Buddha . . . beautiful views.

Meo Hilltribe and Wat Prathat • 3½ hours, daily . . . 8:30 a.m. and 1:30 p.m. . . . see colorful costumes . . . and most famous temple . . . Bhubing Palace also toured on weekends.

Home Industries • 3½ hours, daily . . . 8:30 a.m. and 1:30 p.m. . . . visit local weaving factories at Sankampaeng . . . umbrella making village of Bor Sarng . . . Thai celadon kiln . . . teak carvings . . . laquerware and silverware.

City Tour • 3½ hours, daily . . . 8:30 a.m. and 1:30 p.m. . . . visit Wat Chiang Man . . . Wat Jedi Luang . . . Wat Pra Singh . . . Wat Suan Dork . . . Wat Jed Yod.

New Meo Hilltribe • 3½ hours daily . . . 8:30 a.m. and 1:30 p.m. . . . also stop at Mae Sa waterfalls and largest Orchid Farm in Chiang Mai.

White Karen Hilltribe and Pasang and Lamphun • 3½ hours daily . . . 8:30 a.m. and 1:30 p.m. . . . visit hilltribe village at Mae Tha . . . beautiful people at Pasang . . . Wat Prathat Haripoonchai and Wat Jamathevi in Lamphun.

Red Karen Hilltribe • 8½ hours daily . . . visit Red Karen Hilltribe village in Hod district . . . see Wat Prathat Chom Thong . . . then Mae Klang waterfall . . . and village where pottery is made.

Lamphun and Pasang • 3½ hours daily . . . 8:30 a.m. and 1:30 p.m. . . . visit historic town of Lamphun . . . see important Wat Prathat Haripoonchai . . . Wat Jamathevi . . . both over 1000 years old . . . see Pasang village of beautiful girls and weavers.

Lisu Hilltribe • 8½ hours daily . . . visit also elephants at work in jungle . . . Lisu are tribe of Tibens and Bhurmese origin.

Mae Sa Waterfall and Orchid Farm • 3½ hours daily . . . 8:30 a.m. only . . . northern area of Chiang Mai . . . demonstration of elephants at work on timber . . . also beautiful Mae Sa waterfall and orchid farm.

Chiang Dao Shrine and Elephants • 8½ hours daily . . . visit demonstration of elephants at work in jungle . . . also Chiang Dao cave and shrine with Buddha images . . . Mae Sa waterfall.

Meo Tribal Village and Elephants • 8½ hours daily . . . elephants in jungle setting . . . Meo village and Mae Sa waterfall . . . also orchid farm.

Mekong River and Elephants • 11 hours daily . . . elephants at work in northern jungle areas . . . drive to Tha Ton landing on Burmese border . . . boat trip on Mekong River to see Lahu and Yao hilltribe villages.

Doi Indhanon National Park • 8½ hours daily . . . visit Thailand's highest mountain . . . for most beautiful views in the land . . . visit also Meo and Karen hilltribe villages . . . Mae Klang waterfalls and Wat Prathat Chom Thong built in 1451.

Chiang Rai and Chiang Saen and Golden Triangle • 12 hours daily . . . full day by car from Chiang Mai . . . Mae Sai to see Burmese border and jade factory . . . Chiang Saen to see Golden Triangle . . . visit Akha and Yao hilltribe villages.

Chiang Rai Tour • 2 days . . . by car for Chiang Rai via Karen and Black Lahu and Meo hilltribe villages . . . overnight in Chiang Rai . . . visit Mae Sai to see Burmese border and jade factory . . . also Akha and Yao hilltribe villages.

Mae Kok/Chiang Rai Tour • 2 days . . . visit Tha Ton landing and elephants at work in jungle . . . boat trip along Mekong River . . . visit various hilltribe villages . . . full day tour to Mae Sai and jade factory . . . see Akha and Yao hilltribe villages . . . also Chiang Saen and Golden Triangle.

Sukhotai and Si Satchanalai • 2 days . . . visit Thailand's first capital and oldest city . . . old town and museum and overnight in

Swankaloke . . . after breakfast at hotel visit ancient town of Si-satchanalai . . . rich in historic ruins and pottery made around 1300.

HOTELS

★★★**Chiang Inn** • *100 Chang Klan Rd. Tel: 235655. Cable: CHIANGIN. Telex: TH 4303* • 175 rooms . . . charming accommodation in the heart of town . . . walk around the corner to the Night Bazaar . . . northern Thailand decor.
Facilities: Romthong coffee shop. Hill Tribe Grill. Lobby lounge. Mae Ping lounge. Wall nightclub. Convention facilities. Swimming pool.
Manager: K. Suvannasurt. *Reservations:* TAT.

★★**Chiang Mai Hills Hotel** • *18 Huay Kaew Rd. Tel: 221255. Cable: CHIANGMAI HILLS. Telex: TH 4332* • 82 rooms . . . situated between city center and Doi Suthep monastery . . . 5-story building overlooking lovely grounds and ponds . . . pleasant setting.
Facilities: Orchid Room coffee shop. Chiang Doi Thai and Japanese restaurant in garden. Saturn discotheque. Swimming pool and health club.
Manager: K. Thernburintr. *Reservations:* Bangkok Tel: 235–0240.

★★★**Dusit Inn** • *112 Chang Klan Rd. Tel: 236835. Telex: TH 49325* • 198 rooms . . . nine-story high rise in center of Chiang Mai . . . extensive renovations.
Facilities: Coffee shop. Golden Lotus Chinese restaurant. Top floor cocktail lounge with panoramic view of city. Basement nightclub. Swimming pool.
Manager: K. Gunatilaka. *Reservations:* UTELL.

★★★★★**Chiang Mai Orchid** • *100-102 Huay Kaew Rd. Tel: 222099. Cable: HYATTOR. Telex: TH 4337* • 267 rooms . . . a beautiful hotel . . . decor emphasizes the essence of Thai-Burmese design . . . lovely woods, carvings, and weavings throughout . . . lobby is a Meo hilltribe experience . . . hotel is a showcase for northern culture and crafts.
Facilities: Le Pavillon French restaurant. Kamogawa Japanese cuisine. 3-tiered Mae Rim coffee shop. Opium Den bar. Lobby bar. Warehouse disco. Convention facilities. Swimming pool and health club. Orchid Club with private lounge for executive clientele. Squash court.
Manager: K. Suwanzinsur. *Reservations:* Direct.

★★★★**Rincome Hotel** • *301 Huay Kaew Rd. Tel: 221044. Cable: RINCOME. CHIANGMAI. Telex: TH 4314* • 158 rooms . . . quiet, established small hotel . . . open since 1969 . . . same ownership and management as Nipa and Orchid Lodges in Pattaya . . . pleasant and casual atmosphere . . . a few minutes from city center.

Facilities: Thong Kwow restaurant in traditional setting. Lanna coffee shop overlooking swimming pool. Lobby lounge. Byblos disco-theque. Large and small swimming pools. Conference facilities. Tennis court.

Manager: H. Stocker. *Reservations:* Robert Jose Assoc.

WINING AND DINING

Thai food in Chiang Mai tends to be less fiery than the central and southern areas of the country and the restaurants are far more casual and quiet. A specialty of Chiang Mai is the Lanna Khantoke dinner, which features northern dishes along with songs and dances of the hill-tribes. The setting is a lovely carved teakwood background and the whole evening lasts about three hours, for a set price of around $10 a person.

European and other Asian food can be enjoyed with great pleasure in Chiang Mai, although hardly with the same degree of variety as in Bangkok. However, there are some popular standbys worthy of a stop.

EUROPEAN

The Chalet • *71 Charoen Prathet Rd., near Diamond Hotel* • European dishes in charming setting.

Hans Munchen • *115/3 Loi Claw Rd., off Chang Klan Rd.* • A German/pub/restaurant . . . all dishes personally prepared by owner Franz.

Hill Tribe Grill • *Chiang Inn Hotel* • You could buy out the Night Bazaar for what a dinner costs here . . . intimate surroundings.

Le Pavillon • *Hyatt Orchid Chiang Mai* • French cuisine in superb setting . . . quite the best in town . . . expensive, too.

The Pub • *Huay Kaew Rd., near Rincome Hotel* • A fun native hut . . . managed by charming English fellow and Thai wife . . . tap beer and steak and kidney pie plus other worthy delectables . . . lunch and dinner, except Monday noon.

Thong Kwow • *Rincome Hotel* • European and westernized Thai dishes in lovely, old-world setting . . . a beautiful, airy dining room.

THAI AND ASIAN

Baan Suan • *51/3 Chiang Mai, San Kampaeng Rd.* • Authentic restaurant out near umbrella-making center . . . if you're in the area.

Bua Tong • *Grand Palace Hotel* • Good Chinese food.

Chiang Mai Coca • *Huay Kaew Rd.* • More casual Chinese.

Golden Lotus • *Chiang Mai Palace Hotel* • Good Chinese buffet.

Hong Yok • *Muangmai Hotel* • Chinese cuisine.

Kamogawa • *Hyatt Orchid Hotel* • Japanese . . . but watch for tour groups.

Lanna Khantoke • *Diamond Hotel* • Most impressive restored house of wealthy Burmese teak trader of a century ago . . . local dishes and performances . . . Meo boy sings in 7 languages.

Mrs. K • *Garnet Chiang Mai Hills Hotel* • She will make anything! Chinese, Japanese, Thai, or European.

Old Chiang Mai Khantoke • *Chiang Mai Cultural Center, Wua Lai Rd.* • New cultural hall in traditional design . . . typical northern dishes with hilltribe entertainment . . . nightly from 7 p.m.–10 p.m.

Whole Earth Vegetarian • *88 Sridonchai Rd.* • Just for something different.

NIGHTLIFE

Yes, there is some . . . although considerably tamer than the new experiences available in the wicked capital down south. However, those who can't do without their massages will find plenty of parlors around the Chiang Mai area . . . in a region noted for its beautiful women! There are also plenty of bars for the lonely traveler as well as some fairly swinging nightclubs and discos:

Byblos Disco • *Rincome Hotel* • Lots of pillows . . . very chic.

Crystal Club • *Suriwongse Hotel* • A supper club . . . if you like that sort of thing.

Saturn • *Garnet Chiang Mai Hills Hotel* • Swinging disco.

The Wall Club • *Chiang Inn* • Very popular and fun.

The Warehouse Disco • *Chiang Mai Orchid Hotel* • The best in town.

SHOPPING

Shopping in this Rose of the North is yet another of its many cultural attractions, for the Chiang Mai area is undoubtedly one of the world's largest centers of cottage industries. These people are true artisans as they work at the craft of silk weaving, wood carving, silverware, and pottery making. Temple bells, paper manufactured by ancient processes and handpainted umbrellas are also produced here. At least one day should be spent on an organized tour, or in a hired car, visiting the many small industries that employ thousands of skilled labor to manufacture charming and inexpensive items completely by hand. For less than $2 each, you can stock up on small lacquered boxes, temple bells, and handmade umbrellas as gifts and souvenirs. (One of my friends insisted I write how much she loves her temple bell, now swinging in the breeze in our nation's capital. "It tinkles just the right amount," Fran told me recently.)

The **Umbrella Village** is located at Bo Sang, along the highway to Sankampaeng. It was founded in 1978 to consolidate the umbrella makers of the area, to preserve the intricate processes of this ancient craft and improve the living conditions of the artisans. Each small factory has a colorful display of new umbrellas drying in the sun, made of cotton, silk or sa-paper *(Brossonetia papyrifera)*. The paper is also handmade from the bark of mulberry trees, which are so abundant in the forest of northern Thailand. The frames are all handmade of bamboo and the covering material is waterproofed by the application of a paste that includes the juice of persimmons. The handpainted designs are both traditional and modern, and custom orders are accepted. And if you feel the umbrellas are too cumbersome to carry home, shipping can be arranged but it's a crime to pay more for postage than the handmade item.

Just south of the Umbrella Village and along the same Sankampaeng Road is **SaiThong, House of Antiques.** The Lanna-style house is worthy of a stop, for it is one of the most stunningly carved structures in all of Thailand, and a very very interesting place to browse. Thai silk is another cottage industry along this road, but I would suggest making such purchases in Bangkok where the quality is more reliable.

Wua Lai Road near Chiang Mai Gate is famous for its silverware and wood carving home industries but the lacquerware is really the most impressive here. Ornately painted trunks are the *piece de resistance* but the small black and gold boxes are sold for a song (less then $2) and make lovely gifts. Highway No. 108, about 5 km. from town, is the center of pottery production and Highway No. 107 is well known for its celadon industry. At each small community, you can tour the facilities and watch the process before surveying the inevitable showroom.

However, some of the best shopping in Chiang Mai is located along **Tha Phae and Witchayanon roads,** right in the center of town. Here, you can find those delightful temple bells as well as other brass and bronze ornaments. Here, too, you can find a vast variety of hilltribe clothing, made to fit the Western frame. Dresses, jackets, shirts in black and red patterns are in all the shops and cost only a few dollars—with a little serious bargaining. Another amusing place to bargain and buy is along both sides of the steps up to Wat Phra That Doi Suthep, for along with the tourist items are mixed some unusual pieces brought in from Burma. There is also a fabulous covered **Night Bazaar,** situated near the Suriwong and Chiang Inn hotels, that features stalls and stalls of clothing and accessories. Great buys here with a little bargaining savvy!

HUA HIN

HUA HIN IN A CAPSULE

Thailand's oldest beach resort . . . now making a bid as an alternative to the touristy Pattaya . . . first established in the 1920s . . . long popular with locals and visitors from surrounding countries . . . can now boast some deluxe accommodations suitable for taste of North Americans . . . located on western shores of Gulf of Thailand . . . same latitude as Pattaya . . . and 105 miles south of Bangkok . . . sandy beaches . . . picturesque backdrop of green hills . . . lovely bay . . . a wonderful place for a relaxing family-type holiday.

Two deluxe hotels are now open for business . . . the 180-room **Royal Garden Resort** on a beach ½ mile from town . . . facilities include deluxe rooms, coffee shop, barbecue terrace, cocktail lounge,

Hua Hin's one and only discotheque and meeting rooms. There are beach, pool, tennis courts and sports center amenities as well as windsurfing and water-skiing. An 18-hole golf course is nearby.

Other competitor is the 100-room **Railway Hotel,** owned by the State Railways of Thailand . . . this property dates from the 1920s, when King Rama VII set up a royal residence here . . . hotel is built in Edwardian style . . . large rooms with ceiling fans and teakwood shutters . . . old-world charm . . . but no air conditioning.

Coming on the horizon here is a large hotel developed by the Central Department Store Group of Bangkok, which is said to be investing about $7.5 million in a new structure . . . this is definitely the Pattaya of two decades ago and the king still spends the months of May and June here.

Hua Hin is accessible from Bangkok by 3½-hour bus daily as well as good train service. The Royal Garden Resort is also arranging its own air-conditioned train cars for incentive and business groups. Get there now—while it is still a unique resort in Thailand!

PATTAYA

PATTAYA IN A CAPSULE

A sleepy fishing village until the late 1960s . . . now a sophisticated beach resort with over 5000 hotel rooms . . . a paradise for swingers and water sport fanciers . . . 3 hours-plus by air-conditioned bus from Bangkok . . . but book early in season and on weekends . . . strictly a recreation area with tennis, waterskiing, parasailing, snorkeling and scuba diving, sailing and fishing . . . walking the beach and ogling the bikini crowd . . . foodstalls and restaurants offering endless variety of international cuisines . . . glamorous nightspots and discos for after dark . . . nonstop entertainment . . . plenty of bars and local companionship if you've forgotten your own.

HOTELS

★★★★**Grand Palace** • *Corner Pattaya Beach, Cholburi. Tel: 418541. Cable: GRANPAT. Telex: 81917.* • 500 rooms (40 suites) . . . new Y-shaped structure at northern end of the beach . . . located on 15 acres of lovely gardens . . . great views . . . contains Thailand's largest convention facilities . . . modern lobby with open courtyard behind . . . plus rooms and suites . . . 30 duplex suites near pool, with own butler . . . the tops in personal comfort and privacy . . . an unbeatable resort hotel.

Facilities: Food market featuring stalls of different cuisines. Nouvelle cuisine dining room. Country & Western saloon. Jazz lounge. Chinese den. Thai music bistro. Discotheque/nightclub. 24-hour coffee shop. 2 swimming pools. 2 tennis courts. 2 private beaches for guests. Recreation center and children's playground. Health club.

Manager: P. Dangrojana. *Reservations:* Distinguished Hotels.

★★**Merlin Pattaya** • *Pattaya Beach, Cholburi. Tel: 428755. Cable: MERLIN PATTAYA. Telex 81905* • 360 rooms . . . also Y-shaped to maximize sea views . . . built in 1975 as a Holiday Inn property . . . dark commercial lobby area . . . overly air-conditioned for my tastes . . . motel-mentality guest room decor . . . has own rock garden and sea frontage.

Facilities: La Veranda bar. Sontaya seafood restaurant. Sea Breeze Cafe. Rhine Continental grillroom. La Concha lounge. Cookie Jar pastry shop. Surfside nightclub. Large swimming pool. Small putting green. 2 tennis courts. Children's playground.

Manager: E. Yeo. *Reservations:* Merlin Hotels.

★★★★**Montien Pattaya** • *Pattaya Beach, Cholburi. Tel: 418155. Cable: MONTELP. Telex: 81906* • 320 rooms . . . one of this resort's most attractive hotels . . . located in 9 acres of tropical gardens . . . all rooms have full sea view and balcony . . . beautifully decorated and recently refurbished . . . open-air public areas . . . centrally located . . . same ownership and management as Bangkok hotel.

Facilities: Veranda coffee shop. Hokkaido Japanese restaurant. Grillroom. Siam Room cocktail lounge/nightclub. Swimming pool and sundeck. 2 tennis courts. Private beach and watersports. Thai classical dancing programs. Massage service.

Manager: M. Intrayota. *Reservations:* UTELL.

★★★**Nipa Lodge** • *Pattaya Beach, Cholburi. Tel: 428195. Cable: NIPALODGE. Telex: 81903* • 150 rooms . . . low-rise built in 1965 . . . one of oldest resort hotels in the area . . . casual atmosphere

. . . simple accommodations . . . interesting amenities . . . sister hotel of Orchid Lodge and Chiang Mai's Rincome Hotel.

Facilities: Oriental Den Asian specialties. Buccaneer Terrace charcoal grill/seafood restaurant. Hafen Stuble German food. Orient Express French restaurant (in 2 former Thai railway cars). Cou Cou Club. Video room. Orchid Terrace coffee shop. Swimming pool and snack bar. Friday night Thai-style barbecue party, with dances and hilltribe fashion show.

Manager: J. Raess. *Reservations:* UTELL.

★★★**Orchid Lodge** • *Pattaya Beach, Cholburi. Tel: 428161. Cable: ORCHID-LODGE PATTAYA. Telex 81903* • 236 rooms . . . casual, low-rise structure opened in 1963 . . . sister of Nipa Lodge and Rincome Hotel in Chiang Mai . . . located in over 10 acres of tropical gardens.

Facilities: Crow's Nest coffee terrace. La Gritta Italian restaurant. Lobby bar. Byblos piano lounge. Garden bar. Orchid grill. Red Baron English/German specialties. Olympic-size swimming pool.

Manager: J. Raess. *Reservations:* UTELL.

★★**Pattaya Palace** • *Pattaya Beach, Cholburi. Tel: 428066. Cable: PALPAT. Telex: 81904* • 291 rooms (17 suites) . . . built in 1970 as a Hyatt property . . . renovated in 1980 . . . half of the guest rooms have sea views . . . large double-height lobby . . . spacious junior suites.

Facilities: Coffee shop. Marlin seafood restaurant. Captain's bar. Evergreen cocktail lounge. Kontiki nightclub. Buo Thong Chinese restaurant. Large swimming pool and terrace cafe. Children's playground. 6 tennis courts. Sauna and massage. Businessmen's club. Miniature putting green.

Manager: P. Dangrojana. *Reservations:* RAMADA HOTELS.

★★★★**Royal Cliff** • *Pattaya Beach, Cholburi. Tel: 418344. Cable: CLIFF PATTAYA. Telex: 81907* • 786 rooms (128 suites) . . . self-contained resort . . . on southern end of Pattaya . . . overlooks own mile-long stretch of private beach . . . reachable only by long flight of stairs or elevator . . . rather out of the way from the mainstream . . . so be prepared to stay awhile . . . taxi rides can be expensive! New Royal Wing with 86 suites . . . its own swimming pool, another restaurant/bar and open-air dining terrace . . . hotel will arrange local fishing boats and equipment for guests. The Royal Cliff was chosen the best resort in Asia for 1988 by *Asia Business Week* magazine.

Facilities: Terrace grill. Lobster Pot seafood restaurant. Piano bar. Coffee shop. Supper club. Sunset bar. 3 swimming pools. Massage parlor. Beach bar. Meeting/conference rooms. 800-hotel personnel. 6 tennis courts. Bowling alley. Jogging track. Squash courts. Watersports. Golf course nearby.

Manager: A. Fassbind. *Reservations:* UTELL.

★★★★**Siam Bayshore** • *Pattaya Beach, Cholburi. Tel: 428678. Cable: BAYSHORE PATTAYA. Telex: 82820* • 274 rooms . . . situated on 20 acres at southern end . . . beginning of the crescent beach . . . 14 low-rise buildings connected by covered walkways . . . lots of greenery and privacy . . . futuristic in feeling . . . many facilities, including professional tennis club on premises . . . all rooms with private balconies . . . also private beach club.

Facilities: Bali Hai seafood and Chinese restaurant. Midships coffee shop. Speakeasy lounge. Ocean Floor nightclub. The Greenery lounge. Bayshore Rotisserie. Meeting and conference facilities. 4 tennis courts. 2 swimming pools. Beach club.

Manager: K. S. Clapp. *Reservations:* UTELL.

★★★★**Siam Bayview** • *Pattaya Beach, Cholburi. Tel: 428728. Cable: BAYVIEW PATTAYA. Telex: 82820* • 300 rooms . . . spring 1983 opening . . . new development by owners of Siam Bayshore . . . designed for upscale market . . . 3-story Bayside wing with 87 rooms . . . 12-story tower with plush rooms . . . all with private balcony . . . stylish, antique-decorated lobby . . . destined to become one of the resort's finest hostelries.

Facilities: Coffee shop. Specialty restaurant. Cocktail lounge. 2 swimming pools. Seafood restaurant. Nightclub and discotheque. Tennis courts.

Manager: S. Narong. *Reservations:* UTELL.

★★**Hotel Tropicana** • *North Pattaya Beach, Cholburi. Tel: 418516. Cable: TROPICANA PATTAYA. Telex: 81910* • 200 rooms . . . tropical garden atmosphere in 7 lush acres . . . plenty of seclusion in the midst of Pattaya's sweeping shoreline . . . low-rise structure with guest rooms recently upgraded . . . located between Merlin and Pattaya Palace high rises . . . relaxing, casual atmosphere . . . all rooms with balcony or terrace setting . . . cabana-style also available.

Facilities: South Seas cafe. Mai Kai grill. Boat bar. Seahorse disco. 2 swimming pools. Conference facilities. Polynesian nightclub. Tennis courts. Watersports.

Manager: P. Phornprapha. *Reservations:* UTELL.

★★★★**Wong Amat** • *Naklua Rd. Pattaya Beach, Cholburi. Tel: 418118. Cable: WONGVILLA PATTAYA. Telex: 81908* • 229 rooms . . . pronounced "Wong-a-mat" and meaning "Noble Family" in Thai . . .

this 229-room-and-bungalow hotel is Pattaya's oldest and most delightful small resort . . . set in a 35-acre garden right on the beachfront . . . mostly low-rise construction . . . clean and charming everywhere . . . new wing open April 1981 . . . well designed . . . balconies overhang the beach . . . peaceful and beautiful . . . try also the honeymoon suite in a houseboat on the beach!

Facilities: Casibo coffee shop. Lobby bar. Beachside barbecue on Fri. Maris Stella grill. Annabella disco. Convention facilities. 4 swimming pools. 2 tennis courts. Watersports. Golf nearby.

Manager: C. Chungsathaporn. *Reservations:* UTELL.

WINING AND DINING

Pattaya is known for its unlimited charms of sun, sand, and sex, where singles and swingers can commingle for the time of their lives. The beach and an exciting nightlife are the pulse of Pattaya. This is a place noted for its commercialization, resulting pollution, and not an insignificant amount of prostitution, although family groups can enjoy the atmosphere of some of the better hotels. And after a full day in the sun, visitors can choose from French, German, Italian, Hungarian, Swiss, Japanese, Chinese, Indonesian, Indian, Arabic, Mexican, and many Thai restaurants for a little repast. (Not to mention the bars, discos, nightclubs, and massage parlors that would keep the devil himself hopping to and fro.) But, speaking of eating . . . the seafood is superb!

EUROPEAN

Alt Heidelberg • *273 Beach Rd.* • German specialties.

Alter Bier Garten • *Soi 7, Pattaya Beach Rd.* • More beer and sauerbraten . . . also Thai dishes and fresh seafood.

Buccaneer Terrace • *Nipa Lodge* • Excellent grilled lobster and filets . . . known for Swiss and Continental menu.

Cartier's Restaurant • *South Pattaya, opposite Beach Inn Hotel* • Steaks cooked to order . . . and fresh seafood . . . combo dinners, too.

Chalet Swiss • *South Pattaya* • Fondues and other delicacies.

Chez Jean • *Pattay Naklua Rd., opposite post office* • Filet steaks are popular here.

Coral Reef • *South Pattaya* • Crab souffle . . . seafood royal . . . lobster au pernod.

Dolf Riks • *South Pattaya Rd.* • Run by Indonesian-born Dutchman . . . hearty dishes plus Indonesian *rijsttafel* on Sun. and Wed. . . . classical music too.

Grill Room • *Royal Cliff Beach Hotel* • U.S. steaks and local seafood . . . expensive and very dressy.

Hafen Stuble • *Nipa Lodge* • More Deutschland dishes.

Haus Munchen • *next to Merlin Pattaya* • Roasted and suckling pigs.

Hideaway Grill Room • *South Pattaya* • Escargots . . . duck in orange sauce . . . New Zealand lamb.

John's Hungarian Inn • *South Pattaya* • Spicy Hungarian dishes and fresh fish.

La Gritta • *Orchid Lodge* • Rock lobster . . . seafood . . . pizza.

Maris Stella Grill • *Wongse Amatya* • Charming grill room in low-rise hotel complex.

Milano • *South Pattaya* • One of many popular pizza and spaghetti places.

Rhine Grillroom • *Merlin Pattaya* • More German and Contentinal specialties in former Baron's Grill.

Rotisserie Grill Room • *Siam Bayshore Hotel* • Very elegant and expensive.

Seafood Restaurant • *South Pattaya* • All combinations of fresh fruits from the sea.

Suthep Kitchen • *Pattaya Beach Rd.* • Excellent lobster and prawns . . . veal also a specialty.

Trade Winds • *Pattaya Beach Rd.* • English food prepared with a Scottish touch.

Viking Restaurant • *South Pattaya* • Seafood in the Scandinavian manner.

THAI AND ASIAN

Al Shahab (Moti Mahal) • *South Pattaya* • Indian, Pakistani, Arabic, Iranian and Thai food . . . take your choice.

Balihai • *Siam Bayshore Hotel* • Peking duck, bird's nest soup, and other Chinese specialties.

Cafe India • *183/9 Soi Chaiyasit, South Pattaya* • Moslem and Arab dishes . . . branch of Bangkok restaurant.

Chalam • *South Pattaya* • Fried fish with chili sauces, Chinese noodles.

Cliff Top Seafood Pavilion • *Asia Pattaya Hotel* • Seafood in many excellent guises . . . spectacular view.

Dee's Pattaya • *next to Palm Garden Hotel* • Thai and Chinese at reasonable prices.

Hokkaido • *Montien Pattaya Hotel* • Japanese dishes in a teahouse atmosphere . . . elegant and soothing.

Latif Restaurant • *109/15 M 10, South Pattaya* • Tandoor cooking and Indian kabobs.

Layla • *South Pattaya* • Arab and Moslem dishes.

Nang Nual Restaurant • *South Pattaya* • Seafood grills and other Thai food.

Palm Kitchen • *near Palm Lodge* • Thai-style seafood and steaks.

Sontaya • *Merlin Pattaya Hotel* • Excellent seafood restaurant with Thai dishes.

Tai Hee Restaurant • *South Pattaya* • Hot fish-tail soup and other Chinese delicacies.

Talay Tong • *Ocean View Hotel* • Chinese/Thai restaurant.

Thai Garden • *South Pattaya* • Seafood and Chinese/Thai dishes.

The Oriental Den • *Nipa Lodge* • Seafood and Chinese-style barbecues.

Villa Restaurant • *South Pattaya* • Chinese restaurant.

Yamato • *Soi Yamato* • Japanese.

NIGHTLIFE

Alcazar Cabaret • *78/14 Pattaya 2nd Rd.* • 2 shows every evening . . . with 35-member transvestite troupe.

Annabella • *Wongse Amatya Hotel* • Pop-rock band . . . disco.

Byblos • *Orchid Lodge* • Disco music and lights.

Cou Cou Club • *Nipa Lodge* • Disco music and lights.

Grace • *South Pattaya* • Disco music . . . girls.

Kontiki • *Pattaya Palace Hotel* • Disco and pop music.

Mai Kai Supper Club • *Tropicana Hotel* • Dinner and dancing.

Neptune Nightclub • *Asia Pattaya Hotel* • Disco and rock group.

Ocean Floor • *Siam Bayshore Hotel* • Rock and pop group.

Simon Club • *South Pattaya* • Disco music and lights.

Supper Club • *Royal Cliff Beach Hotel* • Dinner and dancing . . . floor show Tue. and Fri.

Surf Side • *Merlin Pattaya Hotel* • Pop and rock group.

Tahiti • *Sea View Hotel* • Disco/rock/soul group.

The Marine Disco • *South Pattaya* • Disco and girls.

The Wall Club • *Chiang Inn Hotel* • Disco music and lights.

PHUKET

PHUKET IN A CAPSULE

360-square-mile island off west coast of Isthmus of Kra . . . which separates Gulf of Thailand and Andaman Sea . . . equidistant from Burmese and Malaysian borders . . . one of most beautiful places in all of Thailand . . . economy based on tin and rubber . . . plus natural beauty that local officials are preserving . . . no high-rises . . . local temples and waterfalls for visiting . . . popular spot.

HOTELS

★★★★★**Amanpuri** • *P.O. Box 196, Surin Beach, Phuket. Tel: 2500746/7* • 42 luxury bungalows . . . This is the most expensive and, many say, the most beautiful hotel in Thailand . . . huge bungalows with sea views, restaurants serving Italian and Thai food.

Facilities: Swimming pool, beach, tennis, squash, sailing, and fishing.

★★★★**Club Med-Phuket Island** • opened December 1985. 90-acre resort village . . . two-story accommodations for 600 people curved along protected stretch of white sand. Center of village resembles Thai palace . . . all rooms double occupancy with individual sleeping areas separated by sliding doors . . . all have balconies overlooking sea.

Facilities: Nightclub. Huge sundeck. Windsurfing. Swimming pool. Theater/dance floor complex. Several open-air dining pavilions. Arts and Crafts workshop. Boutique. Annex seafood restaurant up on hilltop perch. 7 tennis courts. 4 squash courts. Tai Chi and other martial arts. Deep-sea fishing (extra charge). Archery. Volleyball. Picnics to off-shore islands. Miniclub and conference center. Boat trips. One-week programs at village and 15-day Siamese Smiles excursions. Open to everyone on a membership basis.

Manager: Changes every six months. *Reservations:* CLUB MED.

★★★★**Coral Beach Hotel** • *104 Moo4, Patong Beach, Kathu District, Phuket 83120. Tel: (076) 321106* • 203 rooms. All rooms air-conditioned . . . facing sea in secluded setting . . . excellent location . . . a member of Siam Lodge Hotels.

Facilities: Giant swimming pool. Chao Lay coffee shop and ter-race. Rimtalay specialty/seafood restaurant. Conference rooms. Health Center. Music lounge. Video films. Tennis. Squash. Badminton. Jogging trails. Nature walks. Water sports.

Manager: K. Kitchakarn. *Reservations:* UTELL.

★★★★**Meridien Phuket** • *P.O. Box 277, Phuket. Tel: 321480-5* • 460 rooms . . . One of several luxury hotels contributing a European flair to the cosmopolitan beach life in Phuket . . . new property with excellent credentials.

Facilities: Four restaurants, tennis/squash courts, fitness center, and two swimming pools.

★★★**Patong Beach Hotel** • *Phuket P.O. Box 25, Phuket. Tel: (076) 321301. Telex: 69521 PATONG. Cable: PATONG HOTEL* • 103 rooms.

Facilities: Located right on Patong Beach. Dining room, bar. Swimming pool. Tennis. Shops. Video Lounge.

General Manager: C. N. Lampoon. *Reservations:* Direct.

★★★★**Phuket Island Resort** • *73/2 Rasda Rd., Phuket. Tel: (076) 212676. Telex: 69555 ISLAND TH. Cables: ISLAND PHUKET* • 194 rooms.

Facilities: All rooms and bungalows with views from hillock. Golf. Tennis. Swimming. Beach Club. 2 restaurants. Outdoor dining terraces. 2 bars. Shop. Games Center. Deepsea fishing and underwater sports.

General Manager: W. Schuller. *Reservations:* UTELL.

Hotel Quick-Reference Charts

BRUNEI DARUSSALAM
Bandar Seri Begawan

Hotel	Telephone	Telex	Cable	No. of Rooms	Page No.
Sheraton-Utama Jalan Bendahara	27272	(809) BU2306	SHERATON BRUNEI	170	7

BURMA (Union of Myanmar)
Rangoon (Yangon)

Hotel	Telephone	Telex	Cable	No. of Rooms	Page No.
Dagon (Orient) 256-260 Sule Pagoda Rd.	71140		CAFETERIA	12	25
Inya Lake Hotel Kaba Aye Pagoda Rd., P.O. Box 1045	50644	BM BM21520 INYAHO	INYA LAKEHO	222	25
Thamada Hotel (President) No. 5, Signal Pagoda Rd.	71499		THAMADAHO	58	26
Strand Hotel 92 Strand Rd.	81533		STRANDHO	100	26

Mandalay

Hotel	Telephone	Telex	Cable	No. of Rooms	Page No.
Htun La Hotel 27th Rd.	21283		HOTELMANDALAY	10	32
Mandalay Hotel 26 B Rd.	21004, 22499		MANHOTEL	68	32

Pagan

Hotel	Telephone	Telex	Cable	No. of Rooms	Page No.
Irra Inn located near Bupaya Pagoda about a mile from Thiripyitsaya Hotel	24			27	37
Thiripyitsaya Hotel located overlooking Irrawaddy River in the midst of the ruins	28			36	38

HONG KONG

Hotel	Telephone	Telex	Cable	No. of Rooms	Page No.
The Excelsior Causeway Bay	5–767365	HX74550	CONVENTION HONG KONG	923	70
Furama Inter-Continental 1 Connaught Rd.	5–255111	HX73081	FURAM H.X.	522	77
Grand Hyatt				575	71

Hong Kong Hilton 2 Queen's Rd. Central	5–233111	HX73355	HILTEL HONG KONG	755	71
Hong Kong Marriott Queensway, Central	5–8101366	66899 MARTT HX		605	72
Lee Gardens Hotel Hysan Ave., Causeway Bay	5–9853311	75601 LEGAR	LEE GARDENS	800	72
The Mandarin Connaught Rd., Central	5–220111	HX73653	MANDARIN HONG KONG	577	72
Victoria Connaught Rd., Central	5–407228	86608 HTLVT HX	HOTELVC	540	73

Kowloon

Park Lane Hotel 310 Gloucester Rd.	5–8903355	75343 PHL EX	PARKLANE	850	73
Holiday Inn Golden Mile 46–52 Nathan Rd.	3–693111	HX56332	HOLIDAYINN HONG KONG	598	73
Holiday Inn Harbour View 70 Mody Rd.	3–7215161	HK38670	INNVIEW	597	74
Hyatt Regency Hong Kong 67 Nathan Rd.	3–3111234	HX43127	HYATT HONG KONG	763	74
Kowloon Hotel 19–21 Nathan Rd.	3–698698	47604 KLNHL	KLN HOTEL HX	708	74
Kowloon Shangri-la 64 Mody Rd.	3–7212111	36718 SHALA HX		719	74

Hotel	Telephone	Telex	Cable	No. of Rooms	Page No.
New World New World Centre, 22 Salisbury Rd.	3–694111	NWHTL HX35860	NWHOTEL	719	75
Omni Prince Hotel	3–7361888	50950 OPHX HX	OMNIPH	401	75
The Omni Hongkong Harbour City	3–7360088	43838 HK	OMNIKH	610	75
Omni The Marco Polo	3–7360888	40077 HX	OMNIP HONG KONG	439	76
The Peninsula Salisbury Rd.	3–666251	HX43821	PENHOTE	181	76
Ramada Renaisance 8 Peking Rd.	3–3113311	81252 RAMDA HX		502	76
Regal Airport 30–38 Sa Po Rd.	3–7180333	40950 HOMRA HX	HOMRA	384	77
Regal Meridien Mody Rd., Tsimshatsui	3–7221818	HX4095HOMRO	HOMRO	623	77
The Regent Salisbury Rd.	3–7211211	HX37134	REGENTEL HONG KONG	602	77
Royal Garden Tsimshatsui East	3–7215215	HX39539	ROYALHOTEL	433	78
Royal Pacific Hotel & Towers, China Hong Kong City	3–7361188	44111 ROPAC HX		650	78
Sheraton Hong Kong Hotel & Towers 20 Nathan Rd.	3–691111	HX45813	SHERATON HONG KONG	860	86

INDONESIA

Jakarta

Hotel	Telephone	Telex	Cable	No. of Rooms	Page No.
Borobudur Intercontinental Jalan Lapangan Banteng Selatan P.O. Box 329	370108	44156 BDO-IA	BOROBUDUR IA	866	119
Horizon Hotel Taman Impian Jaya Ancol, Jakarta Utara	680008	42824 HORIZ JKT	HOTELHORIZON	350	119
Hyatt Aryaduta Jakarta Jalan Prapatan Raya 44—46 P.O. Box 3287	376008	46220	ARYADUTA JAKARTA	220	119
Hotel Indonesia Jalan M.H. Thamrin 58 P.O. Box 54	320008	44233 HIPA JKT	INHOTELCOR	575	119
Jakarta Hilton International Jalan Jend. Subroto (Senayan)	583051	46673	HILTELS-JAKARTA	468	119
Mandarin Oriental Jakarta Jalan M.H. Thamrin P.O. Box 3392	321307	45755 MANDA JKT	MANDAHOTEL JAKARTA	455	120
Kartika Plaza Jalan M.H. Thamrin P.O. Box 2081	321008	45793 ROKAR IA	KARTIKAPLAZA	331	120
Sahid Jaya Hotel Jalan Jen. Sudirman 86	587031	JKT 46331	SAHIDHOTEL	514 (600 exten.)	120
Sari Pacific Hotel Jalan M.H. Thamrin P.O. Box 3138	323707	44514 HTLSARI IA	HOTLSARIPACIFIC	500	120

Bali

Hotel	Telephone	Telex	Cable	No. of Rooms	Page No.
Bali Beach Sanur, Denpasar	8511	035129 HBB DPR		605	134
Bali Hyatt Jalan Tanjun Sari Sanur	8271–7	35127	BALIHYATT	387	134
Bali Oberoi Jalan Kahyu Aya, Legion Beach	51061	35125	BALIOBEROI	75	134
Bali Sanur Bungalows Jalan Raya Sanur, Denpasar	8421	35178 GRIYA BSB DPR	BALI BUNGALOWS	161	134
Kuta Beach Hotel Kuta P.O. Box 393, Denpasar	51461		KUBEHOT	32	135
Nusu Dua Beach Hotel P.O. Box 1028, Denpasar	71210	35107		450	135
Pertamina Cottages Kuta Beach, P.O. Box 121, Denpasar	51161	35131	PERCOT DPS	178	135
Sanur Beach Hotel and Seaside Bungalows P.O. Box 279, Denpasar	8011	35135	AEROPACIFIC	320	135
Segara Village Hotel Jalan Segara Ayu, Sanur	8407	35143		100	135
Tandjung Sari Hotel P.O. Box 25, Denpasar	8441	35157	TANDJUNGSARI	24	136

Yogyakarta

Ambarrukmo Palace P.O. Box 10	88488	APHYO GYA 25111	HOTELAMBAR	251	142
Garuda Hotel 72 Jalan Malioboro	2112–4		GARUDA	120	143
Mutiara Hotel P.O. Box 87	3272		MUTIARA HOTEL YOGYAKARTA	90	143
Puri Artha Cottage Jalan Cendrawasih 9	3752	25147 ARTHA YK		60	143
Sri Wedari Hotel & Cottage Laksamana Adisucipto	88288	25148 SRWHOT	SRI WEDARI HOTEL	70	143

Solo

Kusuma Sahid Prince Hotel P.O. Box 20, Solo	6356	22274 KSPH SOLO	SAHIDPRINCE	100	143
Mangkunegaran Palace Hotel Istana Mangkunegaran, Solo	5683	HIPA JKT 44233	PURI SALA INDONESIA	50	143

Surabaya

Bumi Hyatt 1240128 Jalan Basuki Rakhmat	470875	HYATT BUMI 31391	HYATTSURABAYA	268	147
Jane's House 100 Jalan Dinoyo	67722	31459	JANE'S HOUSE	50	147

Hotel	Telephone	Telex	Cable	No. of Rooms	Page No.
Mirama Hotel 68–74 Jalan Dinoyo	69501	31485 MIRAMA SB	MIRAMA HOTEL	123	147
Ramayana Hotel 67–69 Jalan Basuki Rakhmat	46321	31-202	RAMAYANAHOTEL	100	147
Sumatra Medan					
Danau Toba International Hotel Jalan Imam Bonjol	327000	51167	HOTEL DANAU TOBA	300	150
Dirga Surya Jalan Imam Bonjol	323645		HOTELDIRIGASURYA MEDAN	60	150
Dharma Deli Hotel Jalan Balai Kota	327011	516 GMC	GAP LAZTEL	103	151
Tiara Medan Jalan Cut Mutia	51600	51721 GRIYA MEDAN	GAYA MEDAN		151
Lake Toba					
Hotel Danau Toba Jalan Pulau Samosir	41583	51157	HDTI MEDAN	50	151
Hotel Parapat Jalan Marlhat	41012		HO PAR	75	151
Hotel Patra Jasa Parapet Jalan Suikar 1	41766		PATRAJASA PARAPAT	34	151

JAPAN
Hakodate

Hotel	Telephone	Telex	Cable	No. of Rooms	Page No.
Hakodate Kokusai Hotel 5–10 Otemachi	(0138) 23–8751	9926-04 HAKUHO	HAKODATE KOKUSAI HOTEL JAPAN	131	187
Hakodate-Ohnuma Prince Cottages 148 Nishi-Ohnuma, Nanae-cho	(0138) 67–3211	9925–11 ONPRIN J.		155	187
Hotel Rich Hakodate 16–18 Matsukaze-cho	(0138) 25–2561	9928–15		88	187

Sapporo

Hotel	Telephone	Telex	Cable	No. of Rooms	Page No.
Keio Plaza Hotel Sapporo 7–2 Nishi, Kita-5, Chuo-ku	(011) 271–0111	933–271 KPHSPH	KEIOPLATEL SAPPORO	525	191
Sapporo Grand Hotel 1 Kita, Chuo-ku	(011) 261–3311	932–613 GRAPHO	GRAHO SAPPORO	521	191
Sapporo Park Hotel 3–11 Nishi, Minami-Jujo	(011) 511–3131	932–264 PRKHL	PARK HOTEL SAP	223	191
Sapporo Prince Hotel 11 Nishi, Minami-Jujo, Chuo-ku	(011) 231–5310	933–949 SAPRI	SAPRINCEHOTEL	227	191
Sapporo Royal Hotel Higashi 1-chome, Minami 7–jo, Chuo-ku	(011) 511–2121	923–330 SROYL		88	191
Sapporo Tokyu Hotel Nishi 4–chome, Kita 4–yo, Chuo-ku	(011) 231–5611	934–510 THCSAP		263	192

Karuizawa

Hotel	Telephone	Telex	Cable	No. of Rooms	Page No.
Karuizawa Prince Hotel 1016–75 Karuizawa-machi	(02674) 2–5211			240	197
Karuizawa Prince Hotel Seizan Honkan 1016 Karuizawa-machi	(02674) 2–5211			299	197
Karuizawa Mampei Hotel 925 Sakuranosawa	(02674) 2–2771			127	197

Fuji/Hakone/Izu

Hotel	Telephone	Telex	Cable	No. of Rooms	Page No.
Hotel Grand Fuji 8–1 Heigaki-Honcho Fuji Shizuoka Pref. 416	(0545) 61–0360			25	198
Fuji-View Hotel 511 Katsuyama-mura Minamitsuru-gun Yamanashi Pref. 401–04	(05558) 2–2211		FUJIVIEW KATSUYAMA	66	198
Hotel Mt. Fuji Yamanaka, Yamanakako-mura, Yamanashi Pref. 401–05	(05556) 2–2111		MTFUJI YOSHIDA	110	199
New Yamanakako Hotel Yamanaka, Yamanakako-mura, Yamanashi Pref. 401–05	(05556) 2–2311	3385–478 OMNIA J		66	199
Yamanakako Hotel 506–1 Yamanakako-mura, Yamanashi Pref. 401–05	(05556) 2–2511	3385–492 J YAMHTL J	YAMANAKAKO HOTEL	71	199

Hakone

Hotel	Phone	Telex	Cable	Rooms	Page
Hotel De Yama 80 Moto-Hakone, Hakone-machi	(0460) 3-6321	3892-734		93	201
Fujiya Hotel 359 Miyanoshita, Hakone-machi	(0460) 2-2211	3892-718 FUJIYA J	FUJIYAHOTEL	150	201
Hakone Hotel 65 Hakone-machi	(0460) 3-6311	3892-765	HAKONE HOTEL	34	202
Hakone Prince Hotel 144 Moto-Hakone, Hakone-machi	(0460) 3-7111	3892-609 HAKPRI J		154	202
Hotel Kowaki-En 1297 Ninotaira, Hakone-machi	(0460) 2-4111	3892-730 HAKKWK J	HTLKWK	257	202
Odakyu Hakone Highland Hotel 940 Shinanoki, Sengokuhara, Hakone-machi	(0460) 4-8541			60	202
Yumoto Fujiya Hotel 256 Yumoto, Hakone	(0460) 5-6111	3892-631 YUFUYA J		100	202

Izu Peninsula and Seven Islands

Hotel	Phone	Telex	Cable	Rooms	Page
Chateau Tel Akanezaki Aza Akane, Kamitaga, Atami	(0557) 67-1111	3927-631		550	204
New Fujiya Hotel 1-16 Ginza, Atami	(0557) 81-0111	3917-681 NEFTEL J	NEFTEL ATAMI	320	205
Kawana Hotel 1459 Kawana, Ito—City, Shizuoka Pref.	(0557) 45-1111		KATEL ITO	140	205

Hotel	Telephone	Telex	Cable	No. of Rooms	Page No.
Shimoda Prince Hotel 1547–1 Shirahama, Shimoda	(05582) 2–7575	3929–754		135	205
Shimoda Tokyu Hotel 5–12–1 Shimoda	(05582) 2–2411	3929–732	TOKYUTEL SHIMODA	120	205

Japan Sea Coast

Hotel	Telephone	Telex	Cable	No. of Rooms	Page No.
Hagi Grand Hotel 25, Huruhagi-cho, Hagi, Yamaguchi Pref. 758	(08382) 5–1211			150	208
Kanazawa Miyako Hotel 6–10 Konohanacho, Kanazawa, Ishikawa Pref. 920	(0762) 31–2202	5122–203 MIYAKO J		192	208
Kanazawa Holiday Inn 1–10 Horikawa-cho	(0762) 23–1111	5122–288		180	208
Kanazawa New Grand 1–50 Takaoka-machi, Kanazawa, Ishikawa Pref. 920	(0762) 33–1311	5122–357 KANGHL J		122	208
Kanazawa Sky Hotel 15–1 Musashi-machi, Kanazawa, Ishikawa Pref. 920	(0762) 33–2233	5122–716 KSKYHL J		137	208
Kanazawa Tokyu Hotel 2–1 Korinbo, Kanazawa	(0762) 312–411			250	208

Hotel / Address	Phone	Telex / Cable		
Hotel Ichibata 30, Chidoricho, Matsue, Shimane Pref. 690	(0852) 22–0188		138	208
The New Otani Tottori 2–153, Ima-machi, Tottori City 680	(0857) 23–1111		143	209

Kobe

Hotel / Address	Phone	Telex / Cable		
Hotel Okura Kobe 48 Hatoba-cho	(078) 333–0111		491	,212
Kobe Portopia Hotel 10–1, 6-chome, Nakamachi Minatojima	(078) 302–1111	KOPTEL J 5622112	PORTOPIA KOBE	533	212
New Port Hotel 6–3–13 Hamabe-dori, Chuo-ku	(078) 231–4171	5623–058 NEPEL J	NEPOTEL KOBE	208	212
Oriental Hotel Kyomachidori 25	(078) 331–8111	5622–327 J	ORIENT KOB	190	212

Kyoto

Hotel / Address	Phone	Telex / Cable		
International Hotel Kyoto 284 Nijo Aburanokoji, Nakagyo-ku	(075) 222–1111	5422–158 INTCHO	INTERHO KYOTO	332	222
Hotel Fujita Kyoto Kamo Riverside, Nishizume, Nijo-Ohashi, Nakagyo-ku	(075) 222–1511		HOTELFUJITA KYOTO	195	222

Hotel	Telephone	Telex	Cable	No. of Rooms	Page No.
Kyoto Hotel Oike, Kawara-machi, Nakagyo-ku	(075) 211–5111	5422–126	KYOHO KYOTO	507	222
Kyoto Grand Hotel Shiokoji Horikawa, Shimogkyo-ku	(075) 341–2311	5422–551 KYOGRA	KYOTOGRAND KYOTO	577	223
Kyoto Royal Hotel Kawaramachi Sanjo	(075) 223–1234	5422–888 ROYALH	KYOTOROYAL, KYOTO	395	223
Kyoto Park Hotel 644–2 Sanjusangenda, Mawari-machi	(075) 525–3111	5422–777 J PARKHTL	KYOTO PARK	307	223
Kyoto Tokyu Hotel Horikawa, 5 Jyo-Ave	(075) 341–2411	5422459 THCKYO		433	223
Miyako Hotel Sanjo-Keage, Higashiyama-ku, Kyoto 605	(075) 771–7111	5422–132 MIYAKO J	MIYAKO KYOTO	480	223
New Miyako Hotel across from Kyoto Station	(075) 661–7111	5423–211 NEWMYK		715	223
Takara-ga-ike Prince Hotel Sakyo-ku	(81–75) 712–1111	542–3261 KYTPRHJ		322	224

Nagoya

Hotel	Telephone	Telex	Cable	No. of Rooms	Page No.
International Hotel Nagoya 3–23–3 Nishiki, Naka-ku, Nagoya 460	(052) 961–3111	444–3720 INTERPH J	INTERHOTEL NAGOYA	263	230
Meitetsu Grand Hotel 2–4 Meiki–1–chome, Nakamaura-ku, Nagoya 450	(052) 582–2211	442–2031 HGHOTE J	MGHOTEL NAGOYA	242	230

Hotel	Phone	Telex	Cable	Rooms	Page
Hotel Nagoya Castle 3–19 Hinokuchi-cho, Nishi-ku	(052) 521–2121	J 59787 CASTLE	HOTENACASTLE NAGOYA	253	230
Nagoya Kanko Hotel 1–19–30 Nishiki, Naka-ku, Nagoya 460	(052) 231–7711	J5–9946 KANHO	KANHO NAGOYA	505	230
Nagoya Miyako Hotel 9–10, 4–chome Meieke, Nakamura-ku	(052) 571–3211	442–2086 MIYAKO J	HONA MIYAKO	400	230

Nara

Hotel	Phone	Telex	Cable	Rooms	Page
Kikusui-ro 1130 Bodai-cho, Sanjo-dori	(0742) 23–2007			17	234
Hotel Yamatosanso 27 Kawakami-cho	(0742) 26–1011	5522–202		51	234
Nara Hotel 1096 Takabatake-cho, Nara 630	(0742) 26–3300	5522–108 NARAHO	NARAHOTEL	107	234

Osaka

Hotel	Phone	Telex	Cable	Rooms	Page
International Hotel Osaka 58 Hashizume-cho, Uchihon-machi	(06) 941–2661	529–3415 INTHTL J	INTERHOTEL	400	238
Hotel New Hankyu 1–35, Shibata 1–chome, Kita-ku	(06) 372–5101	523–3830 HTLNH J	NEWHANKYU OSAKA	1029	238
Hotel New Otani Osaka 4 Shiromi 1-chome, Higashi-ku	(06) 362–1111	63068 OTANI OSK J		610	238

Hotel	Telephone	Telex	Cable	No. of Rooms	Page No.
Hotel Osaka Castle 2–35–7 Kyobashi, Higashi-ku	(06) 942–1401	529–8505 CASTLE	HOTEL OSKCASTLE	90	239
Hotel Osaka Grand 3–18, 2–chome Nakanoshima, Kita-ku	(06) 202–1212	522–2301 OGRND	OSAKAGRAND OSAKA	358	239
Osaka Dai-ichi Hotel 1–9–20 Umeda Kita-ku	(06) 341–4411	523–4423 ITHLO J		478	239
Miyako Hotel Osaka 6–1–55 Uehonmachi, Tenngi-ku, Osaka 543	(06) 773–1111	527–7555 MYKOSA	MIYAKOHOTEL OSAKA	601	239
The Plaza Hotel ABC Center, 2–49 Oyodo-minami, 2–chome, Oyodo-ku	(06) 453–111	524–5557 PLAOSA J	PLAZAHOTEL OSAKA	575	239
Royal Hotel 5–3–68 Nakanoshima, Kita-ku	(06) 448–1121	J63350 ROYAL HTL	ROYALHOTEL OSAKA	1500	240
Osaka Terminal Hotel 3–1–1 Umeda, Kita-ku	(06) 344–1235	523–3739 OSATER J		671	240

Tohoku

Hotel	Telephone	Telex	Cable	No. of Rooms	Page No.
Hotel Aomori 1–1–23 Tsutsumi-machi, Aomori City	(0177) 75–4141	812755 HTLAOM J		102	243
Aomori Grand Hotel 1–1–23 Shin-machi, Aomori City	(0177) 23–1011			150	243

Hotel	Telephone	Telex / Cable		Page
Myoko Pine Valley Prince Hotel, Okemi, Myoko-Mura, Nakakubiki, Niigata 949–22	(0255) 82–4111		138	243
Naeba Prince Hotel Mikuni, Yuzawa-machi Minami-Uonuma-gun, Niigata 949-62	(0257) 89–2211	3238–370 NAEBA J	1444	243
Okura Hotel Niigata 6–53, Kawabata-cho, Niigata City 951	(0252) 24–6111	3122–815 OKRNIT J	OKURAHOTEL NIIGATA	303	244
The Italia-Ken 7–1574 Nishibori, Niigata City 951	(0252) 24–5111	ITALIAKEN 3122–888	101	244
Hotel Rich Sendai 2–2 Kokubun-cho, 2–chome, Sendai 980	(0222) 62–8811	853–483 RICHSB	242	244
Hotel Sendai Plaza 2–20–1 Honcho, Sendai 980	(0222) 62–7111	852–965	PLAZA SENDAI	221	244
Sendai Tokyu Hotel 2–9–25 Ichiban-cho, Sendai 980	(0222) 62–2411	852–393 THCSEN	THCSEN	302	244

Tokyo

Hotel	Telephone	Telex / Cable		Page
Akasaka Prince Hotel 1–2, Kioi-cho, Chiyoda-ku, Tokyo 102	234–1111		PRINCEAT TOKYO	761	259
Capitol Tokyu Hotel 10–3, Nagata-cho 2-chome, Chiyoda-ku	(03) 581–4511	24290	CAPITOL TOKYUTEL	479	259
Century Hyatt Tokyo 2–7–2 Nishi-Shinjuku, Shinjuku-ku	349–0111	J29411 CENHYATT	CENHYATT	762	259

Hotel	Telephone	Telex	Cable	No. of Rooms	Page No.
Imperial Hotel 1–1–1 Uchisaiwai-cho, Chiyoda-ku	504–1111	222–2346 IMPHO J	IMPHO TOKYO	1133	259
Hotel Kayu Kaikan 8–1 Sanban-cho, Chiyoda-ku, Tokyo 102	230–1111	232–3318	KAYUKAIKAN TOKYO	128	260
Keio Plaza Inter-Continental Hotel 2–1 Nishi Shinjuku, 2–chome, Shinjuku-ku, Tokyo 160	344–0111	J26874 KOPTEL	KEIOPLATEL TOKYO	1500	260
Miyako Hotel 1–50 Shiroganedai, 1–chome Minato-ku, Tokyo 108	447–3111	242–3222 MYKTKY-J	MIYAKO TKY	500	260
New Otani Hotel & Tower 4–1 Kioi-cho, Chiyoda-ku	265–1111	J24719 HTLOTANI	HOTELNEWOTANITOKYO	2047	260
Hotel Okura 10–4 Toranomon 2–chome, Minato-ku, Tokyo 105	582–0111	J22790 HTLOKURA	HOTELOKURA TOKYO	910	260
Hotel Pacific Meridien Tokyo 3–13–3 Takanawa, Minato-ku, Tokyo 108	445–6711	J22861 HOTELPAC	HOTELPACIFIC TOKYO	954	261
Palace Hotel 1–1 Marunouchi 1–chome, Chiyoda-ku, Tokyo	211–5211	222–2580 PALACE	PALACEHOTEL TOKYO	407	261
Roppongi Prince Hotel 2–7 Roppongi 3-chome, Minato-ku, Tokyo 106	587–1111	242–7231 RPNPRH J		216	261
Shinagawa Prince Hotel 4–10–30 Takanawa, Minato-ku, Tokyo 108	440–1111	242–5178 SNAPRH J		1273	261

Hotel	Phone	Telex/Cable	Cable		
Shinjuku Prince Hotel 1–30–1 Kabukicho, Shinjuku-ku, Tokyo 160	205–1111	232–4733 SHIPRH		571	262
Takanawa Prince Hotel and New Takanawa Prince Hotel 3–13–1 Takanawa, Minato-ku, Tokyo 108	447–1111	242–3232 TAKPRH	PRINSOTEL	1510	262
Tokyo Hilton Intl. 6–6–2 Nishi-Shinjuku, Shinjuku-ku, Tokyo 160	344–5111	HILTON J2324515	HILTELS TOKYO	842	262
Tokyo Prince Hotel 3–1 Shiba Park 3–chome, Minato-ku, Tokyo 105	432–1111	242–2488 TYOPRH	HOTELPRINCE	510	262

Tokyo Environs

Hotel	Phone	Telex/Cable	Cable		
Kamakura Park Hotel 33–6 Sakanoshita, Kamakura, Kanagawa Pref. 248	(0467) 25–5121			41	263
Chuzenji Kanaya Hotel 2482 Chugushi, Nikko, Tochigi Pref. 321–6	(0288) 5–0356		CHUZENJI KANAYA	32	263
Nikko Kanaya Hotel 1300 Kami-Hatsuishi, Nikko, Tochigi Pref. 321–4	(0288) 4–0001	3544–451 KANAYA J	KANAYA NIKKO	82	263
Nikko Lakeside Hotel 2482 Chugushi, Nikko, Tochigi Pref. 321–6	(0288) 5–0321			100	263

Hotel	Telephone	Telex	Cable	No. of Rooms	Page No.
Nikko Prince Hotel Shobugahama, Chugushi, Nikko, Tochigi Pref. 321–16	(0288) 5–0661			78	263
Inland Sea					
Hotel Hiroshima Grand 4–4 Kami-Hatchobori, Naka-ku	(0822) 27–1313	652–666 HGH	GRANDHOTEL HIROSHIMA	385	274
Hiroshima Riverside Hotel 7–14, Kaminobori-cho, Naka-ku	(0822) 28–1251	652–554 HRH J		92	274
Hiroshima Tokyu Inn 3–17 Komachi, Naka-ku	(0822) 244–0109			286	274
Hotel New Hiroden 14–9 Osuga-cho, Minami-ku	(0822) 63–3456	653–884	HOHIRODEN	353	274
Ivy Square Hotel 2–7 Honmachi				180	274
Kusashiki Kokusai Hotel 1–44 Chuo 1–chome	(0864) 22–5141	5933–258 KKHTL	KURAHOTEL	70	274
Mizushima Kokusai Hotel 4–20, Mizushima-Aoba-cho	(0864) 44–4321			74	274
Hotel New Okayama 1–25, 1–chome	(0862) 23–8211		HOTELNEWOKAYAMA	82	275

Hotel	Phone	Telex/Fax	Code	Rooms	Page
Okayama Kokusai Hotel 1–16, 4–chome, Kadota Honmachi	(0862) 73–7311	5922–669 OKAKOK	OKAKOKU	194	275
Okayama Plaza Hotel 116 Hama 703	(0862) 72–1201			85	275
Okayama Royal Hotel 2–4 Ezu-cho	(0862) 54–1155			198	275
Shimonoseki Tokyu Inn 4–4–1 Takezaki-cho, Shimonoseki	(0832) 33–0109	6823–15		128	275

Fukuoka

Hotel	Phone	Telex/Fax	Code	Rooms	Page
Hakata Miyako Hotel 2–1–1 Hakataeki Higashi, Hakata-ku	(092) 441–3111		HAMIHO J	300	279
Hakata Tokyu Hotel 1–16–1 Tenjin Chuo-ku	(092) 781–7111	723–295	HAKATATOKYUTEL	266	279
Kitakyushu Prince 3–1 Higashimagari-machi, Yahatanishi-ku	(093) 631–1111			220	279
New Otani Hakata Watanabe-Dori, Chuo-ku	(092) 714–1111	726–567		436	280
Nishitetsu Grand Hotel 2–6–60 Daimyo, Chuo-ku	(092) 771–7171	723351 NGHJ		308	280
Tokyo Dai-Ichi Hotel Fukuoka 2–18, Nakasu 5–chome, Hakata-ku	(092) 281–3311	724–823		221	280

Kagoshima

Hotel	Telephone	Telex	Cable	No. of Rooms	Page No.
Kagoshima Sun Royal Hotel 8–10, Yojiro 1–chome	(0992) 53–2020	7822–91		337	283
Shiroyama Kanko Hotel 41–1 Shinshoin-cho	(0992) 24–2211	7825–48	SHIROYAMA KANKO	621	283
Hotel Plaza Miyazaki 1–1 Kawahara-cho, Miyazaki	(0985) 27–1111	7779–77		183	283
Sun Hotel Phoenix 3083 Hamayama Shioji, Miyazaki	(0985) 39–3131	7778–58	SUNPHENIX	302	283

Kumamoto

Hotel	Telephone	Telex	Cable	No. of Rooms	Page No.
Kijima Kogen Grand Hotel Kijima-Kogen, Beppu	(0977) 22–1161	7734–74	BING HOTEL BEPPU	111	286
Suginoi Hotel Kankaiji, Beppu	(0977) 24–1141		SUGINOI	606	286
Hotel Hokke Club 20–1, Torimachi Kumamoto-shi	(0963) 22–5001	7626–76		152	286
New Sky Hotel 2 Higashi Amidaji-machi, Kumamoto	(0963) 54–2111			201	286

Nagasaki

	Phone	Telex	Cable		
Nagasaki Grand Hotel 5–3 Manzai-machi	(0958) 23–1234		NAGASAKI GRAND HOTEL	126	289
Nagasaki Tokyu Hotel 18–1 Minami Yamate-cho	(0958) 25–1501	752762 THECNGA		225	289

Okinawa

Naha Tokyu Hotel 1002 Ameku, Naha	(0988) 68–2151		TOKYUHOTEL NAHA	280	292
Okinawa Grand Castle 1–132–1 Shuri Yamagawa-cho, Naha	(0988) 86–5454	795375 OKAOGCJ		305	292
Okinawa Miyako Hotel 40 Matsukawa, Naha	(0988) 87–1111			318	292
Pacific Hotel Okinawa 3–5–1 Nishi, Naha	(0988) 68–5162			380	292

Shikoku

Imabari Kokusai Hotel 4–6, 1–chome, Asahi-machi	(0898) 22–3355			144	298
Kochi Dai-Ichi Hotel 2–2–12 Kitahon-machi, Kochi City 780	(0888) 83–1441			120	298

Hotel	Telephone	Telex	Cable	No. of Rooms	Page No.
Hotel Oku Dogo 267 Suemachi	(0899) 77–1111			303	298
Keio Plaza Hotel 5–11, Chuo-cho	(0878) 34–5511	5822–725 KPHT J		180	298
Takamatsu Grand Hotel 10–5–1 Kotobuki-cho	(0878) 51–5757	5822–557 TGRAND J		136	298
Hotel Astoria 2–26 Ichiban-cho, Tokushima 770	(0886) 53–6151			25	299
Awa Kanko Hotel 3–16–3, Ichiban-cho 770	(0886) 22–5161			35	299
Tokushima Park Hotel 2 Tokushima–cho 770	(0886) 25–3311	5862–345 PRKHTL J		82	299

KOREA
Seoul

Hotel	Telephone	Telex	Cable	No. of Rooms	Page No.
Chosun Hotel 87 Sokong dong, Chung-ku (CPO Box 3706)	771–05	K2456 SEOUL	WESTCHOSUN	471	333
Hyatt Regency Seoul 747–7 Hannam-dong, Yongsan-ku (CPO Box 3438)	797–1234	K24136	HYATT SEOUL	607	333

	Phone	Telex	Cable	Rooms	Page
Hotel Inter-Continental 159–1 Samsung-dong, Kangnam-lu	553–8181	K34254		600	334
Hôtel Lotte 1 Sokong-dong, Chung-ku (CPO Box 3500)	771–10	K28313	HOTELOTTE	1353	334
Ramada Renaissance Seoul 676 Yoksam-dong, Dagnam-ku	555–0501	K34392	RAMDAS	500	334
Seoul Hilton 411, 5–Ka, Namdaemun Ro, Jung-ku	753–7788	K26695	HILTELS	712	335
Seoul Plaza 23, 2–ka, T'aep'yong-ro, Chung-ku	771–22	K26215	PLAZA HTL SEOUL	493	335
Sheraton Walker Hill San 21, Kwangjang-dong, Song-dong-ku (CPO Box 714)	453–0121	K28517	WALKERHILL	804	335
Hotel Shilla 202, 2–ka, Changchung-dong, Chung-ku	233–3131	K24160	HOTEL SHILLA	672	336

Pusan (Busan)

	Phone	Telex	Cable	Rooms	Page
Chosun Beach Hotel 737 Woo 1–dong Haeundae-ku, Pusan 607–04	742–7411	CHOSUNB K3718	WESTCHOSUN PUSAN	350	336
Commodore Dynasty Hotel 743–80 Yongju-dong, Chung-ku (P.O. Box 407)	44–9101	COMOTEL K3717	COMMODORE PUSAN	320	337

Hotel	Telephone	Telex	Cable	No. of Rooms	Page No.
Hyatt Regency Pusan 1405–16 Chung-dong, Haeundae-gu	797–7819	K52668		363	337
Kyongju					
Kolon Hotel 64 Ma-dong, Kyongju, Kyongsangbuk-do (CPO Box 7009)	2–9001	K–4469	KOLHT	240	337
Kyongju Chosun Hotel 410 Sinpyong-dong, Kyongju-si, Kyongsangbuk-do (P.O. Bcx Kyongju 35)	2–9600	K4467	CHOSUNKYO	304	337
Kyongju Tokyu Hotel 410 Sinpyong-dong, Kyongju (P.O. Box Kyongju 6)	2–9901/6	K4328	KYONGJU TOKYU	300	338
Cheju Island					
Cheju Grand Hotel 263 Youn-Dong, Cheju-City (P.O. Box 45).	7–2131/41	K712	CHEJUGRANHTL	522 (200 planned)	338
Cheju KAL Hotel 1691–9 Idoil-dong, Cheju-si (CPO Box Cheju 62)	2–6151	K744	CHEJUKALHTEL	310	339
Hyatt Regency Cheju 3039–1 Saekdal-dong, Seogwipo-si	33–1234	66749		225	339

Mt. Sorak National Park area

Hotel	Telephone	Telex	Cable	No. of Rooms	Page No.
New Sorak Hotel 106–1 Sorak-dong, Sokcho-si, Kang-won-do	7131–50	K24983	NEWSORAK HOTEL	120	339
Sorak Park Hotel 74–3, Sorak-dong, Sokcho-si		24142		121	339

MACAU

Hotel	Telephone	Telex	Cable	No. of Rooms	Page No.
Bela Vista 8 Rua Comendador Kou Ho Neng	573821		VISTA	23	368
Hyatt Regency Macau C.P.O. Box 3008, Taipa Island	27000	88512 HYMAC OM		356	368
Hotel Lisboa Avenida da Amizade	77666	88203 HOTELOM	HOTELISBOA	750	368
Mandarin Oriental Macau Avenida da Amizade	567888	88588 OMA OM	ORIENTAL	406	369
Pousada de Coloane Praia de Cheoc Van, Coloane	28143	88690 PDC OM		22	369
Pousada de Sao Tiago Avenida da Republica	78111	88376 TIAGO OM		23	369
Hotel Presidente Avenida da Amizade	553888	88440HPM OM		333	370
Hotel Royal Estrada da Vitoria	552222	88514ROYAL OM		380	370

MALAYSIA

Johor Bahru

Hotel	Telephone	Telex	Cable	No. of Rooms	Page No.
Desaru Merlin Inn P.O. Box 50, Kotatinggi, Tanjung Penawar	(07) 838101			100	392
Holiday Inn Johor Bahru Jalan Dato Sulai-man Century Gardens	(07) 323800			200	393
Merlin Johor Bahru 10 Jalan Bukit Meldrum	(07) 225811		MERLIN JOHOR BAHRU	104	393

Mersing

Mersing Merlin Inn 1½ Mile, Jalan Endau	791312			34	393
Rawa Island Chalets Rawa Safaris Tourist Center	791204			20	393
Tioman Island Resort Pulau Tioman Island	44544-5			170	393

Kota Bharu

Hotel Perdana Jalan Mahmud, P.O. Box 222	785000	MA 53143	HOTDANA KOTA BHARU	136	393

Name / Address	Phone	Telex	Cable	Rooms	Page
Resort Pantai Cinta Berahi Kota Bharu, P.O. Box 131	781307			38	393
Kuantan					
Club Mediterranee Holiday Village Cherating, near Kuantan	591131			300	394
Hyatt Kuantan Telok Chempedak	525211	MA 50252	HYATT KUANTAN	185	394
Merlin Kuantan Telok Chempedak	522388	MA 50285	MERLINKUANTAN	106	394
Kuala Trengganu					
Pantai Primula Hotel Jalan Persinggahan, P.O. Box 43	622100	PANTAI MA 51403	PAN MOTEL	260	394
Rantau Abang Visitor Centre 13th Mile, off Dungan	841533	JARA MA 51449		10	394
Tanjong Jara Beach Hotel 8 Mile, off Dungan	841801–3	MA 51449	PEMRESORT	100	395
Cameron Highlands					
Cameron Highlands Merlin P.O. Box 4, Tanah Rata	941205	MA 30487	CAMHOTEL CAMERONHIGHLANDS	60	397

Hotel	Telephone	Telex	Cable	No. of Rooms	Page No.
Fosters Lakehouse Hotel Ringlet	948680			12	397
Golf Course Inn Tanah Rata	941411			30	397

Fraser's Hill

Hotel	Telephone	Telex	Cable	No. of Rooms	Page No.
Fraser's Hill Development Corp. Holiday Bungalows Fraser's Hill	382201		KEBUKIT FRASERSHILL	69	397
Fraser's Hill Merlin Hotel Fraser's Hill	382247	MA 30487		109	397

Genting Highlands

Hotel	Telephone	Telex	Cable	No. of Rooms	Page No.
Genting Hotel, Genting Highlands Resort Jalan Ismail 50250, Kuala Lumpur	2613833	MA 30482	GENTOTEL K.L.	1070	398

Kuala Lumpur

Hotel	Telephone	Telex	Cable	No. of Rooms	Page No.
Equatorial Hotel Jalan Sultan Ismail	2422022	EQATOR MA 30263	EQUATORIAL	300	405

Hotel	Telephone	Telex	Cable	Rooms	Page
Federal Hotel 35 Jalan Bukit Bintang	2489166	FEDTEL MA 30429	FEDEROTEL	450	405
Holiday Inn City Center Raja Laut	939333	HOLIDAYINN		200	405
Hyatt Saujana Hotel and Country Club Subang International Airport Hwy.	7461188			250	405
Kuala Lumpur Hilton Jalan Sultan Ismail (P.O. Box 577)	2422222	MA 30495	HILTELS KUALA LUMPUR	589	405
Kuala Lumpur Merlin Hotel 2 Jalan Sultan Ismail	2480033	MA 30487	MERLIN	687	406
Ming Court Jalan Ampang	2619066			447	406
Pan Pacific Kuala Lumpur Jalan Chow Kitbaru, P.O. Box 11468	4225555	MA 33706 PPHTKL	PANPACKUL	571	406
Petaling Jaya Hilton 2 Jalan Barat Petaling, Jaya	7553533	MA 37542	JAYAPURI PJ	388	406
Shangri-la Kuala Lumpur 11 Jalan Sultan Ismail	2322388	SHNGKL MA 30021		722	406
Ming Court Beach Hotel Port Dickson, Negri Sembilan	405244	MA 63952	MUIPORTSON	165	407
Si-Rusa Inn 7th Mile, Coast Rd., P.O. Box 31, Port Dickson, Negri Sembilan	405244	MA 63865		160	407

Malacca

Hotel	Telephone	Telex	Cable	No. of Rooms	Page No.
Malacca Straits Inn 37A Jalan Badar Hilir	21101			45	415
Malacca Village Resort Ayer Keroh	313600	MA 62854		147	415
Ramada Renaissance Hotel Melaka Jalan Bendahara P.O. Box 105	248888	RAMADA MA 62966	RAMADARENA	295	415
Shah's Beach Motel 6th Mile, Tanjong Keling	26222	HMSHAH MA 62808	SHAH'S	50	415

Penang

Hotel	Telephone	Telex	Cable	No. of Rooms	Page No.
Bayview Beach Hotel Batu Ferringhi	811311	MA 40004	BAYBEACH PENANG	74	421
Casuarina Beach Hotel Batu Ferringhi	811711	MOON MA 40137	CASUARINA PENANG	175	421
Eastern & Oriental Hotel 10 Farquhar St.	375322	MA 40270	HOTELEANDO	100	421
Hotel Equatorial 1 Jalan Bukit Jambul, 11900	838000			415	421
Ferringhi Beach Hotel Batu Ferringhi Rd., 11100, Batu Ferringhi	805999	MA 40634	FERTEL	350	421

Golden Sands Hotel P.O. Box 222, Batu Ferringhi	811911	MA 40627	GOLDSANDS PENANG	310	422
Holiday Inn Hotel Penang Batu Ferringhi	811601	MA 40281 HOLINN	HOLIDAYINN PEN	165	422
Orchard Sun Penang Tanjung Bungah, Penang	891111	MA 33139 SUNTEL		323	422
Palm Beach Hotel Batu Ferringhi	811621	MA 40404	PALMHOTEL	145	422
Penang Merlin 25–A Farquhar St., Georgetown	23301	MA 40632	MERLIN PENANG	295	422
Rasa Sayang Hotel Batu Ferringhi Beach	811811	MA 40065	RASAYANG/PENANG	305	423
Shangri-la Inn Victoria Street, Penang	612148	MA 40878		452	423

Sabah

Hotel Capital P.O. Box 23, Jalan Haji Saman	53433		CAPITAL	102	428
Hyatt Kinabalu International	51777	KITA MA 80036	HYATTKI	345	428
Hotel Shangrila P.O. Box 1718, Bandaran Berjaya	56100	HOSHAN MA 80001	SHANGRILA	120	428

Sarawak

Hotel	Telephone	Telex	Cable	No. of Rooms	Page No.
Aurora Beach Hotel Jalan Tanjong Batu, Bintulu	20281	MA 73150	AURORA BINTULU	108	431
Holiday Inn Kuching Jalan Tunku Abdul Rahman, Kuching	23111	MA 70086	HOLIDAY INN	165	431
Hotel Long House Abell Rd., Kuching	55333	MA 70039	LONGHOUSE	50	431

PHILIPPINES
Manila

Hotels	Telephone	Telex	Cable	No. of Rooms	Page No.
Century Park Sheraton corner of Vito Cruz and M. Adriatico avenues	50–60–41	CPH 27791	CENPARK MANILA	510	458
Holiday Inn 3001 Roxas Blvd.	59–79–61	63487	HOLIDAY INN MANILA	370	459
Hyatt Regency Manila 2702 Roxas Blvd.	80–26–11	PN 3344	HYATT MANILA	265	459
Manila Pavilion United Nations Ave., Ermita	57–37–11	722–3387		416	459
Manila Hotel Rizal Park	47–00–11	3496	MANILHOTEL	570	460

Hotel / Address	Phone	Cable / Telex	Telex answer	Rooms	Page
Manila Inter-Continental Ayala Ave., Makati Commercial Center	89–40–11	RCA 7222212	INHOTELCOR	420	460
Mandarin Oriental Manila corner Makati Ave. and Paseo de Roxas	81–36–01	63756 MANDA PN	MANDAHOTEL MANILA		461
Manila Peninsula Ayala and Makati avenues	85–77–11	22507 PEN PH	PENHOT MANILA	537	461
Philippine Plaza Cultural Center complex, Roxas Blvd.	832–0701	742–0443	PHILPLAZA MLA	676	461
Silahis International Hotel 1990 Roxas Blvd.	57–38–11	63163 SILTEL PN	SILATEL MANILA	600	462

Banaue

Hotel / Address	Phone	Cable / Telex	Telex answer	Rooms	Page
Banaue Hotel and Youth Hostel Banaue, Ifugao				20 (30 beds)	462

Baguio

Hotel / Address	Phone	Cable / Telex	Telex answer	Rooms	Page
Baguio Park Hotel Harrison Rd./P. Claudio St., Baguio City	56–26	7420329 RAJAH PM		65	462
Cresta Ola Beach Resort Hotel Bauang, La Union	09–2983			20	463
Hyatt Terraces Baguio South Drive, Baguio City	56–70/57–80	2920 TERRACES PU	HYATT MANILLA	303	463

Hotel	Telephone	Telex	Cable	No. of Rooms	Page No.
International Spiritual Center and Resorts (ISCR) Lucnab, Baguio City	69–06	27955 ISCR PH		55-plus	463
Pagsanjan Falls Lodge and Summer Resort Pagsanjan	645–1251			28	463
Pagsanjan Rapids Hotel Pagsanjan	645–1258			38	463
Mt. Data Lodge Mt. Data (100 km) Mountain Province				8	464
Puerto Azul Beach and Country Club Ternate, Cavite		64546 AZUTEL, PN	TERNATEL MANILA	350	464
Ruff Inn 1 Maryhills, Loakan Airport, Baguio City	22–18			30	464
Taal Vista Lodge Tagaytay City, c/o Resort Hotels Corp., Alco Bldg., 391 Buendia Ave.	818–0811 or 88–23–82			25	464

Mindanao Islands

Hotel	Telephone	Telex	Cable	No. of Rooms	Page No.
Alta Tierra Hotel Carmen St., Cagayan de Oro City	36–61; 36–62			32	468
Caprice Hotel by the Sea Lapasan St., Cagayan de Oro City	48–80			23	468

Hotel	Phone	Telex	Cable		
Mindanao Hotel corner Chavez and Corrales streets, Cagayan de Oro City	30–10; 35–51			53	468
Apo View Hotel J. Camus St., Davao City	7–48–61			86	468
Davao Insular Inter-Continental Inn Lanang, Davao City	7–60–61	ITT 48209	DAVINS	153	469
Imperial Hotel Claro M. Recto Ave., Davao City	7–84–81		DAVAO IMPERIAL HOTEL	52	469
Lantaka by the Sea Mayor Valderoza St., Zamboanga City	39–31			132	469
Zamboanga Plaza Hotel Pasonanca Park	20–51			210	469

The Visayas

Hotel	Phone	Telex	Cable		
Argao Beach Club Casay, Dalaguete, Cebu Island		22482 PTI PH	BAYVIEW MANILA	77	474
Cebu Plaza Barrio Nivel, Lahug, Cebu City	611–29	24861 CEPLA PH	BAYVIEW MANILA	450	474
Magellan International Hotel Gorordo Ave., Cebu City	7–46–11	24729 MIH PH	MAGELLAN CEBU	200	474
Montebello Resort Hotel Banilad, Cebu City	7–76–81/3	6232 MONTE PU		142	474

Hotel	Telephone	Telex	Cable	No. of Rooms	Page No.
Tambuli Beach Resort Buyong Beach, Mactan Island, Cebu City	7–00–52			52	475
Hotel Del Rio M. H. del Pilar, Molo Iloilo City	7–55–85			57	475

SINGAPORE

Hotel	Telephone	Telex	Cable	No. of Rooms	Page No.
Century Park Sheraton 16 Nassim Hill, Singapore 1025	7321222	CPHSIN RS21817	CENPARK SINGAPORE	462	511
Crown Prince Hotel 270 Orchard Rd., Singapore 0923	7321111	RS 22819	HCROWN	303	511
The Dynasty 320 Orchard Rd., Singapore 0923	7349900	RS36633 DYNTEL	DYNASTY SINGAPORE	400	511
Glass Hotel 317 Outram Rd., Singapore 0316	7330188	50141		509	512
Goodwood Park Hotel 22 Scotts Rd., Singapore 0922	7377411	RS24377 GOODTEL	GOODWOOD	235	512
Hilton International Singapore 581 Orchard Rd., Singapore 0923	7372233	RS21491	HILTELS SINGAPORE	435	512
Holiday Inn Hotel 25 Scotts Rd., Singapore 0922	7377966	RS21818	HOLIDAYINN	600	513

Hotel	Phone	Telex	HOLIDEX		
Holiday Inn Park View 11 Cavenagh Rd., Singapore 0922	7338333			320	513
Hyatt Regency Singapore 10–12 Scotts Rd., Singapore 0922	7331188	RS24415	HYATTSIN	1174	513
The Mandarin Singapore 6 Raffles Blvd., Singapore 0103	3383388	RS21528 MANOTEL	MANRINOTEL	1200	513
Marina Mandarin Marina Square, Singapore	7379155	MANOTEL RS 21528	MARMANRINHOTEL	640	514
The Marco Polo Singapore Tanglin Rd., Singapore 1024	4747141	RS21476 BEDTEL	HOMARCPOLO	603	514
Hotel Meridien Singapore 100 Orchard Rd., Singapore 0923	7338855	RS50163 HOMERI	HOMERI SINGAPORE	419	515
Hotel Meridien Changi-Singapore 1 Netheravon Rd., Singapore 1750	5427700	RS36042 HOMRA	SINGAPORE ORIENTAL	280	515
The Oriental Marina Square, Singapore 01–200	3380066	RS 29117 ORSIN	SINGAPORE	402	515
Pan Pacific Hotel 7 Raffles Blvd., Singapore 0103	3368111	RS38821		800	516
The Regent Singapore 1 Cuscaden, Singapore 1024	7338888	RS37248 SINIHC	INHOTELCOR	443	516
Raffles Hotel 1/3 Beach Rd., Singapore 0718	Currently under renovation; will reopen to its former glory in 1992.				
Shangri-la Singapore 22 Orange Grove Rd., Singapore 1025	7373644	RS21505	SHANGRI LA SINGAPORE	809	516

Hotel	Telephone	Telex	Cable	No. of Rooms	Page No.
Sheraton Towers 39 Scotts Rd., Singapore 0922	7376888	RS37750 SHINSIN		443	517
The Westin Plaza 2 Stamford Rd., Singapore 0617	3388585	RS22206 RCHTLS		796	517
The Westin Stamford 2 Stamford Rd., Singapore 0617	3338585	RS2206 RCHTLS		1253	517

TAIWAN
Taipei

Hotel	Telephone	Telex	Cable	No. of Rooms	Page No.
Grand Hotel 1 Chungshan North Rd., Section 4	596–5565	11646; 11647	GRANDHTEL	530	550
Hilton International Taipei 38 Chung Siao Rd. West, Section 1	311–5151	785–11699	HILTELS TAIPEI	527	550
Howard Plaza Hotel 160 Jen Air Rd., Sec. 3, Taipei	(02) 700–2323	10702 HOPLATEL TAIPEI		606	550
Lai Lai Sheraton Hotel 12 Chung Hsiao East Rd., Section 1, Taipei	321–5511	23939	SHANGTEL	705	551
Ritz Taipei Hotel 155 Min Chuan East Rd., Taipei 104	597–1234	27345 THE RITZ	THERITZ, TAIPEI	220	551

	Phone	Telex	Cable		
The Regent of Taipei 41 Chung Shan North Rd., Sec. 2	542–1024	23466	REGENT TAIPEI	560	551

Kaohsiung

	Phone	Telex	Cable		
Ambassador Hotel 202 Minsheng 2nd Rd.	(07) 211–5211	72105	AMTELKAO	457	552
Grand Hotel Cheng Ching Lake 833	(07) 383–5911	71231	GRAND HOTEL	108	552
Holiday Garden Hotel Kaoshiung 279 Liuho 2nd Rd.	(07) 241–0121	81948 GARDEN	GARDEN KAOHSIUNG	313	552

Hualien

	Phone	Telex	Cable		
Hotel Astar Sea View Ave., Mei-Lun	(038) 326–111	11540	ASTAR	170	552
China Trust Hualien 2 Yonng-Shing Rd.	(038) 221–171	11144	CTCOM	327	553
Marshal Hotel 36 Kungyuan Rd.	(038) 326–123	21656	MARSHALHTL	350	553

Sun Moon Lake

	Phone	Telex	Cable		
China Trust Sun Moon Lake Tourist Hotel 23 Chung Cheng Rd., Nantou	(049) 855–911	11144 CITC TAIPEI	SOMOTEL NANTOU	116	553

Taichung

Hotel	Telephone	Telex	Cable	No. of Rooms	Page No.
Hotel National 257 Taichung Kong Rd., Section 1	(04) 321–3111	51393	NATALHTL NATIONALHTL	404	553
Park Hotel 17 Kung Yuan Rd., Taichung 40007	(04) 220–581	51525 PARKTEL	PARKHOTEL	124	553

Tainan

Hotel	Telephone	Telex	Cable	No. of Rooms	Page No.
Hotel Tainan 1 Cheng Kung Rd., 70001 Tainan	(06) 228–9101	71365 TAN HOTEL		152	554

Pingtung

Hotel	Telephone	Telex	Cable	No. of Rooms	Page No.
Caesar Park Hotel-Kenting 6 Kenting Rd., Henchung Town, Ping Tung Hsien	(08) 889–5222	71882 CAESARKT		250	554

THAILAND
Bangkok

Hotel	Telephone	Telex	Cable	No. of Rooms	Page No.
Ambassador Hotel 171 Sukhumvit Rd.	254–0444	TH 82910 AMTEL	AMTELBANGKOK	942	588

666

Hotel	Phone	Telex	Cable		Page
Dusit Thani Rama IV Rd.	236–0450	TH 81170	DUSITOTEL	525	589
Hilton International Bangkok 2 Wireless Rd., off Ploenchit Rd.	253-0123	TH 72206 HILBKK		389	589
Holiday Inn Bangkok 981 Silom Rd.	234–1010	82998 TH 82998	RAMATOW	360	589
Imperial Hotel Wireless Rd., Bangkok 5	254–0023	TH 2301	IMPERHOTEL	400	590
Indra Regent Hotel Rajprarob Rd.	252–1111	82723 INDRATH	INDRAHOTEL	500	590
Mandarin Hotel 662 Rama IV Rd., Bangkok 10110	233–4980	TH 87689	MANOTEL	343	590
The Menam 2074 New Rd., Yannawa	289–1148	87423TH	MENAMHOTEL	727	590
Montien 54 Suriwongse Rd.	234–8060	TH 81038	MONTEL BKK	600	591
Novotel Bangkok Siam Swuare, Soi 6, Bangkok 10500	255–2444			350	591
The Oriental Oriental Ave.	236–0400	TH 2997	ORIENHOTEL	402	591
The Regent of Bangkok 155 Rajadamri Rd.	251–6127	TH 20004	REGHO	424	591
The Royal Orchid Sheraton Captain Bush Lane, off Siphya Rd.	234–5599	84491	RAYORCH-BANGKOK	698	592

Hotel	Telephone	Telex	Cable	No. of Rooms	Page No.
Shangri-la Hotel 89 Soi Wat Suan Plu, New Rd., Bangkok	235–6210/2	TH 84265	SHANGRILA BANGKOK	650	592
Siam Inter-Continental Srapatum Palace Property, Rama 1 Rd.	252–9040	TH 81155	INHOTELCOR	411	592
Tawana Ramada 80 Surawongse Rd.	236–0631	TH 81167	SHERATON	265	593
Chiang Mai					
Chiang Inn 100 Chang Klan Rd.	235655	TH 4303	CHIANGIN	175	610
Chiang Mai Hills Hotel 18 Huay Kaew Rd.	221255	TH 4332	CHINGMAI HILLS	82	610
Rincome Hotel 301 Huay Kaew Rd.	221044	TH 4314	RINCOME CHIANGMAI	158	610
Dusit Inn 112 Chang Klan Rd.	236835	TH 4338	GRANPAL	198	610
Chiang Mai Orchid 100-102 Huay Kaew Rd.	222099	TH 4337	HYATTOR	267	610
Pattaya					
Grand Palace Corner Pattaya Beach, Cholburi	418541	81917	GRANPAL	500	616

Merlin Pattaya Pattaya Beach, Cholburi	428755	81905		360	616
Montien Pattaya Pattaya Beach, Cholburi	418155	81906	MONTELP	320	616
Nipa Lodge Pattaya Beach, Cholburi	428195	81903	NIPALODGE	150	616
Orchid Lodge Pattaya Beach, Cholburi	428161	81903	ORCHID-LODGE	236	617
Pattaya Palace Pattaya Beach, Cholburi	428066	81904	PALPAT	291	617
Royal Cliff Pattaya Beach, Cholburi	418344	81907	CLIFF PATTAYA	786	617
Siam Bayshore Pattaya Beach, Cholburi	428678	82820	BAYSHORE PATTAYA	274	618
Siam Bayview Pattaya Beach, Cholburi	428728	82820	BAYVIEW PATTAYA	300	618
Hotel Tropicana North Pattaya Beach, Cholburi	418516	81910	TROPICANA PATTAYA	200	618
Wong Amat 90 Naklua Rd., Pattaya Beach, Cholburi	418118	81908	WONGVILLA PATTAYA	229	618

Phuket

Amanpuri P.O. Box 196, Surin Beach, Phuket	250-0746			42	623

Hotel	Telephone	Telex	Cable	No. of Rooms	Page No.
Club Med-Phuket Island				300	623
Coral Beach Hotel 104 Moo4, Patong Beach Kathu District, Phuket 83120	2526045			600	623
Meridien Phuket P.O. Box 277, Phuket	321–4805			460	624
Patong Beach Hotel Phuket P.O. Box 25	321301	TH 69521 PATONG	PATONG HOTEL	103	624
Phuket Island Resort 73/2 Rasda Road, Phuket	212676	69555 ISLAND TH	ISLAND PHUKET	194	624

670

INDEX